W9-ATU-040

CHEATS
ACHIEVEMENTS
AND
TROPHIES
2013

PLUS

DOWNLOAD A FREE COPY OF THE
BRADYGAMES CHEAT CODE OVERLOAD APP

THE BEST DIGITAL COMPANION FOR ALL THE MOST POPULAR HANDHELD, CONSOLE, MOBILE, AND PC GAMES ALL IN ONE PLACE!

GET YOUR FREE APP!

Visit the App Store to download your free copy of the BradyGames Cheat Code Overload app. Using your Apple device, go to the App Store and enter "Cheat Code Overload" in the search bar. Simply tap the icon to install the app and prepare to take your gaming experience further!

Please note that the free app is only available in iOS format. Offer valid through 12/31/13.

007 LEGENDS

UNLOCK MOONRAKER SKIN

Select Online Multiplayer in the Mutliplayer menu and then Promotional Codes. Type in the code astr0b0y to unlock the Moonraker skin.

2010 FIFA WORLD CUP

ACHIEVEMENTS & TROPHIES

NAME	GOAL/REQUIREMENT	POINT VALUE	TROPHY VALUE
Single Star Group Stage	Finish the Group Stage in the Online 2010 FIFA World Cup™ with a 1/2 - 1 star team.	30	Bronze
Two Star Group Stage	Finish the Group Stage in the Online FIFA World Cup™ with a 1.5 - 2 star team.	20	Bronze
Three Star Group Stage	Finish the Group Stage in the Online FIFA World Cup™ with a 2.5 - 3 star team.	5	Bronze
Against all odds	Win the Online 2010 FIFA World Cup™ with a 1/2 - 1 star team.	75	Gold
Ultimate Underdogs	Win the Online 2010 FIFA World Cup™ with a 1.5 - 2 star team.	50	Silver
Played well as a team	Win the Online FIFA World Cup™ with a 2.5 - 3 star team.	15	Bronze
Dream Come True	Advance past the group stage in the Online FIFA World Cup™ with a team rated 3 stars or lower.	5	Bronze
Undefeated Group Stage	Win all three group games and advance to the knockout stage in the Online FIFA World Cup™.	15	Silver
Hospitality and Victories	As the lead profile advance through the group stage as South Africa in 2010 FIFA World Cup™.	10	Bronze
We'll just score more	As the lead profile Concede 14+ In the Finals & Win the World Cup™. Semi-Pro or higher difficulty.	10	Bronze
Concede No Goals	As the lead profile Advance to the round of 16 without conceding a goal: Semi-pro+ difficulty.	10	Bronze
Defend, Defend, Defend	Lift the World Cup™ Trophy in the 2010 FIFA World Cup™ scoring 11 or fewer total goals :Lead Profile.	10	Bronze
Second Trip, First Goal	Qualify & Score in the finals using any team that's been to the finals & not scored : Lead profile.	10	Bronze
First Team Selection	Get promoted to the First team and play a match in Captain your Country.	15	Bronze
Managers First Choice	With a Virtual Pro play a game as the #1 ranked squad member in Captain your Country.	15	Silver
Co-op Success	All four co-op players get a match rating of 7 or above in a captain your country match.	5	Bronze

NAME	GOAL/REQUIREMENT	POINT VALUE	TROPHY VALUE
Practice Penalty Kicks	Score at least 5 penalty Kicks in Penalty Shootout Practice.	10	Bronze
Masterful Performance	Finish a Captain your Country where one of the players wins an end of tournament award.	20	Silver
The Captain	In a Captain your Country campaign play a game as the captain for your country's first team.	10	Bronze
Solid Performer	Achieve an average match rating of 8 at the end of a single Captain your Country campaign.	10	Bronze
Fair Play	In a single Captain your Country campaign Receive no match bans.	5	Silver
Hold the Line	Earn a match rating of 8 or above as a Defender in Captain your Country.	5	Bronze
Most Hat-tricks	In Captain your Country score 2 or more hat-tricks in the Finals to beat the standing record.	20	Bronze
2010 FIFA World Cup™ Mastery	Defeat all 32 teams that qualified for the 2010 FIFA World Cup™.	125	Silver
2006 FIFA World Cup™ Final	Beat France using Italy on Semi-Pro or Higher Difficulty.	10	Bronze
2002 FIFA World Cup™ Final	Beat Germany using Brazil on Semi-Pro or Higher Difficulty.	10	Bronze
1998 FIFA World Cup™ Final	Defeat Brazil using France on Semi-Pro or Higher Difficulty.	10	Bronze
Lightning Quick Strike	Score in under 90 seconds to beat the standing record for fastest goal in a World Cup™ finals match.	20	Silver
Europe Qualifier	As the lead profile qualify as a team from Europe in 2010 FIFA World Cup™.	20	Bronze
Asia Qualifier	As the lead profile qualify as a team from Asia in 2010 FIFA World Cup™.	20	Bronze
Oceania Qualifier	As the lead profile qualify as a team from Oceania in 2010 FIFA World Cup™.	20	Bronze
CONCACAF Qualifier	As the lead profile qualify as a team from CONCACAF in 2010 FIFA World Cup™.	20	Bronze
South America Qualifier	As the lead profile qualify as a team from South America in 2010 FIFA World Cup™.	20	Bronze
Africa Qualifier	As the lead profile qualify as a team from Africa in 2010 FIFA World Cup™.	20	Bronze
World Cup™ Winner	As the lead profile win the FIFA World Cup™ Final in 2010 FIFA World Cup™.	125	Gold
Victorious!	Win the FIFA World Cup™ in a Captain your Country campaign.	100	Gold
Shameful	I've quit out of at least 5 ranked matches while losing.	0	—

SECRET ACHIEVEMENTS & TROPHIES

NAME	GOAL/REQUIREMENT	POINT VALUE	TROPHY VALUE
First time on the world stage	Play with a team in the Online FIFA World Cup™ that's never qualified for the real World Cup Finals.	15	Bronze
adidas Golden Shoe	Beat the standing record by scoring 10 goals in an Online FIFA World Cup™ with a single player.	25	Bronze
Better luck needed next time	Finish the group stage without advancing to the Knockout stage of the Online 2010 FIFA World Cup™	20	Bronze
Practice Makes Perfect	Enter the training grounds to practice after a loss.	5	Bronze
Pressure Cooker	Score in a penalty shootout using your Virtual Pro and win the game.	15	Bronze
2 Button Mentor	Play and win a co-op game where at least one user is on 2 Button Controls.	10	Bronze
2010 FIFA World Cup™ Fever	Challenge and defeat someone with this achievement in the Online FIFA World Cup™.	10	Bronze

2010 FIFA WORLD CUP SOUTH AFRICA

XBOX 360

ADIDAS U11 TEAM

Go to EA Extras in My 2010 FIFA World Cup. Select Unlockable Code Entry and enter WSBJPJYODFYQIIGK.

FINAL MATCH BALL

Go to EA Extras in My 2010 FIFA World Cup.
Select Unlockable Code Entry and enter FGWIXGFXTNSICLSS

ADIDAS ADIPURE III TRX (BLACK/SUN)

Go to EA Extras in My 2010 FIFA World Cup.
Select Unlockable Code Entry and enter HHDOPWPMIXZQOJOZ

ADIDAS F50 ADIZERO (BLACK/SUN/SUN)

Go to EA Extras in My 2010 FIFA World Cup.
Select Unlockable Code Entry and enter SGFSTZPPXCHHMJMH

ADIDAS F50 ADIZERO (CHAMELEON)

Go to EA Extras in My 2010 FIFA World Cup.
Select Unlockable Code Entry and enter VOKMNEZTJOQPULUT

ADIDAS F50 ADIZERO (SUN/ BLACK/GOLD)

Go to EA Extras in My 2010 FIFA World Cup.
Select Unlockable Code Entry and enter YOZCCVIFJGKQJWTW

ADIDAS PREDATOR X (BLACK/SUN)

Go to EA Extras in My 2010 FIFA World Cup.
Select Unlockable Code Entry and enter OCEGZCUHXOBSBNFU

COCA-COLA CELEBRATIONS

Go to EA Extras in My 2010 FIFA World Cup.
Select Unlockable Code Entry and enter the following:

CELEBRATION	CODE	HOW TO PERFORM
Baby Cradle	UGSIMLBHLFPUBFJY	Left Trigger + A
Dance	KBRRWKUIRSTWUJQW	Left Trigger + B
Dying Fly	DVMNJPBTLHJZGECP	Left Trigger + X
Flying Dive	DBQDUXQTRWTVXYDC	Left Trigger + Y
Prancing Bird	TWVBIXYACAOLGOWO	Right Bumper + B
River Dance	MIKAKPUMEEWNTQVE	Right Bumper + X
Side Slide	VNDWDUDLMGRNHDNV	Right Bumper + Y
Speed Skating	LHEHJZTPYYQDJQXB	Right Bumper + A

NINTENDO WII

WORLD CLASSIC XI TEAM

Earn at least Bronze against each team in Kazumi's Dream Team to play the World Classic XI Team. Defeat them in a best of three match to play as the team in Hit the Pitch.

3D CLASSICS: TWINBEE

NINTENDO 3DS

10 LIVES

When starting a game, hold Up + Right and press A.

3D DOT GAME HEROES

PLAYSTATION 3

HIDE SHIELD

Pause the game and press Up, Up, Down, Down, Left, Right, Left, Right, ●, ●. Re-enter the code to reveal the shield again.

TOGGLE SWAY IN WALKING

Pause the game and press L1, R1, L1, R1, L1, L1, R1, R1, ●. Re-enter to turn the code back on.

SPELUNKER MODE

Enter your name as SPELUNKER. In this mode, you will die with one hit.

THE 3RD BIRTHDAY

PSP

After you complete the game and save, you can load up that save and start a new game with your weapons and Over Energy still intact. You also get the ability to unlock cheat codes from the start menu. Press Start and select Cheat Codes to access them. Obtain more cheat codes by fulfilling certain conditions. Rank and Feat results are not recorded while cheat codes are turned on.

ASSIST CODES

CHEAT	HOW TO OBTAIN IT	DESCRIPTION
High Regen	10,000 BP	Greatly accelerates Aya's LIFE recovery rate.
Free Crossfire	10,000 BP	NPCs can join a crossfire even if not taking cover.
Infinite Ammo	Clear the game 10 times at any level.	All guns can shoot unlimited bullets.

CHEATS, ACHIEVEMENTS, AND TROPHIES

#

CHEATS, ACHIEVEMENTS, AND TROPHIES

CHEAT	HOW TO OBTAIN IT	DESCRIPTION
No Armor	Accomplish 4 or more Episode 1 feats at the Hard difficulty level.	Protective gear is always at max damage.
No Evasion Assist	Accomplish 4 or more Episode 2 feats at the Hard difficulty level.	No invulnerability while evading.
No Regen	Accomplish 3 or more Episode 3 feats at the Hard difficulty level.	LIFE does not recover automatically.
No Info	Accomplish 3 or more Episode 4 feats at the Hard difficulty level.	No on-screen battle info.
Critical Disease	Accomplish 5 or more Episode 5 feats at the Hard difficulty level.	The Liberation gauge refills at half speed.
No Over Energy	Accomplish at least 75 percent of all feats at the Hard difficulty level.	Unable to unleash Over Energy.
Static LIFE	Accomplish 4 or more Episode 1 feats at the Deadly difficulty level.	Aya gains the max LIFE amount of the NPC she dives into, regardless of her level.
Limited Weapons	Accomplish 4 or more Episode 2 feats at the Deadly difficulty level.	Unable to carry any weapon apart from the starting handgun (76SA).
Level Hold	Accomplish 3 or more Episode 3 feats at the Deadly difficulty level.	Aya is permanently at level 1 and gains no experience.
Critical Illness	Accomplish 3 or more Episode 4 feats at the Deadly difficulty level.	Constantly receive damage.
Half Ammo	Accomplish 5 or more Episode 5 feats at the Deadly difficulty level.	Ammo capacity of all guns is halved.
NPC One-Hit Death	Accomplish at least 75 percent of all feats at the Deadly difficulty level.	NPCs die with one hit.
No Haste	Complete the game at the Insane difficulty level.	Time does not slow during an Overdive.
Maintain LIFE	Complete the game at the Insane difficulty level.	LIFE doesn't increase or decrease, even during an Overdive.
Friendly Fire	Complete the game at the Insane difficulty level.	Can be damaged by allies.
No Cover	Accomplish at least 75 percent of all feats at the Hard and higher difficulties.	No barricades or plateaus.
One-Hit Death	Obtain all cheat codes.	Aya dies with one hit.

AAH IMPOSSIBLE RESCUE

NARRATOR

At the main menu, enter the following codes to change the narrator.

NARRATOR	CODE
Anime-L22	Y, Y, Y, Y, X
Carole Clark	X, Y, Y, Y, X
Geoff-Li	X, Y, X, X, X
Hoegoeshinseki	Y, X, X, X, Y
Lilfirebender	X, X, Y, Y, X
Lucas Wilheim	Y, X, Y, X, Y
Meika	X, X, X, X, X
Michelle Rakar	X, X, X, X, Y
Ofebriso	Y, Y, X, X, X
Pia Lehtinen	X, X, Y, X, X
Sanjikunsgirl	X, Y, X, Y, X
Skimlines	Y, Y, X, X, Y
Teisei	Y, X, X, X, X

ADVANCE WARS: DAYS OF RUIN

UNLOCK COS

Complete the following missions to unlock the corresponding CO.

COMPLETE MISSION	CO UNLOCKED
12	Tasha
13	Gage
14	Forthsythe
20	Waylon
21	Greyfield
24	Penny
25	Tabitha
26	Caulder

ADVENTURE TIME: HEY ICE KING! WHY'D YOU STEAL OUR GARBAGE?!

NEW GAME+

Complete the game to unlock New Game+, which can be selected by choosing the arrow next to the "plus" symbol on the file select screen.

SOUND TEST

Complete New Game+ to unlock the Sound Test mode.

SECRET SCREEN

At the title select screen, input Up, Up, Down, Down, Left, Right, Left, Right, B, A to see a Secret Screen.

CHEATS, ACHIEVEMENTS, AND TROPHIES

A

AGE OF EMPIRES II HD

CHEAT CODES

Press Enter and enter the following codes to enable the desired cheats.

EFFECT	CODE
1000 Food	CHEESE STEAK JIMMY'S
1000 Gold	ROBIN HOOD
1000 Stone	ROCK ON
1000 Wood	LUMBERJACK
Birds Become Super Dogs	WOOF WOOF
Cobra Car	HOW DO YOU TURN THIS ON
Control Animals	NATURAL WONDERS
Defeat Everyone	BLACK DEATH
Destroy Individual Enemy Empire	TORPEDO# (# is the empire you want to destroy)
Destroy Yourself	WIMPYWIMPYWIMPY
Fast Build	AEGIS
Furious the Monkey	FURIOUS THE MONKEY BOY
Instant Loss	RESIGN
Instant Win	I R WINNER
Remove Fog of War	POLO
Reveal Full Map	MARCO
Saboteur Unit	TO SMITHEREENS
VDML	I LOVE THE MONKEY HEAD

ALAN WAKE

ACHIEVEMENTS

NAME	GOAL/REQUIREMENT	POINT VALUE
Follow the Light	Take a night course of light education.	10
Nordic Walking	Take a walk through the logging area, meet one of the quirky locals.	10
Bright Falls' Finest	Call for help.	20
Boob Tube	See what's on TV.	5
Under a Thin Layer of Skin	Defy the park ranger.	10
Park Ranger	Enjoy the sounds and sights of Elderwood National Park.	15
Heavy Metal	Survive the bulldozer attack.	10
Iron Horse	Encounter a steam engine.	10
Wheels Within Wheels	Meet the kidnapper.	20
Medical Opinions	Listen to Hartman's recordings.	10
Child of the Elder God	Have a rock'n'roll moment without dropping to a low health state.	10
Perchance to Dream	Take a moment to reflect on past events.	20
Drink 'Em Both Up	Put de lime in de coconut twice.	10
Gatekeeper	Cut the power to the transformer yard.	10
The Lady of the Light	Discover the secret she guards.	20
Tornado Wrangler	Defeat the tornado.	20
Departure	Complete the game on Normal difficulty.	40
Hardboiled Writer	Complete the game on Hard difficulty.	40
Alan, Wake Up	Complete the game on Nightmare difficulty.	50

NAME	GOAL/REQUIREMENT	POINT VALUE
If It Flies, It Burns	Burn 1,000 birds.	20
They're Heeeeeere!	Inanimate objects shouldn't move of their own accord. Put a stop to this affront, oh, say, 20 times.	20
The Six-Gun Scribe	Defeat 100 Taken with the revolver.	20
Taken Season	Defeat 50 Taken with the hunting rifle.	20
It's Not Just a Typewriter Brand	Defeat 50 Taken with a shotgun.	20
What Light Through Yonder Window	Defeat 50 Taken with the flaregun, the way Shakespeare intended.	20
Thunder and Lightning	Defeat 50 Taken with flashbang grenades.	20
Collateral Carnage	Defeat 20 Taken with indirect means.	20
Come One, Come All	Kill four Taken with a single shot from the flaregun.	10
Sound and Fury	Kill four Taken with a single flashbang.	10
Two For the Price of One	Kill two Taken with a single shotgun blast.	10
Back! Back, I Say!	Save yourself with a flare.	10
Float Like a Butterfly	Perform a cinematic dodge.	15
Missed by a Mile	Perform a cinematic dodge 20 times.	25
Energized!	Use 100 batteries.	10
Let There Be Light	Get a generator running.	10
Carny	Knock over five can pyramids.	10
Meet the Deadline	In "Mirror Peak," make it from the Coal Mine Museum to Cauldron Lake in 30 minutes.	30
An Idyllic Small Town	Make it through "Night Life in Bright Falls" in one go without dying or restarting even once.	30
Gunless Wonder	Make it to Cauldron Lake without firing a single shot in "On the Road to Cauldron Lake."	30
Right of Way	Drive over 15 Taken.	10
Finders Keepers	Discover 5 hidden chests.	20
Every Nook and Cranny	Discover all of the hidden chests.	30
Paging Mr. Wake	Find 25 manuscript pages.	20
Picking Up After Yourself	Find all of the manuscript pages in Normal mode.	30
Collector's Edition	Find all of the manuscript pages in the game, including the ones in Nightmare mode.	50
Damn Good Cup of Coffee	Discover 25 coffee thermoses.	20
Hypercaffeinated	Discover all coffee thermoses.	30
KBF-FM	Listen to all of the radio shows.	30
Couch Potato	Watch every single TV show.	30
Bright Falls Aficionado	Absorb every bit of local history and culture.	30

ALAN WAKE'S AMERICAN NIGHTMARE

XBOX 360

AVATAR AWARDS

AVATAR	EARNED BY
American Nightmare Hoodie	Purchase the Game and Meet Emma in the Game.
Night Springs T-Shirt	Unlock the first Nightmare Difficulty Arcade Level.
Old Gods of Asgard Tour T-Shirt	Complete Story Mode.

ALICE IN WONDERLAND

DORMOUSE COAT

Enter 3676 as a cheat code.

RED GUARD SHIELD

Enter 7453 as a cheat code.

RED QUEEN MASK

Enter 7675 as a cheat code.

TAN ALICE BOOK

Enter 2625 as a cheat code.

TWEEDLE OUTFIT

Enter 8946 as a cheat code.

ALICE: MADNESS RETURNS

DRESSES

Completing each chapter unlocks a new dress—each with a special ability.

DRESS	COMPLETE THIS CHAPTER	DRESS ABILITY
Steamdress	Chapter 1	Breakables drop more Teeth and Roses.
Siren	Chapter 2	Enemies drop twice as many Roses.
Silk Maiden	Chapter 3	Enemies drop twice as many Teeth.
Royal Suit	Chapter 4	Health limited to 4 Roses total.
Misstitched	Chapter 5	Shrink Sense duration is doubled.
Classic	Chapter 6	Regain health while shrunk.

ALIENS: COLONIAL MARINES

ACHIEVEMENTS & TROPHIES

NAME	GOAL/REQUIREMENT	POINT VALUE	TROPHY VALUE
Another Day in the Corps!	Complete Distress	20	Bronze
Bad Feeling About This Drop	Complete Sulaco Falls	20	Bronze
Quoth the Raven	Complete The Raven	20	Bronze
Still Got a Job to Do	Complete Rampart	20	Bronze
Dragged Queen	Complete Home	20	Bronze
Game Over, Man!	Complete all Campaign levels on any difficulty	30	Silver
Not Bad For a Human	Complete all Campaign levels on Hardened difficulty	40	Silver
State of the Badass Art	Complete all Campaign levels on Ultimate Badass difficulty	50	Gold
Short, Controlled Bursts	Defeat all Xenomorphs in the Sulaco hangar bay without them crossing your barricade	20	Bronze
Fire Drill	Arm the emergency release and escape in under 2:30 on Sulaco Falls	20	Bronze
Mostly Come at Night...	Find Newt's doll	20	Bronze
Just a Grunt	Complete Hope in Hadley's	20	Bronze

NAME	GOAL/REQUIREMENT	POINT VALUE	TROPHY VALUE
No Need For Alarm	Complete One Bullet without setting off the alarm	20	Bronze
Heavy Lifting	Defeat the Raven in under 1:10 on Soldier difficulty or higher	20	Bronze
Adios, Muchachos	Gib two enemies at once	20	Bronze
Field Promotion	Earn Rank 2 as a Marine	10	Bronze
Lean and Mean	Earn Rank 20 as a Marine	20	Bronze
I Love the Corps!	Earn Rank 60 as a Marine	40	Gold
Oorah to Ashes	Collect a Dog Tag	10	Bronze
Remember the Fallen	Collect all 35 Dog Tags	30	Silver
Personal Friend of Mine	Collect a Legendary Weapon	10	Bronze
I Like to Keep These Handy	Collect all 6 Legendary Weapons	30	Silver
Another Bug Hunt	Complete a Challenge	5	Bronze
Stay Frosty	Complete an entire Challenge category	20	Bronze
Distinguished Service Medal	Complete all Challenges	30	Silver
I Feel Safer Already	Have another player join your party	10	Bronze
Don't Count Me Out	Revive a teammate	5	Bronze
Ready to Fry Half a City	Edit a Marine Loadout	5	Bronze
Structural Perfection	Edit a Xenomorph Loadout	5	Bronze
Perfect Killing Machine	Upgrade every Loadout slot for a Xenomorph class	20	Bronze
Field Modified, Kill Certified	Upgrade every slot for a weapon	20	Bronze
You Look Just Like I Feel	Upgrade every Appearance slot once for your Marine	30	Silver
Adaptive Morphology	Upgrade every Appearance slot once for a Xenomorph class	30	Silver
I Can Handle Myself	Purchase all Upgrades for a weapon	40	Silver
Majority Shareholder	Spend 30 Commendations	25	Bronze
I Heard THAT	Collect all 12 Audio Logs	25	Bronze
Entry Prohibited	Kill 10 Xenomorphs that are using vents	20	Bronze
Let's Rock!	Kill 10 Xenomorphs in a game with the M56A2 Smart Gun	20	Bronze
Need a Deck Of Cards?	Set up a UA 571-C Remote Sentry	5	Bronze
Micro Changes in Air Density	Track 100 hostile targets with the Motion Tracker	10	Bronze
It's a Dry Heat	Kill 3 enemies with a single U4 Firebomb	20	Bronze
Eat This!	Kill a Xenomorph with a shotgun at very close range	10	Bronze
Coming Outta the Walls!	Kill a Xenomorph climbing on the walls or ceiling	10	Bronze
Secreted from What?	Kill 5 Splitters without being damaged by acid	20	Bronze
No Offense	Melee a Lurker that is pouncing towards you	20	Silver
Arbitrarily Exterminated	Kill 2179 Xenomorphs	30	Silver
Anytime, Anywhere	Kill a Crusher without it damaging you	20	Bronze
Love at First Sight	Survive a Close Encounter with a Facehugger	10	Bronze
… But No Cigar	Rescue a teammate from a Close Encounter	20	Bronze
Easter Egg	Find the Easter Egg	5	Bronze

ALIENS VS. PREDATOR

ACHIEVEMENTS & TROPHIES

NAME	GOAL/REQUIREMENT	POINT VALUE	TROPHY VALUE
Not Bad for A Human	Get all the Aliens vs Predator achievements	50	Platinum
Game Over, Man!	Complete all three Campaigns	30	Silver
Club hopper	Survive The 'Party' at The Club	15	Bronze
Exit Strategy	Escape from C-Block	15	Bronze
You Have My Sympathies	Help Van Zandt	15	Bronze
Regicide	Defeat the Matriarch	15	Bronze
I Will Never Leave You...	Locate Tequila	15	Bronze
...That's A Promise	Get Tequila to surgery	15	Bronze
One Big Bug	Defeat the Praetorian	15	Bronze
Get To The Chopper!	Recover Weyland's datapad	30	Silver
Come to Mama	Liberate the Matriarch	15	Bronze
Breaking Quarantine	Escape from the Research Lab	15	Bronze
Grunt Hunt	Wipe out all of the Marines in the Colony	15	Bronze
Under Pressure	Solve the riddle of the Ruins	15	Bronze
Grim Reaper	Harvest all available civilians in the Alien Campaign	15	Bronze
Alien vs Predator	Create a new species	30	Silver
It Uses The Jungle	Find a way through Gateway	15	Bronze
Fallen Comrade	Find the Youngbloods in the Jungle	15	Bronze
Matter of Honor	Discover the Elite Predator's fate	15	Bronze
Eyes of The Demon	Retrieve the ancient mask	15	Bronze
World of Hurt	Survive trial by combat	15	Bronze
Breaking and Entering	Find a way into the Research Lab	15	Bronze
Reclaimer	Retrieve the second artifact	15	Bronze
Extinction Agenda	Destroy the Abomination	30	Silver
Stay Frosty	Complete Marine Campaign on Hard difficulty setting	15	Bronze
I Admire its Purity	Complete Alien Campaign on Hard difficulty setting	15	Bronze
It Ain't No Man	Complete Predator Campaign on Hard difficulty setting	15	Bronze
I LOVE the Corps!	Complete Marine Campaign on Nightmare difficulty setting	30	Silver
Magnificent, Isn't It?	Complete Alien Campaign on Nightmare difficulty setting	30	Silver
One Ugly Mother	Complete Predator Campaign on Nightmare difficulty setting	30	Silver
Harsh Language	Discover all 67 Audio Diaries	15	Silver
Quite A Specimen	Destroy all 50 Royal Jelly Containers	15	Bronze
Fortune and Glory	Find all 45 Predator trophy belts	15	Bronze
Scatter Shot	As a team, kill 20 enemies in under 60 seconds in a Survivor match.	15	Bronze
I Like to Keep This Handy	Kill 2 enemies with one shot with the shotgun	15	Bronze
Spin Doctor	Kill two enemies with one throw of the Battle Disc	15	Bronze
Let's Rock!	Kill 5 enemies with one burst from the smartgun	15	Bronze

NAME	GOAL/REQUIREMENT	POINT VALUE	TROPHY VALUE
Elite Sniper	Kill 10 enemies with head shots from the scoped rifle	15	Bronze
Stick Around	Kill 20 enemies with the Combi Stick	15	Bronze
Gunslinger	Kill 30 enemies with the pistol	30	Silver
Welcome to The War	Play and complete your first Ranked Match in standard Deathmatch mode	15	Bronze
Killer Instinct	Win your first Ranked Match in standard Deathmatch mode	15	Bronze
Serial Killer	Win 10 Ranked Matches in any Deathmatch mode	30	Silver
Very Tough Hombre	Kill 10 enemies in a row without dying in a Ranked Match	15	Bronze
Persecution Complex	Achieve Persecutor status more than once in any Ranked Match	15	Bronze
The Six Pack	Play with six friends in a Ranked Match	30	Silver
Ain't Got Time to Bleed	Heal or regenerate 30 blocks of health in Survivor	15	Bronze
The Uninfected	Finish a Ranked Infestation match as the only remaining prey	30	Silver
Welcome to The Party	Get 6000 XP in Ranked Matches	30	Silver
Real Nasty Habit	Get 18060 XP in Ranked Matches	50	Gold

ALPHA PROTOCOL

XBOX 360/PS3

ACHIEVEMENTS & TROPHIES

NAME	GOAL/REQUIREMENT	POINT VALUE	TROPHY VALUE
Operation True Heirs	Complete Operation True Heirs.	75	Silver
Basic Training	Complete the Training Mission.	50	Bronze
Alpha Protocol	Complete Operation Desert Spear.	75	Silver
Operation Blood Feud	Complete Operation Blood Feud.	75	Silver
Operation Deus Vult	Complete Operation Deus Vult.	75	Silver
Full Circle	Complete Alpha Protocol.	125	Gold
Hardcore	Complete Alpha Protocol on Hard difficulty setting.	25	Gold
Evolution of an Action Hero	Complete the Alpha Protocol using the Recruit background.	10	Silver
Desert Spear	Assassinate Sheikh Shaheed.	25	Bronze
Ask Questions First, Shoot Later	Refrain from killing in cold blood.	15	Bronze
Judge, Jury, and Executioner	Let your gun do the talking.	15	Bronze
Thorton, Inc.	Turn all your enemies into allies in one single career.	10	Silver
Ladies' Man	Romance all the ladies in Alpha Protocol in a single career.	10	Bronze
No Time For Love	Complete the game without being seduced.	20	Bronze
Hard to Read	Use each stance at least 25% across 90 dialogue stance choices.	10	Bronze

NAME	GOAL/REQUIREMENT	POINT VALUE	TROPHY VALUE
Social Butterfly	Gain Liked reputation status of 3 people (who must all Like you at the same time).	10	Bronze
Antisocial	Get 3 people to hate you (who must all hate you at the same time).	10	Bronze
Ready For Anything	Acquire the vast majority of Intel available in the game.	5	Bronze
Pistol Mastery	Score 100 Critical Hits with the Pistol.	5	Bronze
SMG Havoc	Achieve the maximum SMG Critical Hit Multiplier 7 times in your career.	5	Bronze
Shotgun Crowd Control	Score 100 Critical Hits with the Shotgun.	5	Bronze
Assault Rifle Marksmanship	Score 100 head shots with the Assault Rifle.	5	Bronze
Black Belt	Defeat 50 enemies with CQC.	5	Bronze
Lurker	Evade or Takedown 75 enemies across your career.	5	Bronze
One With The Shadows	Complete 3 missions with less than 5 kills and with no enemies alerted to your presence.	5	Bronze
Technophile	Complete 5 missions wherein 6 different gadgets are used.	5	Bronze
Building a Deadlier Mousetrap	Have 100 placed devices detonate.	5	Bronze
Breaking and Entering	Pick 10 locks.	5	Bronze
Circuit Breaker	Bypass 20 electronic devices.	5	Bronze
Data Theft	Hack 10 computers.	5	Bronze

SECRET ACHIEVEMENTS & TROPHIES

NAME	GOAL REQUIREMENTS	POINT VALUE	TROPHY VALUE
Friends Before Strangers	You saved Madison Saint James from certain death.	25	Bronze
Hard Choices	The Roman History Museum is safe, thanks to your efforts.	25	Bronze
Keeping the Peace	You prevented a riot from killing hundreds in Taipei.	25	Bronze
Secret Service	You prevented the assassination of President Ronald Sung.	25	Bronze
Stay of Execution	You allowed Sheikh Shaheed to live.	25	Bronze
No Compromise, No Mercy	Choosing your own path, you put an end to Halbech and Alpha Protocol.	25	Silver
Savage Love	You gained the affection of SIE and allowed her to consummate her lust.	5	Bronze
Exclusive Interview	You and Scarlet Lake had a romantic trist.	5	Bronze
Crime Buster	You reconciled with Alpha Protocol and put Halbech out of business.	25	Silver
Rising Star	You joined Halbech and put an end to Alpha Protocol.	25	Silver
Price For Lying	You killed Surkov for lying to you.	5	Bronze
Russian Alliance	You forged a partnership with Sergei Surkov.	5	Bronze
A Price On Mercy	You spared Konstantin Brayko.	25	Bronze
One Less Gangster	Konstantin Brayko is dead by your hand.	25	Bronze

NAME	GOAL REQUIREMENTS	POINT VALUE	TROPHY VALUE
Youth Trumps Experience	By carefully pushing his buttons, you provoked Marburg into fighting to the death.	5	Bronze
Respected Enemies	You gained Marburg's respect and bested him in battle.	5	Bronze
Never Trust A Sociopath	You successfully alienated "secret agent" Steven Heck.	5	Bronze
A Plot Uncovered	You discovered the identity of Sung's assassin.	5	Bronze
Office Romance	Your working relationship with Mina Tang turned into something more.	5	Bronze
Rome-ance	You became more than friends with Madison Saint James.	5	Bronze

AMAZING SPIDER-MAN

XBOX 360/PS3

UNLOCKABLE SUITS

Perform the following tasks to unlock new suits.

SUIT	REQUIREMENT
Big Time Suit	Found in Times Square, behind the red bleachers, on the glass.
Classic Black Suit	Under the Gazebo in the park left of the main Oscorp Building.
Cross Species Spider-Man	Complete the game on any difficulty.
Future Foundation Suit	One block right of the north bridge, behind a gas station in a small alley.
Negative Zone Suit	On top of the Beenox building, the second building inwards from the Brooklyn Bridge.
New Black Suit	Complete the game 100%.
Scarlet Spider Suit	Go to fountain in Central Park, then move north until you see a bridge. Use the camera.

XBOX 360/PS3

ACHIEVEMENTS & TROPHIES

NAME	GOAL/REQUIREMENT	POINT VALUE	TROPHY VALUE
Gladiator	Completed all Oscorp Secret Research Labs	15	Bronze
A Dash of Spider	Completed all XTreme Race challenges	15	Bronze
The Camera Loves You	Completed all XTreme Video challenges	15	Bronze
Friendly Neighbor	Saved a hostage caught in a petty crime	15	Bronze
Call Interrupted	Destroyed a Seeker before it could call a Hunter	15	Bronze
Negotiator	Resolved all police deadlocks	15	Bronze
Car Hopper	Cleared all car chases	15	Bronze
Peace of Mind	Returned all escapees to the police	15	Bronze
Sanitized	Rescued all infected civilians	15	Bronze
Sky Captain	Chained 10 Web-Rushes in the city	15	Bronze
Amazing Spider-Man	Unlocked all concept art	20	Bronze
Ultimate Spider-Man	Acquired all upgrades	20	Bronze
Heavyweight Champion	Defeated 1000 enemies	30	Gold
Middleweight Champion	Defeated 500 enemies	20	Silver

NAME	GOAL/REQUIREMENT	POINT VALUE	TROPHY VALUE
Lightweight Champion	Defeated 100 enemies	15	Bronze
The Sky Is the Limit	Defeated the S-01 without touching the ground	20	Silver
Clean Victory	Defeated a Hunter without using your Web-Shooters	20	Silver
All Tied Up	Defeated 100 enemies by performing Stealth Takedowns	15	Silver
Stick to the Plan	Defeated 50 enemies by performing Stealth Takedowns	15	Bronze
Keep It Together	Immobilized 6 enemies simultaneously with web	15	Bronze
Haymaker	Performed a Web-Rush punch	10	Bronze
FYI I'm Spider-Man	Performed 25 Signature Moves	10	Bronze
I'm on a Roll!	Achieved a combo streak of 42	15	Silver
Journalist	Collected all audio evidence	15	Bronze
Corporate	Collected all Oscorp Manuals	15	Bronze
Tech Savvy	Collected all hidden Tech Pieces	15	Bronze
Librarian	Collected all magazines	15	Bronze
On the Fly	Collected all 700 Spider-Man Comic Pages	25	Bronze
Spider-Man	Completed the game on super hero difficulty	100	Gold
Vigilante	Completed the game on hero difficulty	50	Silver
Peter Parker	Completed the game on human difficulty	25	Bronze

SECRET ACHIEVEMENTS & TROPHIES

NAME	GOAL/REQUIREMENT	POINT VALUE	TROPHY VALUE
Pest Control	Defeated Scorpion in the city	20	Bronze
Speed Bump Ahead	Defeated Rhino in the city	20	Bronze
Welcome Back, Friend	Defeated Lizard	30	Silver
Deeply Sorry	Defeated Nattie	20	Bronze
Smell You Later	Defeated Vermin	20	Bronze
Jinxed	Defeated Felicia	20	Bronze
Tail? You Lose	Defeated Scorpion in quarantine	20	Bronze
Down for the Count	Defeated Rhino in the sewers	20	Bronze
Switched Off	Rescued Alistaire Smythe	25	Silver
Apparent Defeat	Defeated Iguana	20	Bronze
Tomorrow Is Saved	Defeated the S-03	30	Silver
Big Apple, Big Worm	Defeated the S-02	30	Silver
Siege Averted	Defeated the S-01	30	Silver
Beating the Odds	Cleared the second fight against the Hunter robots	30	Bronze
Who's the Prey?	Cleared the first fight against the Hunter robots	30	Bronze
Does everything a spider can!	Unlock all Trophies	—	Platinum

AMAZING SPIDER-MAN: ULTIMATE EDITION

NINTENDO WII U

UNLOCKABLE SUITS

Perform the following tasks to unlock new suits.

SUIT	REQUIREMENT
Big Time Costume Suit	Complete the first Iguana Mission.
Classic Black Suit	Unlocks after Chapter 5.
Future Foundation Suit	Complete all Oscorp Secret Lab Side Missions.
Negative Zone Suit	Complete all Rescue Missions.
Scarlet Spider Suit	Collect 700 Comics.

ANARCHY REIGNS

XBOX 360/PS3

UNLOCK GARGOYLE

Gargoyle can be unlocked as a playable character by completing the Campaign twice: once on White Side and once on Black Side. You can also unlock Gargoyle by reaching Rank 22 in Multiplayer.

XBOX 360/PS3

ACHIEVEMENTS & TROPHIES

NAME	GOAL/REQUIREMENT	POINT VALUE	TROPHY VALUE
Max Anarchy	Complete the game without using retries on any difficulty.	60	Gold
Anarchy Recognizes Anarchy	Unlock all player characters in the game.	30	Bronze
Burnt Out Anarchy	Defeat all the bosses while in a Rampage. (Campaign Mode)	40	Silver
Anarchy's Executioner	Defeat all the bosses with your Killer Weapon. (Campaign Mode)	40	Silver
Ultimate Weapon of Anarchy	Defeat Cthulhu within 5 minutes. (Campaign Mode)	60	Gold
Anarchy in the Calamari	Defeat the Kraken within 5 minutes. (Campaign Mode)	60	Gold
Minefield of Anarchy!	Shock 3 enemies at once with a Supercharged Trap. (Campaign Mode)	20	Bronze
Lake of Fire? Lake of Anarchy!	Defeat 5 enemies at once with an incendiary grenade. (Campaign Mode)	20	Bronze
Anarchist's Tomato Cookbook	Defeat 50 enemies with the Rifle. (Campaign Mode)	20	Bronze
Machine Gun Anarchy	Defeat 15 enemies with the Gatling gun. (Campaign Mode)	15	Bronze
Backyard Barbeque (With Anarchy)	Fry 50 enemies with the Flying Platform. (Campaign Mode)	15	Bronze
Baron von Anarchy	Defeat 50 enemies while riding a Helicopter Drone. (Campaign Mode)	15	Bronze
Someone Set Up Us The Anarchy!	Defeat 10 enemies by throwing an explosive Pyro Killseeker before they explode. (Campaign Mode)	15	Bronze
Anarchy Clockwork Drone	Defeat 5 enemies by throwing a self-destructing Drone before they explode. (Campaign Mode)	15	Bronze
Frozen in Time for Anarchy	Defeat a frozen enemy. (Campaign Mode)	15	Bronze

CHEATS, ACHIEVEMENTS, AND TROPHIES

A

NAME	GOAL/REQUIREMENT	POINT VALUE	TROPHY VALUE
Throw The Anarchy Already!	Defeat 20 enemies with thrown objects. (Campaign Mode)	15	Bronze
Guy Dead Missile Anarchy	Destroy a Helicopter Drone by throwing its missile back at it. (Campaign Mode)	20	Bronze
The Plural of Ninja is Anarchy	Throw 10 enemies from behind using stealth. (Campaign Mode)	20	Bronze
Meet the Anarchy Butcher	Kill 20 mutants via the mutant execution technique. (Campaign Mode)	20	Bronze
Big Combo Anarchy	Defeat an enemy with a combo of 100 hits or longer. (Campaign Mode)	40	Silver
Massage with an Anarchy Ending	Evade 5 throws. (Campaign Mode)	15	Bronze
Duel of the Anarchies	Counter 5 enemy attacks. (Campaign Mode)	15	Bronze
Rage! Rampage! Anarchy?	Defeat 50 enemies while in Rampage mode. (Campaign Mode)	15	Bronze
Anarchy is a Killer Weapon!	Defeat 50 enemies with Killer Weapon attacks. (Campaign Mode)	15	Bronze
Path of the Weak isn't Anarchy	Defeat 30 enemies with throw attacks. (Campaign Mode)	15	Bronze
In Anarchy, Timing is Everything	Evade 10 times. (Campaign Mode)	10	Bronze
The Best Defense is Anarchy	Defend against an enemy attack 10 times. (Campaign Mode)	10	Bronze
Elite Force of Anarchy	Starting on White Side, complete all Campaign and free missions on any difficulty. (Stage Select OK)	20	Bronze
Chasing Anarchy	Starting on Black Side, complete all Campaign and free missions on any difficulty. (Stage Select OK)	20	Bronze
Mad Anarchy	Starting on White Side, complete the Campaign on hard difficulty.	30	Silver
Bari Shur Loves Anarchy	Complete White Side stage 4 on hard difficulty.	15	Bronze
All of the Lights of Anarchy	Complete White Side stage 3 on hard difficulty.	15	Bronze
Anarchy Carrier	Complete White Side stage 2 on hard difficulty.	15	Bronze
Broken Bottles of Anarchy	Complete White Side stage 1 on hard difficulty.	15	Bronze
Anarchy Reigns is an Oxymoron	Starting on Black Side, complete the Campaign on hard difficulty.	30	Silver
Anarchy in the Dunes	Complete Black Side stage 4 on hard difficulty.	15	Bronze
Shining a Light on Anarchy	Complete Black Side stage 3 on hard difficulty.	15	Bronze
Anarchy in the Navy	Complete Black Side stage 2 on hard difficulty.	15	Bronze
Knockdown, Drag Out Anarchy	Complete Black Side stage 1 on hard difficulty.	15	Bronze
Dead Anarchy	Starting on White Side, complete the Campaign on normal difficulty.	20	Bronze
Sandstorm of Anarchy	Complete White Side stage 4 on normal difficulty.	10	Bronze
Bright Side of Anarchy	Complete White Side stage 3 on normal difficulty.	10	Bronze
Defending Coastal Anarchy	Complete White Side stage 2 on normal difficulty.	10	Bronze
Drunken Anarchy	Complete White Side stage 1 on normal difficulty.	10	Bronze

NAME	GOAL/REQUIREMENT	POINT VALUE	TROPHY VALUE
Ending Anarchy is Endless	Starting on Black Side, complete the Campaign on normal difficulty.	20	Bronze
The Rude Sandstorm of Anarchy	Complete Black Side stage 4 on normal difficulty.	10	Bronze
Filling Dark Souls with Anarchy	Complete Black Side stage 3 on normal difficulty.	10	Bronze
Anarchy Coast Guard	Complete Black Side Stage 2 on normal difficulty.	10	Bronze
Pub Crawl Anarchy	Complete Black Side stage 1 on normal difficulty.	10	Bronze
Anarchy Training Complete	Complete all tutorials.	10	Bronze
Platinum Anarchist	Obtain all Trophies.	—	Platinum

ANGRY BIRDS

MOBILE

GOLDEN EGGS

#	LOCATION	DESCRIPTION
1	World Select	At the world select, tap the sun until another Golden Egg pops out.
2	Credits	Select I from the Options and scroll up to find the Golden Egg.
3	Help Screen	This Golden Egg becomes available once you unlock the white bird. Then, during any level, pause the game and select the question mark. At the white bird help screen, touch the Golden Egg.
4	Poached Eggs	Earn three stars on all of the Poached Eggs levels.
5	Poached Eggs 1-8	Simply tap the treasure chest until you get the egg.
6	Poached Eggs 2-2	Destroy the beach ball that sits among the ice cubes.
7	Mighty Hoax	Earn three stars on all of the Mighty Hoax levels.
8	Mighty Hoax 4-7	Zoom out to spot the egg on the right cliff. Launch the yellow bird into a high arc and tap when it lines up with the egg.
9	Mighty Hoax 5-19	The egg is located above the rocket ship. Zoom out and use a yellow or white bird to get it. Fire the yellow bird almost straight up and then tap when it reaches the clouds. If done correctly, the bird will get the egg as it comes back down.
10	Danger Above Level Select	Select Danger Above and scroll the level select screens as far as you can to the right to find this egg.
11	Danger Above	Earn three stars on all of the Danger Above levels.
12	Danger Above 6-14	Pop the yellow balloon floating below the structure on the right to get this one. Send the boomerang bird over the house and tap to have it come back to the balloon. This requires very good timing with the boomerang.
13	Danger Above 8-15	The golden egg is located behind the two boxes below the slingshot. Zoom out to see it. Bounce a yellow bird off the pink cushion located to the right.
14	The Big Setup	Earn three stars on all of The Big Setup levels.
15	The Big Setup 9-14	This egg hides under a hard hat on the far side of the area. Send a bird over or through the structure to get it.
16	The Big Setup 10-3	Destroy the rubber duck located below the bridge to get another Golden Egg.
17	The Big Setup 11-15	Zoom out to spot an egg below and to the left of your location. Fire the boomerang bird to the left and tap the screen to bring it back to the egg.
18	Ham 'Em High	Earn three stars on all of Ham 'Em High levels.
19	Ham 'Em High 12-12	Destroy the cup that sits on the small platform below the big structure. Destroy the building and then send a bird through the opening to get it.

CHEATS, ACHIEVEMENTS, AND TROPHIES

#	LOCATION	DESCRIPTION
20	Ham 'Em High 13-10	Zoom out to see the egg hanging on the far side of the map. Send the white bird toward the middle of the structure, just above the two concrete bars on top. At this time, tap the screen to send the bird into the egg.
21	Ham 'Em High 13-12	You cannot see this egg until you get it. Zoom out so that you see the entire hill that you sit upon. Send a white bird to the left and quickly drop an explosive egg to reveal the Golden Egg.
22	Ham 'Em High 14-4	Zoom out so that you can see the Golden Egg that sits high on the mountain in the upper-right corner. Launch the yellow bird at about a 60 degree angle and then tap the screen to send it toward the egg.
23	Mine and Dine 15-12	Zoom out and an egg becomes visible in the top-right corner. Getting this one is very similar to 20. Send the yellow bird up and tap when it lines up with the egg.
24	Mine and Dine 16-9	Zoom out to spot the egg on the rock formation to the right. Aim a yellow bird just to the left of the first platform above the slingshot. Immediately tap the screen and if done correctly, the bird will reach the egg on the descent.
25	Mine and Dine	Earn three stars on all Mine and Dine levels.
26	Mine and Dine 17-12	Zoom out and a treasure chest can be seen on a rock high above. The first two birds cannot reach it, so use them up. Then fire the yellow bird at about a sixty degree angle up and to the right. As it lines up with the chest, tap the screen to get it.

ANGRY BIRDS HD

UNLOCKING WORLD THE EASY WAY

At the world select, center on a locked world. Back out all the way out of the game. Go back into Angry Birds. At the Play button, tap it very quickly. Pass the first level to unlock the world.

SOUND BOARD

Earn three stars for all levels on world 1 through 3.

ANGRY BIRDS SPACE

GOLDEN EGGSTEROID

Golden Eggsteroids are hidden in six levels. These unlock bonus levels that are based on classic video games.

EGGSTEROID	WORLD	LEVEL	LOCATION
1	Pig Bang	1-9	In brush below two pigs in bubbles.
2	Pig Bang	1-20	In brush on top of the planet.
3	Cold Cuts	2-13	In brush on planet below slingshot.
4	Cold Cuts	2-25	Under slingshot.
5	Cold Cuts	2-28	Hidden in snow, being pointed out by arrow.
6	Fry Me to the Moon	3-10	In bush on west side of planet.

ANGRY BIRDS STAR WARS

GOLDEN DROID LOCATIONS

STAGE	INSTRUCTIONS
Tatooine 1-13	Located at the top of the screen. Deflect blaster shots into the Golden Droid using the Black bird's force push. Throw away the Red bird so you don't accidentally kill the pig shooting lasers.
Tatooine 1-25	Located at the bottom of the screen. Fling the Red bird to the bottom, destroying the bush in front of the metal bit, then use the Black bird to force-push the metal bit onto the Golden Droid.
Tatooine 1-31	Located at the back of the stage. Force-push the asteroids to the right, then fling another bird upwards and force-push the asteroid onto the Golden Droid.
Death Star 2-18	Located at the bottom of the screen. Shoot your Yellow bird off-screen to the left. He won't be gone yet. There is a tunnel below the area where the egg is; wait until your Yellow bird is below the entrance of the tunnel and have him shoot his blaster to reflect the shot into the egg.
Death Star 2-33	Located above the main structure. Use one or two Yellow birds through the small gap on the north side of the level, shooting the Droid and its enclosure with the blaster.
Hoth 3-17	Located at the top-right corner of the level. Bounce Han's blaster off the miniature tower way above the AT-AT.
Hoth 3-36	Located at the top-right corner of the level. Use the Pink bird's tractor beam to lift the stone slab right of the Golden Droid, then use the Yellow Bird's blaster to shoot the Droid.
Cloud City 4-14	Located in the middle of the level. Toss the Chewbacca bird nearly vertically to cause him to fall onto the Golden Droid.

GREEN LIGHT SABER

Complete the Path of the Jedi episode to unlock the Green Light Saber.

OBI-WAN FORCE UPGRADE

Complete level 25 of the Death Star to get the Obi-Wan Force Upgrade.

PATH OF THE JEDI EPISODE

Earn a 3-star rating on all Tatooine and Death Star levels to unlock Path of the Jedi.

STRATEGIES & TIPS

- Use the Force—In Angry Birds Star Wars, each bird has special abilities that can help you clear areas better. After you throw your bird, tap the screen to use their special power.
- Look at Your Surroundings—Many puzzles are too big to see at a glance. Pinch the screen to zoom out and see more of the level instead of wasting a bird on an exploratory mission.
- Don't Always Avoid Obstacles—Enemy lasers can impede your flight path and send you flying in different ways. This isn't always a bad thing—you can use these to send your birds flying in ways you might not have thought of before!

ANOMALY: WARZONE EARTH

AVATAR AWARDS

AVATAR	EARNED BY
Anomaly Battle Pants	Complete any tactical trial mission to unlock these pants.
Anomaly Battle Shirt	Complete 1st mission to unlock the battle shirt.
Anomaly Commander's Helmet	Finish the campaign to unlock the commander's helmet.

ARMORED CORE V

ACHIEVEMENTS & TROPHIES

NAME	GOAL/REQUIREMENT	POINT VALUE	TROPHY VALUE
Rookie	Awarded for joining a team.	5	Bronze
Assembler	Awarded for assembling an AC.	5	Bronze
Color Customizer	Awarded for setting an AC's coloring.	5	Bronze
Emblem Designer	Awarded for editing an emblem.	5	Bronze
Communicator	Awarded for editing a message.	5	Bronze
AC Wrecker	Awarded for winning a battle against an AC.	15	Bronze
Charge Master	Awarded for destroying an enemy with a boost charge.	5	Bronze
Complete Custom Part	Awarded for continuing to use an arm unit to maximize its performance.	15	Bronze
Story 00	Awarded for completing Story Mission 00.	10	Bronze
Story 01	Awarded for completing Story Mission 01.	10	Bronze
Story 02	Awarded for completing Story Mission 02.	10	Bronze
Story 03	Awarded for completing Story Mission 03.	10	Bronze
Story 04	Awarded for completing Story Mission 04.	10	Bronze
Story 05	Awarded for completing Story Mission 05.	10	Bronze
Story 06	Awarded for completing Story Mission 06.	10	Bronze
Story 07	Awarded for completing Story Mission 07.	10	Bronze
Story 08	Awarded for completing Story Mission 08.	10	Bronze
Story 09	Awarded for completing Story Mission 09.	10	Bronze
Complete Story Missions	Awarded for completing all Story Missions.	50	Silver
Story Master	Awarded for completing all Story Missions with Rank S.	50	Gold
Order Mission	Awarded for completing at least one Order Mission.	10	Bronze
Complete Order Missions	Awarded for completing all Order Missions.	40	Bronze
Subquests 30%	Awarded for completing 30% of all Story Mission and Order Mission subquests.	20	Bronze
Subquests 50%	Awarded for completing 50% of all Story Mission and Order Mission subquests.	20	Bronze
Subquest Master	Awarded for completing all Story Mission and Order Mission subquests.	50	Gold
Emblem Master	Awarded for getting all emblems and emblem pieces by buying them at the shop and/or destroying ACs.	30	Bronze
Mercenary	Awarded for accepting and going on a job as a mercenary.	5	Bronze
A Job Well Done	Awarded for successfully completing a job as a mercenary.	10	Bronze

NAME	GOAL/REQUIREMENT	POINT VALUE	TROPHY VALUE
Team Sortie	Awarded for going on a Conquest Mission or Territory Mission with four or more team members.	15	Bronze
Operator	Awarded for leading your team to victory on a Conquest Mission or Territory Mission.	15	Bronze
Territory Mission Sortie	Awarded for going on a Territory Mission.	5	Bronze
Accomplish Territory Mission	Awarded for claiming victory on a Territory Mission.	10	Bronze
Territory Mission Victory	Awarded for claiming victory on a Territory Mission in an emergency state.	30	Silver
Conquest Mission Sortie	Awarded for going on a Conquest Mission.	5	Bronze
Conquest Mission Victory	Awarded for claiming victory on a Conquest Mission.	30	Bronze
Territorial Claim	Awarded for claiming victory on a Conquest Mission as an Invasion Mission.	30	Silver
Customize Territory	Awarded for acquiring territory and uploading custom gun battery positions.	10	Bronze
Perfect Mission	Awarded for completing emergency Territory/Conquest Mission w/four or more members, all surviving.	30	Bronze
Team Level 10	Awarded for belonging to a team with a team level of 10 or higher.	15	Bronze
Team Level 50	Awarded for belonging to a team with a team level of 50 or higher.	40	Silver
Migrant	Awarded for raising your money to 10 million Au or more.	20	Bronze
Overlord	Awarded for belonging to a team that holds ten different territories at the same time.	30	Bronze
Ruler	Awarded for belonging to a team that holds one or more territories in all areas.	50	Gold

ARMY CORPS OF HELL

PLAYSTATION VITA

The following passwords unlock mantles that allow you to change the background music and give an effect of Help/Recover Radius +7.

GHOULS ATTACK!

Enter G75i8K8a as a password.

GXSXD

Enter GUK218Jh as a password.

KING'S-EVIL

Enter KB2p3tAs as a password.

KNIGHTS OF ROUND

Enter K77w3P5a as a password.

RACHEL MOTHER GOOSE

Enter RJ53z42i as a password.

REBEL-SURVIVE

Enter S4R29dlu as a password.

UNITED

Enter U541337k as a password.

ARMY OF TWO: THE DEVIL'S CARTEL

XBOX 360/PS3

ACHIEVEMENTS & TROPHIES

NAME	GOAL/REQUIREMENT	POINT VALUE	TROPHY VALUE
Sir, yes sir!	Level up to Rank 5	20	Bronze
Keep it up!	Level up to Rank 15	30	Silver
Blood, Sweat and Guns	Level up to Rank 25	50	Gold
My Baby	Fully customize a weapon with 6 customizable parts or more	10	Bronze
Overkiller	200 targets killed in single Overkill (Triggered by you)	20	Bronze
Whack-A-Mask	500 targets killed while in cover	20	Bronze
Double Trouble	200 targets killed in double Overkill	50	Silver
Moocher	200 targets killed in single Overkill (Triggered by your partner)	20	Bronze
Let 'er Rip	100 targets killed using either an MMG or an MGL	20	Bronze
Barbarian	Destroyed 500 objects	10	Bronze
Armed to the Teeth	Buy All Guns	25	Silver
Look at you!	Buy All Outfits	25	Silver
Look mom, I made it!	Complete the game on Insane	100	Gold
Deep Pockets	Buy all Weapons, Tattoos, Masks and Outfits	100	Gold
Army Of Two	Perform 250 Flank, Surprise and/or Tag Team kills	75	Silver
Aggro-er	You took the Aggro for 100 Flank kills	40	Silver
Headache	Perform 100 Headshots	30	Bronze
Blood Sport	Perform 100 melee kills	25	Bronze
Just a scratch	You didn't go wounded once in a mission (medium, hard or insane)	25	Bronze
Combo Master	Perform a x10 Co-op Combo	30	Silver
Melee all day!	Perform a melee kill while you're in Overkill	10	Bronze
Cover Hopper	Perform 10 cover to cover transition in a row	10	Bronze
TWO heads	Complete a mission (excluding New Blood) with a human partner	10	Bronze

SECRET ACHIEVEMENTS & TROPHIES

NAME	GOAL/REQUIREMENT	POINT VALUE	TROPHY VALUE
Let's do this	Complete New Blood	10	Bronze
Now what?	Complete Cause and Effect	10	Bronze
FUBAR	Complete Rally Point	10	Bronze
From bad to worse	Complete Outside Contact	10	Bronze
Massacre in Paradise	Complete Last Resort	10	Bronze
Forgive our sins	Complete Salvation	10	Bronze
Behind enemies lines	Complete Enemy Territory	10	Bronze
Drugs are for losers	Complete Narco Hell	10	Bronze
War comes home	Complete Assault	10	Bronze
Revenge is a bitch	Complete Confrontation	10	Bronze
And now what?	Complete the Campaign	25	Silver

NAME	GOAL/REQUIREMENT	POINT VALUE	TROPHY VALUE
David vs. Goliath	Kill 10 Brutes in Physical Confrontation	10	Bronze
Party Pooper	Kill 3 targets with 1 grenade	10	Bronze
Environmentalist	Kill 3 targets or more using an explosive object in any level	10	Bronze
Backstabbing Bastard	Perform 50 Backstabs	10	Bronze
Art is not a crime	Create your own Custom Mask	10	Bronze
Michelangelo	Apply the maximum number of layers on a customized mask	10	Bronze
Demolition Derby	Destroy 50 cars	10	Bronze
Money Shot	Headshot a target while blind firing	10	Bronze
And stay down	Perform 10 melee kills on wounded targets	10	Bronze
Fashion Police	Perform 50 Hat Shots	10	Bronze
1-2-3-GO!	Players simultaneously killed 2 unaware targets	10	Bronze
First Blood	Make your first kill as a rookie (in Cause and Effect mission)	10	Bronze

ASSASSIN'S CREED III

WII U/XBOX 360/PS3

OUTFIT	REQUIREMENTS
Achilles' Original Outfit	Complete the Achilles' Painting mission.
Altaïr's Outfit	Complete all story missions with all Optional Objectives.
Baltimore Outfit	Purchased in shops at the start of Sequence 09.
Boston Outfit	Purchased in shops at the start of Sequence 06.
Captain Kidd's Outfit	Complete the Oak Island Naval Location.
Charleston Outfit	Purchased in shops at the start of Sequence 06.
Ezio Outfit	Redeem from Uplay.
Jamestown Outfit	Purchased in shops at the start of Sequence 06.
Kanienkeha:ka Outfit	Collect all Feathers.
New York Outfit	Purchased in shops at the start of Sequence 09.
Philadelphia Outfit	Purchased in shops at the start of Sequence 09.
Prisoner Outfit	Finish the prison sequence.

XBOX 360/PS3

ACHIEVEMENTS & TROPHIES

NAME	GOAL/REQUIREMENT	POINT VALUE	TROPHY VALUE
Rude Awakening	Re-Enter the Animus.	10	Bronze
No Good Deed Goes Unpunished	Open the Temple Door and learn Desmond's fate.	20	Silver
Mystery Guest	Complete Sequence 1 & 2.	20	Bronze
How D'ya Like Them Apples	Complete Sequence 3.	20	Bronze
Heroes are Born	Complete Sequence 4.	20	Bronze
The Day the Templars Cried	Complete Sequence 5.	20	Bronze
Tea is for Englishmen	Complete Sequence 6.	20	Silver

NAME	GOAL/REQUIREMENT	POINT VALUE	TROPHY VALUE
The Whites of Their Eyes	Complete Sequence 7.	20	Silver
Caged Wolf	Complete Sequence 8.	20	Bronze
Two if by Sea	Complete Sequence 9.	20	Silver
Grim Expectations	Complete Sequence 10.	20	Bronze
Difficult End	Complete Sequence 11.	20	Bronze
The Sum of Truth	Complete Sequence 12.	50	Gold
Perfectionist	Complete 100% of all main mission constraints.	50	Silver
An Extraordinary Man	Complete the Encyclopedia of the Common Man.	10	Bronze
Patent Not Pending	Craft one of Franklin's inventions to decorate your Manor.	10	Bronze
House Party	Recruit any of the Artisans and see them settled on the Homestead.	10	Bronze
A Complete Set	See all the optional characters settled at the Homestead.	20	Silver
Original Gamer	Win a game of Fanorona, Morris and Bowls on the Homestead.	20	Bronze
Bring Down the House	Explore Fort Wolcott.	20	Bronze
Kidd Gloves	Uncover the mystery of Oak Island.	30	Bronze
All Washed Up	Complete all Naval Missions aboard the Aquila.	40	Silver
Entrepreneur, not Pirate!	Complete all 12 Privateer Contracts.	20	Bronze
Tumblehome	Upgrade the Aquila.	10	Bronze
By Invitation Only	Be invited to join a Club.	20	Bronze
In Good Standing	Complete all challenges for any of the Clubs.	30	Silver
Man of the People	Liberate all districts in Boston OR New York.	20	Silver
Monopoly Man	Send a convoy to Boston, New York and the Frontier.	10	Bronze
Blowing in the Wind	Retrieve every page for one of Ben Franklin's Almanacs.	20	Bronze
Completionist	Complete ALL Progress Tracker grid entries.	50	Silver
Multitasking	Complete 50% of the Progress Tracker entries.	20	Bronze
Spit Roast	Perform a double assassination using a musket.	20	Bronze
Circus Act	Kill 15 guards with a single cannon shot.	10	Bronze
Predator	Hang 5 enemies by using rope darts.	10	Bronze
Prince of Thieves	Loot a convoy without killing any of its guards.	10	Bronze
Whit's fur ye'll no go by ye!	Block a firing line 5 times by using a human shield.	10	Bronze
Jager Bomb	After becoming fully Notorious, kill 10 Jagers before losing your notoriety.	20	Bronze
Magna cum Laude	Have a Trainee reach the Assassin Rank.	20	Bronze
Coureur des Bois	Exchange undamaged pelts at all different general stores.	10	Bronze
Eye Witness	Witness a predator killing an enemy.	10	Bronze
Fin	Complete each of the epilogue missions unlocked after the credits roll.	30	Silver

NAME	GOAL/REQUIREMENT	POINT VALUE	TROPHY VALUE
Abstergo Entertainment	Reach level 20 in the multiplayer mode.	10	Silver
Hunter/Killer	Reach Sequence 10 in a map on Wolfpack multiplayer mode.	20	Bronze
Winning Team	Be on the winning team at the end of a multiplayer game session.	20	Bronze
Personalized	Customize your multiplayer Profile and Character.	10	Bronze
The Truth Will Out	Unlock a hacked version of one of the Abstergo videos in the story quest.	20	Silver
Master Assassin	Get every trophy.	—	Platinum

SECRET ACHIEVEMENTS & TROPHIES

NAME	GOAL/REQUIREMENT	POINT VALUE	TROPHY VALUE
Daddy Dearest	Complete Present – Stadium.	20	Bronze
Criss Cross	Complete Present – Skyscraper.	20	Bronze
The End is Night	Complete Present – Abstergo.	20	Silver
Head in the Cloud	Find all pivots and sync the Animus to the Cloud.	20	Silver

BATTLE HARDENED PACK DLC

NAME	GOAL/REQUIREMENT	POINT VALUE	TROPHY VALUE
One for All	With any of the additional characters, perform 20 'Revive' actions.	25	Silver
A New Challenger Appears	Finish a multiplayer game session with each of the additional characters.	25	Silver
Stubborn Stunner	Stun 3 pursuers without dying, playing with any of the additional characters.	25	Silver
Wolves for Lambs	Complete a Wolfpack multiplayer session on any of the additional maps.	25	Silver

THE TYRANNY OF KING WASHINGTON, PART 1: INFAMY DLC

NAME	GOAL/REQUIREMENT	POINT VALUE	TROPHY VALUE
Uniquely Familiar	Receive an unexpected gift.	15	Bronze
A Wolf in Sheep's Clothing	Kill 25 enemies while staying cloaked.	15	Silver
Frontiersman	Reach 100% synchronization in the Frontier.	40	Silver

SECRET ACHIEVEMENTS & TROPHIES

NAME	GOAL/REQUIREMENT	POINT VALUE	TROPHY VALUE
West Point Payback	Defeat Benedict Arnold.	20	Silver

THE TYRANNY OF KING WASHINGTON, PART 2: BETRAYAL DLC

NAME	GOAL/REQUIREMENT	POINT VALUE	TROPHY VALUE
Frequent Flyer	Use Eagle Flight to travel 1 km.	15	Silver
The New Tea Party	Reach 100% synchronization in Boston.	40	Silver

SECRET ACHIEVEMENTS & TROPHIES

NAME	GOAL/REQUIREMENT	POINT VALUE	TROPHY VALUE
Blindsided	Defeat Putnam.	20	Silver

THE TYRANNY OF KING WASHINGTON, PART 3: REDEMPTION DLC

NAME	GOAL/REQUIREMENT	POINT VALUE	TROPHY VALUE
Aftershock	Kill 125 enemies using Bear Might.	15	Silver
If I Can Make It There	Reach 100% synchronization in New York.	40	Silver

SECRET ACHIEVEMENTS & TROPHIES

NAME	GOAL/REQUIREMENT	POINT VALUE	TROPHY VALUE
First in the Hearts	Defeat George Washington	30	Silver

ASSASSIN'S CREED: BROTHERHOOD

XBOX 360/PS3

CAPES

Select Outfits from the Inventory screen to access.

CAPE	HOW TO OBTAIN
Auditore Cape	100% Rebuilding Rome
Borgia Cape	Collect 100 Borgia Flags
Medici and Venetian Capes	Complete Auditore Trail Mnemonic in Assassin's Creed: Project Legacy

CHEATS

Select Cheats from the Options menu when replaying a memory.

CHEAT	OBTAIN 100% SYNC IN THIS SEQUENCE
Ride the Unicornç	1
Buns of Steel	2
Killing Spree	3
Sisterhood	4
Ultimate Guild	5
Unlimited Assassins Signals	6
Desmond	8

ASSASSIN'S CREED: REVELATIONS

XBOX 360/PS3

100% SYNC CHEATS

Completing the sequences with 100% sync unlocks various cheats. They can be used when replaying a memory and are accessed through the Options.

CHEAT	COMPLETE SEQUENCE WITH 100% SYNC
Buns of Steel	2
Killing Spree	3
Ultimate Guild	4
Calling All Assassins	5
Permanent Secrecy	6
Infinite Ammunition	7
The Old Eagle Outfit	8

ACHIEVEMENTS & TROPHIES

NAME	GOAL/REQUIREMENT	POINT VALUE	TROPHY VALUE
Mastering the Art	Earn the INCOGNITO bonus (Multiplayer).	30	Silver
Tools of the Templar	Purchase your first ABILITY in the Abstergo Store (Multiplayer).	10	Bronze
Achiever	Complete a Challenge (Multiplayer).	10	Bronze
True Templar	Reach level 20 (Multiplayer).	20	Silver
Looking Good	Customize a PERSONA (Multiplayer).	10	Bronze
There Is No I in Team	Win a session of a team mode (Multiplayer).	20	Bronze
Make the Headlines	Obtain 12 different Accolades (Multiplayer).	30	Silver
The Way I Like It	Edit your TEMPLAR PROFILE to change your title, emblem, and patron (Multiplayer).	20	Bronze
Explorer	Finish a session of each game mode (Multiplayer).	20	Silver
Tactician	Score at least 2500 points in a session (Multiplayer).	30	Silver
The Early Years	Complete Desmond Sequence 1.	20	Bronze
Best Served Cold	Complete DNA Sequence 1.	20	Silver
The Reluctant Assassin	Complete Desmond Sequence 2.	20	Bronze
Istanbul and Constantinople	Complete DNA Sequence 2.	20	Silver
Escape To New York	Complete Desmond Sequence 3.	20	Bronze
Seal the Deal	Complete DNA Sequence 3.	20	Silver
The Prince	Complete DNA Sequence 4.	20	Silver
The Plot Thickens	Complete DNA Sequence 5.	20	Silver
Successes and Failures	Complete DNA Sequence 6.	20	Silver
The Rotten Apple	Complete Desmond Sequence 4.	20	Bronze
Old Boss, New Boss	Complete DNA Sequence 7.	20	Silver
Priorities	Complete DNA Sequence 8.	20	Silver
Are You Desmond Miles?	Complete Desmond Sequence 5.	20	Bronze
Revelations	Complete DNA Sequence 9.	50	Gold
Fond Memories	Achieve 100% Synchronization in all Sequences.	20	Silver

NAME	GOAL/REQUIREMENT	POINT VALUE	TROPHY VALUE
Holy Wisdom	Complete the Hagia Sofia challenge level.	20	Silver
Capped	Collect all animus data fragments.	20	Bronze
Worth A Thousand Words	Collect all of Ishak Pasha's memoir pages.	20	Bronze
Pyromaniac	Complete all Bomb Missions.	20	Bronze
Armchair General	Control all cities (except Rhodes) simultaneously in the Mediterranian Defense game.	20	Bronze
Iron Curtain	Perform a perfect den defense without using the cannon.	20	Bronze
Spider Assassin	Climb Hagia Sofia, from the ground to the pinnacle, in under 25 seconds.	20	Bronze
A Friend Indeed	Complete all Faction Creed Challenges from a single faction.	20	Bronze
Tax Evasion	Get your money back from a Templar tax collector.	10	Bronze
The Mentor	Have seven trainees reach the rank of Master Assassin.	20	Silver
Lightning Strikes	Kill 5 guards in 5 seconds using only your hidden blades.	20	Bronze
Overkiller	Assassinate 50 guards with the hidden blade.	20	Bronze
Show-Off	Parachute onto a zipline.	20	Bronze
Sage	Collect all available books.	20	Bronze
Fast Fingers	Loot 50 dead guards with thief looting.	20	Bronze
Mosh Pit	Have 10 guards poisoned at the same time.	20	Bronze
Mouse Trap	Kill 5 guards with a scaffold after they have been stunned by caltrops.	20	Bronze
Craft Maniac	Craft 30 bombs.	20	Bronze
My Protégé	Have one trainee reach the rank of Master Assassin.	20	Bronze
Almost Flying	Parachute directly from the top of the Galata Tower to the golden horn.	20	Bronze
Silent But Deadly	Kill three guards simultaneously with only throwing knives.	20	Bronze
I can see you	Kill 5 guards while under the cover of a smoke screen bomb.	20	Bronze
Monster's Dance	Have a guard incapacitate 3 civilians while he's poisoned.	20	Bronze
Bully	Find and beat up Duccio.	20	Bronze

THE ANCESTORS CHARACTER PACK

ACHIEVEMENTS & TROPHIES

NAME	GOAL/REQUIREMENT	POINT VALUE	TROPHY VALUE
Stopped Dead	Obtain 3 Hidden Gun kills during a session of Steal The Artifact as The Corsair (Multiplayer).	20	Bronze
The Vulture	Perform 5 Ground Finish in Manhunt during a session as The Brigand (Multiplayer).	20	Bronze
Pirate's bravery	Use the Bodyguard against your pursuer as The Privateer (Multiplayer).	30	Silver
The Juggernaut	Perform 3 kills using the Charge as The Gladiator (Multiplayer).	20	Bronze

MEDITERRANEAN TRAVELER MAP PACK

ACHIEVEMENTS & TROPHIES

NAME	GOAL/REQUIREMENT	POINT VALUE	TROPHY VALUE
Carnival	Stay blended for 3 minutes during a Wanted session in Siena (Multiplayer).	20	Bronze
Wild Rage	Perform 3 Stuns without dying in Jerusalem (Multiplayer).	30	Silver
Restrained Violence	Obtain 5 Kill Assist bonuses during a session of any Team Mode in Dyers (Multiplayer).	20	Bronze
Straw Hat	Perform 2 kills from haystacks during a session in San Donato (Multiplayer).	30	Silver
The Spice of Life	Obtain 2 Variety bonuses during a session in Firenze (Multiplayer).	30	Silver
Up and Down	Perform 5 Leaps of Faith during a session of Assassinate in Imperial District (Multiplayer).	20	Bronze

LOST ARCHIVE

ACHIEVEMENTS & TROPHIES

NAME	GOAL/REQUIREMENT	POINT VALUE	TROPHY VALUE
Part of the Creed	Take the induction leap of faith	10	Bronze
Jump they say	Reach the Animus memo	10	Bronze
Enter the Animus	Enter the Animus simulation	10	Bronze
Meet your maker	Finish memory five	10	Bronze
Find all Pieces	Find all decipher fragments	50	Silver
Save yourself	Land on a block after falling more than 25 meters	10	Bronze
Impress Warren Vidic	Complete the Animus testing sequence without failing	50	Bronze
Cross Styx without dying	Make it across the river Styx without failing	25	Bronze

SECRET ACHIEVEMENTS

NAME	GOAL/REQUIREMENT	POINT VALUE	TROPHY VALUE
The Loop	Experience the loop	25	Silver
Breaking the Loop	Break the loop, escape the cycle	50	Silver

ASTRO BOY: THE VIDEO GAME

INVULNERABLE

Pause the game and press Up, Down, Down, Up, 1, 2.

MAX STATS

Pause the game and press Left, Left, 2, Down, Down, 1.

INFINITE SUPERS

Pause the game and press Left, 1, Right, 1, Up, Down.

INFINITE DASHES

Pause the game and press 2, 2, 1, 2, Left, Up.

DISABLE SUPERS

Pause the game and press 1, 1, 2, 2, 1, Left.

COSTUME SWAP (ARENA AND CLASSIC COSTUMES)

Pause the game and press 2, Up, 1, Up, Down, 2.

UNLOCK LEVELS

Pause the game and press Up, 1, Right, 1, Down, 1. This allows you to travel to any level from the Story menu.

INVULNERABLE

Pause the game and press Up, Down, Down, Up, L1, R.

MAX STATS

Pause the game and press Left, Left, R, Down, Down, L1.

INFINITE SUPERS

Pause the game and press Left, L1, Right, L1, Up, Down.

INFINITE DASHES

Pause the game and press R, R, L1, R, Left, Up.

DISABLE SUPERS

Pause the game and press L1, L1, R, R, L1, Left.

COSTUME SWAP (ARENA AND CLASSIC COSTUMES)

Pause the game and press R, Up, L1, Up, Down, R.

UNLOCK LEVELS

Pause the game and press Up, L1, Right, L1, Down, L1. This allows you to travel to any level from the Story menu.

ATELIER TOTORI PLUS: THE ADVENTURER OF ARLAND

COSTUME PIECES

COSTUME	REQUIREMENT
Dress Ribbon	Obtain the Normal Ending.
Medical Dress	Obtain the Normal Ending.
Nurse Cap	Obtain the Normal Ending.
Rose Ornament	Obtain the Normal Ending.

AVATAR: THE LAST AIRBENDER

UNLIMITED HEALTH

Select Code Entry from Extras and enter 94677.

UNLIMITED CHI

Select Code Entry from Extras and enter 24463.

UNLIMITED COPPER

Select Code Entry from Extras and enter 23637.

NEVERENDING STEALTH

Select Code Entry from Extras and enter 53467.

ONE-HIT DISHONOR

Select Code Entry from Extras and enter 54641.

DOUBLE DAMAGE

Select Code Entry from Extras and enter 34743.

ALL TREASURE MAPS

Select Code Entry from Extras and enter 37437.

THE CHARACTER CONCEPT ART GALLERY

Select Code Entry from Extras and enter 97831.

AVATAR: THE LAST AIRBENDER — THE BURNING EARTH

NINTENDO WII

DOUBLE DAMAGE

Go to the code entry section and enter 90210.

INFINITE LIFE

Go to the code entry section and enter 65049.

INFINITE SPECIAL ATTACKS

Go to the code entry section and enter 66206.

MAX LEVEL

Go to the code entry section and enter 89121.

ONE-HIT DISHONOR

Go to the code entry section and enter 28260.

ALL BONUS GAMES

Go to the code entry section and enter 99801.

ALL GALLERY ITEMS

Go to the code entry section and enter 85061.

XBOX 360/PS3

UNLIMITED HEALTH

Select Code Entry from the Extras menu and enter 65049.

DOUBLE DAMAGE

Select Code Entry from the Extras menu and enter 90210.

MAXIMUM LEVEL

Select Code Entry from the Extras menu and enter 89121.

UNLIMITED SPECIALS

Select Code Entry from the Extras menu and enter 66206.

ONE-HIT DISHONOR

Select Code Entry from the Extras menu and enter 28260.

ALL BONUS GAMES

Select Code Entry from the Extras menu and enter 99801.

UNLOCKS GALLERY

Select Code Entry from the Extras menu and enter 85061.

AVATAR: THE LAST AIRBENDER— INTO THE INFERNO

NINTENDO WII

After you have defeated the first level, The Awakening, go to Ember Island. Walk to the left, past the volleyball net, to a red and yellow door. Select Game Secrets and then Code Entry. Now you can enter the following cheats:

MAX COINS

Enter 66639224.

ALL ITEMS AVAILABLE FROM SHOP

Enter 34737253.

ALL CHAPTERS

Enter 52993833.

UNLOCK CONCEPT ART IN GALLERY

Enter 27858343.

BAG IT!

MOBILE

COMBOS

There are combos that get you extra rewards when bagging the groceries. Place the following items next to each other to create the combo. The characters names are as follows: Lucky is the cereal, Spilt is the milk, Sunshine is juice, Crusteau is the baguette, Chia Sister is either of the bananas, Sir Eggward is the carton of eggs, Nacho is the chips and Seedy is the watermelon.

COMBO NAME	REQUIRED ITEMS
Balanced Breakfast	Spilt + Sunshine + Lucky + Sir Eggward
Banana Split	Both Chica Sisters
Breakfast Club	Lucky (x3)
Crusty Rivals	Sir Eggward + Crusteau
Double Date	Spilt (x2) + Sunshine (x2)
Eggcelent	Sir Eggward (x4)
Fiesta of Flavor	Nacho (x6)
Milky Way	Spilt (x4)
Mutiny!	Seedy (x5)
Nice Melons	Seedy (x2)
Scallywags	Seedy (x4)
Slumber Party	Sunshine (x3)
Sweethearts	Spilt + Sunshine
Three Amigops	Nacho (x3)
Well Bread	Crusteau (x4)

BAJA: EDGE OF CONTROL

CAREER COMPLETE 100%

Select Cheat Codes from the Options menu and enter SHOWTIME.

INSTALL ALL PARTS

Select Cheat Codes from the Options menu and enter SUPERMAX.

BAKUGAN BATTLE BRAWLERS

1,000 BP

Start a new game and enter the name as 180978772269.

5,000 BP

Start a new game and enter the name as 332044292925.

10,000 BP

Start a new game and enter the name as 423482942968.

BRONZE WARIUS

Start a new game and enter the name as 449824934071.

1,000 BP

Enter 33204429 as your name.

5,000 BP

Enter 42348294 as your name.

10,000 BP

Enter 46836478 as your name.

100,000 BP

Enter 18499753 as your name.

500,000 BP

Enter 26037947 as your name.

BRONZE WARIUS

Enter 44982493 as your name.

1,000 BP

Enter 33204429 as your name.

5,000 BP

Enter 42348294 as your name.

10,000 BP

Enter 46836478 as your name.

100,000 BP

Enter 18499753 as your name.

500,000 BP

Enter 26037947 as your name.

BAKUGAN: DEFENDERS OF THE CORE

HIDDEN ITEMS

Select Unlock Codes from Collection and enter HXV6Y7BF. Now you can enter up to 8 of your unique Bakugan Dimensions codes.

The codes unlock the following:

- 10,000 Core Energy
- Ten Vexos Passes
- Earthen Armor
- Fire Spirit
- Light Arrow
- Tornado Vortex
- Water Pillar
- Zorch Thunder

Here are 8 codes:

- 2FKRRMNCDQ
- 82D77YK6P8
- HUUH8ST7AR
- JJUZDEACXX
- QY8CLD5NJE
- TD4UMFSRW3
- YJ7RGG7WGZ
- YQLHBBSMDC

BAND HERO

MOST CHARACTERS UNLOCKED

Select Input Cheats from the options and enter Blue, Yellow, Green, Yellow, Red, Green, Red, Yellow.

ELECTRIKA STEEL UNLOCKED

Select Input Cheats from the options and enter Blue, Blue, Red, Yellow, Red, Yellow, Blue, Blue.

ALL HOPO MODE

Select Input Cheats from the options and enter Red, Green, Blue, Green, Blue, Green, Red, Green.

ALWAYS SLIDE

Select Input Cheats from the options and enter Yellow, Green, Yellow, Yellow, Yellow, Red, Blue, Red.

AUTO KICK

Select Input Cheats from the options and enter Yellow, Green, Yellow, Blue, Blue, Red, Blue, Red.

FOCUS MODE

Select Input Cheats from the options and enter Yellow, Yellow, Green, Green, Red, Red, Blue, Blue.

HUD FREE MODE

Select Input Cheats from the options and enter Green, Red, Green, Red, Yellow, Blue, Green, Red.

PERFORMANCE MODE

Select Input Cheats from the options and enter Yellow, Yellow, Blue, Green, Blue, Red, Red, Red.

AIR INSTRUMENTS

Select Input Cheats from the options and enter Blue, Yellow, Blue, Red, Red, Yellow, Green, Yellow.

INVISIBLE ROCKER

Select Input Cheats from the options and enter Green, Red, Yellow, Green, Yellow, Blue, Yellow, Green.

BANJO-TOOIE

XBOX 360

REGAIN ENERGY

Go to the Code Chamber in the Mayahem Temple and access the scroll on the wall. If you have been awarded this cheat by Cheato, enter HONEYBACK. If not, enter CHEATOKCABYENOH.

FALLS DON'T HURT

Go to the Code Chamber in the Mayahem Temple and access the scroll on the wall. If you have been awarded this cheat by Cheato, enter FALLPROOF. If not, enter CHEATOFOORPLLAF.

HOMING EGGS

Go to the Code Chamber in the Mayahem Temple and access the scroll on the wall. If you have been awarded this cheat, enter HOMING. If not, enter CHEATOGNIMOH.

DOUBLES MAXIMUM EGGS

Go to the Code Chamber in the Mayahem Temple and access the scroll on the wall. If you have been awarded this cheat by Cheato, enter EGGS. If not, enter CHEATOSGGE.

DOUBLES MAXIMUM FEATHERS

Go to the Code Chamber in the Mayahem Temple and access the scroll on the wall. If you have been awarded this cheat by Cheato, enter FEATHERS. If not, enter CHEATOSREHTAEF.

JOLLY ROGER LAGOON'S JUKEBOX

Go to the Code Chamber in the Mayahem Temple and access the scroll on the wall. If you have been awarded this cheat, enter JUKEBOX. If not, enter CHEATOXOBEKUJ.

SIGNS IN JIGGYWIGGY'S TEMPLE GIVE HINTS TO GET EACH JIGGY

Go to the Code Chamber in the Mayahem Temple and access the scroll on the wall. If you have been awarded this cheat, enter GETJIGGY. If not, enter CHEATOYGGIJTEG.

ALL LEVELS

Go to the Code Chamber in the Mayahem Temple and enter JIGGYWIGGYSPECIAL.

SPEED BANJO

Go to the Code Chamber in the Mayahem Temple and enter SUPERBANJO.

SPEED ENEMIES

Go to the Code Chamber in the Mayahem Temple and enter SUPERBADDY.

INFINITE EGGS & FEATHERS

Go to the Code Chamber in the Mayahem Temple and enter NESTKING.

INFINITE HONEY

Go to the Code Chamber in the Mayahem Temple and enter HONEYKING.

BATMAN: ARKHAM CITY

PLAYSTATION 3

ALL BATMAN SKINS

This code allows you to start the campaign with all of the skins that you have downloaded, purchased, or unlocked. After selecting your save slot, press Left, Left, Down, Down, Left, Left, Right, Up, Up, Down at the main menu. You are then given the opportunity to select a skin.

BIG HEAD MODE

In the game, select the Cryptographic Sequencer. Hold L2 and then hold R2 to get Batman to use the device. Next, rotate the right analog stick clockwise while rotating the left analog stick counter-clockwise. Eventually, you notice Batman's head enlarge. Enemies and other characters' heads are also big. This works in Normal, Hard, and New Game +.

CHEATS, ACHIEVEMENTS, AND TROPHIES

B

ALL BATMAN SKINS

This code allows you to start the campaign with all of the skins that you have downloaded, purchased, or unlocked. After selecting your save slot, press Left, Left, Down, Down, Left, Left, Right, Up, Up, Down at the main menu. You are then given the opportunity to select a skin.

BIG HEAD MODE

In the game, select the Cryptographic Sequencer. Hold Left Trigger and then hold Right Trigger to use the device. Next, rotate the right Thumbstick clockwise while rotating the left Thumbstick counter-clockwise. Eventually, you notice Batman's head enlarge. Enemies and other characters' heads are also big. This works in Normal, Hard, and New Game +.

ACHIEVEMENTS & TROPHIES

NAME	GOAL/REQUIREMENT	POINT VALUE	TROPHY VALUE
I'm Batman	Become the Bat	10	Bronze
Acid Bath	Save the damsel, but is she in distress?	10	Bronze
Savior	Save the medical volunteers	10	Bronze
Chimney Sweep	There is only one way in	10	Bronze
One Armed Bandit	Hammer the point home	10	Bronze
Communication Breakdown	Clear the airwaves	10	Bronze
Gladiator	Last man standing	10	Bronze
Wrecking Ball	Stop the unstoppable	25	Silver
Lost And Found	Uncover the secret of Arkham City	10	Bronze
Sand Storm	We are legion	25	Silver
Hide And Seek	A deadly game of hide and seek	25	Silver
Ghost Train	Fight for survival	25	Silver
Freefall	Don't look down	25	Bronze
Exit Stage Right	All the world is a stage	50	Silver
Forensic Expert	Collect enough evidence to locate the gun for hire	10	Bronze
Contract Terminated	Stop the contract operative	25	Silver
Serial Killer	Track down the serial killer	25	Silver
Mystery Stalker	Reveal the mystery watcher	15	Bronze
Distress Flare	Answer the call for help	5	Bronze
Broken Toys	Destroy it all	25	Silver
Ring Ring	Answer a ringing phone	5	Bronze
Dial Z For Murder	Stop the phone booth killer	25	Silver
Stop the Clock	Time is running out	15	Bronze
Bargaining Chip	Reunite the separated couple	15	Bronze
AR Knight	Complete all augmented reality training exercises	25	Silver
Fully Loaded	Collect all of Batman's gadgets and upgrades	10	Bronze
Aggravated Assault	Stop all assaults in Arkham City	10	Bronze
IQ Test	Solve the first riddle	10	Bronze
Conundrum	Rescue the first hostage from Riddler	20	Bronze
Mastermind	Rescue the second hostage from Riddler	20	Bronze
Puzzler	Rescue the third hostage from Riddler	30	Bronze

NAME	GOAL/REQUIREMENT	POINT VALUE	TROPHY VALUE
Intellectual	Rescue the fourth hostage from Riddler	30	Bronze
Brainteaser	Rescue the fifth hostage from Riddler	40	Silver
Genius	Rescue all the hostages from Riddler	50	Silver
Bronze Revenge	Obtain 24 medals on the original Arkham City ranked maps (as Batman)	10	Bronze
Silver Revenge	Obtain 48 medals on the original Arkham City ranked maps (as Batman)	20	Bronze
Gold Revenge	Obtain all 72 medals on the original Arkham City ranked maps (as Batman)	40	Silver
Campaign Bronze	Obtain 24 medals on the original Arkham City campaigns (as Batman)	10	Bronze
Campaign Silver	Obtain 72 medals on the original Arkham City campaigns (as Batman)	20	Bronze
Campaign Gold	Obtain all 108 medals on the original Arkham City campaigns (as Batman)	40	Silver
Flawless Freeflow Fighter 2.0	Complete one combat challenge without taking damage (any character)	5	Bronze
Twice Nightly	Complete New Game Plus	75	Silver
Gotham Base Jumper	Jump off the tallest building in Arkham City and glide for 1 minute without touching the ground	5	Bronze
Pay Your Respects	A moment of remembrance	5	Bronze
Story Teller	Have 12 murderous dates with Calendar Man	10	Bronze
Catch	Find someone to play remote Batarang catch with	5	Bronze
50x Combo	Complete a combo of 50 moves (any play mode, any character)	5	Bronze
Perfect Freeflow 2.0	Perform a perfect combo including all of Batman's combat moves (any play mode)	5	Bronze
Gadget Attack	Use 5 different Quickfire gadgets in one fight (any play mode)	5	Bronze
Perfect Knight - Day 2	Main Story, Side Missions, Upgrades, Collectables, New Game Plus and Riddlers Revenge (as Batman)	75	Gold

B

CATWOMAN BUNDLE PACK
ACHIEVEMENTS & TROPHIES

NAME	GOAL/REQUIREMENT	POINT VALUE	TROPHY VALUE
Sphinx' Riddle	Complete all 40 of the Catwoman Riddler grid items	10	Bronze
Arkham City Sirens	Drop in on an old friend	25	Silver
Pick Pocket	Steal the score of a lifetime	25	Silver
Family Jewels	Retrieve your stolen goods	40	Silver
Feline Revenge	Obtain all 72 medals on the original Arkham City ranked maps (as Catwoman)	25	Bronze
Campaign Kitty	Obtain all 108 medals on the original Arkham City campaigns (as Catwoman)	25	Bronze

ROBIN BUNDLE PACK
ACHIEVEMENTS & TROPHIES

NAME	GOAL/REQUIREMENT	POINT VALUE	TROPHY VALUE
Robin Revenge	Obtain 78 medals on the original Arkham City and Robin Bundle Pack ranked maps (as Robin)	25	Bronze
Campaign Wonder	Obtain 114 medals on the original Arkham City and Robin Bundle Pack campaigns (as Robin)	25	Bronze

NIGHTWING BUNDLE PACK
ACHIEVEMENTS & TROPHIES

NAME	GOAL/REQUIREMENT	POINT VALUE	TROPHY VALUE
Nightwing Revenge	Obtain 78 medals on the original Arkham City and Nightwing Bundle Pack ranked maps (as Nightwing)	25	Bronze
Campaign Nightwing	Obtain 114 medals on the original Arkham City and Nightwing Bundle Pack campaigns (as Nightwing)	25	Bronze

HARLEY QUINN'S REVENGE
ACHIEVEMENTS & TROPHIES

NAME	GOAL/REQUIREMENT	POINT VALUE	TROPHY VALUE
Lost Property	No crimefighter should be without this	20	Bronze
Breaking and Entering	Find a way into the secret base	20	Bronze
How's It Hanging?	Clean up the Dry Docks	20	Silver
The Last Laugh	The joke's on who?	40	Silver
Frequent Flyer	Zip Kick 5 different thugs	10	Bronze
Battering Ram	Shield Bash 5 different thugs	10	Bronze
Snap To It	Snap Flash an unarmed thug, an armed thug, an environmental object and a Titan	20	Bronze
Bomb Squad	Defuse all bombs in 3 minutes or less	40	Bronze
A Few New Tricks	Use 5 different Quickfire gadgets in one fight as Robin in Harley Quinn's Revenge	20	Bronze
Party's Over	Destroy all Harley Balloons	50	Silver

BATMAN: ARKHAM CITY—
ARMORED EDITION

NINTENDO WII U

ALL BATMAN SKINS

This code allows you to start the campaign with all of the skins that you have downloaded, purchased, or unlocked. After selecting your save slot, press Left, Left, Down, Down, Left, Left, Right, Up, Up, Down at the main menu. You are then given the opportunity to select a skin.

BIG HEAD MODE

In the game, select the Cryptographic Sequencer. Hold ZL and then hold ZR to get Batman to use the device. Next, rotate the right Thumbstick clockwise while rotating the left Thumbstick counter-clockwise. Eventually, you notice Batman's head enlarge. Enemies and other characters' heads are also big. This works in Normal, Hard and New Game +.

BATMAN: THE BRAVE AND THE BOLD —
THE VIDEOGAME

NINTENDO WII/3DS

Access the terminal on the left side of the Batcave and enter the following:

BATMAN COSTUMES

COSTUME	CODE
Dark Batsuit	3756448
Medieval Batsuit	5644863
Rainbow Suit	7629863

CHALLENGE MAPS

CHALLENGE MAP	CODE
Gotham 1 & 2	4846348
Proto Sparring	6677686
Science Island 1 & 2	7262348

WEAPONS

WEAPON	CODE
Barrier	2525655
Belt Sword	2587973
Flashbangs	3527463
Smoke Pellets	7665336

BATTLE OF GIANTS: DRAGONS

NINTENDO 3DS

Select Unlock Gold Gems from the Extras Menu and enter the following passwords:

BREATH ATTACK GOLD GEMS

LEVEL	ATTACK	PASSWORD
1	NAMGILIMA	ISAM SKNF DKTD
2	NIGHHALAMA	ZNBN QOKS THGO
3	KUGDIM	AWBF CRSL HGAT
4	KUZEN	ACLC SCRS VOSK
5	SUGZAG	XSPC LLSL KJLP

CLAW ATTACK GOLD GEMS

LEVEL	ATTACK	PASSWORD
1	USUD	NAKF HLAP SDSP
2	ULUH	SAPO RLNM VUSD
3	NIGHZU	POZX MJDR GJSA
4	GHIDRU	GPGE SMEC TDTB
5	MUDRU	ABLP CGPG SGAM

HEAD ATTACK GOLD GEMS

LEVEL	ATTACK	PASSWORD
1	MEN	PQTM AONV UTNA
2	SAGHMEN	TNAP CTJS LDUF
3	KINGAL	FHSK EUFV KALP
4	DALLA	EPWB MPOR TRTA
5	AGA	GPKT BBWT SGNR

TAIL ATTACK GOLD GEMS

LEVEL	ATTACK	PASSWORD
1	AASH	LSSN GOAJ READ
2	ASH	FUTY HVNS LNVS
3	ASH SAR	LPAQ KOYH TGDS
4	AHS BALA	VLQL QELB IYDS
5	NAMTAGTAG	VLDB DDSL NCJA

BATTLE OF GIANTS: MUTANT INSECTS

NINTENDO 3DS

UNLOCK REWARDS

Select Unlock Rewards from the Options and enter the following passwords:

REWARD	PASSWORD
500 Golden Gems	SRKC RDZR KZAE
500 Golden Gems	HDTQ JCLO SSUU
750 Golden Gems	OAZN CEYQ XRDT
750 Golden Gems	FBRY CMTR KXUQ
Claw Upgrade	PLQO ILQJ YKEQ
Cyan Color	LYYD UAXR IPRT
Green Color	LCYH FVQZ XEVB
Head Upgrade	TDFS ZITF BKYE
Ice upgrade	PLAL TALG JPZV
Mutant Wasp	CHYV UEMJ QVGM
Red Color	QODI LHGH HNBN
Shock Upgrade	WLUA DZCN ZNKE
Yellow Color	TZCK AXZJ VSTW

BATTLE: LOS ANGELES

HOLLYWOOD MODE (BIG HEADS)

Complete Campaign mode on easy difficulty.

DOUBLE-PHYSICS (INCREASES EXPLOSIONS)

Complete Campaign mode on medium difficulty.

TOUGH GUYS (INCREASES ENEMY HEALTH)

Complete Campaign mode on hard difficulty.

BATTLEBLOCK THEATER

AVATAR AWARDS

AVATAR	EARNED BY
Cat Guard Mask	Complete a Featured Adventure Playlist.
Cat Guard Outfit	Beat the final Finale!
Hatty Mask	Awarded by the Cast Member Achievement.

SECRET HEADS

HEAD	REQUIREMENT
Alien Hominid Head	Install Alien Hominid HD.
Behemoth Head	Complete Furbottom's Features.
Castle Crashers Knight Head	Install Castle Crashers.
Donuts Head	Complete the first Singleplayer Furbottom's Features.
Purrham Furbottom Head	Sign-in to Furbottom's Features.
Winston Head	Complete the first Co-Op Furbottom's Features.

ACHIEVEMENTS

NAME	GOAL/REQUIREMENT	POINT VALUE
Cast Member	Complete the story's opening sequence in any mode.	5
Seasoned Performer	Complete the first four finales in any mode.	10
Virtuoso	Get an A++ in 10 levels.	15
Solo Star	Get a letter grade in every level (except Encores) in Normal Solo Story Mode.	20
Co-op Star	Get a letter grade in every level (except Encores) in Normal Co-op Story Mode.	20
Insane Solo Star	Get a letter great in every level (except Encores) in Normal Co-op Story Mode.	30
Insane Co-op Star	Get a letter grade in every level (except Encores) in insane co-op story mode.	30
Crowd Pleaser	Complete all the Encores in any mode.	15
Secret Hat Hunter	Collect 10 Golden Hats.	10
Hats Off	Get a letter grade in all eight finales in any mode.	20
The Professional	Be on the winning team in 100 arena matches.	15
All Around Joe	Be on the winning team in one arena match of every mode.	15
Nailfile Cake	Free a fellow prisoner.	5
Black Marketeer	Get yourself a cool new weapon.	5
Jail Breaker	Free 50 prisoners in the Gift Shop.	10
Social Butterfly	Collect all the prisoners of one head shape.	15
Freedom Hero	Free all the prisoners in the Gift Shop by unlocking or trading.	30

NAME	GOAL/REQUIREMENT	POINT VALUE
Armed and Dangerous	Collect all the weapons in the Gift Shop by unlocking or trading.	10
First Time Trader	Make a trade with someone.	5
Global Trader	Trade online with ten different players.	10
Deadly Performer	Get 100 kills.	10
Chicken Toucher	Play with the Behemoth or someone with this achievement in an online game.	15
Melee Master	Successfully use every melee attack move.	15
Weapons Master	Use each weapon successfully.	15
Theater Critic	Play and rate 10 user-created levels.	10
Theater Manager	Download and host a game of user-created levels.	10

SECRET ACHIEVEMENTS & TROPHIES

NAME	GOAL/REQUIREMENT	POINT VALUE
Secret Finder	Find a secret level.	10
Traitor	Kill your teammate 50 times.	5
Consolation Prize	Die enough times and we give you a prize.	10
Prison Food	Get eaten alive.	5

BATTLEFIELD 2: MODERN COMBAT

XBOX 360

ALL WEAPONS

During a game, hold Right Bumper + Left Bumper and quickly press Right, Right, Down, Up, Left, Left.

BATTLEFIELD 3

XBOX 360/PS3

ACHIEVEMENTS & TROPHIES

NAME	GOAL/REQUIREMENT	POINT VALUE	TROPHY VALUE
Not on my watch	Protect Chaffin from the soldiers in the street in Operation Swordbreaker	25	Bronze
Involuntary Euthanasia	Kill the 2 soldiers before the building falls on them in Uprising	25	Bronze
The Professional	Complete the street chase in Comrades in under 2 minutes 30 seconds without dying	30	Bronze
Army of Darkness	Shoot out the 4 lights with 4 bullets in Night Shift	30	Bronze
Practice makes perfect	Headshot each of the targets in the gun range in Kaffarov	15	Bronze
What the hell *are* you?	Take a russian Dog Tag in the forest ambush in Rock And A Hard Place	20	Bronze
Roadkill	Kick the car to kill the soldiers in Uprising	20	Bronze
You can be my wingman anytime	Complete Going Hunting in a perfect run	30	Bronze
Scrap Metal	Destroy 6 enemy tanks before reaching the fort in Thunder Run	25	Bronze

NAME	GOAL/REQUIREMENT	POINT VALUE	TROPHY VALUE
Butterfly	Take down the jet in one attempt in Rock And A Hard Place	25	Bronze
Twofor	Take down 2 enemies with 1 bullet in Night Shift	15	Bronze
Ooh-rah!	Complete the campaign story	30	Silver
Between a rock and a hard place	Beat Solomon, flawlessly, in The Great Destroyer	15	Bronze
Semper Fidelis	Complete the campaign story on Hard	50	Gold
Push On	Reach the garage without going into man-down state in Hit and Run	20	Bronze
Two-rah!	Complete all co-op missions	30	Silver
Lock 'n' Load	Unlock all unique co-op weapons	30	Silver
Car Lover	Complete the mission without losing a humvee in Operation Exodus	20	Bronze
In the nick of time	Disarm the bomb in under 20 seconds in The Eleventh Hour	20	Bronze
Bullseye	Reach and save the hostages without alerting any enemies in Drop 'em Like Liquid	20	Bronze
Untouchable	Complete the mission without using the fire extinguisher in Fire From The Sky	20	Bronze
Army of Two	Complete all co-op missions on Hard	50	Gold
Ninjas	Reach the VIP without setting off the alarm in Exfiltration	20	Bronze
Vehicle Warfare	Obtain all 3 vehicle warfare ribbons	30	Bronze
Infantry Efficiency	Obtain all 4 weapon efficiency ribbons	30	Bronze
Decorated	Obtain one of each ribbon in the game	50	Gold
It's better than nothing!	Finish as 3rd MVP in a ranked match	30	Silver
Support Efficiency	Obtain all 4 support efficiency ribbons	30	Bronze
Colonel	Achieve rank 45	50	Gold
1st Loser	Finish as 2nd MVP in a ranked match	30	Silver
Most Valuable Player	Finish as MVP in a ranked match	30	Silver
M.I.A	Obtain your first enemy Dog Tag	20	Bronze

BATTLEFIELD: BAD COMPANY

XBOX 360/PS3

M60

Select Unlocks from the Multiplayer menu, press Start, and enter try4ndrunf0rcov3r.

QBU88

Select Unlocks from the Multiplayer menu, press Start, and enter your3mynextt4rget.

UZI

Select Unlocks from the Multiplayer menu, press Start, and enter cov3r1ngthecorn3r.

FIND ALL FIVE WEAPONS

SNIPER RIFLE

You received a weapon unlock code for this gun if you pre-ordered the game.

MACHINE GUN

Receive a weapon unlock code for this gun after signing up for the newsletter at www.findallfive.com.

SUB-MACHINE GUN

Download the demo and reach rank 4 to receive an unlock code for this weapon.

ASSAULT RIFLE

Go to veteran.battlefield.com and register your previous Battlefield games to receive an unlock code for this weapon.

SEMI-AUTOMATIC SHOTGUN

Check your online stats at www.findallfive.com to get an unlock code for this weapon.

BATTLEFIELD: BAD COMPANY 2

ACHIEVEMENTS & TROPHIES

NAME	GOAL/REQUIREMENT	POINT VALUE	TROPHY VALUE
I knew we'd make it	Campaign: finish Operation Aurora	15	Bronze
Retirement just got postponed.	Campaign: finish Cold War	15	Bronze
It's bad for my karma man!	Campaign: finish Heart of Darkness	15	Bronze
They got all your intel?	Campaign: finish Upriver	15	Bronze
Salvage a vehicle.	Campaign: finish Crack the Sky	15	Bronze
Alright, here it is.	Campaign: finish Snowblind	15	Bronze
Nobody ever drowned in sweat	Campaign: finish Heavy Metal	15	Bronze
Ghost rider's here!	Campaign: finish High Value Target	15	Bronze
Sierra Foxtrot 1079	Campaign: finish Sangre del Toro	15	Bronze
Thanks for the smokes, brother!	Campaign: finish No One Gets Left Behind	15	Bronze
Save me some cheerleaders.	Campaign: finish Zero Dark Thirty	15	Bronze
Turn on a light.	Campaign: finish Force Multiplier	15	Bronze
P.S. Invasion cancelled, sir.	Campaign: finish Airborne	30	Silver
It sucks to be right.	Campaign: finish Airborne on Hard	50	Bronze
New Shiny Gun	Campaign: find 5 collectable weapons	15	Bronze
Guns Guns Guns	Campaign: find 15 collectable weapons	50	Silver
Link to the Past	Campaign: destroy 1 satellite uplink	15	Bronze
Communication Issues	Campaign: destroy 15 satellite uplinks	15	Bronze
Complete Blackout	Campaign: destroy all satellite uplinks	50	Silver
Ten Blades	Campaign: 10 melee kills	15	Bronze
Taxi!	Campaign: drive 5 km in any land vehicle	15	Bronze
Destruction	Campaign: destroy 100 objects	15	Bronze

NAME	GOAL/REQUIREMENT	POINT VALUE	TROPHY VALUE
Destruction Part 2	Campaign: destroy 1000 objects	30	Silver
Demolish	Campaign: demolish 1 house	15	Bronze
Demolish Part 2	Campaign: demolish 50 houses	30	Bronze
Assault Rifle Aggression	Campaign: 50 kills with assault rifles	15	Bronze
Sub Machine Gun Storm	Campaign: 50 kills with sub machine guns	15	Bronze
Light Machine Gun Lash Out	Campaign: 50 kills with light machine guns	15	Bronze
Sniper Rifle Strike	Campaign: 50 kills with sniper rifles	15	Bronze
Wall of Shotgun	Campaign: 50 kills with shotguns	15	Bronze
Multiplayer Knowledge	Online: reach Rank 10 (Sergeant I)	15	Bronze
Multiplayer Elite	Online: reach Rank 22 (Warrant Officer I)	50	Silver
Assault Expert	Online: unlock 3 weapons in the Assault kit	15	Bronze
Engineer Expert	Online: unlock 3 weapons in the Engineer kit	15	Bronze
Medic Expert	Online: unlock 3 weapons in the Medic kit	15	Bronze
Recon Expert	Online: unlock 3 weapons in the Recon kit	15	Bronze
Battlefield Expert	Online: obtain all unlocks in any kit or all Vehicle unlocks	50	Gold
15 Minutes of Fame	Online: play for 15 minutes	15	Bronze
Mission... Accomplished.	Online: in a round do one kill with the knife, the M60 and the RPG-7	15	Bronze
Pistol Man	Online: get 5 kills with every handgun in the game	15	Bronze
Airkill	Online: roadkill an enemy with any helicopter	15	Bronze
Et Tu, Brute?	Online: knife 5 friends	15	Bronze
Demolition Man	Online: get 20 demolish kills	15	Bronze
Careful Guidance	Online: destroy an enemy helicopter with a stationary RPG	15	Bronze
The Dentist	Online: do a headshot kill with the repair tool	15	Bronze
Won Them All	Online: win a round in all online game modes	15	Bronze
Squad Player	Online: obtain the Gold Squad Pin 5 times	30	Bronze
Combat Service Support	Online: do 10 resupplies, repairs, heals, revives and motion mine spot assists	15	Bronze
Award Aware	Online: obtain 10 unique awards	15	Bronze
Award Addicted	Online: obtain 50 unique awards	30	Silver

DOWNLOADABLE CONTENT: WEAPONS PACK 1

NAME	GOAL/REQUIREMENT	POINT VALUE	TROPHY VALUE
SPECACT Assault Elite	Get all SPECACT Assault awards	15	Bronze
SPECACT Engineer Elite	Get all SPECACT Engineer awards	15	Bronze
SPECACT Medic Elite	Get all SPECACT Medic awards	15	Bronze
SPECACT Recon Elite	Get all SPECACT Recon awards	15	Bronze

DOWNLOADABLE CONTENT: ONSLAUGHT

NAME	GOAL/REQUIREMENT	POINT VALUE	TROPHY VALUE
Valpariso Conquered	Successfully complete Valpariso in Onslaught mode on any difficulty	10	Bronze
Valpariso Veteran	Successfully complete Valpariso in Onslaught mode on Hardcore difficulty	20	Silver
Isla Inocentes Conquered	Successfully complete Isla Inocentes in Onslaught mode on any difficulty	10	Bronze
Isla Inocentes Veteran	Successfully complete Isla Inocentes in Onslaught mode on Hardcore difficulty	20	Silver
Atacama Desert Conquered	Successfully complete Atacama Desert in Onslaught mode on any difficulty	10	Bronze
Atacama Desert Veteran	Successfully complete Atacama Desert in Onslaught mode on Hardcore difficulty	20	Silver
Nelson Bay Conquered	Successfully complete Nelson Bay in Onslaught mode on any difficulty	10	Bronze
Nelson Bay Veteran	Successfully complete Nelson Bay in Onslaught mode on Hardcore difficulty	20	Silver

BATTLESHIP CRAFT

MOBILE

MIKASA

Go to options, select Code, and enter JMSDF.

BAYONETTA

PLAYSTATION 3

In Chapter 2 after Verse 3, find the phones in the plaza area. Stand in front of the appropriate phone and enter the following codes. The left phone is used for Weapons, the right phone is for Accessories, and the far phone is for Characters.

These codes require a certain amount of halos to be used. You will lose these halos immediately after entering the code.

WEAPONS

BAZILLIONS

Required Halos: 1 Million

Up, Up, Up, Up, Down, Down, Down, Down, Left, Right, Left, Right, ●

PILLOW TALK

Required Halos: 1 Million

Up, Up, Up, Up, Down, Down, Down, Down, Left, Right, Left, Right, ✖

RODIN

Required Halos: 5 Million

Up, Up, Up, Up, Down, Down, Down, Down, Left, Right, Left, Right, L1

ACCESSORIES

BANGLE OF TIME

Required Halos: 3 Million

Up, Up, Up, Up, Down, Down, Down, Down, Left, Right, Left, Right, L2

CLIMAX BRACELET

Required Halos: 5 Million

Up, Up, Up, Up, Down, Down, Down, Down, Left, Right, Left, Right, R2

ETERNAL TESTIMONY

Required Halos: 2 Million

Up, Up, Up, Up, Down, Down, Down, Down, Left, Right, Left, Right, R1

CHARACTERS

JEANNE

Required Halos: 1 Million

Up, Up, Up, Up, Down, Down, Down, Down, Left, Right, Left, Right, ●

LITTLE ZERO

Required Halos: 5 Million

Up, Up, Up, Up, Down, Down, Down, Down, Left, Right, Left, Right, ●

XBOX 360

In Chapter 2, after Verse 3, find the phones in the plaza area. Stand in front of the appropriate phone and enter the following codes. The left phone is used for Weapons, the right phone is for Accessories, and the far phone is for Characters.

These codes require a certain amount of halos to be used. You will lose these halos immediately after entering the code.

WEAPONS

BAZILLIONS

Required Halos: 1 Million

Up, Up, Up, Up, Down, Down, Down, Down, Left, Right, Left, Right, Y

PILLOW TALK

Required Halos: 1 Million

Up, Up, Up, Up, Down, Down, Down, Down, Left, Right, Left, Right, A

RODIN

Required Halos: 5 Million

Up, Up, Up, Up, Down, Down, Down, Down, Left, Right, Left, Right, Left Bumper

ACCESSORIES

BANGLE OF TIME

Required Halos: 3 Million

Up, Up, Up, Up, Down, Down, Down, Down, Left, Right, Left, Right, Left Trigger

CLIMAX BRACELET

Required Halos: 5 Million

Up, Up, Up, Up, Down, Down, Down, Down, Left, Right, Left, Right, Right Trigger

ETERNAL TESTIMONY

Required Halos: 2 Million

Up, Up, Up, Up, Down, Down, Down, Down, Left, Right, Left, Right, Right Bumper

CHARACTERS

JEANNE

Required Halos: 1 Million

Up, Up, Up, Up, Down, Down, Down, Down, Left, Right, Left, Right, B

LITTLE ZERO

Required Halos: 5 Million

Up, Up, Up, Up, Down, Down, Down, Down, Left, Right, Left, Right, X

BEJEWELED 3

PLAYSTATION 3

BUTTERFLIES MODE

Reach Level 5 in Zen Mode.

DIAMOND MINE MODE

In Quest Mode, unlock the second relic by completing four challenges of the first.

ICE STORM MODE

Score over 100,000 points in Lightning Mode.

POKER MODE

Reach Level 5 in Classic Mode.

BEN 10: ALIEN FORCE: THE GAME

PSP

LEVEL LORD

Enter Gwen, Kevin, Big Chill, Gwen as a code.

INVINCIBILITY

Enter Kevin, Big Chill, Swampfire, Kevin as a code.

ALL COMBOS

Enter Swampfire, Gwen, Kevin, Ben as a code.

INFINITE ALIENS

Enter Ben, Swampfire, Gwen, Big Chill as a code.

BEN 10: ALIEN FORCE VILGAX ATTACKS

NINTENDO WII/XBOX 360/PSP

LEVEL SKIP

Pause the game and enter Portal in the Cheats menu.

UNLOCK ALL SPECIAL ATTACKS (ALL FORMS)

Pause the game and enter Everythingproof in the Cheats menu.

UNLOCK ALL ALIEN FORMS

Pause the game and enter Primus in the Cheats menu.

TOGGLE INVULNERABILITY ON AND OFF

Pause the game and enter XImrsmoothy in the Cheats menu.

FULL HEALTH

Pause the game and enter Herotime in the Cheats menu.

QUICK ENERGY REGENERATION

Pause the game and enter Generator in the Cheats menu. Pause the game and enter Generator in the Cheats menu.

BEN 10: GALACTIC RACING

PLAYSTATION VITA

KINECELERATOR KART

Enter the code Ben, Spidermonkey, Kevin, Ultimate Echo Echo.

BEN 10: OMNIVERSE

NINTENDO 3DS/WII/WII U/XBOX 360/PS3

UPGRADE CODES

In the Extras menu select Promotions and then select the alien images to upgrade XLR8, Gravattack and Wildvine.

UPGRADE	CODE
Gravattack	Feedback—Fourarms—Diamondhead—Bloxx
Wildvine	Gravattack—Eye Guy—Arctiguana—Wildmutt
XLR8	XLR8—Shocksquatch—Gravattack—Arctiguana—Diamondhead

ACHIEVEMENTS & TROPHIES

NAME	GOAL/REQUIREMENT	POINT VALUE	TROPHY VALUE
Smoothie Operator	Collected all Smoothie power-ups.	70	Gold
Codon Collector	Collected all Codon Crystal power-ups.	70	Gold
Omnitrix To The Max	Fully upgraded all of Ben's alien forms.	100	Gold
Plumber Power	Fully upgraded all of Rook's Proto-Tool functions.	60	Silver
Open Season	Opened 75 Tech Repositories over the course of the game.	40	Bronze
Focused Destruction	Destroyed 8 crates in a single attack.	30	Bronze
Mass Destruction	Destroyed 150 crates in the game.	45	Gold
15-Hitter	Performed a 15-hit combo.	10	Bronze
25-Hitter	Performed a 25-hit combo.	15	Bronze
35-Hitter	Performed a 35-hit combo.	20	Silver
Up In The Air	Defeated 30 enemies while they were in the air.	30	Bronze
Human Power	Defeated 20 enemies as Young Ben or Teen Ben (not in alien form).	10	Bronze
Omni What?	Defeated 30 enemies as Young Ben or Teen Ben (not in alien form).	20	Bronze
Look, Grandpa—No Aliens!	Defeated 50 enemies as Young Ben or Teen Ben (not in alien form).	30	Silver
Feedback Frenzy	Defeated 50 enemies as Feedback.	20	Bronze
Think Fast	Defeated 50 enemies as XLR8.	20	Bronze
The Eyes Have It	Defeated 50 enemies as Eye Guy.	10	Bronze
Shockingly Effective	Defeated 50 enemies as Shocksquatch.	10	Bronze
Gravattackitics	Defeated 50 enemies as Gravattack.	10	Bronze
Battle Bloxx	Defeated 50 enemies as Bloxx.	15	Bronze
Four Times The Fun	Defeated 50 enemies as Four Arms.	10	Bronze
Cannon Fodder	Defeated 50 enemies as Cannonbolt.	15	Bronze
Diamond In The Rough	Defeated 50 enemies as Diamondhead.	10	Bronze
Branching Out	Defeated 50 enemies as Wildvine.	15	Bronze
Heated Exchange	Defeated 50 enemies as Heatblast.	10	Bronze
Goin' Mutts	Defeated 50 enemies as Wild Mutt.	10	Bronze
Just Chillin'	Defeated 50 enemies as Arctiguana.	10	Bronze
Not A Scratch	Completed an entire level without being defeated and reset.	25	Bronze
It's Hero Time	Completed the entire game on Hero difficulty.	50	Bronze

CHEATS, ACHIEVEMENTS, AND TROPHIES

B

SECRET ACHIEVEMENTS & TROPHIES

NAME	GOAL/REQUIREMENT	POINT VALUE	TROPHY VALUE
Training Time	Completed the training simulation… and wrecked the timeline.	10	Bronze
The Galvanic Butterfly Effect	Escaped from Malware… for now.	10	Bronze
Future Malformed	Defeated Mucilator.	10	Bronze
Technical Difficulties	Took out Psyphon and rescued Blukic and Driba.	10	Bronze
Past Due	Defeated the Queen Ant and rescued Grandpa Max.	10	Bronze
Extreme Earth Makeover	Discovered the morphic generator.	10	Bronze
That Was Then…	Planted the explosives in the past.	10	Bronze
…This Is Now	Set off the explosives in the present.	10	Bronze
Weird Scientist	Stole Animo's tech and lured Malware to the cavern.	10	Bronze
Plumb Crazy	Lured Malware into the Plumber Training Room.	10	Bronze
Two Malwares… No Waiting	Defeated both Malwares and fixed the timeline.	20	Bronze
Muttin' To It	Unlocked Wildmutt.	15	Bronze
Have A Ball	Unlocked Cannonbolt.	15	Bronze
Constructive Feedback	Unlocked Feedback.	15	Bronze
Heavy Duty	Unlocked Gravattack.	15	Bronze
Building Bloxx	Unlocked Bloxx.	15	Bronze
Super Cool	Unlocked Artiguana.	15	Bronze

BEN 10: PROTECTOR OF EARTH

NINTENDO 3DS

GALACTIC ENFORCER SKINS
At the level select, press A, B, X, Y, L, R, SELECT.

GWEN 10 SKINS
At the level select, press Left, Right, Left, Right, L, R, SELECT.

ULTRA BEN SKINS
At the level select, press Up, Right, Down, Left, A, B, SELECT.

UPCHUCK
At the level select, press A, Left, Y, Right, X, Up, B, Down, SELECT.

BONUS MISSION
At the level select, press Left, L, Right, R, Up, Down, SELECT.

NINTENDO WII

INVINCIBILITY
Select a game from the Continue option. Go to the Map Selection screen, press Plus and choose Extras. Select Enter Secret Code and enter XLR8, Heatblast, Wildvine, Fourarms.

ALL COMBOS
Select a game from the Continue option. Go to the Map Selection screen, press Plus and choose Extras. Select Enter Secret Code and enter Cannonblot, Heatblast, Fourarms, Heatblast.

ALL LOCATIONS
Select a game from the Continue option. Go to the Map Selection screen, press Plus and choose Extras. Select Enter Secret Code and enter Heatblast, XLR8, XLR8, Cannonblot.

DNA FORCE SKINS

Select a game from the Continue option. Go to the Map Selection screen, press Plus and choose Extras. Select Enter Secret Code and enter Wildvine, Fourarms, Heatblast, Cannonbolt.

DARK HEROES SKINS

Select a game from the Continue option. Go to the Map Selection screen, press Plus and choose Extras. Select Enter Secret Code and enter Cannonbolt, Cannonbolt, Fourarms, Heatblast.

ALL ALIEN FORMS

Select a game from the Continue option. Go to the Map Selection screen, press Plus and choose Extras. Select Enter Secret Code and enter Wildvine, Fourarms, Heatblast, Wildvine.

MASTER CONTROL

Select a game from the Continue option. Go to the Map Selection screen, press Plus and choose Extras. Select Enter Secret Code and enter Cannonbolt, Heatblast, Wildvine, Fourarms.

PSP

INVINCIBILITY

Select a game from the Continue option. Go to the Map Selection screen, press Start and choose Extras. Select Enter Secret Code and enter XLR8, Heatblast, Wildvine, Fourarms.

ALL COMBOS

Select a game from the Continue option. Go to the Map Selection screen, press Start and choose Extras. Select Enter Secret Code and enter Cannonblot, Heatblast, Fourarms, Heatblast.

ALL LOCATIONS

Select a game from the Continue option. Go to the Map Selection screen, press Start and choose Extras. Select Enter Secret Code and enter Heatblast, XLR8, XLR8, Cannonblot.

DNA FORCE SKINS

Select a game from the Continue option. Go to the Map Selection screen, press Start and choose Extras. Select Enter Secret Code and enter Wildvine, Fourarms, Heatblast, Cannonbolt.

DARK HEROES SKINS

Select a game from the Continue option. Go to the Map Selection screen, press Start and choose Extras. Select Enter Secret Code and enter Cannonbolt, Cannonbolt, Fourarms, Heatblast.

ALL ALIEN FORMS

Select a game from the Continue option. Go to the Map Selection screen, press Start and choose Extras. Select Enter Secret Code and enter Wildvine, Fourarms, Heatblast, Wildvine.

MASTER CONTROL

Select a game from the Continue option. Go to the Map Selection screen, press Start and choose Extras. Select Enter Secret Code and enter Cannonbolt, Heatblast, Wildvine, Fourarms.

CHEATS, ACHIEVEMENTS, AND TROPHIES

B

BEN 10 ULTIMATE ALIEN: COSMIC DESTRUCTION

To remove the following cheats, you must start a new game.

1,000,000 DNA

Pause the game, select Cheats, and enter Cash.

REGENERATE HEALTH

Pause the game, select Cheats, and enter Health.

REGENERATE ENERGY

Pause the game, select Cheats, and enter Energy.

UPGRADE EVERYTHING

Pause the game, select Cheats, and enter Upgrade.

ALL LEVELS

Pause the game, select Cheats, and enter Levels.

DAMAGE

Pause the game, select Cheats, and enter Hard. With this code, enemies cause double damage while you cause half damage.

Note that these cheats will disable Trophies! To remove the cheats, you will need to start a new game.

1,000,000 DNA

Pause the game, select Cheats, and enter Cash.

REGENERATE HEALTH

Pause the game, select Cheats, and enter Health.

REGENERATE ENERGY

Pause the game, select Cheats, and enter Energy.

UPGRADE EVERYTHING

Pause the game, select Cheats, and enter Upgrade.

ALL LEVELS

Pause the game, select Cheats, and enter Levels.

DAMAGE

Pause the game, select Cheats, and enter Hard. When entered, the enemies cause double damage while the player inflicts about half damage.

UNLOCK FOUR ARMS

Pause the game, select Cheats, and enter Classic.

To remove these cheats, you must start a new game.

1,000,000 DNA

Pause the game, select Cheats, and enter Cash.

REGENERATE HEALTH

Pause the game, select Cheats, and enter Health.

REGENERATE ENERGY

Pause the game, select Cheats, and enter Energy.

UPGRADE EVERYTHING

Pause the game, select Cheats, and enter Upgrade.

ALL LEVELS

Pause the game, select Cheats, and enter Levels.

DAMAGE

Pause the game, select Cheats, and enter Hard. Enemies cause double the damage, while you inflict half damage.

START A ROOKIE WITH HIGHER STATS

When you create a rookie, name him HOT DOG. His stats will be higher than when you normally start.

THE BINDING OF ISAAC

UNLOCKABLE CHARACTERS

CHARACTER	REQUIREMENT
???	Defeat It Lives (complete the game 10 times)
Cain	Collect all 55 coins in one playthrough
Eve	Make two deals with the devil in one playthrough
Judas	Complete the second playthrough
Magdalene	Have seven heart containers in one playthrough
Samson	Defeat Mom and skip two treasure chest rooms (Wrath of the Lamb DLC only)

CHEAT CODES

First, enable the console by going to the directory "C:\Users\(**your user name here**)\ Documents\My Games\Runic Games\Torchlight 2\save\(**save number**) (the number differs from person to person but it will be a string of numbers. Open that folder and then open "settings.txt" in Notepad. Change "Console:0" to "Console:1". Once in the game, press Insert and enter these codes to enable cheats.

EFFECT	CODE
Add a friend by their Torchlight 2 username or email address.	ADDFRIENDBYUSER
Toggle monster AI on and off.	AIFREEZE
Spawn all items.	ALLITEMS
Give all stats (depending on the number entered).	ALLSTATS (number)
Every attack will be a critical hit.	ALWAYSCRIT
Move down a floor.	ASCEND
Clear Console History.	CLS
Give defense points.	DEFENSE (number)
Move up a floor.	DESCEND
Give ranged points.	DEXTERITY (number)
Display the current game difficulty.	DIFFICULTY
Disable your pet.	DISABLEPET
Give fame points.	FAME (number)
Show frame rate.	FPS
Turn on God Mode (Invincibility).	GOD
Turn on God Mode and Speed Mode.	GODSPEED
Show list of commands.	HELP
Decreases your health by the specified percentage.	HURTME (percentage)
Identifies all items in your inventory.	IDENTIFYALL
Gives an item and the specified number of an item.	ITEM (Item Name), (count)
Kill all monsters.	KILLALL
Increase XP to the next level.	LEVELUP
Gives magic points.	MAGIC (number)

EFFECT	CODE
Gives gold.	MONEY (number)
You won't gain XP.	NOXP
Makes monsters not target the player.	PLAYERNOTTARGET
Complete a specified Quest.	QUESTCOMPLETE (questname)
Reset pet level to 1.	RESETPETLEVEL
Reset your stats, skills and level.	RESETPLAYER
Reset your level to 1.	RESETPLAYERLEVEL
Reset your skills.	RESETSKILL
Reset your stat points.	RESETSTATS
Restart the current level.	RESTARTLEVEL
Set the current difficulty.	SETDIFFICULTY (difficulty)
Set your pet's level.	SETPETLEVEL (level)
Set the time of day.	SETTIME (time)
Set the timescale for time of day.	SETTIMESCALE (number)
Gives skill points.	SKILLPOINTS (number)
Toggle blood.	SHOWBLOOD
Toggles player speed.	SPEED
Gives stat points.	STATPOINTS (number)
Gives melee points.	STRENGTH (number)

BIONIC COMMANDO REARMED

PLAYSTATION 3

The following challenge rooms can be found in the Challenge Room list. Only one code can be active at a time.

AARON SEDILLO'S CHALLENGE ROOM (CONTEST WINNER)

At the Title screen, Right, Down, Left, Up, L1, R1, ●, ●, ⊗, ⊗, Start.

EUROGAMER CHALLENGE ROOM

At the Title screen, press Down, Up, Down, Up, Left, L1, ●, L1, ●, ●, Start.

GAMESRADAR CHALLENGE ROOM

At the Title screen, R1, ●, ●, ●, Up, Down, L1, L1, Up, Down, Start.

IGN CHALLENGE ROOM

At the Title screen, Up, Down, ●, ●, ●, ●, Down, Up, L1, L1, Start.

XBOX 360

The following challenge rooms can be found in the Challenge Room list. Only one code can be active at a time.

AARON SEDILLO'S CHALLENGE ROOM (CONTEST WINNER)

At the Title screen, press Right, Down, Left, Up, Left Bumper, Right Bumper, Y, Y, X, X, Start.

EUROGAMER CHALLENGE ROOM

At the Title screen, press Down, Up, Down, Up, Left, Left Bumper, X, Left Bumper, X, Y, Start.

GAMESRADAR CHALLENGE ROOM

At the Title screen, press Right Bumper, Y, X, X, Up, Down, Left Bumper, Left Bumper, Up, Down, Start.

IGN CHALLENGE ROOM

At the Title screen, press Up, Down, Y, X, X, Y, Down, Up, Left Bumper, Left Bumper, Start.

MAJOR NELSON CHALLENGE ROOM

At the Title screen, press Left Bumper, X, X, X, Right, Down, Left Bumper, Left, Y, Down, Start.

BIOSHOCK 2

XBOX 360/PS3

ACHIEVEMENTS & TROPHIES

NAME	GOAL/REQUIREMENT	POINT VALUE	TROPHY VALUE
Bought a Slot	Buy one Plasmid or Tonic Slot at a Gatherer's Garden.	5	Bronze
Max Plasmid Slots	Fully upgrade to the maximum number of Plasmid Slots.	10	Bronze
Upgraded a Weapon	Upgrade any weapon at a Power to the People Station.	10	Bronze
Fully Upgraded a Weapon	Install the third and final upgrade to any of your weapons.	10	Bronze
All Weapon Upgrades	Find all 14 Power to the People weapon upgrades in the game.	20	Bronze
Prolific Hacker	Successfully hack at least one of every type of machine.	20	Bronze
Master Hacker	Hack 30 machines at a distance with the Hack Tool.	20	Bronze
First Research	Research a Splicer with the Research Camera.	5	Bronze
One Research Track	Max out one Research Track.	20	Bronze
Research Master	Max out research on all 9 research subjects.	20	Bronze
Grand Daddy	Defeat 3 Big Daddies without dying during the fight.	25	Silver
Master Gatherer	Gather 600 ADAM with Little Sisters.	30	Silver
Fully Upgraded a Plasmid	Fully upgrade one of your Plasmids to the level 3 version at a Gatherer's Garden.	10	Bronze
All Plasmids	Find or purchase all 11 basic Plasmid types.	20	Bronze
Trap Master	Kill 30 enemies using only Traps.	15	Bronze
Master Protector	Get through a Gather with no damage and no one getting to the Little Sister.	15	Bronze
Big Spender	Spend 2000 dollars at Vending Machines.	15	Bronze
Dealt with Every Little Sister	Either Harvest or Save every Little Sister in the game.	50	Silver
Against All Odds	Finish the game on the hardest difficulty level.	30	Bronze
Big Brass Balls	Finish the game without using Vita-Chambers.	25	Silver
Rapture Historian	Find 100 audio diaries.	40	Silver
Unnatural Selection	Score your first kill in a non-private match.	10	Bronze
Welcome to Rapture	Complete your first non-private match.	10	Bronze
Disgusting Frankenstein	Become a Big Daddy for the first time in a non-private match.	10	Bronze
"Mr. Bubbles-- No!"	Take down your first Big Daddy in a non-private match.	20	Bronze
Mother Goose	Save your first Little Sister in a non-private match.	20	Bronze
Two-Bit Heroics	Complete your first trial in a non-private match.	10	Bronze
Parasite	Achieve Rank 10.	10	Bronze
Little Moth	Achieve Rank 20.	20	Bronze
Skin Job	Achieve Rank 30.	20	Bronze

CHEATS, ACHIEVEMENTS, AND TROPHIES

NAME	GOAL/REQUIREMENT	POINT VALUE	TROPHY VALUE
Choose the Impossible	Achieve Rank 40.	50	Gold
Proving Grounds	Win your first non-private match.	20	Silver
Man About Town	Play at least one non-private match on each multiplayer map.	10	Bronze

SECRET ACHIEVEMENTS & TROPHIES

NAME	GOAL/REQUIREMENT	POINT VALUE	TROPHY VALUE
Daddy's Home	Found your way back into the ruins of Rapture.	10	Bronze
Protector	Defended yourself against Lamb's assault in the train station.	20	Bronze
Sinclair's Solution	Joined forces with Sinclair in Ryan Amusements.	20	Bronze
Confronted Grace	Confronted Lamb's lieutenant in Pauper's Drop.	10	Bronze
Defeated the Preacher	Defeated the Preacher.	20	Bronze
Nose for News	Uncovered the secret of Dionysus Park.	20	Bronze
Found Lamb's Hideout	Gained access to Lamb's stronghold.	20	Bronze
Reunion	Reunited with your original Little Sister.	50	Silver
Heading to the Surface	Headed to the surface on the side of Sinclair's escape pod.	25	Bronze
Escape	Escaped Rapture.	100	Gold
9-Irony	Paid your respects to the founder of Rapture.	5	Bronze
Distance Hacker	Used the Hack Tool to hack an object at a distance.	5	Bronze
Unbreakable	Defended yourself against the Big Sister without dying.	20	Bronze
Look at You, Hacker	Killed 50 enemies using only hacked Security.	15	Bronze
Adopted a Little Sister	Adopted a new Little Sister for the first time.	5	Bronze
Savior	Saved every Little Sister and spared Grace, Stanley and Gil.	25	Silver
Counterattack	Killed an enemy with its own projectile.	5	Bronze

DOWNLOADABLE CONTENT: RAPTURE METRO PACK

NAME	GOAL/REQUIREMENT	POINT VALUE	TROPHY VALUE
Aqua Incognita	Play at least one non-private match on each downloadable content map.	25	Silver
Territorial	Win a non-private match in each of the 6 new maps.	25	Silver
Reincarnation	Use Rebirth to start again!	100	Gold

DOWNLOADABLE CONTENT: THE PROTECTOR TRIALS

NAME	GOAL/REQUIREMENT	POINT VALUE	TROPHY VALUE
Litmus Test	Earn 6 stars in the Protector Trials	5	Bronze
Acid Test	Earn 18 stars in the Protector Trial	10	Bronze
Trial By Fire	Earn 36 stars in the Protector Trials	15	Silver

NAME	GOAL/REQUIREMENT	POINT VALUE	TROPHY VALUE
Enemy of the Family	Earn an A rank in all Protector Trials	15	Silver
Perfect Protector	Collect 100% of the ADAM in a single Protector Trial	20	Silver
Get a Bigger Bucket	Collect 50% of the ADAM available in all Protector Trials	25	Silver

SECRET ACHIEVEMENTS & TROPHIES

NAME	GOAL/REQUIREMENT	POINT VALUE	TROPHY VALUE
Guardian Angel	Completed all bonus Protector Trials.	10	Silver

DOWNLOADABLE CONTENT: MINERVA'S DEN

NAME	GOAL/REQUIREMENT	POINT VALUE	TROPHY VALUE
Garbage Collection	Destroy all 10 Vacuum Bots in Minerva's Den	10	Bronze
Lancer Killer	Kill a Lancer Big Daddy	10	Bronze
ADAM Addict	Resolve all the Little Sisters in Minerva's Den	10	Bronze

SECRET ACHIEVEMENTS & TROPHIES

NAME	GOAL/REQUIREMENT	POINT VALUE
Login	Reached Rapture Central Computing Operations	20
Root Access Granted	Reached Computer Core Access	20
Logout	Escaped Minerva's Den	50
SUDO	Wrested control of the Thinker from Reed Wahl	20
High Score	Get 9999 points in a single game of spitfire	10

BIOSHOCK INFINITE

PLAYSTATION 3

UNLOCK 1999 MODE EARLY

At the Title Screen, enter Up, Up, Down, Down, Left, Right, Left, Right, O, X to unlock 1999 Mode immediately.

XBOX 360

UNLOCK 1999 MODE EARLY

At the Title Screen, enter Up, Up, Down, Down, Left, Right, Left, Right, B, A to unlock 1999 Mode immediately.

XBOX 360/PS3

ACHIEVEMENTS & TROPHIES

NAME	GOAL/REQUIREMENT	POINT VALUE	TROPHY VALUE
Tin Soldier	Completed the game on Easy difficulty or above.	10	Bronze
Saw the Elephant	Completed the game on Normal difficulty or above.	25	Bronze
Stone Cold Pinkerton	Completed the game on Hard difficulty or above.	50	Silver
Auld Lang Syne	Completed the game on 1999 mode.	75	Silver
Should Auld Acquaintance…	Unlocked 1999 mode.	10	Bronze

NAME	GOAL/REQUIREMENT	POINT VALUE	TROPHY VALUE
Industrial Accident	Killed 20 enemies with a Sky-Hook Execution.	5	Bronze
Aerial Assassin	Killed 20 enemies with a Sky-Line Strike.	5	Bronze
A Real Pistol	Killed 25 enemies with the Broadsider Pistol.	5	Bronze
Passionately Reciprocated	Killed 150 enemies with the Founder Triple R Machine Gun or Vox Repeater.	5	Bronze
Street Sweeper	Killed 50 enemies with the Founder China Broom Shotgun or Vox Heater.	5	Bronze
Big Game Hunter	Killed 100 enemies with the Founder Huntsman Carbine or Vox Burstgun.	5	Bronze
Loose Cannon	Killed 25 enemies with the Paddywhacker Hand Cannon.	5	Bronze
On a Clear Day…	Killed 30 enemies with the Bird's Eye Sniper Rifle.	5	Bronze
Here Little Piggy	Killed 30 enemies with the Founder Pig Volley Gun or Vox Hail Fire.	5	Bronze
Master of Pyrotechnics	Killed 20 enemies with the Barnstormer RPG.	5	Bronze
Seasoned to Taste	Killed 30 enemies with the Peppermill Crank Gun.	5	Bronze
Well Rounded	Used all 8 Vigors against enemies.	10	Bronze
Vigorous Opposition	Killed 75 enemies either with a Vigor or while the enemy is under the effects of a Vigor.	50	Bronze
More for Your Money	Lured 3 enemies into a single Vigor trap 5 times.	25	Silver
Combination Shock	Performed all 8 of the Vigor combinations.	50	Silver
Mind Over Matter	Killed 20 enemies using Possessed machines.	10	Silver
Tear 'em a New One	Opened 30 Tears.	25	Bronze
Strange Bedfellows	Killed 20 enemies using allies brought in through a Tear.	10	Silver
On the Fly	Killed 30 enemies while riding a Sky-Line.	10	Bronze
Bolt From the Blue	Killed 5 enemies with a headshot while riding a Sky-Line.	25	Silver
Hazard Pay	Killed 10 enemies by utilizing environmental hazards.	25	Silver
Bon Voyage	Killed 20 enemies by knocking them off Columbia.	25	Silver
Skeet Shoot	Killed 5 enemies while they are falling.	25	Silver
Lost Weekend	Killed 5 enemies while you are drunk.	10	Silver
David & Goliath	Killed 20 "Heavy Hitter" enemies.	10	Bronze
Heartbreaker	Killed a Handyman by only shooting his heart.	50	Bronze
Dress for Success	Equipped a piece of Gear in all four slots.	5	Silver
Kitted Out	Fully upgraded one weapon and one Vigor.	10	Bronze
Raising the Bar	Upgraded one attribute (Health, Shield, or Salts) to its maximum level.	10	Bronze
Infused with Greatness	Collected every Infusion upgrade in a single game.	25	Bronze

NAME	GOAL/REQUIREMENT	POINT VALUE	TROPHY VALUE
Sightseer	Used all telescopes and Kinetoscopes in the game.	50	Bronze
The Roguish Type	Used Elizabeth to pick 30 locks.	25	Silver
Eavesdropper	Collected every Voxophone.	50	Silver
Grand Largesse	Spent $10,000 at the vending machines of Columbia.	10	Bronze
Coins in the Cushion	Looted 200 containers.	10	Silver
Scavenger Hunt	Completed the game in 1999 mode without purchasing anything from a Dollar Bill vending machine.	75	Gold
Platinum Columbia	Acquire all other trophies.	—	Platinum

SECRET ACHIEVEMENTS & TROPHIES

NAME	GOAL/REQUIREMENT	POINT VALUE	TROPHY VALUE
Written in the Clouds	Completed Lighthouse.	5	Bronze
Welcome to Monument Island	Reached Monument Island.	10	Bronze
Shock Tactics	Retrieved Shock Jockey.	10	Bronze
First Class Ticket	Boarded The First Lady.	10	Bronze
Armed Revolt	Assisted the Gunsmith.	10	Bronze
Working Class Hero	Completed Factory.	25	Bronze
Blood in the Streets	Completed Emporia.	25	Bronze
Higher Learning	Completed Comstock House.	25	Bronze
The Bird or The Cage	Completed The Hand of the Prophet.	25	Bronze

BIT.TRIP PRESENTS RUNNER 2: FUTURE LEGEND OF RHYTHM ALIEN

XBOX 360/PS3

ACHIEVEMENTS & TROPHIES

NAME	GOAL/REQUIREMENT	POINT VALUE	TROPHY VALUE
First Steps	Completed 10 Rewards.	10	—
On Your Way	Completed 20 Rewards.	10	—
Jogging Along	Completed 30 Rewards.	10	Bronze
Going Somewhere	Completed 40 Rewards.	15	—
Sir Trots-A-Lot	Completed 50 Rewards.	15	—
Running Steady	Completed 60 Rewards.	15	Bronze
Good Stride	Completed 70 Rewards.	20	—
Sprint!!	Completed 80 Rewards.	20	—
You are AWESOME	Completed all 90 Rewards.	30	Bronze
Cloud King	What were those giant things in the background of World 1? You are pretty sure you have no idea.	10	Bronze
Water Slider	Mucked through the Emerald Brine.	15	Bronze
Super Tree Hugger	Evolved past the Supernature.	20	Bronze
Feel the Burn	How did you manage to get through the Mounting Sadds?	25	Bronze
Future Legend	Back on track to your FATE.	30	Bronze
Hardcore	Beat all levels on hard. That's something!	20	Bronze
Perfectionist	Perfect Runned each level.	10	Bronze

NAME	GOAL/REQUIREMENT	POINT VALUE	TROPHY VALUE
Perfect Perfectionist	Triple Perfect+ed the entire game. Holy crap!	50	Gold
A New Challenger	Checkpoints are for suckers!	5	—
Who Dat!?	You made a new friend.	10	Bronze
Better Than Perfect	Got 5 Perfect+s, one in each World.	5	Bronze
Double Perfectionist	Double Double Perfected once in each World.	10	Bronze
Triple Perfectionist	Triple Triple Perfected once in each World.	20	Bronze

SECRET ACHIEVEMENTS & TROPHIES

NAME	GOAL/REQUIREMENT	POINT VALUE	TROPHY VALUE
Multiple Personalities	Beat 30 levels as alternate characters. Way to go!	10	—
Dancing Fool	You got the fever and danced 100 times.	5	Bronze
Bullseye!	Perfect+?! That's unpossible!	5	—
Marathoner	You warned the Athenians of the oncoming Persian army!	5	—

BLACK KNIGHT SWORD

PLAYSTATION 3

ARCADE MODE

Finish the game on any difficulty to unlock Arcade mode.

NEW GAME +

Finish the game once to unlock New Game+.

TRUE ENDING

Complete the game on New Game+ to obtain the True Ending.

BLACKLIGHT: TANGO DOWN

XBOX 360/PS3

UNLOCK CODES

Select Unlock Code from the Help & Options menu, then enter the following. These tags can be used on your customized weapons.

TAG	UNLOCK CODE
Alienware Black	Alienwarec8pestU
Alienware	Al13nwa4re5acasE
AMD VISION	4MDB4quprex
AMD VISION	AMD3afrUnap
ATi	AT1hAqup7Su
Australian Flag	AUS9eT5edru
Austria Flag	AUTF6crAS5u
Belgium Flag	BELS7utHAsP
Blacklight	R41nB0wu7p3
Blacklight	Ch1pBLuS9PR
Canada Flag	CANfeprUtr5
Denmark Flag	DENdathe8HU
E3 Dog Tags	E3F6crAS5u
Famitsu Magazine	Fam1tsuprusWe2e
Finland Flag	FINw3uthEfe

TAG	UNLOCK CODE
France Flag	FRApRUyUT4a
Germany Flag	GERtRE4a4eS
Holland Flag	HOLb8e6UWuh
Hong Kong Flag	HOKYeQuKuw3
India Flag	INDs4u8RApr
Ireland Flag	IRE8ruGejec
Italy Flag	ITAQ7Swu9re
Jace Hall Show	J4ceH4llstuFaCh4
Japan Flag	JPNj7fazebR
Korea Flag	KORpaphA9uK
Mexico Flag	MEX5Usw2YAd
New Zealand Flag	NZLxut32eSA
Norway Flag	NOR3Waga8wa
Orange Scorpion	Ch1pMMRSc0rp
Order Logo Chip	Ch1p0RD3Ru02
Pink Brass Knuckles	H4rtBr34kerio4u
Portugal Flag	PORQ54aFrEY
Razer	R4z3erzu8habuC
Russia Flag	RUS7rusteXe
Singapore Flag	SINvuS8E2aC
Spain Flag	ESPChE4At5p
Storm Lion Comics	StormLion9rAVaZ2
Storm Lion Comics	St0rmLi0nB4qupre
Sweden Flag	SWEt2aPHutr
Switzerland Flag	SWIsTE8tafU
Taiwan Flag	TAW8udukUP2
United Kingdom Flag	UKv4D3phed
United States Flag	USAM3spudre
Upper Playground	UPGr0undv2FUDame
Upper Playground	UPGr0undWupraf4u
UTV Lightning Logo chip	Ch1p1GN1u0S
Yellow Teddy Bear	Denek1Ju3aceH7
Zombie Studios Logo Chip	Ch1pZ0MB1Et7

BLADES OF TIME

XBOX 360/PS3

ACHIEVEMENTS & TROPHIES

NAME	GOAL/REQUIREMENT	POINT VALUE	TROPHY VALUE
Too Hot For You	Kill Brutal Maul without being frozen by his shockwave.	15	Bronze
Brutal Kill	Kill 5 enemies at once.	15	Bronze
Annihilation Kill	Kill 10 enemies at once.	30	Silver
Famous Hunter	Kill 1000 enemies in total.	15	Bronze
Faster Than You!	Use Counterattack 100 times.	15	Bronze
Grasshopper	Use Dash 30 times without touching the ground.	15	Bronze
Curious	Find half of the notes.	15	Bronze
Collector	Find all notes.	30	Silver
Ready To Fight	Find all types of equipment.	15	Bronze
Unstoppable	Win any Outbreak match.	15	Bronze
Out of My Way	Kill an enemy player in Outbreak match.	15	Bronze

NAME	GOAL/REQUIREMENT	POINT VALUE	TROPHY VALUE
Outbreak Hero	Kill each Outbreak boss at least once.	30	Silver
Experienced	Play 5 Outbreak matches.	10	Bronze
I'm Rich	Find all the chests in story mode on the Normal difficulty level.	15	Bronze
Treasure Hunter	Find all the chests in story mode on the Hard difficulty level.	30	Silver
Double Attack	Kill 25 heavy enemies using the Time Rewind double attack.	15	Bronze
Angry	Kill 100 enemies during your Time Rewind Berserk buff.	15	Bronze
Rain of Bullets	Shoot off Magic Armor from 50 enemies using Time Rewind clones.	15	Bronze

SECRET ACHIEVEMENTS & TROPHIES

NAME	GOAL/REQUIREMENT	POINT VALUE	TROPHY VALUE
Gather Chi	Get the ability to gather Chi.	15	Bronze
Rifle	Find the rifle.	15	Bronze
Coral Dash	Get the ability to dash to corals.	15	Bronze
Enemy Dash	Get the ability to dash to enemies.	15	Bronze
Time Rewind	Get the ability to rewind time.	15	Bronze
Order Spell	Survive Chaos event.	15	Bronze
Free to go!	Kill Gateguard.	30	Silver
Clear the Jungle	Kill Shaman Boss.	30	Silver
Your Fire Is Nothing	Kill Shaman Boss without taking damage from his massive fire spell.	15	Bronze
Old Temple	Reach the Sanctuary.	15	Bronze
World of Order	Defeat Skyguard Commander.	30	Silver
Big Corpse	Defeat Giant Worm.	90	Gold
Sky Islands	Leave the Sky Islands.	90	Gold
Brutal Lands	Kill the Vicar of Chaos.	90	Gold
Dragon	Ayumi gets Dragon form.	15	Bronze
Keeper Is Dead	Finish game on any difficulty.	90	Gold
Hard Times Are Over	Finish game on Hard difficulty.	90	Gold

BLITZ: THE LEAGUE II

TOUCHDOWN CELEBRATIONS

Press these button combinations when given the chance after scoring a touchdown

CELEBRATION	CODE
Ball Spike	A, A, A, B
Beer Chug	A, A, B, B
Dance Fever	Y, Y, Y, A
Get Down	B, A, B, Y
Golf Putt	A, X, Y, B
Helmet Fling	A, X, A, X
Knockout	X, X, Y, Y
Man Crush	X, X, X, Y
Nut Shot	Y, Y, B, A
Pylon Darts	A, B, A, B
The Pooper	Y, X, A, B

BLUR

BMW CONCEPT 1 SERIES TII CHROME

In the Multiplayer Showroom, highlight the BMW Concept 1 Series tii and press L2, R2, L2, R2.

FULLY UPGRADED FORD BRONCO

In the Multiplayer Showroom, highlight the Ford Bronco and press L2, R2, L2, R2.

BMW CONCEPT 1 SERIES TII CHROME

In the Multiplayer Showroom, highlight the BMW Concept 1 Series tii and press Left Trigger, Right Trigger, Left Trigger, Right Trigger.

FULLY UPGRADED FORD BRONCO

In the Multiplayer Showroom, highlight the Ford Bronco and press Left Trigger, Right Trigger, Left Trigger, Right Trigger.

AVATAR AWARDS

AWARD	EARNED BY
Wreck Tee	Earn the Been there, got the T-shirt Achievement
Friend Rechallenge Tee	Defeat a friends rechallenge.
Legend Tee	Unlock first Legend Rank in multiplayer.
Showdown Tee	Complete Showdown
Sticker Tee	Complete the Sticker Book.

BOLT

Many of the following cheats can be toggled on/off by pausing the game and selecting Cheats.

LEVEL SELECT

Select Cheats from the Extras menu and enter Right, Up, Left, Right, Up, Right.

ALL MINIGAMES

Select Cheats from the Extras menu and enter Right, Up, Right, Right.

UNLIMITED ENHANCED VISION

Select Cheats from the Extras menu and enter Left, Right, Up, Down.

UNLIMITED GROUND POUND

Select Cheats from the Extras menu and enter Right, Up, Right, Up, Left, Down.

UNLIMITED INVULNERABILITY

Select Cheats from the Extras menu and enter Down, Down, Up, Left.

UNLIMITED GAS MINES

Select Cheats from the Extras menu and enter Right, Left, Left, Up, Down, Right.

UNLIMITED LASER EYES

Select Cheats from the Extras menu and enter Left, Left, Up, Right.

UNLIMITED STEALTH CAMO

Select Cheats from the Extras menu and enter Left, Down (x3).

UNLIMITED SUPERBARK

Select Cheats from the Extras menu and enter Right, Left, Left, Up, Down, Up.

BORDERLANDS 2

BORDERLANDS 1 SKIN

With a Borderlands save game on your system, veteran skins from the first game is unlocked. Find them in the Extras menu.

MINECRAFT SKINS

Go to Caustic Caverns, which is reached by cutting through Sanctuary Hole. Find the train tracks to the northwest and follow them to a big door. Move around it, turn right and hop over the blocks. Move along the left wall until you find Minecraft dirt. Break through them until a Badass Creeper appears. Defeat it to unlock the skins.

EXTRA WUBS

At the title screen, press Up, Up, Down, Down, Left, Right, Left, Right, B, A, Start. This is a pretty useless code as Wubs do not do anything.

BOOM BLOX BASH PARTY

At the title screen, press Up, Right, Down, Left. Now you can enter the following codes:

UNLOCK EVERYTHING

Enter Nothing But Hope.

1 MILLION BOOM BUX

Enter Bailout.

TURN ON BLOX TIME

Enter Freeze Frame.

TURNS ALL SOUND EFFECTS INTO VIRUS BLOX SOUND EFFECTS

Enter Musical Fruit.

ALL COLORED BLOX

Enter Rainbow Blox.

BRAIN AGE: CONCENTRATION TRAINING

TRAINING EXERCISES

Complete these tasks to unlock these game exercises. After 40 days of attendance, all initial game modes will be unlocked.

EXERCISE	REQUIREMENT
Brain Training: Klondike	Raise attendance to 3 days.
Brain Training: Piano Player	Raise attendance to 5 days.
Brain Training: Spider Solitaire Easy and Normal Mode	Raise attendance to 8 days.
Brain Training: Peg Solitaire Normal Mode	Raise attendance to 15 days.
Brain Training: Word Blend	Raise attendance to 19 days.
Brain Training: Golf Solitaire	Raise attendance to 25 days.
Brain Training: Low to High	Raise attendance to 31 days.
Brain Training: Mahjong Solitaire	Raise attendance to 40 days.
Brain Training: Block Head Hard Mode	Complete 15 stages of Block Head.

EXERCISE	REQUIREMENT
Brain Training: Block Head Very Hard Mode	Complete 35 stages of Block Head.
Brain Training: Peg Solitaire Hard Mode	Complete 15 stages of Peg Solitaire.
Brain Training: Peg Solitaire Very Hard Mode	Complete 35 stages of Peg Solitaire.
Brain Training: Spider Solitaire Hard Mode	Win one game of Spider Solitaire Normal Mode.
Brain Training: Spider Solitaire Very Hard Mode	Win one game of Spider Solitaire in Hard mode.
Brain Training: Spider Solitaire Super Hard Mode	Win one game of Spider Solitaire in Very Hard mode.
Concentration Challenge: Hard Mode	Play Concentration Challenge and last for 10 minutes.
Devilish Training: Devilish Mice	Raise attendance to 2 days.
Devilish Training: Devilish Reading	Raise attendance to 3 days.
Devilish Training: Devilish Shapes	Raise attendance to 4 days.
Devilish Training: Devilish Cups	Raise attendance to 6 days.
Devilish Training: Devilish Listening	Raise attendance to 9 days.
Relaxation Mode: Germ Buster	Raise attendance to 9 days.
Relaxation Mode: Music Appreciation	Raise attendance to 13 days.
Settings: Stamp Design	Raise attendance to 11 days.
Settings: Change Outfit	Raise attendance to 14 days.
Supplemental Training: Word Attack	Raise attendance to 2 days.
Supplemental Training: By the Numbers	Raise attendance to 4 days.
Supplemental Training: Sum Totaled Battle	Raise attendance to 7 days.
Supplemental Training: Word Attack Space	Raise attendance to 12 days.
Supplemental Training: Change Maker	Raise attendance to 17 days.
Supplemental Training: Calculations x 100	Raise attendance to 22 days.
Supplemental Training: Sum Totaled	Raise attendance to 28 days.
Supplemental Training: Time Lapse	Raise attendance to 35 days.

BRAIN AGE EXPRESS: ARTS & LETTERS

NINTENDO 3DS

ELIMINATE ENEMIES IN WORD ATTACK

In Word Attack, during the Space mode, press A, Y, X, B. You can use this once each training session.

BRAIN QUEST GRADES 5 & 6

NINTENDO 3DS

MAD COW STICKER

Select Cheats from the Options and enter MADCOW.

BRAIN VOYAGE

NINTENDO 3DS

ALL GOLD MEDALS

At the World Map, press A, B, Up, L, L, Y.

INFINITE COINS

At the World Tour Mode, press L, Up, X, Up, R, Y.

CHEATS, ACHIEVEMENTS, AND TROPHIES

B

BRINK

ACHIEVEMENTS & TROPHIES

NAME	GOAL/REQUIREMENT	POINT VALUE	TROPHY VALUE
That's how you win a match	While on defense, take down an attacker who's completing a Primary Objective	10	Silver
Not over till the fat lady sings	Take down an enemy with gunfire while knocked down	10	Bronze
Cut 'em off at the pass	Close an enemy team's shortcut	10	Silver
Oh I'm sorry, was that yours?	Capture an enemy Command Post	10	Bronze
Not so sneaky now, are you?	Reveal an enemy in disguise	10	Bronze
You shall not pass!	While on defense, prevent the attackers from completing their first objective	20	Silver
Was it the red or the blue wire?	Disarm an HE charge	10	Silver
Great shot kid! One in a million	Take down an enemy by shooting a grenade	10	Bronze
They never knew what hit them	While on offense, win the match in less than 30% of the time limit	20	Silver
The story has just begun	Win both story campaigns (not including What-If missions)	100	Silver
You've escaped the Ark	Win all main missions of the Resistance campaign (not including What-If missions)	75	Bronze
The start of something big	Win any mission, whether campaign or What-If	20	Bronze
You've saved the Ark	Win all main missions of the Security campaign (not including What-If missions)	75	Bronze
Viva la revolution!	Win every Resistance campaign mission, including What-If missions	50	Silver
Use the wheel, earn more XP	Complete an objective after first selecting it on the Objective Wheel	10	Bronze
I think I know a shortcut	Open a shortcut for your team	10	Silver
To serve and protect	Win every Security campaign mission, including What-If missions	50	Silver
Tough as nails	Win all storyline campaign missions (exc. What-If missions) in either Online Versus, or in Hard mode	80	Gold
Well done!	Complete your first 1 Star Challenge	10	Silver
Very well done indeed!	Complete your first 3 Star Challenge	20	Silver
No I insist, you take it	Use the last of your Supplies to refill a teammate's ammo rather than your own	5	Silver
It's a trap!	Take down an enemy with a Satchel Charge	10	Bronze
Who's bad?	Complete all 1 Star Challenges	25	Silver
You're going places, kid!	Reach Rank 2	20	Silver
Time to start a new character	Reach Rank 5	100	Gold
King of the world!	Complete all 3 Star Challenges	100	Gold
Well that was educational	Collect all Audio Logs	50	Silver

NAME	GOAL/REQUIREMENT	POINT VALUE	TROPHY VALUE
Smart decisions win battles	Attempt to Revive an objective-class teammate over a non-objective teammate near a Primary Objective	10	Silver
I live... again!	Revive yourself	5	Bronze
You can place another mine now	Take down an enemy with a mine	10	Bronze
Pump up the volume!	Upgrade your team's Command Post	10	Bronze
T'is better to give than receive	As a Medic, using the Transfer Supplies ability, give the last of your Supplies away	10	Bronze
A bit of a headache	Take down an enemy with a Cortex Bomb	5	Bronze
Boom!	Detonate a HE Charge	10	Silver
That mine you found? Disarmed!	Spot a mine which is later defused by another Engineer	10	Silver
Brinksmanship	Complete an Operative Primary Objective within 5 seconds of breaking disguise	10	Silver

BROTHERS IN ARMS: HELL'S HIGHWAY

XBOX 360/PS3

ALL CHAPTERS

Select Enter Codes from the Options and enter GIMMECHAPTERS.

ALL RECON POINTS

Select Enter Codes from the Options and enter 0ZNDRBICRA.

KILROY DETECTOR

Select Enter Codes from the Options and enter SH2VYIVNZF.

TWO MULTIPLAYER SKINS

Select Enter Codes from the Options and enter HI9WTPXSUK.

BUBBLE BOBBLE REVOLUTION

NINTENDO 3DS

BONUS LEVELS IN CLASSIC MODE

At the Classic Mode title screen, press L, R, L, R, L, R, Right, Select. Touch the door at Level 20.

POWER UP! MODE IN CLASSIC VERSION

At the Classic Mode title screen, press Select, R, L, Left, Right, R, Select, Right.

SUPER BUBBLE BOBBLE IN CLASSIC VERSION

You must first defeat the boss with two players. Then at the Classic Mode title screen, press Left, R, Left, Select, Left, L, Left, Select.

CHEATS, ACHIEVEMENTS, AND TROPHIES

B

BULLETSTORM

ACHIEVEMENTS & TROPHIES

NAME	GOAL/REQUIREMENT	POINT VALUE	TROPHY VALUE
Weed Killer	Tidy up the back yard	15	Bronze
Minced Meat	Take out the Mall's biggest customer	15	Bronze
Grilled Meat	Prepare a big meal using an improvised electric stove	15	Bronze
Size Matters	Use your biggest weapon	15	Bronze
Damsel in Distress	Rescue the princess	15	Bronze
Destroyer of Worlds	Cause major destruction	15	Bronze
Disco Inferno	Kill all enemies without leaving the dance floor in the city outskirts	10	Bronze
Chop-Chopper	Kill the enemy inside the airborne helicopter in the park	30	Bronze
Red Barrels	Explode all the red barrels on the rooftop while in a helicopter	10	Bronze
Armed and Dangerous	Grow as a person, experience betrayal. Again.	15	Bronze
Stowaway	Catch a ride	15	Bronze
Pointless	Execute at least 10 Headshots before you find the first DropKit	10	Bronze
All Bow To Heavy Metal	Big head, big headache	15	Bronze
Blood Symphony	Complete the Campaign on Very Hard Difficulty	50	Bronze
Major Malfunction	Destroy 50% of the Newsbots in the Single Player Campaign	10	Bronze
Total Malfunction	Destroy all Newsbots in the Single Player Campaign	20	Silver
Destructive Beat	Complete the Campaign on Very Easy or Easy Difficulty	20	Bronze
Violent Melody	Complete the Campaign on Normal Difficulty	30	Bronze
Brutal Chorus	Complete the Campaign on Hard Difficulty	40	Silver
Straight Edge	Destroy at least 20 bottles of Nom Juice in the Single Player Campaign	10	Bronze
Fits Like a Glove	Meet your new best friend	15	Bronze
Patched Up	Receive a software update for your leash	15	Bronze
Insecticide	Destroy 50% of the Electroflies in the Single Player Campaign	10	Bronze
Pest Control	Destroy all Electroflies in the Single Player Campaign	20	Silver
Space Pirate	Drink at least 20 bottles of Nom Juice in the Single Player Campaign	10	Bronze
Old School	Finish an Echo round without executing a single Skillshot	15	Bronze
Enforcer	Get at least 15,000 points in one Echo round	20	Bronze
Star struck	Get 3 Stars on 10 different Echoes	10	Bronze
Bounty Hunter	Have a total of at least 75,000 points in Echoes Mode's total high score	20	Bronze
Guerrilla Tactics	Execute at least 25 different Skillshots in one Echo round	10	Bronze

NAME	GOAL/REQUIREMENT	POINT VALUE	TROPHY VALUE
Halfway There	Get at least 21 stars in Echoes Mode	15	Bronze
Team Player	Complete 200 team challenges in your career in Anarchy mode	10	Bronze
Final Echo	Achieve level 65 in Anarchy mode	40	Bronze
Environment Master	Perform every Anarchy environmental Skillshot	20	Bronze
Hoarder	Have a total of at least 150,000 points in Echoes Mode's total high score	40	Gold
Like A Boss	Defeat a miniboss in Anarchy mode	5	Bronze
Anarchy Master	Achieve a score of at least 50,000 as a team in Anarchy mode	30	Bronze
Supernova	Get 3 stars on each of the first 14 Echoes	40	Silver
Om Nom Nom!	Feed a flytrap with a Nom parasite	10	Bronze
Wannabe	Perform 10 different Single Player Skillshots	10	Bronze
Somebody	Perform 25% of the Single Player Skillshots	20	Bronze
No Man Left Behind	Kill all enemies while escaping from the collapsed building	20	Bronze
I might be late	Kill all enemies during the sprint to the jumpship	20	Bronze
Just one last thing	Kill all enemies before you reach the escape capsule	20	Bronze
Master of Disaster	Earn 2000 points or more at once	40	Silver
Remembrance	Play three different Echoes	10	Bronze
Shooting Star	Get at least 1 star on each of the first 14 Echoes	10	Bronze
Big Cheese	Perform 50% of the Single Player Skillshots	30	Bronze
Celebrity	Perform 75% of the Single Player Skillshots	40	Bronze
Golden Idol	Perform every Single Player Skillshot in the game	50	Gold

DOWNLOADABLE CONTENT: GUN SONATA

NAME	GOAL/REQUIREMENT	POINT VALUE	TROPHY VALUE
Bell End	Kill five enemies at the same time using "Dung" in the Villa map.	10	Bronze
Extinguisher	In the Sewer map, kill five enemies in one wave by setting them on fire then extinguishing them.	20	Silver
Heart Attack	Killa Boss using the Hot Dog cart in the Hotel Elysium map.	40	Gold
Hell Razor	Kill a Burnout using the helicopter that arrives in Crash Site	25	Silver
Last Blood	At the end of Guns of Stygia, kill all enemies on the walkways before the explosions do.	30	Silver

BULLY: SCHOLARSHIP EDITION

FULL HEALTH

During a game and with a second controller, hold Left Bumper and press Right Trigger, Right Trigger, Right Trigger.

MONEY

During a game and with a second controller, hold Left Bumper and press Y, X, B, A.

INFINITE AMMO

During a game and with a second controller, hold Left Bumper and press Up, Down, Up, Down. Re-enter code to disable it.

ALL WEAPONS

During a game and with a second controller, hold Left Bumper and press Up, Up, Up, Up.

ALL GYM GRAPPLE MOVES

During a game and with a second controller, hold Left Bumper and press Up, Left, Down, Down, Y, X, A, A.

ALL HOBO MOVES

During a game and with a second controller, hold Left Bumper and press Up, Left, Down, Right, Y, X, A, B

BURNOUT PARADISE

BEST BUY CAR

Pause the game and select Sponsor Product Code from the Under the Hood menu. Enter Bestbuy. Need the A License to use this car offline.

CIRCUIT CITY CAR

Pause the game and select Sponsor Product Code from the Under the Hood menu. Enter Circuitcity. Need Burnout Paradise License to use this car offline.

GAMESTOP CAR

Pause the game and select Sponsor Product Code from the Under the Hood menu. Enter Gamestop. Need the A License to use this car offline.

WALMART CAR

Pause the game and select Sponsor Product Code from the Under the Hood menu. Enter Walmart. Need the Burnout Paradise License to use this car offline.

"STEEL WHEELS" GT

Pause the game and select Sponsor Product Code from the Under the Hood menu. Enter G23X 5K8Q GX2V 04B1 or E60J 8Z7T MS8L 51U6.

LICENSES

LICENSE	NUMBER OF WINS NEEDED
D	2
C	7
B	16
A	26
Burnout Paradise	45
Elite License	All events

BUST-A-MOVE DS

DARK WORLD

Complete the game then press A, Left, Right, A at the Title screen.

SOUND TEST

At the Main menu, press Select, A, B, Left, Right, A, Select, Right.

CABELA'S DANGEROUS HUNTS 2013

ACHIEVEMENTS & TROPHIES

NAME	GOAL/REQUIREMENT	POINT VALUE	TROPHY VALUE
Survived!	Completed the Story Mode.	30	Silver
Just Like a Pro	Completed the Story Mode without dying once or restarting checkpoints.	50	Gold
Scratchless	Passed any Story Mode level except the Take the Shot level without taking damage.	30	Bronze
Stealth Approach	Passed any Story Mode level using only the crossbow.	15	Bronze
They Call Me Long Barrel	Hunted an animal from beyond 200 meters with a scope in any Story Mode level.	15	Bronze
Eagle Eye	Hunted a bird or bat using a crossbow in any Story Mode level.	10	Bronze
Who Needs Glasses?	Hunted an animal from at least 100 meters, without using the scope in any Story Mode level.	15	Bronze
Dodge This	Dodged an animal attack 30 times in Story Mode.	10	Bronze
Primary Target: Alpha	Hunted 5 Alpha males in Marksman Opportunity situations in Story Mode.	15	Bronze
Collector	Picked up all Collectibles in Story Mode.	50	Silver
In Father's Memory	Hunted 10 different hidden Big Game trophy animals in Story Mode.	30	Bronze
Brave or Crazy?	Used only a pistol to hunt a hippopotamus in the Keep Moving Story Mode level.	30	Silver
Always Fresh	Didn't empty the whole stamina bar during one Story Mode level.	15	Bronze
Two Birds, One Stone	Hunted two predators with one shotgun shot in any Story Mode level.	30	Silver
Newton's Apple	Hunted a predator while it is in a tree in any Story Mode level.	15	Bronze
Hunter's Quality	Shot 50 animals using Killer Instinct in Story Mode.	10	Bronze
Gunsmith	Found special ammunition for all firearms in Story Mode.	20	Bronze
Bullet-man	Picked up 500 rounds of any ammunition in Story Mode.	10	Bronze
Ambulance-man	Picked up 50 health packs in Story Mode.	10	Bronze
Heavy Breather	Shot 25 predators while holding your breath in Story Mode.	15	Bronze

NAME	GOAL/REQUIREMENT	POINT VALUE	TROPHY VALUE
Gallery Addict	Passed all Reflex and Arcade Plus Shooting Gallery levels in single player.	60	Gold
Hunter of Hunters	Shot all predators that you encounter in any Shooting Gallery level in single player.	15	Bronze
Now We're Even	During a co-op Shooting Gallery, scored within 3500 points of y our teammate.	30	Bronze
Reflex Master	Won any Reflex Shooting Gallery hunting all animals in order in single player.	30	Silver
Combo Wizard	In Single Player Arcade Plus, kept the 2x Damage Hunter Award from the first checkpoint to the end.	30	Bronze
Overtime	Got at least 10,000 points in Free Shooting phases of any Reflex Plus gallery in single player.	30	Bronze
Dare-devil	Took all the dangerous paths in all Arcade Plus levels in single player.	20	Bronze
Run Piggie, Run!	Shot 75 warthogs in Reflex Plus galleries in single player.	15	Bronze
Steel Hunter	Completed 10 rounds in Maneater in single player.	40	Silver
Locked and Loaded	In Maneater single player, collected 25 special ammunition boxes (repeated play needed).	15	Bronze
Untouchable	Passed round 1 to 5 of any Maneater level in single player without receiving a single hit.	30	Silver
Eater of Maneaters	Passed all Maneater levels in single player.	60	Gold
Sub Zero	Froze 20 animals by shooting away ice floes in Breakthrough Maneater level in single player.	15	Bronze
Booom!	In Maneater single player, blew up 10 TNT crates.	15	Bronze
Got Your Back	In Maneater single player, protected an injured friend so that no predator attacked them.	15	Bronze
Repeating Fun	Finished one Maneater level in single player only using the repeating crossbow.	15	Bronze
Double Fun	Hunted 25 elite animals with the double barrel shotgun in single player Maneater levels.	15	Bronze
Semi-Automatic Fun	Shot 3 animals in 5 seconds with the semi-auto rifle in single player Maneater.	15	Bronze
Abyss	Hunted 20 animals by opening the trapdoor in the Trap Door Maneater level in single player.	15	Bronze
Unlocker	Unlocked all unlockable content.	50	Silver
Adrenaline Junkie	Hunted 5 predators in less than 5 seconds in single player.	15	Bronze
Hair Away from Death	With less than 5% health, hunted an attacking predator less than 2 meters away in single player.	15	Bronze

CALL OF DUTY: BLACK OPS

NINTENDO WII/PS3

ACCESS TERMINAL

At the main menu, alternately press aim and fire until you break free of the restraints. Find the terminal behind the chair. Here you can enter the following.

TERMINAL COMMANDS

EFFECT	COMMAND
List Commands	Help
Root directory (use ls to list codes)	cd .. [enter] cd .. [enter] cd bin [enter]
List directory	ls
List audio files and pictures	DIR
Open file	CAT [filename found from DIR command]
View a file	TYPE (filename.extension)
List CIA e-mail	mail
List login names (does not give passwords)	WHO
FI FIE FOE	FOOBAR
All Intel	3ARC INTEL
Dead Ops Arcade	DOA
Dead Ops Arcade and Presidential Zombie Mode	3ARC UNLOCK
Virtual Therapist Software	Alicia
Zork I: The Great Underground Adventure	ZORK

CIA DATA SYSTEM LOGINS

Use the following IDs and Passwords to access users' files and mail.

USER ACCOUNT	ID	PASSWORD
Alex Mason	amason	PASSWORD
Bruce Harris	bharris	GOSKINS
D. King	dking	MFK
Dr. Adrienne Smith	asmith	ROXY
Dr. Vannevar Bush	vbush	MANHATTAN
Frank Woods	fwoods	PHILLY
Grigori "Greg" Weaver	gweaver	GEDEON
J. Turner	jturner	CONDOR75
Jason Hudson	jhudson	BRYANT1950
John McCone	jmccone	BERKLEY22
Joseph Bowman	jbowman	UWD
President John Fitzgerald Kennedy	jfkennedy	LANCER
President Lyndon Baines Johnson	lbjohnson	LADYBIRD
President Richard Nixon	rnixon	CHECKERS
Richard Helms	rhelms	LEROSEY
Richard Kain	rkain	SUNWU
Ryan Jackson	rjackson	SAINTBRIDGET
T. Walker	twalker	RADIO
Terrance Brooks	tbrooks	LAUREN
William Raborn	wraborn	BROMLOW

CHEATS, ACHIEVEMENTS, AND TROPHIES

C

ACCESS TERMINAL

At the main menu, alternately press aim and fire until you break free of the restraints. Find the terminal behind the chair. Here you can enter the following.

TERMINAL COMMANDS

EFFECT	COMMAND
List Commands	Help
Root directory (use ls to list codes)	cd .. [enter] cd .. [enter] cd bin [enter]
List directory	ls
List audio files and pictures	DIR
Open file	CAT [filename found from DIR command]
View a file	TYPE (filename.extension)
List CIA e-mail	mail
List login names (does not give passwords)	WHO
FI FIE FOE	FOOBAR
All Intel	3ARC INTEL
Dead Ops Arcade	DOA
Dead Ops Arcade and Presidential Zombie Mode	3ARC UNLOCK
Virtual Therapist Software	Alicia
Zork I: The Great Underground Adventure	ZORK

CIA DATA SYSTEM LOGINS

Use the following IDs and Passwords to access users' files and mail.

USER ACCOUNT	ID	PASSWORD
Alex Mason	amason	PASSWORD
Bruce Harris	bharris	GOSKINS
D. King	dking	MFK
Dr. Adrienne Smith	asmith	ROXY
Dr. Vannevar Bush	vbush	MANHATTAN
Frank Woods	fwoods	PHILLY
Grigori "Greg" Weaver	gweaver	GEDEON
J. Turner	jturner	CONDOR75
Jason Hudson	jhudson	BRYANT1950
John McCone	jmccone	BERKLEY22
Joseph Bowman	jbowman	UWD
President John Fitzgerald Kennedy	jfkennedy	LANCER
President Lyndon Baines Johnson	lbjohnson	LADYBIRD
President Richard Nixon	rnixon	CHECKERS
Richard Helms	rhelms	LEROSEY
Richard Kain	rkain	SUNWU
Ryan Jackson	rjackson	SAINTBRIDGET
T. Walker	twalker	RADIO
Terrance Brooks	tbrooks	LAUREN
William Raborn	wraborn	BROMLOW

FRANK WOODS GAMER PICTURE

Escape from interrogation chair by pressing the aim and fire buttons at the main menu.

JASON HUDSON GAMER PICTURE

Use the terminal to login as Jason Hudson.

ACHIEVEMENTS & TROPHIES

NAME	GOAL/REQUIREMENT	POINT VALUE	TROPHY VALUE
Death to Dictators	Take down Castro with a headshot.	15	Bronze
Sacrifice	Ensure your squad escapes safely from Cuba.	10	Bronze
Vehicular Slaughter	Destroy all enemies on vehicles during the prison break.	25	Silver
Slingshot Kid	Destroy all slingshot targets in 3 attempts.	15	Bronze
Give me liberty	Escape Vorkuta.	10	Bronze
VIP	Receive orders from Lancer.	10	Bronze
A safer place	Sabotage the Soviet space program.	10	Bronze
Tough Economy	Use no more than 6 TOW guided missiles to destroy the tanks in the defense of Khe Sanh.	15	Bronze
Looks don't count	Break the siege in the battle of Khe Sanh.	10	Bronze
Raining Pain	Rack up a body count of 20 NVA using air support in Hue City.	15	Bronze
The Dragon Within	Kill 10 NVA with Dragon's Breath rounds.	15	Bronze
SOG Rules	Retrieve the dossier and the defector from Hue City.	10	Bronze
Heavy Hand	Use the Grim Reaper to destroy the MG emplacement.	15	Bronze
Up close and personal	Silently take out 3 VC.	15	Bronze
Double Trouble	Use only dual wield weapons to escape Kowloon.	10	Bronze
Broken English	Escape Kowloon.	10	Bronze
Lord Nelson	Destroy all targets and structures while making your way up the river.	25	Silver
Never get off the boat	Find the Soviet connection in Laos.	10	Bronze
Pathfinder	Guide the squad through the Soviet outpost without them getting killed.	50	Bronze
Mr. Black OP	Enter the Soviet relay station undetected.	50	Silver
With extreme prejudice	Get to the POW compound in the Hind using only rockets.	25	Silver
Russian bar-b-q	Incinerate 10 enemies with the flamethrower attachment in the POW compound.	15	Bronze
Light Foot	Escape the ship with 2:15 left on the timer in Veteran.	30	Silver
Some wounds never heal	Escape the Past.	10	Bronze
I hate monkeys	Kill 7 monkeys in under 10 seconds in the Rebirth labs.	15	Bronze
No Leaks	Make it through the NOVA 6 gas without dying on Rebirth Island.	50	Silver
Clarity	Crack the code.	10	Bronze
Double Whammy	Destroy both helicopters with one Valkyrie rocket from the deck of the ship.	15	Bronze
Stand Down	Complete the campaign on any difficulty.	35	Silver
BLACK OP MASTER	Complete the campaign on Hardened or Veteran difficulty.	100	Gold

CHEATS, ACHIEVEMENTS, AND TROPHIES

C

NAME	GOAL/REQUIREMENT	POINT VALUE	TROPHY VALUE
Frag Master	Kill 5 enemies with a single frag grenade in the campaign.	15	Bronze
Sally Likes Blood	Demonstrate killer economic sensibilities by taking down 3 enemies with a single bullet.	15	Bronze
Unconventional Warfare	Use the explosive bolts to kill 30 enemies in the campaign.	15	Bronze
Cold Warrior	Complete "Operation 40," "Vorkuta," and "Executive Order" on Veteran difficulty.	25	Silver
Down and Dirty	Complete "SOG" and "The Defector" on Veteran difficulty.	25	Silver
It's your funeral	Complete "Numbers," "Project Nova," and "Victor Charlie" on Veteran difficulty.	25	Silver
Not Today	Complete "Crash Site," "WMD," and "Payback" on Veteran difficulty.	25	Silver
Burn Notice	Complete "Rebirth" and "Redemption" on Veteran difficulty.	25	Silver
Closer Analysis	Find all the hidden intel.	15	Bronze
Date Night	Watch a film or clip with a friend.	15	Bronze
In The Money	Finish 5 Wager Matches "in the money."	20	Bronze
Ready For Deployment	Reach rank 10 in Combat Training.	15	Bronze
The Collector	Buy every weapon off the walls in a single Zombies game.	20	Silver
Hands Off the Merchandise	Kill the Pentagon thief before it can steal your load-out.	20	Bronze
Sacrificial Lamb	Shoot at or be shot by an ally with a Pack-a-Punch crossbow and kill six zombies with the explosion.	15	Bronze
"Insert Coin"	Access the terminal and battle the forces of the Cosmic Silverback in Dead Ops Arcade.	5	Bronze
Easy Rhino	In Dead Ops Arcade, use a Speed Boost to blast through 20 or more enemies at one time.	10	Silver

SECRET ACHIEVEMENTS

NAME	GOAL/REQUIREMENT	POINT VALUE	TROPHY VALUE
See Me, Stab Me, Heal Me	Fire a Pack-a-Punched Ballistic Knife at a downed ally to revive them from a distance.	15	Bronze
Just ask me nicely	Break free from the torture chair.	15	Bronze
Eaten by a Grue	Play Zork on the terminal.	15	Bronze

CALL OF DUTY: BLACK OPS — ANNIHILATION

XBOX 360

DEMPSEY & RICHTOFEN GAMER PICTURES

Earn the Time Travel Will Tell Achievement.

CALL OF DUTY: MODERN WARFARE 2

XBOX 360/PS3

ACHIEVEMENTS & TROPHIES

NAME	GOAL/REQUIREMENT	POINT VALUE	TROPHY VALUE
Back in the Saddle	Help train the local militia.	15	Bronze
Danger Close	Get hand picked for Shepherd's elite squad.	15	Bronze
Cold Shoulder	Infiltrate the snowy mountain side base.	15	Bronze
Tag 'em and bag 'em	Find Rojas in the Favelas.	15	Bronze
Royale with Cheese	Defend Burger Town.	15	Bronze
Soap on a Rope	Storm the gulag.	15	Bronze
Desperate Times	Execute the plan to help the Americans.	15	Bronze
Whiskey Hotel	Take back Whiskey Hotel.	15	Bronze
The Pawn	Assault Makarov's safe house.	15	Bronze
Out of the Frying Pan…	Complete the mission in the airplane graveyard.	15	Bronze
For the Record	Complete the Single Player campaign on any difficulty.	35	Silver
The Price of War	Complete the single player campaign on Hardened or Veteran Difficulty.	90	Gold
First Day of School	Complete 'S.S.D.D' and 'Team Player' on Veteran Difficulty.	25	Bronze
Black Diamond	Complete 'Cliffhanger' on Veteran Difficulty.	25	Bronze
Turistas	Complete 'Takedown' and 'The Hornet's Nest' on Veteran Difficulty.	25	Silver
Red Dawn	Complete 'Wolverines!' and 'Exodus' on Veteran Difficulty.	25	Silver
Prisoner #627	Complete 'The Only Easy Day… Was Yesterday' and 'The Gulag' on Veteran Difficulty.	25	Silver
Ends Justify the Means	Complete 'Contingency' on Veteran Difficulty	25	Bronze
Homecoming	Complete 'Of Their Own Accord', 'Second Sun', and 'Whiskey Hotel' on Veteran Difficulty.	25	Silver
Queen takes Rook	Complete 'Loose Ends' and 'The Enemy of My Enemy' on Veteran Difficulty.	25	Silver
Off the Grid	Complete 'Just Like Old Times' and 'Endgame' on Veteran Difficulty.	25	Bronze
Pit Boss	Run The Pit in 'S.S.D.D' and finish with a final time under 30 seconds.	10	Bronze
Ghost	Plant the C4 in 'Cliffhanger' without alerting or injuring anyone in the blizzard.	10	Bronze
Colonel Sanderson	Kill 7 chickens in under 10 seconds in 'The Hornet's Nest'.	10	Bronze
Gold Star	Earn 1 star in Special Ops.	20	Bronze
Hotel Bravo	Earn 4 stars in Special Ops.	20	Bronze
Charlie On Our Six	Earn 8 stars in Special Ops.	20	Bronze
It Goes to Eleven	Earn at least 1 star in 11 different Special Op missions.	20	Bronze
Operational Asset	Earn all 3 stars in at least 5 different Special Op missions.	20	Bronze
Blackjack	Earn 21 stars in Special Ops.	20	Bronze

C

NAME	GOAL/REQUIREMENT	POINT VALUE	TROPHY VALUE
Honor Roll	Earn at least 1 star in each Special Op mission.	20	Silver
Operative	Earn all 3 stars in at least 10 different Special Op missions.	30	Silver
Specialist	Earn 30 stars in Special Ops.	30	Silver
Professional	Earn all 3 stars in at least 15 different Special Op missions.	30	Silver
Star 69	Earn 69 stars in Special Ops.	90	Gold
Downed but Not Out	Kill 4 enemies in a row while downed in Special Ops.	10	Bronze
I'm the Juggernaut…	Kill a Juggernaut in Special Ops.	10	Bronze
Ten plus foot-mobiles	Kill at least 10 enemies with one Predator missile in Single Player or Special Ops.	10	Bronze
Unnecessary Roughness	Use a riot shield to beat down an enemy in Single Player or Special Ops.	10	Bronze
Knock-knock	Kill 4 enemies with 4 shots during a slow-mo breach in Single Player or Special Ops.	10	Bronze
Some Like it Hot	Kill 6 enemies in a row using a thermal weapon in Single Player or Special Ops.	10	Bronze
Two Birds with One Stone	Kill 2 enemies with a single bullet in Single Player or Special Ops.	10	Bronze
The Road Less Traveled	Collect 22 enemy intel items.	10	Bronze
Leave No Stone Unturned	Collect 45 enemy intel items.	10	Bronze
Drive By	Kill 20 enemies in a row while driving a vehicle in Single Player or Special Ops.	10	Bronze
The Harder They Fall	Kill 2 rappelling enemies in a row before they land on their feet in Single Player or Special Ops.	10	Bronze
Desperado	Kill 5 enemies in a row using 5 different weapons or attachments in Single Player or Special Ops.	10	Bronze
Look Ma Two Hands	Kill 10 enemies in a row using akimbo weapons in Single Player or Special Ops.	10	Bronze
No Rest For the Wary	Knife an enemy without him ever knowing you were there in Single Player or Special Ops.	10	Bronze
Three-some	Kill at least 3 enemies with a single shot from a grenade launcher in Single Player or Special Ops.	10	Bronze

CALL OF DUTY: MODERN WARFARE 3

NINTENDO WII

NAME COLOR FOR PROFILE

When entering your name for your Multiplayer Profile, click Shift and then ^. Now enter the number as given below to change the color. The ^ will be removed and the text that you enter will be the color you chose.

FONT COLOR	NUMBER
Black	0
Red	1
Green	2
Yellow	3
Blue	4
Dark Blue	5
Pink	6
Orange	7
Grey	8
Dark Grey	9

XBOX 360/PS3

ARCADE MODE

After a complete playthrough of the game, Arcade Mode becomes available from the Main menu.

UNLOCKABLE CHEATS

After completing the game, cheats are unlocked based on how many intelligence pieces were gathered. These cheats cannot be used during Arcade Mode. They may also disable the ability to earn Achievements.

CHEAT	INTEL ITEMS	DESCRIPTION
CoD Noir	2	Black and white
Photo-Negative	4	Inverses colors
Super Contrast	6	Increases contrast
Ragtime Warfare	8	Black and white, scratches fill screen, double speed, piano music
Cluster Bombs	10	Four extra grenade explosions after frag grenade explodes
A Bad Year	15	Enemies explode into a bunch of old tires when killed
Slow-Mo Ability	20	Melee button enables/disables slow-motion mode
Infinite Ammo	30	Unlimited ammo and no need to reload. Doesn't work for single-shot weapons such as RPG.

ACHIEVEMENTS & TROPHIES

NAME	GOAL/REQUIREMENT	POINT VALUE	TROPHY VALUE
Back in the Fight	Start the Single Player Campaign on any difficulty.	5	Bronze
Too Big to Fail	Destroy the Jamming Tower. Complete "Black Tuesday" on any difficulty.	10	Bronze
Wet Work	Take back New York Harbor. Complete "Hunter Killer" on any difficulty.	10	Bronze
Carpe Diem	Escape the mountain safe house. Complete "Persona Non Grata" on any difficulty.	10	Bronze
Frequent Flyer	Defend the Russian President. Complete "Turbulence" on any difficulty.	10	Bronze

CHEATS, ACHIEVEMENTS, AND TROPHIES

C

NAME	GOAL/REQUIREMENT	POINT VALUE	TROPHY VALUE
Up to No Good	Infiltrate the village. Complete "Back on the Grid" on any difficulty.	10	Bronze
One Way Ticket	Make it to Westminster. Complete "Mind the Gap" on any difficulty.	10	Bronze
Welcome to WW3	Save the US Vice President. Complete "Goalpost" on any difficulty.	10	Bronze
Sandstorm!	Assault the shipping company. Complete "Return to Sender" on any difficulty.	10	Bronze
Back Seat Driver	Track down Volk. Complete "Bag and Drag" on any difficulty.	10	Bronze
We'll Always Have Paris	Escape Paris with Volk. Complete "Iron Lady" on any difficulty.	10	Bronze
Vive la Révolution!	Reach the church. Complete "Eye of the Storm" on any difficulty.	10	Bronze
Requiem	Escape the city. Complete "Blood Brothers" on any difficulty.	10	Bronze
Storm the Castle	Discover Makarov's next move. Complete "Stronghold" on any difficulty.	10	Bronze
Bad First Date	Find the girl. Complete "Scorched Earth" on any difficulty.	10	Bronze
Diamond in the Rough	Rescue the Russian President. Complete "Down the Rabbit Hole" on any difficulty.	10	Bronze
The Big Apple	Complete "Black Tuesday" and "Hunter Killer" on Veteran difficulty.	25	Silver
Out of the Frying Pan…	Complete "Persona Non Grata", "Turbulence", and "Back on the Grid" on Veteran difficulty.	25	Silver
Payback	Complete "Mind the Gap", "Goalpost", and "Return to Sender" on Veteran difficulty.	25	Silver
City of Lights	Complete "Bag and Drag" and "Iron Lady" on Veteran difficulty.	25	Silver
The Darkest Hour	Complete "Eye of the Storm", "Blood Brothers", and "Stronghold" on Veteran difficulty.	25	Silver
This is the End	Complete "Scorched Earth", "Down the Rabbit Hole", and "Dust to Dust" on Veteran difficulty.	25	Silver
Who Dares Wins	Complete the campaign on any difficulty.	40	Silver
The Best of the Best	Complete the campaign on Hardened or Veteran difficulty.	100	Gold
Strike!	Kill 5 enemies with a single grenade in Single Player or Special Ops.	20	Bronze
Jack the Ripper	Melee 5 enemies in a row in Single Player or Special Ops.	20	Bronze
Informant	Collect 22 Intel Items.	20	Bronze
Scout Leader	Collect 46 Intel Items.	35	Silver
This Is My Boomstick	Kill 30 enemies with the XM25 in "Black Tuesday."	20	Bronze
What Goes Up…	Destroy all the choppers with only the UGV's grenade launcher in "Persona Non Grata."	20	Bronze

NAME	GOAL/REQUIREMENT	POINT VALUE	TROPHY VALUE
For Whom the Shell Tolls	Destroy all targets during the mortar sequence with only 4 shells in "Back on the Grid."	20	Bronze
Kill Box	Kill 20 enemies with the Chopper Gunner in a single run in "Return to Sender."	20	Bronze
Danger Close	Take down a chopper with an AC-130 smoke grenade in "Bag and Drag."	20	Bronze
Ménage à Trois	Destroy 3 tanks with a single 105mm shot in "Iron Lady."	20	Bronze
Nein	Kill 9 enemies with A-10 strafing runs in "Scorched Earth."	20	Bronze
50/50	Complete a Special Ops Mission Mode game with the same number of kills as your partner.	20	Bronze
Birdie	Kill 2 enemy helicopters without getting hit in a Special Ops Survival game.	20	Bronze
Serrated Edge	Finish a Juggernaut with a knife in Special Ops.	15	Bronze
Arms Dealer	Buy all items from the Survival Weapon Armory.	20	Bronze
Danger Zone	Buy all items from the Survival Air Support Armory.	20	Bronze
Defense Spending	Buy all items from the Survival Equipment Armory.	20	Bronze
Get Rich or Die Trying	Have $50,000 current balance in a Special Ops Survival game.	25	Silver
I Live	Survive 1 wave in a Special Ops Survival game.	10	Bronze
Survivor	Reach Wave 10 in each mission of Special Ops Survival mode.	20	Silver
Unstoppable	Reach Wave 15 in each mission of Special Ops Survival mode.	40	Silver
No Assistance Required	Complete a Special Ops Mission Mode game on Hardened or Veteran with no player getting downed.	20	Bronze
Brag Rags	Earn 1 star in Special Ops Mission Mode.	10	Bronze
Tactician	Earn 1 star in each mission of Special Ops Mission Mode.	20	Bronze
Overachiever	Earn 48 stars in Special Ops Mission Mode.	40	Silver

SECRET ACHIEVEMENTS & TROPHIES

NAME	GOAL/REQUIREMENT	POINT VALUE	TROPHY VALUE
Flight Attendant	Kill all 5 enemies during the zero-g sequence in "Turbulence."	20	Bronze

COLLECTION 1
ACHIEVEMENTS

NAME	GOAL/REQUIREMENT	POINT VALUE	TROPHY VALUE
Shotgun Diplomacy	Complete the Special Ops mission "Negotiator" on any difficulty.	15	Bronze
Not on My Watch	Rescue all the hostages in the Special Ops mission "Negotiator."	35	Silver
Skilled Negotiator	Complete the Special Ops mission "Negotiator" on V eteran difficulty.	25	Silver
Slippery Slope	Complete the "Black Ice" Special Ops mission on any difficulty.	15	Bronze
A Baker's Dozen	Run over and kill 13 enemies with the snowmobile in the "Black Ice" Special Ops mission.	35	Silver
Ice in Your Veins	Complete the "Black Ice" Special Ops mission on Veteran difficulty.	35	Silver

CALL OF DUTY: MODERN WARFARE: MOBILIZED

NINTENDO 3DS

SURVIVAL MODE

Select Options from the War Room and press SELECT, L, R, SELECT, Y, Y, X, R, L, X, R, Y

CALL OF DUTY: WORLD AT WAR

NINTENDO 3DS

ALL CAMPAIGN AND CHALLENGE MISSIONS

At the War Room Options screen, press Y, X, Y, Y, X, Y, X, X, Y.

PLAYSTATION 3

ZOMBIE MODE

Complete Campaign mode.

USER ACCOUNT	ID	PASSWORD
Richard Helms	rhelms	LEROSEY
Richard Kain	rkain	SUNWU
Ryan Jackson	rjackson	SAINTBRIDGET
T. Walker	twalker	RADIO
Terrance Brooks	tbrooks	LAUREN
William Raborn	wraborn	BROMLOW

XBOX 360

ZOMBIE MODE

Complete Campaign mode.

CAPCOM ARCADE CABINET

1943 CHEATS

These cheats can be input at the beginning of a stage in 1943 to instantly gain a power-up.

EFFECT	PLAYER 1 CODE	PLAYER 2 CODE
Activate 3-Way in Stage 05	Hold A	Hold Up
Activate 3-Way in Stage 08	Hold Left + A + B	Hold A + B
Activate 3-Way in Stage 12	Hold Right + A + B	Hold A + Right + Up
Activate Auto in Stage 06	Hold Left	Hold Right + B
Activate Auto in Stage 11	Hold Up + Left	Hold Right + A
Activate Auto in Stage 13	Hold Up	Hold Down
Activate Auto in Stage 16	Hold Right + A	Hold Left
Activate Laser in Stage 03	Hold Up +_Right + A + B	Hold Down + B
Activate Laser in Stage 09	Hold Down + Right + A + B	Hold Right + Down + A + B
Activate Laser in Stage 14	Hold Up + Left + A + B	Hold Right + A + B
Activate Shell in Stage 07	Hold Up + Left	Hold Down
Activate Shell in Stage 10	Hold Up + Right + B	Hold Down + Right
Activate Shell in Stage 15	Hold Down + Right + A	Hold Left
Activate Shotgun in Stage 01	Hold Down	Hold A
Activate Shotgun in Stage 02	Hold A	Hold B
Activate Shotgun in Stage 04	Hold Down + Left + B	Hold Left + Up

CAPCOM CLASSICS COLLECTION REMIXED

UNLOCK EVERYTHING

At the title screen, press Left on D-pad, Right on D-pad, Left on Analog stick, Right on Analog stick, ●, ●, Up on D-pad, Down on D-pad.

CAPCOM PUZZLE WORLD

SUPER BUSTER BROS.

LEVEL SELECT IN TOUR MODE

At the Main menu, highlight Tour Mode, hold Down and press ●.

SUPER PUZZLE FIGHTER

PLAY AS AKUMA

At the character select, highlight Hsien-Ko and press Down.

PLAY AS DAN

At the character select, highlight Donovan and press Down.

PLAY AS DEVILOT

At the character select, highlight Morrigan and press Down.

PLAY AS ANITA

At the character select, hold L + R and choose Donovan.

PLAY AS HSIEN-KO'S TALISMAN

At the character select, hold L + R and choose Hsien-Ko.

PLAY AS MORRIGAN AS A BAT

At the character select, hold L + R and choose Morrigan.

CARNIVAL GAMES: MONKEY SEE, MONKEY DO!

XBOX 360

AVATAR AWARDS

AWARD	EARNED BY
Barker Bowler	Purchase Barker Bowler Prize.
Barker's Best	Purchase Barker's Best Prize.
Monkey Barker	Purchase Monkey Barker Prize.

CARS

XBOX 360

UNLOCK EVERYTHING

Select Cheat Codes from the Options and enter IF900HP.

ALL CHARACTERS

Select Cheat Codes from the Options and enter YAYCARS.

ALL CHARACTER SKINS

Select Cheat Codes from the Options and enter R4MONE.

ALL MINI-GAMES AND COURSES

Select Cheat Codes from the Options and enter MATTL66.

FAST START

Select Cheat Codes from the Options and enter IMSPEED.

INFINITE BOOST

Select Cheat Codes from the Options and enter VROOOOM.

ART

Select Cheat Codes from the Options and enter CONC3PT.

VIDEOS

Select Cheat Codes from the Options and enter WATCHIT.

CARS 2: THE VIDEO GAME

NINTENDO WII/XBOX 360/PS3

ALL MODES AND TRACKS

Select Enter Codes from the Options and enter 959595.

UNLIMITED ENERGY

Select Enter Codes from the Options and enter 721953. Select Cheats to toggle the cheat on and off.

LASER GUIDED

Select Enter Codes from the Options and enter 123456. Select Cheats to toggle the cheat on and off.

CARS: MATER-NATIONAL

ALL ARCADE RACES, MINI-GAMES, AND WORLDS

Select Codes/Cheats from the options and enter PLAYALL.

ALL CARS

Select Codes/Cheats from the options and enter MATTEL07.

ALTERNATE LIGHTNING MCQUEEN COLORS

Select Codes/Cheats from the options and enter NCEDUDZ.

ALL COLORS FOR OTHERS

Select Codes/Cheats from the options and enter PAINTIT.

UNLIMITED TURBO

Select Codes/Cheats from the options and enter ZZOOOOM.

EXTREME ACCELERATION

Select Codes/Cheats from the options and enter 0TO200X.

EXPERT MODE

Select Codes/Cheats from the options and enter VRYFAST.

ALL BONUS ART

Select Codes/Cheats from the options and enter BUYTALL.

CARTOON NETWORK: PUNCH TIME EXPLOSION

BATTLE MODE CHARACTERS

In Battle Mode, win the following number of matches to unlock the corresponding characters.

CHARACTER	# OF MATCHES
Captain Knuckles	3
Bubbles	7
Blossom	12
Monkey	18
Grim	25
Samurai Jack	33
Father	42
Vilgax	52
Mojo Jojo	63
Captain Planet	75

CASTLEVANIA: THE ADVENTURE REBIRTH

LEVEL SELECT

Select Game Start and hold Right for a few seconds. You can play any level you have already played.

CASTLEVANIA: HARMONY OF DESPAIR

HARD MODE

Complete Chapter 6 to unlock Hard Mode for Chapter 1.

ALUCARD GAMERPIC

Complete Chapter 6 in single player.

JAPANESE VOICES

At the character's color select, hold Right Trigger and press A.

CASTLEVANIA: LORDS OF SHADOW

CHEAT MENU

At a loading screen, press Up, Up, Down, Down, Left, Right, Left, Right, ●, ✕. The cheats can be found in the Extra Options. Activating any cheats disables saving and Trophies.

SNAKE OUTFIT

After completing the game, go to the Extras menu and toggle on Solid Eye and Bandanna.

VAMPIRE WARGAME

During Chapter 6-3, Castle Hall, complete the Vampire Wargame to unlock this mini-game in the Extras menu.

CHEAT MENU

At a loading screen, press Up, Up, Down, Down, Left, Right, Left, Right, B, A. The cheats can be found in the Extra Options. Activating any cheats disables saving and Achievements.

SNAKE OUTFIT

Defeat the game. In the Extras menu, toggle Solid Eye and Bandanna on.

VAMPIRE WARGAME

During Chapter 6-3: Castle Hall, beat the Vampire Wargame to unlock it in the Extras menu.

CASTLEVANIA: LORDS OF SHADOW— MIRROR OF FATE

EXTRA CUTSCENE

Complete the game with 100% completion to unlock an extra cutscene.

HARDCORE MODE

Complete the game once to unlock Hardcore Mode.

STAFF CREDITS

Complete the game once to unlock the Staff Credits in the main menu.

CASTLEVANIA: PORTRAIT OF RUIN

JAPANESE VOICEOVERS

At the Main menu, hold L and press A.

CASTLEVANIA: SYMPHONY OF THE NIGHT

XBOX 360

Before using the following codes, complete the game with 170%.

PLAY AS RICHTER BELMONT

Enter RICHTER as your name.

ALUCARD WITH AXELORD ARMOR

Enter AXEARMOR as your name.

ALUCARD WITH 99 LUCK AND OTHER STATS ARE LOW

Enter X-X!V"Q as your name.

CASTLEVANIA: THE DRACULA X CHRONICLES

PSP

ORIGINAL RONDO OF BLOOD

LEVEL SELECT

Enter X-X!V"Q as your player name

SYMPHONY OF THE NIGHT

PLAY AS ALUCARD WITH 99 LUCK AND LAPIS LAZULI

Start a new game with the name X-X!V"Q.

PLAY AS ALUCARD WITH AXE LORD ARMOR

After clearing the game once, start a new game with the name AXEARMOR.

PLAY AS MARIA RENARD

After clearing the game once, start a new game with the name MARIA.

PLAY AS RICHTER BELMONT

After clearing the game once, start a new game with the name RICHTER.

CATAPULT MADNESS

MOBILE

ACHIEVEMENTS

ACHIEVEMENT	REQUIREMENT
Addicted	Play for an hour.
Air Control	Hit 20 birds.
Bombardier	Hit 100 bombs.
Camping Freak	Destroy 50 tents.
Fat Lover	Bounce on 100 fat trolls.
Long Jumper	Get 10,000 feet distance in a single throw.
Sky's the Limit	Get 1,500 feet height in a single throw.
Super Jumper	Get 30,000 feet distance in a single throw.
Troll Lover	Hit 50 Trolls.
Veteran	Play for 30 minutes.

CATHERINE

XBOX 360/PS3

NEW RAPUNZEL STAGES

At the title screen, press Up, Down, Down, Up, Up, Up, Down, Down, Down, Down, Right. Re-enter the code to disable.

C

CENTIPEDE: INFESTATION

NINTENDO 3DS

PLAY AS RIVET WITH RIVETER GUN

Select Code Entry from Extras and enter 121213.

NINTENDO WII

MISSILE COMMAND PACK

Select Enter Code from Extras and enter 111771.

CHU CHU ROCKET HD

MOBILE

HARD PUZZLES

Complete all 25 Normal puzzles.

SPECIAL PUZZLES

Complete all 25 Hard puzzles.

MANIA PUZZLES

Complete all 25 Special puzzles.

CITY LIFE DS

NINTENDO 3DS

1,000,000

Pause the game and press A, B, Y, L, R.

ALL BUILDINGS

Pause the game and hold B + Y + X + R for 2 seconds.

CLASH OF CLANS

MOBILE

STRATEGIES & TIPS

- Properly Plan for Battle—No matter what happens at the end of a battle, every troop you take with you into battle will be lost at the end, even if they are unharmed by fighting. Think carefully about your opponent's strength and send out soldiers accordingly before deploying your troops for battle.

- Scout Ahead—Even though you can't see what troops the enemy will have in single-player mode, you can scout ahead by sending a few weak units at an encounter. Send some expendable troops at your enemy to learn their layout, then send your real force out after you know what they're capable of.

- Balance Your Attack—Try not to stretch yourself too far towards offense or defense. Even if you can easily destroy any enemy, it won't matter if others can quickly destroy you! Make sure your town hall and resource gatherers are guarded by cannon-fire so you can protect yourself while your army attacks.

- Clear Smart Space—Removing larger objects requires more resources and sometimes isn't the best way to advance. Try to clear out smaller objects and use that space instead.

- Boring Upgrades—While they aren't very exciting, upgrading your resource collectors over your armies will give you more total resources, giving you a stronger army overall.

CLUB PENGUIN: ELITE PENGUIN FORCE

FLOWER HUNT MISSION

Change your system's date to April 1st.

APRIL ITEMS IN CATALOG

Change your system's date to April 1st.

SUMMER PARTY MISSION

Change your system's date to June 21st.

FIESTA HAT ON FROZEN POND

Change your system's date to June 21st.

JUNE ITEMS IN CATALOG

Change your system's date to June 21st.

HALLOWEEN PARTY MISSION

Change your system's date to October 31st.

FISH COSTUME IN LODGE ATTIC

Change your system's date to October 31st.

DELIVER THE PRESENTS MISSION

Change your system's date to December 25th.

ICE SKATES ON THE ICEBERG

Change your system's date to December 25th.

CODE LYOKO

CODELYOKO.COM SECRET FILES

Enter the following as Secret Codes on the My Secret Album page of www.codelyoko.com:

SECRET FILE	CODE
Dark Enemies Wallpaper	9L8Q
Desert Sketch	6G7T
Fight Video	4M9P
FMV Ending	5R5K
Forest Sketch	8C3X
Ice Sketch	2F6U
Mountain Sketch	7E5V
Overbike	3Q4L
Overboard	8P3M
Overwing	8N2N
Scorpion Video	9H8S
Scorpion Wallpaper	3D4W
Sector 5 Sketch	5J9R
Ulrich	9A9Z
Yumi	4B2Y

C

CODE LYOKO: QUEST FOR INFINITY

UNLOCK EVERYTHING

Pause the game and press 2, 1, C, Z, 2, 1.

UNLIMITED HEALTH AND POWER

Pause the game and press 2, 2, Z, Z, 1, 1.

INCREASE SPEED

Pause the game and press Z, 1, 2, 1 (x3).

INCREASE DAMAGE

Pause the game and press 1, Z, Z, C (x3).

CONFIGURATION A

Pause the game and press 2, Z, 1, Z, C, Z.

CONFIGURATION B

Pause the game and press C, C, 1, C, Z, C.

ALL ABILITIES

Pause the game and press Z, C, Z, C (x3).

ALL BONUSES

Pause the game and press 1, 2, C, 2 (x3).

ALL GOODIES

Pause the game and press C, 2, 2, Z, C, Z.

COMMAND & CONQUER 3: TIBERIUM WARS

FREE NOD SHADOW SQUADS

During a NOD game, pause and press Left, Right, Up, Up, Up, Down, RB, LB, LB, B. This code does not work in Skirmish or Career.

CONDUIT 2

EYE OF RA ASE

Select Promotional Codes from the Extras menu and enter EYEOFRA.

GOLDEN DESTROYER ARMOR (ONLINE ONLY)

Select Promotional Codes from the Extras menu and enter 14KARMOR.

CONTRA 4

SUPER C

10 LIVES

At the title screen, press Right, Left, Down, Up, B, Y.

SOUND TEST

As the logo fades in to the title screen, hold Y + B and press Start

CONTRA

30 LIVES

At the title screen, press Up, Up, Down, Down, Left, Right Left, Right, Y, B.

UPGRADE WEAPONS

Pause the game and press Up, Up, Down, Down, Left, Right Left, Right, B, A, Start. This code can be used once per life. If you enter it a second time, you will die.

CONTRA REBIRTH

DEBUG MENU

At the title screen, press Plus + 1 + 2.

CORALINE

UNLIMITED LEVEL SKIP

Select Cheats from the Options menu and enter beldam.

UNLIMITED HEALTH

Select Cheats from the Options menu and enter beets.

UNLIMITED FIREFLIES

Select Cheats from the Options menu and enter garden.

FREE HALL PASSES

Select Cheats from the Options menu and enter well.

BUTTON EYE CORALINE

Select Cheats from the Options menu and enter cheese.

CRACKDOWN 2

AVATAR AWARDS

AWARD	EARNED BY
Orb Shirt (Male and Female)	Have First Blood achievement from Crackdown
Freaky Slippers (Male and Female)	Earn First Hurdle achievement
Ruffian Hat	Earn Hope Springs Savior achievement
Level 1 Agent Suit (Male and Female)	Earn Light Bringer achievement
Official Agency Hoodie (Male and Female)	Earn Jack of all Trades achievement

DOWNLOADABLE CONTENT: TOY BOX

AVATAR AWARDS

AWARD	EARNED BY
Green Agent Helmet	Download Toy Box DLC
Green Agent Suit	Earn Rocketeer achievement

CRASHMO

CRASHMO STUDIO

Complete 10 lessons in Crashmo Park to unlock the Crashmo Studio, which allows you to create your own levels.

GADGETS

Clearing challenges unlocks Gadgets in Crashmo Studio.

GADGETS	REQUIREMENT
Floating Block Gadget	Complete Challenge 2-1.
Manholes	Complete Challenge 3-1.
Doors	Complete Challenge 4-1.
Move Switches	Complete Challenge 5-1.

PROTOTYPE MODE

Complete Challenge 5-10 to unlock Prototype Mode.

PROTOTYPES

Prototypes are unlocked after 70 puzzles have been cleared.

TRAINING MODE

After completing 20 lessons in Crashmo Park you'll unlock Trainin Mode, which contains additional puzzles.

CRAZY TAXI

EXPERT MODE

In Crazy Box, complete 1-x stages. Select Special from Help & Options to access this option.

TOGGLE ARROW AND DESTINATION MARK ON AND OFF

In Crazy Box, complete 2-x stages. Select Special from Help & Options to access this option.

ANOTHER DAY MODE

In Crazy Box, complete all 1-x stages Select Special from Help & Options to access this option.

RICKSHAW BIKE

In Crazy Box, complete all 3-x stages Select Special from Help & Options to access this option.

THE CREEPS! HD

DOODLER FROM DOODLE JUMP TOWER

Look at the Credits and click on the word AWESOME 100 times. Doodler shows up on the right side. Tap him to enable the secret. Now you can toggle Doodler on and off in the help menu.

PYGMIES FROM POCKET GOD ENEMIES

Look at the Credits and click on the egg on the left side to enable this secret. Now you can toggle the Pygmies on and off in the help menu.

CRIMSON ALLIANCE

XBOX 360

AVATAR AWARDS

AWARD	EARNED BY
Pocket Shaman	Defeat a Primitive Shaman.
Death Knight Helm	Collect 20 Treasures.

CRIMSON DRAGON

XBOX 360

AVATAR AWARDS

AVATAR	EARNED BY
Bloodskin Helmet	Complete the First Mission.
Bloodskin Suit (Top)	Raise the level of Bloodskin.
Bloodskin Suit (Bottom)	Get an S rank five times with Bloodskin.

CRIMSON DRAGON: SIDE STORY

MOBILE

AVATAR AWARDS

AVATAR	EARNED BY
White T-Shirt	Clear the First Level.
Dragon Head	Clear the Second Level.

CRISIS CORE—FINAL FANTASY VII

PSP

NEW GAME+

After completing the game, you'll be prompted to make a new save. Loading a game from this new save will begin a New Game+, starting the game over while allowing Zack to retain almost everything he's earned.

The following items transfer to a New Game+: Level, Experience, SP, Gil, Playtime, Non-Key Items, Materia, and DMW Completion Rate

The following items do not transfer: Key Items, Materia/Accessory Slot Expansion, Ability to SP Convert, DMW Images, Mission Progress, Mail, and Unlocked Shops

CRYSIS 2

NINTENDO WII

HIDDEN MINIGAME

At the credits, press R2 five times.

HIDDEN MINIGAME

At the credits, press Right Trigger five times.

ACHIEVEMENTS & TROPHIES

NAME	GOAL/REQUIREMENT	POINT VALUE	TROPHY VALUE
Can it run Crysis?	Complete In at the Deep End	10	Bronze
Foreign Contaminant	Escape the Battery Park evacuation center	10	Bronze
More than Human	Assimilate alien tissue at the crash site	15	Bronze
False Prophet	Find Nathan Gould	15	Bronze
Internal Affairs	Infiltrate the CELL facility at Wall Street	15	Bronze
Into the Abyss	Infiltrate the alien hive	20	Bronze
Once a Marine, Always a Marine	Assist the Marines in Madison Square	20	Bronze
Hung Out to Dry	Reach the Hargreave-Rasch building	20	Bronze
Fire Walker	Assist the evacuation at Bryant Park	25	Bronze
Dark Night of the Soul	Defend Central Station	25	Bronze
Crossroads of the World	Complete the evacuation at Times Square	25	Bronze
Theseus at Last	Locate Jacob Hargreave	25	Bronze
Home Stretch	Reach Central Park	25	Silver
Start Spreading the News	Finish the single player campaign on any difficulty	35	Silver
City That Never Sleeps	Complete 6 levels on Veteran difficulty	25	Silver
Evolution	Complete 12 levels on Veteran difficulty	25	Silver
Heart of Darkness	Complete 6 levels on Supersoldier difficulty	25	Silver
Medal of Honor	Complete 12 levels on Supersoldier difficulty	25	Silver
Men of Destiny	Complete the single player campaign on Veteran difficulty	45	Silver
Supersoldier	Complete the single player campaign on Supersoldier	65	Gold
Close Encounters	Single Player: Stealth kill 25 enemies	15	Bronze
The Tourist	Find all New York Souvenirs	15	Bronze
Fastball	Kill 10 enemies by throwing an object at them	15	Bronze
Death Grip	Kill 10 enemies with grab and throw	15	Bronze
Popcorn	Single Player: Kill 20 enemies with the Microwave cannon	15	Bronze
Two Heads Are Better Than One	Single Player: Kill two enemies with a single bullet	15	Bronze
Blast Radius	Single Player: Kill at least 3 enemies with a single grenade	15	Bronze
Headhunter	Single Player: Kill 4 enemies in a row with headshots	15	Bronze
Death Slide	Single Player: Kill 5 enemies while sliding	15	Bronze
Food for thought	Kill a CELL operator with a giant donut in Lower Manhattan	10	Bronze
Hole in One	Throw an alien down the sinkhole in Dark Heart	10	Bronze

NAME	GOAL/REQUIREMENT	POINT VALUE	TROPHY VALUE
Band of Brothers	Keep all marines alive during the rescue in Semper Fi or Die	15	Bronze
Literary Agent	Scan all of Richard Morgan's books in the NY public library	10	Bronze
Stealth Assassin	Re-route the power in Eye of the Storm without being detected	15	Bronze
Crysis, What Crysis?	Multiplayer: Reach Rank 50	35	Gold
League of Your Own	Multiplayer: Finish top of the Scoreboard	25	Silver
Dressed to Kill	Multiplayer: Fully level the Nanosuit	30	Silver
Tooled Up	Multiplayer: Unlock all the weapons	30	Silver
The Cleaner	Get 1 of each Skill Kill	25	Bronze
Cry Spy	Multiplayer: Get 30 Spot Assists	25	Bronze
Jack of all Trades	Multiplayer: Win a match of every game mode	25	Bronze
Dedication	Play online 6 months after your first time	25	Bronze
Modern Art	Unlock 150 Dog Tag displays	5	Bronze
Try Me	Complete 3 Xbox LIVE matches	10	Bronze
The Collector	Collect 20 Dog Tags	15	Bronze
Maximum Module	Multiplayer: Fully level a Suit Module	20	Bronze
Team Player	Be in a squad of at least 3 people and play a full game	10	Bronze
Nomad	Multiplayer: Play a full game on every map	10	Bronze
I Am Not A Number	Create your first custom class	10	Bronze

SECRET ACHIEVEMENTS & TROPHIES

NAME	GOAL/REQUIREMENT	POINT VALUE	TROPHY VALUE
Speeding Ticket	Break the speed limit in front of 10 speed cameras	10	Bronze

CRYSIS 3

XBOX 360/PS3

ACHIEVEMENTS & TROPHIES

NAME	GOAL/REQUIREMENT	POINT VALUE	TROPHY VALUE
Staying Sharp	Complete Tutorial	20	Bronze
Welcome to the Jungle!	Complete Post-Human	15	Bronze
A Flawless Getaway	Complete Welcome to the Jungle	15	Bronze
Off the Grid	Complete The Root of All Evil	15	Bronze
Turning the Tide	Complete Safeties Off	15	Bronze
Brink of Apocalypse	Complete Red Star Rising	20	Bronze
Belly of the Beast	Complete Only Human	20	Bronze
The True Measure of a Hero	Complete Gods and Monsters	20	Bronze
Nanosuit Veteran	Complete 3 of 7 levels on Veteran difficulty	25	Silver
Halfway to Hell	Complete 3 of 7 levels on Supersoldier difficulty	25	Silver
World Saver	Finish the campaign on any difficulty	35	Silver

NAME	GOAL/REQUIREMENT	POINT VALUE	TROPHY VALUE
Bring it On	Complete the campaign on Veteran difficulty	45	Silver
Professional Superhero	Complete the campaign on Supersoldier difficulty	65	Gold
Perk Of The Job	Single Player: Save a Nanosuit module package	15	Bronze
Geared-up	Single Player: Unlock all weapon attachments	25	Silver
Suited-up	Single Player: Upgrade all Nanosuit modules to Maximum level	20	Silver
Be a Pro, use a Bow!	Single Player: Kill 10 enemies with each arrow type	20	Bronze
Maximum Strength	Single Player: Kill 25 enemies using only the Nanosuit's enhanced powers instead of guns	15	Bronze
Hunter-Gatherer	Single Player: Retrieve 10 arrows from pinned enemies	15	Bronze
The Gibson	Single Player: Complete 20 hacking challenges	15	Bronze
I'll Have That!	Single Player: Rip off and use all alien weapon types	15	Bronze
Taste Of Your Own Medicine	Single Player: Kill 25 enemies while supercharged	15	Bronze
Breaking the Lore	Single Player: Retrieve all CELL Intel	10	Bronze
Bang For The Buck	Single Player: Kill a deer using explosive arrows	10	Bronze
Can You Hear Me Now?	Welcome to the Jungle: Disable the Nanosuit Jammer	20	Bronze
Who Needs Rockets?	Post-Human: Take out an attack helicopter using the Predator Bow	20	Bronze
White Rider	The Root of All Evil: Surf the donut down the river for 20 seconds	20	Bronze
Roadkill	Red Star Rising: Crush 5 enemies with the Buggy	20	Bronze
Ping Pong!	Only Human: Kill all Pingers	20	Bronze
Inside Job	Single Player: Kill 10 enemies using hacked sentry guns	25	Silver
Post-Human Warrior	Single Player: Kill 10 enemies in a single Supercharge boost	25	Silver
Arrow to the Knee!	Single Player: End an enemy's career as a CELL operative by wounding him in the knee with an arrow!	20	Bronze
Improviser	Single Player: Kill two enemies in one strike using the environment	15	Bronze
Nanosuit Ninja	Single Player: Perform 20 Stealth Kills without alerting nearby enemies	15	Bronze
Stick Around	Single Player: Using the Predator Bow, pin 10 enemies to walls with arrows	15	Bronze
Clever Girl!	Single Player: Stealth kill a Ceph Stalker	15	Bronze
Poltergeist	Single Player: Kill 10 enemies with thrown objects without being detected	10	Bronze
Rising Star	Reach Rank 20	15	Bronze
Block Party	Complete a match in every location in New York (Public Match only)	20	Silver

NAME	GOAL/REQUIREMENT	POINT VALUE	TROPHY VALUE
Odd Job	Get two kills with one throw-able object in the same match (Public Match only)	25	Silver
Lord of the Pings	Kill 25 enemies with the Pinger (Public Match only)	15	Bronze
The Specialist	Get a stealth kill, a rip and a throw kill and an air stomp kill in the same match (Public Match only)	30	Silver
Bird of Prey	Air stomp someone from a height of 15 meters (Public Match only)	15	Bronze
Going Commando	Get a primary weapon, secondary weapon and explosive kill in one life (Public Match only)	30	Silver
Hit me baby one more time	Melee someone with a ripped off shield in Spears (Public Match only)	15	Bronze
Rudely Interrupted	Rip an enemy player out of a Pinger (Public Match only)	20	Silver
I See Cloaked People	Kill 10 Hunters as a C.E.L.L. operative (Public Match only)	20	Silver
Would you kindly …	Accept and complete 25 unique challenges	20	Silver
Aerial Support	Kill 10 enemies using the mounted weapon on the VTOL (Public Match only)	15	Bronze
Kicking off the training wheels	Complete a match using manual armor mode only (Public Match only)	10	Bronze

CUT THE ROPE

MOBILE

OM NOM'S DRAWINGS

In 12 levels, if you tap on a certain spot of the background a drawing will be revealed. This spot can be something like a caution exclamation point or a peeling wallpaper. Just look for something that looks a little off in the following levels: 1-16, 2-18, 3-3, 3-20, 4-14, 5-1, 5-15, 6-7, 7-3, 7-21, 8-17 and 9-21. Select Om Nom's Drawings to look at your collection.

DAMNATION

PLAYSTATION 3

INSANE DIFFICULTY

Select Enter Code from Unlockables and enter Revenant.

VORPAL MECHANICAL REPEATER

Select Enter Code from Unlockables and enter BlowOffSomeSteam.

BIG HEAD MODE

Select Enter Code from Unlockables and enter LincolnsTopHat.

CUSTOM CHARACTERS

Select Enter Code from Unlockables and enter PeoplePerson.

CUSTOM LOADOUT

Select Enter Code from Unlockables and enter LockNLoad.

CHEATS, ACHIEVEMENTS, AND TROPHIES

D

DANCE CENTRAL 2

ANGEL'S DC CLASSIC OUTFIT

Select Gameplay Settings from the Options, choose Enter Cheats and enter Y, Right, Left, Up, X, X, Down, Y.

EMILIA'S DC CLASSIC OUTFIT

Select Gameplay Settings from the Options, choose Enter Cheats and enter Left, Left, Up, Right, Right, X, Down, Y.

MISS AUBREY'S DC CLASSIC OUTFIT

Select Gameplay Settings from the Options, choose Enter Cheats and enter Left, Down, X, X, Down, Right.

TAYE'S DC CLASSIC OUTFIT

Select Gameplay Settings from the Options, choose Enter Cheats and enter Up, Left, Y, X, Left, Up, X, Y.

AVATAR AWARDS

AWARD	EARNED BY
Bring It Tee	Play every song in the game in Perform It mode.
Neon Tee	Get a solo score of at least 2,000,000 points on a song.
Ribbon Tee	Earn Gold Stars on a song.

DANTE'S INFERNO

UNLOCK EARTHLY REWARDS FOR YOUR COMPUTER

Go to www.hellisnigh.com and enter the following passwords:

- Password #1: excommunicate
- Password #2: scythe
- Password #3: grafter
- Password #4: styx
- Password #5: unbaptized
- Password #6: alighieri

THE DARKNESS

DARKLING OUTFITS

Even Darklings can make a fashion statement. Support your mini minions with an ensemble fit for murderous monsters by collecting these fun and colorful outfits.

OUTFIT	MENTIONED IN	AREA	LOCATION
Potato Sack	Chapter 1	Chinatown	Sitting against alley wall near metro exit
Jungle	Chapter 1	Hunters Point Alley	Inside hidden room
Roadworker	Chapter 3	City Hall station	Inside train car
Lumberjack	Side Objectives	Cutrone objective	Inside Cutrone's apartment
Fireman	Side Objectives	Pajamas objective	Inside room 261
Construction	Side Objectives	Mortarello objective	Inside room of last mission
Baseball	N/A	Dial: 555-4263	N/A
Golfshirt	N/A	Dial: 555-5664	N/A

PHONE NUMBERS

Dialing 'D' for Darkness isn't the only number to punch on a telephone. Sure, you called every number you found on those hard-to-get Collectibles, but you certainly haven't found all of the phone numbers. Pay close to attention to the environment as you hunt down Uncle Paulie. Chances are, you overlooked a phone number or two without even knowing it as you ripped out a goon's heart. All 25 'secret' phone numbers are scattered throughout New York and can be seen on anywhere from flyers and storefronts to garbage cans and posters. Dial 18 of the 25 numbers on a phone—in no specific order—to unlock the final secret of the game.

555-6118	555-1847	555-6667	555-4569
555-9985	555-1037	555-1206	555-9528
555-3285	555-5723	555-8024	555-6322
555-9132	555-6893	555-2402	555-6557
555-2309	555-4372	555-9723	555-5289
555-6205	555-7658	555-1233	555-3947
555-9562	555-7934	555-7892	555-8930
555-3243	555-3840	555-2349	555-6325
555-4565	555-9898	555-7613	555-6969

DARKSIDERS

XBOX360/PS3

HARVESTER FOR 0 SOULS

Pause the game and select Enter Code from the Options. Enter The Hollow Lord.

DARKSTALKERS RESURRECTION

XBOX 360/PS3

VAMPIRE SAVIOR

EXTRA BATTLE

If you defeat three enemies in Arcade Mode with an EX Finish and don't lose a round you will be challenged by a midboss.

SOUL MODE

On the character select screen, move your cursor to the Random Select box and press Start five times then any punch or kick.

ALTERNATE SOUL MODE

On the character select screen, move your cursor to any character and press Start 3 times, then go to the Random Select box and press Start 5 times then any punch or kick.

DARK TALBAIN

On the character select screen, move your cursor to J. Talbain and press Start & all three punch buttons simultaneously.

DE BLOB

MOBILE

INVULNERABILITY

During a game, hold C and press 1, 1, 1, 1. Re-enter the code to disable.

LIFE UP

During a game, hold C and press 1, 1, 2, 2.

TIME BONUS

During a game, hold C and press 1, 2, 1, 2. This adds 10 minutes to your time.

ALL MOODS

At the Main menu, hold C and press B, B, 1, 2, 1, 2, B, B.

ALL MULTIPLAYER LEVELS

At the Main menu, hold C and press 2, 2, B, B, 1, 1, B, B.

DEAD BLOCK

XBOX 360

AVATAR AWARDS

AWARD	EARNED BY
Construction Worker Helmet	Collect the helmet in the tutorial.
Dead Block Shirt	Beat all singleplayer levels.

DEAD ISLAND

XBOX360/PS3

ACHIEVEMENTS & TROPHIES

NAME	GOAL/REQUIREMENT	POINT VALUE	TROPHY VALUE
Rootin' Tootin' Lootin'	Loot 5 Exceptional Weapons.	30	Gold
'Tis but a flesh wound!	Sever 100 limbs.	10	Bronze
There and back again	Explore the entire island.	30	Silver
Catch!	Kill an Infected with a grenade blast.	10	Bronze
Road Trip	Drive a total distance of 10 kilometers.	10	Bronze
Cardio	Travel a distance of 20 kilometers on foot.	10	Bronze
Swing them sticks	Kill 150 enemies using Analog Fighting controls.	25	Silver
Gesundheit!	Heal yourself with a medkit 100 times.	10	Bronze
Light my fire	Set 10 zombies on fire simultaneously.	20	Bronze
10 heads are better than 1	Kill 10 zombies in a row with headshots.	15	Bronze
A taste of everything	Kill a zombie with 10 different melee weapons.	25	Bronze
One is all I need	Kill 5 Infected in a row with a single blow.	20	Bronze
Can't touch this	Use a hammer to kill a series of 15 zombies without taking damage.	20	Bronze
Humanitarian	Kill 50 human enemies.	15	Bronze
Tae Kwon Leap	Kill 25 zombies with your bare fists.	25	Bronze
I want one of those	Customize 25 weapons.	30	Silver
Karma-geddon	Kill 50 zombies using a vehicle.	15	Bronze
To put it bluntly	Kill 250 zombies using blunt melee weapons.	25	Bronze
Hack & slash	Kill 250 zombies using edged melee weapons.	25	Bronze
Guns don't kill but they help	Kill 250 zombies using firearms.	25	Bronze
Need a hand?	Join another player's game.	10	Bronze
Warranty Void if Used	Create a customized weapon.	10	Bronze
Gotta find'em all	Find 60 collectibles.	20	Bronze
Nearly there	Find 120 collectibles.	25	Bronze
Steam Punk	Create weapons to rival the gods of fire or thunder.	30	Silver
Originality	Play in a co-op team of 4 different playable characters.	10	Bronze
Together in the light	Complete 5 quests in a single co-op game with the same partners.	10	Bronze

NAME	GOAL/REQUIREMENT	POINT VALUE	TROPHY VALUE
Going steady	Complete 25 quests while playing with at least one co-op partner.	25	Bronze
Rageman	Kill 100 enemies with Fury attacks.	25	Bronze
People Person	Play with 10 different co-op partners for at least 15 minutes each.	10	Bronze
Ménage à trois	Complete 5 quests with 3 co-op partners.	25	Bronze
Right 4 Life	Complete act I with 4 different characters.	30	Silver
A very special day	Kill 250 zombies with modified weapons.	30	Bronze
School of hard knocks	Reach level 50.	30	Silver
Knock, knock	Breach a locked door with the first blow.	15	Bronze
Busy, busy, busy	Finish 75 quests cumulatively.	60	Silver
Learning the ropes	Reach level 10.	10	Bronze
Dedicated student	Reach level 25.	25	Bronze

SECRET ACHIEVEMENTS & TROPHIES

NAME	GOAL/REQUIREMENT	POINT VALUE	TROPHY VALUE
Everybody lies	Use a large medkit to heal an injury of 5% or less.	20	Bronze
Hell in paradise	Complete act I.	30	Silver
Ah! Spoiled meat!	Kill a Butcher using an axe.	10	Bronze
Oh, no you don't	Kill a Ram using tackle skill.	10	Bronze
Savior	Save 5 people besieged by zombies.	20	Bronze
How many days exactly?	Play Dead Island at least 28 days after starting it for the first time.	10	Bronze
No raccoons in here	Complete act II.	30	Silver
King of the jungle	Complete act III.	30	Silver
Banoi Redemption	Complete act IV.	30	Silver
First!	Kill a Suicider with a grenade.	15	Bronze

DEAD ISLAND: RIPTIDE

XBOX 360/PS3

ACHIEVEMENTS & TROPHIES

NAME	GOAL/REQUIREMENT	POINT VALUE	TROPHY VALUE
Achiever	Finish all quests in the game	100	Gold
Mystery solved	Find all the secret files	15	Bronze
Obtain level 50	Obtain level 50	30	Silver
Obtain level 70	Obtain level 70	90	Gold
Siege Hammer	Install a total of 5 barricades during hub defense	15	Bronze
Dream Team	Complete all the main quests cooperatively with any number of partners	15	Bronze
The Collector	Find 50% of collectibles	15	Bronze
The Hoarder	Find all collectibles	30	Silver
Professional Tourist	Find all pages from the guide book	30	Silver
Twins	Kill the Twins	30	Silver

NAME	GOAL/REQUIREMENT	POINT VALUE	TROPHY VALUE
News junkie	Find all the volunteer's voice recordings	30	Silver
At Your Service	Rescue 20 NPCs that have been grabbed by monsters	15	Bronze
The Hurt Mine Locker	Kill 10 monsters with one mine	15	Bronze
BrainLess	Kill 50 monsters by smashing, decapitating or shooting them in the head	15	Bronze
Hurler	Kill 100 monsters with thrown melee weapons	15	Bronze
Bully	Kill 100 monsters with a kick	15	Bronze
Jetboat	Kill 100 monsters using the boat's speed boost	90	Gold
Juggernaut	Kill 100 enemies using charge attacks	15	Bronze
Better than the arm	Kill 25 monsters with a chainsaw	30	Silver
It's an Order	Mark 100 opponents which were then killed by your co-op partners	15	Bronze
King among Kings	Kill special enemies: Grenadier, Thug, Wrestler, Infected, Suicider, Screamer, Butcher, Floater.	30	Silver
Hunter-Seeker	Find and kill all named champion monsters located in dead zones	90	Gold
The Whole World Went Away	Collect all other trophies	—	Platinum

SECRET ACHIEVEMENTS & TROPHIES

NAME	GOAL/REQUIREMENT	POINT VALUE	TROPHY VALUE
Heart of Darkness	Find a boat for use in the jungle	15	Bronze
Breaching the Tunnels	Successfully defend the tunnel entrance	15	Bronze
The Cinema	Clear out the cinema	15	Bronze
Military Base	Gain access to a long-range radio station	30	Silver
Combat on the roof	Survive the horde on the roof	15	Bronze
Henderson Town	Reach Henderson	15	Bronze
Meeting Serpo	Make pact with Serpo	15	Bronze
The Docks	Enter the docks in Quarantine Zone	15	Bronze
You've tricked me once	Finish the game	30	Silver
Serving Science	Finish quests for Dr. Kessler	30	Silver
First Do No Harm	Finish hospital quests for Cecil	30	Silver
Defeat Harlow	Defeat Harlow	15	Bronze
The Storm	Escape from the ship	15	Bronze

DEAD OR ALIVE 5 PLUS

OMG MODE

Perform 5,000 taps total in Touch Matches to unlock OMG-level physics.

DEAD RISING 2

KNIGHT ARMOR

Wearing this armor doubles Chuck's health. When his health falls below half, though, the armor is destroyed.

ARMOR NAME	OBTAIN
Full Beard Moustache	Found in the back of Wave of Style, located in Royal Flush Plaza.
Knight Armor	Finish the game with an "S" ending.
Knight Boots	Purchase for $2,000,000 at Moe's Maginations pawnshop on the Platinum Strip.
Knight Helmet	Rescue Jack in "Meet the Family" and win at poker in "Ante Up."

UNLOCKABLE OUTFITS

The following items are unlocked by performing the corresponding task.

ITEM	OBTAINED BY
Bowling Shirt, Diner Waitress, Hunting Jacket, and Overalls	Import a save game from Case Zero.
Champion Jacket	Earn the Win Big! Trophy. Get this by finishing in first place in a TIR Episode.
Dealer Outfit	Earn Chuck Greene: Cross Dresser? Trophy. Get this by changing into all the clothes in the game.
Hockey Mask	Earn the Head Trauma Trophy. Get this by using every type of melee weapon on a zombie.
Orange Prison Outfit	Earn the Judge, Jury and Executioner Trophy. Get this by killing 10 psychos.
Tattered Clothes	Earn the Zombie Fu Trophy. Get this by killing 1000 zombies barehanded.
TIR Helmet	Earn $1,000,000 in Terror is Reality.
TIR Outfit	Earn $5,000,000 in Terror is Reality.
Willamette Mall Security Uniform	Earn Hero of Fortune City Trophy. Get this by rescuing 50 survivors.

DEAD SPACE 2

ACHIEVEMENTS & TROPHIES

NAME	GOAL/REQUIREMENT	POINT VALUE	TROPHY VALUE
Mission Impossible	Complete the game on Zealot setting	50	Gold
Romper Stomper	Stomp 10 Containers	25	Bronze
Vacuum Cleaner	Decompress 20 Necromorphs without getting sucked out yourself	30	Bronze
Made Us Whole	Complete the game on any difficulty setting	10	Bronze
Frozen in Time	Kill 50 Necromorphs while they are in Stasis (single player only)	10	Bronze
First Aid	Use Quick Heal ten times (single player only)	10	Bronze
Epic Dismemberment	Dismember 2,500 Necromorph Limbs (single player only)	50	Silver
...And Stay Down	Kill 25 crawling enemies with Stomp (single player only)	10	Bronze

NAME	GOAL/REQUIREMENT	POINT VALUE	TROPHY VALUE
Think Fast	Kill 30 Necromorphs with Kinesis objects	15	Bronze
The Nanny	Kill 30 Crawlers without detonating them	10	Bronze
C-Section	Knock down an enemy with Contact Beam Alt-Fire then kill it with Primary Fire before it stands up	10	Bronze
Going for Distance	Impale an enemy and make him fly through the air for 17 meters—it must stick to the surface	20	Bronze
Taste of your own Medicine	TK Impale a live Slasher to a surface using a Slasher's arm—it must stick to the surface	20	Bronze
It's a Trap!	Kill 20 enemies with Detonator Mines in a deployed state	20	Bronze
Necro Flambé	Kill 50 enemies using the Flamethrower	10	Bronze
Peek a Boo!	Kill a Stalker with the Seeker Rifle while in Zoom Mode	20	Bronze
Brute Juke	Kill a Brute without taking damage	10	Bronze
Shoot the Limbs!	Dismember 25 Necromorph Limbs (single player only)	10	Bronze
Bouncing Betty	Kill a Cyst by catching its Mine and throwing it back	10	Bronze
Skewered in Space	Impale an enemy into a Decompression Window to cause it to blow out	15	Bronze
Hard to the Core	Complete the game on Hard Core setting	50	Gold
Clean Cut	Sever all three tentacles of a Lurker with one Line Gun Primary Fire shot (single player only)	10	Bronze
Lawnmower Man	Kill 4 enemies with the same Ripper blade	10	Bronze
Fully Loaded	Simultaneously have four completely upgraded weapons	50	Bronze
The Sampler Platter	Kill a Necromorph with every Weapon in the game (single player only)	20	Bronze
Lightspeed de Milo	Dismember the Lightspeed Boy Statue	10	Bronze
Looking good	Purchase the Advanced Suit	10	Bronze
Fully Outfitted	Upgrade your RIG and Stasis completely	30	Bronze
Picking favorites	Upgrade 1 Weapon completely	30	Bronze
The Engineer	Collect 10 Schematics	10	Silver
My Boom Stick	Kill 6 enemies at once with Line Gun's Alt-Fire (single player only)	20	Bronze
Shock Therapy	Impale an enemy with the Javelin Gun and use its Alt-Fire to shock 3 others (single player only)	10	Bronze
Collect Peng	Find the Peng treasure	20	Silver
The Librarian	Collect 100 logs	10	Bronze
The Electrician	Collect 10 Semiconductors	10	Silver

SECRET ACHIEVEMENTS & TROPHIES

NAME	GOAL/REQUIREMENT	POINT VALUE	TROPHY VALUE
The Fugitive	Escape the Facility	50	Gold
Cross your Heart, Hope to Die	Survive the Eye Poke Machine	30	Bronze
The Final Sacrifice	Destroy the Marker	50	Bronze
Clever Girls	Survive your first encounter with Stalkers	10	Bronze
Torment Me No More	Kill the Tormenter	20	Bronze
The Graduate	Win the fight at the School	20	Bronze
Patient on the Loose	Get your first Suit	15	Bronze
Derailed	Survive the Train Sequence	20	Bronze
One Small Step	Get through the first Zero-G area	10	Bronze
Hornet's Nest	Destroy the Tripod Nest	30	Bronze
Operation!	Snare the Shard with the Ishimura	15	Bronze
Knock Knock	Complete the Drill Ride	25	Bronze
Elevator Action	Knock off every Tripod during the Elevator Sequence	15	Bronze
Shut Down	Defeat the AI	10	Bronze
Powered Up	Complete the Solar Array Puzzle	15	Bronze

DOWNLOADABLE CONTENT: SEVERED

NAME	GOAL/REQUIREMENT	POINT VALUE	TROPHY VALUE
Grind House	Severed: In the grinder room, cause an enemy to die in the grinders.	20	Bronze
King of the Hill	Severed: Defend the quarry platform until the door unlocks.	20	Bronze
Peng Me Again	Severed: Find the Peng treasure in Severed.	20	Bronze
Remember the Alamo	Severed: Kill 16 or more enemies in the final last stand combat sequence.	20	Bronze
The Veteran	Severed: Complete on Zealot difficulty.	50	Silver

SECRET ACHIEVEMENTS

NAME	GOAL/REQUIREMENT	POINT VALUE	TROPHY VALUE
The Betrayal	Severed: Complete Chapter 1.	50	Silver
The Sacrifice	Severed: Complete Chapter 2.	50	Silver
Ship Shape	Severed: Take out the gunship within 30 seconds.	20	Silver

DEAD SPACE 3

XBOX 360/PS3

SAVE FILE BONUSES

If you've completed Mass Effect 3 or Dead Space 2 and have a save file on your console, you can unlock an additional Suit and Weapon.

UNLOCKABLES

UNLOCKABLE	REQUIREMENT
Devil's Horns	Complete the game on Classic Mode.
Flight Suit	Collect all 40 artifacts.
Retro Mode	Complete Hardcore Mode.
S.C.A.F. Deep Dig Suit	Collect all weapon parts.

ACHIEVEMENTS & TROPHIES

NAME	GOAL/REQUIREMENT	POINT VALUE	TROPHY VALUE
Get On My Level	Complete the game on any difficulty setting.	10	Bronze
The Explorer	Complete all optional missions.	25	Bronze
Aren't You Thankful?	Complete the game on Hardcore Mode.	50	Gold
Epic Tier 4 Engineer	Complete the game in Classic Mode.	40	Silver
Survivalist	Complete the game in Pure Survival Mode.	40	Silver
Gun Collector	Collect all Weapon Parts.	25	Bronze
The Professor	Collect all Artifacts.	25	Bronze
The Librarian	Collect all Logs.	25	Bronze
The Armorer	Collect all Circuits.	25	Bronze
There's Always Peng!	Find Peng.	50	Silver
My Buddy	Retrieve Resources from a Scavenger Bot at a Bench.	10	Bronze
Metal Detector	Successfully deploy Scavenger Bots to 15 Resource Areas.	30	Bronze
Strapped	Craft a Weapon.	10	Bronze
Circuit's Edge	Add a Circuit to a Weapon.	10	Bronze
EMT	Craft a Large Med Pack.	25	Bronze
Full House	Craft a Weapon with 2 Tools, Tips, and Attachments with all Circuit slots filled.	25	Bronze
RIG Master	Fully upgrade your RIG.	50	Silver
Master Plan	Create a Blueprint that needs at least 2000 resources worth of parts and Circuits to build.	25	Bronze
From the Jaws	Save your Co-Op partner from an execution by killing the attacker.	10	Bronze
Share and Share Alike	Use the RIG to give an item to your Co-Op partner.	10	Bronze
Medic!	Revive your Co-Op partner 10 times.	10	Bronze
Ghosts of the Past	Face all of Carver's demons by completing all Co-Op only optional missions.	25	Silver
Architect	Share a Blueprint with your Co-Op partner.	10	Bronze
Axes High	Kill 30 enemies using Fodder axes.	20	Bronze
Payback	Kill a Soldier by TK'ing a grenade or rocket back at them.	15	Bronze
Go for the Limbs!	Dismember 500 limbs from living enemies.	10	Bronze
And Then We Doubled It!	Dismember 1000 lims from living enemies.	10	Bronze
Slow Mo	Kill 50 enemies while they are in stasis.	10	Bronze
Blast Corps	Kill 30 enemies with explosion damage.	10	Bronze
Shootbang	Kill 30 Soldiers with head shots.	10	Bronze
Empty Chamber	Kill 30 enemies using melee strikes or a melee Weapon Part.	10	Bronze
Dropping Acid	Dissolve 50 enemies with acid.	10	Bronze
Electric Lawnmower	Kill 30 enemies using an electrified Ripper blade.	10	Bronze
Overpowered Healing	Use quick heal to heal yourself 20 times.	10	Bronze
Brave New World	Obtain all trophies.	—	Platinum

SECRET ACHIEVEMENTS & TROPHIES

NAME	GOAL/REQUIREMENT	POINT VALUE	TROPHY VALUE
Stranger in a Strange Land	Complete the Prologue.	10	Bronze
Space Odyssey	Survive your first spacewalk.	15	Bronze
Critical Mass	Recover the shuttle.	15	Bronze
Snow Crash	Reach Tau Volantis.	15	Bronze
Intestinal Fortitude	Defeat the Hive Mind.	25	Silver
Hydra	Kill the Snowbeast.	15	Bronze
Together as One	Reassemble Rosetta.	15	Bronze
Infernal Machine	Reach the Alien Machine.	15	Silver
Shoot for the Moon	Defeat the Moon.	50	Gold
Under a Buck	Shoot the deer head trophy in the Admiral's Quarters.	10	Bronze
Space Ace	Shoot at least 70 targets during the ride to Tau Volantis.	20	Bronze
Hungry	Reach the pump room of the Waystation without alerting any Feeders.	20	Bronze
Drill Sergeant	Complete the Drill Room without taking any damage.	30	Bronze
Weedkiller	Kill 5 Cysts in the Biology Building with a single poison gas cloud.	30	Silver
Aliens	Collect all Alien Artifacts.	15	Bronze
Close Encounter	Kill 10 alien Necromorphs.	10	Bronze

AWAKENED DLC

NAME	GOAL/REQUIREMENT	POINT VALUE	TROPHY VALUE
Pure Lunacy	Complete Dead Space 3 Awakened in Pure Survival Mode.	50	Silver
Just the Tip	Awakened: Craft a weapon using a MK-II Weapon Tip.	20	Silver
Heaven Can Wait	Awakened: Stasis your Co-Op partner when he is downed to slow his bleed out timer.	20	Bronze
Supercharger	Awakened: Finish charging the reactor in under 90 seconds.	20	Bronze

SECRET ACHIEVEMENTS & TROPHIES

NAME	GOAL/REQUIREMENT	POINT VALUE	TROPHY VALUE
Bad Moon Rising	Complete Dead Space 3 Awakened.	50	Silver
Heretic	Awakened: Kill the Unitologist Cult Leader.	20	Bronze
True Believer	Awakened: Allow the Unitologist Cult Leader to survive.	20	Bronze
Get to the Chopper!	Awakened: Escape from Tau Volantis to the Terra Nova.	50	Silver

DEAD TO RIGHTS: RETRIBUTION

XBOX 360

AVATAR AWARDS

AWARD	EARNED BY
GAC Armor	Earn the Best cop this city's ever had Achievement. Get this by completing the game on Officer difficulty.
GAC Helmet	Earn the Boom! Achievement. Get this by getting 30 headshots in any level, on Officer or greater difficulty.
GCPD Shirt	Earn the Brawler Achievement. Get this by completing any level (excluding the Prologue) without firing a shot.
Jack and Shadow Shirt	Earn the Finish him Shadow! Achievement. Get this by combining Jack and Shadow to kill 20 enemies in any level, on Officer or greater.
Logo Shirt	Earn the Protect the Innocent Achievement. Get this by saving the hostages.

DEADLIEST WARRIOR: LEGENDS

XBOX 360

AVATAR AWARDS

AWARD	EARNED BY
Sun Tzu's Costume	Complete arcade mode with any warrior on any difficulty level.
Sun Tzu's Helmet	Complete arcade mode as each warrior on the Deadliest difficulty.

KOI WEAPON

Kill 25 enemies in Survival Slice.

DEADLY CREATURES

NINTENDO WII

ALL CHAPTERS

At the chapter select, press Right, Right, Up, Down, 2, 1, 1, 2. When you jump to a later chapter, you get any move upgrades you would have, but not health upgrades.

DEATHSPANK

XBOX 360

AVATAR AWARDS

AWARD	EARNED BY
Dragon Hatchling	Complete Ms. Heybenstances quest to rescue the hatchlings.
Unicorn Poop T-shirt	Kill the twin dragons guarding the artifact.

DEFEND YOUR CASTLE

GIANT ENEMIES

Select Credits and click SMB3W4 when it appears.

TINY UNITS

Select Credits and click Chuck Norris when it appears.

EASY LEVEL COMPLETE

Pause the game and wait for the sun to set. Unpause to complete the level.

DEFIANCE

ACHIEVEMENTS & TROPHIES

NAME	GOAL/REQUIREMENT	POINT VALUE	TROPHY VALUE
Legend of Defiance	Your reputation is sure to spread far beyond the borders of Paradise; Defiance!	70	Platinum
Holy Shtako!	New Freedom has crashed, you've made a few new friends and one of them lives inside your head	15	Bronze
Skruggin' Ark Core	Von Bach is alive, he has an Ark Core, and Cass is not happy about it	15	Bronze
Wrong Hands	Cooper and Ara are good people and you'll need them now that Dark Matter has the Matrix	15	Bronze
That Hagisi Lied	Rosa had revenge and is grateful for the help, but the Matrix is still missing, no thanks to Varus	15	Bronze
Everyone Will Die	Torc's a badass, but so's Nim, as Von Bach learned too late; It'll take everyone to bring Nim down	15	Bronze
Who… Are You?	Nim is dead, again, and the secrets of Defiance will remain; If only Karl could see you now	15	Bronze
Overdosing	Piercer needed an intervention	15	Bronze
Broom Closet	Varus killed a monster	15	Bronze
Save Your Ganchis	That darn Varus	15	Bronze
Call Me Psycho	Poor Peter Nardone	15	Bronze
Ha! Ha! Ha! Ha! Ha!	Wait… Motherlode is a dude?	15	Bronze
Not Bad at All	You can't destroy energy	15	Bronze
Super Excited	Now… which core was that again?	15	Bronze
Individual Pursuit	You completed your first pursuit in the Bay Area	15	Bronze
Hot Pursuit	You completed 5 pursuits in the Bay Area	15	Bronze
Pursuit of Happiness	You completed 10 pursuits in the Bay Area	15	Bronze
High Speed Pursuit	You completed 15 pursuits in the Bay Area	15	Bronze
Pursuit of Excellence	You completed 20 pursuits in the Bay Area	15	Bronze
Executive Wash Room	On the cutting edge, Von Bach Industries is one of the few corporations with truly global reach	15	Bronze

NAME	GOAL/REQUIREMENT	POINT VALUE	TROPHY VALUE
Private Booth	While the gulanite boom put it on the map, Soleptor Enterprises has its fingers in many pies	15	Bronze
Office in Back	Top Notch Toolworks is all about family tradition and custom craftsmanship	15	Bronze
Secure Channel	Despite the violence, Echelon is still a business; Because of the violence, business is good	15	Bronze
Seven Days a Week	Your contributions to the Bay Area have not gone unnoticed	15	Bronze
Key to Paradise	It's thanks to people like you that the community of Paradise might actually incorporate some day	15	Bronze
Widely Regarded	You are a true professional and well respected by the movers and shakers in Paradise	30	Silver
Arkhunting	Valuabloe relics from the destroyed Votan arks frequently and dangerously rain from the sky	10	Bronze
Arkhunting Party	Arkfalls draw quite a crowd for as dangerous as they are; Risk vs. reward, or so they say	10	Bronze
Arkhunting Safari	The amount of debris still in the Ark Belt is nearly limitless; Talk about job security	15	Bronze
Freight Magnate	Arkfall really did a number on shipping costs	15	Bronze
Stargazer	That dark, dead spot in the sky is the Votanis System	15	Bronze
Wharfie	Raiders shut down sea lanes faster than E-Rep can open them	15	Bronze
Bit of an EGO	Von Bach has unlocked the secrets of EGO technology for commercial use; You are proof	10	Bronze
Abundance of Ego	The evolution of your EGO is a testament to the genius of Von Bach and his mastery of Votan tech.	40	Silver
Stroking Your EGO	EGO hosts a Votan artificial intelligence, the implications of which are not fully understood	15	Bronze
EGO Maniac	Both the Earth Republic and the Votanis Collective are behind the curve in regulating EGO research	30	Silver
Powerful EGO	EGO integrates at the genetic level, boosting the capabilities of the host beyond natural limits	15	Bronze
EGOTistical	As your EGO evolves, so does your ability to handle diverse tactical situations	20	Bronze
EGOcentric Arkhunter	Your EGO has evolved past VBI's most optimistic forecasts	60	Gold
Wait For It...	You have found an extremely rare and valuable weapon; Make good use of it	50	Gold
Shoot to Skill	While it's good to specialize, it's wise to pick up a variety of skills	50	Gold
Calculated Killer	To your enemies across the new frontier, your name is "Death"	25	Silver
A Friend in Need	Arkhunting can be a lonely vocation without trusted friends	5	Bronze
Chasing Shadows	Echelon values experienced Shadow Operatives like yourself	15	Bronze

NAME	GOAL/REQUIREMENT	POINT VALUE	TROPHY VALUE
Vehicular Manslaughter	Normally Echelon hires drivers for non-combat contracts; For you, they make exceptions	15	Bronze
Brain Surgeon	When Echelon needs a skilled assassin, they know who to call	15	Bronze
Upper Echelon	Quantity over quality, but dead is still dead	15	Bronze
Yeeeeeeehaaaaawww!	It would be more impressive if you did it in a single jump…	30	Silver
Good Cardio	Sure, it's fun. But swimming's not the most effective means of travel…	35	Silver
Monolithic Landmark	Some gatekeepers are not to be trifled with	15	Bronze

DESPICABLE ME: THE GAME

PSP

MINIONETTES COSTUME SET

In Gru's Lab, select Cheats from the Bonus menu and enter ●, ●, ●, ●, ⊗.

VILLAGE FOLK COSTUME SET

In Gru's Lab, select Cheats from the Bonus menu and enter ●, ⊗, ⊗, ●, ⊗.

TAFFY WEB GUN

In Gru's Lab, select Cheats from the Bonus menu and enter ⊗, ●, ●, ●, ●.

DESTROY ALL HUMANS! BIG WILLY UNLEASHED

NINTENDO WII

Pause the game and go to the Unlockables screen. Hold the analog stick Up until an Enter Unlock Code window appears. You can now enter the following cheats with the directional-pad. Press A after entering a code.

Use this menu to toggle cheats on and off.

UNLOCK ALL GAME WORLDS
Up, Right, Down, Right, Up

CAN'T BE KILLED
Left, Down, Up, Right, Up

LOTS OF GUNS
Right, Left, Down, Left, Up

INFINITE AMMO
Right, Up, Up, Left, Right

UNLIMITED BIG WILLY BATTERY
Left, Left, Up, Right, Down

UNLIMITED JETPACK FUEL
Right, Right, Up, Left, Left

PICK UP HEAVY THINGS
Down, Up, Left, Up, Right

STEALTH SPACE NINJA
Up, Right, Down, Down, Left

CRYPTO DANCE FEVER SKIN
Right, Left, Right, Left, Up

KLUCKIN'S CHICKEN BLIMP SKIN
Left, Up, Down, Up, Down

LEISURE SUIT SKIN
Left, Down, Right, Left, Right

PIMP MY BLIMP SKIN
Down, Up, Right, Down, Right

DEUS EX: HUMAN REVOLUTION

ACHIEVEMENTS & TROPHIES

NAME	GOAL/REQUIREMENT	POINT VALUE	TROPHY VALUE
Cloak & Daggers	Deal with the man in the shadows.	10	Bronze
Smash the State	Help Officer Nicholas take out the trash.	10	Bronze
Acquaintances Forgotten	Follow Pritchard's lead to uncover the truth.	10	Bronze
Doctorate	Read all 29 unique XP books within a single playthrough.	50	Silver
Lesser Evil	Deal with Mr. Carella's indiscretion.	10	Bronze
Motherly Ties	Put a grieving mother's doubts to rest.	10	Bronze
Corporate Warfare	Protect a client's interests by performing a less-than-hostile takeover.	10	Bronze
Talion A.D.	Descend into the bowels of an urban jungle and confront a warrior-priest.	10	Bronze
Gun Nut	Fully upgrade one of your weapons.	20	Bronze
Bar Tab	Help the Hive Bartender settle a tab.	10	Bronze
Rotten Business	Help a lady in the oldest of professions clean house.	10	Bronze
Shanghai Justice	It may take some sleuthing, but justice must be served.	10	Bronze
Hax0r1!	Successfully hack 50 devices within the same playthrough.	15	Bronze
Transhumanist	Fully upgrade your first augmentation of choice.	5	Bronze
Consciousness is Over-rated	Knock out 100 enemies in a single playthrough.	15	Bronze
First Takedown	Perform your first Takedown. Civilians don't count, so be nice.	5	Bronze
Opportunist	Perform 50 takedowns within the same playthrough. (Civilians don't count.)	15	Bronze
First Hack	Perform your first Hack successfully.	5	Bronze
Deus Ex Machina	Experience all the different endings that Deus Ex: Human Revolution has to offer.	50	Silver
Pacifist	Complete Deus Ex: Human Revolution without anyone dying by your hand. (Boss fights don't count.)	100	Gold
Foxiest of the Hounds	Complete Deus Ex: Human Revolution without setting off any alarms.	100	Gold
Up the Ante!	Upgrade your first weapon of choice.	15	Silver
Trooper	Complete Deus Ex: Human Revolution.	50	Gold
Legend	Complete Deus Ex: Human Revolution at its hardest setting without ever changing the difficulty.	100	Gold

SECRET ACHIEVEMENTS & TROPHIES

NAME	GOAL/REQUIREMENT	POINT VALUE	TROPHY VALUE
Ghost	You made it through an entire hostile area without so much as a squeak.	15	Bronze
Sentimental Value	You kept Megan's bracelet for yourself. Apparently, letting go really is the hardest part.	10	Bronze
The Take	Greedy bastard. You accepted O'Malley's blood money and let him go.	10	Bronze
Guardian Angel	You paid poor Jaya's debt in full. How very… humane… of you.	10	Bronze
The D Project	You watched the entire credit list and saw the surprise at the end.	15	Silver
Good Soul	Against all odds, you saved Faridah Malik's life.	15	Bronze
Hangar 18	You found and read the secret message. Now you know too much…	10	Bronze
Super Sleuth	You really nailed your case against Lee Hong.	10	Bronze
Ladies Man	You convinced Mengyao to spill the beans on the mysterious Hyron Project.	10	Bronze
Balls	Seems you like playing with balls, eh?	5	Bronze
Lucky Guess	Next time, Jacob better use a more complex code to arm his bombs.	10	Bronze
Kevorkian Complex	You granted a dying man his final request.	10	Bronze
The Fall	You sent Diamond Chan on the trip of a lifetime.	10	Bronze
The End	You defeated Zhao Yun Ru and destroyed the Hyron Project.	25	Bronze
Old School Gamer	You found all the hidden story items in Megan's office. Point and Click much?	10	Bronze
Unforeseen Consequence	You convinced Zeke Sanders to let his hostage go.	15	Bronze
The Bull	You defeated Lawrence Barrett, elite member of a secret mercenary hit squad.	25	Bronze
The Mantis	You defeated Yelena Fedorova, elite member of a secret mercenary hit squad.	25	Bronze
The Snake	You defeated Jaron Namir, Leader of Belltower's Elite Special Operations Unit.	25	Bronze
The Throwdown	You convinced the smooth-talking politician Bill Taggart to tell the truth in public.	15	Bronze
The Last Straw	You talked Doctor Isaias Sandoval out of suicide.	15	Bronze
The Final Countdown	You showed millionaire Hugh Darrow that his logic was flawed.	15	Bronze
The Desk Job	You convinced Wayne Haas to let you into the morgue.	15	Bronze

NAME	GOAL/REQUIREMENT	POINT VALUE	TROPHY VALUE
Yes Boss	You had an argument with your boss, David Sarif, and won.	15	Bronze
Darker Shades	You convinced a fast-talking bartender to let you see Tong Si Hung.	15	Bronze

DLC: THE MISSING LINK

ACHIEVEMENTS & TROPHIES

NAME	GOAL/REQUIREMENT	POINT VALUE	TROPHY VALUE
Factory Zero	You survived The Missing Link using no Praxis kits, weapons, or explosives. Whoa.	70	Silver
Never Stop Looking	You escaped Rifleman Bank Station. Nothing will stop you from finding Megan now.	20	Silver

SECRET ACHIEVEMENTS & TROPHIES

NAME	GOAL/REQUIREMENT	POINT VALUE	TROPHY VALUE
Good Samaritan	You replaced the power supply on a damaged stasis pod, saving the occupants life.	20	Bronze
Never Forget	You revisited the site where Belltower discovered and captured you.	20	Bronze
Out of the Frying Pan	You made it off the boat… but to what end?	20	Bronze
The learn'd Scholar	When the proofs, the figures, were ranged in columns before me…	20	Bronze
All of the Above	You managed to save Dr. Kavanagh and all the prisoners, too.	20	Bronze
Back Stage Pass	You gained access to Quinn's secret store.	20	Bronze
Apex Predator	You performed a takedown on Burke without being detected.	20	Bronze
That Old Adage	Apparently, your CASIE augmentation doesn't work on everyone…	20	Bronze

DINOSAUR KING

STONE CIRCLE PASSWORDS

Defeat the game to unlock the Stone Circle in South Euro. Now you can enter the following passwords to unlock dinosaurs. Find the level 1 dinosaur in a chest at the shrine.

009 DASPLETEOSARUS

Enter Grass, Water, Lightning, Lightning, Earth, Earth, Water, Wind.

012 SIAMOTYRRANUS

Enter Fire, Wind, Fire, Water, Wind, Grass, Fire, Water.

025 JOBARIA

Enter Water, Lightning, Lightning, Earth, Fire, Earth, Fire, Wind.

029 TRICERATOPS

Enter Lightning, Fire, Lightning, Fire, Water, Lightning, Grass, Earth.

038 MONOCLONIUS

Enter Lightning, Earth, Water, Water, Grass, Fire, Earth, Wind.

046 EUOPLOCEPHALUS

Enter Earth, Earth, Grass, Water, Wind, Earth, Wind, Fire.

058 ALTIRHINUS

Enter Wind, Fire, Fire, Fire, Lightning, Earth, Water, Grass.

061 CARNOTAURUS

Enter Earth, Wind, Water, Lightning, Fire, Wind, Wind, Water.

EX ACE/EX CHOMP

Enter Lightning, Grass, Fire, Earth, Water, Water, Lightning, Fire. This gives you Ace if you are playing as Rex and Chomp as Max.

EX MINI-KING

Enter Lightning, Wind, Earth, Lightning, Grass, Wind, Fire, Water.

EX PARIS

Enter Grass, Water, Water, Earth, Wind, Grass, Lightning, Lightning.

EX SAUROPHAGANAX

Enter Fire, Water, Earth, Grass, Wind, Lightning, Fire, Water.

EX SPINY

Enter Water, Earth, Fire, Water, Fire, Grass, Wind, Earth.

EX TANK

Enter Earth, Grass, Earth, Water, Wind, Water, Grass, Fire.

EX TERRY

Enter Fire, Lightning, Wind, Wind, Water, Fire, Fire, Earth.

DIRT 3

XBOX 360

AVATAR AWARDS

AVATAR	EARNED BY
Racing Shoes	Reach Fan Level 12.
Racing Gloves	Reach Fan Level 24.
Racing Suit	Complete Season 1.
Rally Helmet	Complete Season 2.

DISGAEA: AFTERNOON OF DARKNESS

PSP

ETNA MODE

At the Main menu, highlight New Game and press ●, ●, ●, ●, ●, ●, ●, ⊗.

DISGAEA DS

NINTENDO 3DS

ETNA MODE

At the Main menu, highlight New Game and press X, Y, B, X, Y, B, A.

DISGAEA 2: DARK HERO DAYS

AXEL MODE

Highlight New Game and press , , , , , , .

DISGAEA 3: ABSENCE OF DETENTION

GET ACCESS TO NEW VITA CONTENT

Highlight Continue and press ●, ●, ●, ●, ●, ●, ●. Talk to the Parallel Worlder under the stairs in the lower levels of the base.

DISGAEA 4: A PROMISE UNFORGOTTEN

EXTRA CHARACTERS

After completing the story, extra battles become available from the Senate. Clear these to unlock the following characters.

CHARACTER	CLEAR EXTRA BATTLE
Axel	1
Flonne	2
Raspberyl	3
Etna	4
Laharl	5
Asagi	6
Kurtis	7
Zetta	9

DISNEY EPIC MICKEY 2: THE POWER OF TWO

ACHIEVEMENTS & TROPHIES

NAME	GOAL/REQUIREMENT	POINT VALUE	TROPHY VALUE
Apprentice Pin Collector	Acquired a Collectible Pin for the first time	10	Bronze
Clear!	Mickey revived Oswald while playing co-op	10	Bronze
Devoted Pin Collector	Found 88 Collectible Pins	25	Bronze
Dressed to Impress	Collected every Costume	30	Silver
Dress-up	Changed costumes for the first time	10	Bronze
Fall From Grace	Entered Angel Falls, exited Devil Falls	20	Bronze
Film Buff	Collected every 2D Film Reel	30	Silver
Who Left These Lying Around?	Rescued all the gremlins	10	Bronze
Get with the Program	Reprogrammed a Beetleworx	10	Bronze
Heads Up	Matched Seth's flowers to OsTown's statue	20	Bronze
Heroes of Wasteland	Built both statues in OsTown	25	Bronze
Junker	Destroyed 50 enemies	10	Bronze
Lab Tested	Finished Yen Sid's Lab	20	Bronze

NAME	GOAL/REQUIREMENT	POINT VALUE	TROPHY VALUE
Make Your Own Way	Ignored Daisy AND Smee's suggestions	25	Bronze
Master Pin Collector	Collected 176 Collectible Pins	75	Gold
Not-So-Sleepy Hollow	Revealed every knothole surprise	10	Bronze
Off Track	Shuttered all four train stations	25	Silver
Oswald's New Groove	Finished Dark Beauty Castle with two players	10	Bronze
Perfectionist	Finished all quests	75	Gold
Picture Perfect	Got all three of Metairie's pictures	10	Bronze
Prince Charming	Befriended 100 enemies	25	Silver
Projector Corrector	Restarted the Rainbow Falls Substation	20	Bronze
Recycler	Befriended 50 enemies	10	Bronze
Rogues Gallery	Photographed every enemy	20	Bronze
Staff Photographer	Got all Adelle's photos from the official Picture Spots	30	Silver
Statue Garden	Awakened every Spirit	50	Gold
Thinderella	Destroyed 100 enemies	25	Silver
Tunnel Mouse	Played through every D.E.C.	10	Bronze
Walking the Mean Streets	Navigated both halves of Mean Street	20	Bronze
We've Got Spirit, Yes We Do!	Awakened a Spirit	10	Bronze
When You Wish Upon a Star	Painted every star and comet in Yen Sid's Lab	10	Bronze
Can I Get a Pin of That?	Earned all other trophies in the game	—	Platinum

SECRET ACHIEVEMENTS & TROPHIES

NAME	GOAL/REQUIREMENT	POINT VALUE	TROPHY VALUE
Blot Alley Superstar	Befriended the Blotworx and helped Petetronic	10	Bronze
Dragon Defeat	Defeated the Blotworx Dragon	30	Silver
Fortified	Scouted a path through Fort Wasteland	20	Bronze
Full-court Prescott	Chased Prescott through the Floatyard	20	Bronze
Go with the Flow	Solved OsTown's Thinner problem	20	Bronze
Hard Hat Area	Got through Ventureland's construction area	20	Bronze
Race the Autotopia Speedway	Completed a race in Autotopia	10	Bronze
Running the Gauntlet	Got through Blot Alley by any means	20	Bronze
Siphon...Siphoff...	Dealt with all the Guardian Siphons	20	Bronze
The Bigger They Are...	Defeated Prescott's mechanical creation	30	Silver
Things Are Worxing Out	Opened the way to Blot Alley	20	Bronze
Trailblazer	Braved Disney Gulch	20	Bronze
Tryptic	Dealt with all 3 dioramas	20	Bronze
You Must be This Tall to Ride	Defeated the Mad Doctor's new ride	30	Silver
Your Conscience Be Your Guide	Found a way through the Rainbow Caverns	20	Bronze

DISNEY FAIRIES: TINKER BELL

TINKERBELL MAGIC BOOK CODES

Talk to Queen Clarion about the Magic Book to enter the following codes.

UNLOCK	CODE
Augustus	5318 3479 7972
Baden	1199 2780 8802
Blair	6899 6003 4480
Cera	1297 0195 5747
Chipper	7980 9298 9818
Dewberry	0241 4491 0630
Elwood	3527 5660 3684
Fawn	9556 0047 1043
Idalia	2998 8832 2673
Iridessa	0724 0213 6136
Luminaria	8046 5868 5678
Magnolia	1697 4780 6430
Mariana	5138 8216 9240
Minister Autumn	2294 0281 6332
Minister Spring	2492 1155 4907
Minister Summer	2582 7972 6926
Minister Winter	2618 8587 2083
Nollie	5905 2346 9329
Olwen	7629 0545 7105
One Black Shell	1234 5678 9012
One Blue Dewdrop	0987 6543 2109
One Fairy Medal	1111 1111 1111
One Green Leaf	4444 4444 4444
One Pink Petal	2222 2222 2222
One Red Leaf	5555 5555 5555
One Snow Grain	7777 7777 7777
One Weak Thread	9999 9999 9999
One White Feather	8888 8888 8888
One Yellow Leaf	6666 6666 6666
One Yellow Petal	3333 3333 3333
Party Shoes	1390 5107 4096
Party Skirt	6572 4809 6680
Party Tiara	8469 7886 7938
Party Top	0977 4584 3869
Queen Clarion	1486 4214 8147
Rosetta	8610 2523 6122
Rune	3020 5768 5351
Silvermist	0513 4563 6800
Terence	8606 6039 6383
Tinkerbell	2495 7761 9313
Vidia	3294 3220 0349

DISSIDIA: FINAL FANTASY

PSP

SECRET PASSWORDS

The following passwords can be entered into the personal message section of your Friend Card to make the following items appear in the shop. Use the NA Version passwords for the North American version of the game and use the EU Ver. Passwords for the European version of the game.

REWARDS	NA VER.		EU VER.	
Player Icon: Chocobo (FF5)	58205	2436	62942	36172
Player Icon: Moogle (FF5)	13410	3103	84626	93120
Capricorn Recipe	87032	2642	6199	27495
Aquarius Recipe	39275	40667	3894	27509
Pisces Recipe	5310	62973	15812	2748
Friend Card: Matoya	39392	58263	1849	16360
Friend Card: Ninja	27481	73856	46490	11483
Friend Card: Fusoya	2943	2971	2971	2943
Friend Card: Siegfried	2015	1231	25496	12772
Friend Card: Vivi	37842	27940	70271	8560
Friend Card: Auron	12982	28499	33705	59603

DJ HERO

NINTENDO WII

Select Cheats from Options and enter the following. Some codes will disable high scores and progress. Cheats cannot be used in tutorials and online.

UNLOCK ALL CONTENT

Enter tol0.

ALL CHARACTER ITEMS

Enter uNA2.

ALL VENUES

Enter Wv1u.

ALL DECKS

Enter LAuP.

ALL HEADPHONES

Enter 62Db.

ALL MIXES

Enter 82xl.

AUTO SCRATCH

Enter IT6j.

AUTO EFFECTS DIAL

Enter ab1L.

AUTO FADER

Enter SL5d.

AUTO TAPPER

Enter ZitH.

AUTO WIN EUPHORIA

Enter r3a9.

BLANK PLINTHS

Enter ipr0.

HAMSTER SWITCH

Enter 7geo.

HYPER DECK MODE

Enter 76st.

SHORT DECK

Enter 51uC.

INVISIBLE DJ

Enter oh5T.

PITCH BLACK OUT

Enter d4kR.

PLAY IN THE BEDROOM

Enter g7nH.

ANY DJ, ANY SETLIST

Enter 0jj8.

DAFT PUNK'S CONTENT

Enter d1g?.

DJ AM'S CONTENT

Enter k07u.

DJ JAZZY JEFF'S CONTENT

Enter n1fz.

DJ SHADOW'S CONTENT

Enter oMxV.

DJ Z-TRIP'S CONTENT

Enter 5rtg.

GRANDMASTER FLASH'S CONTENT

Enter ami8.

CHEATS, ACHIEVEMENTS, AND TROPHIES

D

XBOX 360/PS3

Select Cheats from Options and enter the following. Some codes will disable high scores and progress. Cheats cannot be used in tutorials and online.

UNLOCK ALL CONTENT

Enter tol0.

ALL CHARACTER ITEMS

Enter uNA2.

ALL VENUES

Enter Wv1u.

ALL DECKS

Enter LAuP.

ALL HEADPHONES

Enter 62Db.

ALL MIXES

Enter 82xl.

AUTO SCRATCH

Enter it6j.

AUTO EFFECTS DIAL

Enter ab1l.

AUTO FADER

Enter sl5d.

AUTO TAPPER

Enter zith.

AUTO WIN EUPHORIA

Enter r3a9.

BLANK PLINTHS

Enter ipr0.

HAMSTER SWITCH

Enter 7geo.

HYPER DECK MODE

Enter 76st.

SHORT DECK

Enter 51uc.

BLACK AND WHITE

Enter b!99.

EDGE EFFECT

Enter 2u4u.

INVISIBLE DJ

Enter oh5t.

MIDAS

Enter 4pe5.

PITCH BLACK OUT

Enter d4kr.

PLAY IN THE BEDROOM

Enter g7nh.

RAINBOW

Enter ?jy!.

ANY DJ, ANY SETLIST

Enter 0jj8.

DAFT PUNK'S CONTENT

Enter d1g?.

DJ AM'S CONTENT

Enter k07u.

DJ JAZZY JEFF'S CONTENT

Enter n1fz.

DJ SHADOW'S CONTENT

Enter omxv.

DJ Z-TRIP'S CONTENT

Enter 5rtg.

GRANDMASTER FLASH'S CONTENT

Enter ami8.

DJ HERO 2

XBOX 360/PS3

ALL BONUS CONTENT

Select Cheats from the Options. Choose Retail Cheats and enter VIP Pass.

DAVID GUETTA

Select Cheats from the Options. Choose Retail Cheats and enter Guetta Blaster.

DEADMAU5

Select Cheats from the Options. Choose Retail Cheats and enter Open The Trap.

INVISIBLE DJ

Select Cheats from the Options. Choose Retail Cheats and enter Now You See Me.

AUTO CROSSFADE

Select Cheats from the Options. Choose Retail Cheats and enter I Hate Crossfading. This disables Leaderboards.

AUTO SCRATCH

Select Cheats from the Options. Choose Retail Cheats and enter Soothing. This disables Leaderboards.

AUTO TAP

Select Cheats from the Options. Choose Retail Cheats and enter Look No Hands! This disables Leaderboards.

DJ MAX TECHNIKA TUNE

CLUB MODE SETS

Additional sets in Club Mode can be unlocked by raising your DJ Level.

REQUIREMENT	LEVEL
Instrumental	Reach Lv10
Rock to the Rhythm	Reach Lv20
Nostalgia Set	Reach Lv30
Freaky Garden Set	Reach Lv40
Dark Abyss	Reach Lv50

DMC: DEVIL MAY CRY

RARE ARTWORK

ART	REQUIREMENT
Rare Art #1	Activate Devil Trigger 666 times.
Rare Art #2	Play for 50 hours.
Rare Art #3	Deal 5,000,000 points of damage.
Rare Art #4	Complete any 60 missions with SSS Rank.

UNLOCKABLE COSTUMES & PERKS

BONUS	REQUIREMENT
Original Costume	Complete the game on Human, Devil Hunter or Nephilim difficulty.
Son of Sparda Costume	Complete the game on Son of Sparda difficulty.
Super Dante	Complete the game on Dante Must Die difficulty.

UNLOCKABLE DIFFICULTIES

DIFFICULTY	REQUIREMENT
Dante Must Die	Complete the game on Son of Sparda difficulty.
Heaven or Hell	Complete the game on Son of Sparda difficulty.
Hell and Hell	Complete the game on Heaven or Hell difficulty.
Son of Sparda	Complete the game on any difficulty.

RARE ARTWORK

ART	REQUIREMENT
Rare Art #1	Activate Devil Trigger 666 times.
Rare Art #2	Play for 50 hours.
Rare Art #3	Deal 5,000,000 points of damage.
Rare Art #4	Complete any 60 missions with SSS Rank.

UNLOCKABLE COSTUMES & PERKS

BONUS	REQUIREMENT
Original Costume	Complete the game on Human, Devil Hunter or Nephilim difficulty.
Son of Sparda Costume	Complete the game on Son of Sparda difficulty.
Super Dante	Complete the game on Dante Must Die difficulty.

UNLOCKABLE DIFFICULTIES

DIFFICULTY	REQUIREMENT
Dante Must Die	Complete the game on Son of Sparda difficulty.
Heaven or Hell	Complete the game on Son of Sparda difficulty.
Hell and Hell	Complete the game on Heaven or Hell difficulty.
Son of Sparda	Complete the game on any difficulty.

XBOX 360/PS3

ACHIEVEMENTS & TROPHIES

NAME	GOAL/REQUIREMENT	POINT VALUE	TROPHY VALUE
Time to go to work guys!	You purchased your first upgrade	10	Bronze
Come on Puppy. Let's go!	You have defeated the Hunter	20	Bronze
Thing drives me crazy	You have acquired Osiris	10	Bronze
Only kind of gift worth giving	You have acquired the Angel Boost ability	10	Bronze
Flock off, feather-face!	You have defeated the Tyrant	20	Bronze
It's got to stay in the family	You have acquired Arbiter	10	Bronze
This baby sure can pack a punch	You have acquired Eryx	20	Bronze
He's a demon too	You helped Phineas by retrieving his eye	10	Bronze
You are not a Human, are you?	You have acquired the Devil Trigger ability	10	Bronze
No talking!	You have acquired Aquila	20	Bronze
More than just a few sparks	You have acquired Revenant	10	Bronze
Whatever, Lady	You have defeated Mundus' spawn	20	Bronze
You're not going to shoot me	You have acquired Kablooey	10	Bronze
It's time to finish this!	You helped Vergil open the Vault	10	Bronze
Cleaning up his Dad's mess	You have defeated Mundus	20	Bronze
The end? Don't bet on it	You defeated Vergil on any difficulty	40	Silver
Looks like it's your lucky day	You completed a level without taking any damage	10	Bronze
Every hero has a weakness	You completed Furnace of Souls without taking damage from the furnace	10	Bronze
It's only the rain	You Killed 10 enemies by pushing them into the Hurricane ride	10	Bronze
A man with guts and honor	You reached the end of the descent on Mission 6 having killed all of the enemies	10	Bronze
Now my coat's all charred	You navigated the Sky Bridge without hitting the lasers	10	Bronze

NAME	GOAL/REQUIREMENT	POINT VALUE	TROPHY VALUE
Where does the time go?	You completed a level in 2 minutes or less	10	Bronze
For Tony Redgrave	You killed 50 enemies using nothing but firearms	10	Bronze
In the name of my father	You killed 100 enemies using nothing but Demon weapons	10	Bronze
You'll never have her fire	You killed 100 enemies using nothing but Angel weapons	10	Bronze
Impressive	You have slayed 100 Demons	10	Bronze
Bring it on!	You have slayed 1,000 Demons	20	Bronze
Looks like we have a winner	You have slayed 5,000 Demons	30	Silver
Sensational!	You gained a SSS Style Rank during combat	10	Bronze
It's showtime. Come on!	You earned 1,500 Style Bonuses	20	Bronze
This is my kind of rain	You have spent 10,000 Red Orbs	10	Bronze
Absolutely crazy about it	You have Spent 50,000 Red Orbs	20	Bronze
Let's rock, baby!	You have upgraded Dante's health to maximum	10	Bronze
You can't handle it	You have upgraded Dante's Devil Trigger to maximum	10	Bronze
Power… Give me more power!	You have purchased all of Dante's combat upgrades	20	Silver
Dude, the show's over!	You have found all 21 Keys	10	Bronze
Let's welcome chaos!	You have opened all 21 Secret Doors	10	Bronze
And you are set free	You have found half of the Lost Souls	10	Bronze
Fill your dark soul with light	You have found all of the Lost Souls	20	Silver
Keeps getting better and better	You have been awarded a 100% completion rank on all missions	40	Silver
Stylish!	Completed a mission with a SSS rank	10	Bronze
Too easy!	Completed all missions on the Son of Sparda difficulty	40	Silver
Devils never cry	Completed all missions on the Dante Must Die difficulty	100	Gold
This is what I live for!	Completed all missions on Heaven Or Hell difficulty	10	Bronze
And welcome to Hell!	Completed all missions on Hell and Hell difficulty	100	Gold
Jackpot!	Completed all missions on the Nephilim difficulty with a SSS rank	80	Gold
This party's just getting crazy!	You have completed 10 of the Secret Missions	20	Bronze
One hell of a party!	You have completed all of the Secret Missions	50	Silver

VERGIL'S DOWNFALL DLC

NAME	GOAL/REQUIREMENT	POINT VALUE	TROPHY VALUE
We have an uninvited guest	Defeat a Wisp	10	Bronze
You don't belong here	Defeat an Imprisoner	10	Bronze
Our souls are at odds brother	Complete Vergil's downfall	20	Bronze
I've come to retrieve my power	Acquire all of Vergil's health, Devil trigger and combat upgrades	30	Bronze

NAME	GOAL/REQUIREMENT	POINT VALUE	TROPHY VALUE
I'll try it your way for once	Complete all missions in Vergil's downfall on the Nephilim difficulty with a SSS rank	50	Silver
I need more power!	Complete Vergil's downfall on Son of Sparda difficulty	20	Bronze
This is the power of Sparda!	Complete Vergil's downfall on Vergil Must Die difficulty	40	Silver
Now I'm a little motivated!	Complete Vergil's downfall on Heaven or Hell difficulty	10	Bronze
You're not worthy as my opponent	Complete Vergil's downfall on Hell on Hell difficulty	40	Silver
Might controls everything	Gain a 100% completion rank on all missions in Vergil's downfall (difficulty doesn't matter)	20	Bronze

DOKAPON KINGDOM

NINTENDO WII

DOUBLE THE TAXES FROM A TOWN

After saving a town, hold the controller sideways and press A, A + 2.

DOLLAR DASH

XBOX 360

AVATAR AWARDS

AWARD	REQUIREMENT
Dollar Dash Beanie	Buy a shop item.
Dollar Dash Shirt	Win 10 online games in Dollar Dash mode.

DOODLE JUMP

MOBILE

OOG FROM POCKET GOD

After falling, enter OOGA, KLIK or KLAK as your name. This only works with version 1.2.1 or later.

MONSTERS FROM THE CREEPS!

After falling, enter CREEPS as your name.

EASTER LEVEL

After falling, enter E.B., HOP or BUNNY as your name.

SNOW THEME

After falling, enter SNOW as your name.

HALLOWEEN THEME

After falling, enter BOO as a name.

DRAGLADE

CHARACTERS

CHARACTER	TO UNLOCK
Asuka	Defeat Daichi's story
Gyamon	Defeat Guy's story
Koki	Defeat Hibito's story
Shura	Defeat Kairu's story

HIDDEN QUEST: SHADOW OF DARKNESS

Defeat Story Mode with all of the main characters. This unlocks this hidden quest in Synethesia.

ZEKE

Complete all of the quests including Shadow of Darkness to unlock Zeke in wireless battle.

DRAGON AGE II

ACHIEVEMENTS & TROPHIES

NAME	GOAL/REQUIREMENT	POINT VALUE	TROPHY VALUE
Master Craftsman	Crafted all of the items from a single crafting tree.	25	Silver
Mogul	Had 100 or more sovereigns in your purse.	25	Bronze
Crowning Glory	Became the viscount of Kirkwall.	25	Silver
Dedicated	Reached Level 10.	15	Bronze
A Friend in Need	Upgraded the armor of one of your party members.	5	Bronze
Enchanter	Enchanted an item.	5	Bronze
Immigrant	Became a resident of Kirkwall.	5	Bronze
Delver of the Deep	Explored the Deep Roads.	10	Bronze
Birthright	Kicked the slavers out of your ancestral mansion.	15	Bronze
Specialized	Learned two class specializations.	25	Bronze
I Got Your Back	Completely upgraded the armor of one of your party members.	25	Bronze
Legendary	Reached Level 20.	50	Silver
Financier	Became a partner in a Deep Roads expedition.	10	Bronze
Talented	Upgraded a spell or talent.	5	Silver
Tag Team	Used teamwork to perform a cross-class combo.	5	Bronze
That Thing Has Legs	Found and killed a varterral.	25	Silver
Weapon Master	Mastered a weapon style.	25	Silver
Unstoppable	Completed a full year in Kirkwall without any party member being knocked unconscious.	50	Silver
Craftsman	Acquired your first crafting recipe.	5	Silver
Dragon Slayer	Found and killed a high dragon.	25	Bronze
Exorcist	Found and killed the undying Xebenkeck.	25	Bronze
Demon Slayer	Found and killed the ancient demon, Hybris.	25	Bronze

NAME	GOAL/REQUIREMENT	POINT VALUE	TROPHY VALUE
Chantry Historian	Found all four chapters of "The History of the Chantry," by Brother Genitivi.	25	Gold
A Worthy Rival	Earned the Arishok's respect.	25	Silver
Great Minds Think Alike	Earned the friendship or rivalry of four party members.	50	Bronze
Friend	Earned the friendship of one of your party members.	25	Bronze
Rival	Earned the rivalry of one of your party members.	25	Bronze
Romantic	Completed a romance with one of your party members.	25	Bronze
Epic	Completed Dragon Age II twice, or completed it once with a save imported from Dragon Age Origins.	50	Bronze
Champion of Kirkwall	Completed Dragon Age II.	20	Silver
Mercenary	Allied yourself with the mercenaries upon arriving in Kirkwall.	10	Bronze
Nefarious	Allied yourself with the smugglers upon arriving in Kirkwall.	10	Bronze
Flirtatious	Flirted with one of your party members to begin a romance.	5	Bronze
Mass Exodus	Reached Kirkwall with each character class across multiple playthroughs.	25	Bronze
Knowledgeable	Unlocked 100 codex entries.	25	Bronze
Treasure Hunter	Opened 50 chests.	25	Bronze
Darkness Falls	Toggled the map from day to night.	5	Silver
Explorer	Left Kirkwall to explore the outlying regions.	5	Silver
Spelunker	Visited 10 caves in Kirkwall and the surrounding area.	25	Bronze
Full House	Recruited four party members.	10	Bronze
Friends in High Places	Met Grand Cleric Elthina, Viscount Dumar, Knight-Commander Meredith, and First Enchanter Orsino.	15	Bronze
Gift Giver	Gave a gift to one of your party members.	5	Bronze
Supplier	Found every variety of crafting resources.	25	Silver
Archeologist	During each year in Kirkwall, discovered 3 secret messages from the Band of Three.	50	Silver
Tale Within a Tale	Listened to Varric begin his tale of the Champion of Kirkwall.	5	Bronze

SECRET ACHIEVEMENTS & TROPHIES

NAME	GOAL/REQUIREMENT	POINT VALUE	TROPHY VALUE
Stone Cold	Defeated the rock wraith on your expedition into the Deep Roads.	5	Bronze
King of the Hill	Defeated the Arishok.	10	Bronze
Conqueror	Defeated Meredith, knight-commander of Kirkwall's templars.	15	Bronze
Arcane Defender	Sided with the mages five times.	25	Silver
Mage Hunter	Sided with the templars five times.	25	Silver

DOWNLOADABLE CONTENT: THE EXILED PRINCE

NAME	GOAL/REQUIREMENT	POINT VALUE	TROPHY VALUE
Avenged	Confront the culprit behind the Vael family's murder.	25	Bronze
Cloak and Dagger	Meet secretly with the agent of the Divine	25	Bronze
Loyalty of the Prince	Earn either a friendship or rivalry with Sebastian.	30	Bronze
Memento	Give Sebastian a family heirloom.	25	Bronze

SECRET ACHIEVEMENTS

NAME	GOAL/REQUIREMENT	POINT VALUE	TROPHY VALUE
Retribution	Dealt with the mercenaries that killed the Vael family.	25	Bronze

DRAGON AGE II

PLAYSTATION 3

STAFF OF PARTHALAN

Create a BioWare Social account and sign up for the newsletter.

HAYDER'S RAZOR

Complete the Dragon Age II demo while logged in to your EA Account.

HINDSIGHT

Visit the Penny Arcade page from the Dragon Age 2 website and click on "Get your DAII Penny Arcade Belt."

SER ISAAC'S ARMOR

Put in Dead Space 2, sign in with your EA Account and then insert Dragon Age II and sign in with that same EA Account.

BLOOD DRAGON ARMOR

Have a save game from Dragon Age Origins with the Blood Dragon Armor unlocked on your hard drive.

DRAGON BALL Z: BUDOKAI HD COLLECTION

PLAYSTATION 3

DRAGON BALL Z BUDOKAI HD

NEW TITLE SCREENS

SCREEN	REQUIREMENT
Frieza Title Screen	Complete the Saiyan saga.
Cell Title Screen	Complete the Namek saga.
Everyone Title Screen	Complete the game.

UNLOCKABLE CHARACTERS

CHARACTER	REQUIREMENT
#16	Defeat #16 in the Android saga.
#17	Defeat #17 in the Android saga.
#18	Defeat #18 in the Android saga.
#19	Defeat #19 in the Android saga.
Captain Ginyu	Defeat Ginyu in Story Mode after he takes over Goku's body.
Cell	Defeat Cell in Story Mode.
Dodoria	Defeat Frieza with Vegeta in Story Mode.
Frieza	Defeat Frieza in Story Mode.

CHARACTER	REQUIREMENT
Great Saiyaman	Defeat the World Tournament in Advanced Mode.
Hercule	Defeat World Tournament in Adept Mode.
Nappa	Defeat Nappa in Story Mode.
Raditz	Defeat Raditz in Story Mode.
Recoome	Defeat Recoome the first time as Vegeta in Story Mode.
Teen Gohan	Complete A Warrior Beyond Goku.
Trunks	Complete Perfect Cell.
Vegeta	Defeat Vegeta in Story Mode.
Yamcha	Defeat Yamcha as Cell in Story Mode.
Zarbon	Defeat Zarbon with Vegeta in Story Mode.

UNLOCKABLE MODES

MODE	REQUIREMENT
Adept and Advanced World Tournaments	Beat the Novice World Tournament then buy them from Popo's shop.
Legend of Hercule Mode	Beat the World Tournament on Adept then buy from Popo's shop.

UNLOCKABLE SIDE-QUESTS

SIDE-QUEST	REQUIREMENT
Cell	Complete the Android Saga.
Frieza	Complete the Namekian Saga.
Vegeta	Complete Story Mode.

DRAGON BALL Z BUDOKAI 3 HD

EXTRA DIFFICULTY LEVELS

DIFFICULTY	REQUIREMENT
Z Mode—Goku's Wish	Complete Dragon Universe on Very Hard once.
Z2 Mode—The Path to Power	Complete Dragon Universe on Z Mode.
Z3 Mode—Endless Path to Power	Complete Dragon Universe on Z2 Mode.

WORLD TOURNAMENT DIFFICULTIES

DIFFICULTY	REQUIREMENT
Adept	Unlock 16 or more characters and complete Novice level, then buy it from the shop.
Advanced	Unlock 32 or more characters and complete Adept level, then buy it from the shop.
Cell Games Rules	Defeat Cell after he has "broken in" during Dragon Arena.

STORY REENACTMENTS

REENACTMENT	CHARACTER	REQUIREMENT
000	Goku	Use Kamehameha vs. Raditz.
001	Piccolo	Use Special Beam Cannon vs. Raditz.
002	Tien	Use Ki Blast Cannon vs. Nappa.
003	Kid Gohan	Use Masenko vs. Nappa.
004	Krillin	Use Destructo Disk vs. Frieza Form 2.
005	Goku	Turn Super Saiyan vs. Frieza.
006	Yamcha	When your life is red, use a Senzu Bean vs. Dr. Gero.
007	Piccolo	Use Fuse with Kami vs. Cell
008	Vegeta	Have at least 50% life remaining vs. 17 Absorption Cell
009	Vegeta	Use Final Flash vs. Perfect Cell.
010	Teen Gohan	Turn Super Saiyan vs. Goku.
011	Teen Gohan	Use Father Son Kamehameha vs. Super Perfect Cell.

REENACTMENT	CHARACTER	REQUIREMENT
012	Vegeta	Use Final Explosion vs. Majin Buu.
013	Goku	Turn Super Saiyan 3 vs. Majin Buu.
014	Piccolo	Fight vs. Super Buu for more than 60 seconds.
015	Gohan	Turn Mystic Gohan vs. Super Buu.
016	Goku	Use Super Spirit Bomb (normal state with Super Saiyan 1 & 2 equipped) vs. Kid Buu.
017	Vegeta	Turn Super Saiyan 4 vs. Super Saiyan 4 Goku.
018	Goku	As Super Saiyan 4 Gogeta use 100x Big Bang Kamehameha vs. Omega Shenron.
019	Broly	Use Gigantic Meteor vs. Gohan for the first time.
020	Uub	Use Ki Cannon vs. Goku for the first time.

UNLOCKABLE STAGES

STAGE	REQUIREMENT
Cell Ring	Defeat Perfect Cell in Goku's Dragon Universe.
Grandpa Gohan's House	Instead of fighting Piccolo in the Mountains, go to Grandpa Gohan's House and defeat Goku with Kid Gohan in the 2nd playthrough of Dragon Universe.
Grandpa Gohan's House	In Adult Gohan's Dragon Universe, go to Grandpa Gohan's House and defeat Goten, then Videl then return to Grandpa Gohan's House and enter it.
Inside Buu	Beat Super Buu inside of Buu with Goku and Vegeta.
Planet Namek	Play the Namek Saga.
Red Ribbon Army Base	Unlock Dragon Arena mode.
Supreme Kai's World	Beat Kid Buu in Goku and Vegeta's Dragon Universes in Supreme Kai's World.
Urban Level	Go to Central City in Teen Gohan's Dragon Universe.

UNLOCKABLE CHARACTERS

CHARACTER	REQUIREMENT
Android 16	Find him at the Plains around the South Island and bring him to Bulma in West City during the 2nd playthrough of Krillin's Dragon Universe.
Android 17	Defeat Android 17 in Piccolo's Dragon Universe.
Android 18	Complete Dragon Universe with Krillin.
Bardok	In the beginning of Dragon Universe fly to Raditz's Spaceship and enter the ??? area.
Captain Ginyu	Defeat Captain Ginyu in Goku's Dragon Universe.
Cell	Defeat Cell in Teen Gohan's Dragon Universe.
Cell Jr.	Defeat Piccolo in Dragon Arena when he breaks in.
Cooler	After defeating Frieza in Dragon Universe, defeat Super Saiyan Vegeta then move to Cooler's red mark and defeat him.
Dabura	Defeat Dabura in Adult Gohan's Dragon Universe.
Dr. Gero	Defeat Dr. Gero in Yamcha's Dragon Universe.
Fat Buu	Complete Goku's Dragon Universe.
Frieza	Defeat Frieza in Goku's Dragon Universe.
Gogeta (SSJ2)	After defeating Broly in Dragon Universe, defeat Gotenks at the World Tournament Arena.

D

CHARACTER	REQUIREMENT
Gogeta (SSJ4)	In Vegeta's Dragon Universe instead of fighting Kid Buu defeat Super Saiyan 4 Goku.
Gogeta (Vegeta)	Buy it from Skill Shops with the Black Membership Card.
Gogeta Capsule	Instead of fighting Uub or Brolly fight Goten and Trunks instead.
Gohan	Complete Teen Gohan's Dragon Universe.
Goku (SSJ4)	Defeat Kid Buu with a Super Spirit Bomb. Then go to the islands next to the goal and select ???.
Goten	Defeat Goten in Gohan's Dragon Universe.
Gotenks	Purchase from the Capsule Shop.
Great Saiyaman	Defeat Cell in Teen Gohan/Kid Gohan's Dragon Universe.
Hercule	Help him in Piccolo's Dragon Universe then talk to Videl at Central City.
Kid Buu	Defeat Kid Buu in Goku's Dragon Universe.
Kid Goku	Complete Broly's Dragon Universe.
Kid Trunks	Defeat Majin Buu in Vegeta's Dragon Universe.
Majin Buu	Defeat Majin Buu in Goku's Dragon Universe.
Omega Shenron	After being invited to fight Gotenks at the World Tournament, visit Bulma in West City then defeat Gotenks.
Recoome	Defeat Recoome in Goku's Dragon Universe.
Saibamnan	Beat Nappa when he breaks into the Dragon Arena.
Super Buu	Defeat Super Buu in Goku's Dragon Universe.
Supreme Kai	Find him at the plains before the last battle in Gohan's Dragon Universe.
Teen Gohan	Complete Kid Gohan's Dragon Universe.
Trunks	Complete Vegeta's Dragon Universe.
Uub	Defeat Kid Buu with a Spirit Bomb in Goku's Dragon Universe.
Vegeta	Defeat Vegeta in Goku's Dragon Universe.
Vegeta (SSJ4)	Buy it from the Capsule Shop with the Black Membership Card.
Vegito (Goku)	Defeat Super Buu in Buu's Body in Goku's Dragon Universe.
Vegito (Vegeta)	Defeat Super Buu in Buu's Body in Vegeta's Dragon Universe.
Videl	Go to the Plains (Point 4 on the map) in Gohan's Dragon Universe.

XBOX 360

DRAGON BALL Z BUDOKAI HD
NEW TITLE SCREENS

SCREEN	REQUIREMENT
Frieza Title Screen	Complete the Saiyan saga.
Cell Title Screen	Complete the Namek saga.
Everyone Title Screen	Complete the game.

UNLOCKABLE CHARACTERS

CHARACTER	REQUIREMENT
#16	Defeat #16 in the Android saga.
#17	Defeat #17 in the Android saga.

CHARACTER	REQUIREMENT
#18	Defeat #18 in the Android saga.
#19	Defeat #19 in the Android saga.
Captain Ginyu	Defeat Ginyu in Story Mode after he takes over Goku's body.
Cell	Defeat Cell in Story Mode.
Dodoria	Defeat Frieza with Vegeta in Story Mode.
Frieza	Defeat Frieza in Story Mode.
Great Saiyaman	Defeat the World Tournament in Advanced Mode.
Hercule	Defeat World Tournament in Adept Mode.
Nappa	Defeat Nappa in Story Mode.
Raditz	Defeat Raditz in Story Mode.
Recoome	Defeat Recoome the first time as Vegeta in Story Mode.
Teen Gohan	Complete A Warrior Beyond Goku.
Trunks	Complete Perfect Cell.
Vegeta	Defeat Vegeta in Story Mode.
Yamcha	Defeat Yamcha as Cell in Story Mode.
Zarbon	Defeat Zarbon with Vegeta in Story Mode.

UNLOCKABLE MODES

MODE	REQUIREMENT
Adept and Advanced World Tournaments	Beat the Novice World Tournament then buy them from Popo's shop.
Legend of Hercule Mode	Beat the World Tournament on Adept then buy from Popo's shop.

UNLOCKABLE SIDE-QUESTS

SIDE-QUEST	REQUIREMENT
Cell	Complete the Android Saga.
Frieza	Complete the Namekian Saga.
Vegeta	Complete Story Mode.

DRAGON BALL Z BUDOKAI 3 HD

EXTRA DIFFICULTY LEVELS

DIFFICULTY	REQUIREMENT
Z Mode—Goku's Wish	Complete Dragon Universe on Very Hard once.
Z2 Mode—The Path to Power	Complete Dragon Universe on Z Mode.
Z3 Mode—Endless Path to Power	Complete Dragon Universe on Z2 Mode.

WORLD TOURNAMENT DIFFICULTIES

DIFFICULTY	REQUIREMENT
Adept	Unlock 16 or more characters and complete Novice level, then buy it from the shop.
Advanced	Unlock 32 or more characters and complete Adept level, then buy it from the shop.
Cell Games Rules	Defeat Cell after he has "broken in" during Dragon Arena.

STORY REENACTMENTS

REENACTMENT	CHARACTER	REQUIREMENT
000	Goku	Use Kamehameha vs. Raditz.
001	Piccolo	Use Special Beam Cannon vs. Raditz.
002	Tien	Use Ki Blast Cannon vs. Nappa.
003	Kid Gohan	Use Masenko vs. Nappa.
004	Krillin	Use Destructo Disk vs. Frieza Form 2.
005	Goku	Turn Super Saiyan vs. Frieza.

CHEATS, ACHIEVEMENTS, AND TROPHIES

D

REENACTMENT	CHARACTER	REQUIREMENT
006	Yamcha	When your life is red, use a Senzu Bean vs. Dr. Gero.
007	Piccolo	Use Fuse with Kami vs. Cell
008	Vegeta	Have at least 50% life remaining vs. 17 Absorption Cell
009	Vegeta	Use Final Flash vs. Perfect Cell.
010	Teen Gohan	Turn Super Saiyan vs. Goku.
011	Teen Gohan	Use Father Son Kamehameha vs. Super Perfect Cell.
012	Vegeta	Use Final Explosion vs. Majin Buu.
013	Goku	Turn Super Saiyan 3 vs. Majin Buu.
014	Piccolo	Fight vs. Super Buu for more than 60 seconds.
015	Gohan	Turn Mystic Gohan vs. Super Buu.
016	Goku	Use Super Spirit Bomb (normal state with Super Saiyan 1 & 2 equipped) vs. Kid Buu.
017	Vegeta	Turn Super Saiyan 4 vs. Super Saiyan 4 Goku.
018	Goku	As Super Saiyan 4 Gogeta use 100x Big Bang Kamehameha vs. Omega Shenron.
019	Broly	Use Gigantic Meteor vs. Gohan for the first time.
020	Uub	Use Ki Cannon vs. Goku for the first time.

UNLOCKABLE STAGES

STAGE	REQUIREMENT
Cell Ring	Defeat Perfect Cell in Goku's Dragon Universe.
Grandpa Gohan's House	Instead of fighting Piccolo in the Mountains, go to Grandpa Gohan's House and defeat Goku with Kid Gohan in the 2nd playthrough of Dragon Universe.
Grandpa Gohan's House	In Adult Gohan's Dragon Universe, go to Grandpa Gohan's House and defeat Goten, then Videl then return to Grandpa Gohan's House and enter it.
Inside Buu	Beat Super Buu inside of Buu with Goku and Vegeta.
Planet Namek	Play the Namek Saga.
Red Ribbon Army Base	Unlock Dragon Arena mode.
Supreme Kai's World	Beat Kid Buu in Goku and Vegeta's Dragon Universes in Supreme Kai's World.
Urban Level	Go to Central City in Teen Gohan's Dragon Universe.

UNLOCKABLE CHARACTERS

CHARACTER	REQUIREMENT
Android 16	Find him at the Plains around the South Island and bring him to Bulma in West City during the 2nd playthrough of Krillin's Dragon Universe.
Android 17	Defeat Android 17 in Piccolo's Dragon Universe.
Android 18	Complete Dragon Universe with Krillin.
Bardok	In the beginning of Dragon Universe fly to Raditz's Spaceship and enter the ??? area.
Captain Ginyu	Defeat Captain Ginyu in Goku's Dragon Universe.
Cell	Defeat Cell in Teen Gohan's Dragon Universe.
Cell Jr.	Defeat Piccolo in Dragon Arena when he breaks in.
Cooler	After defeating Frieza in Dragon Universe, defeat Super Saiyan Vegeta then move to Cooler's red mark and defeat him.
Dabura	Defeat Dabura in Adult Gohan's Dragon Universe.

CHARACTER	REQUIREMENT
Dr. Gero	Defeat Dr. Gero in Yamcha's Dragon Universe.
Fat Buu	Complete Goku's Dragon Universe.
Frieza	Defeat Frieza in Goku's Dragon Universe.
Gogeta (SSJ2)	After defeating Broly in Dragon Universe, defeat Gotenks at the World Tournament Arena.
Gogeta (SSJ4)	In Vegeta's Dragon Universe instead of fighting Kid Buu defeat Super Saiyan 4 Goku.
Gogeta (Vegeta)	Buy it from Skill Shops with the Black Membership Card.
Gogeta Capsule	Instead of fighting Uub or Brolly fight Goten and Trunks instead.
Gohan	Complete Teen Gohan's Dragon Universe.
Goku (SSJ4)	Defeat Kid Buu with a Super Spirit Bomb. Then go to the islands next to the goal and select ???.
Goten	Defeat Goten in Gohan's Dragon Universe.
Gotenks	Purchase from the Capsule Shop.
Great Saiyaman	Defeat Cell in Teen Gohan/Kid Gohan's Dragon Universe.
Hercule	Help him in Piccolo's Dragon Universe then talk to Videl at Central City.
Kid Buu	Defeat Kid Buu in Goku's Dragon Universe.
Kid Goku	Complete Broly's Dragon Universe.
Kid Trunks	Defeat Majin Buu in Vegeta's Dragon Universe.
Majin Buu	Defeat Majin Buu in Goku's Dragon Universe.
Omega Shenron	After being invited to fight Gotenks at the World Tournament, visit Bulma in West City then defeat Gotenks.
Recoome	Defeat Recoome in Goku's Dragon Universe.
Saibamnan	Beat Nappa when he breaks into the Dragon Arena.
Super Buu	Defeat Super Buu in Goku's Dragon Universe.
Supreme Kai	Find him at the plains before the last battle in Gohan's Dragon Universe.
Teen Gohan	Complete Kid Gohan's Dragon Universe.
Trunks	Complete Vegeta's Dragon Universe.
Uub	Defeat Kid Buu with a Spirit Bomb in Goku's Dragon Universe.
Vegeta	Defeat Vegeta in Goku's Dragon Universe.
Vegeta (SSJ4)	Buy it from the Capsule Shop with the Black Membership Card.
Vegito (Goku)	Defeat Super Buu in Buu's Body in Goku's Dragon Universe.
Vegito (Vegeta)	Defeat Super Buu in Buu's Body in Vegeta's Dragon Universe.
Videl	Go to the Plains (Point 4 on the map) in Gohan's Dragon Universe.

XBOX 360/PS3

ACHIEVEMENTS & TROPHIES

NAME	GOAL/REQUIREMENT	POINT VALUE	TROPHY VALUE
The Ultimate Warrior	You earned all achievements (trophies)	65	Platinum

CHEATS, ACHIEVEMENTS, AND TROPHIES

NAME	GOAL/REQUIREMENT	POINT VALUE	TROPHY VALUE
Special Beam Cannon	You cleared "Mysterious Alien Attack!!" in Dragon Ball Z: Budokai	15	Bronze
Focus Your Ki!	You cleared "A Mutually Deadly Foe" in Dragon Ball Z: Budokai	15	Bronze
Saibaman Hunter	You cleared "Saiyan Attack!!" in Dragon Ball Z: Budokai	15	Bronze
Saiyan Saga Clear	You cleared "Vegeta, Saiyan Prince" and completed the Saiyan Saga in Dragon Ball Z: Budokai	15	Bronze
Intensive Training	You cleared "Let's Go To Namek!" in Dragon Ball Z: Budokai	15	Bronze
Retrieval	You cleared "Goku's Arrival!!" in Dragon Ball Z: Budokai	15	Bronze
Super Saiyan	You cleared "The Legendary Super Sayain" in Dragon Ball Z: Budokai	15	Bronze
Namekian Saga Clear	You cleared "The True Ruler" and completed the Namekian Saga in Dragon Ball Z: Budokai	15	Bronze
Beat The Illness	You cleared "A New Threat" in Dragon Ball Z: Budokai	15	Bronze
Fusion With Kami	You cleared "A Wicked Omen" in Dragon Ball Z: Budokai	15	Bronze
Super Saiyan 2	You cleared "Gohan Explodes!!" in Dragon Ball Z: Budokai	15	Bronze
Android Saga Complete	You cleared "A Cold-Blooded Assassin" and completed the Android Saga in Dragon Ball Z: Budokai	30	Silver
Budokai Novice Champion	You won World Tournament mode on Novice in Dragon Ball Z: Budokai	10	Bronze
Budokai Adept Champion	You won World Tournament mode on Adept in Dragon Ball Z: Budokai	20	Bronze
Budokai Advanced Champion	You won World Tournament mode on Advanced in Dragon Ball Z: Budokai	50	Silver
Budokai 3 Goku	You cleared Dragon Universe in Dragon Ball Z: Budokai 3 with Goku	15	Bronze
Budokai 3 Kid Gohan	You cleared Dragon Universe in Dragon Ball Z: Budokai 3 with Kid Gohan	15	Bronze
Budokai 3 Teen Gohan	You cleared Dragon Universe in Dragon Ball Z: Budokai 3 with Teen Gohan	15	Bronze
Budokai 3 Gohan	You cleared Dragon Universe in Dragon Ball Z: Budokai 3 with Gohan	15	Bronze
Budokai 3 Vegeta	You cleared Dragon Universe in Dragon Ball Z: Budokai 3 with Vegeta	15	Bronze
Budokai 3 Krillin	You cleared Dragon Universe in Dragon Ball Z: Budokai 3 with Krillin	15	Bronze
Budokai 3 Piccolo	You cleared Dragon Universe in Dragon Ball Z: Budokai 3 with Piccolo	15	Bronze
Budokai 3 Tien	You cleared Dragon Universe in Dragon Ball Z: Budokai 3 with Tien	15	Bronze
Budokai 3 Yamcha	You cleared Dragon Universe in Dragon Ball Z: Budokai 3 with Yamcha	15	Bronze

NAME	GOAL/REQUIREMENT	POINT VALUE	TROPHY VALUE
Budokai 3 Uub	You cleared Dragon Universe in Dragon Ball Z: Budokai 3 with Uub	15	Bronze
Budokai 3 Broly	You cleared Dragon Universe in Dragon Ball Z: Budokai 3 with Broly	15	Bronze
Budokai 3 Novice Champion	You won World Tournament mode on Novice in Dragon Ball Z: Budokai 3	10	Bronze
Budokai 3 Adept Champion	You won World Tournament mode on Adept in Dragon Ball Z: Budokai 3	20	Bronze
Budokai 3 Advanced Champion	You won World Tournament mode on Advanced in Dragon Ball Z: Budokai 3	30	Silver
Budokai 3 Cell Games Champion	You won the Cell Games in Dragon Ball Z: Budokai 3	40	Gold
Budokai 3 Dragon Arena	You unlocked Dragon Arena mode in Dragon Ball Z: Budokai 3	30	Silver

SECRET ACHIEVEMENTS & TROPHIES

NAME	GOAL/REQUIREMENT	POINT VALUE	TROPHY VALUE
Budokai Team Earth	You unlocked Great Saiyaman, Trunks, Yamcha, and Hercule in Dragon Ball Z: Budokai	30	Silver
Budokai Team Frieza	You unlocked Zarbon and Dodoria in Dragon Ball Z: Budokai	30	Silver
Budokai Team Android	You unlocked #16, #18, and #19 in Dragon Ball Z: Budokai	30	Silver
Budokai Legend of Hercule	You unlocked Legend of Hercule in Dragon Ball Z: Budokai	30	Silver
Budokai 3 Goku's Family	You unlocked Goku (Kid), Gohan (Teen, Adolescent, Saiyaman), and Goten in Dragon Ball Z: Budokai 3	35	Silver
Budokai 3 Vegeta's Family	You unlocked Vegeta and Trunks (Future and Kid) in Dragon Ball Z: Budokai 3	35	Silver
Budokai 3 Team Earthlings	You unlocked Hercule, Videl, and Uub in Dragon Ball Z: Budokai 3	35	Silver
Budokai 3 Team Frieza	You unlocked Ginyu, Recoome, Frieza, and Saibamen in Dragon Ball Z: Budokai 3	35	Silver
Budokai 3 Team Android	You unlocked #16, #17, #18, Dr. Gero, Cell, and Cell Jr. in Dragon Ball Z: Budokai 3	35	Silver
Budokai Buu Saga	You unlocked Buu (Majin, Super, and Kid), Dabura, and Supreme Kai in Dragon Ball Z: Budokai 3	35	Silver
Budokai 3 Fierce Warriors	You unlocked Cooler, Bardock, Broly, and Omega Shenron in Dragon Ball Z: Budokai 3	35	Silver

DRAGON BALL Z: BUDOKAI TENKAICHI 3

NINTENDO WII

SURVIVAL MODE

Clear 30 missions in Mission 100 mode.

DRAGON BLADE: WRATH OF FIRE

ALL LEVELS

At the Title screen, hold Plus + Minus and select New Game or Load game. Hold the buttons until the stage select appears.

EASY DIFFICULTY

At the Title screen, hold Z + 2 when selecting "New Game."

HARD DIFFICULTY

At the Title screen, hold C + 2 when selecting "New Game."

To clear the following codes, hold Z at the stage select.

DRAGON HEAD

At the stage select, hold Z and press Plus. Immediately Swing Wii-mote Right, swing Wii-mote Down, swing Nunchuck Left, swing Nunchuck Right.

DRAGON WINGS

At the stage select, hold Z and press Plus. Immediately Swing Nunchuck Up + Wii-mote Up, swing Nunchuck Down + Wii-mote Down, swing Nunchuck Right + Wii-mote Left, swing Nunchuck Left + Wii-mote Right.

TAIL POWER

At the stage select, hold Z and press Plus. Immediately Swing your Wii-mote Down, Up, Left, and Right

DOUBLE FIST POWER

At the stage select, hold Z and press Plus. Immediately swing your Nunchuck Right, swing your Wii-mote left, swing your Nunchuck right while swinging your Wii-mote left, then swing both Wii-mote and Nunchuck down

DRAGON QUEST HEROES: ROCKET SLIME

KNIGHTRO TANK IN MULTIPLAYER

While inside the church, press Y, L, L, Y, R, R, Y, Up, Down, Select.

THE NEMESIS TANK IN MULTIPLAYER

While inside the church, press Y, R, R, Up, L, L, Y, Down, Down, Down, Y, Select.

DRAGON QUEST IX: SENTINELS OF THE STARRY SKIES

MINI MEDAL REWARDS

Trade your mini medals with Cap'N Max Meddlin in Dourbridge. The effects are cumulative, so giving him 80 medals unlocks all of the rewards.

# MINI MEDALS	REWARD
4	Thief's Key
8	Mercury Bandanna
13	Bunny Suit
18	Jolly Roger Jumper
25	Transparent Tights
32	Miracle Sword
40	Sacred Armor
50	Meteorite Bracer
62	Rusty Helmet
80	Dragon Robe

After giving him 80 mini medals, he will sell the following items for mini medals.

# MINI MEDALS	ITEM
3	Prayer Ring
5	Elfin Elixir
8	Saint's Ashes
10	Reset Stone
15	Orichalcum
20	Pixie Boots

DOURBRIDGE SECRET SHOP

In Dourbridge, there is a secret shop behind the Dourbridge Item Shop. You need the Ultimate Key to access the shop.

DRAGON QUEST MONSTERS: JOKER

NINTENDO 3DS

CAPTAIN CROW

As you travel between the islands on the sea scooters, you are occasionally attacked by pirates. Find out which route the pirates are located on the bulletin board in any scoutpost den. When you face them between Infant Isle and Celeste Isle, Captain Crow makes an appearance. Defeat him and he forces himself into your team.

SOLITAIRE'S CHALLENGE

After completing the main game, load your game back up for a new endeavor. The hero is in Solitaire's office where she proposes a new non-stop challenge known as Solitaire's Challenge.

METAL KING SLIME

Acquire 100 different skills for your library and talk to the woman in Solitaire's office.

METAL KAISER SLIME

Acquire 150 different skills for your library and talk to the woman in Solitaire's office.

LEOPOLD

Acquire all of the skills for your library and talk to the woman in Solitaire's office.

LIQUID METAL SLIME

Collect 100 monsters in your library and talk to the man in Solitaire's office.

GRANDPA SLIME

Collect 200 monsters in your library and talk to the man in Solitaire's office.

EMPYREA

Collect all of the monsters in your library and talk to the man in Solitaire's office.

TRODE AND ROBBIN' HOOD

Complete both the skills and monster libraries and talk to both the man and woman in Solitaire's office.

DRAGON QUEST MONSTERS: JOKER 2

NINTENDO 3DS

UNLOCK MONSTERS

MONSTER	OWN THIS MANY DIFFERENT MONSTERS
Great Argon Lizard	50
Drakularge	100
Metal King Slime	150
Grandpa Slime	200

CHEATS, ACHIEVEMENTS, AND TROPHIES

D

MONSTERS FROM DRAGON QUEST VI: REALMS OF REVELATION

Activate Dreamsharing on Dragon Quest VI and then turn on Tag Mode on Dragon Quest Monsters: Joker 2. This unlocks Malevolamp, Mottle Slime, Noble Gasbagon, and Overkilling Machine.

MONSTERS FROM DRAGON QUEST IX: SENTINELS OF THE STARRY SKIES

Activate Tag Mode on Dragon Quest IX and then turn on Tag Mode on Dragon Quest Monsters: Joker 2. This unlocks Shogum, Slime Stack, and Teeny Sanguini.

DRAGON'S DOGMA

XBOX 360/PS3

ACHIEVEMENTS & TROPHIES

NAME	GOAL/REQUIREMENT	POINT VALUE	TROPHY VALUE
The Patron	Helped Madeleine open her shop.	15	Bronze
The Coin Collector	Earned a total of 10,000,000G.	30	Silver
The Ever-Turning Wheel	Completed the adventure a second time.	50	Gold
The Explorer	Visited 150 locations.	35	Silver
The Vagabond	Visited 100 locations.	20	Bronze
The Tourist	Visited 50 locations.	10	Bronze
Into the Frontier Caverns	Entered the southwestern caves.	15	Bronze
Into the Manse	Entered the duke's manse.	20	Bronze
Into Soulflayer Canyon	Entered the Soulflayer Canyon.	15	Bronze
Into the Ancient Quarry	Entered the ancient quarry.	10	Bronze
Into Dripstone Cave	Entered the azure caverns.	10	Bronze
Affinity and Beyond	Raised a person's affinity to the maximum.	10	Bronze
The Escort	Acted as a reliable travel companion.	10	Bronze
The Philanthropist	Gave 50 presents.	15	Bronze
A Queen's Regalia	Dressed a male party member in women's clothing.	20	Bronze
Well Equipped	Obtained 350 pieces total of weapons and armor.	30	Bronze
The Artisan	Combined two materials to make an item.	10	Bronze
The Knave	Obtained a forgery.	15	Bronze
The Savior	Used a Wakestone to restore the dead to life.	10	Bronze
Inhuman Resources	Changed your main pawn's vocation.	20	Bronze
The Captain	Enlisted a large number of pawns.	15	Bronze
Foreign Recruit	Enlisted a pawn to your party from beyond the rift.	5	Bronze
Local Recruit	Directly enlisted a pawn to your party.	5	Bronze
The Veteran	Defeated 3,000 enemies.	35	Bronze

NAME	GOAL/REQUIREMENT	POINT VALUE	TROPHY VALUE
The Specialist	Learned all the skills of a single vocation.	40	Silver
Human Resources	Changed your vocation.	20	Bronze
The Hero	Completed all pre-planned, non-notice board quests.	40	Silver
The Laborer	Completed 50 notice board quests.	20	Bronze

SECRET ACHIEVEMENTS & TROPHIES

NAME	GOAL/REQUIREMENT	POINT VALUE	TROPHY VALUE
Dragon Forged	Strengthened equipment in wyrmfire.	30	Silver
The Messiah	Defeated the Ur-Dragon.	50	Gold
Serpents' Bane	Defeated a drake, wyrm, and wyvern.	40	Bronze
Eye Contact	Defeated an evil eye.	30	Bronze
Headshunter	Defeated a hydra or archydra.	30	Bronze
Closure	Put an end to all things.	40	Gold
Peace	Took refuge in an illusion.	20	Bronze
Servitude	Soar unto a new world.	20	Bronze
Solitude	Obtained the almighty power of sovereignty.	20	Bronze
Mercy	Dealt the blow of deliverance.	30	Bronze
Freedom	Escaped the yoke of eternity.	10	Bronze
Treacherous	Peered into the very depths of the world.	10	Bronze
Destiny	Accepted the Godsbane blade.	25	Bronze
Rough Landing	Completed the urgent mission.	10	Bronze
The Message	Received the duke's commendation.	15	Bronze
Come Courting	Attended an audience with the duke.	15	Bronze
Writ Large	Received a writ from the castle.	10	Bronze
The Courier	Entered Gran Soren.	10	Bronze
Getting a Head	Earned the approval of the Enlistment Corps.	15	Bronze
A New Ally	Summoned your own pawn.	10	Bronze
Onward	Departed from Cassardis.	5	Bronze
It Begins	Completed the prologue.	5	Bronze

DRAGON'S LAIR

XBOX 360

AVATAR AWARDS

AWARD	EARNED BY
Dragon's Lair Logo T-Shirt	Free with your purchase of Dragon's Lair!
Dragon's Lair Castle T-Shirt	Unlock the Secret Achievement.
Dirk the Daring's Helmet	Beat the Game.

DRAWN TO LIFE

HEAL ALL DAMAGE
During a game, press Start, hold L and press Y, X, Y, X, Y, X, A.

INVINCIBLITY
During a game, press Start, hold L and press A, X, B, B, Y.

ALIEN TEMPLATES
During a game, press Start, hold L and press X, Y, B, A, A.

ANIMAL TEMPLATES
During a game, press Start, hold L and press B, B, A, A, X.

ROBOT TEMPLATES
During a game, press Start, hold L and press Y, X, Y, X, A.

SPORTS TEMPLATES
During a game, press Start, hold L and press Y, A, B, A, X.

DRAWN TO LIFE: SPONGEBOB SQUAREPANTS EDITION

NINTENDO 3DS

EXTRA REWARD COINS
Select Cheat Entry and enter Down, Down, B, B, Down, Left, Up, Right, A.

DRAWN TO LIFE: THE NEXT CHAPTER

NINTENDO 3DS

TEMPLATES
At the Creation Hall, hold L and press X, Y, B, A, A to unlock the following Templates.

- Astronaut Template
- Knight Template
- Ninja Girl Template
- Spartan Template
- Super Girl Template

DRIVER: PARALLEL LINES

NINTENDO WII

ALL VEHICLES
Pause the game, select cheats and enter carshow.

ALL WEAPONS
Pause the game, select cheats and enter gunrange.

INVINCIBILITY
Pause the game, select cheats and enter steelman.

INFINITE AMMUNITION
Pause the game, select cheats and enter gunbelt.

INFINITE NITROUS
Pause the game, select cheats and enter zoomzoom.

INDESTRUCTIBLE CARS
Pause the game, select cheats and enter rollbar.

WEAKER COPS
Pause the game, select cheats and enter keystone.

ZERO COST
Pause the game, select cheats and enter tooledup. This gives you free upgrades.

DRIVER: SAN FRANCISCO

MOVIE SCENE CHALLENGES

As you collect the 130 Movie Tokens in the game, Movie Scene Challenges are unlocked as shown below.

MOVIE SCENE CHALLENGE	VEHICLE GIVEN	# MOVIE TOKENS
Gone In 60 Seconds	1973 Ford Mustang Mach I	10
Starsky & Hutch	1974 Dodge Monaco Cop	20
Bullitt	1968 Ford Mustang GT Fastback	30
The French Connection	1971 Pontiac LeMans	40
Blues Brothers	1974 Dodge Monaco	50
Cannonball Run	1978 Lamborghini Countach LP400S	60
Dukes of Hazard	1969 Dodge Charger R/T	70
Vanishing Point	1970 Dodge Challenger R/T	80
The Driver	1965 Chevrolet S-10	90
Redline	2011 McLaren MP4-12C	100
Smokey & The Bandit	1977 Pontiac TransAm Firebird	110
Test Drive	1987 RUF CT-R Yellow Bird	120
The Italian Job	1972 Lamborghini Miura	130

DUKE NUKEM FOREVER

CLUB DOOR CODE

Behind the bar in the club, there is a door that requires a code to get in. Enter 4768.

CHEATS

Defeating the game gives you the ability to activate the following cheats in Extras.

- Duke 3D Freeze Ray
- Grayscale Mode
- Head Scale
- Infinite Ammo
- Instagib
- Invincibility
- Mirror Mode

DUNGEON SIEGE: THRONE OF AGONY

ITEM CODES

Talk to Feydwer and Klaars in Seahaven and enter the following codes. Enter the Master Code and one of the item codes.

ITEM	CODE
Master Code	MPJNKBHAKANLPGHD
Bloodstained Warboots	MHFMCJIFNDHOKLPM
Bolt Flingers	OBMIDNBJNPFKADCL
Enkindled Cleaver	MJPOBGFNLKELLLLP
Malignant Force	JDGJHKPOLNMCGHNC
Polychromatic Shiv	PJJEPCFHEIHAJEEE
Teasha's Ire	GDIMBNLEIGNNLOEG
Traveler's Handbook	PIJNPEGFJJPFALNO

ELITE MODE

Defeat the game to unlock this mode.

EA REPLAY

B.O.B.

PASSWORDS

LEVEL	PASSWORD
Anciena 1	672451
Anciena 2	272578
Anciena 3	652074
Anciena 4	265648
Anciena 5	462893
Anciena 6	583172
Goth 2	171058
Goth 3	950745
Goth 4	472149
Ultraworld 1	743690
Ultraworld 2	103928
Ultraworld 3	144895
Ultraworld 4	775092
Ultraworld 5	481376

DESERT STRIKE

10 LIVES

At the Desert Strike menu, press ● to bring up the Password screen. Enter BQQQAEZ.

JUNGLE STRIKE

PASSWORDS

Press ● at the Jungle Strike menu to bring up the Password screen. Enter the following:

LEVEL	PASSWORD
Mountains	7LSPFBVWTWP
Night Strike	X4MFB4MHPH4
Puloso City	V6HGY39XVXL
Return Home	N4MK9N6MHM7
River Raid	TGB76MGCZCC
Training Ground	9NHDXMGCZCG
Washington D.C	BXYTNMGCYDB

WING COMMANDER

INVINCIBILITY AND STAGE SELECT

At the Wing Commander menu, press ⊗, ●, ⊗, ●, ⊗, ●, L, ●, R, ●, Start.

ROAD RASH 2

WILD THING MOTORCYCLE

At the title screen, hold Up + ● + ● and press Start.

EA SPORTS NBA JAM

Hold the Wii Remote vertically when entering the following codes. To access the teams, press + at the Team Select screen.

BEASTIE BOYS

At the Title screen, press Up, Up, Down, Down, Left, Right, Left, Right, B, +. This team includes Ad Rock, MCA, and Mike D.

J.COLE & 9TH WONDER

At the Title screen, press Up, Left, Down, Right, Up, Left, Down, Right, 1, 2.

DEMOCRAT TEAM

At the Title screen, press Left (x13), +. This team includes Barack Obama, Joe Biden, Bill Clinton, and Hillary Clinton.

REPUBLICAN TEAM

At the Title screen, press Right (x13), +. The team includes George W. Bush, Sarah Palin, and John McCain.

ESPN'S SPORTSNATION

Select Play Now. When entering the initials, enter ESP for P1 and NSN for P2. Advance to the Choose Teams screen and use + to find the team. This team includes the hosts of the show, Colin Cowherd and Michelle Beadle.

NBA MASCOTS

Select Play Now. When entering the initials, enter MAS for P1 and COT for P2. Advance to the Choose Teams screen and use + to find the team.

ORIGINAL JAM

Select Play Now. When entering the initials, enter MJT for P1. Advance to the Choose Teams screen and use + to find the team. This team includes Mark Turmell and Tim Kitzrow.

EARTH DEFENSE FORCE: INSECT ARMAGEDDON

HIDDEN IMAGES IN GALLERY

Select Gallery from the Extras menu. At the gallery press ●, ●, ●, ●, L1, R1.

HIDDEN IMAGES IN GALLERY

Select Gallery from the Extras menu. At the gallery press X, X, Y, X, Left Bumper, Right Bumper.

EARTHWORM JIM

CHEAT MENU

Pause the game and press Y + Left, B, B, Y, Y + Right, B, B, Y. Notes that these are the button presses for the classic controller.

E

ELEBITS: THE ADVENTURES OF KAI & ZERO

BIG RED BONUS OMEGA

Select Download Additional Omegas from the Extra menu. Choose Download Data and press B, Y, Up, L, Right, R, Down, Left, X, A.

F1 RACE STARS

ACHIEVEMENTS & TROPHIES

NAME	GOAL/REQUIREMENT	POINT VALUE	TROPHY VALUE
Taste of Victory	You won an event	5	Bronze
Red Carpet	You took a locked shortcut	10	Bronze
Career is GO!	You completed the first championship of your career	10	Bronze
Career 25%	You completed 8 different championships in your career	10	Bronze
Career 50%	You completed 15 different championships in your career	25	Bronze
Career 75%	You completed 23 different championships in your career	50	Silver
Career 100%	You completed 30 different championships in your career	100	Gold
Shelf Promotion	You filled your career trophy cabinet	25	Silver
Your Friends are Cool	You completed a championship in your career in a splitscreen team	10	Bronze
Internet Famous	You won an online event	25	Bronze
Fish in a Barrel	You used power-ups against 3 drivers who are within range of the safety car (globals not included)	10	Bronze
Heavyweight	You affected 3 drivers with a single Pulse	10	Bronze
Fully Automatic	You hit the same driver three times with a 3x Ricochet Bubble	10	Bronze
Scientific Method	You made an impact with each type of power-up	10	Bronze
Nailed the Jump	You triggered a jump boost	5	Bronze
Jump Boost Expert	You triggered 50 jump boosts	25	Bronze
Slipstreamer	You slipstreamed past a driver	5	Bronze
Slipstream Expert	You slipstreamed past 50 drivers	25	Bronze
Shortcut Expert	You took every shortcut in the game	10	Bronze
Abu Dhabi Expert	You won an Abu Dhabi event at 3,000cc	10	Bronze
Australia Expert	You won an Australia event at 3,000cc	10	Bronze
Belgium Expert	You won a Belgium event at 3,000cc	10	Bronze
Brazil Expert	You won a Brazil event at 3,000cc	10	Bronze
Germany Expert	You won a Germany event at 3,000cc	10	Bronze
Great Britain Expert	You won a Great Britain event at 3,000cc	10	Bronze
Italy Expert	You won an Italy event at 3,000cc	10	Bronze

NAME	GOAL/REQUIREMENT	POINT VALUE	TROPHY VALUE
Japan Expert	You won a Japan event at 3,000cc	10	Bronze
Monaco Expert	You won a Monaco event at 3,000cc	10	Bronze
Singapore Expert	You won a Singapore event at 3,000cc	10	Bronze
USA Expert	You won a USA event at 3,000cc	10	Bronze
Around the World	You won an event on every track at 3,000cc	50	Silver
Qualifying Lap	You set a Time Trial record	10	Bronze
Bronze Time	You earned a bronze Time Trial record on all tracks	25	Bronze
Silver Time	You earned a silver Time Trial record on all tracks	50	Silver
Gold Time	You earned a gold Time Trial record on all tracks	100	Gold
Player of Games	You completed one event in each race mode	25	Bronze
Exhibition Rush	You earned 1,000 Exhibition points in under 5 seconds	25	Silver
Vapours	You won a Refuel event with an empty tank	25	Silver
My House	You owned the whole track in Sector Snatch	25	Silver
Causing Trouble	You hit another driver after being eliminated	25	Bronze
Shakedown	You made a nearby driver drop 600 points in Trophy Chase	25	Silver
Ecto-won	You beat a friend's Time Trial lap	10	Bronze
Prince of the Screen	You reached King of the Screen level 3	10	Bronze
King of King of the Screen	You reached King of the Screen level 6	25	Silver
Social Butterfly	You completed one event with each constructor	10	Bronze
Pitmaster	You repaired in the pits 10 times	10	Bronze
Bingo!	You used a power-up against every opponent on the track (globals not included)	25	Silver

SECRET ACHIEVEMENTS & TROPHIES

NAME	GOAL/REQUIREMENT	POINT VALUE	TROPHY VALUE
Whoops!	You hit yourself with your own Ricochet Bubble	10	Bronze
They See You Rollin'	You earned 3,141 badges	25	Silver

CANADA TRACK DLC

NAME	GOAL/REQUIREMENT	POINT VALUE	TROPHY VALUE
Canadian Gold	Earn a Gold Time Trial record on Canada	25	Gold
Road Trip: Canada	Win an online race on Canada (no teams)	25	Silver
Trophy Hunter	Collect 200 trophies on Canada	20	Bronze
Canada Expert	Win a Canada event at 3,000cc (no teams)	20	Bronze
Maple Highway	Take the locked shortcut on Canada	10	Bronze

CHEATS, ACHIEVEMENTS, AND TROPHIES

F

CHINA TRACK DLC

NAME	GOAL/REQUIREMENT	POINT VALUE	TROPHY VALUE
Chinese Gold	Earn a Gold Time Trial record on China	25	Gold
Road Trip: China	Win an online race on China (no teams)	25	Silver
Gate Hunter	Pass through 100 gates on China	20	Bronze
China Expert	Win a China event at 3,000cc (no teams)	20	Bronze
Dragon Dance	Take the locked shortcut on China	10	Bronze

INDIA TRACK

NAME	GOAL/REQUIREMENT	POINT VALUE	TROPHY VALUE
Indian Gold	Earn a Gold Time Trial record on India	25	Gold
Road Trip: India	Win an online race on India (no teams)	25	Silver
Fuel Hunter	Collect 50 fuel cans on India	20	Bronze
India Expert	Win a India event at 3,000cc (no teams)	20	Bronze
Lotus Garden	Take the locked shortcut on India	10	Bronze

F.E.A.R.

ALL MISSIONS

Sign in with F3ARDAY1 as your Profile Name. Using this cheat will disable Achievements.

FABLE 3

ACHIEVEMENTS

NAME	GOAL/REQUIREMENT	POINT VALUE
The Guild Seal	Unleash your heroic potential.	10
And So It Begins	Win the support of the Dwellers.	20
Swift Justice	Win the support of the Swift Brigade.	20
The Resistance	Win the support of Bowerstone.	50
Distant Friends	Win the support of Aurora.	20
The Ruler of Albion	Become the ruler of Albion.	80
For Albion!	This is where you *spoiler* the great, big *spoiler* and then it all *spoiler*.	80
Save The Princess!	Rescue the princess from the evil Baron.	10
Ghost Brothers	Make sure Max and Sam get home in time for tea.	10
Tragical-Comical-Historical	Help the celebrated thespians Lambert and Pinch put on the world's greatest play.	10
The Dark Sanctum	Reinstate an ancient, evil temple.	10
Island Paradise	Establish the island of Driftwood.	10

NAME	GOAL/REQUIREMENT	POINT VALUE
Knight Jumps Chesty	Defeat Chesty at his own game.	10
Coronation Chicken	Perform a royal judgment while dressed as a chicken.	10
Spellweaver	Combine two gauntlets to cast a "woven" spell.	5
Archmage	Cast all 15 possible spell combinations.	20
Total Warrior	Kill enemies with melee, ranged and spell attacks.	10
Pull!	Send an enemy flying into the air and kill him while he's airborne.	10
Gunning For Glory	Kill 500 enemies using firearms.	20
If It Bleeds, We Can Kill It	Kill 500 enemies using melee weapons.	20
Wizard's Revenge	Kill 500 enemies using magic.	20
Super Hero	Fully upgrade your Melee, Ranged, and Magic abilities on the Road to Rule.	50
You Can't Bring Me Down	Complete Fable III without being knocked out in combat.	50
My Weapon's Better Than Yours	Complete 3 unique upgrades on one of the legendary weapons found around Albion.	25
I Am The Keymaster	Collect all 50 Silver Keys and 4 Gold Keys.	30
Flower Power	Collect all 30 Auroran flowers.	30
Gnome Invasion	Destroy all 50 gnomes.	30
Brightwall Book Club	Collect all 30 rare books for the Brightwall Academy.	30
Digger	Dig up 50 items.	15
We Need Guns, Lots Of Guns	Collect all 50 legendary weapons. They won't all appear in your world, so trade with other Heroes!	20
Fashion Victim	Collect every item of clothing.	20
He's a Woman. She's a Man	Wear a full set of clothing intended for the opposite sex.	5
Dye Hippie, Dye	Dye each part of an outfit you're wearing a different color and have long hair.	5
Hand in Hand	Hold hands with someone.	5
Long Distance Relationship	Get married to another Xbox LIVE player.	10
Cross-Dimensional Conception	Have a child with another Xbox LIVE player.	10
Online Merger	Enter into a business partnership with another Xbox LIVE player.	10
Barrel of Laughs	Kill 30 enemies with explosive barrels.	10
We Can Be Heroes	Earn 1,000 gold in henchman wages in another Hero's world.	10
Kaboom!	Score 2000 on the Mourningwood Fort mortar game.	10
Lute Hero Tour	Play in each town as a 5 star lute player.	10
Touched By A Hero	Use touch expressions to interact with 20 different people.	10
Popularity Contest	Make 20 Friends.	15
Remodelling	Remodel 5 different houses by changing the furniture.	10
Magnate Personality	Build a property empire worth 2,000,000 gold.	50
Crime Spree	Get a 15,000 gold bounty placed on your head.	10
Henry VIII	As ruler of Albion, get married 6 times and kill 2 of your spouses.	10
Chest Grandmaster	Unlock all of the chests on the Road To Rule.	40
Tough Love	Save the maximum amount of Albion citizens.	10
Adopt Or Die	Adopt a child.	5

F

FABLE HEROES

AVATAR AWARDS

AVATAR	EARNED BY
Heroes T-Shirt	Unlock the Heroes T-Shirt by completing the Millfields level.
Jack of Blades Mask	Unlock the Jack of Blades Mask by purchasing all the abilities for the Jack of Blades puppet.

ACHIEVEMENTS

NAME	GOAL/REQUIREMENT	POINT VALUE
Rolled the Dice	Visit a tile on the Abilities Board. This also unlocks a tile on the Inner Board.	5
Better When Shared	Complete a level as part of a four-player team. This also unlocks a tile on the Inner Board.	5
Cast Party	Unlock all the playable characters. This also unlocks a tile on the Inner Board.	20
Rule the Dice	Purchase all abilities for one puppet. This also unlocks a tile on the Inner Board.	10
Bully	Kick a hobblet, then shoot it out of the air. This also unlocks a tile on the Inner Board.	5
Veg Head	Hit an enemy with its own head. This also unlocks a tile on the Inner Board.	5
Traitor	Kill a Hobbe while disguised as a Hobbe. This also unlocks a tile on the Inner Board.	5
Can't See the Future	Complete a 'Challenging' level in 'No HUD' mode. This also unlocks a tile on the Inner Board.	5
One Down	Buy all abilities on a single tile. This also unlocks a tile on the Inner Board.	5
Puppet Beats Chicken	Complete the Chicken Bomb Mini-Game without getting hurt. This unlocks a tile on the Inner Board.	10
Fast & Furious	Complete the Mine Cart Mini-Game in under 13 seconds. This unlocks a tile on the Inner Board.	5
World Champion	Achieve a Gold Medal in every level. This also unlocks a tile on the Inner Board.	20
Heroes of Millfields	Complete Millfields in the world of Albion.	10
Heroes of Gravestone	Complete Gravestone in the world of Albion.	10
Heroes of Mistpeak	Complete Mistpeak in the world of Albion.	10
Ruler of Albion	Complete all levels in the world of Albion.	20
Heroes of Bowerstone	Complete Bowerstone in the world of Albion.	10
Heroes of Aurora	Complete Aurora in the world of Albion.	10
Heroes of The Credits	Complete The Credits in the world of Albion.	10
Ruler of Dark Albion	Complete all levels in the world of Dark Albion.	40
Heroes of The Cloud	Complete The Cloud in the world of Albion.	10
Heroes of Hobbe Caves	Complete Hobbe Caves in the world of Albion.	10
Heroes of Dark Millfields	Complete Millfields in Dark Albion without being hit!	20
Heroes of Dark Gravestone	Complete Gravestone in Dark Albion with Big Heads mode enabled!	20
Heroes of Dark Mistpeak	Complete Mistpeak in Dark Albion with a Perk activated!	20
Heroes of Dark Hobbe Caves	Complete Hobbe Caves in Dark Albion and finish in first place!	20
Heroes of Dark Bowerstone	Complete Bowerstone in Dark Albion on Challenging and without dying!	20
Heroes of Dark Aurora	Complete Aurora in Dark Albion and use at least three Power-Ups!	20

NAME	GOAL/REQUIREMENT	POINT VALUE
Heroes of The Dark Credits	Complete The Credits in Dark Albion and smash 20 Lionhead developers!	20
Heroes of The Dark Cloud	Complete The Cloud in Dark Albion and make your head POP!	20

FANTASTIC PETS

AVATAR AWARDS

AWARD	EARNED BY
Fantastic T-Shirt	Reach Fantastic Pet trainer rank 2.
Cute Hat (Female)	Reach Fantastic Pet trainer rank 3.
Fierce Hat (Male)	Reach Fantastic Pet trainer rank 3.
Fantastic Gloves	Reach Fantastic Pet trainer rank 4.
Fantastic Shoes	Reach Fantastic Pet trainer rank 5.
Fantastic Pet	Reach Fantastic Pet trainer rank 6.

FAR CRY 3

SIGNATURE WEAPONS

Signature weapons are powerful weapons that are unlocked by completing in-game challenges.

WEAPON	REQUIREMENT
AMR (Sniper Rifle)	Find 20 Relics.
Bull (Shotgun)	Find 10 Relics.
Bushman (Assault Rifle)	Activate all Radio Towers.
Japanese Tanto (Melee Weapon)	Find six Letters of the Lost.
Ripper (Light Machine Gun)	Survive 6 Trials of the Rakyat.
Shadow (Pistol)	Take over 17 Encampments.
Shredder (Sub-Machine Gun)	Collect 10 Memory Cards.

ACHIEVEMENTS & TROPHIES

NAME	GOAL/REQUIREMENT	POINT VALUE	TROPHY VALUE
Free Fall	Freefall more than 100m and live (Single Player only).	5	Bronze
Inked Up	Earn 5 skill tattoos.	5	Bronze
Fully Inked	Earn every tattoo by learning all the skills.	30	Gold
Money to Burn	Spend $5000 at the shop.	15	Bronze
Aftermarket Junkie	Buy all attachments and paint jobs for one weapon.	20	Bronze
Rebel With a Cause	Liberate 3 outposts.	10	Bronze
Island Liberator	Liberate all outposts.	40	Silver
Unheard	Liberate an outpost without triggering an alarm.	20	Bronze
Full Bars	Activate 9 radio towers.	20	Silver
Archeology 101	Gather a total of 60 relics.	20	Silver
Dead Letters	Gather all "Letters of the Lost".	20	Silver
Memory to Spare	Gather all the memory cards.	20	Silver
Jungle Journal	Unlock 50 entries in the Survivor Guide.	20	Silver

F

NAME	GOAL/REQUIREMENT	POINT VALUE	TROPHY VALUE
Bagged and Tagged	Complete a Path of the Hunter quest.	10	Bronze
Road Trip	Complete a Supply Drop quest.	10	Bronze
In Cold Blood	Complete a WANTED Dead quest.	10	Bronze
Let the Trials Begin	Beat any Trial of the Rakyat score.	10	Bronze
Poker Bully	Win $1500 playing poker.	20	Silver
Hunter Hunted	Lure and kill a predator.	10	Bronze
Poacher	Hunt and skin a rare animal.	20	Bronze
Artsy Craftsy	Craft 5 upgrades for your equipment.	10	Bronze
Needle Exchange	Craft 25 syringes.	15	Bronze
The Good Stuff	Craft a special syringe.	15	Bronze
Say Hi to the Internet	Find the lost Hollywood star.	10	Bronze
Heartless Pyro	Kill 50 enemies with the flamethrower (Single Player only).	10	Bronze
Love the Boom	Kill 4 enemies simultaneously with one explosion (Single Player only).	10	Bronze
Rock Always Wins	Fully distract 25 enemies with rocks (Single Player only).	10	Bronze
Island Paparazzi	Tag 25 enemies using the camera (Single Player only).	15	Bronze
Fearless or Stupid	Dive more than 60m (Single Player only).	15	Bronze
Never Saw it Coming	Kill an enemy with a takedown from above from a glider, zipline or parachute (Single Player only).	20	Bronze
Improper Use	Kill an enemy with the Repair Tool (Single Player only).	5	Bronze
Toxophilite	Kill a target from 70m or more with the bow (Single Player only).	10	Bronze
Here We Come	Complete "Ready or Not" Co-op map (Online/Offline).	20	Bronze
Return to Sender	Complete "Sidetracked" Co-op map (Online/Offline).	20	Bronze
Rocking the Boat	Complete "Overboard" Co-op map (Online/Offline).	20	Bronze
Hide and Seek	Complete "Lights Out" Co-op map (Online/Offline).	20	Bronze
Late Night Pick-up	Complete "Rush Hour" Co-op map (Online/Offline).	20	Bronze
Getting Even	Complete "Payback" Co-op map (Online/Offline).	20	Bronze

SECRET ACHIEVEMENTS & TROPHIES

NAME	GOAL/REQUIREMENT	POINT VALUE	TROPHY VALUE
First Blood	Escape the pirates and survive in the wilderness.	10	Bronze
Magic Mushroom	Return to the doctor with the cave mushrooms.	20	Bronze
Worst Date Ever	Rescue Liza from the burning building.	20	Bronze
One of Us	Complete the Rakyat initiation.	20	Bronze
Hands Off My Stoner	Rescue Oliver from the pirates.	20	Bronze
Retake Wallstreet	Rescue Keith from Buck.	20	Bronze

NAME	GOAL/REQUIREMENT	POINT VALUE	TROPHY VALUE
Have I Told You?	Survive the encounter with Vaas and escape.	50	Silver
Taken for Granted	Kill Vaas.	50	Silver
Higher Than a Kite	Use your wingsuit to reach the Southern island.	20	Bronze
Deep Cover	Complete Riley's interrogation.	20	Bronze
Poker Night	Kill Hoyt.	50	Silver
What a Trip	Attend the final ceremony.	100	Gold

FAR CRY 3: BLOOD DRAGON

ACHIEVEMENTS & TROPHIES

NAME	GOAL/REQUIREMENT	POINT VALUE	TROPHY VALUE
Blood Dragon Down	Kill Your First Dragon	20	Bronze
Derp	Jump Down from 50 Meters	20	Bronze
Dragon Slayer	Kill 25 Dragons	20	Bronze
Hail to the King	Reach Maximum Level and Become the Ultimate Badass	40	Bronze
Just the Tip	Kill a Dragon with the Bow	15	Bronze
Kill Them All	Finish all the Predator's Path Quests	20	Bronze
Murder Nature	Kill all the Animal Types	30	Bronze
Nice Like Jesus	Finish all the Hostages Situations	5	Bronze
Running man	After saving Darling, enter Combat Mode with a Dragon and Return to Stealth	30	Bronze
Set Them Free	Destroy 5 Braincages	5	Bronze
The Drug of the Nation	Find all TV SETS to Decrypt the Hidden Message	20	Bronze
The Greatest Format of all Time	Find all VHS Tapes	20	Bronze
The Only True Stopper	Headshot Every Type of Enemy	15	Bronze
Tooled Up	Own all Weapons Attachments	20	Bronze
Way to Go, Garri-Son	Finish all the Garrisons	20	Bronze
What are You Reading For?	Find all of Dr. Carlyle's Notes	20	Bronze

SECRET ACHIEVEMENTS & TROPHIES

NAME	GOAL/REQUIREMENT	POINT VALUE	TROPHY VALUE
End Game	Finished Final Showdown	50	Silver
One Small Step	Finished First Garrison	20	Bronze
Welcome to the Party, Pal	Finished Helicopter Entry	10	Bronze

FATAL FURY SPECIAL

CHEAT MENU

During a game, hold Start and push A + X + Y.

FEZ

FLY

In New Game + at any time, press Up, Up, Up, Up + A.

FIFA 12

ACHIEVEMENTS & TROPHIES

NAME	GOAL/REQUIREMENT	POINT VALUE	TROPHY VALUE
Precision Tackler	Obtain a successful tackle percentage of 80% with a minimum of 5 tackles in a game	15	Bronze
Megged	Successfully dribble the ball through a defender's legs	30	Silver
Riding Bikes	Score with a bicycle kick	50	Silver
Legendary	Win a game vs. the CPU on legendary difficulty against a club of the same or higher star level	30	Silver
Don't Blink	Score within the first 5 minutes of a game in a game vs the CPU	10	Bronze
Comeback Kid	Win after being down 3 goals in the 2nd half in a game vs. the CPU	15	Bronze
10 vs 11	Win from a draw or behind while down a man in a game vs the CPU	10	Bronze
Ruud Boy	Score a goal on a volley	15	Bronze
Block Party	Manually block 5 shots while defending in a single game	10	Bronze
Century of Goals	Score 100 goals in FIFA 12 match play	45	Silver
All My Own Work	Win a Match with Manual Controls (including Tactical Defending)	10	Bronze
Warrior	Score a goal after suffering a non-contact injury with a player	20	Bronze
Quickly Now!	Score shortly after a quick throw-in	20	Bronze
EAS FC Youth Academy	Reach level 5 in the EA SPORTS Football Club	10	Bronze
EAS FC Starting 11	Reach level 20 in the EA SPORTS Football Club	30	Silver
Challenge Accepted	Complete an EA SPORTS Football Club Game Scenario Challenge	15	Bronze
Path to the Cup	Win a cup game in Head to Head Seasons	20	Bronze
Campaign Complete	Complete a Season in Head to Head Seasons	50	Silver
Friends now Enemies?	Win an Online Friendlies season	25	Bronze
Being Social	Play an Online Friendlies Match	10	Bronze
3 Points	Win a season game in Head to Head Seasons	10	Bronze

NAME	GOAL/REQUIREMENT	POINT VALUE	TROPHY VALUE
Virtual Debut	Play an online Pro Club or Pro Ranked match with your Virtual Pro	10	Bronze
New Club in Town	Create your FIFA 12 Ultimate Team club	5	Bronze
Legends start with Victories	Win a match with your FIFA 12 Ultimate Team club	10	Bronze
Tournament Victory	Win a tournament in FIFA 12 Ultimate Team	10	Bronze
I'll have that one	Open your first pack in FIFA 12 Ultimate Team	10	Bronze
Friendly	Finish a match against a Friend in FIFA 12 Ultimate Team	10	Bronze
Marquee Signing	Purchase a Gold Player from the trade market for 15,000 or more coins using Buy now	30	Silver
Growing Club	Achieve a club value of 85,000,000 in FIFA 12 Ultimate Team	30	Bronze
Big Cup Squad	Enter an Ultimate Team tournament and finish a match with an overall squad rating of 85 or higher	30	Silver
Pack King	Open 100 packs in FIFA 12 Ultimate Team	50	Gold
We'll need a larger trophy case	Win your 10th trophy in FIFA 12 Ultimate Team	30	Silver
Club Legend	Play 100 matches with any player in FIFA 12 Ultimate Team	15	Bronze
Trophy Time	Win the league title in any league in Career Mode	50	Silver
Procrastinator	Sign a player on Deadline Day in the transfer window in Career Mode	15	Bronze
Fully Formed	Have three players be in full form at the same time on your club in Career Mode	30	Silver
Massive Signing	Sign a player better than anyone else on your club during the transfer window	20	Bronze
Youth is Served	Sign a player to your youth squad in Career Mode	20	Bronze
Puppet Master	Talk to the Press in Career Mode	10	Silver
Sweet Music	Set up some Custom Audio in FIFA 12	10	Silver
Virtual Legend	Play 50 Matches with your Virtual Pro	50	Bronze
FIFA for Life	Spend 50 hours on the pitch	50	Bronze
Happy 20th EA SPORTS!	Score 20 match goals in FIFA 12 to celebrate 20 years of EA SPORTS!	20	Bronze

SECRET ACHIEVEMENTS

NAME	GOAL/REQUIREMENT	POINT VALUE	TROPHY VALUE
No Draw for You!	Score a 90th minute winner in a game vs. the CPU	15	Bronze
How Great is that?	Find a team of the week player in an Ultimate Team pack	20	Bronze

FIFA 13

ACHIEVEMENTS & TROPHIES

NAME	GOAL/REQUIREMENT	POINT VALUE	TROPHY VALUE
Bronzed	Complete the Bronze stage of all Skills	30	Bronze
Skill Legend	Become Legendary on one of the Skill Challenges	50	Gold
Road to Mastery	Unlock a Skill Challenge	30	Silver
Trolling for Goals	Score on a free kick after running over the ball	15	Bronze
No Goal for You!	Goal Line Clearance	30	Bronze
Creeping on the Down Low	Wall creep, free kick is blocked by wall	5	Bronze
Body Control	Score an off balance shot	5	Bronze
Cheeky	Chip the Keeper	5	Bronze
Get In!	Score a Diving Header	15	Bronze
Brains and Brawn	Shield the ball out of play for a goal kick	15	Bronze
Road to Promotion	Win a FUT Seasons Match	10	Bronze
Get Physical	Seal out an attacking player to gain possession of the ball	5	Bronze
1 week	Win all the EAS FC Match Day Games of the Week in a single week	15	Bronze
Go Live!	Win an EAS FC Match Day Live Fixture	15	Bronze
Getting Real	Play 25 EAS FC Match Day Games	30	Bronze
Division King	Win a Division title in Season	50	Silver
Filling Cabinets	Win a Cup in Seasons	30	Silver
Hello World	Play your first match with your Online Pro	5	Bronze
On the Rise	Earn a Promotion in Seasons	25	Bronze
One of the Bros	Be part of a Club win	15	Bronze
Bros	Play a Seasons game with a Guest	15	Bronze
Good Start	Unlock 10% of the accomplishments with your Online Pro	30	Bronze
Well on Your Way	Unlock 25% of the accomplishments with your Online Pro	50	Silver
Still Friends?	Win an Online Friendlies Season	30	Bronze
Mr. Manager	Take Control of your own FIFA Ultimate Team	10	Bronze
Silverware	Win a Trophy in a FUT Competition	10	Bronze
Building My Club	Claim your first FUT Pack	10	Bronze
Press Conference	Purchase a gold player in the Auction House for 15,000 or more coins using buy it now	30	Silver
I Love This Club	Achieve a club value of 85,000,000	30	Bronze
Promoted!	Earn promotion in FUT Seasons	30	Silver
Pack King	Open 50 FUT Packs	50	Gold
Challenge Accepted	Win a match against the team of the week	30	Silver
So Euro	Enable European competition in the first season of Career	5	Bronze

NAME	GOAL/REQUIREMENT	POINT VALUE	TROPHY VALUE
For Country	Become manager of an international team	20	Bronze
Way with Words	Successfully request additional funds from your board in Career	5	Bronze
National Pride	Get called up to the national team as a player	30	Silver
Wheeling and Dealing	Complete a Player + cash deal in Career	15	Bronze
Impressive	Achieve one of your season objectives as a player at any point in your career	50	Silver
Nice Form	Achieve your match set objective as player at any point in your career	30	Bronze
Digi-Me	Start your Player Career with a Created Pro	5	Bronze
Packing Bags	Go out on loan or transfer to another club with your Pro in Play as Player	15	Bronze
Master Negotiator	Sell a player by getting your counter offer accepted by the CPU	10	Bronze
Maxed Out	Reach the daily limit of XP in the EA SPORTS Football Club	10	Bronze
EASFC Youth Academy	Reach level 5 in the EA SPORTS Football Club	10	Bronze
EASFC Starting 11	Reach level 20 in the EA SPORTS Football Club	30	Silver
Challenging	Complete an EA SPORTS Football Club Challenge	10	Silver
Big Spender	Redeem an item with EASFC Football Club Credits.	10	Bronze
Football Legend	Unlock all other trophies (excluding additional content trophies)	—	Platinum

SECRET ACHIEVEMENT & TROPHY

NAME	GOAL/REQUIREMENT	POINT VALUE	TROPHY VALUE
In Form!	Find a team of the week player in a pack	20	Bronze

FIFA STREET

XBOX 360/PS3

ACHIEVEMENTS & TROPHIES

NAME	GOAL/REQUIREMENT	POINT VALUE	TROPHY VALUE
Got any Nutmeg?	Panna your first Opponent	15	Bronze
Rush Keepers!	Score a goal while controlling your Goal Keeper	25	Silver
Very Entertaining	Earn at least 1500 Style Points without losing possession	25	Silver
Sightseer	In any game mode win a match/event in 50% of the venues as the lead profile	25	Silver
Globetrotter	In any game mode win a match/event in every venue as the lead profile	95	Gold
Geometry was good for something	Score a goal by deflecting the ball off a wall	20	Bronze
Ultimate Humiliation	Score a goal with a Panna	15	Bronze

CHEATS, ACHIEVEMENTS, AND TROPHIES

F

NAME	GOAL/REQUIREMENT	POINT VALUE	TROPHY VALUE
Are we there yet?	Reach the World Tour map screen for the first time as the lead profile	10	Bronze
New Champion	Win a World Tour Tournament for the first time as the lead profile	15	Bronze
Regional Street Champion	Win stage 1 of World Tour as the lead profile	20	Bronze
National Street Champion	Win stage 2 of World Tour as the lead profile	25	Silver
European Champion	Win stage 3 of World Tour as the lead profile	50	Silver
World Grand Champion	Win stage 4 of World Tour as the lead profile	100	Gold
World Tour Around the World	Win any World Tour tournament Online as the lead profile	30	Silver
Challenge the pros	Win a street challenge against an authentic club team in stage 4 of world tour as the lead profile	20	Bronze
Street Legend	Defeat Messi in a street challenge game as the lead profile	20	Silver
Local Heroes	Win the final national tournament with at least 8 created players on your team as the lead profile	25	Bronze
Who brought the snacks?	Win a tournament with a local Co-Op player as the lead profile	15	Bronze
Mighty Heroes	Have a team with at least 8 created players that are level 50 or higher as the lead profile	40	Silver
Career Milestone	Score 100 goals with your created player in any game modes as the lead profile	25	Silver
Mister Entertainment	Earn 100,000 Style Points with your created player in any game mode as the lead profile	25	Silver
Attributed Success	Upgrade one of your created players attributes to Max as the lead profile	25	Silver
It's Tricky	Unlock 10 tricks on a created player as the lead profile	20	Silver
5 Tool Player	Upgrade 5 attributes on a created player to maximum as the lead profile	50	Gold
Time to Celebrate	Unlock a created player celebration and perform it in game as the lead profile	15	Bronze
Shopping Spree	Wear an Unlocked item in any game mode as the lead profile	10	Bronze
Moving on up	In a street season obtain promotion to the next division as the lead profile	25	Silver
Online Enthusiast	Win a game of 5 a side, 6 a side and Futsal online as the lead profile	20	Bronze
Online Cup Champion	Win any Online Cup as the lead profile	25	Silver
Online Dominance	Win all 9 online cups as the lead profile	100	Gold
Video Proof	Upload a saved video as the lead profile	20	Bronze
Friendly Publicity	Watch a video posted by one of your Friends as the lead profile	15	Bronze
Making new friends	Add a new Friend using the Friend Recommendation feature as the lead profile	15	Bronze
Watching Film	Watch a gameplay tutorial video as the lead profile	20	Bronze

FIGHTING STREET

+4 CREDITS, SIMPLIFIED SPECIAL MOVES, AND STAGE SELECT

After getting a high score, enter .SD as your initials. Then, at the title screen, hold Left + 1 + 2, and press Minus.

+4 CREDITS

After getting a high score, enter .HU as your initials. Then, at the title screen, hold Left + 1 + 2, and press Minus.

SIMPLIFIED SPECIAL MOVES

After getting a high score, enter .LK as your initials. Then, at the title screen, hold Left + 1 + 2, and press Minus.

STAGE SELECT

After getting a high score, enter .AS as your initials. Then, at the title screen, hold Left + 1 + 2, and press Minus.

FINAL FANTASY FABLES: CHOCOBO TALES

OMEGA – WAVE CANNON CARD

Select Send from the Main Menu and then choose Download Pop-Up Card. Press L, L, Up, B, B, Left.

FINAL FANTASY TACTICS: THE WAR OF THE LIONS

MUSIC TEST MODE

Enter the main character's name as PolkaPolka at the name entry screen.

FINAL FANTASY XIII-2

LIGHTNING THEME

This theme is unlocked if you have a save game for Final Fantasy XIII on your console.

ANOTHER LIGHTNING THEME

Earn the Master of Time Trophy.

MOG THEME

Earn the Fair Fighter Trophy.

NOEL THEME

Earn the Chronosavior Trophy.

SERAH THEME

Earn the Defragmented Trophy.

LIGHTNING GAMER PICTURE

This gamer picture is unlocked if you have a save game for Final Fantasy XIII on your console.

ANOTHER LIGHTNING GAMER PICTURE

Earn all of the Achievements.

MOG GAMER PICTURE

Earn the Fair Fighter Achievement.

NOEL GAMER PICTURE

Earn the Chronosavior Achievement.

SERAH GAMER PICTURE

Earn the Defragmented Achievement.

FIRE EMBLEM: AWAKENING

LUNATIC+ MODE

Complete the game on Lunatic difficulty to unlock Lunatic+ difficulty.

EXTRAS MENU

Complete the game once to unlock the Support Log, Theater and Unit Gallery/Sound Test in the Extras Menu.

FIST OF THE NORTH STAR: KEN'S RAGE 2

DREAM MODE CHARACTERS

CHARACTER	REQUIREMENT
Bat	Finish Legendary Mode.
Fudo	Finish all of Fudo's segments in Legendary Mode.
Jagi	Defeat Jagi in Legendary Mode as Kenshiro.
Juda	Defeat Juda in Legendary Mode as Rei.
Juuza	Finish all of Juuza's segments in Legendary Mode.
Kenshiro	Finish Legendary Mode.
Mamiya	Defeat Juda in Legendary Mode as Rei.
Rei	Defeat Juda in Legendary Mode as Rei.
Rin	Finish Legendary Mode.
Ryuga	Defeat Ryuga as Ken in Legendary Mode.

ACHIEVEMENTS & TROPHIES

NAME	GOAL/REQUIREMENT	POINT VALUE	TROPHY VALUE
Eviscerate Zeed	Defeated Zeed in the Legend Mode episode "Zeed Attacks."	15	Bronze
Slay Shin	Defeated Shin in the Legend Mode episode "The Flames of Obsession."	15	Bronze
Crush the Colonel	Defeated the Colonel in the Legend Mode episode "The Tears to End Ambition."	15	Bronze
Destroy Devil Rebirth	Defeated Devil Rebirth in the Legend Mode episode "The Incarnation of Indra."	15	Bronze
Dethrone Fang King	Defeated Fang King in the Legend Mode episode "The Stone-Shattering Fist."	15	Bronze
Finish Jagi	Defeated Jagi in the Legend Mode episode "Blood Feud."	15	Bronze
Annihilate Amiba	Defeated Amiba in the Legend Mode episode "Tragic Genius."	15	Bronze
Inhume Uighur	Defeated Uighur in the Legend Mode episode "The Quiet Giant."	15	Bronze
Overcome Raoh	Defeated Raoh in the Legend Mode episode "The Harbinger of Death."	15	Bronze
Humiliate Juda	Defeated Juda in the Legend Mode episode "Into the Flames of Hell."	15	Bronze
Subjugate Shew	Defeated Shew in the Legend Mode episode "The Star of Benevolence Awakens."	15	Bronze

NAME	GOAL/REQUIREMENT	POINT VALUE	TROPHY VALUE
Thrash Thouzer	Defeated Thouzer in the Legend Mode episode "The Empire Crumbles."	35	Silver
Maul Ryuga	Defeated Ryuga in the Legend Mode episode "Tears of the Wolf."	15	Bronze
Repel Raoh	Defeated Raoh in the Legend Mode episode "The Moment Has Come."	15	Bronze
Ruin Raoh	Defeated Raoh in the Legend Mode episode "Farewell, My Rival."	35	Silver
Outlast Ein	Defeated Ein in the Legend Mode episode "A Fearless Smile."	15	Bronze
Foil Falco	Defeated Falco in the Legend Mode episode "A Duel to Split the Heavens."	35	Silver
Smash the Nameless Shura	Defeated the Nameless Shura in the Legend Mode episode "Those Who Would Consume Death."	15	Bronze
Quash Keiser	Defeated Keiser in the Legend Mode episode "The Most Evil Art on Earth."	15	Bronze
Hammer Han	Defeated Han in the Legend Mode episode "A Fated Legacy."	15	Bronze
Vanquish Hyou	Defeated Hyou in the Legend Mode episode "Brother Against Brother."	15	Bronze
Conquer Kaioh	Defeated Kaioh in the Legend Mode episode "A Destined Encounter."	35	Silver
True Successor	Completed all Legend Mode episodes.	60	Gold
Post-Apocalyptic Savior	Completed Dream Mode with Kenshiro.	15	Bronze
Miracle Maker	Completed Dream Mode with Toki.	15	Bronze
Absolute Ruler	Completed Dream Mode with Raoh.	15	Bronze
Twisted Brute	Completed Dream Mode with Jagi.	15	Bronze
Star of Righteousness	Completed Dream Mode with Rei.	15	Bronze
Star of Martyrdom	Completed Dream Mode with Shin.	15	Bronze
Emperor of Nanto	Completed Dream Mode with Thouzer.	15	Bronze
Star of Enchantment	Completed Dream Mode with Juda.	15	Bronze
Blind General of Valor	Completed Dream Mode with Shew.	15	Bronze
Towering Mountain	Completed Dream Mode with Fudo.	15	Bronze
Keeper of the Hokuto Spirit	Completed Dream Mode with Bat.	15	Bronze
The One True Hope	Completed Dream Mode with Rin.	15	Bronze
Warrior of Eternal Love	Completed Dream Mode with Shachi.	15	Bronze
Passionate Shura General	Completed Dream Mode with Hyou.	15	Bronze
Crazed Demonic Fiend	Completed Dream Mode with Kaioh.	15	Bronze

NAME	GOAL/REQUIREMENT	POINT VALUE	TROPHY VALUE
Proud Maiden Warrior	Completed Dream Mode with Mamiya.	15	Bronze
Wolf of Anarchy	Completed Dream Mode with Ryuga.	15	Bronze
Free-Spirited Cloud	Completed Dream Mode with Juza.	15	Bronze
Bounty Hunter	Completed Dream Mode with Ein.	15	Bronze
Golden Guardian General	Completed Dream Mode with Falco.	15	Bronze
Quest Master	Completed all Dream Mode challenges in Free Mode.	35	Silver
True Savior	Completed all Dream Mode quests with the highest Level.	60	Gold
Fists of Persistence	Played for over 50 hours in total.	35	Silver
True Master of the Apocalypse	Defeated 100,000 enemies.	35	Silver
Ultimate Nexus Master	Collected all scrolls and completed an Ultimate Nexus.	35	Silver
Co-op Play Veteran	Participated in 10 online Co-op Play games.	15	Bronze
Team Match Master	Claimed victory in 10 online Team Matches.	15	Bronze

FLATOUT: HEAD ON

PSP

1 MILLION CREDITS

Select Enter Code from the Extras menu and enter GIVECASH.

ALL CARS AND 1 MILLION CREDITS

Select Enter Code from the Extras menu and enter GIEVEPIX.

BIG RIG

Select Enter Code from the Extras menu and enter ELPUEBLO.

BIG RIG TRUCK

Select Enter Code from the Extras menu and enter RAIDERS.

FLATMOBILE CAR

Select Enter Code from the Extras menu and enter WOTKINS.

MOB CAR

Select Enter Code from the Extras menu and enter BIGTRUCK.

PIMPSTER CAR

Select Enter Code from the Extras menu and enter RUTTO.

ROCKET CAR

Select Enter Code from the Extras menu and enter KALJAKOPPA.

SCHOOL BUS

Select Enter Code from the Extras menu and enter GIEVCARPLZ.

FLATOUT: ULTIMATE CARNAGE

MOB CAR IN SINGLE EVENTS

Select Enter Code from Extras and enter BIGTRUCK.

PIMPSTER IN SINGLE EVENTS

Select Enter Code from Extras and enter RUTTO.

ROCKET IN SINGLE EVENTS

Select Enter Code from Extras and enter KALJAKOPPA.

FLIGHT CONTROL

ACHIEVEMENTS

ACHIEVEMENT	REQUIREMENT
Safety Card	Read the Game Tutorial.
First Flights	Land an aircraft on each airfield.
Jet Power	Land 20 jets in a game.
Centurion	Reach 100 Total Aircraft landed.
Helicopter Love	Land 5 helicopters in a row.
Rush Hour	Land 7 aircraft within 12 seconds.
Holding Pattern	Keep the same aircraft in the sky for 5 minutes.
Restrainer	Land no aircraft for 1.5/2 minutes.
Perfect Timing	Land 3 aircraft at the same time.
Crowded Sky	Reach 15/20 Most Aircraft on Screen.
Veteran	Play 250 games in total.
Wings	Land 200 aircraft in a game.

FORZA MOTORSPORT 4

AVATAR AWARDS

AVATAR	EARNED BY
Autovista T-Shirt	Fully explore any car in Autovista.
Stopwatch Cap	Post a time in every Rivals Mode Event.

FRACTURE

EXCLUSIVE PRE-ORDER SKIN

Pause the game and press Up, Right, Left, Down, Up, Left, Right, Down.

FROGGER

BIG FROGGER

At the One/Two-Player screen, press Up, Up, Down, Down, Left, Right, Left, Right, B, A.

FROM DUST

AVATAR AWARDS

AVATAR	EARNED BY
The Tribal Mask	Retrieve this mask by unlocking the complete version of "From Dust".

FRUIT NINJA

ACHIEVEMENTS

ACHIEVEMENT	REQUIREMENT
Almost a Century	Failed with a score of 99.
Are you kidding me?!	Failed with the same score as my personal best.
Bomb Magnet	Hit three bombs and scored over 250 after all bonuses in Arcade Mode.
Combo Mambo	Slice 6 fruits in one combo.
Connected Ninja	Post a score to Facebook or Twitter.
Déjà vu	Kill 4 of the same type of fruit in a row in Classic Mode.
Fruit Annihilation	Kill 10,000 Fruit total.
Fruit Blitz	Kill 500 Fruit total.
Fruit Fight	Kill 150 Fruit total.
Fruit Frenzy	Kill 1,000 Fruit total.
Fruit Ninja	Get a score of 50 in Classic Mode.
Fruit Rampage	Kill 5,000 Fruit total.
Go Banana	Kill 10 Bananas in one round of Classic Mode.
Great Fruit Ninja	Get a score of 100 in Classic Mode.
It's all Pear Shaped!	Kill 3 Pears in a row in Classic Mode.
Lovely Bunch	Get the Lovely Bunch star in Zen Mode.
Lucky Ninja	Get 6 criticals in one round of Classic Mode.
Mango Magic	Get a critical hit with a Mango.
Moment of Zen	Achieve a score of 200 in Zen mode.
Night Shift	Completed 3 games between the hour of 2 A.M. and 5 A.M.
No Doctors Here	Kill 15 Apples in one round of Classic Mode.
Over Achiever	Get a score over 400 after all bonuses in Arcade Mode.
Patience is a Virtue	Slice 10 Coming Soon Fruits.
Perfectionist	Retired a game 3 times in a row.
Purple is a Fruit	Kill 20 Plums in one round of Classic Mode.
Tee Hee Hee	Failed with a score of 69.
Ultimate Fruit Ninja	Get a score of 200 in Classic Mode.
Under Achiever	Got a score less than 20 after all bonuses in Arcade Mode.
Wake Up	Failed with a score of 0.
Year of the Dragon	Sliced the secret fruit!

BLADES

Unlock the following blades by completing the task. These can be found in Sensei's Swag in the Dojo.

BLADE	EARNED BY
Disco Blade	Slice 50 bananas.
Mr. Sparkle	Slice 3 pineapples in a row in Classic Mode.
Old Glory	Finish a game with a score matching the number of stars on the U.S. Flag.
Butterfly Knife	Get a combo with a strawberry 40 times.
Flame Blade	Slice a combo after the timer ends in Zen Mode.
Ice Blade	Slice 20 freeze bananas in Arcade Mode to unlock.
The Shadow	Get a score of exactly 234 in Arcade Mode.
Pixel Love	Get 50 combos in classic mode.
Piano Blade	Slice 100 criticals to unlock.
Party Time	Slice every strawberry (and nothing else) in a game of Arcade Mode!
The Firecracker	Get the same score as the year of the Battle of Red Cliffs (208).
Bamboo Shoot	Play a full game of Zen Mode every day, 5 days in a row.

BACKGROUNDS

Unlock the following backgrounds by completing the task. These can be found in Sensei's Swag in the Dojo.

BACKGROUND	EARNED BY
Fruit Ninja	Get 125 points without dropping a fruit in Classic Mode.
I Heart Sensei	Read 3 of Sensei's Fruit Facts that are about strawberries.
Great Wave	Slice 250 watermelons.
Yin Yang	Slice 75 passion fruit.
Chinese Zodiac	Slice 384 peaches.

FRUIT NINJA KINECT

XBOX 360

AVATAR AWARDS

AVATAR	EARNED BY
Fruit Ninja T-Shirt	Equip an Item in Sensei's Swag.
Kung Fu Pants	Complete 3 Multplayer Games.
Kung Fu Sensei Shirt	Complete 5 games of Classic, Zen or Arcade.

FULL AUTO 2: BATTLELINES

PSP

ALL CARS

Select Cheats from the Options and press Up, Up, Up, Up, Left, Down, Up, Right, Down, Down, Down, Down.

ALL EVENTS

Select Cheats from the Options and press Start, Left, Select, Right, Right, ●, ⊗, ●, Start, R, Down, Select.

FULL HOUSE POKER

AVATAR AWARDS

AWARD	EARNED BY
Hoodie	Level up
Bulldog Helmet	Level up to 50

G.I. JOE: THE RISE OF COBRA

CLASSIC DUKE

At the Title screen, press Left, Up, Minus, Up, Right, Plus.

CLASSIC SCARLETT

At the Title screen, press Right, Up, Down, Down, Plus.

CLASSIC DUKE

At the Main menu, press Left, Up, ●, Up, Right, ●.

CLASSIC SCARLET

At the Main menu, press Right, Up, Down, Down, ●.

GAME OF THRONES

ACHIEVEMENTS & TROHPIES

NAME	GOAL/REQUIREMENT	POINT VALUE	TROPHY VALUE
Clever dog	Gain all the skills linked to the dog with Mors	30	Bronze
Master of light and flame	Gain all the skills linked to R'hllor's fire with Alester	30	Bronze
Master-at-arms	Learn all skills within a character's stance tree	25	Bronze
Warlord	Reach the maximum level	30	Silver
Great teamwork	Finish the game without a single ally (except Mors and Alester) being KO'd	30	Silver
Merciless	Mete out 5 deathblows	20	Bronze
True warrior	Kill 400 enemies	20	Bronze
Man's best friend	Kill 10 enemies with Mors' dog in skinchanger mode	20	Bronze
Golden touch	Acquire 1 golden dragon	30	Silver
R'hllor sees all	Find 10 secrets with the vision of R'hllor	30	Silver
Fetch!	Use Mors' dog's sense of smell to find 5 secret objects	30	Silver
Thorough	Complete all the secondary objectives of the story	40	Gold

SECRET ACHIEVEMENTS & TROPHIES

NAME	GOAL/REQUIREMENT	POINT VALUE	TROPHY VALUE
Devout follower	Find all the statues of the Seven	30	Silver
Pimp	Convince Bethany to return to Chataya's brothel with Alester	30	Silver
Collector	Seize the three objects of value from the Collector with Alester	30	Silver
Endless watch	Send 10 recruits to the Wall with Mors	30	Silver
The Greatest	Emerge triumphant in the final arena combat	30	Silver
The true face of the Spider	Lose the final battle	10	Bronze
My darkest hour	Chapter 15: execute the judgement passed down on the Westfords	10	Bronze
Lesser of two evils	Chapter 14: come to the aid of the Reapers	15	Bronze
Quiet as a shadow	Chapter 13: reach Jeyne's room without ever being seen	35	Silver
Unrivaled strategist	Chapter 12: take back Riverspring with a total victory	35	Silver
Swift and deadly	Chapter 11: bring an end to the trial by combat in under 2 minutes	35	Silver
'Tis but a scratch !	Chapter 9: suffer all the physical abuse during the torture sequence	20	Bronze
The butcher comes to dinner	Chapter 9: kill 6 of Lord Harlton's soldiers during the fight at dinner	35	Silver
Desecration	Chapter 8: find the key in Alester's father's tomb	15	Bronze
Am I not merciful?	Chapter 8: save Orys from the City Watch	15	Bronze
Once more unto the breach	Chapter 7: attack the camp without killing the sentries at the start	35	Silver
Bloodhound	Chapter 7: find all the corrupt brothers of the Night's Watch	25	Bronze
End of the line	Chapter 6: don't lose pursuit of the bastard	20	Bronze
Man of the people	Chapter 2: protect the people with Alester	15	Bronze
Know your place	Chapter 2: protect the nobility with Alester	15	Bronze
Disciplinarian	Chapter 1: confront the four recruits during the training session with Mors	10	Bronze
Sworn brother	Finish Mors' Story	10	Bronze
Red priest of R'hllor	Finish Alester's story	10	Bronze
The night is dark…	Finish chapter 15	10	Bronze
Valar morghulis	Finish chapter 14	10	Bronze
Growing strong	Finish chapter 13	10	Bronze
As high as honor	Finish chapter 12	10	Bronze
Come try me	Finish chapter 11	10	Bronze
Fire and blood	Finish chapter 10	10	Bronze
Unbowed, unbent, unbroken	Finish chapter 9	10	Bronze
Family, duty, honor	Finish chapter 8	10	Bronze
Here we stand	Finish chapter 7	10	Bronze
Dead men sing no songs	Finish chapter 6	10	Bronze
Proud to be faithful	Finish chapter 5	10	Bronze
Hear me roar	Finish chapter 4	10	Bronze
Dark wings, dark words	Finish chapter 3	10	Bronze
Family is hope…	Finish chapter 2	10	Bronze
Winter is coming	Finish chapter 1	10	Bronze

CHEATS, ACHIEVEMENTS, AND TROPHIES

G

GAME ROOM

SWAP KONAMI AND ASTEROIDS CABINET STYLES

During a game or at a menu, press Up, Up, Down, Down, Left, Right, Left, Right, B, A.

GAMERBOTS: THIRD-ROBOT SHOOTING

300,000 GP

Enter 24162444 as a gift code.

DEMON SWORD

Enter 39121412 as a gift code.

DUAL FLAME

Enter 34094035 as a gift code.

SPIKED CLUB

Enter 56095802 as a gift code.

STAR SLICER

Enter 55122302 as a gift code.

GEARS OF WAR 3

AVATAR AWARDS

AVATAR	EARNED BY
Marcus Doo-Rag	Complete campaign on any difficulty.
Horde Shirt	Earn "Welcome to Horde Mode" achievement.
Locust Drone Mask	Earn "Welcome to Beast Mode" achievement.

MUTATORS

Mutators are special rules that can have…unusual effects on the battlefield. You can enable Mutators for private matches, or watch for playlists from Epic when they turn them on for special events and holidays.

EASY

These Mutators give you an easier time in game.

MUTATOR	DESCRIPTION	HOW TO UNLOCK
Comet	When you Roadie Run, you build up energy until you ignite into a fireball that you can unleash on impacting enemies.	Gold "Shock Trooper" medal. (Versus mode)
Instagib Melee	Melee causes instant death.	Kill 200 enemies while playing a wretch in Beast. (Beast Mode)
Super Reload	Easier active reloads.	Bronze "Master at Arms" Medal. (Versus Mode)
Infinite Ammo	Unlimited clips of ammo, though you still must reload between clips.	Earn 100 "Combat Engineer" Ribbons. (Horde Mode)
Big explosions	Explosions have bigger blast radius.	Earn 100 "Hail Mary" Ribbons. (Arcade, Beast, Horde, Versus Modes)

HARD

These Mutators make the game a little tougher.

MUTATOR	DESCRIPTION	HOW TO UNLOCK
No Ammo Pickups	Gets rid of ammo boxes on map.	Unlocked at start.
Enemies Regeneration	Enemy's health regenerates.	Silver "Afficionado" medal. (Arcade Mode)
Vampire	Health does not regenerate, but every point of damage you inflict heals you in kind.	Earn 100 "Executioner" ribbons. (Versus Mode)
Must Active Reload	You must achieve an Active Reload to reload your weapon.	Silver "Active Reloader" Medal.
Friendly fire	Gunfire hurts your own team.	Complete the campaign in 4-player co-op. (Co-op Campaign)

FUN

These Mutators create fun effects with no effect on gameplay.

MUTATOR	DESCRIPTION	HOW TO UNLOCK
Big Head	Everyone's head (and other key features) are inflated to comical proportrions.	Gold "Horder" Medal (Horde Mode)
Piñata	Special tokens from every kill; collect them to earn points.	Gold "Investor" Medal (Beast Mode)
Flower Blood	Blood looks like flowers.	Silver "King of Cog" medal. (Arcade Mode)
Headless Chicken	Enemies attack each other for several seconds after they lose their heads.	Unlocked at start.
Laugh Track	Play as if your game was filmed before a live studio audience.	Bronze "Tour of Duty", "For the Horde", "I'm a Beast", and "Warmonger" Medals.

MULTIPLAYER CHARACTERS

Unlock the following characters for use in Multiplayer.

LOCUST (23 CHARACTERS)

CHARACTER	HOW TO UNLOCK
Drone	Available from start
Grenadier Elite	Available from start
Savage Drone	Available from start
Savage Grenadier	Available from start
Armored Myrrah	Available from start
Savage Grenadier Elite	Available as preorder from WalMart
Savage Kantus	Available as preorder from Amazon
Miner	Unlocks at XP Level 3
Beast Rider	Unlocks at XP Level 5
Hunter	Unlocks at XP Level 8
Theron Guard	Unlocks at XP Level 12
Spotter	Unlocks at XP Level 20
Flame Grenadier	Unlocks at XP Level 26
Grenadier	Unlocks at XP Level 39
Hunter Elite	Unlocks at XP Level 60
Golden Miner	Unlock with "Rifleman" Gold Medal.
Golden Hunter	Unlock with "Master at Arms" Gold Medal.
Sniper	Unlock with "Headshot" Bronze Medal.
Kantus	Unlock with "Medic" Gold Medal.
Savage Theron Guard	Unlock with Onyx "I'm a Beast" Medal.

COG (33 CHARACTERS)

CHARACTER	HOW TO UNLOCK
Marcus Fenix	Available from start
Dominic Santiago	Available from start
Damon Baird	Available from start
Augustus Cole	Available from start
Anya Stroud	Available from start
Commando Dom	Available as preorder from GameStop
Mechanic Baird	Available as preorder from Best Buy
Soldier Adam	Available as preorder with Gears of War 3 Limited Collector's Edition
COG Gear	Unlocks at XP Level 2
Samantha Byrne	Unlocks at XP Level 4
Dizzy Wallin	Unlocks at XP Level 7
Jace Stratton	Unlocks at XP Level 10
Clayton Carmine	Unlocks at XP Level 14
Classic Dom	Unlocks at XP Level 17
Classic Cole	Unlocks at XP Level 23
Classic Baird	Unlocks at XP Level 30
Benjamin Carmine	Unlocks at XP Level 34
Civilian Anya	Unlocks at XP Level 45
Victor Hoffman	Unlocks at XP Level 50
Anthony Carmine	Unlocks at XP Level 75
Cole Train	Unlocked with participation in Beta.
Classic Marcus	Unlock with "Veteran" Silver Medal.
Superstar Cole	Unlock with "MVP" Gold Medal.
Golden Gear	Unlock with "War Supporter" Bronze Medal.
Aaron Griffin	Unlock with "Big Money" Onyx Medal.
Chairman Prescott	Unlock with "Allfather" Silver Medal.
Underarmor Marcus	Complete the campaign on any difficulty.

ACHIEVEMENTS

NAME	GOAL/REQUIREMENT	POINT VALUE
Marcus, It's Your Father	Story Progression in Prologue (Standard or Arcade).	5
Swimmin' in Glowie Gravy	Story Progression in Act 1 Chapter 2 (Standard or Arcade).	10
We Struck Gold, Son!	Story Progression in Act 1 Chapter 3 (Standard or Arcade).	10
My Turf! Cougars Territory!	Story Progression in Act 1 Chapter 5 (Standard or Arcade).	10
Putting it Scientifically…	Story Progression in Act 1 Chapter 6 (Standard or Arcade).	10
Okay, Now We Find Hoffman	Story Progression in Act 2 Chapter 1 (Standard or Arcade).	10
Oh Yeah, It's Pirate Time	Story Progression in Act 2 Chapter 5 (Standard or Arcade).	10
Thanks For Flying GasBag Airways	Story Progression in Act 2 Chapter 7 (Standard or Arcade).	10
Anvil Gate's Last Resort	Story Progression in Act 3 Chapter 1 (Standard or Arcade).	10
Was it Good For You?	Story Progression in Act 3 Chapter 2 (Standard or Arcade).	10
Lost Your Good Driver Discount	Story Progression in Act 3 Chapter 3 (Standard or Arcade).	10
Brothers to the End	Story Progression in Act 3 Chapter 5 (Standard or Arcade).	10
Think You Can Handle That?	Story Progression in Act 4 Chapter 3 (Standard or Arcade).	10

NAME	GOAL/REQUIREMENT	POINT VALUE
Baird's Favorite Kind of Toy	Story Progression in Act 4 Chapter 5 (Standard or Arcade).	10
Welcome To -redacted-	Story Progression in Act 4 Chapter 6 (Standard or Arcade).	10
Look at That, Instant Summer.	Story Progression in Act 5 Chapter 2 (Standard or Arcade).	10
Ok. Faith. Yeah. Got It.	Story Progression in Act 5 Chapter 5 (Standard or Arcade).	10
You're Dead! Now Stay Dead!	Story Progression in Act 5 Chapter 6 (Standard or Arcade).	10
Ready for More	Complete all campaign Acts on Casual or Normal Difficulty (Standard or Arcade).	50
Ain't My First Rodeo	Complete all campaign Acts on Hardcore Difficulty (Standard or Arcade).	50
That's Just Crazy	Complete all campaign Acts on Insane Difficulty (Standard or Arcade).	75
Collector	Recover 5 Campaign Collectibles (any difficulty, Standard or Arcade).	5
Pack Rat	Recover 20 Campaign Collectibles (any difficulty, Standard or Arcade).	10
Hoarder	Recover all 42 Campaign Collectibles (any difficulty, Standard or Arcade).	15
Remember the Fallen	Recover all 15 COG Tags during the Campaign (any difficulty, Standard or Arcade).	15
My Fellow Gears	Complete all Campaign Acts in Co-op (any difficulty, Standard or Arcade).	50
We Few, We Happy Few…	Complete all Campaign Acts in 4 player Co-op (any difficulty, Standard or Arcade).	50
Level 5	Reach level 5.	5
Level 10	Reach level 10.	10
Level 15	Reach level 15.	15
Level 25	Reach level 25.	25
Level 50	Reach level 50.	50
Judge, Jury and Executioner	Get a kill with every possible execution finishing move (any mode).	10
Wreaking Locust Vengence	Get a kill with every Locust monster in Beast mode (any difficulty).	10
Enriched and Fortified	Complete all 50 waves of Horde mode (any difficulty, any map).	10
It's All About the Loot!	Earn the Bronze "Loot Courtesan" medal.	25
All for One, One for All	Earn the Bronze "Force Multiplier" medal.	10
First Among Equals	Earn the Silver "Number 1" medal.	25
Award Winning Tactics	Earn at least one Onyx medal.	25
Seriously 3.0	Reach level 100 and earn every Onyx medal.	100
Welcome to Versus	Kill 10 enemies in Team Deathmatch (Standard or Casual).	10
The Versus Sampler Platter	Complete one match of all six Versus game modes (Standard or Casual).	10
Welcome to Horde Mode	Survive the first 10 waves of Horde mode (any difficulty, any map).	10
Welcome to Beast Mode	Survive all 12 waves of Beast mode (any difficulty, any map).	10
Welcome to Arcade Mode	Complete 5 Arcade Campaign chapters in co-op (any difficulty).	10
Welcome to the Big Leagues	Demonstrate your skill in Casual Versus multiplayer.	0
Wait, What Time is it?	Earn the maximum Consecutive Match Bonus in Versus multiplayer (Standard or Casual).	10
Lambency	Execute an Epic employee, or someone who already has Lambency, in Versus multiplayer (any mode).	50
Socialite	Earn the Onyx "War Supporter" medal.	70

SECRET ACHIEVEMENTS

NAME	GOAL/REQUIREMENT	POINT VALUE
Respect for the Dead	Your respect for the dead earned you access to Griffin's special weapons stash.	5

DLC: HORDE COMMAND PACK

NAME	GOAL/REQUIREMENT	POINT VALUE
The Host with the Most	Host a private Horde Match with a party of 5 players on any Horde Command Pack map (any difficulty).	25
Places to See, People to Destroy	Host a private Beast Match with a party of 5 players on any Horde Command Pack map (any difficulty).	25
What Does This Button Do?	Get 500 Silverback rocket kills in Horde (any map, any difficulty).	50
It's Hammer Time!	Achieve Level 4 in Horde Command Center fortifications.	50
Kill Locust (Like a Boss)	Defeat a Boss Wave as 5 Onyx Guards (Hardcore difficulty).	100

GEARS OF WAR: JUDGMENT

XBOX 360

EXTRA CAMPAIGN MISSION

Earn 40 Stars in Campaign Mode to unlock the Aftermath mission which takes place towards the end of Gears of War 3.

UNLOCK COLE IN MULTIPLAYER

Survive the 10th wave in Survival mode to unlock Cole in Multiplayer.

UNLOCK TAI IN MULTIPLAYER

Gain 126 Stars in Campaign Mode to unlock Tai in Multiplayer.

ACHIEVEMENTS

NAME	GOAL/REQUIREMENT	POINT VALUE
They Called Him Karn	Completed Museum Of Military Glory	10
Open Arms	Completed Halvo Bay Military Academy	10
The Real Thing	Completed Seahorse Hills	10
Take Back This City	Completed Onyx Point	10
I Told You	Completed Downtown Halvo Bay	10
This One's Not Over	Completed Courthouse	10
Friends	Completed Aftermath	10
Determined	Completed all Campaign Chapters on at least Casual difficulty	10
Steel Nerves	Completed all Campaign Chapters on at least Normal difficulty	10
Iron Fist	Completed all Campaign Chapters on at least Hardcore difficulty	25
Lion Heart	Completed all Campaign Chapters on at least Insane difficulty	50
Party People	Played any section in 4 player Co-Op	10
Blood Brothers	Completed all Campaign Chapters in Co-op	50
Challenge Accepted	Completed your first Declassified mission	5
Never Give Up	Completed at least 20 Declassified missions	10
Quality Soldiering	Completed all Declassified missions	50
A Peek into the Future	Watched Aftermath teaser	10
The Aftermath	Unlocked Aftermath	20
Rising Star	Attained 50 Stars on at least Casual Difficulty	10
Shooting Star	Attained 75 Stars on at least Normal Difficulty	20
Star Struck	Attained 100 Stars on at least Hardcore Difficulty	50

NAME	GOAL/REQUIREMENT	POINT VALUE
Superstar	Attained all Stars on Insane Difficulty	50
Never Forgotten	Recovered 10 COG Tags during the Campaign	10
Veteran Remembrance	Recovered 25 COG Tags during the Campaign	10
Respect for the Fallen	Recovered all 48 COG Tags during the Campaign	20
Ribbon Master	Earned 3 unique Ribbons in any section	10
Proud Wearer	Equipped your first Medal	5
Ready for War	Earned at least one Onyx medal	20
Sybarite	Earned the Onyx "War Supporter" medal	50
Seriously Judgmental	Completed all Declassified Missions on Insane difficulty	75
Level 5	Reached level 5	5
Level 10	Reached level 10	10
Level 20	Reached level 20	10
Level 30	Reached level 30	15
Level 40	Reached level 40	25
Level 50	Reached level 50	25
Let's Do This	Achieved level 50 and chose to re-up for another tour of duty	50
Fearless	Achieved level 50 a second time and chose to re-up for another tour	50
Unstoppable	Achieved level 50 a third time and chose to re-up for another tour	50
Death to Locust	Killed with all classes of COG in Overrun or Survival	10
Death to the COG	Killed with all classes of Locust in Overrun	10
Survivor	Completed wave 10 on all maps in Survival mode	10
Globe Trotter	Won a match on every map in all Versus modes	10
Jack of All Trades	Won 10 matches of Overrun	10
Team Leader	Won 10 rounds of Team Deathmatch	10
All Rounder	Won one match in Free For All, Team Deathmatch, and Domination	10
Roaming Free	Won one match on every map in Free For All	10
Team On Tour	Won one match on every map in Team Deathmatch	10
Overran	Won one match on every map in Overrun	10
Dominator	Won one match on every map in Domination	10

CALL TO ARMS DLC

NAME	GOAL/REQUIREMENT	POINT VALUE
BOOSHKA!	Earn 50 Double ribbons with the Booshka on Terminal (Public/Ranked)	50
Don't you die on me!	Revive 100 total teammates on Terminal as a Medic (Public/Ranked)	25
Surprise!	Get a Double while emerging as a Corpser (Public/Ranked)	10
Professional Locust	Kill 100 enemies with each Locust	75
All Aboard!	Win Hardcore Survival on Terminal with 5 Soldiers	25
Captain Sera	Earn a killing spree with the Boomshield on Boneyard (Public/Ranked)	10
Long Bomb	Earn the You're It ribbon on Boneyard (Public/Ranked)	10
Old School Marathon	Play 10 matches total on BloodDrive (Public/Ranked)	10
Like A Boss	Place first in Free For All in Boneyard 5 times (Public/Ranked)	15
You Looking At Me	Win a Team Death Match game with the entire team wearing the Car 13 Armor skin (Public/Ranked)	20

CHEATS, ACHIEVEMENTS, AND TROPHIES

GHOST RECON: FUTURE SOLDIER

XBOX 360/PS3

ACHIEVEMENTS & TROPHIES

NAME	GOAL/REQUIREMENT	POINT VALUE	TROPHY VALUE
Doing Work	Kill 1000 enemies while in Guerrilla mode	10	Bronze
Quality Beats Quantity	Defeat all 50 enemy waves on Guerrilla mode (any difficulty, any map)	30	Silver
Good Effect on Target	In Guerrilla mode, kill more than 5 enemies with an airstrike	10	Bronze
Just a Box	While in Guerrilla mode, complete an infiltration sequence without being detected	10	Bronze
Good Enough for Government Work	Achieve a Ghost skill rating above 80% for all missions	10	Bronze
Qualified	Achieve a Ghost skill rating of above 90% on one mission	25	Bronze
Master Tactician	Complete 100% of the Tactical challenges	25	Silver
Tactician	Complete 50% of the Tactical challenges	10	Bronze
Battle Buddies	Complete the campaign in Co-op	30	Bronze
Future Soldier	Complete the campaign in Elite	50	Gold
Advanced Warfighter	Complete the campaign in Veteran	40	Silver
Just Another Day at the Office	Complete the campaign for the first time	30	Silver
…I Can Do Better	Complete 20 Daily Friend Challenges	5	Bronze
Anything You Can Do…	Complete a Daily Friend Challenge through all return fire volleys	20	Bronze
Total Domination	Complete all of the Domination achievements	40	Bronze
Saboteur Domination	Be part of a squad match where your team takes the bomb into the enemy base in under 2 minutes	10	Bronze
Decoy Domination	In squad matches your team completes the key objective first, five times.	10	Bronze
Siege Domination	Be part of a squad match where your team captures the objective in under 2 minutes	10	Bronze
Conflict Domination	Be part of a squad match where your team wins by a margin of 500 points or more	10	Bronze
Cross-trained	Reach Level 10 on one Rifleman, one Scout, and one Engineer character	10	Bronze
Backup	Complete 5 Savior Kills in Quick Matches	5	Bronze
Actionable Intel	Complete 10 Coordinated Kills	10	Bronze
Mod Pro	Spend 50 Attachment Credits to add attachments to various guns	40	Silver
Tuned Up	Customize all the internal parts of one weapon	25	Bronze
Field Tested	Play 5 MP matches of each game type	5	Bronze

NAME	GOAL/REQUIREMENT	POINT VALUE	TROPHY VALUE
Counter-Intelligence	Interrupt an enemy's attempt to data hack a teammate 5 times, by killing or stunning the enemy	10	Bronze
True Ghost	Get 10 consecutive kills in one Quick Match without dying	10	Bronze
Recon Specialist	Complete 5 Intel Assists in Quick Matches	25	Bronze
Kitted Out	Customize 1 weapon with an external attachment at every attachment point	25	Bronze
Mod Rookie	Add an attachment to any gun	5	Bronze
High-Value Target	Kill a member of the dev team, or kill someone who has	5	Bronze
Coordinated Assault	Use the Coordination System to reach an objective	5	Bronze
Armorer	Spend 25 Attachment Credits with each role	35	Silver
High Speed, Low Drag	Reach Level 50 on any character	50	Gold
Call, Answered	Complete all Tours of Duty	35	Silver
Tour of Duty: North Sea	Win 3 MP matches of any game type on each: Harbor, Cargo, and Rig maps	25	Bronze
Tour of Duty: Arctic	Win 3 MP matches of any game type on each: Underground, Mill, and Alpha maps	25	Bronze
Tour of Duty: Nigeria	Win 3 MP of any game type on each: Pipeline, Market, Sand Storm, and Overpass maps	25	Bronze

SECRET ACHIEVEMENTS & TROPHIES

NAME	GOAL/REQUIREMENT	POINT VALUE	TROPHY VALUE
No Loose Ends	Eliminate the leader of the Raven's Rock faction	20	Bronze
Relieved of Command	Kill the general commanding the Moscow defenses	20	Bronze
Special Election	Rescue Russian President Volodin from the prison camp	20	Bronze
Breathing Room	Destroy the second piece of enemy artillery	20	Bronze
Fuel for the Fire	Secure the drilling ships and complete the mission	20	Bronze
Blood Brother	Rescue the Georgian Spec Ops	20	Bronze
…Must Come Down.	Destroy the plane with the weapons system on board while it is in flight	20	Bronze
EOD	Destroy the Russian weapons transfer station	20	Bronze
Source Control	Secure the VIP and transfer them to the exfiltration team	20	Bronze
Precious Cargo	Secure the VIP and transfer him to the exfiltration team	20	Bronze
What Goes Up…	Shoot down the cargo plane	20	
Loose Thread	Secure Gabriel Paez	20	

GHOST SQUAD

COSTUMES

Reach the following levels in single player to unlock the corresponding costume.

LEVEL	COSTUME
07	Desert Camouflage
10	Policeman
15	Tough Guy
18	Sky Camouflage
20	World War II
23	Cowboy
30	Urban Camouflage
34	Virtua Cop
38	Future Warrior
50	Ninja
60	Panda Suit
99	Gold Uniform

NINJA MODE

Play through Arcade Mode.

PARADISE MODE

Play through Ninja Mode.

GHOUL PATROL

PASSWORDS

LEVEL	PASSWORD
5	CP4V
9	7LBR
13	KVCY

GOD OF WAR III

TREASURES OF THE GODS

These items can be turned on and off after you've completed the game. Note, however, that using these items disables Trophies.

TREASURE	DESCRIPTION	LOCATION
Zeus' Eagle	Grants infinite Rage of Sparta.	Climb the vines on the wall east of Gaia's heart. The treasure is located beneath an ancient mural.
Hades' Helm	Maxes Health, Magic, and Item Meters.	After defeating Hades and diving into the River Styx, search the bottom for this treasure.
Helios' Shield	Triples the number on the Hits Counter.	After defeating Helios, search the area to the right.
Hermes' Coin	Kratos collects 10 times the amount of Red Orbs.	After Kratos and Hermes fall and land in the damaged room, search behind the head of the demolished Athena Statue.

TREASURE	DESCRIPTION	LOCATION
Hercules' Shoulder Guard	Decreases damage taken by one-third.	After defeating Hercules, search the bottom of the pool beneath his body.
Poseidon's Conch Shell	Grants infinite Magic.	After freeing the frightened Princess, this treasure is near an item chest.
Aphrodite's Garter	Lets Kratos continue to use Athena's Blades.	Fly behind Aphrodite's bed to find this rare treasure.
Hephaestus' Ring	Kratos automatically wins all context-sensitive attacks.	Finish off Hephaestus and search his cooling pool for the ring.
Daedalus' Schematics	Grants infinite item use.	Found in Daedalus' Workshop after lowering two item chests with a pull of a lever.
Hera's Chalice	Causes your Health Meter to slowly drain over time; it never completely empites.	It's located to the left of where Kratos enters Hera's Garden and a Save Altair.

CHAOS DIFFICULTY, CHALLENGES OF OLYMPUS, & FEAR KRATOS COSTUME

Complete the game on any difficulty.

COMBAT ARENA

Complete the Challenges of Olympus.

GOD OF WAR: ASCENSION

PLAYSTATION 3

TITAN MODE

Complete the game on any difficulty to unlock the Titan Difficulty Mode.

UNLOCKABLE COSTUMES

Complete the game and start New Game+ to unlock the Battle Armor of Ares, Battle Armor of Zeus, Fury Armor, Kraken Armor, Olive Skin Kratos, Skorpian Armor and War Armor of Hades costumes.

TROPHIES

NAME	GOAL/REQUIREMENT	TROPHY VALUE
Big Spender	Upgrade any Magic to the next level.	Bronze
Champion of the Gods	Unlock all Trophies.	Platinum
Fireproof	Complete the Screw of Archimedes without getting hit by the Fire Traps.	Silver
Fully Loaded	Completely Upgrade Kratos.	Silver
Handyman	Reconstruct the Water Wheel of Kirra.	Bronze
If it ain't broke…	Reconstruct all of the Decayed Chests.	Gold
Light as a Feather	Collect all of the Phoenix Feathers.	Silver
Lubed up	Complete the slide in the Statue of Apollo without dying.	Silver
No Drake. You can't have these.	Collect all Artifacts in the game.	Gold
Swinger	Ring out an enemy with the Club.	Bronze
Tell Me How You Really Feel	Kill 25 Enemies using the Rage of the Gods.	Bronze
That's Gonna Leave a Mark	Spill 500 buckets of blood on Kratos.	Bronze
The Eyes have It	Collect all of the Gorgon Eyes.	Silver
Tools of the Trade	Use All 5 World Weapons in Combat.	Bronze
You Bastards!	Treat the Martyr of Hecatonchires poorly.	Bronze

CHEATS, ACHIEVEMENTS, AND TROPHIES

G

SECRET TROPHIES

NAME	GOAL/REQUIREMENT	TROPHY VALUE
Biting the Hand that Feeds You	Defeat Megaera and the Titan Hecatonchires.	Silver
Blind Justice	Use the Eyes of Truth successfully.	Silver
Blood Oath	Complete the MP Training in Olympus.	Bronze
Bond Broken	Complete the game.	Gold
Bros before Foes	Escape the Fury Ambush.	Silver
Can't Stop, Won't Stop. BadBoy!	Perform a 1000 Hit Combo.	Bronze
Gateway Gas	Breathe the toxic gases within the Oracle's Temple.	Bronze
Gotta Hand It To You	Defeated the infected Hand of Aegaeon.	Bronze
Hello, Friend	Use the Oath Stone of Orkos in Combat 10 Times.	Bronze
Hold Still Please	Slow 100 Enemies with the Amulet of Uroborus.	Bronze
Hot Lunch	Win the Buttonless MiniGame against a Manticore.	Bronze
Legendary Warrior	Complete the game on Hard Difficulty.	Gold
Maybe you should call a Doctor?	Keep the Rage Meter Filled for 2+ Minutes.	Silver
Next time use the stairs	Complete the Gauntlet of Archimedes.	Gold
Open Minded	Win the Buttonless MiniGame against a Juggernaut.	Bronze
Prison Break	Free Kratos from his imprisonment.	Bronze
Quaid!!!	Defeat Pollux.	Silver
Round and Round	Solve the Rolling Crusher Puzzle.	Bronze
Snakes on a Train	Ride the snake back to the Tower of Delphi.	Bronze
Tag Teamed	Hit 100 Enemies with the Oath Stone of Orkos.	Bronze
Unleashed	Throw, Slam and Ram a grappled enemy.	Bronze

THE GODFATHER: THE GAME

XBOX 360

FULL AMMO

Pause the game and press Y, Left, Y, Right, X, Right Thumbstick.

FULL HEALTH

Pause the game and press Left, X, Right, Y, Right, Left Thumbstick.

UNLOCK ENTIRE FILM ARCHIVE

After loading a game and before joining the family, press Y, X, Y, X, X, Left Thumbstick. Select Film Archive to view the films.

THE GODFATHER II

XBOX 360

These codes can only be used once every few minutes.

$5,000

While in Don view, press X, Y, X, X, Y, click Left Analog Stick.

FULL HEALTH

While in Don view, press Left, X, Right, Y, Right, click Left Analog Stick.

FULL AMMO

While in Don view, press Y, Left, Y, Right, X, click Right Analog Stick.

THE GODFATHER: BLACKHAND EDITION

The following pause screen codes can be used only once every five minutes.

$5,000

Pause the game and press Minus, 2, Minus, Minus, 2, Up.

FULL AMMO

Pause the game and press 2, Left, 2, Right, Minus, Down.

FULL HEALTH

Pause the game and press Left, Minus, Right, 2, Right, Up.

FILM CLIPS

After loading your game, before selecting Play Game, press 2, Minus, 2, Minus, Minus, Up.

GODZILLA UNLEASHED

UNLOCK ALL

At the Main menu, press A + Up to bring up the cheat entry screen. Enter 204935.

90000 STORE POINTS

At the Main menu, press A + Up to bring up the cheat entry screen. Enter 031406.

SET DAY

At the Main menu, press A + Up to bring up the cheat entry screen. Enter 0829XX, where XX represents the day. Use 00 for day one.

SHOW MONSTER MOVES

At the Main menu, press A + Up to bring up the cheat entry screen. Enter 411411.

VERSION NUMBER

At the Main menu, press A + Up to bring up the cheat entry screen. Enter 787321.

MOTHERSHIP LEVEL

Playing as the Aliens, destroy the mothership in the Invasion level.

GOLDENEYE 007

BIG HEADS IN LOCAL MULTIPLAYER

Select Cheat Codes from the Extras menu and enter <477MYFR13NDS4R3SP13S>.

INVISIBILITY MODIFIER IN LOCAL MULTIPLAYER

Select Cheat Codes from the Extras menu and enter Inv1s1bleEv3ryth1ng.

TAG MODIFIER IN LOCAL MULTIPLAYER

Select Cheat Codes from the Extras menu and enter NotIt!!!11.

GOLDENEYE 007: RELOADED

BLACK MOONRAKER SKIN IN MULTIPLAYER

Select Cheat Codes from the Extras menu and enter las3r3ras3r.

INVISIBILITY AND TAG IN MULTIPLAYER

Select Cheat Codes from the Extras menu and enter f11ypr3load3ed.

PAINTBALL MODE IN MULTIPLAYER

Select Cheat Codes from the Extras menu and enter wr1t1ng1s0nth3wa11.

ALL MI6 OPS WITH 4-STAR RATINGS

Select Cheat Codes from the Extras menu and enter Quimbecile. Then, play one of the missions. Any missions you had already play will remain the rating that you earned.

BLACK MOONRAKER SKIN IN MULTIPLAYER

Select Cheat Codes from the Extras menu and enter las3r3ras3r.

INVISIBILITY AND TAG IN MULTIPLAYER

Select Cheat Codes from the Extras menu and enter f11ypr3load3ed.

PAINTBALL MODE IN MULTIPLAYER

Select Cheat Codes from the Extras menu and enter wr1t1ng1s0nth3wa11.

ACHIEVEMENTS & TROPHIES

NAME	GOAL/REQUIREMENT	POINT VALUE	TROPHY VALUE
MI6 Ops Recruit	Earn 10 stars in MI6 Ops.	10	Bronze
MI6 Ops Specialist	Earn 25 stars in MI6 Ops.	25	Silver
MI6 Ops Elite	Earn 44 stars in MI6 Ops.	45	Gold
Operative	Complete all objectives for every mission on Operative difficulty.	10	Bronze
Agent	Complete all objectives for every mission on Agent difficulty.	15	Bronze
007	Complete all objectives for every mission on 007 difficulty.	25	Silver
Classic	Complete all objectives for every mission on 007 Classic difficulty.	40	Gold
Arkhangelsk Dossier	Complete all objectives in Arkhangelsk on 007 difficulty or higher.	40	Bronze
Barcelona Dossier	Complete all objectives in Barcelona on 007 difficulty or higher.	15	Bronze
Dubai Dossier	Complete all objectives in Dubai on 007 difficulty or higher.	15	Bronze
Severnaya Dossier	Complete all objectives in Severnaya on 007 difficulty or higher.	30	Silver
St. Petersburg Dossier	Complete all objectives in St. Petersburg on 007 difficulty or higher.	40	Silver
Nigeria Dossier	Complete all objectives in Nigeria on 007 difficulty or higher.	40	Silver
Phone a Friend	Get 20 kills with hacked drone guns in 'Jungle'.	15	Bronze
Bullet Dance	Get 40 kills with the Wolfe .44 in 'Nightclub'.	20	Bronze
Emblem Hunter	Single Player: Find and destroy a Janus emblem.	5	Bronze
Emblem Marksman	Single Player: Find and destroy 20 Janus emblems.	10	Bronze

NAME	GOAL/REQUIREMENT	POINT VALUE	TROPHY VALUE
Emblem Elite	Single Player: Find and destroy 50 Janus emblems.	15	Silver
I am INVINCIBLE!	Single Player: Complete any mission without taking any damage.	25	Bronze
Dressed to Kill	Single Player: Complete any mission without collecting any body armor on 007 Classic difficulty.	20	Bronze
Going Dark	Get to master engineering in 'Facility' without reinforcements getting called in.	15	Bronze
Choppers Down	Shoot down 15 helicopters in 'Tank'.	15	Bronze
Invisible Descent	Get to the server room in 'Bunker' without reinforcements getting called in.	15	Bronze
Secret Servers	Destroy all the servers in 'Archives' within 40 secs of the first being damaged.	10	Bronze
Haven't Got Nine Minutes	Complete 'Airfield' in under 4:35 (007 Classic difficulty).	15	Silver
Made you feel it, did he?	Single Player: Silently subdue 30 enemies.	10	Bronze
Master at Arms	Single Player: Make a kill with every weapon.	10	Bronze
Get to the Chopper	Complete 'Carrier' in under 11:00 (007 difficulty or higher).	15	Silver
Russian Escape	Complete 'Archives' in under 15:10 (Agent difficulty or higher).	15	Silver
Solar Agitated	Complete 'Solar' in under 13:00 (007 Classic difficulty).	15	Silver
Orbis Non Suffict	Public Match: Complete a match on every map.	15	Bronze
Butter Hook	Public Match: As Tee Hee, get the most kills with a melee strike (min 3 melee kills).	15	Bronze
Au-ned	Public Match: Achieve 79 kills with the Golden Gun in Golden Gun mode.	30	Bronze
Clobbering	Public Match: Achieve 64 melee kills with the KL-033 Mk2.	30	Bronze
Hat Trick	Public Match: In one life, make three kills with Oddjob's hat.	20	Bronze
Braced for Impact	Public Match: As Jaws, survive a shot to the head which would otherwise have killed you.	15	Bronze
The Man Who Cannot Die	Public Match: As Baron Samedi, survive a bullet which would otherwise have killed you.	15	Bronze
Console Compliancy	Public Match: Capture and defend the most consoles in one match of GoldenEye mode.	30	Bronze
For England, Alec	Public Match: As Bond, kill 006 with an explosive device.	20	Bronze
The Other Cheek	Public Match: As Bond, kill Zukovsky with a melee strike.	20	Bronze
Full Deck	Public Match: Play at least one complete match of Classic Conflict with every character.	15	Bronze
Boys with Toys	Public Match: Kill 50 enemies with Proximity Mines.	50	Bronze
Lucky Seven	Public Match: Defuse a planted bomb which has exactly 0:07 seconds remaining on its fuse.	40	Bronze

NAME	GOAL/REQUIREMENT	POINT VALUE	TROPHY VALUE
Boxing Clever	Public Match: Earn all accolades specific to Black Box.	30	Bronze
Had Your Six	Public Match: Kill six enemies with the Wolfe .44 or Gold Plated Revolver without reloading.	30	Bronze

SECRET ACHIEVEMENTS

NAME	GOAL/REQUIREMENT	POINT VALUE	TROPHY VALUE
Rocket Man	Kill an enemy with the RPG in 'Dam'.	15	Bronze
Royal Flush	In 'Facility', successfully kill the enemy in the toilet cubicle without any shots being fired.	2	Bronze
Dance Commander	Surrender to the music in 'Nightclub'.	5	Bronze
Welcome to Russia	Make the initial rendezvous with 006 in 'Dam'.	5	Bronze
Cheated	Public Match: Get killed the most times by Oddjob's hat (min 3 deaths).	3	Bronze

GRADIUS COLLECTION

PSP

AALL WEAPONS & POWER-UPS

Pause the game and press Up, Up, Down, Down, Left, Right, Left, Right, L, R. This code can be used once per level.

GRADIUS REBIRTH

NINTENDO WII

4 OPTIONS

Pause the game and press Up, Up, Down, Down, Left, Right, Left, Right, Fire, Powerup. This code can be used once for each stage you have attempted.

GRAN TURISMO 5

PLAYSTATION 3

B LICENSE TESTS

Buy a car.

A LICENSE TESTS

Reach Level 3 and complete the B License Tests.

INTERNATIONAL C LICENSE TESTS

Reach Level 6 and complete the A License Tests.

INTERNATIONAL B LICENSE TESTS

Reach Level 9 and complete the International C License Tests.

INTERNATIONAL A LICENSE TESTS

Reach Level 12 and complete the International B License Tests.

S LICENSE TESTS

Reach Level 15 and complete the International A License Tests.

TOP GEAR TEST TRACK

Complete Top Gear Challenge Beginner with gold.

NÜRBURGRING NORDSCHLEIFE

Complete all AMG Challenge Intermediate with at least bronze.

NÜRBURGRING NORDSCHLEIFE 4-HOUR CIRCUIT WITHOUT TIME AND WEATHER CHANGE

Complete all AMG Challenge Intermediate with at least silver.

NÜRBURGRING NORDSCHLEIFE 24-HOUR CIRCUIT WITH TIME AND WEATHER CHANGE

Complete all AMG Challenge Intermediate with gold.

GRAND THEFT AUTO: CHINATOWN WARS

MOBILE

$10,000

In the safe house at the mission replay board, move the letters around to enter CASHIN.

FULL HEALTH

In the safe house at the mission replay board, move the letters around to enter LIFEUP.

FULL ARMOR

In the safe house at the mission replay board, move the letters around to enter SHELLY.

WEAPON CHEAT 1

In the safe house at the mission replay board, move the letters around to enter LOADOA. This gives you the Pistol, Nightstick, Minigun, Assault Rifle, Micro SMG, Stubby Shotgun and Grenades.

WEAPON CHEAT 2

In the safe house at the mission replay board, move the letters around to enter LOADOB. This gives you the Twin Pistol, Taser, Flame Thrower, Carbine Rifle, SMG, Double Barreled Shotgun and Molotovs.

WEAPON CHEAT 3

In the safe house at the mission replay board, move the letters around to enter LOADOC. This gives you the Revolver, Chainsaw, Flamethrower, Carbine Rifle, SMG, Double Barreled Shotgun and Proximity Mines.

WEAPON CHEAT 4

In the safe house at the mission replay board, move the letters around to enter LOADOD. This gives you the Pistol, Baseball Bat, Carbine Rifle, RPG, Micro SMG, Shotgun and Flash Bangs.

EXPLOSIVE EAGLE (PISTOL HAS EXPLOSIVE BULLETS)

In the safe house at the mission replay board, move the letters around to enter BOOMCAN.

ALL DRUG DEALER LOCATIONS

In the safe house at the mission replay board, move the letters around to enter TRIPPY.

INCREASE WANTED LEVEL ONE STAR

In the safe house at the mission replay board, move the letters around to enter COPIN.

DECREASE WANTED LEVEL ONE STAR

In the safe house at the mission replay board, move the letters around to enter COPOUT.

ADVANCE TIME AN HOUR

In the safe house at the mission replay board, move the letters around to enter JUMPHR.

ADVANCE TIME SIX HOURS

In the safe house at the mission replay board, move the letters around to enter JUMPHRS.

ADVANCE TIME A DAY

In the safe house at the mission replay board, move the letters around to enter JUMPDAY.

G

FULL HEALTH AND ARMOR

During a game, press L, L, R, A, A, B, B, R.

FULL ARMOR

During a game, press L, L, R, B, B, A, A, R.

INCREASE WANTED LEVEL

During a game, press L, L, R, Y, Y, X, X, R.

DECREASE WANTED LEVEL

During a game, press R, X, X, Y, Y, R, L, L.

EXPLOSIVE PISTOL ROUND

During a game, press L, R, X, Y, A, B, Up, Down.

WEAPONS SET 1

During a game, press R, Up, B, Down, Left, R, B, Right. This gives you the Pistol, Nightstick, Minigun, Assault Rifle, Micro SMG, Stubby Shotgun, and Grenades with max ammo.

WEAPONS SET 2

During a game, press R, Up, A, Down, Left, R, A, Right. This gives you the Twin Pistol, Teaser, Flame Thrower, Carbine Rifle, SMG, Double Barreled Shotgun, and Molotovs with max ammo.

WEAPONS SET 3

During a game, press R, Up, Y, Down, Left, R, Y, Right. This gives you the Revolver, Chainsaw, Flame Thrower, Carbine Rifle, SMG, Double Barreled Shotgun, and Proximity Mines with max ammo.

WEAPONS SET 4

During a game, press R, Up, X, Down, Left, R, X, Right. This gives you the Pistol, Baseball Bat, Carbine Rifle, RPG, Micro SMG, Shotgun, and Flashbangs with max ammo.

WEATHER: SUNNY

During a game, press Up, Down, Left, Right, A, B, L, R.

WEATHER: CLOUDY

During a game, press Up, Down, Left, Right, X, Y, L, R.

WEATHER: RAIN

During a game, press Up, Down, Left, Right, Y, A, L, R.

WEATHER: HEAVY RAIN

During a game, press Up, Down, Left, Right, A, X, R, L.

WEATHER: THUNDERSTORMS

During a game, press Up, Down, Left, Right, B, Y, R, L.

GRAND THEFT AUTO: LIBERTY CITY STORIES

$250,000

During a game, press L, R, ●, L, R, ●, L, R.

FULL HEALTH

During a game, press L, R, ⊗, L, R, ●, L, R.

FULL ARMOR

During a game, press L, R, ●, L, R, ●, L, R.

WEAPON SET 1

During a game, press Up, ●, ●, Down, L, ●, ●, R.

WEAPON SET 2

During a game, press Up, ●, ●, Down, Left, ●, ●, R.

WEAPON SET 3

During a game, press Up, ⊗, ⊗, Down, L, ⊗, ⊗, R.

CHROME PLATED CARS

During a game, press ●, R, L, Down, Down, R, R, ●.

BLACK CARS

During a game, press ●, ●, R, ●, ●, L, ●, ●.

WHITE CARS

During a game, press ⊗, ⊗, R, ●, ●, L, ●, ●.

CARS DRIVE ON WATER

During a game, press ●, ⊗, Down, ●, ⊗, Up, L, L.

PERFECT TRACTION

During a game, press L, Up, L, R, ●, ●, Down, ⊗.

CHANGE BICYCLE TIRE SIZE

During a game, press ●, Right, ⊗, Up, R, ⊗, L, ●.

AGGRESSIVE DRIVERS

During a game, press ●, ●, R, ⊗, ⊗, L, ●, ●.

ALL GREEN LIGHTS

During a game, press ●, ●, R, ●, ●, L, ⊗, ⊗.

DESTROY ALL CARS

During a game, press L, L, Left, L, L, R, ⊗, ●.

RAISE MEDIA ATTENTION

During a game, press L, Up, R, R, ●, ●, Down, ⊗.

RAISE WANTED LEVEL

During a game, press L, R, ●, L, R, ●, L, R.

NEVER WANTED

During a game, press L, L, ●, R, R, ⊗, ●, ●.

CHANGE OUTFIT

During a game, press L, L, L, L, L, Right, ●, ●.

BOBBLE HEAD WORLD

During a game, press Down, Down, Down, ●, ●, ⊗, L, R.

PEOPLE ATTACK YOU

During a game, press L, L, R, L, L, R, Up, ●.

PEOPLE FOLLOW YOU

During a game, press Down, Down, Down, ●, ●, ●, L, R.

PEOPLE HAVE WEAPONS

During a game, press R, R, L, R, R, L, R, ●.

PEOPLE RIOT

During a game, press L, L, R, L, L, R, L, ●.

SPAWN RHINO

During a game, press L, L, L, L, L, R, ●, ●.

SPAWN TRASHMASTER

During a game, press ●, ●, Down, ●, ●, Up, L, L.

FASTER CLOCK

During a game, press L, L, L, L, L, R, ●, ⊗

FASTER GAMEPLAY

During a game, press R, R, L, R, R, L, Down, ⊗

SLOWER GAMEPLAY

During a game, press R, ●, ⊗, R, ●, ●, L, R.

ALL CHARACTERS, CARS, & ENTIRE CITY (MULTIPLAYER)

During a game, press Up (x3), ●, ●, ●, L, R.

43 CHARACTERS & 7 GANGS (MULTIPLAYER)

During a game, press Up (x3), ✕, ●, ●, R, L.

28 CHARACTERS & 4 GANGS (MULTIPLAYER)

During a game, press Up (x3), ●, ●, ✕, L, R.

14 CHARACTERS & 2 GANGS (MULTIPLAYER)

During a game, press Up (x3), ●, ●, ●, R, L.

CLEAR WEATHER

During a game, press Up, Down, ●, Up, Down, ●, L, R.

FOGGY WEATHER

During a game, press Up, Down, ●, Up, Down, ✕, L, R.

OVERCAST WEATHER

During a game, press Up, Down, ✕, Up, Down, ●, L, R.

RAINY WEATHER

During a game, press Up, Down, ●, Up, Down, ●, L, R.

SUNNY WEATHER

During a game, press L, L, ●, R, R, ●, ●, ✕

UPSIDE DOWN

During a game, press Down, Down, Down, ✕, ✕, ●, R, L.

UPSIDE UP

During a game, press ✕, ✕, ✕, Down, Down, Right, L, R.

RIGHT SIDE UP

During a game, press ●, ●, ●, Up, Up, Right, L, R.

COMMIT SUICIDE

During a game, press L, Down, Left, R, ✕, ●, Up, ●.

GAME CREDITS

During a game, press L, R, L, R, Up, Down, L, R.

SUNNY WEATHER

During a game, press L, L, ●, R, R, ●, ●, ✕

UPSIDE DOWN

During a game, press Down, Down, Down, ✕, ✕, ●, R, L.

UPSIDE UP

During a game, press ✕, ✕, ✕, Down, Down, Right, L, R.

RIGHT SIDE UP

During a game, press ●, ●, ●, Up, Up, Right, L, R.

COMMIT SUICIDE

During a game, press L, Down, Left, R, ✕, ●, Up, ●.

GAME CREDITS

During a game, press L, R, L, R, Up, Down, L, R.

CHEAT CODES

If you have a keyboard for your iOS or Android device, you can input these codes to unlock various cheats.

EFFECT	CODE
150 Health	GIVEUSPOWERTOREVENGE
200 Armor	WOWPOWER
Aggressive Drivers	MIAMITRAFFIC
All Heavy Weapons	NUTTERTOOLS
All Light Weapons	THUGSTOOLS
All Medium Weapons	PROFESSIONALTOOLS
All Cars are Black	IWANTITPAINTEDBLACK
All Cars are Pink	AHAIRDRESSERSCAR
All Cars have Nitrous	JUSTALITTLEFASTER
All Traffic Lights are Green	GREENLIGHT
All Weather Effects at Once	WORLDISMAD
Blow Up Nearby Cars	BIGBANG
Cars and Bikes have Nitrous	MEGASPEED
Cars can Drive Over Water	SEAWAYS
Cars Can Fly	COMEFLYWITHME
Change Clothes	STILLLIKEDRESSINGUP
Commit Suicide	ICANTTAKEITANYMORE
Decrease Wanted Level	LEAVEMEALONE
Dense Clouds	ABITDRIEG
Fast Boats Can Fly	AIRSHIP
Foggy Weather	CANTSEEATHING
Full Armor	PRECIOUSPROTECTION
Full Health	ASPIRINE
Full Wanted Level	MOSTWANTED
Girls Carry Guns	CHICKSWITHGUNS
Girls Follow You	FANNYMAGNET
Gives Tommy Small Limbs	PROGRAMMER
Light Clouds	APLEASANTDAY
Make Everything Faster	ONSPEED
Make Everything Slower	BOOOOOORING
Make Tommy Fatter	DEEPFRIEDMARSBARS
No More Money	LOSTALL
Only Wheels of Cars are Visible	WHEELSAREALLINEED
Pedestrians Carry Guns	OURGODGIVENRIGHTTOBEARARMS
Pedestrians Carry Rocket Launchers	GODPOWER
Pedestrians Follow You	STOPTHEMTORUSHAGAINST
Pedestrians Hate You	NOBODYLIKESME
Pedestrians Riot	FIGHTFIGHTFIGHT
Pedestrians Riot w/ Weapons	THEGODHASGIVEUSPOWERTOFIGHT
Pedestrians Without Close	LOLOLDISGUS
Perfect Handling	GRIPISEVERYTHING
Play as Hilary King	ILOOKLIKEHILARY
Play as Ken Rosenberg	MYSONISALAWYER
Play as Lance Vance	LOOKLIKELANCE

CHEATS, ACHIEVEMENTS, AND TROPHIES

G

EFFECT	CODE
Play as Love Fist Dick	WELOVEOURDICK
Play as Love Fist Jezz Torent	ROCKANDROLLMAN
Play as Mercedes	FOXYLITTLETHING
Play as Phil Cassidy	ONEARMEDBANDIT
Play as Ricardo Diaz	CHEATSHAVEBEENCRACKED
Play as Sonny Forelli	IDONTHAVETHEMONEYSONNY
Raise Wanted Level	YOUWONTTAKEMEALIVE
Show Media Level	CHASESTAT
Smoke a Cigarette	CERTAINDEATH
Spawn a Bloodring Banger	TRAVELINSTYLE
Spawn a Bloodring Banger #2	GETTHEREQUICKLY
Spawn a Caddie	BETTERTHANWALKING
Spawn a Hotring Racer	GETTHEREVERYFASTINDEED
Spawn a Hotring Racer #2	GETTHEREAMAZINGLYFAST
Spawn a Hunter	LETSMERISEUP
Spawn a Hunter #2	AIRJUMP
Spawn a Hunter #3	IWILLGETTOMARS
Spawn a Rhino	PANZER
Spawn a Romero's Hearse	THELASTRIDE
Spawn a Sabre Turbo	GETTHEREFAST
Spawn a Trashmaster	RUBBISHCAR
Spawn Love Fist's Limo	ROCKANDROLLCAR
Speed Up Game Clock	LIFEISPASSINGMEBY
Sports Cars Have Big Wheels	LOADSOFLITTLETHINGS
Stormy Weather	CATSANDDOGS
Sunny Weather	ALOVELYDAY
Unlimited Ammo	NOTHINGENDS

GRAND THEFT AUTO: VICE CITY STORIES

PSP

Enter the following cheats during a game.

$250000

Press Up, Down, L, R, ✖, ●, ✖, L, R.

ARMOR

Press Up, Down, L, R, ●, ●, ●, L, R.

HEALTH

Press Up, Down, L, R, ●, ●, ●, L, R.

NEVER WANTED

Press Up, R, ●, ●, Down, L, ●, ●.

LOWER WANTED LEVEL

Press Up, R, ●, ●, Down, L, ✖, ✖.

RAISE WANTED LEVEL

Press Up, R, ●, ●, Down, L, ●, ●.

WEAPON SET 1

Press L, R, ✖, Up, Down, ●, L, R.

WEAPON SET 2

Press L, R, ●, Up, Down, ●, L, R.

WEAPON SET 3

Press L, R, ●, Up, Down, ●, L, R.

SPAWN RHINO

Press Up, L, Down, R, L, L, R, R.

SPAWN TRASHMASTER

Press Down, Up, R, ⬤, L, ⬤, L, ⬤.

BLACK CARS

Press L, R, L, R, L, ⬤, Up, ✖.

CHROME CARS

Press R, Up, L, Down, ⬤, ⬤, L, R.

CARS AVOID YOU

Press Up, Up, R, L, ⬤, ⬤, ⬤, ⬤.

DESTROY ALL CARS

Press L, R, R, L, R, ⬤, Down, R.

GUYS FOLLOW YOU

Press R, L, Down, L, ⬤, Up, L, ⬤.

PERFECT TRACTION

Press Down, Left, Up, L, R, ⬤, ⬤, ✖. Press Down to jump into a car.

PEDESTRIAN GETS INTO YOUR VEHICLE

Press Down, Up, R, L, L, ⬤, Up, L.

PEDESTRIANS ATTACK YOU

Press Down, ⬤, Up, ✖, L, R, L, R.

PEDESTRIANS HAVE WEAPONS

Press Up, L, Down, R, L, ⬤, R, ⬤.

PEDESTRIANS RIOT

Press R, L, L, Down, L, ⬤, Down, L.

SUICIDE

Press R, R, ⬤, ⬤, L, R, Down, ✖.

UPSIDE DOWN 1

Press ⬤, ⬤, ⬤, L, L, R, L, R.

UPSIDE DOWN 2

Press L, L, L, R, R, L, R, L.

FASTER CLOCK

Press R, L, L, Down, Up, ✖, Down, L.

FASTER GAMEPLAY

Press L, L, R, R, Up, ⬤, Down, ✖.

SLOWER GAMEPLAY

Press L, L, ⬤, ⬤, Down, Up, ⬤, ✖.

CLEAR WEATHER

Press L, Down, R, L, R, Up, L, ✖.

FOGGY WEATHER

Press L, Down, ⬤, ✖, R, Up, L, L.

OVERCAST WEATHER

Press L, Down, L, R, R, Up, L, ⬤.

RAINY WEATHER

Press L, Down, L, R, R, Up, Left, ⬤.

SUNNY WEATHER

Press L, Down, R, L, R, Up, L, ⬤.

GRAND THEFT AUTO III

MOBILE

KEYBOARD CHEATS

If you have an external keyboard for your iOS or Android device or are able to bring up the device's keyboard during the game, the following codes can be entered during gameplay. The cheats may not work on your game. Do not save your game after entering cheats as they may also be saved.

EFFECT	CODE
Full Health	GESUNDHEIT
Full Armor	TURTOISE
All Weapons	GUNSGUNSGUNS
More Money	IFIWEREARICHMAN
Higher Wanted Level	MOREPOLICEPLEASE
Lose Wanted Level	NOPOLICEPLEASE
Change to Other Peds	ILIKEDRESSINGUP
Crazy Peds	ITSALLGOINGMAAAD
Peds Attack You	NOBODYLIKESME
All Peds are Armed	WEAPONSFORALL
Blow Up Cars	BANGBANGBANG
Only Wheels are Visible	WHEELSONLYPLEASE
Flying Car	CHITTYCHITTYBB
Spawn Random Vehicle (Including Tank)	GIVEUSATANK
Improved Handling	CORNERSLIKEMAD
Gore Mode	NASTYLIMBCHEAT
Fast Game Clock	MADWEATHER
Faster Game Play	BOOOOORING
Clear Weather	SKINCANCERFORME
Cloudy Weather	ILIKESCOTLAND
Foggy Weather	PEASOUP
Rainy Weather	ILOVESCOTLAND

GRAND THEFT AUTO IV

XBOX 360/PS3

CHEATS

Call the following phone numbers with Niko's phone to activate the cheats. Some cheats may affect the missions and achievements.

VEHICLE	PHONE NUMBER
Change weather	468-555-0100
Get weapons	486-555-0100
Get different weapons	486-555-0150
Raise wanted level	267-555-0150
Remove wanted level	267-555-0100
Restore armor	362-555-0100
Restore health	482-555-0100
Restore armor, health, and ammo	482-555-0100

SPAWN VEHICLES

Call the following phone numbers with Niko's phone to spawn the corresponding vehicle.

VEHICLE	PHONE NUMBER
Annihilator	359-555-0100
Cognoscenti	227-555-0142
Comet	227-555-0175
FIB Buffalo	227-555-0100
Jetmax	938-555-0100
NRG-900	625-555-0100
Sanchez	625-555-0150
SuperGT	227-555-0168
Turismo	227-555-0147

MAP LOCATIONS

Access a computer in game and enter the following URL:
www.whattheydonotwantyoutoknow.com.

GRAND THEFT AUTO IV: THE BALLAD OF GAY TONY

PLAYSTATION 3

CHEATS

Call the following phone numbers with your phone to activate the cheats. Some cheats may affect the missions and achievements.

CHEAT	PHONE NUMBER
Get weapons	486-555-0100
Get different weapons	486-555-0150
Raise wanted level	267-555-0150
Remove wanted level	267-555-0100
Restore armor	362-555-0100
Restore armor, health, and ammo	482-555-0100
Sniper uses exploding bullets	486-555-2526
Super Punch	276-555-2666
Parachute	359-555-7272
Change Weather	468-555-0100

SPAWN VEHICLES

Call the following phone numbers with your phone to spawn the corresponding vehicle.

VEHICLE	PHONE NUMBER
Akuma	625-555-0200
Annihilator	359-555-0100
APC	272-555-8265
Bullet GT	227-555-9666
Buzzard	359-555-2899
Cognoscenti	227-555-0142
Comet	227-555-0175
FIB Buffalo	227-555-0100
Floater	938-555-0150
Jetmax	938-555-0100
NRG-900	625-555-0100
Sanchez	625-555-0150
Super GT	227-555-0168
Turismo	227-555-0147
Vader	625-555-3273

CHEATS

Call the following phone numbers with your phone to activate the cheats. Some cheats may affect the missions and achievements.

CHEAT	PHONE NUMBER
Get weapons	486-555-0100
Get different weapons	486-555-0150
Raise wanted level	267-555-0150
Remove wanted level	267-555-0100
Restore armor	362-555-0100
Restore armor, health, and ammo	482-555-0100
Parachute	359-555-7272
Change Weather	468-555-0100

SPAWN VEHICLES

Call the following phone numbers with your phone to spawn the corresponding vehicle.

VEHICLE	PHONE NUMBER
Akuma	625-555-0200
Annihilator	359-555-0100
APC	272-555-8265
Bullet GT	227-555-9666
Buzzard	359-555-2899
Cognoscenti	227-555-0142
Comet	227-555-0175
FIB Buffalo	227-555-0100
Floater	938-555-0150
Jetmax	938-555-0100
NRG-900	625-555-0100
Sanchez	625-555-0150
Super GT	227-555-0168
Turismo	227-555-0147
Vader	625-555-3273

GRAND THEFT AUTO IV: THE LOST AND DAMNED

SPAWN VEHICLES

Call the following phone numbers with your phone to spawn the corresponding vehicle.

VEHICLE	PHONE NUMBER
Annihilator	359-555-0100
Burrito	826-555-0150
Cognoscenti	227-555-0142
Comet	227-555-0175
Double T	245-555-0125
FIB Buffalo	227-555-0100
Hakuchou	245-555-0199
Hexer	245-555-0150
Innovation	245-555-0100
Jetmax	938-555-0100
NRG-900	625-555-0100
Sanchez	625-555-0150
Slamvan	826-555-0100
Turismo	227-555-0147

CHEATS

Call the following phone numbers with your phone to activate the cheats. Some cheats may affect the missions and achievements.

BONUS	PHONE NUMBER
Get weapons	486-555-0100
Get different weapons	486-555-0150
Raise wanted level	267-555-0150
Remove wanted level	267-555-0100
Restore armor	362-555-0100
Restore armor, health, and ammo	482-555-0100

SPAWN VEHICLES

Call the following phone numbers with your phone to spawn the corresponding vehicle.

VEHICLE	PHONE NUMBER
Annihilator	359-555-0100
Burrito	826-555-0150
Double T	245-555-0125
FIB Buffalo	227-555-0100
Hakuchou	245-555-0199
Hexer	245-555-0150
Innovation	245-555-0100
Slamvan	826-555-0100

GRAVITRONIX

NINTENDO WII

VERSUS OPTIONS AND LEVEL SELECT

At the Options menu, press 1, 2, 2, 2, 1.

GREG HASTINGS PAINTBALL 2

NINTENDO WII

PRO & NEW GUN

Select Career, hold C, and press Up, Up, Down, Right, Left, Left, Right, Up.

GRID

NINTENDO 3DS

UNLOCK ALL

Select Cheat Codes from the Options and enter 233558.

INVULNERABILITY

Select Cheat Codes from the Options and enter 161650.

DRIFT MASTER

Select Cheat Codes from the Options and enter 789520.

PERFECT GRIP

Select Cheat Codes from the Options and enter 831782.

HIGH ROLLER

Select Cheat Codes from the Options and enter 401134.

GHOST CAR

Select Cheat Codes from the Options and enter 657346.

TOY CARS

Select Cheat Codes from the Options and enter 592014.

MM MODE

Select Cheat Codes from the Options and enter 800813.

XBOX 360/PS3

ALL DRIFT CARS

Select Bonus Codes from the Options. Then choose Enter Code and enter TUN58396.

ALL MUSCLE CARS

Select Bonus Codes from the Options. Then choose Enter Code and enter MUS59279.

BUCHBINDER EMOTIONAL ENGINEERING BMW 320SI

Select Bonus Codes from the Options. Then choose Enter Code and enter F93857372. You can use this in Race Day or in GRID World once you've started your own team.

EBAY

Select Bonus Codes from the Options. Then choose Enter Code and enter DAFJ55E01473M0. You can use this in Race Day or in GRID World once you've started your own team.

GAMESTATION BMW 320SI

Select Bonus Codes from the Options. Then choose Enter Code and enter G29782655. You can use this in Race Day or in GRID World once you've started your own team.

MICROMANIA PAGANI ZONDA R

Select Bonus Codes from the Options. Then choose Enter Code and enter M38572343. You can use this in Race Day or in GRID World once you've started your own team.

PLAY.COM ASTON MARTIN DBR9

Select Bonus Codes from the Options. Then choose Enter Code and enter P47203845. You can use this in Race Day or in GRID World once you've started your own team.

THE GRIM ADVENTURES OF BILLY & MANDY

NINTENDO WII

CONCEPT ART

At the Main menu, hold 1 and press Up, Up, Down, Down, Left, Right, Left, Right.

GUACAMELEE!

PLAYSTATION 3

TROPHIES

NAME	GOAL/REQUIREMENT	TROPHY VALUE
A Hero is Born	Save Pueblucho	Bronze
All Cooped Up	Complete the Chicken Hedring quest	Bronze
Belly Flop	Destroy a Block using Slam	Bronze
Big Hearted	Complete a full heart upgrade	Bronze
Boom-Shack-Calaca	Defeat Calaca	Silver
Boomerang	Defeat an enemy with its own projectile	Bronze
Catch the Rainbow!	Connect with all six special attacks without touching the ground	Bronze
Cleaned Out	Buy all the items in the shop	Silver
Cock of the Walk	Defeat an enemy as a chicken	Bronze

NAME	GOAL/REQUIREMENT	TROPHY VALUE
Combo Nerd	Achieve a 150 Hit Combo	Bronze
Delicious	Complete the World's Greatest Enchilada quest	Bronze
Endurance	Complete a full stamina upgrade	Bronze
Flawless	Defeat an arena without taking any damage	Bronze
Giant Killer	Defeat 3 giant skeletons	Bronze
Got to catch them all	Find an orb	Bronze
Green Thumb	Uproot 20 plant enemies	Bronze
Guacamelee! Platinum trophy	Your luchador mask is in the mail	Platinum
Gumshoe	Complete the Chicken Thief quest	Bronze
I AM ERROR	Complete the I AM ERROR quest	Bronze
I swat you	Defeat a Chupacabra using only Slam	Bronze
Licking his Wounds	Defeat Jaguar Javier	Bronze
Lore Master	Complete All Side Quests	Silver
Music to my ears	Complete the Mariachi Band quest	Bronze
My First Power Move	Destroy a Block using Uppercut	Bronze
Nap Time's Over	Wake up an Alebrije	Bronze
Nooks and Crannies	Find 100% of the hidden items in a single area	Bronze
Poncho'd Out	Complete the Combo Chicken quest (Defeat Poncho forever)	Bronze
Pow	Destroy a Block using Dash Punch	Bronze
Reunited	Complete the Missing Doll quest	Bronze
Rocketman	Soar through the air for 12 seconds using "Goat Fly"	Bronze
Shopaholic	Spend $10000 in the store	Bronze
Snuffed Out	Defeat Flame Face	Bronze
Stop squirming	Defeat an Alux using only Headbutt	Bronze
That was Hard Mode?	Defeat the game on Hard mode	Gold
That's one big Gato Frito	Kill the Alebrije	Bronze
That's using your head	Headbutt an enemy off a cliff	Bronze
The Never Ending Combo	Achieve a 300 Hit Combo	Silver
They hit really hard	Defeat 5 arenas in Hard mode	Bronze
Thick headed	Destroy a Block using Headbutt	Bronze
Up Close and Personal	Defeat Calaca using only melee attacks	Silver
Viva La Resurreccion	Become a Luchador	Bronze
What us to untie you?	Talk to a Goat	Bronze
We built this city on Guac and Roll	Discover Santa Luchita	Bronze
Wheeee	Teleport through an Olmec head	Bronze
Who put these here???	Collect every chest in the game	Gold
Why all the long faces?	Enter the world of the dead	Bronze
X'tabay-Bye	Redeem X'tabay	Bronze

GUARDIAN HEROES

XBOX 360

AVATAR AWARDS

AVATAR	EARNED BY
Guardian Heroes Helmet	Scored 360 points in Arcade Mode.
Guardian Heroes T-Shirt	Unlocked at least 30 characters in Story Mode.

GUARDIANS OF MIDDLE-EARTH

XBOX 360/PS3

ACHIEVEMENTS & TROPHIES

NAME	GOAL/REQUIREMENT	POINT VALUE	TROPHY VALUE
Honor in Death	Fall on the Battleground	5	Bronze
Foe's Bane	Achieve a Kill Streak of 3 in any Battlegrounds match	5	—
And My Axe	Achieve an Assist Streak of 5 in any Battlegrounds match	5	—
Drive Them Back	Achieve a Multi-Kill of 2 in any Battlegrounds match	5	—
Ultimate Vengeance	Use an Ultimate Ability to defeat an Enemy Guardian in any Battlegrounds Match	5	Bronze
Master Mason	Upgrade 3 Towers in any single Battlegrounds match	5	—
Rise to the Top	Reach Level 14 in any Battlegrounds Match	5	Bronze
All Falls Before You	Destroy 5 Soldier Upgrades total in Battlegrounds matches	5	—
Rally the Troops	Build 6 Soldier Upgrades total in any Battlegrounds matches	5	—
Win Your Way	Win a Custom Match	5	—
Rule Them All	Win any 3-Lane Battlegrounds or Skirmish match	10	—
Warrior's Mettle	Win with a Warrior-Class Guardian in any Battlegrounds Match	15	Bronze
Strike Hard, Strike Fast	Win with a Striker-Class Guardian in any Battlegrounds match	15	Bronze
Defend to the End	Win with a Defender-Class Guardian in any Battlegrounds match	15	Bronze
Enchanted	Win with an Enchanter-Class Guardian in any Battlegrounds match	15	Bronze
Fortified	Win with a Tactician-Class Guardian in any Battlegrounds Match	15	Bronze
In Command	Use a Tier-4 Command in any Battlegrounds match	15	—
Draught of Courage	Use 4 Potions in any single Battlegrounds Match	15	—
Renowned	Earn 20 Guardian Kills in any single Battlegrounds Match	15	Bronze
(MVG) Most Valuable Guardian	Earn a combined Guardian Kill/Assist Streak of 8 in any Battlegrounds Match	15	Bronze
Seasoned	Earn 5 Accolades from any single Battlegrounds Match	20	Bronze
Collector	Kill or Assist a Guardian from each Class once in any Battlegrounds Match	20	Bronze
Capture the Power	Capture 15 Shrines total in any Battlegrounds matches	20	Bronze
Notches in the Axe	Earn 50 Accolades total in any Battlegrounds matches	20	Silver
In the Light	Play as every Good Guardian once in Battlegrounds matches	25	—
Servant of the Shadows	Play as every Evil Guardian once in Battlegrounds matches	25	—
No Head Left Uncracked	Damage every Guardian once in Battlegrounds matches	25	—
There And Back Again	Win 25 total Battlegrounds Matches	25	Gold
An Unexpected Journey	Win 100 Battlegrounds or Skirmish Matches	25	—

GUILTY GEAR XX ACCENT CORE PLUS

PSP

FIGHT EX CHARACTERS

Highlight Arcade or M.O.M. and hold R while starting the game.

FIGHT GOLD CHARACTERS

Highlight Arcade or M.O.M. and hold L while starting the game.

FIGHT GOLD/EX CHARACTERS

Highlight Arcade or M.O.M. and hold L + R while starting the game.

SPECIAL ILLUSTRATIONS

ILLUSTRATION	REQUIREMENT
Special Illustrations 2-6	Reach level 500 in Survival Mode.
Special Illustration 7	Unlock all Black and Gold colors for every character.
Special Illustration 8	Unlock all Arcade Gallery images.
Special Illustration 9	Unlock all EX Arcade Gallery images.
Special Illustration 10	Reach level 1000 in Survival Mode and defeat Gold EX Order-Sol.

XBOX 360/PS3

BLACK/GOLD CHARACTERS

Clear both Story Mode paths in Survival or defeat a character's Gold version in Survival Mode to unlock them.

EX ARCADE/M.O.M. MODE

After unlocking all EX characters, hold LT while selecting Arcade or M.O.M. Mode.

EX CHARACTERS

Clear a Story Mode path with a character or defeat their Black version in Survival mode to unlock their EX character. Alternatively, complete all 25 missions to unlock them.

EXTRA OPTIONS

Clear missions 26-30 in Mission Mode to unlock an Extra Options menu.

GOLD ARCADE/M.O.M. MODE

After unlocking all Gold and EX characters hold LB+LT while selecting Arcade or M.O.M. Mode.

GUILTY GEAR GENERATIONS MODE

Unlock all Arcade Gallery illustrations or complete all 25 missions.

UNLOCK JUSTICE

Complete Justice's Story Mode or complete 10 missions.

UNLOCK KLIFF

Complete Kliff's Story Mode or complete 5 missions.

SPECIAL ILLUSTRATIONS

ILLUSTRATION	REQUIREMENT
Special Illustrations 2-6	Reach level 500 in Survival Mode.
Special Illustration 7	Unlock all Black and Gold colors for every character.
Special Illustration 8	Unlock all Arcade Gallery images.
Special Illustration 9	Unlock all EX Arcade Gallery images.
Special Illustration 10	Reach level 1000 in Survival Mode and defeat Gold EX Order-Sol.

CHEATS, ACHIEVEMENTS, AND TROPHIES

G

GUITAR HERO III: LEGENDS OF ROCK

NINTENDO WII

To enter the following cheats, strum the guitar with the given buttons held. For example, if it says Yellow + Orange, hold Yellow and Orange as you strum. Air Guitar, Precision Mode and Performance Mode can be toggled on and off from the Cheats menu. You can also change between five levels of Hyperspeed at this menu.

UNLOCK EVERYTHING

Select Cheats from the Options. Choose Enter Cheat and enter Green + Red + Blue + Orange, Green + Red + Yellow + Blue, Green + Red + Yellow + Orange, Green + Yellow + Blue + Orange, Green + Red + Yellow + Blue, Red + Yellow + Blue + Orange, Green + Red + Yellow + Blue, Green + Yellow + Blue + Orange, Green + Red + Yellow + Blue, Green + Red + Yellow + Orange, Green + Red + Yellow + Orange, Green + Red + Yellow + Blue, Green + Red + Yellow + Orange. No sounds play while this code is entered.

An easier way to show this code is by representing Green as 1 down to Orange as 5. For example, if you have 1345, you would hold down Green + Yellow + Blue + Orange while strumming. 1245 + 1234 + 1235 + 1345 + 1234 + 2345 + 1234 + 1345 + 1234 + 1235 + 1235 + 1234 + 1235.

ALL SONGS

Select Cheats from the Options. Choose Enter Cheat and enter Yellow + Orange, Red + Blue, Red + Orange, Green + Blue, Red + Yellow, Yellow + Orange, Red + Yellow, Red + Blue, Green + Yellow, Green + Yellow, Yellow + Blue, Yellow + Blue, Yellow + Orange, Yellow + Orange, Yellow + Blue, Yellow, Red, Red + Yellow, Red, Yellow, Orange.

NO FAIL

Select Cheats from the Options. Choose Enter Cheat and enter Green + Red, Blue, Green + Red, Green + Yellow, Blue, Green + Yellow, Red + Yellow, Orange, Red + Yellow, Green + Yellow, Yellow, Green + Yellow, Green + Red.

AIR GUITAR

Select Cheats from the Options. Choose Enter Cheat and enter Blue + Yellow, Green + Yellow, Green + Yellow, Red + Blue, Red + Yellow, Red + Yellow, Blue + Yellow, Green + Yellow, Green + Yellow, Red + Blue, Red + Blue, Red + Yellow, Yellow, Green + Yellow, Green + Yellow, Red + Yellow, Red + Yellow.

HYPERSPEED

Select Cheats from the Options. Choose Enter Cheat and enter Orange, Blue, Orange, Yellow, Orange, Blue, Orange, Yellow.

PERFORMANCE MODE

Select Cheats from the Options. Choose Enter Cheat and enter Red + Yellow, Red + Blue, Red + Orange, Red + Blue, Red + Yellow, Green + Blue, Red + Yellow, Red + Blue.

EASY EXPERT

Select Cheats from the Options. Choose Enter Cheat and enter Green + Red, Green + Yellow, Yellow + Blue, Red + Blue, Blue + Orange, Yellow + Orange, Red + Yellow, Red + Blue.

PRECISION MODE

Select Cheats from the Options. Choose Enter Cheat and enter Green + Red, Green + Red, Green + Red, Red + Yellow, Red + Yellow, Red + Blue, Red + Blue, Yellow + Blue, Yellow + Orange, Yellow + Orange, Green + Red, Green + Red, Green + Red, Red + Yellow, Red + Yellow, Red + Blue, Red + Blue, Yellow + Blue, Yellow + Orange, Yellow + Orange.

LARGE GEMS

Select Cheats from the Options. Choose Enter Cheat and enter Green, Red, Green, Yellow, Green, Blue, Green, Orange, Green, Blue, Green, Yellow, Green, Red, Green, Green + Red, Red + Yellow, Green + Red, Yellow + Blue, Green + Red, Blue + Orange, Green + Red, Yellow + Blue, Green + Red, Red + Yellow, Green + Red, Green + Yellow.

To enter the following cheats, strum the guitar with the given buttons held. For example, if it says Yellow + Orange, hold Yellow and Orange as you strum. Air Guitar, Precision Mode, and Performance Mode can be toggled on and off from the Cheats menu. You can also change between five different levels of Hyperspeed at this menu.

UNLOCK EVERYTHING

Select Cheats from the Options. Choose Enter Cheat and enter Green + Red + Blue + Orange, Green + Red + Yellow + Blue, Green + Red + Yellow + Orange, Green + Yellow + Blue + Orange, Green + Red + Yellow + Blue, Red + Yellow + Blue + Orange, Green + Red + Yellow + Blue, Green + Yellow + Blue + Orange, Green + Red + Yellow + Blue, Green + Red + Yellow + Orange, Green + Red + Yellow + Orange, Green + Red + Yellow + Blue, Green + Red + Yellow + Orange. No sounds play while this code is entered.

An easier way to show this code is by representing Green as 1 down to Orange as 5. For example, if you have 1345, you would hold down Green + Yellow + Blue + Orange while strumming. 1245 + 1234 + 1235 + 1345 + 1234 + 2345 + 1234 + 1345 + 1234 + 1235 + 1235 + 1234 + 1235.

ALL SONGS

Select Cheats from the Options. Choose Enter Cheat and enter Yellow + Orange, Red + Blue, Red + Orange, Green + Blue, Red + Yellow, Yellow + Orange, Red + Yellow, Red + Blue, Green + Yellow, Green + Yellow, Yellow + Blue, Yellow + Blue, Yellow + Orange, Yellow + Orange, Yellow + Blue, Yellow, Red, Red + Yellow, Red, Yellow, Orange.

NO FAIL

Select Cheats from the Options. Choose Enter Cheat and enter Green + Red, Blue, Green + Red, Green + Yellow, Blue, Green + Yellow, Red + Yellow, Orange, Red + Yellow, Green + Yellow, Yellow, Green + Yellow, Green + Red.

AIR GUITAR

Select Cheats from the Options. Choose Enter Cheat and enter Blue + Yellow, Green + Yellow, Green + Yellow, Red + Blue, Red + Blue, Red + Yellow, Red + Yellow, Blue + Yellow, Green + Yellow, Green + Yellow, Red + Blue, Red + Blue, Red + Yellow, Red + Yellow, Green + Yellow, Green + Yellow, Red + Yellow, Red + Yellow.

HYPERSPEED

Select Cheats from the Options. Choose Enter Cheat and enter Orange, Blue, Orange, Yellow, Orange, Blue, Orange, Yellow.

PERFORMANCE MODE

Select Cheats from the Options. Choose Enter Cheat and enter Red + Yellow, Red + Blue, Red + Orange, Red + Blue, Red + Yellow, Green + Blue, Red + Yellow, Red + Blue.

EASY EXPERT

Select Cheats from the Options. Choose Enter Cheat and enter Green + Red, Green + Yellow, Yellow + Blue, Red + Blue, Blue + Orange, Yellow + Orange, Red + Yellow, Red + Blue.

PRECISION MODE

Select Cheats from the Options. Choose Enter Cheat and enter Green + Red, Green + Red, Green + Red, Red + Yellow, Red + Yellow, Red + Blue, Red + Blue, Yellow + Blue, Yellow + Orange, Yellow + Orange, Green + Red, Green + Red, Green + Red, Red + Yellow, Red + Yellow, Red + Blue, Red + Blue, Yellow + Blue, Yellow + Orange, Yellow + Orange.

BRET MICHAELS SINGER

Select Cheats from the Options. Choose Enter Cheat and enter Green + Red, Green + Red, Green + Red, Green + Blue, Green + Blue, Green + Blue, Red + Blue, Red, Red, Red, Red + Blue, Red, Red, Red, Red + Blue, Red, Red, Red.

GUITAR HERO 5

XBOX 360/PS3/WII

ALL HOPOS

Select Input Cheats from the Options menu and enter Green, Green, Blue, Green, Green, Green, Yellow, Green.

ALWAYS SLIDE

Select Input Cheats from the Options menu and enter Green, Green, Red, Red, Yellow, Blue, Yellow, Blue.

AUTO KICK

Select Input Cheats from the Options menu and enter Yellow, Green, Red, Blue, Blue, Blue, Blue, Red.

FOCUS MODE

Select Input Cheats from the Options menu and enter Yellow, Green, Red, Green, Yellow, Blue, Green, Green.

HUD FREE MODE

Select Input Cheats from the Options menu and enter Green, Red, Green, Green, Yellow, Green, Green, Green.

PERFORMANCE MODE

Select Input Cheats from the Options menu and enter Yellow, Yellow, Blue, Red, Blue, Green, Red, Red.

AIR INSTRUMENTS

Select Input Cheats from the Options menu and enter Red, Red, Blue, Yellow, Green, Green, Green, Yellow.

INVISIBLE ROCKER

Select Input Cheats from the Options menu and enter Green, Red, Yellow, Yellow, Yellow, Blue, Blue, Green.

ALL CHARACTERS

Select Input Cheats from the Options menu and enter Blue, Blue, Green, Green, Red, Green, Red, Yellow.

CONTEST WINNER 1

Select Input Cheats from the Options menu and enter Green, Green, Red, Red, Yellow, Red, Yellow, Blue.

XBOX 360/PS3

ACHIEVEMENTS & TROPHIES

NAME	GOAL/REQUIREMENT	POINT VALUE	TROPHY VALUE
Fest Quartet Quest	Play 10 4-Player RockFest Mode games of any type	20	Bronze
The Grand Tour	Unlock every venue in the world, and then some	30	Silver
Going Gold	Complete 50 of the challenges at Gold or better	20	Silver
Going Platinum	Complete 50 of the challenges at Platinum or better	30	Silver
Going Diamond	Complete 50 of the challenges at Diamond	50	Silver
Iron Lungs	Complete a 25-phrase streak as a Vocalist	20	Bronze
Sampler Plate	Play at least one song in Quickplay, Career and each Competitive game type	30	Silver
Producer	Create a music studio song	10	Bronze
The Fabricated Four	Create a band of 4 created rockers and play a song with them	10	Bronze

NAME	GOAL/REQUIREMENT	POINT VALUE	TROPHY VALUE
Quadruple Threat	Complete at least one challenge for every instrument at Gold level or better	30	Silver
Rocktopus	Make a standard 8 player Band v Band match online, win or lose	20	Bronze
Ménage à Huit	Play an online match with 8 players, all on the same instrument	20	Bronze
Outgoing	Complete 25 Pro Face Off matches online (Win or Lose)	10	Bronze
Barbershop	Play a song with 4 Vocalists	10	Bronze
Drumline	Play a song with 4 Drummers	10	Bronze
String Quartet	Play a song with 4 Lead Guitarists	10	Bronze
All Four Bass Are Belong to Us	Play a song with 4 Bass Guitarists	10	Bronze
Explore the Studio Space	Read 5 Tooltips in GHMix	10	Bronze
Play It To The Bone	Make and complete a setlist which is at least 1 hour long	20	Bronze
Challenge of the Supergroup	Complete 5 band challenges at Gold or better	20	Bronze
Crowd Pleaser	Fill your Rock Meter all the way	5	Bronze
What's an LP?	Complete 14 songs in Quickplay	20	Bronze
Young Star	Collect 25 Stars in Career	10	Bronze
Rising Star	Collect 101 Stars in Career	20	Bronze
Shooting Star	Collect 303 Stars in Career	30	Bronze
Senior Commander	Earn 5 or more Stars on a song in Career or Quickplay	10	Bronze
Super Star	Collect 505 Stars in Career	50	Silver
You Want More?	Play 5 encore gigs	10	Bronze
Synchronized	Complete 20 Band Moments	10	Bronze
The Streak	Complete a 1001 note streak	30	Bronze
Crank It Up To 11	Achieve a maxed out band multiplier as a standard band	20	Silver
What's New?	Complete any tutorial's lesson on a new feature	5	Bronze
No Mistakes Allowed	Streak through the entirety of a song in Quickplay or Career	20	Bronze
Above And Beyond	Complete a song with an average individual multiplier above 4x	10	Bronze
Score Big	Earn 500,000 points in a single song as a solo act	5	Bronze
Score Bigger	Earn 1,000,000 points in a single song as a solo act or band	10	Bronze
Score Biggest	Earn 3,000,000 points in a single song as a band	30	Silver
Our Powers Combined	As a 4 player standard band, all 4 players activate Star Power simultaneously	10	Bronze
Box Set	Complete 100 songs in Quickplay	20	Bronze
Juke Box	Complete 300 songs in Quickplay	30	Silver
Chanteuse	5 Star 'Ex-Girlfriend', 'Send A Little Love Token' and 'Only Happy When It Rains' as a Vocalist	10	Bronze
Star Cluster	Collect 808 Stars in Career	100	Gold
Special Guest	Complete a song with your Xbox 360 Avatar	10	Bronze

NAME	GOAL/REQUIREMENT	POINT VALUE	TROPHY VALUE
Representative	Complete a sponsor gig challenge at Diamond level	5	Bronze

SECRET ACHIEVEMENTS

NAME	GOAL/REQUIREMENT	POINT VALUE	TROPHY VALUE
Over 9000!	Went super	5	Bronze
Open Minded	Gave every one a chance	50	Silver
Starstruck	Had a brush with celebrity	20	Bronze
Did You Finish Like We Did?	Came alive	5	Bronze
The Traditional	Beat the game	50	Silver

GUITAR HERO: AEROSMITH

XBOX 360/PS3

Select Cheats from the Options menu and enter the following. To do this, strum the guitar with the given buttons held. For example, if it says Yellow + Orange, hold Yellow and Orange as you strum. Air Guitar, Precision Mode, and Performance Mode can be toggled on and off from the Cheats menu. You can also change between five different levels of Hyperspeed at this menu.

ALL SONGS

Red + Yellow, Green + Red, Green + Red, Red + Yellow, Red + Yellow, Green + Red, Red + Yellow, Red + Yellow, Green + Red, Green + Red, Red + Yellow, Red + Yellow, Green + Red, Red + Yellow, Red + Blue. This code does not unlock Pandora's Box.

AIR GUITAR

Red + Yellow, Green + Red, Red + Yellow, Red + Yellow, Red + Blue, Red + Blue, Red + Blue, Red + Blue, Red + Blue, Yellow + Blue, Yellow + Blue, Yellow + Orange

HYPERSPEED

Yellow + Orange, Yellow + Orange, Yellow + Orange, Yellow + Orange, Yellow + Orange, Red + Yellow, Red + Yellow, Red + Yellow, Red + Yellow, Red + Blue, Red + Blue, Red + Blue, Red + Blue, Red + Blue, Yellow + Blue, Yellow + Orange, Yellow + Orange.

NO FAIL

Select Cheats from the Options. Choose Enter Cheat and enter Green + Red, Blue, Green + Red, Green + Yellow, Blue, Green + Yellow, Red + Yellow, Orange, Red + Yellow, Green + Yellow, Yellow, Green + Yellow, Green + Red.

PERFORMANCE MODE

Green + Red, Green + Red, Red + Orange, Red + Blue, Green + Red, Green + Red, Red + Orange, Red + Blue.

PRECISION MODE

Red + Yellow, Red + Blue, Red + Blue, Red + Yellow, Red + Yellow, Yellow + Blue, Yellow + Blue, Yellow + Blue, Red + Blue, Red + Yellow, Red + Blue, Red + Blue, Red + Yellow, Red + Yellow, Yellow + Blue, Yellow + Blue, Yellow + Blue, Red + Blue.

Once entered, the cheats must be activated in the Cheats menu.

GUITAR HERO: METALLICA

XBOX 360/PS3/WII

METALLICA COSTUMES

Select Cheats from Settings and enter Green, Red, Yellow, Blue, Blue, Yellow, Red, Green.

HYPERSPEED

Select Cheats from Settings and enter Green, Blue, Red, Yellow, Yellow, Red, Green, Green.

PERFORMANCE MODE

Select Cheats from Settings and enter Yellow, Yellow, Blue, Red, Blue, Green, Red, Red.

INVISIBLE ROCKER

Select Cheats from Settings and enter Green, Red, Yellow (x3), Blue, Blue, Green.

AIR INSTRUMENTS

Select Cheats from Settings and enter Red, Red, Blue, Yellow, Green (x3), Yellow.

ALWAYS DRUM FILL

Select Cheats from Settings and enter Red (x3), Blue, Blue, Green, Green, Yellow.

AUTO KICK

Select Cheats from Settings and enter Yellow, Green, Red, Blue (x4), Red. With this cheat activated, the bass pedal is automatically hit.

ALWAYS SLIDE

Select Cheats from Settings and enter Green, Green, Red, Red, Yellow, Red, Yellow, Blue. All Guitar Notes Become Touch Pad Sliding Notes.

BLACK HIGHWAY

Select Cheats from Settings and enter Yellow, Red, Green, Red, Green, Red, Red, Blue.

FLAME COLOR

Select Cheats from Settings and enter Green, Red, Green, Blue, Red, Red, Yellow, Blue.

GEM COLOR

Select Cheats from Settings and enter Blue, Red, Red, Green, Red, Green, Red, Yellow.

STAR COLOR

Select Cheats from Settings and enter Press Red, Red, Yellow, Red, Blue, Red, Red, Blue.

ADDITIONAL LINE 6 TONES

Select Cheats from Settings and enter Green, Red, Yellow, Blue, Red, Yellow, Blue, Green.

VOCAL FIREBALL

Select Cheats from Settings and enter Red, Green, Green, Yellow, Blue, Green, Yellow, Green.

GUITAR HERO: SMASH HITS

NINENTDO WII

ALWAYS DRUM FILL

Select Cheats from the Options menu and enter Green, Green, Red, Red, Blue, Blue, Yellow, Yellow.

ALWAYS SLIDE

Select Cheats from the Options menu and enter Blue, Yellow, Red, Green, Blue, Green, Green, Yellow.

AIR INSTRUMENTS

Select Cheats from the Options menu and enter Yellow, Red, Blue, Green, Yellow, Red, Red, Red.

INVISIBLE ROCKER

Select Cheats from the Options menu and enter Blue, Red, Red, Red, Red, Yellow, Blue, Green.

PERFORMANCE MODE

Select Cheats from the Options menu and enter Blue, Red, Yellow, Yellow, Red, Red, Yellow, Yellow.

HYPERSPEED

Select Cheats from the Options menu and enter Red, Green, Blue, Yellow, Green, Yellow, Red, Red. This unlocks the HyperGuitar, HyperBass, and HyperDrums cheats.

AUTO KICK

Select Cheats from the Options menu and enter Blue, Green, Red, Yellow, Red, Yellow, Red, Yellow.

GEM COLOR

Select Cheats from the Options menu and enter Red, Red, Red, Blue, Blue, Blue, Yellow, Green.

FLAME COLOR

Select Cheats from the Options menu and enter Yellow, Blue, Red, Green, Yellow, Red, Green, Blue.

STAR COLOR

Select Cheats from the Options menu and enter Green, Red, Green, Yellow, Green, Blue, Yellow, Red.

VOCAL FIREBALL

Select Cheats from the Options menu and enter Green, Blue, Red, Red, Yellow, Yellow, Blue, Blue.

XBOX 360/PS3

ALWAYS DRUM FILL

Select Cheats from the Options menu and enter Green, Green, Red, Red, Blue, Blue, Yellow, Yellow.

ALWAYS SLIDE

Select Cheats from the Options menu and enter Blue, Yellow, Red, Green, Blue, Green, Green, Yellow.

AIR INSTRUMENTS

Select Cheats from the Options menu and enter Yellow, Red, Blue, Green, Yellow, Red, Red, Red.

INVISIBLE ROCKER

Select Cheats from the Options menu and enter Blue, Red, Red, Red, Red, Yellow, Blue, Green.

PERFORMANCE MODE

Select Cheats from the Options menu and enter Blue, Red, Yellow, Yellow, Red, Red, Yellow, Yellow.

HYPERSPEED

Select Cheats from the Options menu and enter Red, Green, Blue, Yellow, Green, Yellow, Red, Red. This unlocks the HyperGuitar, HyperBass, and HyperDrums cheats.

AUTO KICK

Select Cheats from the Options menu and enter Blue, Green, Red, Yellow, Red, Yellow, Red, Yellow.

GEM COLOR

Select Cheats from the Options menu and enter Red, Red, Red, Blue, Blue, Blue, Yellow, Green.

FLAME COLOR

Select Cheats from the Options menu and enter Yellow, Blue, Red, Green, Yellow, Red, Green, Blue.

STAR COLOR

Select Cheats from the Options menu and enter Green, Red, Green, Yellow, Green, Blue, Yellow, Red.

VOCAL FIREBALL

Select Cheats from the Options menu and enter Green, Blue, Red, Red, Yellow, Yellow, Blue, Blue.

EXTRA LINE 6 TONES

Select Cheats from the Options menu and enter Green, Red, Yellow, Blue, Red, Yellow, Blue, Green.

GUITAR HERO: VAN HALEN

ALWAYS DRUM FILL

Select Input Cheats from the Options menu and enter Red, Red, Red, Blue, Blue, Green, Green, Yellow.

ALWAYS SLIDE

Select Input Cheats from the Options menu and enter Green, Green, Red, Red, Yellow, Red, Yellow, Blue.

AUTO KICK

Select Input Cheats from the Options menu and enter Yellow, Green, Red, Blue, Blue, Blue, Blue, Red.

HYPERSPEED

Select Input Cheats from the Options menu and enter Green, Blue, Red, Yellow, Yellow, Red, Green, Green. This allows you to enable Hyperguitar, Hyperbass, and Hyperdrums.

PERFORMANCE MODE

Select Input Cheats from the Options menu and enter Yellow, Yellow, Blue, Red, Blue, Green, Red, Red.

AIR INSTRUMENTS

Select Input Cheats from the Options menu and enter Red, Red, Blue, Yellow, Green, Green, Green, Yellow.

INVISIBLE ROCKER

Select Input Cheats from the Options menu and enter Green, Red, Yellow, Yellow, Yellow, Blue, Blue, Green.

BLACK HIGHWAY

Select Input Cheats from the Options menu and enter Yellow, Red, Green, Red, Green, Red, Red, Blue.

FLAME COLOR

Select Input Cheats from the Options menu and enter Green, Red, Green, Blue, Red, Red, Yellow, Blue.

GEM COLOR

Select Input Cheats from the Options menu and enter Blue, Red, Red, Green, Red, Green, Red, Yellow.

STAR COLOR

Select Input Cheats from the Options menu and enter Red, Red, Yellow, Red, Blue, Red, Red, Blue.

VOCAL FIREBALL

Select Input Cheats from the Options menu and enter Red, Green, Green, Yellow, Blue, Green, Yellow, Green.

EXTRA LINE 6 TONES

Select Input Cheats from the Options menu and enter Green, Red, Yellow, Blue, Red, Yellow, Blue, Green.

GUITAR HERO: WARRIORS OF ROCK

Select Extras from Options to toggle the following on and off. Some cheats will disable Achievements.

ALL CHARACTERS

Select Cheats from the Options menu and enter Blue, Green, Green, Red, Green, Red, Yellow, Blue.

ALL VENUES

Select Cheats from the Options menu and enter Red, Blue, Blue, Red, Red, Blue, Blue, Red.

ALWAYS SLIDE

Select Cheats from the Options menu and enter Blue, Green, Green, Red, Red, Yellow, Blue, Yellow.

ALL HOPOS

Select Cheats from the Options menu and enter Green (x3), Blue, Green (x3), Yellow. Most notes become hammer-ons or pull-offs.

INVISIBLE ROCKER

Select Cheats from the Options menu and enter Green, Green, Red, Yellow (x3), Blue, Blue.

AIR INSTRUMENTS

Select Cheats from the Options menu and enter Yellow, Red, Red, Blue, Yellow, Green (x3).

FOCUS MODE

Select Cheats from the Options menu and enter Green, Yellow, Green, Red, Green, Yellow, Blue, Green. This removes the busy background.

HUD FREE MODE

Select Cheats from the Options menu and enter Green, Green, Red, Green, Green, Yellow, Green, Green.

PERFORMANCE MODE

Select Cheats from the Options menu and enter Red, Yellow, Yellow, Blue, Red, Blue, Green, Red.

COLOR SHUFFLE

Select Cheats from the Options menu and enter Blue, Green, Blue, Red, Yellow, Green, Red, Yellow.

MIRROR GEMS

Select Cheats from the Options menu and enter Blue, Blue, Red, Blue, Green, Green, Red, Green.

RANDOM GEMS

Select Cheats from the Options menu and enter Green, Green, Red, Red, Yellow, Red, Yellow, Blue.

ACHIEVEMENTS & TROPHIES

NAME	GOAL/REQUIREMENT	POINT VALUE	TROPHY VALUE
Tracker of Deeds	Follow any five Hero Feed items (Xbox LIVE only)	10	Bronze
Anthemic Archivist	Expand your song library to at least 115 songs of any type. Be creative!	10	Bronze
Stellar Centurion	Deploy Star Power a total of 100 times (Quest)	20	Bronze
Gem Collector	Hit a cumulative total of 75,000 notes (Quest)	20	Bronze
Gem Hoarder	Hit a cumulative total of 150,000 notes (Quest)	30	Silver

NAME	GOAL/REQUIREMENT	POINT VALUE	TROPHY VALUE
Champion of Challenges	Target another person's score on any Challenge and earn a higher grade than they did (Local QP+)	20	Bronze
Self Improver	Target your own score on a Challenge and earn a higher grade than you did previously (Local QP+)	10	Bronze
Ultimate Answerer	Earn all Stars from any one song (excluding the Power Challenge) (QP+)	30	Silver
Scions of Excess	Earn an 11x Band multiplier with any 4-player Band configuration (QP+)	20	Bronze
Player of the Ear Worm	Play any one non-GH(tm)Tracks song 10 or more times (QP+, Quest, Competitive)	10	Bronze
Patron of the Arts	5-Star any GH(tm)Tracks song containing at least 200 notes (QP+)	10	Bronze
Apostates of Orthodoxy	5-Star any song as a 4-player Non-Standard Band, with all players on Medium or higher (QP+)	10	Bronze
Bearers of the Standard	5-Star any song as a 4-player Standard Band, with all players on Medium or higher (QP+)	10	Bronze
Mythical Millionaire	Earn 1,000,000 points or more in a single play of a song in a Power Challenge (QP+)	20	Bronze
Manager of Fate	Create and play a custom playlist of at least 5 songs, and earn 5 Stars on 5 of the songs (QP+)	10	Bronze
Mocker of Fate	Create and play a 5-song random playlist, earning 5 Stars on each song (QP+)	10	Bronze
Nauseous Numerologist	Beat any song with a final score of 133,337 (QP+, Competitive)	10	Bronze
Mathematic Sharpshooters	Beat any song with a final score ending in 000 as a Band (QP+)	10	Bronze
Gold Master	As a single player, earn Gold or higher on three or more Challenges on a single play of a song (QP+)	20	Bronze
Diamond Master	As a single player, earn Diamond on two or more Challenges on a single play of a song (QP+)	20	Silver
Quick Learner	Full-Combo any tutorial exercise (no missed notes or overstrums)	10	Bronze
The Siren	Recruit Warrior Judy (Quest)	20	Bronze
The Trickster	Unleash Warrior Johnny (Quest)	20	Bronze
The Vigil	Charm Warrior Casey (Quest)	20	Bronze
The Brute	Release Warrior Lars (Quest)	20	Bronze
The Eternal	Awaken Warrior Axel (Quest)	20	Bronze
The Dynamo	Liberate Warrior Echo (Quest)	20	Bronze
Divine Liberator	Free the Demigod of Rock (Quest)	30	Silver
Axe Claimer	Regain the Legendary Guitar (Quest)	30	Silver
Savior of Rock	Defeat the scourge of Rock (Quest)	50	Silver
Amateur Astrologer	Earn a total of 100 Stars (QP+)	10	Bronze
Accomplished Astrologer	Earn a total of 500 Stars (QP+)	10	Bronze
Adept Astrologer	Earn a total of 1000 Stars (QP+)	40	Silver

NAME	GOAL/REQUIREMENT	POINT VALUE	TROPHY VALUE
Pseudo Perfectionist	Dominate any 2 chapters of Quest (Earn all the Power Stars from any 2 chapters of Quest)	20	Bronze
Ace Astrologer	Earn a total of 2000 Stars (QP+)	60	Bronze
Partial Perfectionist	Dominate any 4 chapters of Quest (Earn all the Power Stars from any 4 chapters of Quest)	20	Bronze
Perfect Perfectionist	Earn all the Power Stars from all character chapters (Quest)	60	Silver
Motivated Improviser	Play 100 notes in a single GH(tm)Jam session	10	Bronze
String Twins	Complete a song with only a Guitarist and Bassist, both earning the same score (QP+)	30	Silver
Altered Virtuoso	Earn 40 Power Stars on a single song (Quest)	20	Bronze
Poor Boys	Beat Bohemian Rhapsody as a band with all on Medium or higher, and at least 2 vocalists (QP+)	10	Bronze
The Meek	Beat 2112 Part 4 as a Standard band with 3 or more members, all on Medium or higher difficulty (QP+)	10	Bronze
Giant Slayer	Beat Holy Wars... The Punishment Due as a solo Bassist on Hard or higher difficulty (QP+)	10	Silver
Chosen One	Beat Fury of the Storm as a solo Drummer on Hard or higher difficulty (QP+)	20	Silver
Hand Mutilator	Beat Black Widow of La Porte as a solo Expert Guitarist (QP+, no Powers)	30	Silver
The Recluse	Invoke Warrior Austin (Quest)	20	Bronze
The Exalted	Summon Warrior Pandora (Quest)	20	Bronze
Lucifer's Accountant	Beat any song with a final score which is evenly divisible by 6 (QP+)	10	Bronze
Gold Standard	As a Standard Band, earn Gold or higher on 2 Band Challenges in a single play of a song (QP+)	20	Bronze
Seasoned Competitor	Play Pro Faceoff, Momentum, Momentum+, Streakers, Do or Die, and Perfectionist at least once each	20	Silver

NINTENDO WII/PS3

Select Extras from the Options menu to toggle the following on and off.

ALL CHARACTERS

Select Cheats from the Options menu and enter Blue, Green, Green, Red, Green, Red, Yellow, Blue.

ALL VENUES

Select Cheats from the Options menu and enter Red, Blue, Blue, Red, Red, Blue, Blue, Red.

ALWAYS SLIDE

Select Cheats from the Options menu and enter Blue, Green, Green, Red, Red, Yellow, Blue, Yellow.

ALL HOPOS

Select Cheats from the Options menu and enter Green (x3), Blue, Green (x3), Yellow. Most notes become hammer-ons or pull-offs.

INVISIBLE ROCKER

Select Cheats from the Options menu and enter Green, Green, Red, Yellow (x3), Blue, Blue.

AIR INSTRUMENTS

Select Cheats from the Options menu and enter Yellow, Red, Red, Blue, Yellow, Green (x3).

FOCUS MODE

Select Cheats from the Options menu and enter Green, Yellow, Green, Red, Green, Yellow, Blue, Green. This removes the busy background.

NO HUD MODE

Select Cheats from the Options menu and enter Green, Green, Red, Green, Green, Yellow, Green, Green.

PERFORMANCE MODE

Select Cheats from the Options menu and enter Red, Yellow, Yellow, Blue, Red, Blue, Green, Red.

COLOR SHUFFLE

Select Cheats from the Options menu and enter Blue, Green, Blue, Red, Yellow, Green, Red, Yellow.

MIRROR GEMS

Select Cheats from the Options menu and enter Blue, Blue, Red, Blue, Green, Green, Red, Green.

RANDOM GEMS

Select Cheats from the Options menu and enter Green, Green, Red, Red, Yellow, Red, Yellow, Blue.

GUITAR HERO WORLD TOUR

NINTENDO WII/PS3/XBOX 360

The following cheats can be toggled on and off at the Cheats menu.

QUICKPLAY SONGS

Select Cheats from the Options menu, choose Enter New Cheat and press Blue, Blue, Red, Green, Green, Blue, Blue, Yellow.

ALWAYS SLIDE

Select Cheats from the Options menu, choose Enter New Cheat and press Green, Green, Red, Red, Yellow, Red, Yellow, Blue.

AT&T BALLPARK

Select Cheats from the Options menu, choose Enter New Cheat and press Yellow, Green, Red, Red, Green, Blue, Red, Yellow.

AUTO KICK

Select Cheats from the Options menu, choose Enter New Cheat and press Yellow, Green, Red, Blue (x4), Red.

EXTRA LINE 6 TONES

Select Cheats from the Options menu, choose Enter New Cheat and press Green, Red, Yellow, Blue, Red, Yellow, Blue, Green.

FLAME COLOR

Select Cheats from the Options menu, choose Enter New Cheat and press Green, Red, Green, Blue, Red, Red, Yellow, Blue.

GEM COLOR

Select Cheats from the Options menu, choose Enter New Cheat and press Blue, Red, Red, Green, Red, Green, Red, Yellow.

STAR COLOR

Select Cheats from the Options menu, choose Enter New Cheat and press Red, Red, Yellow, Red, Blue, Red, Red, Blue.

AIR INSTRUMENTS

Select Cheats from the Options menu, choose Enter New Cheat and press Red, Red, Blue, Yellow, Green (x3), Yellow.

HALO: COMBAT EVOLVED ANNIVERSARY

ACHIEVEMENTS

NAME	GOAL/REQUIREMENT	POINT VALUE
The Silent Cartographer	Complete the level "The Silent Cartographer" on any difficulty.	25
Assault on the Control Room	Complete the level "Assault on the Control Room" on any difficulty.	25
Pillar of Autumn	Complete the level "Pillar of Autumn" on any difficulty.	25
Halo	Complete the level "Halo" on any difficulty.	25
Truth and Reconciliation	Complete the level "Truth and Reconciliation" on any difficulty.	25
343 Guilty Spark	Complete the level "343 Guilty Spark" on any difficulty.	25
The Library	Complete the level "The Library" on any difficulty.	25
Two Betrayals	Complete the level "Two Betrayals" on any difficulty.	25
Keyes	Complete the level "Keyes" on any difficulty.	25
The Maw	Complete the level "The Maw" on any difficulty.	25
Tsantsa	Complete any level with at least three skulls active on Heroic difficulty or higher.	50
What have we here?	Read a terminal.	10
Heavy Reading	Read half the terminals hidden throughout the campaign.	25
Dear Diary…	Read all of the terminals hidden throughout the campaign.	50
Looks like the Oddball	Find your first campaign skull.	10
Skulls Taken!	Locate half of the skulls hidden throughout the campaign.	25
Headhunter	Locate all the skulls hidden throughout the campaign.	50
Birth of a Spartan	Complete every level of the game on Normal difficulty.	10
Believe in a Hero	Complete every level of the game on Heroic difficulty.	20
Living Legend	Complete every level of the game on Legendary difficulty.	50
Standard Operating Brocedure	Complete any level on Normal difficulty cooperatively.	10
Bro7ershield	Complete any level on Heroic difficulty cooperatively.	20
Bro Hammer	Complete any level on Legendary difficulty cooperatively.	50
He's Unstoppable!	Complete any level on Heroic difficulty or higher without taking health damage.	20
Overshields are for Sissies	Complete the level "Pillar of Autumn" on Legendary without picking up an Overshield.	10
Walk it Off	Complete the level "Pillar of Autumn" on Legendary without picking up a health kit.	25
No-Fly Zone	Destroy three of the four Banshees on "Halo" on any difficulty during a single play-through.	10
How Pedestrian	Complete the level "Halo" on any difficulty without entering a vehicle.	25
Close Quarters Combat	Complete the level "Truth and Reconciliation" with at least four rounds left in your Sniper Rifle.	25
I'll Be Taking That!	Pilot a Banshee on the level "Assault on the Control Room."	25
This One's for Jenkins!	Kill 50 Flood Combat Forms on the level "343 Guilty Spark" on Heroic difficulty or higher.	10
That Just Happened	Complete the level "The Library" on Heroic difficulty or higher without dying.	10

NAME	GOAL/REQUIREMENT	POINT VALUE
Speed Reader	Complete the level "The Library" on Legendary difficulty in 30 minutes or less.	25
Look Out for the Little Guys	Complete the level "Two Betrayals" on Heroic difficulty or higher without killing any Grunts.	10
Leave It Where It Lay	Complete the level "Two Betrayals" on Legendary difficulty without picking up a new weapon.	25
Popcorn.gif	Kill 100 Flood Infection Forms on the level "Keyes" on Heroic difficulty or above.	25
All According to Plan…	Kill all the enemies in the first encounter of "Truth and Reconciliation" without being detected.	10
Beachhead	Storm the beach of "The Silent Cartographer" with no marine casualties on Heroic or Legendary.	10
Grenadier	Escape the map room in "The Silent Cartographer" without firing a shot on Heroic or Legendary.	25
Wraith Hunter	Destroy four Wraith tanks in "Assault on the Control Room" with the Scorpion tank, in a single play.	10
Breaking Quarantine	Escape the Forerunner facility on the level "343 Guilty Spark" in 21 minutes or less.	25
Tying Up Loose Ends	Kill every Elite on the level "Keyes" on Heroic difficulty or above.	10
This Side Up	Complete the Warthog ride on the level "The Maw" without being forcibly ejected from your vehicle.	10
Never Tell Me the Odds	Escape "The Maw" on Legendary with at least a minute left on the count down.	25

HALO 3

XBOX 360

TOGGLE HIDE WEAPON

During a local game, hold Left Bumper + Right Bumper + Left Stick + A + Down.

TOGGLE SHOW COORDINATES

During a local game, hold Left Bumper + Right Bumper + Left Stick + A + Up.

TOGGLE BETWEEN PAN-CAM AND NORMAL

During a local game, hold Left Stick + Right Stick and press Left when Show Coordinates is active.

HALO REACH

XBOX 360

AVATAR AWARDS

AWARD	EARNED BY
Carter's Helmet	Clear a Campaign mission on Legendary without dying—Save and quit toward the end of a mission. Resume the game and finish mission without dying to earn this award easily.
Emile's Helmet	Earn a Bulltrue medal in either multiplayer or Firefight Matchmaking
Jorge's Helmet	Earn a Killtacular in multiplayer Matchmaking
Jun's Helmet	Kill 100 enemies in a row without dying in either the Campaign or Firefight
Kat's Helmet	Avenge teammate's death in multiplayer Matchmaking

CHEATS, ACHIEVEMENTS, AND TROPHIES

H

ACHIEVEMENTS

NAME	GOAL/REQUIREMENT	POINT VALUE
The Soldier We Need You To Be	Completed the Campaign on Normal difficulty.	25
Folks Need Heroes…	Completed the Campaign on Heroic difficulty.	50
Gods Must Be Strong	Completed the Campaign on Legendary difficulty.	125
A Monument To All Your Sins	Completed every mission in Halo: Reach alone, on Legendary.	150
We're Just Getting Started	Completed the 2nd mission on Normal or harder.	10
Protocol Dictates Action	Completed the 3rd mission on Normal or harder.	10
I Need A Weapon	Completed the 4th mission on Normal or harder.	10
To War	Completed the 5th mission on Normal or harder.	10
You Flew Pretty Good	Completed the 6th mission on Normal or harder.	10
Into The Howling Dark	Completed the 7th mission on Normal or harder.	10
Dust And Echoes	Completed the 8th mission on Normal or harder.	10
This Is Not Your Grave	Completed the 9th mission on Normal or harder.	10
Send Me Out…With A Bang	Completed the 10th mission on Normal or harder.	10
They've Always Been Faster	Cleared the 2nd mission without setting foot in a drivable vehicle.	25
Two Corpses In One Grave	Killed 2 vehicles at once with the Target Locator in the 3rd mission.	25
Banshees, Fast And Low	Hijacked a Banshee during the Reach Campaign.	25
Your Heresy Will Stay Your Feet	Killed the Elite Zealot before he escaped during the 5th mission.	25
If They Came To Hear Me Beg	Performed an Assassination against an Elite to survive a fall that would've been fatal.	25
Wake Up Buttercup	Destroyed the Corvette's engines & escort in under 3 minutes in the 6th mission on Heroic or harder.	25
Tank Beats Everything	Finished the 9th mission on Legendary with the Scorpion intact.	25
Lucky Me	Earned a Triple Kill while Jetpacking in Campaign, Firefight or Matchmaking.	25
KEEP IT CLEAN	Killed 7 Moa during the 2nd mission of the Campaign.	5
I Didn't Train To Be A Pilot	Killed 3 of the anti-aircraft batteries during the 8th mission.	10
Doctor, Doctor	Used a Health Pack to replenish life after taking body damage.	5
That's A Knife	Performed an Assassination on an enemy.	10
I See You Favour A .45	Killed 10 enemies in a Firefight or Campaign session with the M6G pistol.	10
An Elegant Weapon	Killed 10 enemies in a Firefight or Campaign session with the DMR.	10
Swap Meet	Traded weapons with an AI ally in Campaign.	10
A Spoonful Of Blamite	Killed 10 enemies in Firefight or Campaign with a supercombine explosion.	10
Be My Wingman Anytime	Let a teammate spawn on you 5 times in an Invasion Matchmaking game.	5
Yes, Sensei	Earned a First Strike Medal in a Matchmaking game.	10
Skunked	Won a game of Invasion in the 1st phase.	10
What's A Killing Spree?	Earned a Killing Spree in multiplayer Matchmaking.	5
Crowd Control	Earned a Killionaire medal in Firefight.	10
Knife To A Gun Fight	As an Elite, killed 5 Spartan players in Matchmaking.	5
Score Attack	Scored 15,000 points in Score Attack Firefight Matchmaking.	10
Firestarter	Scored 50,000 points in a Firefight game.	10
Blaze Of Glory	Scored 200,000 points in a Firefight game.	25

NAME	GOAL/REQUIREMENT	POINT VALUE
Heat In The Pipe	Scored 1,000,000 points in a Firefight game.	75
Game, Set, Match	Completed a Firefight set on Legendary without dying.	25
Make It Rain	Purchased an item from the Armory that required the rank of Lt. Colonel.	10
The Start Of Something	Reached the rank of Corporal in the UNSC.	15
An Honor Serving	Reached the rank of Captain in the UNSC.	25
A Storage Solution	Used the File Browser to upload a file to your File Share.	5
A New Challenger	Completed all of the Daily Challenges in a given day.	10
Make It Drizzle	Purchased an item from the Armory.	10
Cool File, Bro	Recommended a file to someone.	5
Lemme Upgrade Ya	Advanced a Commendation to a Silver state.	10
One Down, 51 To Go	Completed a Weekly Challenge.	10

HARRY POTTER AND THE DEATHLY HALLOWS: PART 1

PLAYSTATION 3

SUPER STRENGTH POTIONS

Select Unlock Menu from the Options and enter ✖, Left, Right, ✖, R2, R1.

ELITE CHALLENGES

Select Unlock Menu from the Options and enter ●, Up, ✖, L2, R2, ✖.

AUGMENTED REALITY CHEAT FROM BOX (PROTEGO TOTALUM)

Select Unlock Menu from the Options and enter ●, ●, Up, Left, R2, and Right

XBOX 360

SUPER STRENGTH POTIONS

Select Unlock Menu from the Options and enter X, Left, Right, A, Right Trigger, Right Bumper.

ELITE CHALLENGES

Select Unlock Menu from the Options and enter Y, Up, X, Left Trigger, Right Trigger, A.

AUGMENTED REALITY CHEAT FROM BOX (PROTEGO TOTALUM)

Select Unlock Menu from the Options and enter Y, B, Up, Left, Right Trigger, Right.

HARRY POTTER AND THE HALF-BLOOD PRINCE

NINTENDO WII

BONUS TWO-PLAYER DUELING ARENA CASTLE GATES

At the Rewards menu, press Right, Right, Down, Down, Left, Right, Left, Right, Left, Right, +.

CHEATS, ACHIEVEMENTS, AND TROPHIES

H

HAUNT

AVATAR AWARDS

AVATAR	EARNED BY
Haunt Hoodie	Unlock the Full Game.
Haunt Jeans	Defeat one of each type of ghost.
Charger Ghost Mask	Successfully avoid 5 Charger ghost attacks.

HEAD SOCCER

CAMEROON TEAM

In Arcade mode, defeat 12 characters. Alternatively, you can purchase it for 100,000 points.

NIGERIA TEAM

Win 30 times in a tournament. Alternatively, you can purchase it for 200,000 points.

HELLBOY: THE SCIENCE OF EVIL

REFILL HEALTH

During a game, press Right, Down, Left, ●.

REFILL RAGE

During a game, press Left, Down, Right, ●.

REFILL AMMO

During a game, press Left, Down, Right, ●.

THE HIP HOP DANCE EXPERIENCE

ACHIEVEMENTS

NAME	GOAL/REQUIREMENT	POINT VALUE
Welcome!	Play The Hip Hop Dance Experience	10
First Steps	Play 1 song on any difficulty	10
Keep It Rockin'	Play 50 songs in total on any difficulty	40
Rock It Harder!	Play 200 songs in total on any difficulty	60
Risin' Up!	Play 1 song on Go Hard	20
Paid Your Dues	Earn SWAG! On Newbie difficulty in Dance Party	10
Mad Mack Skills	Earn SWAG! On Mack Skills difficulty in Dance Party	20
Goin' All Out	Earn SWAG! On Go Hard difficulty in Dance Party	20
Silver Triple A	Earn SWAG! On 3 Mack Skills songs consecutively in Dance Party	30
Gold Triple A	Earn SWAG! On 3 Go Hard songs conse3cutively in Dance Party	50
Find Your Turf	Dance at all 6 venues in Dance Party	20
Wear Out The Record	Dance all 40 songs	30
Tough Guy	Challenge Dance Marathon for the first time	10

NAME	GOAL/REQUIREMENT	POINT VALUE
Tough Enough	Clear 100 dances in Dance Marathon	30
Stupid Tough	Clear 250 dances in Dance Marathon	60
I Work Out	Cumulatively burn 250 kcal or more in Dance Marathon	30
Sexy And Ya Know It	Cumulatively burn 500 kcal or more in Dance Marathon	60
Rewind! Rewind!	Play the same song 5 times on any difficulty	20
That's My Jam	Play the same song 20 times on any difficulty	40
It Takes Two	Play a song with another player for the first time	10
Meet My Homes	Encounter all reference dancers in single and multiplayer modes	20
Warp Speed Ahead!	Trigger Star Drive before the other player's Star Drive runs out in Dance Party or Dance Battle	10
Got The Swag	Both players earn SWAG! On the same song together in Dance Party	30
Hype Up The Crowd	Both players earn HYPE!! On a dance at the same time in Dance Party	10
B-Boy Stance	Both players strike the final pose together	20
Hype It Harder!	Earn 20 HYPE!! In 1 song	50
Get Schooled	Practice 1 dance in Power Skooling	10
Slow It Down	Activate Slow Tempo Mode in Power Skooling	10
Knowledge Me	Practice 5 songs in Power Skooling	20
You Know My Steez	Customize and save the player avatar for the first time in the Wardrobe	10
Original Flavor	Customize all of your avatar features and styles in the Wardrobe	20
Many Styles	Customize and save features or styles 20 times in the Wardrobe	30
Dress To Impress	Customize and save both male and female avatars in the Wardrobe	10
Look At Me Now	Successfully perform 10 final poses consecutively	50
Everybody In The House!	Watch the Credits to the end	10
Step Up!	Battle someone for the first time in Dance Battle!	10
Beat Down!	Win for the first time in Dance Battle!	10
Bring It!	Win 20 times in Dance Battle	40
Ain't No Stoppin' Me	Win 3 consecutive times in Dance Battle	20
What Handicap?	Win a Dance Battle on a higher difficulty level than your opponent	20

HISTORY LEGEND OF WAR: PATTON

XBOX 360/PS3

ACHIEVEMENTS & TROPHIES

NAME	GOAL/REQUIREMENT	POINT VALUE	TARGET VALUE
New recruit!	Tutorial completed	10	Bronze
First blood!	First mission completed (Campaign Mode)	10	Bronze
Specialist Infantry	First bazooka recruited (Campaign Mode)	10	Bronze
Retrained!	First upgrade made (Campaign Mode)	20	Bronze
Armored support	First tank recruited (Campaign Mode)	20	Bronze
Destroyer!	50 German units destroyed (Campaign Mode)	20	Bronze

NAME	GOAL/REQUIREMENT	POINT VALUE	TARGET VALUE
Battle Hardened Recruit	First operation completed (Campaign Mode)	30	Silver
Skilled warrior	Second operation completed (Campaign Mode)	40	Silver
Assassin!	15 German soldiers killed with knife (Campaign Mode)	40	Silver
Heroic	5 heroic victories achieved (Campaign Mode)	40	Silver
Their worst nightmare!	100 German units destroyed (Campaign Mode)	40	Silver
Air Support	First aircraft recruited (Campaign Mode)	40	Silver
Inspirational General	Max out any of Patton's Skills (Campaign Mode)	50	Gold
Full army!	Third Army completed (Campaign Mode)	60	Gold
Combat veteran	Third operation completed (Campaign Mode)	70	Gold
War Hero	200 German units destroyed (Campaign Mode)	80	Gold
Weapons Tech	All types of units unlocked (Campaign Mode)	80	Gold
When the war is over	Game completed (Campaign Mode)	100	—
Heroic Leader	10 heroic victories achieved (Campaign Mode)	120	Gold
Supreme commander	Fourth operation completed without casualties (Campaign Mode)	120	Gold
Victory!	Complete the game (Campaign Mode)	—	Gold
Legend of War	Complete all trophies	—	Platinum

HITMAN: ABSOLUTION

ACHIEVEMENTS & TROPHIES

NAME	GOAL/REQUIREMENT	POINT VALUE	TROPHY VALUE
Grand Master	You completed 100 challenges	150	Gold
Reach for the Stars	You completed 50 challenges	50	Silver
The Russian Hare	You performed 47 headshots using a sniper rifle	20	Bronze
A Taste for the Game	You completed 10 challenges	20	Bronze
Absolution	You completed Hitman: Absolution as a professional	50	Gold
Jack of All Trades	You collected all 20 play styles	30	Silver
It's All in the Wrist	You successfully performed a lethal throw	50	Bronze
Information is Power	You collected all evidence	30	Silver
Thumbs Up	You liked a contract	20	Silver
Damage Control	You contained a situation gone bad	20	Bronze
Set for Life	You earned 1 million contracts dollars	20	Silver
Self-improvement	You bought an upgrade for a weapon	20	Bronze
First Contract	You completed the Creating Contracts Tutorial	20	Bronze

NAME	GOAL/REQUIREMENT	POINT VALUE	TROPHY VALUE
Blood Money	You completed the Contract Basics Tutorial	20	Bronze
True Potential	You unlocked a technique	20	Bronze
Partners in Crime	You player a contract made by a friend	20	Silver
Competitive Spirit	You created a contract competition	20	Silver
Contender	You participated in a contract competition	20	Silver
One With the Shadows	You escaped the attention of an enemy	20	Silver
Silent Assassin	You achieved Silent Assassin	20	Silver
Inconspicuous	You remained undetected throughout a checkpoint	20	Bronze
Whoops	You made a kill look like an accident	20	Bronze
One of the Guys	You blended in and fooled someone	20	Silver
Rocksteady	You executed a point shooting with at least 3 kills	20	Bronze
Under Wraps	You hid a body	20	Bronze
Sandman	You subdued a person	20	Bronze
Top of Your Game	Collect all trophies	—	Platinum

SECRET ACHIEVEMENTS & TROPHIES

NAME	GOAL/REQUIREMENT	POINT VALUE	TROPHY VALUE
Heavy Burden	You infiltrated the mansion and assassinated Diana Burnwood	10	Bronze
Kingslayer	You fulfilled Birdie's contract and eliminated The King of Chinatown	10	Bronze
Chamber of Secrets	You located the hotel room number 899	10	Bronze
Catch a Ride	You boarded the train and escaped the Chicago PD	10	Bronze
Forepost	You assassinated Wade's men in Chinatown	10	Bronze
All Bark and no Bite	You assassinated Wade	10	Bronze
The Bartender Always Knows	You questioned the bartender	10	Bronze
Signature Weapons	You re-gained your signature Silverballers	10	Bronze
Like Stealing Candy From a Baby	You circumvented Lenny's crew and secured Lenny	10	Bronze
Not Worth It	You left Lenny in the desert	10	Bronze
Step Into the Light	You found your way through the mines	10	Bronze
A Heavy Blow	You assassinated the facility leaders	10	Bronze
Faith Can Move Mountains	You have defeated Sanchez with your bare hands	10	Bronze
The Killing Fields	You eliminated the Saints	10	Bronze
Jailbird	You infiltrated the courthouse and accessed the jail	10	Bronze
Hour of Reckoning	You caught up with Skurky	10	Bronze
True Form	You visited Tommy the Tailor and acquired a new suit and gloves	10	Bronze
Destroying Something Beautiful	You assassinated Dexter's assistant, Layla	10	Bronze
The Final Countdown	You assassinated Blake Dexter	10	Bronze
A Personal Contract	You eliminated Travis and fulfilled Diana's contract	50	Silver

HOLE IN THE WALL

XBOX 360

AVATAR AWARDS

AVATAR	EARNED BY
Spandex Top	Win China Show.
Spandex Trousers	Win Russia Show.
Blue Helmet	Win USA Show.

HOME RUN STARS

XBOX 360

AVATAR AWARDS

AWARD	REQUIREMENT
Home Run League Pants	Defeat Cyclone Williams in the Home Run League.
Home Run Stars League Hat	Defeat Lucky Lee in the Home Run League.
Home Run Stars League Shirt	Defeat Pistol Pete in the Home Run League.

HOMEFRONT

XBOX 360/PS3

ACHIEVEMENTS & TROPHIES

NAME	GOAL/REQUIREMENT	POINT VALUE	TROPHY VALUE
Why We Fight	Complete chapter 1 in the Single Player Campaign	10	Bronze
Freedom	Complete chapter 2 in the Single Player Campaign	10	Bronze
Fire Sale	Complete chapter 3 in the Single Player Campaign	10	Bronze
The Wall	Complete chapter 4 in the Single Player Campaign	10	Bronze
Heartland	Complete chapter 5 in the Single Player Campaign	10	Bronze
Overwatch	Complete chapter 6 in the Single Player Campaign	10	Bronze
Why We Fight - Guerrilla	Complete chapter 1 on the Hardest Difficulty in the Single Player Campaign	25	Bronze
Freedom - Guerrilla	Complete chapter 2 on the Hardest Difficulty in the Single Player Campaign	25	Bronze
Fire Sale - Guerrilla	Complete chapter 3 on the Hardest Difficulty in the Single Player Campaign	25	Bronze
The Wall - Guerrilla	Complete chapter 4 on the Hardest Difficulty in the Single Player Campaign	25	Bronze
Heartland - Guerrilla	Complete chapter 5 on the Hardest Difficulty in the Single Player Campaign	25	Bronze
Overwatch - Guerrilla	Complete chapter 6 on the Hardest Difficulty in the Single Player Campaign	25	Silver
Weapon Expert	Complete an expert challenge for any weapon in Xbox LIVE	25	Bronze
Drone Expert	Complete an expert challenge for any drone in Xbox LIVE	25	Bronze

NAME	GOAL/REQUIREMENT	POINT VALUE	TROPHY VALUE
Vehicle Expert	Complete an expert challenge for any vehicle in Xbox LIVE	25	Bronze
Expert Of War	Complete all challenges for weapons, drones, vehicles, and modes in Xbox LIVE	100	Gold
Over the Hill	Reach experience level 50 in Xbox LIVE	50	Silver
Squad Commander	Enter an Xbox LIVE Ranked match as the Party Leader of a 4-Player Minimum Party	20	Bronze
Medal of Honor	Win an Xbox LIVE Ranked match as the Party Leader of a Party	20	Bronze
Full Boat	Enter an Xbox LIVE Ranked match in a Party with 16 players	30	Silver
3-Star Threat	Become a 3-Star threat in a Battle Commander Xbox LIVE Ranked match	30	Silver
5-Star Threat	Become a 5-Star threat in a Battle Commander Xbox LIVE Ranked match	75	Gold
Iron Man - Why We Fight	Complete chapter 1 in the Single Player Campaign without dying or restarting a checkpoint	25	Bronze
Iron Man - Freedom	Complete chapter 2 in the Single Player Campaign without dying or restarting a checkpoint	25	Bronze
Iron Man - Fire Sale	Complete chapter 3 in the Single Player Campaign without dying or restarting a checkpoint	25	Bronze
Iron Man - The Wall	Complete chapter 4 in the Single Player Campaign without dying or restarting a checkpoint	25	Bronze
Iron Man - Heartland	Complete chapter 5 in the Single Player Campaign without dying or restarting a checkpoint	25	Bronze
Iron Man - Overwatch	Complete chapter 6 in the Single Player Campaign without dying or restarting a checkpoint	25	Silver
Archivist	Find 30 of 61 News Pickups in the Single Player Campaign	10	Bronze
Historian	Find all 61 News Pickups in the Single Player Campaign	30	Gold
Pistol Whipped	Kill 25 enemies with a pistol in Chapter 1: Why We Fight	10	Bronze
Give Him the Stick	Kill 25 enemies with melee attacks in Chapter 1: Why We Fight	10	Bronze
Welcome to Freedom	Talk at least once to each inhabitant of Oasis in Chapter 2: Freedom	10	Bronze
Good Use of Cover	Destroy the first sentry without taking any damage in Chapter 2: Freedom	10	Bronze
Mercy	Kill 5 enemies while they are on fire in Chapter 3: Fire Sale	10	Bronze
Let 'em Burn	Don't kill any of the enemies that are on fire in Chapter 3: Fire Sale	10	Bronze
Chronicler	Find the first of 61 news pickups	10	Bronze
Stairway to Heaven	From the front door of the church, make it to the crow's nest in 240 seconds in Chapter 5: Heartland	10	Bronze

NAME	GOAL/REQUIREMENT	POINT VALUE	TROPHY VALUE
Speed Demon	Hijack the tankers in less than 8 minutes in one life in Chapter 6: Overwatch	10	Bronze
Safer Skies	Destroy all the SAM trucks in the level in Chapter 6: Overwatch	10	Bronze

SECRET ACHIEVEMENTS & TROPHIES

NAME	GOAL/REQUIREMENT	POINT VALUE	TROPHY VALUE
Golden Gate	Complete chapter 7 in the Single Player Campaign	10	Silver
Golden Gate - Guerrilla	Complete chapter 7 on the Hardest Difficulty in the Single Player Campaign	25	Silver
Iron Man - Golden Gate	Complete chapter 7 in the Single Player Campaign without dying or restarting a checkpoint	25	Silver
David Rejected	Complete the street section without Goliath taking any damage in Chapter 4: The Wall	10	Bronze
Fatal and Tragic	Jump off the Golden Gate Bridge in Chapter 7: Golden Gate	10	Bronze
Wilhelm's Nightmare	Knock 10 enemies off of the scaffolding during the helicopter fly-in in Chapter 7: Golden Gate	10	Bronze
Soft Targets	Destroy all vehicles using the UAV in Chapter 7: Golden Gate	10	Bronze

HOT BRAIN

PSP

119.99 TEMPERATURE IN ALL 5 CATEGORIES

Select New Game and enter Cheat.

ICE AGE 2: THE MELTDOWN

NINTENDO WII

INFINITE PEBBLES

Pause the game and press Down, Down, Left, Up, Up, Right, Up, Down.

INFINITE ENERGY

Pause the game and press Down, Left, Right, Down, Down, Right, Left, Down.

INFINITE HEALTH

Pause the game and press Up, Right, Down, Up, Left, Down, Right, Left.

ILOMILO

XBOX 360

ILOMILO SHUFFLE

At the main menu, press Left Trigger, Right Trigger, Left Bumper, Right Bumper.

AVATAR AWARDS

AWARD	EARNED BY
T-Shirt	Complete 3 levels.
Ilo And Milo	Collect enough memory fragments to unlock a full memory.

INDIANA JONES AND THE STAFF OF KINGS

NINTENDO WII

FATE OF ATLANTIS GAME

At the Extras menu, hold Z and press A, Up, Up, B, Down, Down, Left, Right, Left, B.

INFINITE SPACE

NINTENDO 3DS

NEW GAME+ & EXTRA MODE

Complete the game. New Game+ unlocks additional blue prints, while Extra Mode is another game mode with limited resources.

INFINITY BLADE

MOBILE

NEGATIVE BLOODLINE

After starting Bloodline 3, lose to anyone except the God King. Restart from Bloodline 1 to be taken to the tutorial. Lose to the Dark Knight by tapping the shield instead of holding. After you die, select Save and Restart Castle. This takes you to Bloodlines -1 with Dark Mech gear equipped. If you have enough money, this is a good time to purchase some great equipment. When you return to Bloodline 1, you keep anything in your inventory but the Dark gear is gone.

NEW GAME+

After unlocking the Infinity Blade, defeat each monster behind the three doors at the bottom of the castle followed by the final two high-level enemies. Select New Game+ to restart from Bloodline 1 with all of your stats intact. You do lose your inventory, but much better items wait in the Store.

INJUSTICE: GODS AMONG US

WII U/XBOX 360/PS3

UNLOCKABLE COSTUMES

COSTUME	REQUIREMENT
Boss Grundy	Complete Classic Battle.
Godfall Superman	Complete Story Mode.
Kyrptonite Lex	Complete all S.T.A.R. Labs missions.
New 52 Nightwing	Reach Level 30.
New 52 Shazam	Complete all Shazam S.T.A.R. Labs missions.
Yellow Lantern	Win an Online Ranked Match.

XBOX 360/PS3

ACHIEVEMENTS & TROPHIES

NAME	GOAL/REQUIREMENT	POINT VALUE	TROPHY VALUE
Top Rung	Complete Classic Battle with all characters	25	Silver
Rise to the Top	Complete Classic Battle with any character	10	Bronze
Ultimate Battler	Complete Battle Mode	50	Silver
Throwdown!	Perform 8 throws and win in a multiplayer match	10	Bronze
Groundbreaking	Use every interactable and win in a multiplayer match	10	Bronze

CHEATS, ACHIEVEMENTS, AND TROPHIES

NAME	GOAL/REQUIREMENT	POINT VALUE	TROPHY VALUE
Go Sit in the Corner	Win a multiplayer match with a timeout	10	Bronze
I Conquered All	Beat All S.T.A.R. Lab Missions (Excluding DLC)	20	Bronze
Mini-Master	Win all story mode minigames	25	Bronze
Statistical Advantage	View Your Hero Card	10	Bronze
Sidekick	Reach Level 10	10	Bronze
The Hero We Deserve	Reach Level 100	100	Gold
Almost There	Complete 50% of Story Mode	20	Bronze
Justice for All	Complete 100% of Story Mode	80	Silver
Beginner's Luck!	Win a single online match	10	Bronze
Overthrown	Dethrone the King in an online match	10	Bronze
I Voted!	Vote Correctly in a KOTH match	10	Bronze
Streak Ender	Defeat a Survivor	10	Bronze
Breaking Records	Win 100 complete Online Matches	10	Silver
Over The Top!	Play 200 complete Online Matches	10	Silver
Lucky Break	Win 1 complete Ranked match	10	Bronze
Holy Knockout Batman!	Win 10 complete Ranked matches	10	Bronze
Buddy System	Enter Online Practice with someone on your friends list	10	Bronze
Practice Makes Perfect	Enter Practice Mode	10	Bronze
Learning is Fun	Complete Tutorial	10	Bronze
It Has Begun	Complete 1 S.T.A.R. Lab Mission	10	Bronze
Overachiever	Get 3 stars on 1 S.T.A.R. Lab Mission	15	Bronze
All Star	Get 100 Stars in S.T.A.R. Lab Mode	10	Bronze
World's Finest	Complete All S.T.A.R. Lab Missions with 3 Stars	100	Gold
Heavy Hitter	Perform a 10 hit combo with every character	10	Bronze
Unstoppable Force	Win a Clash sequence with any character	10	Bronze
Wrecking Ball	Knock an opponent through a transition	10	Bronze
Around The World	Knock opponent through all transitions across all levels	15	Bronze
FINISHED	Win a match with the super move of any character	10	Bronze
Superhuman!	Perform every character's supermove	10	Silver
Metahuman	Perform every special move of every character	10	Bronze
Feel the Burnb!	Perform every Meter Burn special move of every character	10	Bronze
True Marksman	Win a match with Green Arrow using only arrows	10	Bronze
The Caped Crusader	Win with Batman using every special move and his Supermove	10	Bronze
Around and Around We Go	Perform every level interaction once	20	Bronze
Arkham City Lockdown	Defeat every Villain with Batman	10	Bronze
Only a Real Master	Make a comeback when at low health (10% or less)	10	Bronze

NAME	GOAL/REQUIREMENT	POINT VALUE	TROPHY VALUE
Perfect Aim	Win a match as Deathstroke without missing a shot (minimum 12 shots)	10	Bronze
Tourist	Send an opponent through all three Metropolis transitions in one fight	30	Silver
Cosplay	Unlock a costume in the Archives	5	Bronze
Gonna Need More Closet Space	Unlock all costumes in the Archives	20	Silver
Hoarder	Unlock everything in Archives	50	Silver
I Can Back it Up	Equip a new Background Image	5	Bronze
Iconic Representation	Equip a new Icon	5	Bronze
Looking Good!	Equip a new Character Portrait	5	Bronze
Bull in a China Shop	Cause maximum damage in all Arenas (does not include Practice mode)	100	Silver
Platinum Trophy	You've unlocked all Trophies!	—	Platinum

INSANELY TWISTED SHADOW PLANET

XBOX 360

AVATAR AWARDS

AVATAR	EARNED BY
Shadow Planet Tee T-Shirt	Make it from your Homeworld to the Shadow Planet to unlock!
UFO Hero's Ship	Complete the Single-Player Campaign to unlock!

INVIZIMALS

PSP

SPECIAL INVIZIMAL

At the World Map, press and hold Select and then press Up, Right, Down, Left. At the Big Secret, choose Capture Invizimals.

IRON MAN

PSP

ARMOR SUITS

Iron Man's different armor suits are unlocked by completing certain missions.

COMPLETE MISSION	SUIT UNLOCKED
1, Escape	Mark I
2, First Flight	Mark II
3, Fight Back	Mark III
5, Maggia Compound	Gold Tin Can
8, Frozen Ship	Classic
11, Island Meltdown	Stealth
13, Showdown	Titanium Man

PSP MINI-GAMES

Minigames can be unlocked by completing the following missions. Access the minigames through the Bonus menu.

COMPLETE MISSION	PSP MINI-GAME UNLOCKED
1, Escape	Tin Can Challenge 1 + 2
2, First Flight	DEATH RACE: STARK INDUSTRY
3, Fight Back	BOSS FIGHT: DREADNOUGHT
4, Weapons Transport	DEATH RACE: AFGHAN DESERT BOSS FIGHT: WHIPLASH
5, Maggia Compound	DEATH RACE: MAGGIA MANSION
6, Flying Fortress	SPEED KILL: FLYING FORTRESS SURVIVAL: FLYING FORTRESS
7, Nuclear Winter	DEATH RACE: ARTIC CIRCLE
8, Frozen Ship	SPEED KILL: FROZEN SHIP SURVIVAL: FROZEN SHIP
9, Home Front	BOSS FIGHT: TITANIUM MAN
10, Save Pepper	DEATH RACE: DAM BASSIN
11, Island Meltdown	SPEED KILL: GREEK ISLANDS SURVIVAL: GREEK ISLANDS
12, Battlesuit Factory	SPEED KILL: TINMEN FACTORY SURVIVAL: TINMEN FACTORY
13, Showdown	BOSS FIGHT: IRON MONGER

CONCEPT ART

As you progress through the game and destroy the Weapon Crates, bonuses are unlocked. You can find all of these in the Bonus menu once unlocked.

CONCEPT ART UNLOCKED	NUMBER OF WEAPON CRATES FOUND
Environments Set 1	6
Environments Set 2	12
Iron Man	18
Environments Set 3	24
Enemies	30
Environments Set 4	36
Villains	42
Vehicles	48
Covers	50

IRON MAN 2

XBOX 360/PS3

ACHIEVEMENTS & TROPHIES

NAME	GOAL/REQUIREMENT	POINT VALUE	TROPHY VALUE
Access Denied	Prevent Roxxon from stealing the Stark Archives.	10	Bronze
Deportation	Prevent the Russian separatists from deploying Roxxon Armigers.	15	Bronze
Power Outage	Defeat the Crimson Dynamo.	15	Bronze
Anti-PROTEAN	Destroy Project PROTEAN.	20	Bronze
Improvisation Under Fire	Save Rhodey and the Stark mobile armory from the A.I.M. attack.	20	Bronze
Operation Daybreak	Defeat A.I.M. and save the S.H.I.E.L.D. Helicarrier.	20	Bronze
Stormbreaker	Shut down the GREENGRID power transmitter.	20	Bronze
The Bigger They Are	Defeat ULTIMO.	30	Silver
Shake It Off	Recover from the Roxxon EMP attack.	3	Bronze

NAME	GOAL/REQUIREMENT	POINT VALUE	TROPHY VALUE
Not In My House	Prevent the first wave of Roxxon dropships from deploying their drones.	15	Bronze
Full Flight	Only one S.H.I.E.L.D. transport lost in the canyon run.	15	Bronze
Area Secured	At least 10 S.H.I.E.L.D. units survive the battle for the docks.	20	Silver
Pulling The Plug	Destroy all four Tesla reactor stabilizers in under 60 seconds.	15	Bronze
Anger Management	Destroy most of the structures in Shatalov's base.	15	Bronze
Entrapment	Reach the bottom of the elevator shaft without touching a laser tripline.	15	Bronze
Defensive Player Of The Year	Save all four repulsor lifts and all four stabilizers on the S.H.I.E.L.D. Helicarrier.	20	Bronze
Brute Force	Destroy the A.I.M. Arc Armiger without using missile deflection.	30	Silver
Guardian	Shut down GREENGRID without needing to repair the Arc Armiger.	25	Silver
Switchboard Operator	Reposition all of the GREENGRID relays without being interrupted.	20	Bronze
Not A Scratch	Defeat ULTIMO with no armor damage.	40	Silver
Ultimatum	Complete every mission on Easy difficulty.	15	Bronze
Iron Man	Complete every mission on Normal difficulty.	30	Silver
Invincible	Complete every mission on Formidable difficulty.	100	Gold
Fists Of Iron	Defeat 100 enemies in close combat.	20	Bronze
Storm Of Lead	Defeat 100 enemies with War Machine's minigun.	20	Bronze
Fire And Forget	Defeat 100 enemies with homing missiles.	10	Bronze
Subtle Like A Rocket	Defeat 100 enemies with the rocket launcher.	15	Bronze
Room Broom	Defeat 100 enemies with War Machine's shotgun.	20	Bronze
Extra Crispy	Defeat 100 enemies with Iron Man's laser.	20	Bronze
Pushback	Defeat 100 enemies with Iron Man's repulsor.	20	Bronze
Up Close And Personal	Defeat 100 enemies with Iron Man's blaster.	20	Bronze
Overkill	Defeat 100 enemies with Iron Man's unibeam.	25	Bronze
Hall Of Armors	Unlock all armor suits.	35	Gold
Technical Genius	Invent every module, ammunition, and weapon upgrade.	50	Silver
Gonna Need Some More Bad Guys	Defeat more than 1,000 enemies.	30	Bronze
Unnecessary Force	Defeat a soldier with Iron Man's unibeam.	7	Bronze
Bulletproof	Defeat 50 enemies in melee as Iron Man while Invincible.	30	Bronze
Ultimate Iron Man	Unlock the Ultimate Iron Man armor.	10	Bronze
Classic Iron Man	Unlock the Classic Iron Man armor.	10	Bronze

NAME	GOAL/REQUIREMENT	POINT VALUE	TROPHY VALUE
Classic Mark I	Unlock the Classic Mark I Iron Man armor.	10	Bronze
Extremis	Unlock the Extremis Iron Man armor.	10	Bronze
Mark III	Unlock the Mark III Iron Man armor.	10	Bronze
Mark II	Unlock the Mark II Iron Man armor.	10	Bronze
Mark VI	Unlock the Mark VI Iron Man armor.	10	Bronze
Silver Centurion	Unlock the Silver Centurion armor.	10	Bronze
Two Man Army	Defeat the Russian separatists as both Iron Man and War Machine.	10	Bronze
It Takes Two To Tangle	Defeat Crimson Dynamo as both Iron Man and War Machine.	10	Bronze
Man And Machine	Destroy Project PROTEAN as both Iron Man and War Machine.	10	Bronze
Bipolar	Shut down the GREENGRID power transmitter as both Iron Man and War Machine.	10	Bronze
Omega Man	Defeat 100 enemies as War Machine while using the Omega System.	30	Bronze

JAKE HUNTER: DETECTIVE CHRONICLES

NINTENDO 3DS

PASSWORDS

Select Password from the Main menu and enter the following:

UNLOCKABLE	PASSWORD
1 Password Info	AAAA
2 Visuals	LEET
3 Visuals	GONG
4 Visuals	CARS
5 Movies	ROSE
6 Jukebox	BIKE
7 Hints	HINT

JAKE HUNTER DETECTIVE STORY: MEMORIES OF THE PAST

NIINTENDO 3DS

JAKE HUNTER QUIZ

Select Password and enter NEET.

JAKE HUNTER SERIES

Select Password and enter MISS.

JAKE HUNTER UNLEASHED 01 BONUS

Select Password and enter NONE.

JAKE HUNTER UNLEASHED 02 BONUS

Select Password and enter ANGL.

JAKE HUNTER UNLEASHED 03 BONUS

Select Password and enter SNAP.

JAKE HUNTER UNLEASHED 04 BONUS

Select Password and enter DOOR.

JAKE HUNTER UNLEASHED 05 BONUS

Select Password and enter STOP.

JAKE HUNTER UNLEASHED DS1 BONUS

Select Password and enter KING.

JAKE HUNTER VISUALS 1

Select Password and enter LEET.

JAKE HUNTER VISUALS 2

Select Password and enter GONG.

JAKE HUNTER VISUALS 3

Select Password and enter CARS.

JAKE HUNTER VISUALS 4

Select Password and enter TREE.

JAKE HUNTER VISUALS 5

Select Password and enter PAPA.

JUKEBOX

Select Password and enter BIKE.

MOVIE GALLERY

Select Password and enter ROSE.

PASSWORD HINTS

Select Password and enter HINT.

SIDE CHARACTER'S BONUS STORY

Select Password and enter MINU.

STAFF COMMENTS 1

Select Password and enter AQUA.

STAFF COMMENTS 2

Select Password and enter MOTO.

WHAT IS A PASSWORD?

Select Password and enter AAAA.

JERRY RICE & NITUS' DOG FOOTBALL

NINTENDO WII

3 OF ALL TREATS AND GAME BALLS

At the player select, press Down, A, +, A.

B BUTTON FOR BOOST

At the player select, press Up, Left, +, Right, A.

CPU VS. CPU

At the player select, hold 2 as you select Play.

FIRST PERSON VIEW

At the player select, press Down, A, Right, +.

GENERIC FIELD

While selecting a field, hold 2.

CREDITS

At the title screen, press A, -, -, A.

JETPACK JOYRIDE

ACHIEVEMENTS

ACHIEVEMENT	REQUIREMENT
A Man, My Son	Finish all the missions and start again.
Alpha, Charlie, Echo	Fly over 2km.
Angry Wings	Get the Profit Bird twice in one game.
Another Way In	Start a game without breaking the laboratory wall.
Big Spender	Spend over 50,000 coins.
Blinged Out	Buy a golden vehicle upgrade.
Bullseye	Get a score of exactly 200m.
Class Act	Fly over 1km sporting the Top Hat, Classy Suit and Traditional Jetpack.
Crackling	Blow up a flying pig with a missile.
Crazy Freaking Skills	Get a best distance of over 800m in the CFT.
Dragonfruit	Secret achievement.
Fallout	Win 3 Atom Blasts.
Foam Party	Fly a total of 10km with the Bubble Gun Jetpack.
For Science	Knock over 1,000 scientists.
Fuzzy Locks	Get fried 99 times.
Germaphobe	Fly over 2km without touching coins, tokens or scientists.
Gold Digger	Collect 20 coins while dead.
Good Work, Muscat	Open and close the main menu slider 10 times.
Good Work, Sierra	Stare at the Shop screen for two minutes.
Good Work, Woody	Run into the bottom obstacle three times in a row.
Happy Snap	Save an action shot to your camera roll.
High Roller	Lose the final spin 100 times total.
Hippy	Take a trip in the Rainbow Jetpack and don't collect any coins.
James Who?	Buy two Jetpacks.
Marathon	Fly a total of 50km.
Mix 'N' Match	Equip 50 unique gadget combos.
Not so Green	Complete 10 missions.
Pretty Woman	Buy a matching set of clothes.
Rejected	Fly past the token gift without collecting it.
Road Trip	Accumulate a total of 10km on the Hog.
Romeo, Alpha, Delta	Fly over 5km.
Spice of Life	Take a ride on every vehicle in the game.
Tee Hee Two	Secret achievement.
Toastie	Get toasted by a missile three times in a row.
Veteran	Complete 40 missions.

JIMMIE JOHNSON'S ANYTHING WITH AN ENGINE

PLAYSTATION 3

ALL RACERS

At the main menu, hold Right Trigger + Left Trigger + Right Bumper + Left Bumper and press Up, Right, Down, Left, Up, Left, Down, Right, click the Right Thumbstick, click the Left Thumbstick.

XBOX 360

ALL RACERS

At the main menu, hold R1 + L1 + R2 + L2 and press Up, Right, Down, Left, Up, Left, Down, Right, R3, L3.

JOY RIDE TURBO

XBOX 360

AVATAR AWARDS

AVATAR	EARNED BY
JR Turbo T	Win your first race to receive the official T shirt of the unofficial Joy Ride Turbo fan club.
Victory Pants	Purchase your first car in order to strut out of the dealership wearing a victorious pair of slacks.
Cacti Cap	Win a race on every track to unlock this trendy piece of headwear.

JUICED 2: HOT IMPORT NIGHTS

PLAYSTATION 3

ASCARI KZ1

Select Cheats and Codes from the DNA Lab menu and enter KNOX. Defeat the challenge to earn the car.

AUDI TT 1.8L QUATTRO

Select Cheats and Codes from the DNA Lab menu and enter YTHZ. Defeat the challenge to earn the car.

BMW Z4 ROADSTER

Select Cheats and Codes from the DNA Lab menu and enter GVDL. Defeat the challenge to earn the car.

FRITO-LAY INFINITI G35

Select Cheats and Codes from the DNA Lab menu and enter MNCH. Defeat the challenge to earn the car.

HOLDEN MONARO

Select Cheats and Codes from the DNA Lab menu and enter RBSG. Defeat the challenge to earn the car.

HYUNDAI COUPE 2.7L V6

Select Cheats and Codes from the DNA Lab menu and enter BSLU. Defeat the challenge to earn the car.

INFINITI G35

Select Cheats and Codes from the DNA Lab menu and enter MRHC. Defeat the challenge to earn the car.

KOENIGSEGG CCX

Select Cheats and Codes from the DNA Lab menu and enter KDTR. Defeat the challenge to earn the car.

MITSUBISHI PROTOTYPE X

Select Cheats and Codes from the DNA Lab menu and enter DOPX. Defeat the challenge to earn the car.

NISSAN 350Z

Select Cheats and Codes from the DNA Lab menu and enter PRGN. Defeat the challenge to earn the car.

NISSAN SKYLINE R34 GT-R

Select Cheats and Codes from the DNA Lab menu and enter JWRS. Defeat the challenge to earn the car.

SALEEN S7

Select Cheats and Codes from the DNA Lab menu and enter WIKF. Defeat the challenge to earn the car.

SEAT LEON CUPRA R

Select Cheats and Codes from the DNA Lab menu and enter FAMQ. Defeat the challenge to earn the car.

JUICED 2: HOT IMPORT NIGHTS

NINTENDO 3DS

$5000

At the Cheat menu, enter HSAC.

ALL CARS

At the Cheat menu, enter SRAC.

ALL RACES

At the Cheat menu, enter EDOM.

ALL TRACKS

At the Cheat menu, enter KART.

PSP

LAST MAN STANDING CHALLENGE AND AN ASCARI KZ1

Select Cheats and Challenges from the DNA Lab menu and enter KNOX. Defeat the challenge to earn the Ascari KZ1.

SPECIAL CHALLENGE AND AN AUDI TT 1.8 QUATTRO

Select Cheats and Challenges from the DNA Lab menu and enter YTHZ. Defeat the challenge to earn the Audi TT 1.8 Quattro.

SPECIAL CHALLENGE AND A BMW Z4

Select Cheats and Challenges from the DNA Lab menu and enter GVDL. Defeat the challenge to earn the BMW Z4.

SPECIAL CHALLENGE AND A HOLDEN MONARO

Select Cheats and Challenges from the DNA Lab menu and enter RBSG. Defeat the challenge to earn the Holden Monaro.

SPECIAL CHALLENGE AND A HYUNDAI COUPE 2.7 V6

Select Cheats and Challenges from the DNA Lab menu and enter BSLU. Defeat the challenge to earn the Hyundai Coupe 2.7 V6.

SPECIAL CHALLENGE AND AN INFINITY G35

Select Cheats and Challenges from the DNA Lab menu and enter MRHC. Defeat the challenge to earn the Infinity G35.

SPECIAL CHALLENGE AND AN INFINITY RED G35

Select Cheats and Challenges from the DNA Lab menu and enter MNCH. Defeat the challenge to earn the Infinity G35.

SPECIAL CHALLENGE AND A KOENIGSEGG CCX

Select Cheats and Challenges from the DNA Lab menu and enter KDTR. Defeat the challenge to earn the Koenigsegg CCX.

SPECIAL CHALLENGE AND A MITSUBISHI PROTOTYPE X

Select Cheats and Challenges from the DNA Lab menu and enter DOPX. Defeat the challenge to earn the Mitsubishi Prototype X.

SPECIAL CHALLENGE AND A NISSAN 350Z

Select Cheats and Challenges from the DNA Lab menu and enter PRGN. Defeat the challenge to earn the Nissan 350Z.

SPECIAL CHALLENGE AND A NISSAN SKYLINE R34 GT-R

Select Cheats and Challenges from the DNA Lab menu and enter JWRS. Defeat the challenge to earn the Nissan Skyline R34 GT-R.

SPECIAL CHALLENGE AND A SALEEN S7

Select Cheats and Challenges from the DNA Lab menu and enter WIKF. Defeat the challenge to earn the Saleen S7.

SPECIAL CHALLENGE AND A SEAT LEON CUPRA R

Select Cheats and Challenges from the DNA Lab menu and enter FAMQ. Defeat the challenge to earn the Seat Leon Cupra R.

JUMBLE MADNESS

NINTENDO 3DS

FEBRUARY 31 PUZZLE

For Daily Jumble and Jumble Crosswords, select the square under February 28, 2009.

JUST CAUSE 2

XBOX 360/PS3

ISLAND FROM LOST

Grab a plane and fly to the small island in the northwest corner of the map. The plane explodes and falls to the ground as you fly over. There are several references to the show, including a hatch in the southwest corner of the island.

ACHIEVEMENTS & TROPHIES

NAME	GOAL/REQUIREMENT	POINT VALUE	TROPHY VALUE
Top Agent	Bonus for completing the game on Normal difficulty.	20	Bronze
Heroic Agent	Bonus for completing the game on Experienced difficulty.	30	Bronze
Legendary Agent	Bonus for completing the game on Hardcore difficulty.	40	Bronze
Gaining a Foothold	Complete 3 stronghold takeovers	10	Bronze
Conqueror of Panau	Complete 9 stronghold takeovers.	20	Silver
A Trusted Ally	Complete 49 faction missions.	20	Gold
First Taste of Chaos	Cause chaos for the first time.	10	Bronze
Saboteur	Complete 150 sabotages.	10	Bronze
Destroyer	Complete 1000 sabotages.	20	Bronze
Professional Hitman	Assassinate 25 colonels.	20	Bronze
Up to the Challenge 1	Complete 10 challenges.	10	Bronze
Up to the Challenge 2	Complete 50 challenges.	20	Bronze
Leaving No Rock Unturned	Collect 1000 resource items.	25	Bronze
Finders Keepers	Collect 100 resource items.	15	Bronze

NAME	GOAL/REQUIREMENT	POINT VALUE	TROPHY VALUE
Faction Benefactor	Collect 150 faction items.	20	Bronze
Globetrotter	Discover 100 locations.	20	Bronze
Freeroamer 1	Reach 100% complete in 15 locations.	10	Bronze
Freeroamer 2	Reach 100% complete in 100 locations.	20	Silver
Body Count	Kill 750 enemies.	15	Bronze
Unarmed and Dangerous	Kill 50 enemies using melee attacks.	15	Bronze
Gravity is a Bitch!	Kill 30 enemies by using the grappling hook and making them fall to their death.	15	Bronze
Follow Me!	Kill 5 enemies by dragging them behind a vehicle with the grappling hook.	15	Bronze
Hang 'em High!	Kill 30 enemies while they're suspended in the air with the grappling hook.	15	Bronze
Wrecking Ball	Kill 5 enemies by smashing them with an object tethered to your vehicle with the grappling hook.	15	Bronze
Piñata Party	Kill 5 enemies with the melee attack while they're suspended with the grappling hook.	15	Bronze
Juggler	Kill 30 enemies while they're in mid air.	15	Bronze
Road Rage	Kill 30 enemies by mowing them down with vehicles.	10	Bronze
Marksman	Kill 50 enemies with head shots.	15	Bronze
Killing Frenzy	Kill 20 enemies in 60 seconds.	20	Bronze
Invincible Warrior	Kill 50 enemies in a row with inventory weapons without losing health.	20	Bronze
Destruction Frenzy	Destroy 30 objects in 60 seconds.	10	Bronze
Test Driver	Drive 30 different vehicles.	10	Bronze
Trying Everything Once	Drive all 104 vehicles.	25	Bronze
Road Trip	Travel 75 kilometers by land vehicle.	20	Bronze
Please Step Out of the Vehicle	Hijack 50 enemy vehicles.	10	Bronze
Stunt Driver	Get 100 stunt driver points.	10	Bronze
Halfway there	Reach 50% completion in the normal mode or mercenary mode.	25	Bronze
Parachute Climber	Open the parachute and then land on foot 300 meters above the starting height.	10	Bronze
I Believe I Can Fly	Base jump 1000 meters.	10	Bronze
Bridge Limbo	Fly an airplane under 30 unique bridges in Panau.	20	Bronze
Stunt Flyer	Fly an airplane close to the ground for 30 seconds.	10	Bronze
Perfectionist	Reach 75% completion in the normal mode or mercenary mode.	25	Bronze
Top of the World	Stand on foot on the highest point of Panau	10	Bronze

SECRET ACHIEVEMENTS & TROPHIES

NAME	GOAL/REQUIREMENT	POINT VALUE	TROPHY VALUE
Welcome to Panau	Complete Story Mission 1.	10	Bronze
Casino Bust	Complete Story Mission 2.	20	Bronze
The White Tiger	Complete Story Mission 3.	30	Bronze
Mountain Rescue	Complete Story Mission 4.	40	Bronze
Three Kings	Complete Story Mission 5.	50	Silver
Into the Den	Complete Story Mission 6.	60	Silver
A Just Cause	Complete Story Mission 7.	70	Gold

JUST DANCE: DISNEY PARTY

XBOX 360

ACHIEVEMENTS

NAME	GOAL/REQUIREMENT	POINT VALUE
First Steps	Danced to 1 song in Just Dance.	10
Double Team	Danced to Team High Score with 2 players.	10
Shake It Up	Danced to Freeze & Shake.	10
Just DJ	Created a User Playlist in Playlists mode.	10
Playlist Champ	Danced to 1 preset playlist in Playlists mode.	10
Watch Me Whirl	Created 1 original dance in Just Create mode.	10
Get Creative	Danced to 1 original dance made in Just Create mode.	10
Say Cheese	Had a photo of 2 or more players taken while dancing.	10
Hit the Stage	Danced a total of 10 times in Just Dance.	10
Work the Floor	Danced a total of 50 times in Just Dance.	20
Mix it Up	Danced to all the songs once.	10
Dancing Machine	Danced 25 times in 1 play session (without returning to Title Screen).	10
Taking Notes	Collected 1000 music notes in Team High Score.	10
Reach for the Stars	Earned 10,000 points in a user-recorded dance.	20
Got the Routine	Earned 4 stars in a dance without showing next move icons.	10
Team Spirit	Earned 4 stars in Team High Score without showing next move icons.	30
Photo Frenzy	Had 20 photos taken while dancing.	30
They'll Come to You	Earned 4 stars in The Bare Necessities.	30
A Delicious Feast	Earned 4 stars in Be Our Guest.	30
Magical Moves	Earned 4 stars in Bibbidi Bobbidi Boo.	30
Scary Moves	Earned 4 stars in Calling All The Monsters.	30
Jazz Cat	Earned 4 stars in Ev'rybody Wants To Be A Cat.	30
Dancing Wizardry	Earned 4 stars in Everything Is Not As It Seems.	40
You Can Fly	Earned 4 stars in Fly to Your Heart.	40
Tee Dee!	Earned 4 stars in Following The Leader.	40
The Future's Bright	Earned 4 stars in Hang In There Baby.	20
Wiki Wiki	Earned 4 stars in Hawaiian Roller Coaster Ride.	20
Boom Boom Clock	Earned 4 stars in Hoedown Throwdown.	20
Rhino is Awesome!	Earned 4 stars in I Thought I Lost You.	20
Around the World	Earned 4 stars in It's a Small World.	20
Dance of the Barbarians	Earned 4 stars in I've Got a Dream.	20
Party Everyday	Earned 4 stars in Hey Jessie.	20
Break it Down	Earned 4 stars in Shake It Up.	20

CHEATS, ACHIEVEMENTS, AND TROPHIES

J

NAME	GOAL/REQUIREMENT	POINT VALUE
Tangled Up	Earned 4 stars in Something That I Want.	20
Just Got Served!	Earned 4 stars in S.I.M.P. (Squirrels In My Pants).	20
Say What?	Earned 4 stars in Supercalifragilisticexpialidocious.	20
Now You Know	Earned 4 stars in That's How You Know.	20
Shine on Me	Earned 4 stars in This is Me.	20
Light the Lights	Earned 4 stars in The Muppet Show Theme.	20
Twist it Up	Earned 4 stars in Twist My Hips.	20
Off the Hook	Earned 4 stars in Under the Sea.	20
Wildcats Everywhere	Earned 4 stars in We're All in This Together.	20
Rock the Party	Danced a total of 100 times in Just Dance.	20
Team Player	Danced to songs in Team High Score 50 times in multiplayer.	20
Shakin' Things Up	Danced to songs in Freeze & Shake 50 times.	20
Create-a-thon	Danced to any songs made in Just Create 50 times.	20
My Fave	Danced to the same song 30 times.	20
Go Team!	Earned 30,000 or more points in all songs in Team High Score.	20
Shake Master	Earned 12,000 or more points in all songs in Freeze & Shake.	20
Disney Star	Earned 4 stars in all songs in Just Dance.	20

KARAOKE REVOLUTION GLEE: VOLUME 2

NINTENDO WII

ICE ICE BABY

Select Unlockables from the Options and enter A64112.

PINK HOUSES

Select Unlockables from the Options and enter DD6C62.

KARAOKE REVOLUTION GLEE: VOLUME 3

NINTENDO WII

BORN THIS WAY

Select Unlockables from the Options and enter 60328B.

FIREWORK

Select Unlockables from the Options and enter 41025F.

TOXIC

Select Unlockables from the Options and enter B81120.

KID ICARUS: UPRISING

NINTENDO 3DS

BOSS RUSH MODE

Defeat the Final Boss. Boss Rush Mode can be accessed next to Chapter 25.

DIALOGUE

Complete Solo Mode. Select Other from Options and then Hidden Options to toggle Dialogue on and off.

PALUTENA OR VIRIDI LOOKS OVER MENU

Complete Chapter 21. Select Other from Options and then Hidden Options to access Palutena and Viridi.

KILLZONE HD

PLAYSTATION 3

NAME	GOAL/REQUIREMENT	TROPHY VALUE
1 v 50	Kill 50 Helghast soldiers without dying	Bronze
2 For The Price Of 1	Kill 2 Helghast with 1 shot from the BP-02 Pup launcher	Bronze
3 Birds With One Stone	Kill 3 Helghast with 1 cooked M194 Percussion Grenade	Bronze
4 X 4 X 4	Kill 4 Helghast in under 4 seconds with the EAW-25/4 Chimera	Silver
Abridged Bridge	Collapse the Helghast bridge in the Jungle Valley	Bronze
Anti-Air Specialist	Bring 2 Dropships crashing down in the Mist Waters Firebase	Bronze
Artillery Artist	Kill a Helghast from 100m+ away with the Priv-3 Siska.	Bronze
Backstabber	Get 20 kills with the FSK-7 Fury	Bronze
Beep Beep Beeep	Kill 10 Helghast with the secondary fire on the M327 Grenade Launcher	Bronze
Bounty Hunted	Kill the IFO Bounty Hunter	Bronze
Brouhaha	Kill 30 Helghast soldiers in under a minute	Bronze
Bullheaded	Get 20 headshots with the M4 Semi-Automatic Pistol	Bronze
Burn Baby Burn	Destroy your first enemy APC	Bronze
Call Of The Siren	Kill 25 Helghast soldiers with the VnD-10M Siren	Bronze
Captain	Complete all levels on the easy difficulty	Bronze
Colonel	Complete all levels on the normal difficulty	Silver
Covering Fire	Kill 10 Helghast with the M224 Mounted Machine Gun	Bronze
Designation: Demolition	Destroy 3 Towers using the BDL-23 Dohvat	Bronze
Disproportionate Force	Kill 1 unfortunate Helghast soldier with 3 rockets from the BLR-06 Hadra	Bronze
Eco-Warrior	Hit 15 Helghast soldiers without reloading, using the secondary fire on the M66 SD Submachine gun	Bronze
Economical Soldier	Finish a level above 75% hit efficiency	Bronze
Elite? HA!	Take down your first 2 Helghast Elite	Bronze
Escape	Complete Chapter 5	Bronze
Explosive Consequences	Kill 5 Helghast soldiers with 1 grenade using the attachment on the M82-G Assault Rifle	Bronze
Field Operative	Complete Chapter 5 to 11 playing as Hakha	Bronze
Forging a Path	Complete Chapter 8	Bronze
General	Complete all levels on the hard difficulty	Gold
Generally Better	Kill General Lente and his bodyguards	Bronze
Get Out Of My Comfort Zone!	Kill a Helghast within 1m with the M404-MAW M. Anti Tank Weapon …and don't die	Bronze
Helghast Assault	Complete Chapter 1	Bronze
Helghast Champion	Win a battlefields game playing on the Helghast's side with the enemy AI set to hard	Bronze
Hidden Pasts	Complete Chapter 9	Bronze
Hope	Complete Chapter 11	Bronze
Hunting the Traitor	Complete Chapter 7	Bronze
ISA Regulator	Complete Chapter 4 to 11 playing as Rico	Bronze
ISA Saviour	Win a battlefields game playing on the ISA's side with the enemy AI set to hard	Bronze
Misty Waters	Complete Chapter 6	Bronze

NAME	GOAL/REQUIREMENT	TROPHY VALUE
New Allies	Complete Chapter 3	Bronze
Nobody Hides From Me	Finish a level above 90% hit efficiency	Silver
One For You And One For You	Kill 2 Helghast with 1 Double Shot from the M13 Semi-Automatic Shotgun	Bronze
Onwards and Upwards	Complete Chapter 10	Bronze
Orbital Strike	Take down General Adams with a grenade	Bronze
Platinum	Collect all trophies in Killzone	Platinum
Rapid Reaction Force	Complete Chapter 1 to 11 playing as Templar	Bronze
Right in the Jewels	Use the M224-A3 Heavy Support Weapon to melee 20 Helghast soldiers	Bronze
Scavenger	Pick up 10,000 rounds for the STA-52 LAR rifle	Silver
Shadow Marshal	Complete Chapter 3 to 11 playing as Luger	Bronze
Short Controlled Bursts	Finish a level above 50% hit efficiency	Bronze
Something Borrowed	Kill 20 Helghast soldiers with the VnS-10 Scylla Mounted Machine Gun	Bronze
Strange Company	Complete Chapter 4	Bronze
Supply and Demand	Blow up the ammo dumps in the Forward Logistics Base	Bronze
Tanks For The Good Times	Destroy 2 Helghast Tanks attacking the Industrial level	Bronze
That Got Their Attention	Destroy the Missile launching APCs in the Misty Waters Firebase	Bronze
The Reds Of Their Eyes	Get 10 headshots with the STA-52 SLAR Sniper Rifle	Bronze
They're On Our Side Now	Switch allegiance of Helghast Sentry bots as Hakha	Bronze
Toothpick Master	Get 20 kills with the M32 combat knife	Bronze
Tripletapper	Get 3 headshots with 1 magazine, using the secondary fire on the IvP-18 Tropov pistol	Bronze
Two's Company	Win a battlefields game with another player in split screen	Bronze
Vekta Evacuates	Complete Chapter 2	Bronze

KINECT DISNEYLAND ADVENTURES

XBOX 360

AVATAR AWARDS

AVATAR	EARNED BY
Sorcerer Mickey Mouse Hat	Earn the Happiest Place on Earth Achievement.

KINECT SPORTS

XBOX 360

AVATAR AWARDS

AWARD	EARNED BY
Classic Kinect Sports Cap	Earn the Amateur Sports Badge.
Classic Kinect Sports Tee	Earn the Professional Sports Badge.
I Heart Kinect Sports Tee	Earn the Champion Sports Badge.
Kinect Sports Champ Trophy	Earn the Legendary Sports Badge.
Kinect Sports Star Tee	Earn the Master Sports Badge.

KINECT SPORTS SEASON TWO

AVATAR AWARDS

AVATAR	EARNED BY
Kinect Sports Darts Top Hat	Stay on target throughout your career with this awesome award for reaching level 5. Woohoo!
Kinect Sports Football Hat	Show your love for all things football with this award for reaching fan level 2. I'm so jealous!
Kinect Sports Golf Green Cap	Impress everyone at the clubhouse with this award for reaching the dizzy heights of fan level 10.

THE KING OF FIGHTERS XIII

ALTERNATE COSTUMES AND COLOR PALETTES

Before selecting the color for the following fighters, press Select to get the alternate outfit.

FIGHTER	OUTFIT
Andy	Ninja Mask
Elisabeth	KOF XI
Joe	Tiger-Striped Boxers
K'	Dual-Colored
Kyo	Orochi Saga
Raiden	Big Bear
Ralf	Camouflage
Takuma	Mr. Karate
Yuri	Braided Ponytail

EXTRA COLORS IN COLOR EDIT

Extra colors become available in color edit mode for every ten times you select a specific character.

BILLY KANE

Successfully pull off 2 target actions in each fight in Arcade Mode until Billy Kane challenges you. Defeat him to unlock him.

SAIKI

Successfully pull off 5 target actions in each fight in Arcade Mode until Saiki challenges you. Defeat him to unlock him.

KINGDOM HEARTS: BIRTH BY SLEEP

FINAL EPISODE

Find all of the Xehanort Reports and complete all three stories.

CHEATS, ACHIEVEMENTS, AND TROPHIES

K

TRINITY ARCHIVES

Complete the story using any character.

TROPHY	UNLOCKED BY...
Power Walker	Taking 99,999 steps.
Keyslinger	Defeating 9999 Unversed.
Clockworks	Accumulating 80 hours or more of gameplay.
Arena Sweeper	Completing all arena matches.
Dairy Devotee	Activating Frozen Fortune 30 times.
In the Munny	Earning 33,333 munny.
One Down	Completing the story using any character.
Trinity	Completing all stories in at least Proud Mode.

KINGDOM RUSH

ACHIEVEMENTS

ACHIEVEMENT	REQUIREMENT
First Blood	Kill one Enemy.
Daring	Call 10 early waves.
Constructor	Build 30 Towers.
Bloodlust	Kill 500 Enemies.
Armaggedon	Use Rain of Fire 5 times in a single stage.
Home Improvement	Upgrade all basic Tower types to level 3.
Starry	Earn 15 Stars.
What's That?	Open 10 Enemy information cards.
Supermario	Earn 30 Stars.
Nuts and Bolts	Defeat The Juggernaut.
Engineer	Build 100 Towers.
Is He Dead Yeti?	Defeat J.T.
Slayer	Kill 2500 Enemies.
Death From Above	Kill 100 Enemies with Meteor Shower.
Tactician	Change Soldiers rally point 200 times.
Superstar	Earn 45 Stars.
The architect	Build 150 Towers.
This is the End!	Defeat Vez'nan.
Terminator	Kill 10,000 Enemies.
Die Hard	Have your Soldiers regenerate a total of 50,000 life.
G.I. Joe	Train 1,000 Soldiers.
Cannon Fodder	Send 1,000 Soldiers to their deaths.
Fearless	Call all waves early in a single mission.
Real Estate	Sell 30 Towers.
Indecisive	Sell 5 Towers in a single mission.
Impatient	Call an early wave within 3 seconds of the icon showing up.
Forest Diplomacy	Recruit max Elves at The Silveroak Outpost.
Like a Henderson	Free the Sasquatch on the Icewind Pass.
Sunburner!	Fire the Sunray 20 times.
Imperial Saviour	Complete The Citadel with at least 3 surviving Imperial Guards.
Specialist	Build all 8 Tower specializations.
50 Shots 50 Kills	Snipe 50 Enemies.

ACHIEVEMENT	REQUIREMENT
Toxicity	Kill 50 Enemies by poison damage.
Entangled	Hold 500 or more Enemies with Wrath of the Forest.
Dust to Dust	Disintegrate 50 or more Enemies.
Beam Me Up Scotty	Teleport 250 or more Enemies.
Shepherd	Polymorph 50 Enemies into sheep.
Elementalist	Summon 5 rock elementals in any one stage.
Axe Rain	Throw 500 or more axes.
Are You Not Entertained?	Have a single Barbarian kill 10 Enemies.
Medic	Have your Paladins heal a total of 7,000 life.
Holy Chorus	Have your Paladins perform 100 Holy Strike.
Rocketeer	Shoot 100 Missiles.
Clustered	Drop 1,000 or more bomblets with the cluster bomb.
Energy Network	Build 4 Tesla towers in any stage.
AC/DC	Kill 300 Enemies with electricity.
Ovinophobia	Kill 10 or more Sheep with your hands.
Twin Rivers Angler	Catch a Fish.
Great Defender	Complete all Campaign stages in Normal difficulty.
Heroic Defender	Complete all Heroic stages in Normal difficulty.
Iron Defender	Complete all Iron stages in Normal difficulty.

KINGDOMS OF AMALUR: RECKONING

XBOX 360

REMOVE STOLEN STATUS FROM ITEM

Find a merchant who buys stolen items and sell the one marked stolen (red hand icon). Without exiting the screen, go to Buy and find the item you just sold. Purchase it and it should no longer be marked as stolen.

XBOX 360/PS3

ACHIEVEMENTS & TROPHIES

NAME	GOAL/REQUIREMENT	POINT VALUE	TROPHY VALUE
House of Ballads	Complete the House of Ballads storyline quests.	20	Silver
House of Sorrows	Complete the House of Sorrows storyline quests.	20	Silver
Scholia Arcana	Complete the Scholia Arcana storyline quests.	20	Silver
Travelers	Complete the Travelers storyline quests.	20	Silver
Warsworn	Complete the Warsworn storyline quests.	20	Silver
Reckoning Rampage	Kill 5 enemies with a single Fateshift.	20	Bronze
Niskaru Slayer	Kill 25 Niskaru.	20	Bronze
Out of Your League	Kill an enemy 4 levels higher than you.	20	Bronze
Cleaning Up the Streets	Kill 50 bandits.	20	Bronze

NAME	GOAL/REQUIREMENT	POINT VALUE	TROPHY VALUE
Blades of Glory	Acquire 10 Unique weapons (Special Delivery weapons excluded).	15	Bronze
Foiled Again!	Parry 100 times.	15	Bronze
Trapper	Kill 25 enemies with traps.	15	Bronze
Riposte!	Land 25 special attacks out of Parry.	10	Bronze
Would You Like Fries with that?	Land 100 complete attack chains.	15	Bronze
Shock and Awe	Kill 100 enemies with abilities.	15	Bronze
And Then There Were None	Kill 500 enemies with abilities.	20	Bronze
Juggler	Land 5 consecutive hits on a launched enemy.	20	Silver
Elixir of Fate	Make a potion with the Essence of Fate.	20	Bronze
It Didn't Explode!	Make a stable potion by experimenting.	10	Bronze
Green Thumb	Harvest 10 of each type of reagent.	15	Bronze
Good as New	Repair a piece of equipment.	10	Bronze
Shop Class	Craft a piece of equipment with Blacksmithing.	10	Bronze
Master of the Forge	Craft an item that uses all 5 forge component slots.	20	Bronze
Romancing the Gem	Craft an Epic Gem.	15	Bronze
Diamond in the Rough	Craft a Pristine Shard.	10	Bronze
They Never Saw it Coming	Backstab 20 enemies.	10	Bronze
Cartographer	Discover 100 locations.	20	Bronze
The Great Detective	Detect 25 hidden things.	10	Bronze
Loremaster	Discover all Lorestones.	20	Bronze
Bookworm	Read 50 books.	15	Bronze
Big Spender	Spend 200,000 gold.	15	Bronze
Five Finger Discount	Steal and fence an item.	10	Bronze
Where's My Wallet?	Pickpocket 20 times.	15	Bronze
Jailbreak	Break out of jail.	10	Bronze
A Life of Crime	Get caught committing a crime 25 times.	15	Bronze
Crime Doesn't Pay	Spend over 10,000 gold in crime bribes.	10	Bronze
Some of This, Some of That	Unlock a two-class hybrid destiny.	10	Bronze
It is Your Destiny	Unlock a top tier destiny.	50	Bronze
Jack of All Trades	Unlock a Jack of All Trades destiny.	10	Bronze
Breaking and Entering	Pick 50 locks.	15	Bronze
Open Sesame	Dispel 50 wards.	15	Bronze
A Wink and a Smile	Succeed at 50 Persuasion attempts.	15	Bronze
Bull in a China Shop	Smash 1,000 objects.	15	Bronze

SECRET ACHIEVEMENTS & TROPHIES

NAME	GOAL/REQUIREMENT	POINT VALUE	TROPHY VALUE
Reborn	You were reborn from the Well of Souls, and have escaped Allestar Tower.	10	Bronze
No Destiny, All Determination	You have met High King Titarion, and have been confronted with the true scope of your powers.	15	Bronze
Turning the Tide	A ruse has baited Octienne into betraying the necromantic nature of his experiments.	20	Silver
Hero of Mel Senshir	You have defeated the great Balor.	75	Gold
Destiny Defiant	You have defeated Tirnoch, and defied destiny.	75	Silver
Destiny Dominated	You have won the game on Hard difficulty.	100	Gold
Streaker	You spoke to someone while not wearing clothes.	10	Bronze

THE LEGEND OF DEAD KEL

ACHIEVEMENTS & TROPHIES

NAME	GOAL/REQUIREMENT	POINT VALUE	TROPHY VALUE
Message in a Bottle	Locate all eight message bottles in Gallows End.	25	Bronze
Keep on Rising	Fully restore Gravehal Keep.	50	Gold
Exterminator	Kill 50 Scavs.	25	Bronze

SECRET ACHIEVEMENTS & TROPHIES

NAME	GOAL/REQUIREMENT	POINT VALUE	TROPHY VALUE
Give Her a Hand	Found Aubrey Gilcrest's severed hand.	25	Bronze
Manic Pixie Dream Elf	Wooed Rast Brattigan.	25	Bronze

TEETH OF NAROS

ACHIEVEMENTS & TROPHIES

NAME	GOAL/REQUIREMENT	POINT VALUE	TROPHY VALUE
Murder Most Fowl	Kill 50 Pteryx.	25	Bronze

SECRET ACHIEVEMENTS & TROPHIES

NAME	GOAL/REQUIREMENT	POINT VALUE	TROPHY VALUE
The Harder They Fall	You've bested Kahrunk without killing his attendants.	20	Bronze
We Built this City	You helped the Kollossae in the Teeth of Naros break free from their fate.	50	Gold
Mistaken Identity	You've found a strange Almain who has been hiding in the sewers of Idylla.	25	Bronze
Beam Me Up	Used the Henge to enter Idylla.	25	Bronze
I Regret Nothing	Fell to your death from the Idylla Concourse.	5	Bronze

K

L.A. NOIRE

Select Outfits from the Pause menu to change into the following. Some have special bonuses when worn.

SWORD OF JUSTICE OUTFIT

Reach rank 3.

SUNSET STRIP OUTFIT

Reach rank 8.

THE OUTSIDER OUTFIT

Reach rank 13.

HAWKSHAW OUTFIT

Reach rank 18. This outfit adds some resistance to damage.

GOLDEN BOY OUTFIT

Awarded for reaching Traffic Desk

BUTTON MAN OUTFIT

Complete the Badge Pursuit Challenge. This outfit allows you to carry extra ammo.

CHICAGO LIGHTING OUTFIT

Become a member of Rockstar's Social Club. You must reach Detective to wear the outfit. When worn, accuracy with the BAR, Thompson, and shotgun is increased.

THE SHARPSHOOTER OUTFIT

This outfit and the Nickel Plated Pistol were pre-order bonuses from Best Buy. It gives you better accuracy with rifles and pistols.

THE BRODERICK OUTFIT

This outfit was a pre-order bonus from Amazon.com. It increases fist-fighting capabilities and adds resistance to damage.

ACHIEVEMENTS & TROPHIES

NAME	GOAL/REQUIREMENT	POINT VALUE	TROPHY VALUE
Asphalt Jungle	Chase down and tackle a fleeing suspect on foot as an LAPD Detective.	15	Bronze
Traffic Stop	Disable a suspect vehicle with help from your partner.	15	Bronze
Not So Hasty	Stop a fleeing suspect with a warning shot as an LAPD Detective.	15	Bronze
Shamus To The Stars	Complete all story cases with a five star rating.	80	Gold
The Brass	Achieve maximum rank.	30	Silver
The Plot Thickens	Find and solve an inspection puzzle.	15	Bronze
Golden Boy	Clear a case finding every clue as an LAPD Detective or Investigator.	15	Bronze
The Straight Dope	Use evidence to prove a lie as an LAPD Detective or Investigator.	15	Bronze
One For The File	Find and inspect a clue as an LAPD Detective or Investigator.	15	Bronze
The City Of The Angels	Reach 100% Game Complete.	80	Gold
The Up And Up	Complete a story case with a five star rating.	30	Silver
The Long Arm Of The Law	Complete all street crime cases.	30	Silver
A Cop On Every Corner	Complete a single street crime case.	15	Bronze

NAME	GOAL/REQUIREMENT	POINT VALUE	TROPHY VALUE
Johnny On The Spot	Respond to 20 street crime cases.	30	Silver
Public Menace	Rack up $47,000 in penalties during a single story case.	30	Bronze
The Moose	Follow Candy Edwards without using cover or incognito, except when starting or picking up the tail.	15	Bronze
Star Map	Discover all landmark locations around the city.	15	Bronze
The Third Degree	Correctly branch every question in every interview in a single story case.	30	Silver
The Hunch	Use four intuition points in a single interview session, correctly branching each question.	30	Silver
Auto Fanatic	Drive every vehicle in the city.	30	Silver
Hollywoodland	Find and inspect all gold film reels.	30	Silver
Auto Collector	Drive 40 different vehicles.	15	Bronze
Keep A Lid On	Complete a brawl without losing your hat as an LAPD Detective or Investigator.	15	Bronze
Auto Enthusiast	Drive 5 different vehicles.	15	Bronze
Lead Foot	Keep the needle above 80mph for more than ten seconds while driving.	15	Bronze
Miles On The Clock	Drive more than 194.7 miles.	15	Bronze
Magpie	Find and inspect 95% of all clues.	80	Bronze

LAIR

PLAYSTATION 3

CHICKEN VIDEO

At the Cheat menu, enter chicken.

COFFEE VIDEO

At the Cheat menu, enter 686F7420636F66666565.

UNLOCKS STABLE OPTION FOR ALL LEVELS

At the Cheat menu, enter koelsch. Saving is disabled with this code.

LARA CROFT AND THE GUARDIAN OF LIGHT

XBOX 360/PS3

LARA CROFT HEAVY JUNGLE OUTFIT

Complete the game.

LARA CROFT JUNGLE OUTFIT

Score 1,410,000 points.

LARA CROFT BIKER OUTFIT

Score 1,900,000 points.

LARA CROFT LEGEND OUTFIT

Defeat Xolotl.

DOPPELGANGER OUTFIT

Score 2,400,000 points.

L

LEFT 4 DEAD 2

AVATAR AWARDS

AWARD	EARNED BY
Med Kit	Defeat all campaigns
Left 4 Dead 2 Hat	Play any map in The Passing
Gnome	Play any 6 Mutations
Left 4 Dead 2 Shirt	Win 10 games in Scavenge
Bull Shifters (Ellis) Shirt	Win 10 games in Versus
Depeche Mode (Rochelle) Shirt	Rescue Gnome Chompski from Dark Carnival
Zombie Hand Shirt	Kill 10,000 infected

ACHIEVEMENTS

NAME	GOAL/REQUIREMENT	POINT VALUE
PRICE CHOPPER	Survive the Dead Center campaign.	20
MIDNIGHT RIDER	Survive the Dark Carnival campaign.	20
RAGIN' CAJUN	Survive the Swamp Fever campaign.	20
WEATHERMAN	Survive the Hard Rain campaign.	20
BRIDGE BURNER	Survive the Parish campaign.	20
STILL SOMETHING TO PROVE	Survive all campaigns on Expert.	35
THE REAL DEAL	Survive a campaign on Expert skill with Realism mode enabled.	35
CONFEDERACY OF CRUNCHES	Finish a campaign using only melee weapons.	30
HEAD HONCHO	Decapitate 200 Infected with a melee weapon.	15
CLUB DEAD	Use every melee weapon to kill Common Infected.	15
CHAIN OF COMMAND	Kill 100 Common Infected with the chainsaw.	15
TANK BURGER	Kill a Tank with melee weapons.	30
SHOCK JOCK	Revive 10 dead Survivors with the defibrillator.	30
THE QUICK AND THE DEAD	Revive 10 incapacitated Survivors while under the speed-boosting effects of adrenaline.	30
ARMORY OF ONE	Deploy an ammo upgrade and have your team use it.	15
BURNING SENSATION	Ignite 50 Common Infected with incendiary ammo.	15
DISMEMBERMENT PLAN	Kill 15 Infected with a single grenade launcher blast.	20
SEPTIC TANK	Use a bile bomb on a Tank.	15
CRASS MENAGERIE	Kill one of each Uncommon Infected.	20
DEAD IN THE WATER	Kill 10 swampy Mudmen while they are in the water.	20
ROBBED ZOMBIE	Collect 10 vials of Boomer vomit from infected CEDA agents you have killed.	15
CL0WND	Honk the noses of 10 Clowns.	15
FRIED PIPER	Using a Molotov, burn a Clown leading at least 10 Common Infected.	15
LEVEL A CHARGE	Kill a Charger with a melee weapon while they are charging.	15
ACID REFLEX	Kill a Spitter before she is able to spit.	15
A RIDE DENIED	Kill a Jockey within 2 seconds of it jumping on a Survivor.	15
STACHE WHACKER	Prove you are faster than Moustachio.	15
GONG SHOW	Prove you are stronger than Moustachio.	15
GUARDIN' GNOME	Rescue Gnome Chompski from the Carnival.	30

NAME	GOAL/REQUIREMENT	POINT VALUE
WING AND A PRAYER	Defend yourself at the crashed airliner without taking damage.	30
SOB STORY	Navigate the sugar mill and reach the safe room without killing any Witches.	30
VIOLENCE IN SILENCE	Navigate the impound lot and reach the cemetery safe room without tripping any alarms.	30
BRIDGE OVER TREBLED SLAUGHTER	Cross the bridge finale in less than three minutes.	30
HEARTWARMER	In a Versus round, leave the saferoom to defibrillate a dead teammate.	20
STRENGTH IN NUMBERS	Form a team and beat an enemy team in 4v4 Versus or Scavenge.	15
QUALIFIED RIDE	As the Jockey, ride a Survivor for more than 12 seconds.	15
BACK IN THE SADDLE	As the Jockey, ride the Survivors twice in a single life.	15
RODE HARD, PUT AWAY WET	As the Jockey, ride a Survivor and steer them into a Spitter's acid patch.	20
GREAT EXPECTORATIONS	As the Spitter, hit every Survivor with a single acid patch.	15
A SPITTLE HELP FROM MY FRIENDS	As the Spitter, spit on a Survivor being choked by a Smoker.	15
SCATTERING RAM	As the Charger, bowl through the entire enemy team in a single charge.	20
MEAT TENDERIZER	As the Charger, grab a Survivor and smash them into the ground for a solid 15 seconds.	20
LONG DISTANCE CARRIER	As the Charger, grab a Survivor and carry them over 80 feet.	15
BEAT THE RUSH	In a Survival round, get a medal only using melee weapons.	15
HUNTING PARTY	Win a game of Scavenge.	15
GAS GUZZLER	Collect 100 gas cans in Scavenge.	20
CACHE AND CARRY	Collect 15 gas cans in a single Scavenge round.	20
SCAVENGE HUNT	Stop the enemy team from collecting any gas cans during a Scavenge round.	15
FUEL CRISIS	Make a Survivor drop a gas can during overtime.	15
GAS SHORTAGE	Cause 25 gas can drops as a Special Infected.	20

DOWNLOADABLE CONTENT: THE PASSING

ACHIEVEMENTS

NAME	GOAL/REQUIREMENT	POINT VALUE
TORCH BEARER	Survive The Passing Campaign.	20
WEDDING CRASHER	As the Charger, grab a Survivor and crash them through 8 chairs at the wedding.	30
TIL IT GOES CLICK	Using the M60, kill 25 infected without letting go of the trigger.	20
GRAVE ROBBER	Collect 10 items dropped by a Fallen Survivor.	25
MUTANT OVERLORD	Play 6 Mutations.	30
FORE!	Knock off the heads of 18 infected with the golf club.	25
KILLING 'EM SWIFTLY TO THIS SONG	Play the new Midnight Riders song on a jukebox.	20
KITE LIKE A MAN	Kill a Tank only with damage from the original Survivors.	30
CACHE GRAB	Open 5 foot lockers.	20
PORT OF SCAVENGE	Play 5 full games of Scavenge on The Port.	30

CHEATS, ACHIEVEMENTS, AND TROPHIES

L

THE LEGEND OF SPYRO: DAWN OF THE DRAGON

INFINITE HEALTH

Pause the game, hold Z and move the Nunchuk Right, Right, Down, Down, Left.

INFINITE MANA

Pause the game, hold Z and move the Nunchuk Up, Right, Up, Left, Down.

MAX XP

Pause the game, hold Z and move the Nunchuk Up, Left, Left, Down, Up.

ALL ELEMENTAL UPGRADES

Pause the game, hold Z and move the Nunchuk Left, Up, Down, Up, Right.

UNLIMITED LIFE

Pause the game, hold L1 and press Right, Right, Down, Down, Left with the Left Analog Stick.

UNLIMITED MANA

Pause the game, hold R1 and press Up, Right, Up, Left, Down with the Left Analog Stick.

MAXIMUM XP

Pause the game, hold R1 and press Left, Right, Right, Up, Up with the Left Analog Stick.

ALL ELEMENTAL UPGRADES

Pause the game, hold L1 and press Left, Up, Down, Up, Right with the Left Analog Stick.

UNLIMITED LIFE

Pause the game, hold Left Bumper and press Right, Right, Down, Down, Left with the Left Control Stick.

UNLIMITED MANA

Pause the game, hold Right Bumper and press Up, Right, Up, Left, Down with the Left Control Stick.

MAXIMUM XP

Pause the game, hold Right Bumper and press Up, Left, Left, Down, Up with the Left Control Stick.

ALL ELEMENTAL UPGRADES

Pause the game, hold Left Bumper and press Left, Up, Down, Up, Right with the Left Control Stick.

THE LEGEND OF ZELDA: SKYWARD SWORD

HERO MODE

After completing the main quest, you can choose to play Hero Mode, which is a tougher version of the regular game. Defeat the game on this mode to unlock a Triforce next to the save.

GRATITUDE CRYSTAL REWARDS

There are 80 Gratitude Crystals that can be found and received throughout the game—65 come from completing side quests and the rest must be found. The following lists the rewards you gain by returning these Gratitude Crystals to Batreaux.

REWARD	NUMBER OF GRATITUDE CRYSTALS
Medium Wallet (500 Rupees)	5
Heart Piece	10
Big Wallet (1000 Rupees) and Cursed Medal	30
Gold Rupee	40
Giant Wallet (5,000 Rupees)	50
2 Gold Rupees	70
Tycoon Wallet (9,000 Rupees)	80

LEGENDS OF WRESTLEMANIA

XBOX 360

ANIMAL'S SECOND COSTUME

Select Cheat Codes from the Options menu and enter TheRoadWarriorAnimal.

BRUTUS BEEFCAKE'S SECOND COSTUME

Select Cheat Codes from the Options menu and enter BrutusTheBarberShop!.

IRON SHIEK'S SECOND COSTUME

Select Cheat Codes from the Options menu and enter IronSheikCamelClutch.

JIMMY HART'S SECOND COSTUME

Select Cheat Codes from the Options menu and enter WithManagerJimmyHart.

KOKO B WARE'S SECOND COSTUME

Select Cheat Codes from the Options menu and enter TheBirdmanKokoBWare!.

THE ROCK'S SECOND COSTUME

Select Cheat Codes from the Options menu and enter UnlockTheRockBottom!.

SGT. SLAUGHTER'S SECOND COSTUME

Select Cheat Codes from the Options menu and enter CobraClutchSlaughter.

SHAWN MICHAELS'S SECOND COSTUME

Select Cheat Codes from the Options menu and enter ShawnsSweetChinMusic.

UNDERTAKER'S SECOND COSTUME

Select Cheat Codes from the Options menu and enter UndertakersTombstone.

LEGO BATMAN

NINTENDO WII/XBOX 360/PS3/PSP

BATCAVE CODES

Using the computer in the Batcave, select Enter Code and enter the following codes.

CHARACTERS

CHARACTER	CODE
Alfred	ZAQ637
Batgirl	JKR331
Bruce Wayne	BDJ327
Catwoman (Classic)	M1AAWW
Clown Goon	HJK327
Commissioner Gordon	DDP967
Fishmonger	HGY748
Freeze Girl	XVK541
Joker Goon	UTF782
Joker Henchman	YUN924
Mad Hatter	JCA283
Man-Bat	NYU942

CHARACTER	CODE
Military Policeman	MKL382
Nightwing	MVY759
Penguin Goon	NKA238
Penguin Henchman	BJH782
Penguin Minion	KJP748
Poison Ivy Goon	GTB899
Police Marksman	HKG984
Police Officer	JRY983
Riddler Goon	CRY928
Riddler Henchman	XEU824
S.W.A.T.	HTF114
Sailor	NAV592
Scientist	JFL786
Security Guard	PLB946
The Joker (Tropical)	CCB199
Yeti	NJL412
Zoo Sweeper	DWR243

VEHICLES

VEHICLE	CODE
Bat-Tank	KNTT4B
Bruce Wayne's Private Jet	LEA664
Catwoman's Motorcycle	HPL826
Garbage Truck	DUS483
Goon Helicopter	GCH328
Harbor Helicopter	CHP735
Harley Quinn's Hammer Truck	RDT637
Mad Hatter's Glider	HS000W
Mad Hatter's Steamboat	M4DM4N
Mr. Freeze's Iceberg	ICYICE
The Joker's Van	JUK657
Mr. Freeze's Kart	BCT229
Penguin Goon Submarine	BTN248
Police Bike	LJP234
Police Boat	PLC999
Police Car	KJL832
Police Helicopter	CWR732
Police Van	MAC788
Police Watercraft	VJD328
Riddler's Jet	HAHAHA
Robin's Submarine	TTF453
Two-Face's Armored Truck	EFE933

CHEATS

CHEAT	CODE
Always Score Multiply	9LRGNB
Fast Batarangs	JRBDCB
Fast Walk	ZOLM6N
Flame Batarang	D8NYWH
Freeze Batarang	XPN4NG
Extra Hearts	ML3KHP
Fast Build	EVG26J
Immune to Freeze	JXUDY6
Invincibility	WYD5CP
Minikit Detector	ZXGH9J

CHEAT	CODE
More Batarang Targets	XWP645
Piece Detector	KHJ554
Power Brick Detector	MMN786
Regenerate Hearts	HJH7HJ
Score x2	N4NR3E
Score x4	CX9MAT
Score x6	MLVNF2
Score x8	WCCDB9
Score x10	18HW07

NINTENDO 3DS

ALFRED PENNYWORTH

Use the computer in the Batcave, select Enter Code and enter ZAQ637.

BATGIRL

Use the computer in the Batcave, select Enter Code and enter JKR331.

BRUCE WAYNE

Use the computer in the Batcave, select Enter Code and enter BDJ327.

CLASSIC CATWOMAN

Use the computer in the Batcave, select Enter Code and enter M1AAWW.

CLOWN GOON

Use the computer in the Batcave, select Enter Code and enter HJK327.

COMMISSIONER GORDON

Use the computer in the Batcave, select Enter Code and enter DDP967.

FISHMONGER

Use the computer in the Batcave, select Enter Code and enter HGY748.

FREEZE GIRL

Use the computer in the Batcave, select Enter Code and enter XVK541.

FREEZE HENCHMAN

Use the computer in the Batcave, select Enter Code and enter NJL412.

JOKER GOON

Use the computer in the Batcave, select Enter Code and enter UTF782.

JOKER HENCHMAN

Use the computer in the Batcave, select Enter Code and enter YUN924.

NIGHTWING

Use the computer in the Batcave, select Enter Code and enter MVY759.

TROPICAL JOKER

Use the computer in the Batcave, select Enter Code and enter CCB199.

1 MILLION STUDS

At the Main menu, press X, Y, B, B, Y, X, L, L, R, R, Up, Down, Left, Right, Start, Select.

3 MILLION STUDS

At the Main menu, press Up, Up, B, Down, Down, X, Left, Left, Y, L, R, L, R, B, Y, X, Start, Select.

ALL CHARACTERS

At the Main menu, press X, Up, B, Down, Y, Left, Start, Right, R, R, L, R, R, Down, Down, Up, Y, Y, Y, Start, Select.

ALL EPISODES AND FREE PLAY MODE

At the Main menu, press Right, Up, R, L, X, Y, Right, Left, B, L, R, L, Down, Down, Up, Y, Y, X, X, B, B, Up, Up, L, R, Start, Select.

ALL EXTRAS

At the Main menu, press Up, Down, L, R, L, R, L, Left, Right, X, X, Y, Y, B, B, L, Up, Down, L, R, L, R, Up, Up, Down, Start, Select.

CHEATS, ACHIEVEMENTS, AND TROPHIES

L

LEGO BATTLES

To activate the following cheats, pause the game and tap the red brick.

INVINCIBLE HERO

At the LEGO Store, tap the Red Brick and enter HJCRAWK.

REGENERATING HEALTH

At the LEGO Store, tap the Red Brick and enter ABABLRX.

ONE-HIT KILL (HEROES)

At the LEGO Store, tap the Red Brick and enter AVMPWHK.

LONG-RANGE MAGIC

At the LEGO Store, tap the Red Brick and enter ZPWJFUQ.

SUPER MAGIC

At the LEGO Store, tap the Red Brick and enter DWFTBNS.

DOUBLE LEGO BRICKS

At the LEGO Store, tap the Red Brick and enter BGQOYRT.

FAST BUILDING

At the LEGO Store, tap the Red Brick and enter QMSLPOE.

FAST HARVESTING

At the LEGO Store, tap the Red Brick and enter PQZLJOB.

FAST MAGIC

At the LEGO Store, tap the Red Brick and enter JRTPASX.

FAST MINING

At the LEGO Store, tap the Red Brick and enter KVBPQRJ.

FULL UNIT CAP

At the LEGO Store, tap the Red Brick and enter UMSXIRQ.

SUPER EXPLOSIONS

At the LEGO Store, tap the Red Brick and enter THNBGRE.

UPGRADED TOWERS

At the LEGO Store, tap the Red Brick and enter EDRFTGY.

SHOW ENEMIES

At the LEGO Store, tap the Red Brick and enter IBGOFWX.

SHOW LEGO STUDS

At the LEGO Store, tap the Red Brick and enter CPLYREK.

SHOW MINIKIT

At the LEGO Store, tap the Red Brick and enter LJYQRAC.

SHOW RED BRICKS

At the LEGO Store, tap the Red Brick and enter RTGYPKC.

REVEAL MAP

At the LEGO Store, tap the Red Brick and enter SKQMXPL.

UNLOCK ISLANDER

At the LEGO Store, tap the Red Brick and enter UGDRSQP.

UNLOCK NINJA MASTER

At the LEGO Store, tap the Red Brick and enter SHWSDGU.

UNLOCK SPACE CRIMINAL LEADER

At the LEGO Store, tap the Red Brick and enter ZVDNJSU.

UNLOCK TROLL KING

At the LEGO Store, tap the Red Brick and enter XRCTVYB.

LEGO BATTLES: NINJAGO

SANTA CLAUS

Change your system date to December 25.

PASSWORDS

Select Cheat Codes from the LEGO shop and enter the following:

EFFECT	PASSWORD
Kruncha	HJEKTPU
Spaceman	TSDYHBZ
Show Enemies on Minimap	KMRWLSS

PASSWORDS FOR STUDS

Select Cheat Codes from the LEGO shop and enter the following:

# OF STUDS	PASSWORD
5000	GQBAUJP
10000	GALNAFE
15000	LQMZPBX
20000	PPMSUGS
25000	SLBQFSW
30000	MXQNVQP
35000	SJVPMAA
40000	WZURMZM
45000	UABBMZQ
55000	BGCHKHA
60000	JXULZZW
65000	FBMRSWG
70000	ZZXWUZJ
75000	HXMVRZP
80000	NYUXUZF

LEGO CITY UNDERCOVER

PASSWORDS

New characters, vehicles and game modes can be unlocked with the following passwords.

UNLOCKABLE	PASSWORD
Baseball Player	YCMWKP
Bonus Missions	3D74QF9
Drag Queen	CNCNRH
Drakonas Vehicle	DWJVCT
Gorilla Suit Guy	XKGZVJ
High Speed Chase Missions & Vehicles	N7NN4F9
Justice and Red Sports Car	3GCC7XR
Natalia Kowalski	HVGTPG
Race Car Driver	MHHRHM
Relocator Vehicle	VZHHDM
Samurai Warrior	RJYZHC
Soccer Player	SYFMWJ
Werewolf	GYSTQP

LEGO CITY UNDERCOVER: THE CHASE BEGINS

NINTENDO 3DS

PASSWORDS

These passwords can be inputted in the mainframe in the police station to unlock additional characters and features.

EFFECT	PASSWORD
Circus Clown	YXJRTC
Deep Sea Diver	RMRQFN
Drakonas	VZHHDM
Ninja Warrior	CXPNXX
Sentinel Disguise	MRPHVQ
Zombie	HVGTPG

LEGO HARRY POTTER: YEARS 1-4

NINTENDO WII/XBOX 360/PS 3

RED BRICK EXTRAS

Once you have access to The Leaky Cauldron, enter Wiseacre's Wizarding Supplies from Diagon Alley. Go upstairs to enter the following. Pause the game and select Extras to toggle the cheats on/off.

CHEAT	CODE
Carrot Wands	AUC8EH
Character Studs	H27KGC
Character Token Detector	HA79V8
Christmas	T7PVVN
Disguise	4DMK2R
Fall Rescue	ZEX7MV
Extra Hearts	J9U6Z9
Fast Dig	Z9BFAD
Fast Magic	FA3GQA
Gold Brick Detector	84QNQN
Hogwarts Crest Detector	TTMC6D
Ice Rink	F88VUW
Invincibility	QQWC6B
Red Brick Detector	7AD7HE
Regenerate Hearts	89ML2W
Score x2	74YKR7
Score x4	J3WHNK
Score x6	XK9ANE
Score x8	HUFV2H
Score x10	H8X69Y
Silhouettes	HZBVX7
Singing Mandrake	BMEU6X
Stud Magnet	67FKWZ

WISEACRE SPELLS

Once you have access to The Leaky Cauldron, enter Wiseacre's Wizarding Supplies from Diagon Alley. Go upstairs to enter the following. You need to learn Wingardium Leviosa before you can use these cheats.

SPELL	CODE
Accio	VE9VV7
Anteoculatia	QFB6NR
Calvorio	6DNR6L

SPELL	CODE
Colovaria	9GJ442
Engorgio Skullus	CD4JLX
Entomorphis	MYN3NB
Flipendo	ND2L7W
Glacius	ERA9DR
Herbifors	H8FTHL
Incarcerous	YEB9Q9
Locomotor Mortis	2M2XJ6
Multicorfors	JK6QRM
Redactum Skullus	UW8LRH
Rictusempra	2UCA3M
Slugulus Eructo	U6EE8X
Stupefy	UWDJ4Y
Tarantallegra	KWWQ44
Trip Jinx	YZNRF6

EEYLOPS GOLD BRICKS

After gaining access to the Leaky Cauldron, enter Wiseacre's Wizarding Supplies from Diagon Alley. Go upstairs to enter the following. To access the LEGO Builder, visit Gringott's Bank at the end of Diagon Alley.

GOLD BRICK	ENTER
1	QE4VC7
2	FY8H97
3	3MQT4P
4	PQPM7Z
5	ZY2CPA
6	3GMTP6
7	XY6VYZ
8	TUNC4W
9	EJ42Q6
10	GRJCV9
11	DZCY6G

LEGO HARRY POTTER: YEARS 5-7

NINTENDO WII/XBOX 360/PS3

CHEATS

Pause the game and select Extras. Go to Enter Code and enter the following:

CHEAT	CODE
Carrot Wands	AUC8EH
Character Studs	H27KGC
Character Token Detector	HA79V8
Christmas	T7PVVN
Collect Ghost Studs	2FLY6B
Extra Hearts	J9U6Z9
Fall Rescue	ZEX7MV
Fast Dig	Z9BFAD
Ghost Coins	2FLY6B
Gold Brick Detector	84QNQN
Hogwarts Crest Detector	TTMC6D
Invincibility	QQWC6B
Red Brick Detector	7AD7HE
Score x2	74YKR7

CHEAT	CODE
Score x6	XK9ANE
Score x8	HUFV2H
Score x10	H8X69Y
Super Strength	BMEU6X

XBOX 360/PS3

ACHIEVEMENTS & TROPHIES

NAME	GOAL/REQUIREMENT	POINT VALUE	TROPHY VALUE
Albus Percival Wulfric Brian	Complete "Dark Times"	10	Bronze
Off the Beaten Track	Complete "Dumbledore's Army"	10	Bronze
Attempt to Resist	Complete "Focus!"	10	Bronze
Did Santa Eat That Cake?	Complete "Kreacher Discomforts"	10	Bronze
Accordion to Grawp	Complete "A Giant Virtuoso"	10	Bronze
He's Back!	Complete "A Veiled Threat"	10	Bronze
Phoenix Rising	Complete Year 5	25	Bronze
Chair-ismatic	Complete "Out of Retirement"	10	Bronze
The Slug Club	Complete "Just Desserts"	10	Bronze
Weasleys' Wizard Woes	Complete "A Not So Merry Christmas"	10	Bronze
Sectumsempra	Complete "Love Hurts"	10	Bronze
A Riddle Revealed	Complete "Felix Felicis"	10	Bronze
Dumbledore's Demise	Complete "Horcrux and the Hand"	10	Bronze
I am the Half-Blood Prince	Complete Year 6	25	Bronze
Cake or Death Eater?	Complete "The Seven Harrys"	10	Bronze
A Wise Disguise	Complete "Magic is Might"	10	Bronze
Shedding Skin	Complete "In Grave Danger"	10	Bronze
Soul Searching	Complete "Sword and Locket"	10	Bronze
The Tale of the Three Brothers	Complete "Lovegood's Lunacy"	10	Bronze
Here Lies a Free Elf	Complete "DOBBY!"	10	Bronze
To Be Continued	Complete Year 7	25	Bronze
That's Unfortunate	Complete "The Thief's Downfall"	10	Bronze
Undesirable No. 1	Complete "Back to School"	10	Bronze
You and Whose Army?	Complete "Burning Bridges"	10	Bronze
Wit Beyond Measure…	Complete "Fiendfyre Frenzy"	10	Bronze
Kick the Bucket	Complete "Snape's Tears"	10	Bronze
Voldemort's Demise	Complete "The Flaw in the Plan"	10	Bronze
All Was Well	Complete Year 8	50	Bronze
Collector's dream	Complete the Bonus Level	25	Silver
But… I Am The Chosen One	Complete the game to 100% (Single Player Only)	100	Gold
Hogwarts has Changed	Visit the Hogwarts Foyer in Year 7	30	Silver
Halfway There	Unlocked on hitting 50% game completion (Single Player Only)	30	Silver
Avid Reader	Use a Quibbler dispenser 25 times	25	Silver
Idling	Stand still with no controller input for 5 minutes	20	Bronze
Lessons Learned	Complete all lessons (Single Player Only)	30	Silver

NAME	GOAL/REQUIREMENT	POINT VALUE	TROPHY VALUE
We are the D.A.	Unlock all of the members of Dumbledore's Army (Single Player Only)	30	Silver
Weasley Does It	Use a Weasley box with every Weasley	25	Bronze
O Children	Complete the scene where Hermione and Harry dance in the tent	20	Bronze
Knuts and Vaults	Collect 1 billion studs (Single Player Only)	50	Gold
What if?	Defeat every Harry freeplay variant as Lord Voldemort	20	Silver
Tall Order	Unlock ALL of the Order of the Phoenix character variants (Single Player Only)	40	Silver
A Minifig's Best Friend	Unlock every character with a pet (Single Player Only)	30	Silver
Witch!	Unlock all witch characters (Single Player Only)	50	Bronze
Pyjama Drama	Unlock every pyjama character variant (Single Player Only)	20	Bronze
A Dish Best Served Cold	Defeat Bellatrix with Neville (Waiter) in a duel	20	Bronze
Not "Fun Guys"	Defeat 30 Red Caps	15	Bronze
Dark Times Ahead	Unlock every bad wizard (Single Player Only)	25	Silver
Lighten Up	Use the Deluminator	10	Bronze
A Sirius Family Issue	Defeat Bellatrix as any Sirius Black character variant in a duel	20	Bronze

LEGO INDIANA JONES: THE ORIGINAL ADVENTURES

NINTENDO WII/XBOX 360/PS3

CHARACTERS

Approach the blackboard in the Classroom and enter the following codes.

CHARACTER	CODE
Bandit	12N68W
Bandit Swordsman	1MK4RT
Barranca	04EM94
Bazooka Trooper (Crusade)	MK83R7
Bazooka Trooper (Raiders)	S93Y5R
Belloq	CHN3YU
Belloq (Jungle)	TDR197
Belloq (Robes)	VEO29L
British Commander	B73EUA
British Officer	VJ5TI9
British Soldier	DJ5I2W
Captain Katanga	VJ3TT3
Chatter Lal	ENW936
Chatter Lal (Thuggee)	CNH4RY
Chen	3NK48T
Colonel Dietrich	2K9RKS
Colonel Vogel	8EAL4H
Dancing Girl	C7EJ21
Donovan	3NFTU8

CHARACTER	CODE
Elsa (Desert)	JSNRT9
Elsa (Officer)	VMJ5US
Enemy Boxer	8246RB
Enemy Butler	VJ48W3
Enemy Guard	VJ7R51
Enemy Guard (Mountains)	YR47WM
Enemy Officer	572E61
Enemy Officer (Desert	2MK45O
Enemy Pilot	B84ELP
Enemy Radio Operator	1MF94R
Enemy Soldier (Desert)	4NSU7Q
Fedora	V75YSP
First Mate	0GIN24
Grail Knight	NE6THI
Hovitos Tribesman	H0V1SS
Indiana Jones (Desert Disguise)	4J8S4M
Indiana Jones (Officer)	VJ85OS
Jungle Guide	24PF34
Kao Kan	WMO46L
Kazim	NRH23J
Kazim (Desert)	3M29TJ
Lao Che	2NK479
Maharajah	NFK5N2
Major Toht	13NS01
Masked Bandit	N48SF0
Mola Ram	FJUR31
Monkey Man	3RF6YJ
Pankot Assassin	2NKT72
Pankot Guard	VN28RH
Sherpa Brawler	VJ37WJ
Sherpa Gunner	ND762W
Slave Child	0E3ENW
Thuggee	VM683E
Thuggee Acolyte	T2R3F9
Thuggee Slave Driver	VBS7GW
Village Dignitary	KD48TN
Village Elder	4682E1
Willie (Dinner Suit)	VK93R7
Willie (Pajamas)	MEN4IP
Wu Han	3NSLT8

EXTRAS

Approach the blackboard in the Classroom and enter the following codes. Some cheats need to be enabled by selecting Extras from the pause menu.

CHEAT	CODE
Artifact Detector	VIKED7
Beep Beep	VNF59Q
Character Treasure	VIES2R
Disarm Enemies	VKRNS9
Disguises	4ID1N6
Fast Build	V83SLO
Fast Dig	378RS6
Fast Fix	FJ59WS
Fertilizer	B1GW1F
Ice Rink	33GM7J

CHEAT	CODE
Parcel Detector	VUT673
Poo Treasure	WWQ1SA
Regenerate Hearts	MDLP69
Secret Characters	3X44AA
Silhouettes	3HE85H
Super Scream	VN3R7S
Super Slap	0P1TA5
Treasure Magnet	H86LA2
Treasure x10	VI3PS8
Treasure x2	VM4TS9
Treasure x4	VLWEN3
Treasure x6	V84RYS
Treasure x8	A72E1M

NINTENDO 3DS

You should hear a confirmation sound after the following codes are entered.

ALL CHARACTERS

At the Title screen, press X, Up, B, Down, Y, Left, Start, Right, R, R, L, R, R, Down, Down, Up, Y, Y, Y, Start, Select.

ALL EPISODES AND FREE PLAY MODE

Right, Up, R, L, X, Y, Right, Left, B, L, R, L, Down, Down, Up, Y, Y, X, X, B, B, Up, Up, L, R, Start, Select.

ALL EXTRAS

Up, Down, L, R, L, R, L, Left, Right, X, X, Y, Y, B, B, L, Up, Down, L, R, L, R, Up, Up, Down, Start, Select.

1,000,000 STUDS

At the Title screen, press X, Y, B, B, Y, X, L, L, R, R, Up, Down, Left, Right, Start, Select.

3,000,000 STUDS

At the Title screen, press Up, Up, B, Down, Down, X, Left, Left, Y, L, R, L, R, B, Y, X, Start, Select.

PSP

CHARACTERS

Approach the blackboard in the Classroom and enter the following codes.

CHARACTER	CODE
Bandit	12N68W
Bandit Swordsman	1MK4RT
Barranca	04EM94
Bazooka Trooper (Crusade)	MK83R7
Bazooka Trooper (Raiders)	S93Y5R
Belloq	CHN3YU
Belloq (Jungle)	TDR197
Belloq (Robes)	VEO29L
British Commander	B73EUA
British Officer	VJ5TI9
British Soldier	DJ5I2W
Captain Katanga	VJ3TT3
Chatter Lal	ENW936
Chatter Lal (Thuggee)	CNH4RY
Chen	3NK48T
Colonel Dietrich	2K9RKS
Colonel Vogel	8EAL4H
Dancing Girl	C7EJ21

CHARACTER	CODE
Donovan	3NFTU8
Elsa (Desert)	JSNRT9
Elsa (Officer)	VMJ5US
Enemy Boxer	8246RB
Enemy Butler	VJ48W3
Enemy Guard	VJ7R51
Enemy Guard (Mountains)	YR47WM
Enemy Officer	572E61
Enemy Officer (Desert	2MK45O
Enemy Pilot	B84ELP
Enemy Radio Operator	1MF94R
Enemy Soldier (Desert)	4NSU7Q
Fedora	V75YSP
First Mate	0GIN24
Grail Knight	NE6THI
Hovitos Tribesman	H0V1SS
Indiana Jones (Desert Disguise)	4J8S4M
Indiana Jones (Officer)	VJ85OS
Jungle Guide	24PF34
Kao Kan	WMO46L
Kazim	NRH23J
Kazim (Desert)	3M29TJ
Lao Che	2NK479
Maharajah	NFK5N2
Major Toht	13NS01
Masked Bandit	N48SF0
Mola Ram	FJUR31
Monkey Man	3RF6YJ
Pankot Assassin	2NKT72
Pankot Guard	VN28RH
Sherpa Brawler	VJ37WJ
Sherpa Gunner	ND762W
Slave Child	0E3ENW
Thuggee	VM683E
Thuggee Acolyte	T2R3F9
Thuggee Slave Driver	VBS7GW
Village Dignitary	KD48TN
Village Elder	4682E1
Willie (Dinner Suit)	VK93R7
Willie (Pajamas)	MEN4IP
Wu Han	3NSLT8

LEGO INDIANA JONES 2: THE ADVENTURE CONTINUES

NINTENDO WII/XBOX 360/PS3

Pause the game, select Enter Secret Code from the Extras menu, and enter the following.

CHARACTERS

CHARACTER	CODE
Belloq (Priest)	FTL48S
Dovchenko	WL4T6N
Enemy Boxer	7EQF47
Henry Jones	4CSAKH
Indiana Jones	PGWSEA
Indiana Jones: 2	FGLKYS
Indiana Jones (Collect)	DZFY9S
Indiana Jones (Desert)	M4C34K
Indiana Jones (Desert Disguise)	2W8QR3
Indiana Jones (Dinner Suit)	QUNZUT
Indiana Jones (Kali)	J2XS97
Indiana Jones (Officer)	3FQFKS
Interdimensional Being	PXT4UP
Lao Che	7AWX3J
Mannequin (Boy)	2UJQWC
Mannequin (Girl)	3PGSEL
Mannequin (Man)	QPWDMM
Mannequin (Woman)	U7SMVK
Mola Ram	82RMC2
Mutt	2GKS62
Salah	E88YRP
Willie	94RUAJ

EXTRAS

EFFECT	CODE
Beep Beep	UU3VSC
Disguise	Y9TE98
Fast Build	SNXC2F
Fast Dig	XYAN83
Fast Fix	3Z7PJX
Fearless	TUXNZF
Ice Rink	TY9P4U
Invincibility	6JBB65
Poo Money	SZFAAE
Score x3	PEHHPZ
Score x4	UXGTB3
Score X6	XWLJEY
Score x8	S5UZCP
Score x10	V7JYBU
Silhouettes	FQGPYH
Snake Whip	2U7YCV
Stud Magnet	EGSM5B

CHEATS, ACHIEVEMENTS, AND TROPHIES

L

LEGO THE LORD OF THE RINGS

NINTENDO 3DS/XBOX 360/PS3/PSVITA

PASSWORDS

These passwords can be inputted to unlock new characters or enable cheats and new features.

EFFECT	PASSWORD
8-Bit Music	GD35HC
Action Assist	T1JM4R
Attract Studs	C7FJ7B
Berserker	UE5Z7H
Bilbo Baggins	J4337V
Boromir (Captain)	HTYADU
Boss Disguises	F3H14H
Character Studs	PR3V4K
Denethor	RJV4KB
Disguises	MX26RJ
Easterling	R7XKDH
Elrond (2nd Age)	A9FB4Q
Eomer	U47AOG
Fall Rescue	WS68P2
Fast Build	A2LU58
Galadriel	7B4VWH
Gamling	AJVII1
Gondor Ranger	LG5GI7
Grima Wormtongue	BU95CB
Hama	73HJP6
King of the Dead	IH7E58
Lothlorien Elf	C2A58D
Lutz (Newborn)	QL28WB
Madril	C19F3A
Minikit Chest Finder	A24TVJ
Mithril Brick Finder	B72D7E
Mithril Hearts	2MCRDN
Mouth of Sauron	F4M7FC
Poo Studs	D49TXY
Quest Finder	EY4K32
Radagast the Brown	5LV6EB
Regenerate Hearts	H5L6N6
Ringwraith White	LYQU1F
Shagrat	PJB6MV
Studs x2	1F5YH2

XBOX 360/PS3

ACHIEVEMENTS & TROPHIES

NAME	GOAL/REQUIREMENT	POINT VALUE	TROPHY VALUE
The strength of Men failed.	Complete 'Prologue'.	25	Bronze
It's a dangerous business…	Complete 'The Black Rider'.	25	Bronze
That is no trinket you carry.	Complete 'Weathertop'.	25	Bronze
The long way around.	Complete 'The Pass of Caradhras'.	25	Bronze

NAME	GOAL/REQUIREMENT	POINT VALUE	TROPHY VALUE
This is no mine— it's a tomb.	Complete 'The Mines of Moria'.	25	Bronze
Let's hunt some Orc!	Complete 'Amon Hen'.	25	Bronze
On the Precious…	Complete 'Taming Gollum'.	25	Bronze
Soft and quick as shadows…	Complete 'The Dead Marshes'.	25	Bronze
Safe is where I'll keep you.	Complete 'Track Hobbits'.	25	Bronze
Stinking creatures…	Complete 'Warg Attack'.	25	Bronze
The battle is about to begin…	Complete 'Helm's Deep'.	25	Bronze
A Wizard should know better!	Complete 'Osgiliath'.	25	Bronze
Naughty little fly…	Complete 'The Secret Stairs'.	25	Bronze
We did it, Mr. Frodo.	Complete 'Cirith Ungol'.	25	Bronze
They have been summoned.	Complete 'The Paths of the Dead'.	25	Bronze
You and whose army?	Complete 'The Battle of Pelennor Fields'.	25	Bronze
This day we fight!	Complete 'The Black Gate'.	25	Bronze
It's gone.	Complete 'Mount Doom'.	25	Bronze
My Precious…	Collect all the Mithril Bricks. (Single Player Only)	50	Gold
There's some good in this world.	Complete all the Fetch Quests in Middle-earth. (Single Player Only)	50	Gold
There and Back Again.	Get 100%. (Single Player Only)	75	Gold
I told you he was tricksy.	Collect all the Red Bricks. (Single Player Only)	30	Silver
Of all the inquisitive Hobbits.	Unlock all the Map Stones in Middle-earth. (Single Player Only)	30	Bronze
Here's a pretty thing!	Craft every Mithril item. (Single Player Only)	30	Silver
Not with 10,000 men…	Unlock all characters. (Single Player Only)	30	Silver
Ready for another adventure.	Achieve True Adventurer in every level. (Single Player Only)	30	Silver
The Lord of the Ring.	Complete the Bonus Level.	30	Silver
Delved too greedily…	Collect more than 10,000,000,000 studs. (Single Player Only)	25	Bronze
I'm glad to be with you.	Complete a level in co-op.	10	Bronze
Don't tell the Elf…	Throw Gimli 30 times.	10	Bronze
Our only wish to catch a fish!	Fish perfectly 20 times by pressing the icon as it flashes.	10	Bronze
That is a rare gift.	Reach the top of Amon Hen without being caught once by Boromir. (Single Player Only)	10	Bronze
… And away he goes, Precious!	Defeat Gollum as Gollum.	10	Bronze
What about second breakfast?	Complete 2 cooking puzzles.	10	Bronze
That one counts as mine!	Finish one of Gimli's opponents as Legolas in 'Helm's Deep'.	10	Bronze
I've always been taller!	Use the Ent Draught on Pippin.	10	Bronze
We cannot linger.	Complete 'The Mines of Moria' in under 15 minutes.	10	Bronze
Dance of the dead.	Turn an enemy into a skeleton and make them dance.	10	Bronze
Pointy-eared Elvish princeling.	Defeat 42 Uruk-hai as Legolas.	10	Bronze

NAME	GOAL/REQUIREMENT	POINT VALUE	TROPHY VALUE
Great! …Where are we going?	Form The Fellowship of the Ring.	5	Bronze
Taking the Hobbits to Isengard.	Travel to Isengard as every playable Hobbit.	10	Bronze
An expected journey.	Travel to Trollshaws as Bilbo.	5	Bronze
Return of the Mushroom King.	Equip Aragorn with the Mushroom Crown.	5	Bronze
Worth greater than the Shire.	Dress a character completely in treasure items.	10	Bronze
One Ring to build them all.	Collect every trophy.	—	Platinum

SECRET ACHIEVEMENTS & TROPHIES

NAME	GOAL/REQUIREMENT	POINT VALUE	TROPHY VALUE
One does not simply…	Walk into Mordor.	5	Bronze
That still only counts as one!	Defeat an Oliphaunt as Legolas.	10	Bronze
It won't be that easy!	During 'Prologue', jump into the fires of Mount Doom as Isildur.	5	Bronze
A link to the elements.	Craft the Fire and Ice Bows. (Single Player Only)	5	Bronze

LEGO PIRATES OF THE CARIBBEAN

NINTENDO WII/3DS/XBOX 360/PS3

CODES

Pause the game and select Extras. Choose Enter Code and enter the following codes:

EFFECT	PASSWORD
Ammand the Corsair	EW8T6T
Angelica (Disguised)	DLRR45
Angry Cannibal	VGF32C
Blackbeard	D3DW0D
Clanker	ZM37GT
Clubba	644THF
Davy Jones	4DJLKR
Govorner Weatherby Swann	LD9454
Gunner	Y611WB
Hungry Cannibal	64BNHG
Jack Sparrow (Musical)	VDJSPW
Jacoby	BWO656
Jimmy Legs	13GLW5
King George	RKED43
Koehler	RT093G
Mistress Ching	GDETDE
Phillip	WEV040
Quartermaster	RX58HU
The Spaniard	P861JO
Twigg	KDLFKD

ACHIEVEMENTS & TROPHIES

NAME	GOAL/REQUIREMENT	POINT VALUE	TROPHY VALUE
Welcome to the Caribbean!	Complete Port Royal	12	Bronze
Hello, poppet!	Unlock all Elizabeth characters (Single Player Only)	15	Bronze
The Green Flash	Watch a sunset	15	Bronze
You may throw my hat	Collect all the red hats (Single Player Only)	40	Silver
A weather eye on the horizon	Use a spyglass	15	Bronze
More what you'd call guidelines	Complete the Brethren Court	15	Bronze
A pirate's life for me	Test any custom character	15	Bronze
The worst pirate I've ever seen	Complete Port Royal in Story with zero studs	15	Bronze
The Brethren Court	Unlock all the Pirate Lord characters (Single Player Only)	25	Bronze
The best pirate I've ever seen	Complete Port Royal in Story without dying	15	Bronze
On Stranger Tides	Complete the Film 4 story	20	Bronze
Take what you can	Collect all Gold bricks (Single Player Only)	65	Gold
At World's End	Complete the Film 3 story	20	Bronze
The Curse of the Black Pearl	Complete the Film 1 story	20	Bronze
Dead Man's Chest	Complete the Film 2 story	20	Bronze
Do you fear death?	Unlock all the Flying Dutchman crew characters (Single Player Only)	25	Silver
The pirate all pirates fear	Unlock all the Queen Anne's Revenge crew characters (Single Player Only)	25	Silver
Believing in ghost stories	Unlock all the cursed Black Pearl crew characters (Single Player Only)	25	Silver
Now bring me that horizon	Complete the game to 100% (Single Player Only)	100	Gold
Here there be monsters	Get eaten by a creature in deadly water	15	Bronze
Gents, take a walk	Walk on the sea bed with all possible characters	20	Bronze
I am a bad man	Play a level with all Extras turned on (Single Player Only)	15	Bronze
Sea turtles, mate	Ride on all types of animal in the game	25	Silver
There's the Jack I know	Get True Pirate in all levels (Single Player Only)	25	Silver
Aye-aye, captain!	Play a level in co-op	15	Bronze
You're off the edge of the map	Highlight the secret 6th point on all 4 level select maps (Single Player Only)	15	Bronze
Hello, beastie	Get eaten by the Kraken 10 times	25	Silver
Fire!	Fire 100 cannonballs	15	Bronze
Fight to the bitter end!	Defeat 100 enemies	20	Bronze
Five lashes be owed	As Jimmy Legs, whip Will Turner 5 times	15	Bronze
Hoist the colours!	Sail all the minikits in the hub	50	Gold
Parley!	Unlock all characters (Single Player Only)	25	Silver

NAME	GOAL/REQUIREMENT	POINT VALUE	TROPHY VALUE
What do you want most?	In any level use only the compass to find all its secrets in one go, alone.	25	Silver
You filthy, slimy, mangy cur!	Complete all the Guard Dog levels	15	Bronze
Try wearing a corset	Do 5 lady backflips in a row	15	Bronze
Pieces of Eight	Reach 888,888,888 studs	88	Silver
Did everybody see that?	High dive into the Maelstrom	20	Bronze
Wind in your sails!	Hit a flying parrot on Smuggler's Den	15	Bronze
And really bad eggs	Play as all the Extra Toggle characters	25	Silver
Savvy?	Unlock all the Jack Sparrow characters (Single Player Only)	15	Bronze

LEGO STAR WARS: THE COMPLETE SAGA

NINTENDO WII/XBOX 360/PS3

The following still need to be purchased after entering the codes.

CHARACTERS

ADMIRAL ACKBAR

At the bar in Mos Eisley Cantina, select Enter Code and enter ACK646.

BATTLE DROID (COMMANDER)

At the bar in Mos Eisley Cantina, select Enter Code and enter KPF958.

BOBA FETT (BOY)

At the bar in Mos Eisley Cantina, select Enter Code and enter GGF539.

BOSS NASS

At the bar in Mos Eisley Cantina, select Enter Code and enter HHY697.

CAPTAIN TARPALS

At the bar in Mos Eisley Cantina, select Enter Code and enter QRN714.

COUNT DOOKU

At the bar in Mos Eisley Cantina, select Enter Code and enter DDD748.

DARTH MAUL

At the bar in Mos Eisley Cantina, select Enter Code and enter EUK421.

EWOK

At the bar in Mos Eisley Cantina, select Enter Code and enter EWK785.

GENERAL GRIEVOUS

At the bar in Mos Eisley Cantina, select Enter Code and enter PMN576.

GREEDO

At the bar in Mos Eisley Cantina, select Enter Code and enter ZZR636.

IG-88

At the bar in Mos Eisley Cantina, select Enter Code and enter GIJ989.

IMPERIAL GUARD

At the bar in Mos Eisley Cantina, select Enter Code and enter GUA850.

JANGO FETT

At the bar in Mos Eisley Cantina, select Enter Code and enter KLJ897.

KI-ADI MUNDI

At the bar in Mos Eisley Cantina, select Enter Code and enter MUN486.

LUMINARA

At the bar in Mos Eisley Cantina, select Enter Code and enter LUM521.

PADMÉ

At the bar in Mos Eisley Cantina, select Enter Code and enter VBJ322.

R2-Q5

At the bar in Mos Eisley Cantina, select Enter Code and enter EVILR2.

STORMTROOPER

At the bar in Mos Eisley Cantina, select Enter Code and enter NBN431.

TAUN WE

At the bar in Mos Eisley Cantina, select Enter Code and enter PRX482.

VULTURE DROID

At the bar in Mos Eisley Cantina, select Enter Code and enter BDC866.

WATTO

At the bar in Mos Eisley Cantina, select Enter Code and enter PLL967.

ZAM WESELL

At the bar in Mos Eisley Cantina, select Enter Code and enter 584HJF.

SKILLS

DISGUISE

At the bar in Mos Eisley Cantina, select Enter Code and enter BRJ437.

FORCE GRAPPLE LEAP

At the bar in Mos Eisley Cantina, select Enter Code and enter CLZ738.

VEHICLES

DROID TRIFIGHTER

At the bar in Mos Eisley Cantina, select Enter Code and enter AAB123.

IMPERIAL SHUTTLE

At the bar in Mos Eisley Cantina, select Enter Code and enter HUT845.

TIE INTERCEPTOR

At the bar in Mos Eisley Cantina, select Enter Code and enter INT729.

TIE FIGHTER

At the bar in Mos Eisley Cantina, select Enter Code and enter DBH897.

ZAM'S AIRSPEEDER

At the bar in Mos Eisley Cantina, select Enter Code and enter UUU875.0

NINTENDO 3DS

3,000,000 STUDS

At the main menu, press START, START, Down, Down, Left, Left, Up, Up, SELECT.
This cheat can only be used once.

DEBUG MENUS

At the main menu, press Up, Left, Down, Right, Up, Left, Down, Right, Up, Left, Down, Right, R, L, START, SELECT.

BONUS TOUCH GAME 1

At the main menu, press Up, Up, Down, L, L, R, R.

LEGO STAR WARS II: THE ORIGINAL TRILOGY

10 STUDS

At the Mos Eisley cantina, enter 4PR28U.

OBI WAN GHOST

At the Mos Eisley cantina, enter BEN917.

BEACH TROOPER

At Mos Eisley Canteena, select Enter Code and enter UCK868. You must still select Characters and purchase this character for 20,000 studs.

BEN KENOBI (GHOST)

At Mos Eisley Canteena, select Enter Code and enter BEN917. You must still select Characters and purchase this character for 1,100,000 studs.

BESPIN GUARD

At Mos Eisley Canteena, select Enter Code and enter VHY832. You must still select Characters and purchase this character for 15,000 studs.

BIB FORTUNA

At Mos Eisley Canteena, select Enter Code and enter WTY721. You must still select Characters and purchase this character for 16,000 studs.

BOBA FETT

At Mos Eisley Canteena, select Enter Code and enter HLP221. You must still select Characters and purchase this character for 175,000 studs.

DEATH STAR TROOPER

At Mos Eisley Canteena, select Enter Code and enter BNC332. You must still select Characters and purchase this character for 19,000 studs.

EWOK

At Mos Eisley Canteena, select Enter Code and enter TTT289. You must still select Characters and purchase this character for 34,000 studs.

GAMORREAN GUARD

At Mos Eisley Canteena, select Enter Code and enter YZF999. You must still select Characters and purchase this character for 40,000 studs.

GONK DROID

At Mos Eisley Canteena, select Enter Code and enter NFX582. You must still select Characters and purchase this character for 1,550 studs.

GRAND MOFF TARKIN

At Mos Eisley Canteena, select Enter Code and enter SMG219. You must still select Characters and purchase this character for 38,000 studs.

GREEDO

At Mos Eisley Canteena, select Enter Code and enter NAH118. You must still select Characters and purchase this character for 60,000 studs.

HAN SOLO (HOOD)

At Mos Eisley Canteena, select Enter Code and enter YWM840. You must still select Characters and purchase this character for 20,000 studs.

IG-88

At Mos Eisley Canteena, select Enter Code and enter NXL973. You must still select Characters and purchase this character for 30,000 studs.

IMPERIAL GUARD

At Mos Eisley Canteena, select Enter Code and enter MMM111. You must still select Characters and purchase this character for 45,000 studs.

IMPERIAL OFFICER

At Mos Eisley Canteena, select Enter Code and enter BBV889. You must still select Characters and purchase this character for 28,000 studs.

IMPERIAL SHUTTLE PILOT

At Mos Eisley Canteena, select Enter Code and enter VAP664. You must still select Characters and purchase this character for 29,000 studs.

IMPERIAL SPY

At Mos Eisley Canteena, select Enter Code and enter CVT125. You must still select Characters and purchase this character for 13,500 studs.

JAWA

At Mos Eisley Canteena, select Enter Code and enter JAW499. You must still select Characters and purchase this character for 24,000 studs.

LOBOT

At Mos Eisley Canteena, select Enter Code and enter UUB319. You must still select Characters and purchase this character for 11,000 studs.

PALACE GUARD

At Mos Eisley Canteena, select Enter Code and enter SGE549. You must still select Characters and purchase this character for 14,000 studs.

REBEL PILOT

At Mos Eisley Canteena, select Enter Code and enter CYG336. You must still select Characters and purchase this character for 15,000 studs.

REBEL TROOPER (HOTH)

At Mos Eisley Canteena, select Enter Code and enter EKU849. You must still select Characters and purchase this character for 16,000 studs.

SANDTROOPER

At Mos Eisley Canteena, select Enter Code and enter YDV451. You must still select Characters and purchase this character for 14,000 studs.

SKIFF GUARD

At Mos Eisley Canteena, select Enter Code and enter GBU888. You must still select Characters and purchase this character for 12,000 studs.

SNOWTROOPER

At Mos Eisley Canteena, select Enter Code and enter NYU989. You must still select Characters and purchase this character for 16,000 studs.

STORMTROOPER

At Mos Eisley Canteena, select Enter Code and enter PTR345. You must still select Characters and purchase this character for 10,000 studs.

THE EMPEROR

At Mos Eisley Canteena, select Enter Code and enter HHY382. You must still select Characters and purchase this character for 275,000 studs.

TIE FIGHTER

At Mos Eisley Canteena, select Enter Code and enter HDY739. You must still select Characters and purchase this item for 60,000 studs.

TIE FIGHTER PILOT

At Mos Eisley Canteena, select Enter Code and enter NNZ316. You must still select Characters and purchase this character for 21,000 studs.

TIE INTERCEPTOR

At Mos Eisley Canteena, select Enter Code and enter QYA828. You must still select Characters and purchase this item for 40,000 studs.

TUSKEN RAIDER

At Mos Eisley Canteena, select Enter Code and enter PEJ821. You must still select Characters and purchase this character for 23,000 studs.

UGNAUGHT

At Mos Eisley Canteena, select Enter Code and enter UGN694. You must still select Characters and purchase this character for 36,000 studs.

LEGO STAR WARS III: THE CLONE WARS

Pause the game, select Enter Code from Extras and enter the following:

CHARACTERS

CHARACTER	CODE
Aayla Secura	2VG95B
Adi Gallia	G2BFEN
Admiral Ackbar (Classic)	272Y9Q
Admiral Yularen	NG6PYX
Ahsoka	2VJ9TH
Anakin Skywalker	F9VUYJ
Anakin Skywalker (Geonosian Arena)	9AA4DW
Asajj Ventress	YG9DD7
Aurra Sing	M2V1JV
Bail Organa	GEHX6C
Barriss Offee	BTVTZ5
Battle Droid	5Y7MA4
Battle Droid Commander	LSU4LJ
Bib Fortuna	9U4TF3
Boba Fett (Classic)	TY2BYJ
Boil	Q5Q39P
Bossk	2KLW5R
C-3PO	574226
Cad Bane	NHME85
Captain Antilles (Classic)	D8SNGJ
Captain Rex	MW3QYH
Captain Typho	GD6FX3
Chancellor Palpatine	5C62YQ
Chewbacca (Classic)	66UU3T
Clone Pilot	HQ7BVD
Clone Shadow Trooper (Classic)	7GFNCQ
Clone Trooper	NP5GTT
Commander Bly	7CB6NS
Commander Cody	SMN259
Commander Fil	U25HFC
Commander Ponds	JRPR2A
Commander Stone	5XZQSV
Commando Droid	QEGU64
Count Dooku	EWR7WM
Darth Maul (Classic)	QH68AK
Darth Sidious (Classic)	QXY5XN
Darth Vader (Classic)	FM4JB7
Darth Vader Battle Damaged (Classic)	NMJFBL
Destroyer Droid	9MUTS2
Dr. Nuvo Vindi	MB9EMW
Echo	JB9E5S
Eeth Koth	WUFDYA
Gammorean Guard	WSFZZQ
General Grievous	7FNU4T
Geonosian Guard	GAFZUD
Gold Super Battle Droid	2C8NHP
Gonk Droid	C686PK
Grand Moff Tarkin	NH2405

CHARACTER	CODE
Greedo (Classic)	FUW4C2
Hailfire Droid	T7XF9Z
Han Solo (Classic)	KFDBXF
Heavy Super Battle Droid	G65KJJ
Heavy Weapons Clone Trooper	WXUTWY
HELIOS 3D	4AXTY4
Hevy	EUB8UG
Hondo Ohnaka	5A7XYX
IG-86	EABPCP
Imperial Guard (Classic)	5W6FGD
Jango Fett	5KZQ4D
Jar Jar Binks	MESPTS
Jek	AYREC9
Ki-Adi-Mundi	HGBCTQ
Kit Fitso	PYWJ6N
Lando Calrissian (Classic)	ERAEWE
LEP Servent Droid	SM3Y9B
Lieutenant Thire	3NEUXC
Lok Durd	TKCYUZ
Luke Skywalker (Classic)	PG73HF
Luminara Unduli	MKUYQ8
Lurmen Villager	R35Y7N
Luxury Droid	V4WMJN
Mace Windu	8NVRWJ
MagnaGuard	2KEF2D
MSE-6	S6GRNZ
Nahdar Vebb	ZKXG43
Neimoidian	BJB94J
Nute Gunray	QFYXMC
Obi-Wan Kenobi	J9HNF9
Obi-Wan Kenobi (Classic)	FFBU5M
Obi-Wan Kenobi (Geonosian Arena)	5U9FJK
OG-9 Homing Spider Droid	7NEC36
Onaconda Farr	DB7ZQN
Padmé Amidala (Geonosian Arena)	SZ824Q
Padmé Amidala	8X87U6
Pirate Ruffian	BH2EHU
Plo Koon	BUD4VU
Poggle The Lesser	4592WM
Princess Leia (Classic)	2D3D3L
Probe Droid	U2T4SP
Queen Neeyutnee	ZQRN85
Qui-Gon Jinn (Classic)	LKHD3B
R2-D2	RZ5HUV
R3-S6	Z87PAU
R4-P17	5MXSYA
R6-H5	7PMC3C
Rebel Commando (Classic)	PZMQNK
Robonino	2KLW5R
Rys	4PTP53
Savage Oppress	MELL07
Senate Commando	EPBPLK
Senate Commando (Captain)	S4Y7VW
Senator Kharrus	EA4E9S

L

CHARACTER	CODE
Senator Philo	9Q7YCT
Shahan Alama	G4N7C2
Sionver Boll	5C62YQ
Stormtrooper (Classic)	HPE7PZ
Super Battle Droid	MJKDV5
Tee Watt Kaa	FYVSHD
Turk Falso	HEBHW5
Tusken Raider (Classic)	GC2XSA
TX-20	PE7FGD
Undead Geonosian	QGENFD
Vader's Apprentice (Classic)	EGQQ4V
Wag Too	VRUVSZ
Wat Tambor	ZP8XVH
Waxer	BNJE79
Wedge Antilles (Classic)	DRGLWS
Whorm Loathsom	4VVYQV
Workout Clone Trooper	MP9DRE
Yoda	CSQTMB

VEHICLES

VEHICLE	CODE
Dwarf Spider Droid	NACMGG
Geonosian Solar Sailor	PJ2U3R
Geonosian Starfighter	EDENEC
Slave I	KDDQVD
The Twilight	T4K5L4
Vulture Droid	7W7K7S

RED BRICKS

CHEAT	CODE
Character Studs	QD2C31
Dark Side	X1V4N2
Dual Wield	C4ES4R
Fast Build	GCHP7S
Glow in the Dark	4GT3VQ
Invincibility	J46P7A
Minikit Detector	CSD5NA
Perfect Deflect	3F5L56
Regenerate Hearts	2D7JNS
Score x2	YZPHUV
Score x4	43T5E5
Score x6	SEBHGR
Score x8	BYFSAQ
Score x10	N1CKR1
Stud Magnet	6MZ5CH
Super Saber Cut	BS828K
Super Speeders	B1D3W3

RED BRICK CHEATS

Each level has a Red Brick that when found unlocks a cheat for purchase at the shop.

CHEAT	COST (STUDS)
Auto Pickup	500,000
Fast Build	500,000
Flight Weapon Power Up	2,000,000
Funny Jump	250,000
Infinite Missiles	150,000
Invincibility	4,000,000
Minigames	50,000
Regenerate Hearts	400,000
Score x2	100,000
Score x4	250,000
Score x6	500,000
Score x8	1,000,000
Score x10	2,500,000

LET'S GOLF 2 HD

MOBILE

WIZZY THE WIZARD IN INSTANT PLAY

Select Profile from the Options and then tap Edit. Enter WIZZY10.

LITTLEST PET SHOP: GARDEN

NINTENDO 3DS

GIRAFFE PET

Select Passwords from the Options and enter LPSTRU. It is available in the Meow Market.

LITTLEST PET SHOP: JUNGLE

NINTENDO 3DS

GIRAFFE PET

Select Passwords from the Options and enter LPSTRU. It is available in the Meow Market.

LOCK'S QUEST

NINTENDO 3DS

REPLACE CLOCKWORKS WITH KINGDOM FORCE

After completing the game, hold R and select your profile.

ENDING STORY

After completing the game, hold L and select your profile.

CHEATS, ACHIEVEMENTS, AND TROPHIES

L

LORD OF THE RINGS: WAR IN THE NORTH

XBOX 360/PS3

ACHIEVEMENTS & TROPHIES

NAME	GOAL/REQUIREMENT	POINT VALUE	TROPHY VALUE
Where there's life, there's hope	Revive a fallen ally.	10	Bronze
Foe-hammer	Kill 200 enemies in a single playthrough.	10	Bronze
Sudden Fury	Perform 3 critical hits within 10 seconds.	10	Bronze
Strength of Our Alliance	Slay one enemy together with 2 other players.	25	Bronze
Seeker	Discover 25 secrets in a single playthrough.	20	Bronze
Gem-studded	Slot an elfstone into an item.	10	Bronze
Relentless	While in Hero Mode, perform a streak of 50 hits.	20	Bronze
Now for wrath, now for ruin!	Kill 4 enemies simultaneously.	20	Bronze
Troll's Bane	Slay the wild snow trolls.	10	Bronze
Battle-master	Unlock every active-cast ability in one character's skill tree.	20	Bronze
War-hardened	Achieve at least 1 rank in a tier 3 skill.	10	Bronze
Like a Thunderbolt	Deal 3000 damage with a single ranged strike.	20	Silver
Fell-handed	Deal 1500 damage in a single melee strike.	20	Silver
Living Shield	Absorb 25,000 total damage during the course of 1 level.	20	Silver
Many deeds, great and small	Complete 15 quests in a single playthrough.	20	Bronze
War-machinist	Kill 150 enemies with war machines in a single playthrough.	20	Bronze
Well-arrayed	Equip a complete magical armor set.	25	Bronze
Keen-eyed Marksman	Kill 50 enemies with headshots in a single playthrough.	20	Bronze
Swift-winged Warrior	Summon Beleram 10 times in a single playthrough.	20	Bronze
Warrior Exemplar	For one character unlock every skill that provides a modification to War Cry, Sanctuary or Evasion.	25	Bronze
Defender of the North	Achieve level 10.	10	Bronze
Champion of the North	Achieve level 20.	20	Silver
Herb-master	Create 15 potions in a single playthrough.	10	Bronze
Bane of Mordor	Kill 600 enemies in a single playthrough.	25	Silver
Dragon-hoard	Amass 25,000 coins.	20	Bronze
Expert Treasure-hunter	Locate 5 gilded treasure chests in a single playthrough.	25	Silver
Victorious in Battle	Complete a playthrough on at least Normal difficulty.	25	Silver
Against All Odds	Complete a playthrough on Legendary difficulty.	80	Silver
The Lidless Eye	Complete the investigation of the Cult of the Lidless Eye.	25	Silver
Hero of Legend	Complete a playthrough on Heroic difficulty.	50	Silver

SECRET ACHIEVEMENTS & TROPHIES

NAME	GOAL/REQUIREMENT	POINT VALUE	TROPHY VALUE
Giant-slayer	Slay Bargrisar the stone giant.	20	Bronze
Begone, lord of carrion!	Defeat the Barrow Wight Lord.	20	Bronze

NAME	GOAL/REQUIREMENT	POINT VALUE	TROPHY VALUE
Trusted with the Secret	Learn of the Ring of Power and the plan for its destruction.	10	Bronze
In the Dragon's Den	Meet a dragon and survive.	20	Bronze
Friend of the Woodland Realm	Free the elf from his captors in Mirkwood Marsh.	10	Bronze
Eagle Savior	Defeat Agandaûr without the aid of Beleram.	20	Bronze
Friend to the Ring-bearer	Speak with Frodo in Rivendell.	10	Bronze
Tharzog's Bane	Defeat Agandaûr's lieutenant Tharzog.	20	Bronze
Mountain-breaker	Help destroy the citadel within Mount Gundabad.	25	Silver
Wulfrun's Bane	Defeat the Sorceror Wulfrun.	20	Bronze
Tracker	Discover what happened to the missing Rangers.	10	Bronze
Spider-slayer	Slay Saenathra.	25	Silver
Elf-friend	Join forces with the sons of Elrond.	10	Bronze
Friend to the Eagles	Help free the Great Eagle Beleram.	20	Bronze
Siege-breaker	Help weather the siege of Nordinbad.	35	Silver
Hero of the North	Defeat Sauron's Lieutenant Agandaûr.	80	Gold

LOST IN SHADOW

NINTENDO WII

GOBLIN HAND

While the game is loading, press and hold Z.

KNIFE

While the game is loading, press and hold C.

LOST PLANET 2

XBOX 360/PS3

ACHIEVEMENTS & TROPHIES

NAME	GOAL/REQUIREMENT	POINT VALUE	TROPHY VALUE
Complete Prologue A	Complete Episode 1 Chapter 0-A.	10	Bronze
Complete Prologue B	Complete Episode 1 Chapter 0-B.	10	Bronze
Complete Episode 1	Complete all the chapters in Episode 1.	10	Bronze
Rookie	Complete the game on Easy.	10	Bronze
Soldier	Complete the game on Normal.	10	Bronze
Super Soldier	Complete the game on Hard.	15	Bronze
Snow Pirate	Achieve a Career Level of Lv. 10.	10	Bronze
Welcome to the Battle!	Play one Online match.	10	Bronze

SECRET ACHIEVEMENTS & TROPHIES

NAME	GOAL/REQUIREMENT	POINT VALUE	TROPHY VALUE
Complete Episode 2	Complete all the chapters in Episode 2.	10	Bronze
Complete Episode 3	Complete all the chapters in Episode 3.	10	Bronze
Complete Episode 4	Complete all the chapters in Episode 4.	10	Bronze
Complete Episode 5	Complete all the chapters in Episode 5.	10	Bronze
Complete Episode 6	Complete all the chapters in Episode 6.	10	Bronze
100-Chapter Playback	Play through 100 chapters.	10	Bronze
Instrument of Destruction	Defeat 9999 enemies (Akrid, VS, or enemy soldiers).	20	Bronze
300-Chapter Playback	Play through 300 chapters.	30	Silver
200-Chapter Playback	Play through 200 chapters.	20	Bronze
Ultimate Warrior	Complete the game on Extreme.	20	Silver
Snow Pirate Warrior	Achieve a Career Level of Lv. 30.	15	Bronze
Snow Pirate Leader	Achieve a Career Level of Lv. 50.	20	Bronze
Snow Pirate Commander	Achieve a Career Level of Lv. 80.	25	Bronze
Rounder Chief	Achieve a Career Level of Lv. 99 with the Rounders.	30	Silver
Fight Junkie Berserker	Achieve a Career Level of Lv. 99 with the Fight Junkies.	30	Silver
First Among Snow Pirate Elites	Achieve a Career Level of Lv. 99 with the Snow Pirate Elites.	30	Silver
NEVEC Black Ops Commander	Achieve a Career Level of Lv. 99 with the NEVEC Black Ops.	30	Silver
Femmes Fatales Faction Leader	Achieve a Career Level of Lv. 99 with the Femmes Fatales.	30	Silver
Quintuple Factionalism	Achieve a Career Level of Lv. 99 with all 5 factions.	50	Gold
A Thousand Unmarked Graves	Defeat 1000 enemy soldiers.	15	Bronze
Endangered Species	Defeat 3000 S- and M-sized Akrid.	15	Bronze
VS Graveyard	Destroy 100 enemy VSs.	15	Bronze
It's So Easy	Play any combination of chapters 39 times on Easy.	20	Bronze
Monster Hunter	Defeat 30 bosses.	20	Bronze
Thermal Energy Reactor	Accumulate a combined total of more than 99999 units of thermal energy.	10	Bronze
Me Against the World	Complete 93 areas while online without the help of other players.	10	Bronze
Prove Your Mettle	Unlock all the Abilities.	25	Bronze
Weapons Master	Unlock all regular weapons and grenades.	25	Bronze
Honeymoon Period	Celebrate your six-month anniversary with LOST PLANET 2.	20	Bronze
A Collector's Collector	Unlock all items (weapons, Abilities, Noms de Guerre).	50	Silver
All in a Day's Work	Achieve 100 different Good Job awards.	20	Bronze
Warrior of Many Names	Unlock 100 Noms de Guerre.	20	Bronze
Centurion	Win 100 Online Ranked matches.	15	Bronze
Slayer of a Thousand Men	Achieve 1000 kills in Online matches.	15	Bronze

NAME	GOAL/REQUIREMENT	POINT VALUE	TROPHY VALUE
Hot Shot	Gain promotion to the rank of Gunner.	15	Bronze
Two is Better Than One	Complete 386 areas with one or more other players.	10	Bronze
Let's Go VS Force!	Merge two VS units.	10	Bronze
Professional Turncoat	Fight for a number of different factions in Faction Match.	10	Bronze
War Vet	Play 500 Online matches.	15	Bronze
Death Wish	Die more than 444 times.	10	Bronze
Good Job, Soldier	Earn all the Good Job awards.	40	Silver
Committed 'til the End	Earn all the Good Job awards, items, and Career Levels available in the game.	100	Gold

LOST PLANET 2

PLAYSTATION 3

Go to the Customization screen from My Page and select Character Parts. Press ● to access the LP2 Slot Machine and then press ● to enter the following passwords.

T-SHIRT 1
Enter 73154986.

T-SHIRT 4
Enter 40358056.

T-SHIRT 5
Enter 96725729.

T-SHIRT 6
Enter 21899787.

T-SHIRT 7
Enter 52352345.

T-SHIRT 8
Enter 63152256.

T-SHIRT 9
Enter 34297758.

T-SHIRT 10
Enter 88020223.

T-SHIRT 11
Enter 25060016.

T-SHIRT 12
Enter 65162980.

T-SHIRT 13
Enter 56428338.

T-SHIRT 14
Enter 18213092.

T-SHIRT 15
Enter 26797358.

T-SHIRT 16
Enter 71556463.

T-SHIRT 17
Enter 31354816.

T-SHIRT 18
Enter 12887439.

ALBERT WESKER

To unlock Albert Wesker, you need a save game from Resident Evil 5. Alternately, you can unlock him from the LP2 Slot Machine by entering 72962792. This character model can be found in Customization under Preset Models.

FRANK WEST

To unlock Frank West, you need a save game from Lost Planet. Alternately, you can unlock him from the LP2 Slot Machine by entering 83561942. This character model can be found in Customization under Preset Models.

LUIGI'S MANSION: DARK MOON

BONUS MISSIONS

Capture all the Boos in a Mansion to unlock Bonus Missions.

MISSION	REQUIREMENT
Gradual Infiltration	Capture all 5 Boos in Gloomy Manor.
Hostile Intrusion	Capture all 5 Boos in Haunted Towers.
Outlandish Interruption	Capture all 5 Boos in Old Clockworks.
Severe Infestation	Capture all 3 Boos in Secret Mine.
Terrifying Invasion	Capture all 5 Boos in Treacherous Mansion.

E. GADD MEDALS

You can obtain golden E. Gadd medals on your save file by completing certain requirements.

MEDAL	REQUIREMENT
#1	Complete Dark Moon Quest mode.
#2	Obtain a 3-star rank in every mission in Dark Moon Quest mode.
#3	Complete E. Gadd's Vault Room by collecting all Gems, Boos and Ghosts.

SCARESCRAPER MODE

Complete certain requirements to unlock additional features in Scarescraper Mode.

WEAPON	REQUIREMENT
Scarescraper Mode	Complete the mission "Visual Tricks" in Gloomy Manor.
Hunter Endless	Complete a Hunter mode in a 25F Scarescraper.
Polterpup Endless	Complete a Polterpup mode in a 25F Scarescraper.
Rush Endless	Complete a Rush mode in a 25F Scarescraper.
Surprise Endless	Complete a Surprise mode in a 25F Scarescraper.

LUIGI STATUE

Collect all the Gems in Gloomy Manor to unlock a Luigi Statue in the Vault.

MADDEN NFL 10

UNLOCK EVERYTHING

Select Enter Game Code from the Extras menu and enter THEWORKS.

FRANCHISE MODE

Select Enter Game Code from the Extras menu and enter TEAMPLAYER.

SITUATION MODE

Select Enter Game Code from the Extras menu and enter YOUCALLIT.

SUPERSTAR MODE

Select Enter Game Code from the Extras menu and enter EGOBOOST.

PRO BOWL STADIUM

Select Enter Game Code from the Extras menu and enter ALLSTARS.

SUPER BOWL STADIUM

Select Enter Game Code from the Extras menu and enter THEBIGSHOW.

MADDEN NFL 12

PLAYSTATION 3

MADDEN NFL 12 DEVELOPERS TEAM IN EXHIBITION

Select Exhibition from Play Now. At the team select, press the Random Team button, L2, until the Developers team shows up. Once you have entered a game as the team, they will always be on the list.

MADDEN NFL 13

XBOX 360/PS3

ACHIEVEMENTS & TROPHIES

NAME	GOAL/REQUIREMENT	POINT VALUE	TROPHY VALUE
Single Riders Only	Play a MUT game against the CPU.	5	Bronze
MUT Maniac	Complete 20 MUT games.	20	Bronze
This One is Hard 2.0	Build an 85 rated MUT team.	15	Silver
This One is Easy. We Promise	Create a MUT team.	5	Bronze
Hall Of Famer	As a created player or coach, get inducted into the Hall of Fame in Connected Careers.	100	Gold
All Madden	As a created coach, win 100 games in your first 10 seasons in Connected Careers.	100	Silver
Montana's Mountain	As a created QB, win 4 Super Bowls in Connected Careers.	20	Silver
Vince Lombardi Award	As a created coach, surpass Vince Lombardi on Legacy Score in Connected Careers.	30	Silver
Deion Sanders Award	As a created DB, surpass Deion Sanders on Legacy Score in Connected Careers.	30	Silver
Lawrence Taylor Award	As a created LB, surpass Lawrence Taylor on Legacy Score in Connected Careers.	30	Silver
Reggie White Award	As a created DL, surpass Reggie White on Legacy Score in Connected Careers.	30	Silver
Shannon Sharpe Award	As a created TE, surpass Shannon Sharpe on Legacy Score in Connected Careers.	30	Silver
Jerry Rice Award	As a created WR, surpass Jerry Rice on Legacy Score in Connected Careers.	30	Silver
Emmitt Smith Award	As a created RB, surpass Emmitt Smith on Legacy Score in Connected Careers.	30	Silver
Joe Montana Award	As a created QB, surpass Joe Montana on Legacy Score in Connected Careers.	30	Silver
Peak Performance	As a created player, achieve a player rating of 99 overall in Connected Careers.	30	Gold
90 Overall	As a created player, achieve a player rating of 90 overall in Connected Careers.	20	Bronze

CHEATS, ACHIEVEMENTS, AND TROPHIES

M

NAME	GOAL/REQUIREMENT	POINT VALUE	TROPHY VALUE
85 Overall	As a created player, achieve a player rating of 85 overall in Connected Careers.	15	Bronze
80 Overall	As a created player, achieve a player rating of 80 overall in Connected Careers.	10	Bronze
MVP! MVP! MVP!	Complete the Level 4 season goals in one season in Connected Careers.	30	Silver
Welcome to the Community	Join an Online Community.	5	Bronze
Battle Tested	Score 600 points in Online Ranked Head to Head Games.	20	Gold
Online Level 9	Score 500 points in Online Ranked Head to Head Games.	15	Bronze
Online Level 8	Score 400 points in Online Ranked Head to Head Games.	15	Bronze
Online Level 7	Score 300 points in Online Ranked Head to Head Games.	15	Bronze
Online Level 6	Score 250 points in Online Ranked Head to Head Games.	10	Bronze
Online Level 5	Score 200 points in Online Ranked Head to Head Games.	10	Bronze
Online Level 4	Score 150 points in Online Ranked Head to Head Games.	10	Bronze
Online Level 3	Score 100 points in Online Ranked Head to Head Games.	5	Bronze
Online Level 2	Score 50 points in Online Ranked Head to Head Games.	5	Bronze
Online Level 1	Score 25 points in Online Ranked Head to Head Games.	5	Bronze
Tebowing	Tebow Time! Throw a TD with Tim Tebow on the first play in overtime (no SuperSim, OTP or co-op).	25	Bronze
Gronk Spike	Score a TD with Rob Gronkowski (no SuperSim, OTP or co-op).	25	Bronze
Pass The Salsa	Score a TD with Victor Cruz (no SuperSim, OTP or co-op).	25	Bronze
Verizon Scoreboard Overload	Score 50 points in one game (no SuperSim, OTP or co-op).	50	Bronze
Matt Flynn's Arcade	Score 6 touchdowns with your backup quarterback (no SuperSim, OTP or co-op).	55	Bronze
Let's Get Physical	Tackle an opponent using the Hit Stick (no SuperSim, OTP or co-op).	5	Bronze
Made Ya Look	Abort the play action and complete a pass for a TD (no SuperSim, OTP or co-op).	10	Bronze
Smart Mouth	Complete a successful pre-play adjustment using Kinect (no SuperSim, OTP or co-op).	25	—
Belting	Complete a Madden Moments Live situation.	25	Bronze
The Penitent Man Shall Pass	As a QB, win the game with 4 or fewer completed passes (no SuperSim, OTP or co-op).	20	Bronze
You're In the Game	Download A Game Face in Create-a-Player or in Connected Careers.	10	Bronze
Madden NFL 13 Master	Congratulations on earning every Madden NFL 13 trophy!	—	Platinum

MADSTONE

HIGH GRAVITY

At the Main menu, press Down, Down, Down, Down, Right, Left, Right, Left.

LOW GRAVITY

At the Main menu, press Up, Up, Left, Left, Up, Up, Right, Right.

PLAYER SKULLS, ARCADE MODE

At the Difficulty Select screen, press Up, Right, Down, Left, Up, Right, Down, Left.

SAVANT MODE, ARCADE MODE

At the Difficulty Select screen, press Down (x10).

MAFIA II

ACHIEVEMENTS

NAME	GOAL/REQUIREMENT	POINT VALUE	TROPHY VALUE
Viva la Resistenza!	Complete Chapter 1.	20	Bronze
Home Sweet Home	Complete Chapter 2.	20	Bronze
Back in Business	Do your first job for Mike Bruski.	10	Bronze
Big Brother	Protect Francesca.	10	Bronze
A Real Gentleman	Help the woman fix her car in Home Sweet Home.	10	Bronze
The Price of Oil	Complete Chapter 3.	20	Bronze
The Professional	Obtain the ration stamps without raising the alarm.	10	Bronze
Mail Man	Sell all the gas stamps before the time runs out.	10	Bronze
Night Shift	Complete Chapter 4.	20	Bronze
Good Spirit	Complete Chapter 5.	20	Bronze
Time Well Spent	Complete Chapter 6.	20	Bronze
Last Respects	Complete Chapter 7.	30	Bronze
The Wild Ones	Complete Chapter 8.	30	Bronze
Man of Honor	Complete Chapter 9.	30	Bronze
Checking Out	Complete Chapter 10.	40	Bronze
Our Good Friend	Complete Chapter 11.	20	Bronze
Wake Up Call	Help Leo out of a tricky situation without getting caught.	10	Bronze
Chasing the Dragon	Complete Chapter 12.	40	Bronze
Chop Chop!	Complete Chapter 13.	40	Bronze
Men at Work	Complete Chapter 14.	50	Silver
Finish Him	Finish what you started.	50	Silver
Made Man	Finish the story on Medium difficulty level.	50	Gold
Tough Nut	Finish the story on Hard difficulty level.	100	Gold
Get Rich or Die Flyin'	Get all wheels of your car into the air for at least 20 meters and then touch the ground again.	10	Bronze
Pedal to the Metal	Travel at 125 mph.	10	Bronze
One Careful Owner	Travel a total of 50 miles in one vehicle.	10	Bronze
Proper Scrapper	Sell 5 vehicles to Mike Bruski at the scrapyard.	10	Bronze

NAME	GOAL/REQUIREMENT	POINT VALUE	TROPHY VALUE
Exporter	Sell 5 vehicles to Derek at the dock.	10	Bronze
Cruise Control	Keep any vehicle at 30 mph or over for 5 or more minutes.	10	Bronze
Hairdresser	Kill 5 enemies in rapid succession with a headshot.	10	Bronze
Knucklehead	Kill a total of 30 enemies using melee attacks.	10	Bronze
Stuck Up	Rob 5 stores in under 5 minutes.	10	Bronze
The Enforcer	Kill 50 enemies.	10	Bronze
Sharp Suiter	Buy your first luxury suit.	10	Bronze
Tuned Ride	Upgrade one of your cars one level.	10	Bronze
Dream Handling	Upgrade one of your cars to the maximum level.	10	Bronze
Hard to Kill	The police want you dead. Survive for 10 minutes!	10	Bronze
Collector's Item	Find at least one collectible in the game.	10	Bronze
Petrol Head	Drive at least 30 different vehicles.	30	Bronze
Ladies' Man	Find all of the Playboy magazines.	40	Silver
Card Sharp	Find all of the Wanted posters.	40	Silver
He Who Pays the Barber	Improve the dockworkers' haircuts.	10	Silver
A Lesson in Manners	Show that you know how to treat a lady.	10	Silver
Hey Joe	Clean up after Joe.	10	Silver
End of the Rainbow	Settle the score with the Irish once and for all.	10	Silver
The Mafia Never Forgets	Pay a visit to an old friend.	10	Silver
Out for Justice	Learn what it means to be a Scaletta.	30	Silver

DOWNLOADABLE CONTENT: JIMMY'S VENDETTA

NAME	GOAL/REQUIREMENT	POINT VALUE	TROPHY VALUE
First Step	Complete your first mission in "Jimmy's Vendetta."	10	Bronze
Faster than Light	Achieve a 10x point multiplier in "Jimmy's Vendetta."	10	Bronze
Explorer	Drive a total of 1,000 miles in vehicles in "Jimmy's Vendetta."	10	Bronze
Armament King	Kill your enemies in "Jimmy's Vendetta" with every weapon available in the game.	10	Bronze
Firebug	Destroy 100 vehicles in "Jimmy's Vendetta."	10	Bronze
Sharpshooter	Kill 100 enemies by headshots in "Jimmy's Vendetta."	10	Bronze
Carnapper	Finish all Car Dealer missions in "Jimmy's Vendetta."	50	Bronze
Revenged	Finish "Jimmy's Vendetta" on any difficulty level.	100	Silver
Millionaire	Earn 1,000,000 points in "Jimmy's Vendetta."	20	Silver
Massacre	Kill 1,000 enemies in "Jimmy's Vendetta."	20	Bronze

DOWNLOADABLE CONTENT: JOE'S ADVENTURES

NAME	GOAL/REQUIREMENT	POINT VALUE	TROPHY VALUE
What Witness?	Finish the Witness level in "Joe's Adventures."	10	Bronze
Arctic Grave	Push the chief witness into the ice lake in "Joe's Adventures."	20	Bronze
Dockyard Discord	Finish the Connection level in "Joe's Adventures."	20	Bronze
Five Finger Discount	Finish the Supermarket level in "Joe's Adventures."	30	Bronze
Mind the Goods	Finish the Cathouse level in "Joe's Adventures."	40	Silver
Same Shirt Different Day	Finish Joe's Adventures on any difficulty.	50	Silver
Hypersonic	Reach 2000 points for one velocity run in "Joe's Adventures."	20	Bronze
Jacked Jumper	Reach 200 points for one Jump in "Joe's Adventures."	20	Bronze
Driftin' Daddy-O	Reach 200 points for one Drift in "Joe's Adventures."	20	Bronze
Jack of all Trades	Reach 10 different score actions in one mission in "Joe's Adventures."	20	Bronze

MAGIC: THE GATHERING— DUELS OF THE PLANES WALKERS 2013

MOBILE

PROMO UNLOCK 01

At the Player Status screen, select Promotional Unlocks. Click Enter Code and enter WMKFGC.

PROMO UNLOCK 02

At the Player Status screen, select Promotional Unlocks. Click Enter Code and enter KWPMZW.

PROMO UNLOCK 03

At the Player Status screen, select Promotional Unlocks. Click Enter Code and enter FNMDGP.

PROMO UNLOCK 04

At the Player Status screen, select Promotional Unlocks. Click Enter Code and enter MWTMJP.

PROMO UNLOCK 05

At the Player Status screen, select Promotional Unlocks. Click Enter Code and enter FXGJDW.

PROMO UNLOCK 06

At the Player Status screen, select Promotional Unlocks. Click Enter Code and enter GDZDJC.

PROMO UNLOCK 07

At the Player Status screen, select Promotional Unlocks. Click Enter Code and enter HTRNPW.

M

PROMO UNLOCK 08

At the Player Status screen, select Promotional Unlocks. Click Enter Code and enter NCTFJN.

PROMO UNLOCK 09

At the Player Status screen, select Promotional Unlocks. Click Enter Code and enter PCNKGR.

PROMO UNLOCK 10

At the Player Status screen, select Promotional Unlocks. Click Enter Code and enter GPCRSX.

MAGNA CARTA 2

XBOX 360

ACHIEVEMENTS

NAME	GOAL/REQUIREMENT	POINT VALUE
Battle of Highwind Island	Complete the battle of Highwind Island.	10
Battle of Oldfox Canyon	Complete the battle of Oldfox Canyon.	20
Battle of Cota Mare	Complete the battle of Cota Mare.	30
Battle of Dunan Hill	Complete the battle of Dunan Hill.	40
Battle of Ruhalt Basin	Complete the battle of Ruhalt Basin.	50
First Quest Cleared	Clear the first quest.	5
10 Quests Cleared	Clear 10 quests.	5
50 Quests Cleared	Clear 50 quests.	10
80 Quests Cleared	Clear 80 quests.	20
All Quests Cleared	Clear all quests.	30
Co-op Technique: Juto & Zephie	Learn Co-op Technique for Juto & Zephie.	10
Style Master: 1 Handed Sword	Master Juto's 1 Handed Sword skill tree.	30
Style Master: 2 Handed Sword	Master Juto's 2 Handed Sword skill tree.	30
Style Master: Hammer	Master Argo's Hammer skill tree.	30
Style Master: Axe	Master Argo's Axe skill tree.	30
Style Master: Rod	Master Zephie's Rod skill tree.	30
Style Master: Fan	Master Zephie's Fan skill tree.	30
Style Master: Fireball	Master Crocell's Fireball skill tree.	30
Style Master: Knuckles	Master Crocell's Knuckle skill tree.	30
Style Master: Aroma	Master Celestine's Aroma skill tree.	30
Style Master: Bow	Master Celestine's Bow skill tree.	30
Style Master: Katana	Master Rue's Katana skill tree.	30
Style Master: Shuriken	Master Rue's Shuriken skill tree.	30
Weapon Enhanced	Use Enhancements on a weapon.	5
Obtained Item Recipe	Obtain an item recipe.	5
Obtained 6 Item Recipes	Obtain 6 item recipes.	10
Obtained All Item Recipes	Obtain all item recipes.	30
100 Chain Breaks	Complete 100 chain breaks.	10
300 Chain Breaks	Complete 300 chain breaks.	30
500 Chain Breaks	Complete 500 chain breaks.	50
Viewed Live Drama 1	View Live Drama 1	20

NAME	GOAL/REQUIREMENT	POINT VALUE
Viewed Live Drama 2	View Live Drama 2	20
Viewed Live Drama 3	View Live Drama 3	20
Weapon Collector: Juto	Collect all of Juto's weapons, including downloadable content.	30
Weapon Collector: Zephie	Collect all of Zephie's weapons, including downloadable content.	30
Weapon Collector: Argo	Collect all of Argo's weapons, including downloadable content.	30
Weapon Collector: Crocell	Collect all of Crocell's weapons, including downloadable content.	30
Weapon Collector: Celestine	Collect all of Celestine's weapons, including downloadable content.	30
Weapon Collector: Rue	Collect all of Rue's weapons, including downloadable content.	30

SECRET ACHIEVEMENTS

NAME	GOAL/REQUIREMENT	POINT VALUE
Escape from Belfort	Successfully escaped from Belfort.	60
Assault on Ruhalt Plateau	Completed the assault on Ruhalt Plateau.	70
Game Completed	Completed the game's main story.	80
Co-op Technique: Argo&Celestine	Learned Co-op Technique for Argo & Celestine.	10
Co-op Technique: Zephie & Rue	Learned Co-op Technique for Zephie & Rue.	10
Co-op Technique: Juto & Crocell	Learned Co-op Technique for Juto & Crocell.	20
Co-op Technique: Celestine & Rue	Learned Co-op Technique for Celestine & Rue.	20

MAJOR LEAGUE BASEBALL 2K12

ACHIEVEMENTS & TROPHIES

NAME	GOAL/REQUIREMENT	POINT VALUE	TROPHY VALUE
Home, Sweet Home	Score 193 runs with your user profile.	10	Bronze
Chicks Dig It	Hit 74 home runs with your user profile.	10	Bronze
Almost There	Hit 37 triples with your user profile.	10	Bronze
Fanning the Flames	Strike out 514 batters with your user profile.	10	Bronze
Set the Table	Hit 68 doubles with your user profile.	15	Bronze
Productivity	Get 263 hits with your user profile.	20	Bronze
Domination	Save 63 games with your user profile.	20	Bronze
Production	Drive in 192 RBI with your user profile.	20	Bronze
You Make Your Own Destiny	Steal 139 bases with your user profile.	20	Bronze
As Good as a Hit	Walk 233 times with your user profile.	40	Silver
Down But Not Out	Get a hit with 2 strikes in a non-simulated game.	5	Bronze

NAME	GOAL/REQUIREMENT	POINT VALUE	TROPHY VALUE
Grab Some Pine	Get a strikeout to end the inning in a non-simulated game.	5	Bronze
A Pitcher's Best Friend	Turn a double play in a non-simulated game.	10	Bronze
To the Rescue	Get a save with the tying run on base in a non-simulated game.	10	Bronze
Don't Call it a Comeback	Win after being down by 4 after the 6th inning in a non-simulated game.	10	Bronze
The Start of Something Special	Lead off an inning by hitting a triple in a non-simulated game.	10	Bronze
Stooges	Strikeout all three hitters in the inning in a non-simulated game.	10	Bronze
No Hole too Deep	Battle Back: Down 0-2, get walked in a non-simulated game.	10	Bronze
Throw First and Aim Later	Miss your throw to first base with 2 outs in a non-simulated game.	10	Bronze
Take That	Get an RBI after getting brushed back off the plate in a non-simulated game.	15	Bronze
My Main Squeeze	Bunt the man home in a non-simulated game.	15	Bronze
Dual Threat	Steal base with pitcher in a non-simulated game.	20	Bronze
I Came, I Saw...	Hit a Walk-off Home Run in a non-simulated game.	20	Bronze
He Taketh Away	Rob a Home Run in a non-simulated game.	20	Bronze
State Farm®: The Road to Victory	Get 3 consecutive batters on base in a non-simulated game.	20	Bronze
Mr. Consistency	Get a hit in all 9 innings in a non-simulated game.	20	Silver
A Virtue	Face 10 pitches as the batter in a non-simulated game.	20	Silver
One Man Show	Throw a No-Hitter in a 9 inning, non-simulated game.	80	Gold
The Goal	Accomplish a Team Season Goal in My Player Mode.	10	Bronze
Back to the Cage	Get a Golden Sombrero (strikeout 4 times in 1 game) in My Player Mode.	10	Bronze
Payback	Hit a home run off a former team in My Player Mode.	15	Bronze
Your Day	Win player of the game in an MLB game in My Player Mode.	15	Bronze
This is Why I'm Here	Be successful in a major league clutch moment in My Player Mode.	15	Bronze
The Call	Get called up to the Majors in My Player Mode.	20	Bronze
A Job Well Done	Win 100+ games in a season in My Player Mode.	25	Silver
2-Peat	Win Back to Back World Series® in My Player Mode.	25	Silver
The Top	Become the #1 ranked player in your My Player organization.	30	Silver
The Star	Make the All-Star team in My Player Mode.	40	Silver
The Hall	Make the Hall of Fame in My Player Mode.	75	Silver
What's Your Ring Size?	Win a World Series® in My Player Mode.	80	Gold

NAME	GOAL/REQUIREMENT	POINT VALUE	TROPHY VALUE
You're Special	Win a Season award in Franchise Mode. (play at least 20 games)	20	Bronze
Remember Me	Break a record in Franchise Mode. (play at least 20 games)	20	Bronze
The Champs	Win a World Series® in Franchise Mode. (play at least 20 games)	20	Silver
King of the Hill	Get to the top of the Best of the Best ladder in Home Run Derby® Mode.	20	Bronze
My Fellow Man	Complete and win an online league game.	10	Bronze
Count it	Complete and win a ranked match.	10	Bronze
Upset Alert	Use the Houston Astros in a completed ranked match.	10	Bronze
The Spice of Life	Play 10 ranked matches using 10 different teams.	10	Bronze
The Team to Beat	Beat the St. Louis Cardinals in a completed online match.	15	Bronze
The Road to Greatness	Complete and win 3 ranked matches in a row.	20	Silver

MANHUNT 2

NINTENDO WII

INFINITE AMMO

At the Main menu, press Up, Up, Down, Down, Left, Right, Left, Right.

LEVEL SELECT

At the Main menu, press Up, Down, Left, Right, Up, Down, Left, Right.

PSP

EXTRA LEVEL AS LEO

Defeat the game.

RELIVE SCENE

Defeat the game. This allows you to replay any level.

MARBLE SAGA: KORORINPA

NINTENDO WII

MASTER HIGGINS BALL

Select ??? from the Options. Press A on the right lamp, the left lamp twice, and the right lamp again. Now select the right icon and enter TV, Car, Sunflower, Bike, Helicopter, Strawberry.

MIRROR MODE

Select ??? from the Options. Press A on the right lamp, the left lamp twice, and the right lamp again. Now select the right icon and enter Beetle, Clover, Boy, Plane, Car, Bike.

CHEATS, ACHIEVEMENTS, AND TROPHIES

M

MARIO & SONIC AT THE OLYMPIC GAMES

UNLOCK 4X100M RELAY EVENT

Medal in Mercury, Venus, Jupiter, and Saturn.

UNLOCK SINGLE SCULLS EVENT

Medal in Mercury, Venus, Jupiter, and Saturn.

UNLOCK DREAM RACE EVENT

Medal in Mercury, Venus, Jupiter, and Saturn.

UNLOCK ARCHERY EVENT

Medal in Moonlight Circuit.

UNLOCK HIGH JUMP EVENT

Medal in Stardust Circuit.

UNLOCK 400M EVENT

Medal in Planet Circuit.

UNLOCK DREAM FENCING EVENT

Medal in Comet Circuit.

UNLOCK DREAM TABLE TENNIS EVENT

Medal in Satellite Circuit.

UNLOCK 400M HURDLES EVENT

Medal in Sunlight Circuit.

UNLOCK POLE VAULT EVENT

Medal in Meteorite Circuit.

UNLOCK VAULT EVENT

Medal in Meteorite Circuit.

UNLOCK DREAM PLATFORM EVENT

Medal in Cosmos Circuit.

CROWNS

Get all gold medals in all events with a character to unlock their crown.

MARIO KART 7

CHARACTERS

CHARACTER	FINISH 1ST IN...
Daisy	Mushroom Cup 150cc
Honey Queen	Banana Cup 150cc
Lakitu	Lightning Cup 150cc
Metal Mario	Special Cup 150cc
Rosalina	Star Cup 150cc
Shy Guy	Shell Cup 150cc
Wario	Flower Cup 150cc
Wiggler	Leaf Cup 150cc

MII

Place in all cups in one of the CC levels.

MARIO KART WII

NINTENDO WII

CHARACTERS

CHARACTER	UNLOCK BY...
Baby Daisy	Earn 1 Star in 50cc for Mushroom, Flower, Star, and Special Cups.
Baby Luigi	Unlock 8 Expert Staff Ghost Data in Time Trials.
Birdo	Race 16 different courses in Time Trials or win 250 versus races.
Bowser Jr.	Earn 1 Star in 100cc for Shell, Banana, Leaf, and Lightning Cups.
Daisy	Win 150cc Special Cup.
Diddy Kong	Win 50cc Lightning Cup.
Dry Bones	Win 100cc Leaf Cup.
Dry Bowser	Earn 1 Star in 150cc for Mushroom, Flower, Star, and Special Cups.
Funky Kong	Unlock 4 Expert Staff Ghost Data in Time Trials.
King Boo	Win 50cc Star Cup.
Mii Outfit A	Win 100cc Special Cup.
Mii Outfit B	Unlock all 32 Expert Staff Ghost Data in Time Trials.
Mii Outfit C	Get 15,000 points in Versus Mode.
Rosalina	Have a Super Mario Galaxy save file and she is unlocked after 50 races or earn 1 Star in all Mirror Cups.
Toadette	Race 32 different courses in Time Trials.

KARTS

KART	UNLOCK BY...
Blue Falcon	Win Mirror Lightning Cup.
Cheep Charger	Earn 1 Star in 50cc for Mushroom, Flower, Star, and Special Cups.
Rally Romper	Unlock an Expert Staff Ghost Data in Time Trials.
B Dasher Mk. 2	Unlock 24 Expert Staff Ghost Data in Time Trials.
Royal Racer	Win 150cc Leaf Cup.
Turbo Blooper	Win 50cc Leaf Cup.
Aero Glider	Earn 1 Star in 150cc for Mushroom, Flower, Star, and Special Cups.
Dragonetti	Win 150cc Lightning Cup.
Piranha Prowler	Win 50cc Special Cup.

BIKES

BIKE	UNLOCK BY...
Bubble Bike	Win Mirror Leaf Cup.
Magikruiser	Race 8 different courses in Time Trials.
Quacker	Win 150cc Star Cup.
Dolphin Dasher	Win Mirror Star Cup.
Nitrocycle	Earn 1 Star in 100cc for all cups.
Rapide	Win 100cc Lightning Cup.
Phantom	Win Mirror Special Cup.
Torpedo	Unlock 12 Expert Staff Ghost Data in Time Trials.
Twinkle Star	Win 100cc Star Cup.

M

MARIO PARTY DS

BOSS BASH
Complete Story Mode.

EXPERT CPU DIFFICULTY LEVEL
Complete Story Mode.

MUSIC AND VOICE ROOM
Complete Story Mode.

SCORE SCUFFLE
Complete Story Mode.

TRIANGLE TWISTER PUZZLE MODE
Complete Story Mode.

MARIO TENNIS OPEN

BABY MARIO
In the Super Mario Tennis Special Game, complete 1-3.

BABY PEACH
In the Ring Shot Special Game, complete the Pro Rings.

DRY BOWSER
In the Ink Showdown Special Game, complete Inksplosion.

LUMA
In the Galaxy Rally Special Game, complete Superstar.

STAR CHARACTER
Winning the Champions Cup of the World Open gives the character you used a star. This improves the character.

FIRE MARIO
Give two characters a star.

PRO DIFFICULTY IN EXHIBITION
Complete the Champions Cup.

ACE DIFFICULTY IN EXHIBITION
Complete the Final Cup.

HIDDEN GOODIES
At the Select a File screen, hold Up and press Start. This turns on the camera. If you have found one of the QR Codes online that unlocks something for Mario Tennis Open, scan it with the camera.

MARVEL AVENGERS: BATTLE FOR EARTH

XBOX 360

ACHIEVEMENTS

NAME	GOAL/REQUIREMENT	POINT VALUE
Untouchable	You won a fight without being hit in Campaign.	50
Impressive feet	You performed a Close-Combat.	5
Escapist	You performed a Counter Kick.	5
Dodge this	You dodged a Super Attack.	5
Combo	You chained two Super Attacks.	5
Tag Combo	You chained two Super Attacks by switching characters.	10
Super Tag Combo	You chained 3 Super Attacks by switching characters twice.	15
Maximum Combo	You chained 4 Super Attacks by switching characters twice.	20
Counter	You countered a Super Attack with another Super Attack.	10
Breaker	You used your Breaker to break a Combo.	5
Super charged	You used your ULTRA Attack.	5
Power duo	You won a battle in CO-OP.	5
Symbiosis	You performed a 4x Combo in CO-OP.	5
Trialist	You finished every Trial.	50
Speed and Power	You reached the FAST velocity when doing a Super Attack 5 times in a row.	15
Fashion	You changed the costume of one of your character.	5
Fearless	You won a match without dodging in Campaign.	50
Legend	You unlocked the highest Rank.	200
Experienced	You got 100 000 Experience points.	20
Avengers	You won a battle with Captain America and Iron Man.	5
The X-Men	You won a battle with Wolverine and Phoenix.	5
Brothers	You won a battle with Thor and Loki.	5
Skrulls	You won a battle with Super-Skrull and Veranke.	5
Leading Ladies	You won a battle with Scarlet Witch & Storm.	5
Fire & Ice	You won a battle with Human Torch & Iceman.	5
Ride the lightning	You won a battle with Thor & Storm.	5
Heatwave	You won a battle with Phoenix & Human Torch.	5
Need a Doctor?	You won a battle with Doctor Doom & Doctor Strange.	5
Bad Intentions	You won a battle with Super Skrull & Doctor Doom.	5
Uneasy Alliance	You won a battle with Wolverine & Magneto.	5
S.H.I.E.L.D	You won a battle with Hawkeye & Magneto.	5
Pioneers	You won a battle with Hulk & Iron Man.	5
Part of me	You won a battle with Spider-Man & Venom.	5
Earth United	You finished the first part of the Campaign.	30
Closure	You finished the Campaign mode.	100
Completist	You finished all character's challenge.	150
King of the Hill	You won the arcade mode once.	20
Student	You finished the Tutorial challenges.	30
Army of One	You won a fight without changing characters in Campaign.	50
Adamantium	You obtained an adamantium grade.	30
Here I am!	You won your first battle in Campaign.	5
Team power	You fired projectiles during the ULTRA attack in CO-OP.	10
Champion	You won a Tournament.	20

M

MARVEL SUPER HERO SQUAD

IRON MAN BONUS COSTUME

Select Enter Code from the Options menu and enter 111111. This unlocks the bonus costume "War Machine."

HULK BONUS COSTUMES

Select Enter Code from the Options menu and enter 222222. This unlocks the bonus costumes "Grey Hulk and "Red Hulk."

WOLVERINE BONUS COSTUMES

Select Enter Code from the Options menu and enter 333333. This unlocks the bonus costumes "Wolverine (Brown Costume)" and "Feral Wolverine."

THOR BONUS COSTUMES

Select Enter Code from the Options menu and enter 444444. This unlocks the bonus costumes "Thor (Chain Armor)" and "Loki-Thor."

SILVER SURFER BONUS COSTUMES

Select Enter Code from the Options menu and enter 555555. This unlocks the bonus costumes "Anti-Surfer" and "Gold Surfer."

FALCON BONUS COSTUME

Select Enter Code from the Options menu and enter 666666. This unlocks the bonus costume "Ultimates Falcon."

DOCTOR DOOM BONUS COSTUMES

Select Enter Code from the Options menu and enter 999999. This unlocks the bonus costumes "Ultimates Doctor Doom" and "Professor Doom."

CAPTAIN AMERICA BONUS COSTUME

Select Enter Code from the Options menu and enter 177674. This unlocks the bonus costume "Ultimate Captain America."

A.I.M. AGENT BONUS COSTUME

Select Enter Code from the Options menu and enter 246246. This unlocks the bonus costume "Blue Suit A.I.M."

SUPER KNOCKBACK

Select Enter Code from the Options menu and enter 777777.

NO BLOCK MODE

Select Enter Code from the Options menu and enter 888888.

GROUNDED

Select Enter Code from the Options menu and enter 476863

ONE-HIT TAKEDOWN

Select Enter Code from the Options menu and enter 663448

INFINITE SHARD DURATION

Select Enter Code from the Options menu and enter 742737

THROWN OBJECT TAKEDOWN

Select Enter Code from the Options menu and enter 847936

APOCALYPSE MODE

Select Cheats from the Settings and enter Wolverine, Wolverine, Dr Doom, Abomination, Wolverine. This gives everyone one hit kills.

IRON MAN BONUS COSTUME

Select Enter Code from the
Options menu and enter 111111. This unlocks the bonus costume "War Machine."

HULK BONUS COSTUMES

Select Enter Code from the Options menu and enter 222222. This unlocks the bonus costumes "Grey Hulk" and "Red Hulk."

WOLVERINE BONUS COSTUMES

Select Enter Code from the Options menu and enter 333333. This unlocks the bonus costumes "Wolverine (Brown Costume)" and "Feral Wolverine."

THOR BONUS COSTUMES

Select Enter Code from the Options menu and enter 444444. This unlocks the bonus costumes "Thor (Chain Armor)" and "Loki-Thor."

SILVER SURFER BONUS COSTUMES

Select Enter Code from the Options menu and enter 555555. This unlocks the bonus costumes "Anti-Surfer" and "Gold Surfer."

FALCON BONUS COSTUME

Select Enter Code from the Options menu and enter 666666. This unlocks the bonus costume "Ultimates Falcon."

DOCTOR DOOM BONUS COSTUMES

Select Enter Code from the Options menu and enter 999999. This unlocks the bonus costumes "Ultimates Doctor Doom" and "Professor Doom."

CAPTAIN AMERICA BONUS COSTUME

Select Enter Code from the Options menu and enter 177674. This unlocks the bonus costume "Ultimate Captain America Costume."

A.I.M. AGENT BONUS COSTUME

Select Enter Code from the Options menu and enter 246246. This unlocks the bonus costume "Blue Suit A.I.M."

SUPER KNOCKBACK

Select Enter Code from the Options menu and enter 777777.

NO BLOCK MODE

Select Enter Code from the Options menu and enter 888888.

GROUNDED

Select Enter Code from the Options menu and enter 476863.

ONE-HIT TAKEDOWN

Select Enter Code from the Options menu and enter 663448.

INFINITE SHARD DURATION

Select Enter Code from the Options menu and enter 742737.

THROWN OBJECT TAKEDOWN

Select Enter Code from the Options menu and enter 847936.

MARVEL TRADING CARD GAME

PSP

COMPLETE CARD LIBRARY

At the Deck menu, select new deck and name it BLVRTRSK.

ALL PUZZLES

At the Deck menu, select new deck and name it WHOWANTSPIE.

MARVEL ULTIMATE ALLIANCE

UNLOCK ALL SKINS

At the Team menu, press Up, Down, Left, Right, Left, Right, Plus.

UNLOCKS ALL HERO POWERS

At the Team menu, press Left, Right, Up, Down, Up, Down, Plus.

ALL HEROES TO LEVEL 99

At the Team menu, press Up, Left, Up, Left, Down, Right, Down, Right, Plus.

UNLOCK ALL HEROES

At the Team menu, press Up, Up, Down, Down, Left, Left, Left, Plus.

UNLOCK DAREDEVIL

At the Team menu, press Left, Left, Right, Right, Up, Down, Up, Down, Plus.

UNLOCK SILVER SURFER

At the Team menu, press Down, Left, Left, Up, Right, Up, Down, Left, Plus.

GOD MODE

During gameplay, press Up, Down, Up, Down, Up, Left, Down, Right, Plus.

TOUCH OF DEATH

During gameplay, press Left, Right, Down, Down, Right, Left, Plus.

SUPER SPEED

During gameplay, press Up, Left, Up, Right, Down, Right, Plus.

FILL MOMENTUM

During gameplay, press Left, Right, Right, Left, Up, Down, Up, Plus.

UNLOCK ALL COMICS

At the Review menu, press Left, Right, Right, Left, Up, Up, Right, Plus.

UNLOCK ALL CONCEPT ART

At the Review menu, press Down, Down, Down, Right, Right, Left, Down, Plus.

UNLOCK ALL CINEMATICS

At the Review menu, press Up, Left, Left, Up, Right, Right, Up, Plus.

UNLOCK ALL LOAD SCREENS

At the Review menu, press Up, Down, Right, Left, Up, Up Down, Plus.

UNLOCK ALL COURSES

At the Comic Missions menu, press Up, Right, Left, Down, Up, Right, Left, Down, Plus.

UNLOCK ALL SKINS

At the Team menu, press Up, Down, Left, Right, Left, Right, Start.

UNLOCK ALL HERO POWERS

At the Team menu, press Left, Right, Up, Down, Up, Down, Start.

ALL HEROES TO LEVEL 99

At the Team menu, press Up, Left, Up, Left, Down, Right, Down, Right, Start.

UNLOCK ALL HEROES

At the Team menu, press Up, Up, Down, Down, Left, Left, Left, Start

UNLOCK DAREDEVIL

At the Team Menu, press Left, Left, Right, Right, Up, Down, Up, Down, Start.

UNLOCK SILVER SURFER

At the Team menu, press Down, Left, Left, Up, Right, Up, Down, Left, Start.

GOD MODE

During gameplay, press Up, Down, Up, Down, Up, Left, Down, Right, Start.

TOUCH OF DEATH

During gameplay, press Left, Right, Down, Down, Right, Left, Start.

SUPER SPEED

During gameplay, press Up, Left, Up, Right, Down, Right, Start.

FILL MOMENTUM

During gameplay, press Left, Right, Right, Left, Up, Down, Down, Up, Start.

UNLOCK ALL COMICS

At the Review menu, press Left, Right, Right, Left, Up, Up, Right, Start.

UNLOCK ALL CONCEPT ART

At the Review menu, press Down, Down, Down, Right, Right, Left, Down, Start.

MARVEL VS CAPCOM 3: FATE OF TWO WORLDS

XBOX 360

CHARACTERS

Gain the following amount of player points to unlock each character.

CHARACTER	GAIN THIS AMOUNT OF PLAYER POINTS
Akuma	2000
Sentinel	4000
Hsien-Ko	6000
Taskmaster	8000

XBOX 360/PS3

ACHIEVEMENTS & TROPHIES

NAME	GOAL/REQUIREMENT	POINT VALUE	TROPHY VALUE
Passed the Field Test	Clear 160 missions in Mission mode.	20	Bronze
A New Avenger	Clear 320 missions in Mission mode.	40	Silver
Welcome to Avengers Academy!	Clear 80 missions in Mission mode.	10	Bronze
Leading the Charge	Surpass the rank of Fighter.	30	Silver
Combat Specialist	In Ranked Match, surpass the "1st" class rank, or fight someone who has.	30	Silver
Comic Collector	Unlock all items in the Gallery.	50	Gold
Back at 'Cha!	Perform 10 successful Crossover Counters. (Arcade/Xbox LIVE only)	10	Bronze
Excelsior!	Perform 10 Team Aerial Combos. (Arcade/Xbox LIVE only)	10	Bronze
Be Gone!	Perform 10 Snap Backs. (Arcade/Xbox LIVE only)	10	Bronze
Mega Buster	Use 1,000 Hyper Combo Gauge bars. (Arcade/Xbox LIVE only)	20	Bronze
Ultimate Nullifier	Perform 30 successful Advancing Guards. (Arcade/Xbox LIVE only)	10	Bronze
Playtime Is Over	Surpass the rank of Amateur.	10	Bronze
Herculean Task	Beat Arcade mode on the hardest difficulty.	30	Silver
Saving My Quarters	Beat Arcade mode without using any continues.	20	Bronze

NAME	GOAL/REQUIREMENT	POINT VALUE	TROPHY VALUE
Waiting for the Trade	View all endings in Arcade mode.	50	Gold
Master of Fate	Unlock all achievements.	50	Bronze
I Buy the Issues	View one ending in Arcade mode.	10	Bronze
World Warrior	Earn 5,000 Player Points (PP).	10	Bronze
Brusin' Bruce	Land an Incredible Combo. (Arcade/Xbox LIVE only)	20	Bronze
Charles in Charge	Land an Uncanny Combo. (Arcade/Xbox LIVE only)	30	Silver
Average Joe	Land a Viewtiful Combo. (Arcade/Xbox LIVE only)	10	Bronze
Champion Edition Hero	Earn 30,000 Player Points (PP).	30	Silver
Super Turbo Brawler	Earn 100,000 Player Points (PP).	50	Silver
Big Bang Theory	Perform 30 Hyper Combo Finishes. (Arcade/Xbox LIVE only)	30	Silver
Brave New World	Participate in any mode on Xbox LIVE.	10	Bronze
Steel Battalion	Block 100 times. (Arcade/Xbox LIVE only)	20	Bronze
Fate of the Satsui no Hadou	Decide who is the true master of the fist in an Xbox LIVE match.	20	Bronze
Copy This!	Put an end to this game of spider and fly in an Xbox LIVE match.	20	Bronze
Raccoon City Incident	Settle things between former S.T.A.R.S. members in an Xbox LIVE match.	20	Bronze
Passport to Beatdown Country	Fight in all of the stages.	10	Bronze
Need a Healing Factor	Win a match without blocking. (Arcade/Xbox LIVE only)	10	Bronze
School for the Gifted	Get a 5 game win streak in Ranked Match.	15	Bronze
A Hero Stands Alone	Win a match without calling your partners or switching out. (Arcade/Xbox LIVE only)	10	Bronze
Full Roster	Battle against all characters in an Xbox LIVE match.	40	Silver
Who Will Answer the Call?	Participate in an 8 player Lobby on Xbox LIVE.	10	Bronze
Duty and Deus Ex Machina	Make a match on Xbox LIVE between a national hero and a killing machine a reality.	20	Bronze
One Step Ahead	Land 50 First Attacks in a match. (Arcade/Xbox LIVE only)	30	Silver
Avengers Assemble!	Make a team composed of the Big 3 and win a match. (Arcade/Xbox LIVE only)	15	Bronze
Turn the Tables	Land a Team Aerial Counter in a match. (Arcade/Xbox LIVE only)	10	Bronze
Galactic Smasher	Perform 30 Crossover Combination Finishes. (Arcade/Xbox LIVE only)	40	Silver
Wreak "Havok"	Use X-Factor in a match. (Arcade/Xbox LIVE only)	10	Bronze
Badds to the Bone	Make a team of three who have altered their bodies, and win a match. (Arcade/Xbox LIVE only)	15	Bronze
Whose Side Are You On?	Bring about an end to the Civil War in an Xbox LIVE match.	20	Bronze
Fate of Two Worlds	Make a match on Xbox LIVE between the marquee characters for this game a reality.	20	Bronze

NAME	GOAL/REQUIREMENT	POINT VALUE	TROPHY VALUE
Female Flyers	Make a team composed of women who can fly, and win a match. (Arcade/Xbox LIVE only)	15	Bronze
Darkstalkers	Make a team composed of those who dwell in the darkness, and win a match. (Arcade/Xbox LIVE only)	15	Bronze
Weapon X	Make a team composed of Weapon-X test subjects, and win a match. (Arcade/Xbox LIVE only)	15	Bronze

MARVEL: ULTIMATE ALLIANCE 2

NINTENDO WII

GOD MODE

At any point during a game, press Up, Up, Down, Down, Left, Right, Down.

GIVE MONEY

At the Team Select or Hero Details screen press Up, Up, Down, Down, Up, Up, Up, Down.

UNLOCK ALL POWERS

At the Team Select or Hero Details screen press Up, Up, Down, Down, Left, Right, Right, Left.

ADVANCE ALL CHARACTERS TO L99

At the Hero Details screen press Down, Up, Left, Up, Right, Up, Left, Down.

UNLOCK ALL BONUS MISSIONS

While using the Bonus Mission Simulator, press Up, Right, Down, Left, Left, Right, Up, Up.

ADD 1 CHARACTER LEVEL

During a game, press Down, Up, Right, Up, Right, Up, Right, Down.

ADD 10 CHARACTER LEVELS

During a game, press Down, Up, Left, Up, Left, Up, Left, Down.

PLAYSTATION 3

These codes will disable the ability to save.

GOD MODE

During a game, press Up, Down, Up, Down, Up, Left, Down, Right, Start.

UNLIMITED FUSION

During a game, press Right, Right, Up, Down, Up, Up, Left, Start.

UNLOCK ALL POWERS

During a game, press Left, Right, Up, Down, Up, Down, Start.

UNLOCK ALL HEROES

During a game, press Up, Up, Down, Down, Left, Left, Left, Start.

UNLOCK ALL SKINS

During a game, press Up, Down, Left, Right, Left, Right, Start.

UNLOCK JEAN GREY

During a game, press Left, Left, Right, Right, Up, Down, Up, Down, Start.

UNLOCK HULK

During a game, press Down, Left, Left, Up, Right, Up, Down, Left, Start.

UNLOCK THOR

During a game, press Up, Right, Right, Down, Right, Down, Left, Right, Start.

CHEATS, ACHIEVEMENTS, AND TROPHIES

M

UNLOCK ALL AUDIO LOGS

At the main menu, press Left, Right, Right, Left, Up, Up, Right, Start.

UNLOCK ALL DOSSIERS

At the main menu, press Down, Down, Down, Right, Right, Left, Down, Start.

UNLOCK ALL MOVIES

At the main menu, press Up, Left, Left, Up, Right, Right, Up, Start.

PSP

GOD MODE

At any point during a game, press Up, Up, Down, Down, Left, Right, Down.

GIVE MONEY

At the Team Select or Hero Details screen press Up, Up, Down, Down, Up, Up, Up, Down.

UNLOCK ALL POWERS

At the Team Select or Hero Details screen press Up, Up, Down, Down, Left, Right, Right, Left.

ADVANCE ALL CHARACTERS TO L99

At the Hero Details screen press Down, Up, Left, Up, Right, Up, Left, Down.

UNLOCK ALL BONUS MISSIONS

While using the Bonus Mission Simulator, press Up, Right, Down, Left, Left, Right, Up, Up.

ADD 1 CHARACTER LEVEL

During a game, press Down, Up, Right, Up, Right, Up, Right, Down.

ADD 10 CHARACTER LEVELS

During a game, press Down, Up, Left, Up, Left, Up, Left, Down.

XBOX 360

These codes will disable the ability to save.

GOD MODE

During a game, press Up, Down, Up, Down, Up, Left, Down, Right, Start.

UNLIMITED FUSION

During a game, press Right, Right, Up, Down, Up, Up, Left, Start.

UNLOCK ALL POWERS

During a game, press Left, Right, Up, Down, Up, Down, Start.

UNLOCK ALL HEROES

During a game, press Up, Up, Down, Down, Left, Left, Left, Start.

UNLOCK ALL SKINS

During a game, press Up, Down, Left, Right, Left, Right, Start.

UNLOCK JEAN GREY

During a game, press Left, Left, Right, Right, Up, Down, Up, Down, Start.

UNLOCK HULK

During a game, press Down, Left, Left, Up, Right, Up, Down, Left, Start.

UNLOCK THOR

During a game, press Up, Right, Right, Down, Right, Down, Left, Right, Start.

UNLOCK ALL AUDIO LOGS

At the main menu, press Left, Right, Right, Left, Up, Up, Right, Start.

UNLOCK ALL DOSSIERS

At the main menu, press Down, Down, Down, Right, Right, Left, Down, Start.

UNLOCK ALL MOVIES

At the main menu, press Up, Left, Left, Up, Right, Right, Up, Start.

MASS EFFECT 3

BATTLEFIELD 3 SOLDIER IN MULTIPLAYER

This character is unlocked for multiplayer if you have a Battlefield 3 Online Pass activated on your EA account.

RECKONER KNIGHT ARMOR AND CHAKRAM LAUNCHER

Start the Kingdom of Amalur: Reckoning demo to unlock this armor and weapon in Mass Effect 3.

BATTLEFIELD 3 SOLDIER IN MULTIPLAYER

This character is unlocked for multiplayer if you have a Battlefield 3 Online Pass activated on your EA account.

RECKONER KNIGHT ARMOR AND CHAKRAM LAUNCHER

Start the Kingdom of Amalur: Reckoning demo to unlock this armor and weapon in Mass Effect 3.

AVATAR AWARDS

AVATAR	EARNED BY
N7 Helmet	Return to Active Duty.
Omniblade	Kill 25 Enemies with Melee Attacks.

ACHIEVEMENTS & TROPHIES

NAME	GOAL/REQUIREMENT	POINT VALUE	TROPHY VALUE
Driven	Return to active duty.	5	Bronze
Bringer of War	Chase down an assassin.	10	Bronze
Mobilizer	Bring a veteran officer aboard.	15	Bronze
World Shaker	Destroy an Atlas dropped from orbit.	15	Bronze
Pathfinder	Explore a lost city.	15	Bronze
Tunnel Rat	Survive the swarm.	15	Bronze
Party Crasher	Sabotage a dreadnought.	15	Bronze
Hard Target	Call down an orbital strike.	15	Bronze
Saboteur	Disable a group of fighter squadrons.	15	Bronze
Arbiter	Win a political stand-off.	25	Bronze
Last Witness	Extract ancient technology.	25	Bronze
Executioner	Defeat an old adversary.	25	Bronze
Well Connected	Send a warning across the galaxy.	15	Bronze
Fact Finder	Discover an enemy's monstrous origin.	15	Bronze
Liberator	Stop a Cerberus kidnapping.	15	Bronze
Problem Solver	Evacuate a scientific facility.	15	Bronze
Patriot	Make the final assault.	25	Bronze
Legend	Mission accomplished.	50	Silver
Shopaholic	Visit a store in the single-player campaign.	10	Bronze
Master and Commander	Deliver most of the Galaxy at War assets to the final conflict.	50	Silver
Lost and Found	Dispatch 10 probes to retrieve people or resources in Reaper territory.	25	Bronze
Long Service Medal	Complete Mass Effect 3 twice, or once with a Mass Effect 2 import.	50	Silver

NAME	GOAL/REQUIREMENT	POINT VALUE	TROPHY VALUE
Insanity	Finish the game on Insanity without changing difficulty after leaving Earth.	75	Gold
A Personal Touch	Modify a weapon.	10	Bronze
Paramour	Establish or rekindle a romantic relationship.	25	Bronze
Combined Arms	Perform any combination of 50 biotic combos or tech bursts.	25	Silver
Focused	Evolve any of your powers to rank 6.	25	Bronze
Recruit	Kill 250 enemies.	10	Bronze
Soldier	Kill 1,000 enemies.	15	Bronze
Veteran	Kill 5,000 enemies.	25	Silver
Bruiser	Kill 100 enemies with melee attacks.	10	Bronze
Untouchable	Escape a Reaper in the galaxy map.	10	Bronze
Defender	Attain the highest level of readiness in each theater of war.	25	Bronze
Overload Specialist	Overload the shields of 100 enemies.	15	Bronze
Sky High	Lift 100 enemies off the ground with powers.	15	Bronze
Pyromaniac	Set 100 enemies on fire with powers.	15	Bronze
Eye of the Hurricane	Kill a brute while it's charging you.	10	Bronze
Mail Slot	Kill 10 guardians with headshots from the front while their shields are raised.	10	Bronze
Hijacker	Hijack an Atlas mech.	10	Bronze
Giant Killer	Defeat a harvester.	10	Bronze
Enlisted	Start a character in multiplayer or customize a character in single-player.	5	Bronze
Tour of Duty	Finish all multiplayer maps or all N7 missions in single-player.	20	Bronze
Always Prepared	Obtain two non-customizable suits of armor.	10	Bronze
Tourist	Complete one multiplayer match or two N7 missions.	5	Bronze
Explorer	Complete three multiplayer matches or five N7 missions.	15	Bronze
Gunsmith	Upgrade any weapon to level 10.	25	Silver
Almost There	Reach level 15 in multiplayer or level 50 in single-player.	15	Bronze
Peak Condition	Reach level 20 in multiplayer or level 60 in single-player.	25	Bronze
Battle Scarred	Promote a multiplayer character to the Galaxy at War or import an ME3 character.	25	Bronze
Unwavering	Finish all multiplayer maps on Gold or all single-player missions on Insanity.	50	Gold

FROM ASHES

ACHIEVEMENTS & TROPHIES

NAME	GOAL/REQUIREMENT	POINT VALUE	TROPHY VALUE
Freedom Fighter	Find all required intel to help Eden Prime's colonists.	25	Bronze
Prothean Expert	Learn more about the Prothean Empire.	25	Bronze

MAX PAYNE 3

PLAYSTATION 3

NEW YORK MINUTE IN ARCADE MODE
Complete story mode.

CHARACTER SELECT IN ARCADE MODE
Complete story mode on Medium Difficulty.

OLD SCHOOL DIFFICULTY, HARDCORE DIFFICULTY, AND UNLIMITED PAINKILLERS CHEAT
Complete story mode on Hard Difficulty.

MAX PAYNE ADVANCED CHARACTER MODEL
Complete story mode on Old School Difficulty.

The following cheats can be used when replaying a level with the level select:

BULLET CAM ON EVERY KILL
Find all Clues.

ONE HIT KILL CHEAT
Complete story mode on Hardcore difficulty with Free Aim.

UNLIMITED AMMO
Find all Golden Guns.

UNLIMITED BULLET TIME
Earn a Gold Medal on all levels in Arcade Mode.

UNLIMITED PAIN KILLERS
Complete game on Hard difficulty with Free Aim.

XBOX 360

NEW YORK MINUTE IN ARCADE MODE
Complete story mode.

CHARACTER SELECT IN ARCADE MODE
Complete story mode on Medium Difficulty.

OLD SCHOOL DIFFICULTY, HARDCORE DIFFICULTY, AND UNLIMITED PAINKILLERS CHEAT
Complete story mode on Hard Difficulty.

MAX PAYNE ADVANCED CHARACTER MODEL
Complete story mode on Old School Difficulty.

The following cheats can be used when replaying a level with the level select:

BULLET CAM ON EVERY KILL
Find all Clues.

ONE HIT KILL CHEAT
Complete story mode on Hardcore difficulty with Free Aim.

UNLIMITED AMMO
Find all Golden Guns.

UNLIMITED BULLET TIME
Earn a Gold Medal on all levels in Arcade Mode.

UNLIMITED PAIN KILLERS
Complete game on Hard difficulty with Free Aim.

CHEATS, ACHIEVEMENTS, AND TROPHIES

M

ACHIEVEMENTS & TROPHIES

NAME	GOAL/REQUIREMENT	POINT VALUE	TROPHY VALUE
Feel The Payne	Story Complete [MEDIUM]	30	Bronze
Serious Payne	Story Complete [HARD]	50	Silver
Maximum Payne	Story Complete [OLD SCHOOL]	80	Gold
Payne In The Ass	Story Complete [HARDCORE]	20	Bronze
Part I Complete	Complete Part I Of The Story	20	Bronze
Part II Complete	Complete Part II Of The Story	20	Bronze
Part III Complete	Complete Part III Of The Story	20	Bronze
A New York Minute	Finish In A New York Minute	100	Gold
The Shadows Rushed Me	Unlock And Complete New York Minute Hardcore	10	Silver
Out The Window	Get 6 Kills While Diving Through The VIP Window [FREE AIM]	10	Bronze
The One Eyed Man Is King	Cover Passos With Perfect Aim	10	Bronze
Something Wicked This Way Comes	Get 7 Kills While Jumping From The Rickety Boat [FREE AIM]	10	Bronze
That Old Familiar Feeling	Clear The Hallway Of Lasers	10	Bronze
Amidst The Wreckage	Destroy All The Models In The Boardroom	5	Bronze
So Much For Being Subtle	Get 9 Kills While Being Pulled By A Chain [FREE AIM]	10	Bronze
The Only Choice Given	Get 8 Kills While Dangling From A Chain [FREE AIM]	10	Bronze
Trouble Had Come To Me	Clear Everyone On The Bus Ride	15	Bronze
Along For The Ride	Trigger A Bullet Cam On The Zipline [FREE AIM]	10	Bronze
Sometimes You Get Lucky	Get A Headshot During The Rooftop Tremors	5	Bronze
It Was Chaos And Luck	Get 6 Kills While Riding The Push Cart [FREE AIM]	10	Bronze
The Road-Kill Behind Me	Total Everything On The Runway	10	Bronze
The Fear Of Losing It	Survive A Level Without Painkillers	20	Bronze
It's Fear That Gives Men Wings	10 Bullet Time® Kills In A Row	20	Bronze
You Might Hurt Someone With That	Shoot 10 Airborne Grenades	20	Bronze
One Bullet At A Time	300 Headshots	20	Bronze
You Play, You Pay, You Bastard	100 Kills With Melee	20	Bronze
With Practiced Bravado	100 Kills During Shootdodge.	20	Bronze
Colder Than The Devil's Heart	Kill 30 Enemies In 2 Minutes	15	Bronze
A Few Hundred Bullets Back	Use Every Weapon In The Game	20	Bronze
Past The Point Of No Return	Take 100 Painkillers	10	Bronze
An Echo Of The Past	Find All Clues	35	Bronze
Sure Know How To Pick A Place	Discover All Tourist Locations	10	Bronze
A License To Kill	Collect All Golden Guns	40	Silver
All Of The Above	Finish All Single Player Grinds	100	Gold
Full Monty	Complete One Of Each Game Mode Including All Gang Wars	10	Bronze
Payne Bringer	Kill 100 Other Players	30	Silver

NAME	GOAL/REQUIREMENT	POINT VALUE	TROPHY VALUE
Max Payne Invitational	Invite someone to play through the in-game contact list	5	Bronze
Man Of Many Weapons	Unlock All Weapons	25	Bronze
Man Of Many Faces	Unlock All Faction Characters	25	Bronze
Deathmatch Challenge	Winner In Any Public Deathmatch	20	Bronze
Grave Robber	Looted A Body	5	Bronze
The Gambler	Won A Wager	15	Bronze
Training Complete	Achieve Level Rank 50	25	Silver
Dearest Of All My Friends	Kill Someone On Your Friends List	10	Bronze

SECRET ACHIEVEMENTS & TROPHIES

NAME	GOAL/REQUIREMENT	POINT VALUE	TROPHY VALUE
Sweep	Flawless Team Gang Wars Victory	10	Bronze
You Push A Man Too Far	Don't Shoot The Dis-Armed Man	5	Bronze

MEDAL OF HONOR: VANGUARD

NINTENDO WII

EXTRA ARMOR

Pause the game and press Up, Down, Up, Down to display the words Enter Cheat Code. Then press Right, Left, Right, Down, Up, Right.

DECREASE ENEMY ACCURACY

Pause the game and press Up, Down, Up, Down to display the words Enter Cheat Code. Then press Right, Left, Right, Down, Up, Right.

INVISIBLE

Pause the game and press Up, Down, Up, Down to display the words Enter Cheat Code. Then press Up, Right, Left, Down, Down, Up.

MEDAL OF HONOR: WARFIGHTER

XBOX 360/PS3

ACHIEVEMENTS & TROPHIES

NAME	GOAL/REQUIREMENT	POINT VALUE	TROPHY VALUE
Warfighter	Completed the campaign	40	Silver
Tier 1	Completed the campaign on Tier 1 difficulty	50	Silver
Rain of Terror	Completed Changing Tides	15	Bronze
Monsoon Lagoon	Completed Rip Current	15	Bronze
Unexpected Cargo	Completed Unintended Consequences	15	Bronze
One Shot, Three Kills	Completed Hat Trick	15	Bronze
Hit the Beach	Completed Shore Leave	15	Bronze
Know the Enemy	Completed Through the Eyes of Evil	15	Bronze
Non-Official Cover	Completed Finding Faraz	20	Bronze
Class Dismissed	Completed Connect the Dots	20	Bronze
Pedal to the Medal	Completed Hello and Dubai	20	Bronze
Closing Ceremony	Completed Old Friends	20	Bronze
One Man Mutiny	Completed Bump in the Night	20	Bronze

M

NAME	GOAL/REQUIREMENT	POINT VALUE	TROPHY VALUE
Pit and Pin	Completed Hot Pursuit	20	Bronze
Let Him Rot	Completed Shut It Down	20	Bronze
Preacher's Path	Finished all the Preacher Missions	30	Silver
Stump's No Chump	Finished all the Stump Missions	30	Silver
Double Header	Killed two enemies with one bullet in the Changing Tides mission	10	Bronze
Release the Kraken!	Killed 20 enemies during the boat exfil in Rip Current	15	Bronze
Hardcore	Completed the campaign on Hardcore difficulty	80	Gold
Tag, You're It	Caught Faraz within 15 minutes in Finding Faraz	10	Bronze
Leftover Lead	Completed the sniping section in Shore Leave without missing a shot	15	Bronze
On the Clock	Completed the training in Through the Eyes of Evil in under 18 seconds.	10	Bronze
Storm Watch	Got through the sandstorm without hitting any vehicles in Hello and Dubai	10	Bronze
Vender Bender	Destroyed 90 market stalls in Hot Pursuit	10	Bronze
Dirty Laundry	Found the grenades in the laundry room in Bump in the Night	15	Bronze
Room Service	Unlocked all door breach options	20	Bronze
Master Locksmith	Used each breaching option at least once	15	Bronze
Extreme Realism	Recovered from near-death 5 times without dying	10	Bronze
Tier 1 Imports	Got 50 kills while holding enemy weapons	15	Bronze
Peek-a-Boo	Killed an enemy while using peek and lean in the Campaign	5	Bronze
Lean With It	Killed 25 enemies while using peek and lean during the Campaign	15	Bronze
It's Dangerous to go Alone!	Requested ammo from an Ally in the Campaign	5	Bronze
Lead Farmer	Requested ammo from an Ally 25 times in Campaign	10	Bronze
Tactical Toggler	Killed 25 enemies while using Combat Toggle	15	Bronze
Unstoppable	Completed Shore Leave on Hardcore difficulty	30	Silver
The Axeman	Killed 25 enemies with melee during the Campaign	20	Bronze
MVP	Finished in first place in any online match	20	Silver
All In	Called in Apache support	20	Silver
There IS an I in Fire Team	Finished a round as part of the top Fire Team	15	Bronze
Brothers in Arms	Won a round with a Friend as a Fire Team Buddy	20	Bronze
Warchief	Unlocked all soldiers in multiplayer	35	Silver
Jack of all Guns	Earned the Marksman Pin for all Weapons	20	Silver
Back in the Fight	Completed one tour with all classes.	50	Gold

NAME	GOAL/REQUIREMENT	POINT VALUE	TROPHY VALUE
Honey Badger	Used your Fire Team buddy to re-arm or heal	10	Bronze
Squad Leader	Unlocked a soldier of each class	20	Bronze
Downrange	Played online for 15 minutes	20	Bronze
Job done	Complete 3 Combat Mission objectives	20	Bronze
Global Warfighters	Unlocked a soldier from each unit	25	Silver
For Honor For Country	Collected all other Medal of Honor Warfighter Trophies	—	Platinum

SECRET ACHIEVEMENTS & TROPHIES

NAME	GOAL/REQUIREMENT	POINT VALUE	TROPHY VALUE
Target Practice	Shot down the targets in the training camp caves in Connect the Dots	10	Bronze

MEGA MAN 5

NINTENDO WII

ALL WEAPONS AND ITEMS PASSWORD

Enter Blue B4 D6 F1 and Red C1 D4 F6 as a password.

MEGA MAN STAR FORCE 3: BLACK ACE

NINTENDO 3DS

STARS ON NEW GAME/CONTINUE SCREEN

Do the following to earn each star on the New Game/Continue screen.

NAME	HOW TO EARN
Black Ace	Defeat the game
G Comp	Collect all Giga cards
M Comp	Collect all Mega cards
S Comp	Collect all Standard cards
SS	Defeat Sirius

RANDOM SIGMA BOSSES

At the New Game/Continue screen, hold L and tap S Comp Star, G Comp Star, S Comp Star, M Comp Star, SS Star, SS Star, Black Ace Star.

FIGHT ROGUEZZ

At the New Game/Continue screen, hold L and tap G Comp Star, M Comp Star, M Comp Star, SS Star, G Comp Star, S Comp Star, Black Ace Star. RogueZZ appears in Meteor G Control CC.

MEGA MAN STAR FORCE 3: RED JOKER

STARS ON NEW GAME/CONTINUE SCREEN

Do the following to earn each star on the New Game/Continue screen.

NAME	HOW TO EARN
Red Joker	Defeat the game
G Comp	Collect all Giga cards
M Comp	Collect all Mega cards
S Comp	Collect all Standard cards
SS	Defeat Sirius

RANDOM SIGMA BOSSES

At the New Game/Continue screen, hold L and tap S Comp Star, G Comp Star, S Comp Star, M Comp Star, SS Star, SS Star, Red Joker Star.

FIGHT ROGUEZZ

At the New Game/Continue screen, hold L and tap G Comp Star, M Comp Star, M Comp Star, SS Star, G Comp Star, S Comp Star, Red Joker Star. RogueZZ appears in Meteor G Control CC.

MERCENARIES 2: WORLD IN FLAMES

To use Cheat Mode, you must update the game by being online when the game is started. The cheats will keep you from earning trophies, but anything earned up to that point remains. You can still save with the cheats, but be careful if you want to earn trophies. Quit the game without saving to return to normal.

CHEAT MODE

Access your PDA by pressing Select. Press L2, R2, R2, L2, R2, L2, L2, R2, R2, R2, L2 and close the PDA. You then need to accept the agreement that says trophies are disabled. Now you can enter the following cheats.

INVINCIBILITY

Access your PDA and press Up, Down, Left, Down, Right, Right. This activates invincibility for you and anyone that joins your game.

INFINITE AMMO

Access your PDA and press Up, Down, Left, Right, Left, Left.

GIVE ALL VEHICLES

Access your PDA and press Up, Down, Left, Right, Right, Left.

GIVE ALL SUPPLIES

Access your PDA and press Left, Right, Right, Left, Up, Up, Left, Up.

GIVE ALL AIRSTRIKES (EXCEPT NUKE)

Access your PDA and press Right, Left, Down, Up, Right, Left, Down, Up.

GIVE NUKE

Access your PDA and press Up, Up, Down, Down, Left, Right, Left, Right.

FILL FUEL

Access your PDA and press Up, Up, Up, Down, Down, Down.

ALL COSTUMES

Access your PDA and press Up, Right, Down, Left, Up.

GRAPPLING HOOK

Access your PDA and press Up, Left, Down, Right, Up.

METAL GEAR RISING REVENGEANCE

REVENGEANCE MODE

On the title screen input Up, Up, Down, Down, Left, Right, Left, Right, O, X to unlock Revengeance Mode early.

UNLOCKABLE COSTUMES

COSTUME	REQUIREMENT
Custom Cyborg Body (Blue)	Clear 10 VR Missions.
Custom Cyborg Body (Desperado Ver.)	Complete File R-04.
Custom Cyborg Body (Red)	Clear six VR Missions.
Mariachi Uniform	Complete File R-02.
Standard Body	Complete the game on Hard difficulty or higher.
Suit (Tuxedo & Shades)	Complete File R-00 on Very Hard difficulty.

UNLOCKABLE WEAPONS

WEAPON	REQUIREMENT
High-Frequency Long Sword	Rank first in all VR Missions.
High-Frequency Machete	Collect 10 Data Storage items.
High-Frequency Muramasa Blade	Complete the game on any difficulty.
High-Frequency Wooden Sword	Discover all five soldiers in cardboard boxes.
Stun Blade	Collect all Data Storage items.
Weapons Armor Breaker	Collect all ID Chips.

UNLOCKABLE WIGS

Collect a large number of ID Chips to unlock different Wigs in the Customize Menu.

WIG	REQUIREMENT
Blade Mode Wig	Complete the game on Hard or higher and collect all ID Chips.
Infinite Wig A	Complete the game with at least 10 ID Chips.
Infinite Wig B	Complete the game with at least 20 ID Chips.

REVENGEANCE MODE

On the title screen input Up, Up, Down, Down, Left, Right, Left, Right, B, A to unlock Revengeance Mode early.

UNLOCKABLE COSTUMES

COSTUME	REQUIREMENT
Custom Cyborg Body (Blue)	Clear 10 VR Missions.
Custom Cyborg Body (Desperado Ver.)	Complete File R-04.
Custom Cyborg Body (Red)	Clear six VR Missions.
Mariachi Uniform	Complete File R-02.
Standard Body	Complete the game on Hard difficulty or higher.
Suit (Tuxedo & Shades)	Complete File R-00 on Very Hard difficulty.

CHEATS, ACHIEVEMENTS, AND TROPHIES

UNLOCKABLE WEAPONS

WEAPON	REQUIREMENT
High-Frequency Long Sword	Rank first in all VR Missions.
High-Frequency Machete	Collect 10 Data Storage items.
High-Frequency Muramasa Blade	Complete the game on any difficulty.
High-Frequency Wooden Sword	Discover all five soldiers in cardboard boxes.
Stun Blade	Collect all Data Storage items.
Weapons Armor Breaker	Collect all ID Chips.

UNLOCKABLE WIGS

Collect a large number of ID Chips to unlock different Wigs in the Customize Menu.

WIG	REQUIREMENT
Blade Mode Wig	Complete the game on Hard or higher and collect all ID Chips.
Infinite Wig A	Complete the game with at least 10 ID Chips.
Infinite Wig B	Complete the game with at least 20 ID Chips.

XBOX 360/PS3

ACHIEVEMENTS & TROPHIES

NAME	GOAL/REQUIREMENT	POINT VALUE	TROPHY VALUE
File R-00: Status – Closed	Complete File R-00: Guard Duty.	15	Bronze
File R-01: Status – Closed	Complete File R-01: Coup d'Etat.	15	Bronze
File R-02: Status – Closed	Complete File R-02: Research Facility.	15	Bronze
File R-03: Status – Closed	Complete File R-03: Mile High.	15	Bronze
File R-04: Status – Closed	Complete File R-04: Hostile Takeover.	15	Bronze
File R-05: Status – Closed	Complete File R-05: Escape From Denver.	15	Bronze
File R-06: Status – Closed	Complete File R-06: Badlands Showdown.	15	Bronze
File R-07: Status – Closed	Complete File R-07: Assassination Attempt.	15	Bronze
Becoming a Lightning God	Complete story mode on Revengeance difficulty with all S rankings.	50	Gold
Steel Tail	Cut off Metal Gear RAY's metal tail during File R-00.	15	Bronze
No Flash Photography!	Destroy all the Gun Cameras in File R-01.	15	Bronze
Dwarf Raiden	Incapacitate all the soldiers in File R-02 using a Dwarf Gekko.	15	Bronze
A Walk in the Dark	Complete the sewer sequence in File R-03 without using AR Mode.	15	Bronze
Menace to Society	Cut off the finial at the top of the pagoda in File R-04.	5	Bronze
Great Escape	Complete File R-05 in less than 7 minutes.	20	Bronze
Surprise Attack!	Arrive at the objective in File R-07 without being spotted.	20	Bronze

NAME	GOAL/REQUIREMENT	POINT VALUE	TROPHY VALUE
Anti-Cyborg Sentiment	Destroy a total of 100 Cyborgs during story mode.	5	Bronze
The Bigger They Are…	Destroy a total of 100 Custom Cyborgs during story mode.	15	Bronze
Herpetophobia	Destroy a total of 10 Gekkos during story mode.	15	Bronze
Extinction Level Event	Destroy a total of 10 Raptors during story mode.	20	Bronze
Pond Scum	Destroy a total of 5 Vodomjerka during story mode.	20	Bronze
Wolf Hunter	Destroy a total of 10 Fenrirs during story mode.	20	Bronze
Slider Strike	Destroy a total of 10 Sliders during story mode.	15	Bronze
Jumping the Shark	Destroy a total of 10 Hammerheads during story mode.	20	Bronze
Looking Out for the Little Guys	Destroy a total of 30 Dwarf Gekkos during story mode.	5	Bronze
Tearing Away the Disguise	Destroy all of the humanoid Dwarf Gekkos during story mode.	20	Bronze
Datsu Right	Successfully complete 50 Zandatsus during story mode.	15	Bronze
What Doesn't Kill You…	In story mode, successfully parry 10 attacks in a row in one minute or less.	20	Bronze
Assassin Behind Closed Doors	Successfully complete 30 Ninja Kills during story mode.	15	Bronze
You Don't Run from Chance	Successfully complete 50 Executions during story mode.	15	Bronze
A Lover, Not a Fighter	Successfully complete 10 No Kill battles during story mode.	20	Bronze
Assault with a Deadly Weapon	Dismember three enemies during Blade Mode with a single attack.	20	Bronze
Rip 'Em Apart!	In story mode, kill 100 enemies by cutting them.	15	Bronze
Love at First Sight	While remotely operating a Dwarf Gekko in story mode, find and communicate with all Dwarf Gekkos.	15	Bronze
Ich Liebe Kapitalismus!	Acquire all customization items.	20	Bronze
A Big Fan of Lefties	Acquire all enemy officers' left arms.	20	Bronze
Amateur Radio Operator	Listen to most of the codec conversations.	50	Gold
Peekaboo	Discover all of the soldiers hidden in cardboard boxes.	20	Bronze
Data Mining	Acquire all data storage devices.	20	Bronze
Humanitarian Assistance	Rescue all the civilians.	25	Bronze
Analysis Complete	Unlock every VR Mission.	20	Bronze
VR Master	Complete every VR Mission.	30	Bronze
Virtually a God	Set the highest score on every VR Mission.	50	Gold
Revengeance	Obtain all Trophies.	—	Platinum

CHEATS, ACHIEVEMENTS, AND TROPHIES

M

SECRET ACHIEVEMENTS & TROPHIES

NAME	GOAL/REQUIREMENT	POINT VALUE	TROPHY VALUE
Prodigal Murderer	Defeat Mistral without taking any damage on Hard difficulty or above.	30	Silver
Genius Destroyer	Defeat Monsoon without taking any damage on Hard difficulty or above.	30	Silver
Truly Human	Defeat Sundowner without taking any damage on Hard difficulty or above.	30	Silver
Chosen by History	Defeat Samuel without taking any damage on Hard difficulty or above.	30	Silver
The Politics of Silencing Foes	Defeat Sen. Armstrong without taking any damage on Hard difficulty or above.	30	Silver

VR MISSION EXPANSION DLC

NAME	GOAL/REQUIREMENT	POINT VALUE	TROPHY VALUE
DL-VR Master	Complete every DL-VR Mission.	20	Silver
Hero of the Metaverse	Set the highest score on every DL-VR Mission.	90	Gold

JETSTREAM DLC

NAME	GOAL/REQUIREMENT	POINT VALUE	TROPHY VALUE
DL-Story-01: Status – Closed	Complete DL-Story-01: Jetstream.	15	Bronze
You're Hired	Defeat Sen. Armstrong without taking any damage on Hard difficulty or above.	20	Silver
Master of the Wind	Complete DL-Story-01: Jetstream on Revengeance difficulty in one hour or less.	50	Gold
Draw, Pardner!	Defeat 100 enemies in DL-Story-01: Jetstream's Story Mode using Quick Draw.	15	Bronze

BLADE WOLF DLC

NAME	GOAL/REQUIREMENT	POINT VALUE	TROPHY VALUE
DL-Story-02: Status – Closed	Complete DL-Story-02: Blade Wolf.	15	Bronze
Fangs of Fury	Complete DL-Story-02: Blade Wolf on Revengeance difficulty in one hour or less.	50	Gold
Predatory Instincts	Defeat 30 enemies in DL-Story-02: Blade Wolf via Hunt Kills.	15	Bronze
Wolf's Pride	Defeat Khamsin without taking any damage on Hard difficulty or above.	20	Silver

METAL GEAR SOLID 4 GUNS OF THE PATRIOTS

PLAYSTATION 3

100,000 DREBIN POINTS

At Otacon's computer in Shadow Moses, enter 14893.

OPENING – OLD L.A. 2040 IPOD SONG

At Otacon's computer in Shadow Moses, enter 78925.

POLICENAUTS END TITLE IPOD SONG

At Otacon's computer in Shadow Moses, enter 13462.
You must first defeat the game to use the following passwords.

DESPERATE CHASE IPOD SONG

Select password from the Extras menu and enter thomas.

GEKKO IPOD SONG

Select password from the Extras menu and enter george.

MIDNIGHT SHADOW IPOD SONG

Select password from the Extras menu and enter theodore.

MOBS ALIVE IPOD SONG

Select password from the Extras menu and enter abraham.

DESERT EAGLE—LONG BARREL

Select password from the Extras menu and enter deskyhstyl.

MK. 23 SOCOM PISTOL

Select password from the Extras menu and enter mekakorkkk.

MOSIN NAGANT

Select password from the Extras menu and enter mnsoymsyhn.

TYPE 17 PISTOL

Select password from the Extras menu and enter jmsotsynrn.

ALTAIR COSTUME

Select password from the Extras menu and enter aottrykmyn.

METAL GEAR SOLID: PEACE WALKER

PSP

T-SHIRTS

From the Extras menu, select Network and then Enter Passcode. Now you can enter the following. Note that you need a PSN account and each passcode can only be used once per PSN account.

T-SHIRT	PASSCODE
Black with "Big Boss"	2000016032758
Black with "Peace Walker"	2000016032390
Black with Peace Walker Logo	2000016038415
Gray with Coffee Cup	2000016036022
Gray with MSF	2000016032567
Gray with MSF	2000016032574
Gray with Snake	2000016032338
Navy Blue with MSF	2000016032635
Olive with Snake	2000016035902
Red with Big Boss	2000016537833
Tan	2000016038576
White with Big Boss	2000016756791
White with "Big Boss"	2000016032680
White with Coffee Cup	2000016032964

METAL GEAR SOLID: PORTABLE OPS PLUS

SOLDIER PASSWORDS

Enter the following as a password.

SOLDIER	PASSWORD
Alabama	BB6K768KM9
Alaska	XL5SW5NH9S
Arizona	ZHEFPVV947
Arkansas	VNRE7JNQ8WE
Black Genome	WYNGG3JBP3YS
Blue Genome	9GNPHGFFLH
California	6MSJQYWNCJ8
Colorado	W6TAH498DJ
Connecticut	2N2AB3JV2WA
Delaware	AJRL6E7TT9
Female Scientist 1	3W8WVRGB2LNN
Female Scientist 2	FUC72C463KZ
Female Scientist 3	UCAWYTMXB5V
Female Soldier 1	UZZQYRPXM86
Female Soldier 2	QRQQ7GWKHJ
Female Soldier 3	MVNDAZAP8DWE
Florida	A44STZ3BHY5
Fox Soldier 1	FMXT79TPV4U8
Fox Soldier 2	HGMK3WCYURM
Fox Soldier 3	6ZY5NYW4TGK
Georgia	VD5H53JJCRH
Green Genome	TGQ6F5TUHD
GRU Soldier	9V8S7DVYFTR
Gurlukovich's Soldier	6VWM6A22FSS8
Hawaii	TW7ZMZHCBL
Hideochan Soldier	RU8XRCLPUUT
High Official	ADPS2SE5UC8
High Rank Officer 1	DVB2UDTQ5Z
High Rank Officer 2	84ZEC4X5PJ6
High Ranking Officer 3	DTAZ3QRQQDU
High-Tech Soldier	M4MSJ6R87XPP
Idaho	XAFGETZGXHGA
Illinois	QYUVCNDFUPZJ
Indiana	L68JVXVBL8RN
Iowa	B8MW36ZU56S
Kansas	TYPEVDEE24YT
Kentucky	LCD7WGS5X5
KGB Soldier	MNBVYRZP4QH
Louisiana	EHR5VVMHUSG
Maine	T5GYHQABGAC3
KGB Soldier	MNBVYRZP4QH
Louisiana	EHR5VVMHUSG
Maine	T5GYHQABGAC3
Maintenance Crew Member 1	T8EBSRK6F38
Maintenance Crew Member 2	YHQU74J6LLQ
Maintenance Crew Member 3	MFAJMUXZHHKJ

SOLDIER	PASSWORD
Male Scientist 1	ZFKHJKDEA2
Male Scientist 2	QQ4N3TPCL8PF
Male Scientist 3	CXFCXF4FP9R6
Maryland	L2W9G5N76MH7
Massachusetts	ZLU2S3ULDEVF
Michigan	HGDRBUB5P3SA
Minnesota	EEBBM888ZRA
Mississippi	TBF7H9G6TJH7
Missouri	WJND6M9N738
Montana	9FYUFV29B2Y
Nebraska	MCNB5S5K47H
Nevada	Z9D4UGG8T4U6
New Hampshire	7NQYDQ9Y4KMP
New Jersey	LGHTBU9ZTGR
New Mexico	RGJCMHNLSX
New York	6PV39FKG6X
Normal Soldier Long Sleeve	QK3CMV373Y
Normal Soldier Long Sleeve Magazine Vest	D8RV32E9774
Normal Soldier Short Sleeve	N524ZHU9N4Z
Normal Soldier Short Sleeve Magazine Vest	6WXZA7PTT9Z
North Carolina	JGVT2XV47UZ
North Dakota	T5LSAVMPWZCY
Ocelot Female A	9FS7QYSHZ56N
Ocelot Female B	F94XDZSQSGJ8
Ocelot Female C	CRF8PZGXR28
Ocelot Unit	GE6MU3DXL3X
Ohio	AUWGAXWCA3D
Oklahoma	ZQT75NUJH8A3
Oregon	HKSD3PJ5E5
Pennsylvania	PL8GVVUM4HD
Pink Genome	7WRG3N2MRY2
Red Genome	9CM4SY23C7X8
Rhode Island	MMYC99T3QG
Seal	X56YCKZP2V
South Carolina	ZR4465MD8LK
South Dakota	RY3NUDDPMU3
Tengu Soldier	PHHB4TY4J2D
Tennessee	TD2732GCX43U
Texas	QM84UPP6F3
Tsuhan soldier	A9KK7WYWVCV
USSR Female Soldier A	2VXUZQVH9R
USSR Female Soldier B	HPMRFSBXDJ3Y
USSR Female Soldier C	QXQVW9R3PZ
USSR Female Soldier D	GMC3M3LTPVW7
USSR Female Soldier E	5MXVX6UFPMZ5
USSR Female Soldier F	76AWS7WDAV
Utah	V7VRAYZ78GW
Vermont	L7T66LFZ63C8
Virginia	DRTCS77F5N
Washington	G3S4N42WWKTV
Washington DC	Y5YCFYHVZZW
West Virginia	72M8XR99B6
White Genome	QJ4ZTQSLUT8

SOLDIER	PASSWORD
Wisconsin	K9BUN2BGLMT3
Wyoming	C3THQ749RA
Yellow Genome	CE5HHYGTSSB

METAL GEAR SOLID: SNAKE EATER 3D

BOSS SURVIVAL MODE

Defeat the game on any difficulty.

AUSCAM CAMO

Start a new game and select "I like MGS1!"

BANANA CAMO

Start a new game and select "I like MGS PEACE WALKER!"

DESERT TIGER CAMO AND RAIDEN MASK IN THE INTRO CUTSCENE.

Start a new game and select "I like MGS2!"

DPM CAMO

Start a new game and select "I like MGS4!"

FLECKTARN CAMO, GREEN AND BROWN FACEPAINTS.

Start a new game and select "I like MGS3!"

GRENADE CAMO

Start a new game and select "I like all the MGS games!"

MUMMY CAMO

Start a new game and select "I'm playing MGS for the first time!"

METROID OTHER M

HARD MODE

Finish the game with all items.

THEATER MODE

Defeat the final boss.

CHAPTERS	HOW TO UNLOCK
Unlock Chapters 1-26	Defeat the final boss.
Unlock Chapters 27-30	After the credits, finish the bonus area and defeat the boss.

GALLERY MODE

Defeat the final boss.

GALLERY PAGES	HOW TO UNLOCK
1-4	Defeat the final boss.
5-7	After the credits, finish the bonus area and defeat the boss.
8	Finish the game with all items.

MIDWAY ARCADE ORIGINS

APB: ALL POINTS BULLETIN

WARP CODES

Press Siren and Start to warp to level 1-8 or press Gas & Siren and Start to warp to level 1-16.

ROBOTRON: 2084

PROGRAMMER CREDITS

Start the game normally then quickly input move right, fire up and Player 1 start, then move up, fire down and Player 2 start, then move down and fire up to see the credits appear on screen.

TOTAL CARNAGE

PASSWORDS

Input these passwords on the warp at the beginning of the first mission.

ACHIEVEMENTS & TROPHIES

NAME	GOAL/REQUIREMENT	POINT VALUE	TROPHY VALUE
Gold Medalist	You earned a Gold Medal in an event in 720.	90	Gold
Get Freaky	You took down Freddy Freak in APB.	30	Silver
All-Star	You scored 6 consecutive points in Arch Rivals.	90	Gold
Clean-Up	You swept up a big bug in Bubbles.	15	Bronze
True Champion	You got first place in 3 consecutive races in Championship Sprint.	30	Silver
They Need a Hero	You saved 3 astronauts in Defender.	15	Bronze
Doesn't Need Food Badly	You reached Level 8 in Gauntlet.	30	Silver
Survivor	You reached Level 7 in Gauntlet II.	15	Bronze
Pterrific!	You defeated a Pterodactyl in Joust.	30	Silver
Long Live the Bird	You reached Wave 5 in Joust 2.	30	Silver
High Roller	You defeated the beginner race within 15 seconds in Marble Madness.	15	Bronze
First Rule of Pit Fighting	You defeated 3 consecutive opponents in Pit Fighter.	30	Silver
Monstrous	You defeated 3 consecutive cities in Rampage.	30	Silver
Target Practice	You defeated the first 3 ships in the first level in one battle in Rampart.	15	Bronze
Family Man	You rescued 7 family members without losing a life in Robotron: 2084.	15	Bronze
Savior	You defeated Satan in Satan's Hollow.	30	Silver
You Hunger	You defeated Sinistar in Sinistar.	30	Silver
Reality Show-Off	You defeated the first level in Smash TV.	90	Gold
Score Hunter	You broke 10,000 points in Spy Hunter.	15	Bronze
Saint	You played the game for 15 consecutive minutes in Spy Hunter II.	30	Silver

M

NAME	GOAL/REQUIREMENT	POINT VALUE	TROPHY VALUE
They Need a Hero… Again	You saved 3 astronauts in Defender II.	15	Bronze
X-Treme Off-Road	You got first place in 3 consecutive races in Super Off Road.	30	Silver
Superior Sprint	You got first place in 3 consecutive races in Super Sprint.	30	Silver
Tap that Glass	You cleared 25 customers without dropping a glass in Root Beer Tapper.	15	Bronze
Ride the Wave	You completed Colorado without sinking in Toobin'.	30	Silver
Total Warpage	You used a shortcut in Total Carnage.	15	Bronze
Great Coaching	You scored at least 12 consecutive points in Tournament Cyberball 2072.	30	Silver
On Base	You defeated the first base in Vindicators Part II.	15	Bronze
Worrior	You had at least 10,000 points and 3x your opponent's score at the same time in Wizard of Wor.	85	Gold
Not Afraid	You survived the first level in Xenophobe.	30	Silver
Third-Person Shooter	You survived 3 levels without dying in Xybots.	30	Silver

MINECRAFT

XBOX 360/MOBILE/PC

TIPS & STRATEGIES

- Don't Go Out at Night—Once night comes, the world becomes full of creepers and other monsters. Even with the greatest equipment you can quickly be destroyed outside of your fortress.

- Play with Friends—If you can, play with your friends: you'll be able to build things, gather resources and take out enemies faster, giving you more time to build elaborate fortresses.

- Fortify your Fortress—Obviously, you should be buffing your fortress as much as possible to keep monsters away and keep your fortress lit to keep monsters from spawning inside. Also, try and build a series of rooms separated by doors just in case a monster does appear inside, giving you the chance to run away.

- Bring a Bucket of Water—Be sure to always have a bucket of water with you when you're mining. Build a bucket with three iron ingots in a small "v" shape, and use it to pick up and place water spawn blocks. You can put out fire, extinguish lava and save you if you fall into a lava lake. You can also create a water fall to swim up and down steep cliffs and create a stream to push back monsters!

- Don't Dig Straight Up or Down—When digging, dig at an angle instead of straight at your feet. You might open up a cavern or lake of lava, causing you to fall straight to your death. Also, if you're digging upwards, you might unleash a stream of lava or water, causing you to drown. Dig in an angle and try to form a spiral shape so you can run away or won't plummet straight to your death.

MINECRAFT: XBOX 360 EDITION

XBOX 360

AVATAR AWARDS

AVATAR	EARNED BY
The Pork-Chop T-Shirt	Earn a Cooked Porkchop.
A Minecraft Watch	Play the game for 100 day to night cycles.
The Creeper Cap	Kill a Creeper with Arrows.

STEVE GAMER PICTURE

Mine redstone for the first time.

CREEPER GAMER PICTURE

Defeat 10 Creepers.

MINECRAFT XBOX 360 EDITION PREMIUM THEME

Pause the game, press Y to grab a shot, and upload the image to Facebook.

MIRROR'S EDGE

MOBILE

ALL WALLPAPERS

Earn all 28 Badges.

MONDAY NIGHT COMBAT

XBOX 360

AVATAR AWARDS

AWARD	EARNED BY
Mascot Mask	Meet the Mascot in Monday Night Combat Tutorial-kill the mascot in the tutorial.
Monday Night Combat T-Shirt	Earn the Exhibitor Achievement Get this by completing "Exhibition" Blitz mode.

MONSTER HUNTER 3 ULTIMATE

NINTENDO 3DS

UNLOCKABLE MISSIONS

Increase your HR to unlock hidden missions.

MISSION	REQUIREMENT
Ring of the Golden Lune: Gold Rathian	HR25
Ring of the Silver Sol: Silver Rathalos	HR30
Best of Enemies: Purple Ludroth, Volvidon, Steel Uragaan & Great Wroggi	HR35
Invisible Predator: Lucent Nargacuga	HR40
Rage Match: 2 Deviljhos	HR45
Moonlit Tryst: Gold Rathian & Silver Rathalos	HR50
The Earth Quakers: Pink Rathian, Rust Duramboros, Brachydios & Stygian Zinogre	HR55
The Sea Shakers: Royal Ludroth, Gobul, Plesioth & Lagiacrus	HR60
Abyssal Awakening: Abyssal Lagiacrus	HR70

MONSTER LAIR

CONTINUE

At the Game Over screen, press Left, Right, Down, Up, Select + Left.

UNLIMITED CONTINUES

Enter 68K as your initials.

SOUND TEST

At the Title screen, press and hold 1 + 2 and then press Run.

MONSTER WORLD IV

SOUND TEST

Highlight New Game and press Up, Down, Up, Down, Left, Left, Right, Right.

MORTAL KOMBAT

AUGMENTED REALITY – CHANGE BACKGROUND TO REAR CAMERA VIEW

Select Practice Mode from Training. At the character select, press ● to access the
arena select. Press L + R to enable Augmented Reality. You will hear Shao Kahn if
done correctly.

ACHIEVEMENTS & TROPHIES

NAME	GOAL/REQUIREMENT	POINT VALUE	TROPHY VALUE
Cyber Challenger	Complete 100 Online Matches	20	Bronze
Wavenet…	Win 100 total Online Matches	80	Silver
Humiliation	Get a Flawless Victory in an Online Match	10	Bronze
Tough Guy!	Win an Online Match	10	Bronze
Robots Rule!	Win Arcade Tag Ladder with robot Sektor and Cyrax	10	Bronze
Outstanding!	Win 10 Ranked Online Matches in a row	60	Silver
There Will Be Blood!	Spill 10000 pints of blood	40	Silver
License to Kill	Complete Fatality Trainer	20	Bronze
Ultimate Respect!	Earn 2500 Respect Points via King of the Hill Matches	20	Bronze
You Will Learn Respect!	Earn 1000 Respect Points via King of the Hill Matches	10	Bronze
Undertaker	Unlock 50% of the Krypt	20	Bronze
The Krypt Keeper	Unlock 100% of the Krypt	20	Silver
What Does This Button Do??	Complete Arcade Ladder without blocking (allowed to continue)	10	Bronze
Fatality!	Perform a Fatality!	5	Bronze
Block This!	Perform a 10-hit combo with any fighter	10	Bronze
The Grappler	Perform every fighter's forward and backwards throws	10	Bronze
Halfway There!	Complete Story Mode 50%	5	Bronze
Back In Time…	Complete Story Mode 100%	20	Silver

NAME	GOAL/REQUIREMENT	POINT VALUE	TROPHY VALUE
A For Effort	Complete Tutorial Mode	10	Bronze
The Competitor	Complete 200 Versus matches (online OR offline)	30	Silver
Ladder Master	Complete Arcade Ladder on max difficulty without using a continue	20	Bronze
Don't Jump!	Win A Ranked Online Match without jumping	10	Bronze
Where's The Arcade?	Complete Arcade Ladder with Any Fighter	10	Bronze
Arcade Champion	Complete Arcade Ladder with All Fighters	40	Silver
Finish What You Start!	Perform a Fatality with all playable fighters	60	Silver
Tag, You're It!	Perform and land a Tag Combo	10	Bronze
These Aren't My Glasses!	Complete all Test Your Sight mini-game challenges	20	Bronze
Tower Apprentice	Complete 25 Tower missions	10	Bronze
Tower Master	Complete all Tower missions	20	Silver
Dim Mak!	Complete all Test Your Strike mini-game challenges	20	Bronze
I'm Not Dead Yet!	Comeback with under 10% health in an Online Ranked Match	20	Silver
e-X-cellent!	Successfully land every playable fighter's X-Ray attack	10	Bronze
There Can Be Only One!	Win 10 King of the Hill Matches in a row	20	Silver
Throws Are For Champs	Perform 8 throws in an Online Ranked Match	20	Bronze
Turtle!	Win both rounds with timer running out in an Online Ranked Match	20	Silver
My Kung Fu Is Strong	Gain Mastery of 1 Fighter	20	Silver
My Kung Fu Is Stronger	Gain Mastery of All Fighters	60	Gold
I "Might" Be the Strongest	Complete all Test Your Might mini-game challenges	20	Bronze
Luck Be A Lady	Get all MK Dragons in Test Your Luck	10	Bronze
You've Got Style!	Unlock all Alternate Costumes	20	Silver

SECRET ACHIEVEMENTS & TROPHIES

NAME	GOAL/REQUIREMENT	POINT VALUE	TROPHY VALUE
Complet-ality	Perform 1 of each type of "-ality"	10	Bronze
Finish Him?	Perform any fighter's hidden finishing move	10	Bronze
Hide and Seek	Discover and fight Hidden Kombatant 2 in Arcade Ladder	10	Bronze
Pit Master	Discover and fight Hidden Kombatant 3 in Arcade Ladder	10	Bronze
Brotherhood of Shadow	Discover and fight Hidden Kombatant 4 in Arcade Ladder	20	Bronze
Ultimate Humiliation	Perform every fighter's hidden finishing move	20	Silver
Quan-Tease	Unlock Hidden Fighter "Quan Chi"	20	Bronze
You Found Me!	Discover and fight Hidden Kombatant 1 in Arcade Ladder	10	Bronze
Cold Fusion	Unlock Hidden Fighter "Cyber Sub-Zero"	20	Bronze
Best...Alternate...Ever!	Unlock Mileena's 3rd Alternate Costume	10	Bronze

MORTAL KOMBAT ARCADE KOLLECTION

MORTAL KOMBAT II

NO THROWS OPTION

In a two-player match and before the match begins, hold Down + HP on both controllers.

ULTIMATE MORTAL KOMBAT 3

VS CODES

At the VS screen, each player must use LP, BLK, and LK (A, Right Bumper, B) to enter the following codes:

EFFECT	PLAYER 1	PLAYER 2
Blocking Disabled	020	020
Dark Kombat	688	688
Don't Jump at Me	448	844
Explosive Combat (2 on 2)	227	227
Fast Uppercut Recovery Enabled	688	422
No Fear	282	282
No Powerbars	987	123
Player 1 Half Power	033	N/A
Player 1 Quarter Power	707	N/A
Player 2 Half Power	N/A	033
Player 2 Quarter Power	N/A	707
RandPer Kombat	444	444
Silent Kombat	300	300
Throwing Disabled	100	100
Unikoriv Referri: Sans Power	044	440
Unlimited Run	466	466
Two-Player Mini-Game of Galaga	642	468
Kombat Zone: Bell Tower	910	190
Kombat Zone: The Bridge	077	022
Kombat Zone: The Graveyard	666	333
Kombat Zone: Jade's Desert	330	033
Kombat Zone: Kahn's Kave	004	070
Kombat Zone: Kahn's Tower	880	220
Kombat Zone: Kombat Temple	600	040
Kombat Zone: Noob Saibot Dorfen	050	050
Kombat Zone: The Pit 3	820	028
Kombat Zone: River Kombat	002	003
Kombat Zone: Rooftop	343	343
Kombat Zone: Scislac Busorez	933	933
Kombat Zone: Scorpion's Lair	666	444
Kombat Zone: Soul Chamber	123	901
Kombat Zone: Street	079	035
Kombat Zone: Subway	880	088
Winner of round fights Motaro	969	141
Winner of round fights Noob Saibot	769	342
Winner of round fights Shao Kahn	033	564
Winner of round fights Smoke	205	205
Revision	999	999
See the Mortal Kombat Live Tour !!	550	550

EFFECT	PLAYER 1	PLAYER 2
"Hold Flippers During Casino Run"	987	666
"Rain Can Be Found in the Graveyard"	711	313
"Skunky !!"	122	221
"There Is No Knowledge That Is Not Power"	123	926
"Whatcha Gun Do?"	004	400

UNLOCK CLASSIC SUB-ZERO

Lose a match in arcade mode and let the continue timer run out. Enter the following within 10 seconds on both controllers; HP (x8), LP (x1), BL (x8), LK (x3), HK (x5).

UNLOCK ERMAC

Lose a match in arcade mode and let the continue timer run out. Enter the following within 10 seconds; HP (x1), LP (x2), BL (x3), LK (x4), HK (x4) for player 1 and HP (x4), LP (x4), BL (x3), LK (x2), HK (x1) for player 2.

UNLOCK MILEENA

Lose a match in arcade mode and let the continue timer run out. Enter the following within 10 seconds on both controllers; HP (x2), LP (x2), BL (x2), LK (x6), HK (x4).

HUMAN SMOKE

Select Smoke. For player 1, hold Block + Run + High Punch + High Kick + Left before the fight begins. For player 2, hold Block + Run + High Punch + High Kick + Right before the fight begins.

MORTAL KOMBAT KOMPLETE EDITION

PLAYSTATION 3

VS CODES

At the VS screen, each player must use LP, BLK, and LK to enter the following codes. The numbers represent how many times you must press each button.

EFFECT	PLAYER 1	PLAYER 2
Armless Kombat	911	911
Blocking Disabled	020	020
Breakers Disabled	090	090
Dark Kombat	022	022
Double Dash	391	193
Dream Kombat	222	555
Enhance Moves Disabled	051	150
Explosive Kombat	227	227
Foreground Objects Disabled	001	001
Headless Kombat	808	808
Health Recovery	012	012
Hyper Fighting	091	091
Invisible Kombat	770	770
Jumping Disabled	831	831
Klassik Music	101	101
Kombos Disabled	931	931
No Blood	900	900
Player 1 Half Health	220	000
Player 1 Quarter Health	110	000
Player 2 Half Health	000	220
Player 2 Quarter Health	000	110
Power Bars Disabled	404	404
Psycho Kombat	707	707
Quick Uppercut Recovery	303	303

M

EFFECT	PLAYER 1	PLAYER 2
Rainbow Kombat	234	234
Random Phrase 1	717	313
Random Phrase 2	448	844
Random Phrase 3	122	221
Random Phrase 4	009	900
Random Phrase 5	550	055
Random Phrase 6	031	130
Random Phrase 7	282	282
Random Phrase 8	123	926
Sans Power	044	440
Silent Kombat	300	300
Specials Disabled	731	731
Super Recovery	123	123
Throwing Disabled	100	100
Throwing Encouraged	010	010
Tournament Mode	111	111
Unlimited Super Meter	466	466
Vampire Kombat	424	424
XRays Disabled	242	242
Zombie Kombat	666	666

HIDDEN KING OF THE HILL AVATAR ACTIONS

When viewing a fight as a spectator, highlight your avatar and press ● to get the action menu. Now enter the following to perform some hidden actions:

EFFECT	CODE
"$%#&!"	Up, Up, L
#1	Down, Up, J
Big Clap	Right, Up, J
Cheese	Left, Up, Down, L
Cover Face	Left, Right, L
Devil Horns	Down, Up, I
Diamond	Up, Down, Left, J
Double Devil Horns	Up, Down, J
"FATALITY"	Up, Up, Right, Right, I
"FIGHT!"	Left, Right, I
"Finish Him!"	Left, Right, Left, Right, J
Gather Ice	Right, Right, Right, Left, J
"HA!"	Down, Up, Down, K
Hop	Up, Up, I
"I'm Not Worthy"	Down, Down, J
Lighter	Down, Down, Up, Up, I
Point	Right, Right, I
Raiden Pose	Left, Left, Right, Right, I
Shake Head	Left, Right, K
Skunk	Left, Right, Up, Up K
Skunk (Stench)	Up, Down, Down, L
Sleep	Down, Down, Down, L
Stink Wave	Right, Left, L
Throw Tomato	Down, Down, Down, Up, K

VS CODES

At the VS screen, each player must use LP, BLK, and LK to enter the following codes. The numbers represent how many times you must press each button.

EFFECT	PLAYER 1	PLAYER 2
Armless Kombat	911	911
Blocking Disabled	020	020
Breakers Disabled	090	090
Dark Kombat	022	022
Double Dash	391	193
Dream Kombat	222	555
Enhance Moves Disabled	051	150
Explosive Kombat	227	227
Foreground Objects Disabled	001	001
Headless Kombat	808	808
Health Recovery	012	012
Hyper Fighting	091	091
Invisible Kombat	770	770
Jumping Disabled	831	831
Klassik Music	101	101
Kombos Disabled	931	931
No Blood	900	900
Player 1 Half Health	220	000
Player 1 Quarter Health	110	000
Player 2 Half Health	000	220
Player 2 Quarter Health	000	110
Power Bars Disabled	404	404
Psycho Kombat	707	707
Quick Uppercut Recovery	303	303
Rainbow Kombat	234	234
Random Phrase 1	717	313
Random Phrase 2	448	844
Random Phrase 3	122	221
Random Phrase 4	009	900
Random Phrase 5	550	055
Random Phrase 6	031	130
Random Phrase 7	282	282
Random Phrase 8	123	926
Sans Power	044	440
Silent Kombat	300	300
Specials Disabled	731	731
Super Recovery	123	123
Throwing Disabled	100	100
Throwing Encouraged	010	010
Tournament Mode	111	111
Unlimited Super Meter	466	466
Vampire Kombat	424	424
XRays Disabled	242	242
Zombie Kombat	666	666

CHEATS, ACHIEVEMENTS, AND TROPHIES

M

MOSHI MONSTERS: MOSHLINGS THEME PARK

SECRET PASSWORDS

Input these Passwords to unlock bonuses.

PASSWORD	PASSWORD
1GU4ER58	OGG3VP9D
O2PTZ7OZ	41D5H5LL
0ARNHOA5	ZNIYZAVY
DIMBDF48	A9YEC3NJ
87TEHSFV	SPTIV7H9
A9YE9YEU	X1PI9MZH
WNU4PGVU	T2Y6X7FU

MOTOCROSS MADNESS

AVATAR AWARDS

AWARD	UNLOCKABLE
MX Helmet	Get a medal in every Race event.
MX Pants	Get a medal in every Rivals event.
MX Top	Get a medal in every Exploration event.

MOTORSTORM RC

THUNDER LIZARD VEHICLE

Spend 1 hour in the Playground.

BEELZEBUGGY BOOM VEHICLE

Spend 2 hours in the Playground.

DUNK VEHICLE

Jump through the basketball hoop in the Playground 10 times.

HEADCASE VEHICLE

Jump through the basketball hoop in the Playground 20 times.

PATRIOT TOUCHDOWN VEHICLE

Score 10 soccer goals in the Playground.

NORD GNITRO VEHICLE

Score 20 soccer goals in the Playground.

MTX MOTOTRAX

ALL TRACKS

Enter BA7H as a password.

ALL BONUSES

Enter 2468GOA7 as a password.

SUPER SPEED

Enter JIH345 as a password.

MAXIMUM AIR

Enter BFB0020 as a password.

BUTTERFINGER GEAR

Enter B77393 as a password.

LEFT FIELD GEAR

Enter 12345 as a password.

SOBE GEAR

Enter 50BE as a password.

MUTANT MUDDS

PLAY AS GRANNIE

After collecting all 200 Diamonds and 40 Water Sprites, press L at the title screen to switch to Grannie.

MVP BASEBALL

ALL REWARDS

Select My MVP and create a player with the name Dan Carter.

MX VS. ATV: REFLEX

ACHIEVEMENTS

NAME	GOAL/REQUIREMENT	POINT VALUE
Waypoint Series 1	Place 3rd or higher in the Waypoint Series 1 in the MotoCareer	15
Waypoint Series 2	Place 3rd or higher in the Waypoint Series 2 in the MotoCareer	15
Waypoint Series 3	Place 3rd or higher in the Waypoint Series 3 in the MotoCareer	15
National Series 1	Place 3rd or higher in the National Series 1 in the MotoCareer	15
National Series 2	Place 3rd or higher in the National Series 2 in the MotoCareer	15
National Series 3	Place 3rd or higher in the National Series 3 in the MotoCareer	30
Supercross Series 1	Place 3rd or higher in the Supercross Series 1 in the MotoCareer	15
Supercross Series 2	Place 3rd or higher in the Supercross Series 2 in the MotoCareer	15

NAME	GOAL/REQUIREMENT	POINT VALUE
Supercross Series 3	Place 3rd or higher in the Supercross Series 3 in the MotoCareer	30
Freestyle Series 1	Place 3rd or higher in the Freestyle Series 1 in the MotoCareer	15
Freestyle Series 2	Place 3rd or higher in the Freestyle Series 2 in the MotoCareer	15
Freestyle Series 3	Place 3rd or higher in the Freestyle Series 3 in the MotoCareer	15
Omnicross Series 1	Place 3rd or higher in the Omnicross Series 1 in the MotoCareer	15
Omnicross Series 2	Place 3rd or higher in the Omnicross Series 2 in the MotoCareer	15
Omnicross Series 3	Place 3rd or higher in the Omnicross Series 3 in the MotoCareer	15
Champion Sport Track Series 1	Place 3rd or higher in the Champion Sport Track Series 1 in the MotoCareer	15
Champion Sport Track Series 2	Place 3rd or higher in the Champion Sport Track Series 2 in the MotoCareer	15
Champion Sport Track Series 3	Place 3rd or higher in the Champion Sport Track Series 3 in the MotoCareer	15
Ironman of Offroad	Win all Series in the MotoCareer	75
Champion of Champions	Win all Face-Off Challenges in the MotoCareer	25
Greatest of All Time	Place 1st in all events in the MotoCareer	100
Gold Standard	Earn a Gold medal in any MotoCareer Free Ride Challenge	10
Precious Medals	Earn a Gold medal in all MotoCareer Free Ride Challenges	50
Step Into the Arena	Complete an Xbox LIVE Playlist Match	15
To the Victor…	Place 1st in an Xbox LIVE Playlist Match with 11 human opponents	15
Endurance	Complete 25 Xbox LIVE Playlist Matches	25
Long Live the King	Place 1st in 25 Xbox LIVE Playlist Matches	50
Leveler	Finish ahead of any opponent who has a higher Experience Level in a Xbox LIVE Playlist Match	15
You're It!	Win a Tag Mini-Game in an Xbox LIVE Playlist Match	15
Snake in the Grass	Win a Snake Mini-Game in an Xbox LIVE Playlist Match	15
Moto Skills	Complete MotoSkills 1, 2 and 3	15
Master Skills	Complete MotoSkills 4, 5 and 6	15
Trickster	Perform any airborne Trick and land successfully	15
Hat-Trick!	Perform three consecutive, unique airborne Tricks in one jump	15
Perfection	Earn a judge's score of 10.0 in a Freestyle Event	25
Freestylin'	Win a Freestyle Event in the MotoCareer without repeating a trick	25
Coming on Strong	Lap an Opponent in a Race	15
Ace in the Hole	Win 10 Holeshots	15
Showboat	Pull off three unique tricks in a Race Event	15
Tuning In	Adjust a Tuning Slider and save the new setting	5
Keeping it Clean	Complete a Race in a Machine with all body panels still attached to your vehicle	15
Skeletal Remains	Complete a Race in a Machine with no body panels remaining on your vehicle	15
Wreck-less	Avoid a Wreck in a Race	5
Close Calls!	Avoid 100 Wrecks	25
You are Legend	Place 1st in any Race on All-Time difficulty	25
Long Jumper	Land a jump distance of 300 feet or greater	15
Wheelie King	Hold a Wheelie trick for 150 feet or longer	15
Stoppie Master	Hold a Stoppie trick for 75 feet or longer	15

MX VS. ATV REFLEX

MX VEHICLES FOR PURCHASE

Select Enter Cheat Code from the Options and enter brapbrap.

JUSTIN BRAYTON, KTM MX BIKES AND ATVS IN ARCADE MODE

Select Enter Cheat Code from the Options and enter readytorace.

ALL EVENT LOCATIONS IN ARCADE MODE

Select Enter Cheat Code from the Options and enter whereto.

ALL AI OPPONENTS

Select Enter Cheat Code from the Options and enter allai.

ATV VEHICLES FOR PURCHASE

Select Enter Cheat Code from the Options and enter couches.

ALL AVAILABLE RIDER GEAR

Select Enter Cheat Code from the Options and enter gearedup.

ALL AVAILABLE HELMETS

Select Enter Cheat Code from the Options and enter skullcap.

ALL AVAILABLE BOOTS

Select Enter Cheat Code from the Options and enter kicks.

ALL AVAILABLE GOGGLES

Select Enter Cheat Code from the Options and enter windows.

MX VS. ATV UNTAMED

ALL RIDING GEAR

Select Cheat Codes from the Options and enter crazylikea.

ALL HANDLEBARS

Select Cheat Codes from the Options and enter nohands.

MYSIMS AGENTS

ASTRONAUT SUIT

At the Create-a-Sim screen, press Up, Down, Up, Down, Left, Right, Left, Right.

BLACK NINJA OUTFIT

At the Create-a-Sim screen, press Right, Up, Right, Up, Down, Left, Down, Left.

STEALTH SUIT

At the Create-a-Sim screen, press Left, Right, Left, Right, Up, Down, Up, Down.

MYSIMS KINGDOM

NINTENDO WII

DETECTIVE OUTFIT

Pause the game and press Left, Right, Left, Right, Left, Right.

SWORDSMAN OUTFIT

Pause the game and press Down, Up, Down, Up, Down, Up, Down, Up.

TATTOO VEST OUTFIT

Pause the game and press C, Z, C, Z, B, A, B, A.

NINTENDO 3DS

COW COSTUME

Pause the game and press R, X, L, Y, Up, Right, Left, Down.

COW HEADGEAR

Pause the game and press L, R, Y, X, Left, Down, Left, Right.

PATCHWORK CLOTHES

Pause the game and press Right, Down, Left, Up, L, R, L, R.

PATCHWORK PANTS

Pause the game and press Down, L, Left, R, Up, Y, Right, X.

PUNK BOTTOM

Pause the game and press Left, R, L, Right, Y, Y, X, X.

PUNK TOP

Pause the game and press Up, X, Down, Y, Left, L, Right, R.

SAMURAI ARMOR

Pause the game and press Y, X, Right, Left, L, R, Down, Up.

SAMURAI HELMET

Pause the game and press X, Y, R, L, X, Y, R, L.

N+

NINTENDO 3DS

ATARI BONUS LEVELS

Select Unlockables from the Main menu, hold L + R and press A, B, A, B, A, A, B.

PSP

25 EXTRA LEVELS

At the Main menu, hold L + R and press ✖, ●, ✖, ●, ✖, ✖, ●.

NARUTO POWERFUL SHIPPUDEN

NINTENDO 3DS

INFINITE EXP

When using Naruto, go to the mission Pervy Sage Training 1. In the battle preparation screen, select ninja tools then hold R, press A then press Y. You will be rewarded with 258 EXP. Exit to the Map and repeat again to earn more EXP. This trick only works on this mission.

NARUTO UZUMAKI GOKU COSTUME NINJA INFO CARD

Go into the collection menu and enter the password XCHPT2M1PD to unlock the Naruto Goku Costume Ninja Info Card.

SURVIVAL MODE IN FREE BATTLE

Complete the White Zetsu Subjugation special quest to unlock Survival Mode.

UNLOCKABLE CHARACTERS

CHARACTER	REQUIREMENT
Akatsuchi (Support)	Obtain 310,000 ryo.
Ao (Support)	Defeat Mizukage in Chapter 1 or obtain 320,000 ryo.
Asuma (Reanimation)	Obtain 760,000 ryo.
Cee (Support)	Defeat Raikage in Chapter 1 or obtain 210,000 ryo.
Chiyo	Obtain 520,000 ryo.
Choji (Butterfly Mode)	Complete "The Rumbling Coast" in Chapter 7.
Choji (Great Ninja War)	Obtain 740,000 ryo.
Chojuro (Support)	Defeat Mizukage in Chapter 1 or obtain 320,000 ryo.
Danzo	Defeat Danzo in Chapter 2 or obtain 370,000 ryo.
Darui	Defeat Kinkaku and Ginkaku in Chapter 7 or obtain 690,000 ryo.
Deidara	Obtain 570,000 ryo.
Deidara (Reanimation)	Obtain 560,000 ryo.
Foo (Support)	Defeat Danzo in Chapter 2 or obtain 370,000 ryo.
Fuu	Complete "The Last Battle" in Chapter 10 or obtain 970,000 ryo.
Gaara (5 Kage Summit)	Obtain 280,000 ryo.
Guy (Hirudora)	Obtain 440,000 ryo.
Haku	Complete "Threat of the Seven Swordsman" in Chapter 6 or obtain 660,000 ryo.
Haku (Mask)	Obtain 670,000 ryo.
Haku (Reanimation)	Obtain 680,000 ryo.
Han	Complete "The Last Battle" in Chapter 10 or obtain 930,000 ryo.
Hanzo	Defeat Hanzo in Chapter 6 or obtain 600,000 ryo.
Hidan	Obtain 720,000 ryo.
Hinata (Great Ninja War)	Obtain 490,000 ryo.
Hinata PTS	Obtain 170,000 ryo.
Ino (Great Ninja War)	Obtain 750,000 ryo.
Itachi (Tsukuyomi)	Obtain 790,000 ryo.
Jiraiya	Obtain 410,000 ryo.
Jugo	Defeat Raikage in Chapter 1 or obtain 240,000 ryo.
Kabuto (Snake Cloak)	Defeat Kabuto in Chapter 5 or obtain 460,000 ryo.
Kakashi (Great Ninja War)	Obtain 620,000 ryo.
Kakashi (Lightning Blade)	Obtain 380,000 ryo.
Kakashi (Twin Lightning Shiver)	Obtain 380,000 ryo.
Kakashi (Young)	Obtain 330,000 ryo.
Kakuzu	Obtain 710,000 ryo.
Kankuro (5 Kage Summit)	Obtain 260,000 ryo.
Kankuro (Great Ninja War)	Obtain 550,000 ryo.

CHARACTER	REQUIREMENT
Karin	Defeat Raikage in Chapter 1 or obtain 250,000 ryo.
Kiba (Great Ninja War)	Obtain 470,000 ryo.
Killer Bee (Samehada)	Defeat Kisame in Chapter 5 or obtain 350,000 ryo.
Kimimaro	Obtain 530,000 ryo.
Konan	Defeat Madara in Chapter 5 or obtain 450,000 ryo.
Kurotsuchi (Support)	Defeat Mizukage in Chapter 1 or obtain 310,000 ryo.
Lee (Great Ninja War)	Obtain 630,000 ryo.
Madara (Reanimation)	Defeat Madara in Chapter 10 or obtain 840,000 ryo.
Masked Man	Complete the Prologue or obtain 120,000 ryo.
Mifune	Defeat Hanzo in Chapter 6 or obtain 590,000 ryo.
Minato (Hokage)	Complete the Prologue or obtain 100,000 ryo.
Minato (Jonin)	Obtain 100,000 ryo.
Mizukage	Defeat Mizukage in Chapter 1 or obtain 320,000 ryo.
Nagato (Reanimation)	Defeat Nagato in Chapter 9 or obtain 810,000 ryo.
Naruto (Massive Rasengan Barrage)	Defeat the Nine Tails in Chapter 4 or obtain 430,000 ryo.
Naruto (Sage Mode)	Defeat Yamato in Chapter 1 or obtain 340,000 ryo.
Naruto (Tailed Beast Bomb)	Complete "The Last Battle" in Chapter 10 or obtain 980,000 ryo.
Naruto PTS	Obtain 130,000 ryo.
Neji (Great Ninja War)	Obtain 500,000 ryo.
Neji PTS	Obtain 180,000 ryo.
Obito	Obtain 330,000 ryo.
Orochimaru	Obtain 420,000 ryo.
Pain	Obtain 820,000 ryo.
Raikage (Liger Bomb)	Defeat Raikage in Chapter 1 or obtain 210,000 ryo.
Raikage (Lightning Straight)	Obtain 770,000 ryo.
Rock Lee PTS	Obtain 190,000 ryo.
Roushi	Complete "The Last Battle" in Chapter 10 or obtain 910,000 ryo.
Sai (Great Ninja War)	Obtain 540,000 ryo.
Sakura (Great Ninja War)	Obtain 610,000 ryo.
Sakura PTS	Obtain 160,000 ryo.
Sasori	Obtain 580,000 ryo.
Sasuke (5 Kage Summit)	Obtain 220,000 ryo.
Sasuke (Eternal Mangekyo)	Complete the Fragment or obtain 1,500,000 ryo.
Sasuke (Kirin)	Obtain 390,000 ryo.
Sasuke (Taka)	Obtain 400,000 ryo.
Sasuke PTS	Obtain 140,000 ryo.
Shikamaru (Great Ninja War)	Obtain 730,000 ryo.
Shino (Great Ninja War)	Obtain 480,000 ryo.
Suigetsu	Defeat Raikage in Chapter 1 or obtain 230,000 ryo.
Temari (5 Kage Summit)	Obtain 270,000 ryo.
Temari (Great Ninja War)	Obtain 510,000 ryo.
Tenten (Great Ninja War)	Obtain 700,000 ryo.
The 1st Hokage	Obtain 850,000 ryo.

CHARACTER	REQUIREMENT
The 2nd Hokage	Obtain 850,000 ryo.
The 3rd Hokage	Complete the Prologue or obtain 110,000 ryo.
Tobi	Defeat Madara in Chapter 1 or obtain 200,000 ryo.
Tobi (Great Ninja War)	Complete "The Last Battle" in Chapter 10 or obtain 990,000 ryo.
Torune (Support)	Defeat Danzo in Chapter 2 or obtain 370,000 ryo.
Tsuchikage	Defeat Mizukage in Chapter 1 or obtain 310,000 ryo.
Utakata	Complete "The Last Battle" in Chapter 10 or obtain 950,000 ryo.
Yagura	Complete "The Last Battle" in Chapter 10 or obtain 890,000 ryo.
Yugito	Obtain 870,000 ryo.
Zabuza	Complete "Threat of the Seven Swordsman" in Chapter 6 or obtain 640,000 ryo.
Zabuza (Reanimation)	Obtain 650,000 ryo.

NARUTO SHIPPUDEN: CLASH OF NINJA REVOLUTION III

NINTENDO WII

RYO BONUS

A 50,00 starting Ryo bonus is given if you have a saved data from Naruto Shippuden: Clash of Ninja Revolution 1 or 2 on your Nintendo Wii.

NARUTO SHIPPUDEN: ULTIMATE NINJA HEROES 3

PSP

FIGURES

At the Tree of Mettle, select Enter Password and input the following passwords:

FIGURE	PASSWORD
Gods and Angels	Fire, Sheep, Ox, Tiger
Inheritor of the Will	Water, Dog, Snake, Ox
One Who Lurks in Darkness	Thunder, Dog, Tiger, Boar
Rivals	Earth, Sheep, Boar, Dog
Team Asuma	Fire, Dog, Rabbit, Tiger
Team Guy	Water, Dog, Rat, Rooster
Team Kurenai	Thunder, Snake, Dragon, Monkey
The Hokage's Office	Wind, Rabbit, Dragon, Ox
The Innocent Maiden	Water, Snake, Dragon, Ox
The Three Sand Siblings	Earth, Rooster, Ox, Snake

JUTSUS

At the Tree of Mettle, select Enter Password and input the following passwords:

NINJUTSU	PASSWORD
100m Punch	Thunder, Rat, Snake, Horse
Assault Blade	Wind, Rat, Rabbit, Ox
Bring Down the House Jutsu	Thunder, Sheep, Ox, Rooster
Cherry Blossom Clash	Fire, Monkey, Boar, Rabbit
Dead Soul Jutsu	Thunder, Monkey, Dog, Ox

NINJUTSU	PASSWORD
Detonation Dispersion	Wind, Dragon, Horse, Rat
Dynamic Entry	Fire, Rooster, Rabbit, Boar
Feather Illusion Jutsu	Water, Dragon, Boar, Dog
Fire Style: Burning Ash	Fire, Rat, Rabbit, Monkey
Fire Style: Dragon Flame Bomb	Fire, Snake, Dragon, Rabbit
Fire Style: Fire Ball Jutsu	Fire, Dragon, Rat, Monkey
Fire Style: Yoruho'o	Fire, Horse, Rabbit, Sheep
Genjutsu: Haze	Wind, Dragon, Sheep, Rooster
Genjutsu: Madder Mist	Thunder, Rooster, Boar, Dog
Heaven Defending Kick	Earth, Rat, Boar, Monkey
Intensive Healing	Water, Rat, Tiger, Rat
Leaf Repeating Wind	Wind, Rooster, Ox, Tiger
Lightning Blade	Thunder, Monkey, Rooster, Snake
Lightning Style: Thunderbolt Flash	Thunder, Sheep, Ox, Dog
Slithering Snakes	Thunder, Tiger, Rooster, Dog
Summoning: Rashomon	Earth, Monkey, Boar, Rooster
Tunneling Fang	Wind, Dog, Boar, Horse
Water Style: Ripping Torrent	Water, Ox, Dog, Sheep
Water Style: Water Fang Bomb	Water, Horse, Rat, Ox
Weapon: Flash Kunai Ball	Fire, Sheep, Boar, Ox
Wind Style: Air Bullets	Wind, Ox, Boar, Rabbit

HOKAGE NARUTO WALLPAPER

At the Tree of Mettle, select Enter Password and enter Fire, Ox, Rabbit, Horse.

NARUTO SHIPPUDEN: ULTIMATE NINJA STORM 3

XBOX 360

NARUTO UZUMAKI GOKU COSTUME NINJA INFO CARD

Go into the collection menu and enter the password XCHPT2M1PD to unlock the Naruto Goku Costume Ninja Info Card.

SURVIVAL MODE IN FREE BATTLE

Complete the White Zetsu Subjugation special quest to unlock Survival Mode.

CHARACTER	REQUIREMENT
Akatsuchi (Support)	Obtain 310,000 ryo.
Ao (Support)	Defeat Mizukage in Chapter 1 or obtain 320,000 ryo.
Asuma (Reanimation)	Obtain 760,000 ryo.
Cee (Support)	Defeat Raikage in Chapter 1 or obtain 210,000 ryo.
Chiyo	Obtain 520,000 ryo.
Choji (Butterfly Mode)	Complete "The Rumbling Coast" in Chapter 7.
Choji (Great Ninja War)	Obtain 740,000 ryo.
Chojuro (Support)	Defeat Mizukage in Chapter 1 or obtain 320,000 ryo.
Danzo	Defeat Danzo in Chapter 2 or obtain 370,000 ryo.
Darui	Defeat Kinkaku and Ginkaku in Chapter 7 or obtain 690,000 ryo.
Deidara	Obtain 570,000 ryo.
Deidara (Reanimation)	Obtain 560,000 ryo.

CHARACTER	REQUIREMENT
Foo (Support)	Defeat Danzo in Chapter 2 or obtain 370,000 ryo.
Fuu	Complete "The Last Battle" in Chapter 10 or obtain 970,000 ryo.
Gaara (5 Kage Summit)	Obtain 280,000 ryo.
Guy (Hirudora)	Obtain 440,000 ryo.
Haku	Complete "Threat of the Seven Swordsman" in Chapter 6 or obtain 660,000 ryo.
Haku (Mask)	Obtain 670,000 ryo.
Haku (Reanimation)	Obtain 680,000 ryo.
Han	Complete "The Last Battle" in Chapter 10 or obtain 930,000 ryo.
Hanzo	Defeat Hanzo in Chapter 6 or obtain 600,000 ryo.
Hidan	Obtain 720,000 ryo.
Hinata (Great Ninja War)	Obtain 490,000 ryo.
Hinata PTS	Obtain 170,000 ryo.
Ino (Great Ninja War)	Obtain 750,000 ryo.
Itachi (Tsukuyomi)	Obtain 790,000 ryo.
Jiraiya	Obtain 410,000 ryo.
Jugo	Defeat Raikage in Chapter 1 or obtain 240,000 ryo.
Kabuto (Snake Cloak)	Defeat Kabuto in Chapter 5 or obtain 460,000 ryo.
Kakashi (Great Ninja War)	Obtain 620,000 ryo.
Kakashi (Lightning Blade)	Obtain 380,000 ryo.
Kakashi (Twin Lightning Shiver)	Obtain 380,000 ryo.
Kakashi (Young)	Obtain 330,000 ryo.
Kakuzu	Obtain 710,000 ryo.
Kankuro (5 Kage Summit)	Obtain 260,000 ryo.
Kankuro (Great Ninja War)	Obtain 550,000 ryo.
Karin	Defeat Raikage in Chapter 1 or obtain 250,000 ryo.
Kiba (Great Ninja War)	Obtain 470,000 ryo.
Killer Bee (Samehada)	Defeat Kisame in Chapter 5 or obtain 350,000 ryo.
Kimimaro	Obtain 530,000 ryo.
Konan	Defeat Madara in Chapter 5 or obtain 450,000 ryo.
Kurotsuchi (Support)	Defeat Mizukage in Chapter 1 or obtain 310,000 ryo.
Lee (Great Ninja War)	Obtain 630,000 ryo.
Madara (Reanimation)	Defeat Madara in Chapter 10 or obtain 840,000 ryo.
Masked Man	Complete the Prologue or obtain 120,000 ryo.
Mifune	Defeat Hanzo in Cahpter 6 or obtain 590,000 ryo.
Minato (Hokage)	Complete the Prologue or obtain 100,000 ryo.
Minato (Jonin)	Obtain 100,000 ryo.
Mizukage	Defeat Mizukage in Chapter 1 or obtain 320,000 ryo.
Nagato (Reanimation)	Defeat Nagato in Chapter 9 or obtain 810,000 ryo.
Naruto (Massive Rasengan Barrage)	Defeat the Nine Tails in Chapter 4 or obtain 430,000 ryo.
Naruto (Sage Mode)	Defeat Yamato in Chapter 1 or obtain 340,000 ryo.

CHARACTER	REQUIREMENT
Naruto (Tailed Beast Bomb)	Complete "The Last Battle" in Chapter 10 or obtain 980,000 ryo.
Naruto PTS	Obtain 130,000 ryo.
Neji (Great Ninja War)	Obtain 500,000 ryo.
Neji PTS	Obtain 180,000 ryo.
Obito	Obtain 330,000 ryo.
Orochimaru	Obtain 420,000 ryo.
Pain	Obtain 820,000 ryo.
Raikage (Liger Bomb)	Defeat Raikage in Chapter 1 or obtain 210,000 ryo.
Raikage (Lightning Straight)	Obtain 770,000 ryo.
Rock Lee PTS	Obtain 190,000 ryo.
Roushi	Complete "The Last Battle" in Chapter 10 or obtain 910,000 ryo.
Sai (Great Ninja War)	Obtain 540,000 ryo.
Sakura (Great Ninja War)	Obtain 610,000 ryo.
Sakura PTS	Obtain 160,000 ryo.
Sasori	Obtain 580,000 ryo.
Sasuke (5 Kage Summit)	Obtain 220,000 ryo.
Sasuke (Eternal Mangekyo)	Complete the Fragment or obtain 1,500,000 ryo.
Sasuke (Kirin)	Obtain 390,000 ryo.
Sasuke (Taka)	Obtain 400,000 ryo.
Sasuke PTS	Obtain 140,000 ryo.
Shikamaru (Great Ninja War)	Obtain 730,000 ryo.
Shino (Great Ninja War)	Obtain 480,000 ryo.
Suigetsu	Defeat Raikage in Chapter 1 or obtain 230,000 ryo.
Temari (5 Kage Summit)	Obtain 270,000 ryo.
Temari (Great Ninja War)	Obtain 510,000 ryo.
Tenten (Great Ninja War)	Obtain 700,000 ryo.
The 1st Hokage	Obtain 850,000 ryo.
The 2nd Hokage	Obtain 850,000 ryo.
The 3rd Hokage	Complete the Prologue or obtain 110,000 ryo.
Tobi	Defeat Madara in Chapter 1 or obtain 200,000 ryo.
Tobi (Great Ninja War)	Complete "The Last Battle" in Chapter 10 or obtain 990,000 ryo.
Torune (Support)	Defeat Danzo in Chapter 2 or obtain 370,000 ryo.
Tsuchikage	Defeat Mizukage in Chapter 1 or obtain 310,000 ryo.
Utakata	Complete "The Last Battle" in Chapter 10 or obtain 950,000 ryo.
Yagura	Complete "The Last Battle" in Chapter 10 or obtain 890,000 ryo.
Yugito	Obtain 870,000 ryo.
Zabuza	Complete "Threat of the Seven Swordsman" in Chapter 6 or obtain 640,000 ryo.
Zabuza (Reanimation)	Obtain 650,000 ryo.

PLAYSTATION 3

NARUTO UZUMAKI GOKU COSTUME NINJA INFO CARD

Go into the collection menu and enter the password XCHPT2M1PD to unlock the Naruto Goku Costume Ninja Info Card.

SURVIVAL MODE IN FREE BATTLE

Complete the White Zetsu Subjugation special quest to unlock Survival Mode.

CHARACTER	REQUIREMENT
Akatsuchi (Support)	Obtain 310,000 ryo.
Ao (Support)	Defeat Mizukage in Chapter 1 or obtain 320,000 ryo.
Asuma (Reanimation)	Obtain 760,000 ryo.
Cee (Support)	Defeat Raikage in Chapter 1 or obtain 210,000 ryo.
Chiyo	Obtain 520,000 ryo.
Choji (Butterfly Mode)	Complete "The Rumbling Coast" in Chapter 7.
Choji (Great Ninja War)	Obtain 740,000 ryo.
Chojuro (Support)	Defeat Mizukage in Chapter 1 or obtain 320,000 ryo.
Danzo	Defeat Danzo in Chapter 2 or obtain 370,000 ryo.
Darui	Defeat Kinkaku and Ginkaku in Chapter 7 or obtain 690,000 ryo.
Deidara	Obtain 570,000 ryo.
Deidara (Reanimation)	Obtain 560,000 ryo.
Foo (Support)	Defeat Danzo in Chapter 2 or obtain 370,000 ryo.
Fuu	Complete "The Last Battle" in Chapter 10 or obtain 970,000 ryo.
Gaara (5 Kage Summit)	Obtain 280,000 ryo.
Guy (Hirudora)	Obtain 440,000 ryo.
Haku	Complete "Threat of the Seven Swordsman" in Chapter 6 or obtain 660,000 ryo.
Haku (Mask)	Obtain 670,000 ryo.
Haku (Reanimation)	Obtain 680,000 ryo.
Han	Complete "The Last Battle" in Chapter 10 or obtain 930,000 ryo.
Hanzo	Defeat Hanzo in Chapter 6 or obtain 600,000 ryo.
Hidan	Obtain 720,000 ryo.
Hinata (Great Ninja War)	Obtain 490,000 ryo.
Hinata PTS	Obtain 170,000 ryo.
Ino (Great Ninja War)	Obtain 750,000 ryo.
Itachi (Tsukuyomi)	Obtain 790,000 ryo.
Jiraiya	Obtain 410,000 ryo.
Jugo	Defeat Raikage in Chapter 1 or obtain 240,000 ryo.
Kabuto (Snake Cloak)	Defeat Kabuto in Chapter 5 or obtain 460,000 ryo.
Kakashi (Great Ninja War)	Obtain 620,000 ryo.
Kakashi (Lightning Blade)	Obtain 380,000 ryo.
Kakashi (Twin Lightning Shiver)	Obtain 380,000 ryo.
Kakashi (Young)	Obtain 330,000 ryo.
Kakuzu	Obtain 710,000 ryo.
Kankuro (5 Kage Summit)	Obtain 260,000 ryo.
Kankuro (Great Ninja War)	Obtain 550,000 ryo.
Karin	Defeat Raikage in Chapter 1 or obtain 250,000 ryo.
Kiba (Great Ninja War)	Obtain 470,000 ryo.
Killer Bee (Samehada)	Defeat Kisame in Chapter 5 or obtain 350,000 ryo.
Kimimaro	Obtain 530,000 ryo.
Konan	Defeat Madara in Chapter 5 or obtain 450,000 ryo.
Kurotsuchi (Support)	Defeat Mizukage in Chapter 1 or obtain 310,000 ryo.

N

CHARACTER	REQUIREMENT
Lee (Great Ninja War)	Obtain 630,000 ryo.
Madara (Reanimation)	Defeat Madara in Chapter 10 or obtain 840,000 ryo.
Masked Man	Complete the Prologue or obtain 120,000 ryo.
Mifune	Defeat Hanzo in Cahpter 6 or obtain 590,000 ryo.
Minato (Hokage)	Complete the Prologue or obtain 100,000 ryo.
Minato (Jonin)	Obtain 100,000 ryo.
Mizukage	Defeat Mizukage in Chapter 1 or obtain 320,000 ryo.
Nagato (Reanimation)	Defeat Nagato in Chapter 9 or obtain 810,000 ryo.
Naruto (Massive Rasengan Barrage)	Defeat the Nine Tails in Chapter 4 or obtain 430,000 ryo.
Naruto (Sage Mode)	Defeat Yamato in Chapter 1 or obtain 340,000 ryo.
Naruto (Tailed Beast Bomb)	Complete "The Last Battle" in Chapter 10 or obtain 980,000 ryo.
Naruto PTS	Obtain 130,000 ryo.
Neji (Great Ninja War)	Obtain 500,000 ryo.
Neji PTS	Obtain 180,000 ryo.
Obito	Obtain 330,000 ryo.
Orochimaru	Obtain 420,000 ryo.
Pain	Obtain 820,000 ryo.
Raikage (Liger Bomb)	Defeat Raikage in Chapter 1 or obtain 210,000 ryo.
Raikage (Lightning Straight)	Obtain 770,000 ryo.
Rock Lee PTS	Obtain 190,000 ryo.
Roushi	Complete "The Last Battle" in Chapter 10 or obtain 910,000 ryo.
Sai (Great Ninja War)	Obtain 540,000 ryo.
Sakura (Great Ninja War)	Obtain 610,000 ryo.
Sakura PTS	Obtain 160,000 ryo.
Sasori	Obtain 580,000 ryo.
Sasuke (5 Kage Summit)	Obtain 220,000 ryo.
Sasuke (Eternal Mangekyo)	Complete the Fragment or obtain 1,500,000 ryo.
Sasuke (Kirin)	Obtain 390,000 ryo.
Sasuke (Taka)	Obtain 400,000 ryo.
Sasuke PTS	Obtain 140,000 ryo.
Shikamaru (Great Ninja War)	Obtain 730,000 ryo.
Shino (Great Ninja War)	Obtain 480,000 ryo.
Suigetsu	Defeat Raikage in Chapter 1 or obtain 230,000 ryo.
Temari (5 Kage Summit)	Obtain 270,000 ryo.
Temari (Great Ninja War)	Obtain 510,000 ryo.
Tenten (Great Ninja War)	Obtain 700,000 ryo.
The 1st Hokage	Obtain 850,000 ryo.
The 2nd Hokage	Obtain 850,000 ryo.
The 3rd Hokage	Complete the Prologue or obtain 110,000 ryo.
Tobi	Defeat Madara in Chapter 1 or obtain 200,000 ryo.
Tobi (Great Ninja War)	Complete "The Last Battle" in Chapter 10 or obtain 990,000 ryo.
Torune (Support)	Defeat Danzo in Chapter 2 or obtain 370,000 ryo.

CHARACTER	REQUIREMENT
Tsuchikage	Defeat Mizukage in Chapter 1 or obtain 310,000 ryo.
Utakata	Complete "The Last Battle" in Chapter 10 or obtain 950,000 ryo.
Yagura	Complete "The Last Battle" in Chapter 10 or obtain 890,000 ryo.
Yugito	Obtain 870,000 ryo.
Zabuza	Complete "Threat of the Seven Swordsman" in Chapter 6 or obtain 640,000 ryo.
Zabuza (Reanimation)	Obtain 650,000 ryo.

XBOX 360/PS3

ACHIEVEMENTS & TROPHIES

NAME	GOAL/REQUIREMENT	POINT VALUE	TROPHY VALUE
Burning Hidden Leaf Village	You cleared the prologue.	5	Bronze
Crash the Five Kage Summit	You cleared Chapter 1.	5	Bronze
Promise of a Rematch	You cleared Chapter 2.	5	Bronze
Dark Naruto Conquest	You cleared Chapter 3.	5	Bronze
With Love	You cleared chapter 4.	5	Bronze
Approaching Ninja World War	You cleared Chapter 5.	5	Bronze
The Ninja Alliance Struggle	You cleared Chapter 6.	5	Bronze
End of the Coastline Battle	You cleared Chapter 7.	5	Bronze
Gain the Raikage's Approval	You cleared Chapter 8.	5	Bronze
Nearing the Climax	You cleared Chapter 9.	5	Bronze
Beyond the Ninja World War	You cleared the last chapter.	10	Bronze
Avenger on the Move	You cleared the fragments.	60	Silver
Battle of Hidden Leaf	Got A rank in The Nine Tails' Attack.	10	Bronze
The Almighty Leaf	Got S rank in The Nine Tails' Attack.	20	Bronze
Five Kage Summit Interrupted	Got A rank in The Agitated Five Kage Summit.	10	Bronze
We Are Unstoppable!	Got S rank in The Agitated Five Kage Summit.	20	Bronze
His Answer	Got A rank in Hero and Avenger.	10	Bronze
To Fight a Friend	Got S rank in Hero and Avenger.	20	Bronze
Gaining Power	Got A rank in Overcoming Hatred.	10	Bronze
Nine Tails Overwhelmed	Got S rank in Overcoming Hatred.	20	Bronze
Vs. the Seven Swordsmen	Got A rank in Threat of the Seven Swordsmen.	10	Bronze
3rd Unit Rules!	Got S rank in Threat of the Seven Swordsmen.	20	Bronze
Gedo Statue, Vanished	Got A rank in The Rumbling Coast.	10	Bronze
Fists of Determination	Got S rank in The Rumbling Coast.	20	Bronze
Five Kage at Full Power	Got A rank in Bet the Future.	10	Bronze
Uchiha Against Five Kage	Got S rank in Bet the Future.	20	Bronze
End of the War	Got A rank The Last Battle.	10	Bronze
Hero of the Ninja World	Got S rank in The Last Battle.	20	Bronze
Defeated Formidables	Got four S ranks in boss battles.	60	Silver
Conquered Formidables	Got S rank in all boss battles.	100	Gold
A Hidden Memory	Unlocked a Secret Factor.	10	Bronze
Collected Memories	Unlocked four Secret Factors.	60	Silver
Memories In Your Heart	Saw all Secret Factors.	100	Gold
Hidden Action	Successfully performed a Secret Action.	10	Bronze

NAME	GOAL/REQUIREMENT	POINT VALUE	TROPHY VALUE
Tales That Live In An Instant	Successfully performed all Secret Actions.	100	Gold
Ready to Roll	You customized your ninja tools.	10	Bronze
New Products in Stock	The Tool Shop added to its ninja tool lineup.	10	Bronze
Savvy Shopper	Used a coupon.	10	Bronze
Gem of a Card	Got a *x5 Ninja Info Card.	10	Bronze
Team Ultimate Finisher	Finished a match with Team Ultimate Jutsu.	10	Bronze
Take This!!!	Performed an Ultimate Jutsu Finish.	10	Bronze
Taijutsu Master	Performed a 50-hit combo.	10	Bronze
Magnificent Victory	You won the battle with a full health bar.	10	Bronze
Blasting Off	Performed a Ring-Out KO.	10	Bronze
Creeping Shadow	Used rear attack feature in a mob battle.	10	Bronze
Ninja World Traveler	Visited all villages.	10	Bronze
First Championship	You won your first tournament.	20	Bronze
Historian	Completed the Ninja World Timeline.	60	Silver
Consummate Storm Master	You released all achievements (trophies).	0	Platinum

NARUTO SHIPPUDEN: ULTIMATE NINJA STORM GENERATIONS

PLAYSTATION 3

NINJA CARD PASSWORDS

Select Enter Password from the Collection Screen and enter the following. Each password unlocks one Ninja Info Card.

00HNWGTFV8	BL770WJT70	MKKJMC7CWF
0B7JLNHXA4	BQ7207JT80	MMD4M2BK7K
0CKC96JGVL	BVKHANGBKR	MSJ1BFU4JB
0LP3WPBQ7B	C0DGMFHCCD	MUW7LMT1WG
17769QU0KT	CE8Q9UKG8N	NDD9LG0EV0
1TFLMLP4BE	CJE20EPKWV	PLESLFPVKK
1V8WD29DBJ	CVJVLP6PVS	PQVG0KUCL0
1WQ4WR17VV	D53XB9P4LP	PSA21VB6M2
28G1D0FSBS	DCF515Q8X9	Q8M8P2J295
2DRA0BDFAR	DS1BXA13LD	QCS5D53XBA
2LM5CHLVX1	DX0L0382NT	QEB22X9LNP
2MFFXGNKWL	E23G24EB0B	QTBT1W97M2
39PXPFXEDW	EL52EVS00X	R4C43XB8PD
3ET93PHNNM	ENE5N43M9L	R8JE3QS6QT
3J6R2NS6B4	ERCKGKSN1P	RE6KE7GPCC
3USV86L2HM	F515Q009CE	S5JVSL6DDC
4HB5ELA91R	F6DTQBCXCF	S85PRDRU1T
4LTP2Q6U26	F7T1103JNS	SAUFE2T72U
4RTCRU4BWD	FMBB22KR0J	SKJERP5K15
53HXEB6EQ1	G12P36C5QW	TEP2FTPH4A
5DFQ45CJF0	GB7FS2G8EV	TH9NGBKRFF
5FUU285P1D	GR56DKG1CP	TVQ7HC2PQ5
6PF63C1C35	GWQ8EKCNEG	U3GQH7R65P

6QDPEH0HQL	H3D14HNF2X	U59BHXUEF3
6RQD5KD6GN	HH88SX6Q4P	UCM26NV9TW
6UB06B8FS2	HWR9FKDPFH	UFG3GKQJ5B
794L5RFD5J	HX3CS22CEG	UL4KS3Q2SU
7DEDGW26R1	J22C572J3P	UMK7SHU2QQ
7KXC71MSTS	JFXC608F44	UTG4GWQ65P
8CTCJFSQ6L	JMV3HRHBR7	V9TW64S2JJ
8EJ57XFMJ3	JSB8UFKXHL	VG63VA3W6D
8JPPVC8TUG	JXF97FR2F7	VLGL6FEQSU
8Q1VK79N7B	K1C6VJKXHL	VML7SHV3RR
96XD609G54	KE84GXKREE	W1X6BJWX5C
9FP7L7N1H1	KF4RT7RU4B	W57HWX4B7S
9P8BLJ6FXX	KTS46B3JUP	WH0BJBA5HF
ADUMLGTR7M	L3PAK7BPUM	WV72WQ4B7R
ALNQK2L6VS	L6N0B1XT65	XH5G7ASAHD
AQU0KTTFCB	LMTA6QSEJV	XVN2VPX5TT
B7JHWCTWU3	MB3GA4DK88	XXPF0EMWKV

XBOX 360

9 NARUTO: ULTIMATE NINJA STORM CHARACTERS

As long as you have a save game from the original Naruto: Ultimate Ninja Storm on your system, 9 bonus characters are unlocked. These include: Ino, Shikamaru, Choji, Neji, Tenten, Rock Lee, Kiba, Shino, Hinata, and 50,000 Ryo.

11 NARUTO SHIPPUDEN: ULTIMATE NINJA STORM 2 CHARACTERS

As long as you have a save game from Naruto Shippuden: Ultimate Ninja Storm 2 on your system, 11 bonus characters are unlocked. These include: Ino, Shikamaru, Choji, Neji, Tenten, Rock Lee, Kiba, Shino, Hinata, Asuma, Guy, and 50,000 Ryo.

NINJA CARD PASSWORDS

Select Enter Password from the Collection Screen and enter the following. Each password unlocks one Ninja Info Card.

00HNWGTFV8	BL770WJT70	MKKJMC7CWF
0B7JLNHXA4	BQ7207JT80	MMD4M2BK7K
0CKC96JGVL	BVKHANGBKR	MSJ1BFU4JB
0LP3WPBQ7B	C0DGMFHCCD	MUW7LMT1WG
17769QU0KT	CE8Q9UKG8N	NDD9LG0EV0
1TFLMLP4BE	CJE20EPKWV	PLESLFPVKK
1V8WD29DBJ	CVJVLP6PVS	PQVG0KUCL0
1WQ4WR17VV	D53XB9P4LP	PSA21VB6M2
28G1D0FSBS	DCF515Q8X9	Q8M8P2J295
2DRA0BDFAR	DS1BXA13LD	QCS5D53XBA
2LM5CHLVX1	DX0L0382NT	QEB22X9LNP
2MFFXGNKWL	E23G24EB0B	QTBT1W97M2
39PXPFXEDW	EL52EVS00X	R4C43XB8PD
3ET93PHNNM	ENE5N43M9L	R8JE3QS6QT
3J6R2NS6B4	ERCKGKSN1P	RE6KE7GPCC
3USV86L2HM	F515Q009CE	S5JVSL6DDC
4HB5ELA91R	F6DTQBCXCF	S85PRDRU1T
4LTP2Q6U26	F7T1103JNS	SAUFE2T72U
4RTCRU4BWD	FMBB22KR0J	SKJERP5K15
53HXEB6EQ1	G12P36C5QW	TEP2FTPH4A
5DFQ45CJF0	GB7FS2G8EV	TH9NGBKRFF

CHEATS, ACHIEVEMENTS, AND TROPHIES

N

5FUU285P1D	GR56DKG1CP	TVQ7HC2PQ5
6PF63C1C35	GWQ8EKCNEG	U3GQH7R65P
6QDPEH0HQL	H3D14HNF2X	U59BHXUEF3
6RQD5KD6GN	HH88SX6Q4P	UCM26NV9TW
6UB06B8FS2	HWR9FKDPFH	UFG3GKQJ5B
794L5RFD5J	HX3CS22CEG	UL4KS3Q2SU
7DEDGW26R1	J22C572J3P	UMK7SHU2QQ
7KXC71MSTS	JFXC608F44	UTG4GWQ65P
8CTCJFSQ6L	JMV3HRHBR7	V9TW64S2JJ
8EJ57XFMJ3	JSB8UFKXHL	VG63VA3W6D
8JPPVC8TUG	JXF97FR2F7	VLGL6FEQSU
8Q1VK79N7B	K1C6VJKXHL	VML7SHV3RR
96XD609G54	KE84GXKREE	W1X6BJWX5C
9FP7L7N1H1	KF4RT7RU4B	W57HWX4B7S
9P8BLJ6FXX	KTS46B3JUP	WH0BJBA5HF
ADUMLGTR7M	L3PAK7BPUM	WV72WQ4B7R
ALNQK2L6VS	L6N0B1XT65	XH5G7ASAHD
AQU0KTTFCB	LMTA6QSEJV	XVN2VPX5TT
B7JHWCTWU3	MB3GA4DK88	XXPF0EMWKV

XBOX 360/PS3

ACHIEVEMENTS & TROPHIES

NAME	GOAL/REQUIREMENT	POINT VALUE	TROPHY VALUE
Tale of Naruto Uzumaki complete	Completed Tale of Naruto Uzumaki.	15	Bronze
Tale of Sasuke Uchiha complete	Completed Tale of Sasuke Uchiha.	15	Bronze
Tale of Young Naruto complete	Completed Tale of Young Naruto.	15	Bronze
Substitution Jutsu Master	Substitution Jutsu collected: 80%	15	Bronze
Ninja Info Card Collector	Ninja Info Card images collected: 50%	5	Bronze
Ninja Tool Master	Ninja Tools collected: 80%	15	Bronze
Image Master	Images collected: 80%	15	Bronze
Ultimate Jutsu Movie Master	Ultimate Jutsu scenes collected: 80%	15	Bronze
First S Rank!	You've earned your first S Rank in a battle.	5	Bronze
Introductory Stage Survivor!	You've completed all of Introductory Survival.	15	Bronze
Beginner Survivor!	You've completed all of Beginner Survival.	15	Bronze
Intermediate Survivor!	You've completed all of Intermediate Survival.	15	Bronze
Advanced Survivor!	You've completed all of Advanced Survival.	15	Bronze
10 Down	You've defeated 10 opponents in Ultimate Survival.	30	Silver
Team Seven Tournament Champ!	You've completed the Team Seven Tournament.	15	Bronze
Sand Genin Tournament Champ!	You've completed the Sand Genin Tournament.	15	Bronze
Leaf Genin Tournament Champ!	You've completed all Leaf Genin Tournament battles.	15	Bronze
Boy's Life Tournament Champ!	You've completed the Boy's Life Tournament.	15	Bronze
New Team Seven Tournament Champ!	You've completed the New Team Seven Tournament.	15	Bronze

NAME	GOAL/REQUIREMENT	POINT VALUE	TROPHY VALUE
Leaf Chunin Tournament Champ!	You've completed the Leaf Chunin Tournament.	15	Bronze
Ultimate Ninja Tournament Champ!	You've completed the Ultimate Ninja Tournament.	15	Bronze
Leaf Higher-Up Tournament Champ!	You've completed the Leaf Higher-Up Tournament.	15	Bronze
Shippuden Tournament Champ!	You've completed the Shippuden Tournament.	15	Bronze
Peerless Ninja Tournament Champ!	You've completed the Peerless Ninja Tournament.	15	Bronze
Akatsuki Tournament Champ!	You've completed the Akatsuki Tournament.	15	Bronze
Five Kage Tournament Champ!	You've completed the Five Kage Tournament.	15	Bronze
First Shopping!	You've done your first shopping.	5	Bronze
First Ninja Tool Edit!	You've edited a ninja tool set for the first time.	5	Bronze
Wealthy Ninja	You've earned a total of 1,000,000 Ryo.	50	Silver
I'm the greatest ninja!	You've unlocked all achievements.	0	—

SECRET ACHIEVEMENTS & TROPHIES

NAME	GOAL/REQUIREMENT	POINT VALUE	TROPHY VALUE
Tale of Minato Namikaze complete	Completed Tale of Minato Namikaze.	15	Bronze
Tale of Itachi Uchiha complete	Completed Tale of Itachi Uchiha.	15	Bronze
Tale of Madara Uchiha complete	Completed Tale of Madara Uchiha.	15	Bronze
Tale of Zabuza and Haku complete	Completed Tale of Zabuza Momochi and Haku.	15	Bronze
Tale of Jiraiya complete	Completed Tale of Jiraiya.	15	Bronze
Tale of Gaara complete	Completed Tale of Gaara.	15	Bronze
Tale of Kakashi Hatake complete	Completed Tale of Kakashi Hatake.	15	Bronze
Tale of Killer Bee complete	Completed Tale of Killer Bee.	15	Bronze
Card Collection Master	Ninja Info Card images collected: 80%	100	Gold
Alias Master	Titles collected: 80%	100	Gold
Gimme a hand!	You can now use all support characters.	5	Bronze
Master Survivor!	You've completed all of Survival Mode.	30	Silver
Five Kage Summit	All Kage at the Five Kage Summit can now be used.	5	Bronze
Past Hokages	You can now use all past Hokages.	5	Bronze
Younger Version	You can use all the characters of the Young Version.	15	Bronze
Shippuden	You can use all the characters from Shippuden.	15	Bronze
Game Master!	You've played for a total of over 30 hours.	30	Bronze
Ninja Lover!	You've used all leader characters.	50	Gold
Ultimate Ninja Gathering	You can now use all characters.	50	Silver
Tournament Champ!	You've completed all Challenge Tournaments.	30	Silver

CHEATS, ACHIEVEMENTS, AND TROPHIES

N

NARUTO: PATH OF THE NINJA

NINTENDO 3DS

After defeating the game, talk to Knohamaru on the roof of the Ninja Academy. He allows you go get certain cheats by tapping four successive spots on the touch screen in order. There are 12 different spots on the screen, we have numbered them from left to right, top to bottom as follows:

1	2	3	4
5	6	7	8
9	10	11	12

Now enter the following by touching the four spots in the order given.

UNLOCK	CODE
4th Hokage's Sword	4, 7, 11, 5
Fuji Fan	8, 11, 2, 5
Jiraiya	11, 3, 1, 6
Rajin's Sword	7, 6, 5, 11
Rasengan	9, 2, 12, 7

NARUTO: PATH OF THE NINJA 2

NINTENDO 3DS

CHARACTER PASSWORDS

Talk to Konohamaru at the school to enter the following passwords. You must first complete the game for the passwords to work.

CHARACTER	PASSWORD
Gaara	DKFIABJL
Gai	IKAGDEFL
Iruka	JGDLKAIB
Itachi Uchiha	GBEIDALF
Jiraiya	EBJDAGFL
Kankuro	ALJKBEDG
Kyuubi Naruto	GJHLBFDE
Orochimaru	AHFBLEJG

NASCAR

PSP

ALL CHASE PLATES

Go to Fight to the Top mode. Next, edit the driver's first and last name so that it says ItsAll ForMe. Note that the code is case-sensitive.

$10,000,000

In Fight to the Top mode, enter your driver's name as GiveMe More.

10,000,000 FANS

In Fight to the Top mode, enter your driver's name as AllBow ToMe.

ALL CHASE PLATES

In Fight to the Top mode, enter your driver's name as ItsAll ForMe.

OLD SPICE TRACKS AND CARS

In Fight to the Top mode, enter your driver's name as KeepCool SmellGreat.

NASCAR THE GAME 2011

XBOX 360/PS3

MARK MARTIN PAINT SCHEMES

At the garage main menu, press Down, Down, Up, Up, Right, Left, Right, Left.
Enter godaddy.com.

KYLE BUSH NOS ENERGY DRINK CAR

At the garage main menu, press Down, Down, Up, Up, Right, Left, Right, Left.
Enter drinknos.

ACHIEVEMENTS & TROPHIES

NAME	GOAL/REQUIREMENT	POINT VALUE	TROPHY VALUE
"Let's Go Racin Boys"	You took part in your first online race.	10	Bronze
Hotrod	You created a custom tuning setup.	20	Bronze
Up on the Wheel	You lead 5 consecutive laps in an online race.	10	Bronze
Pedal to the Metal	You achieved the fastest lap of the race during an online race.	10	Bronze
Rubbin is Racin!	You raced online at every track.	20	Bronze
Run the Gauntlet	You won a Gauntlet Invitational Event.	10	Bronze
Last Man Standing	You survived a 43 car eliminator race to the end.	10	Bronze
The Champ is here!	You won the Championship Showdown Invitational Event.	20	Bronze
Give me 4	You performed your first 4-tire pit stop in a race.	20	Bronze
Finishing in First!	You won a race crossing the line in first gear.	10	Bronze
Win on Sunday, Sell on Monday	You won a race in all brands of car.	10	Silver
Boy Scout	You unlocked every NASCAR Pin in the game.	70	Gold
Name to Remember	You unlocked every Gold Legends Coin in the game.	50	Silver
Kingly	You defeated Richard Petty's race win record of 200 wins.	50	Silver
Pit Perfection	You performed a 4-tire pit stop, and went on to win an online race.	20	Silver
Styling 'N' Profiling	You won a race with a personalized Paint Scheme.	10	Bronze
Ride in Style	You've collected 88 Paint Schemes by completing all Invitational Events and reaching rank 29	40	Silver
Surfin' USA	You mastered every track in the game.	40	Silver
Groovy	You mastered a track by completing all the objectives on a Master the Track card.	20	Bronze
Victory Lane	You have won a race at every circuit in the game.	20	Silver
Saddle Up & Hang On	You have qualified in pole position at every circuit in the game in Career Mode.	50	Silver

CHEATS, ACHIEVEMENTS, AND TROPHIES

NAME	GOAL/REQUIREMENT	POINT VALUE	TROPHY VALUE
Race Rivalry	You achieved 20 rival victories.	30	Silver
Star of Tomorrow	You achieved a total of 100 fastest laps.	50	Silver
NXP Challenge	You have achieved over 6,666 NXP in a single race.	20	Bronze
Now ya Talkin'	You reached Rank 10.	20	Bronze
One for the Road	You ranked up for the first time.	20	Bronze
NASCAR Legend	You reached Rank 30.	70	Bronze
Decorated Driver	You reached Rank 20.	30	Silver
Keep Diggin'	You have driven 500 miles.	10	Bronze
VIP	You completed all three objectives for a single sponsor in Career Mode.	20	Bronze
Any Place, Any Time	You competed in every Invitational Event.	20	Silver
Car Stylist	You entered the Create New Paint Scheme Menu	10	Bronze
MVP	You received full sponsorship status for your driver in Career Mode.	20	Silver
Cup Contender	You achieved a top 10 finish in every Career Mode race.	40	Silver
Sprint to the Finish	You won a race in Career Mode and got the full 195 points.	10	Bronze
Tailgating	You performed a draft of 500 yards.	10	Bronze
Series Champion	You finished top of the Career Mode standings and became the Sprint Cup series champion.	70	Gold
Race to the Chase	You achieved enough points in Career Mode to move into The Chase, as one of the top 12 drivers.	20	Silver

SECRET ACHIEVEMENTS & TROPHIES

NAME	GOAL/REQUIREMENT	POINT VALUE	TROPHY VALUE
Celebration Shot	You photographed the driver celebrating on the car after a Career Mode race win.	10	Bronze
Rookie Mistake	You received a drive through or speeding penalty.	0	Bronze

NASCAR KART RACING

JOEY LOGANO

Select Enter Cheat from the Profile Info menu and enter 426378.

NASCAR THE GAME: INSIDE LINE

NEW PAINT SCHEMES

Go to Redeem Codes under My Rewards from the Main Menu and enter these codes to unlock new paint schemes.

REWARD	CODE
FOX Sports Paint Schemes	FOXSPORTS
SPEED Channel Paint Scheme	SPEEDTV
Custom Paint Schemes	GODADDY

NEW PAINT SCHEMES

Go to Redeem Codes under My Rewards from the Main Menu and enter these codes to unlock new paint schemes.

REWARD	CODE
FOX Sports Paint Schemes	FOXSPORTS
SPEED Channel Paint Scheme	SPEEDTV
Custom Paint Schemes	GODADDY

ACHIEVEMENTS & TROPHIES

NAME	GOAL/REQUIREMENT	POINT VALUE	TROPHY VALUE
1%'er	Earned a total of 1,000,000Cr.	25	Silver
First Steps	Took part in a Career or Season Race.	5	Bronze
Treat Yourself	Purchased an item from the Reward Store.	5	Bronze
Passing The Time	Flipped the Track Pass 500 times during loading.	15	Bronze
Draft Dodger	Drafted a total of 1000 yards in a race.	15	Bronze
Newbie	Took part in a Public Online Race.	5	Bronze
Upgrade Complete	Purchased an upgrade.	10	Bronze
Speed Star	Won a Superspeedway race in Career or Season Mode.	25	Bronze
Day At The Beach	Won the Daytona 500.	30	Silver
Startin' on Pole	Qualified on pole in Career or Season Mode.	25	Bronze
Miles Away	Won an Intermediate track race in Career or Season Mode.	25	Bronze
In The Chase	Made the Chase.	25	Silver
Chase Champion	Won the Sprint Cup in Chase Mode.	15	Bronze
Challenging	Completed a Head to Head Challenge.	15	Silver
Short & Sweet	Won a Short track race in Career or Season Mode.	25	Bronze
Season Champion	Won the Sprint Cup in Single Season Mode.	25	Silver
Van Gogh	Created a custom paint scheme.	10	Bronze
Turn Right?	Won a Road Course race in Career or Season Mode.	25	Bronze
Last Man Standing	Won an Eliminator Invitational event.	25	Bronze
Snap Happy	Took a picture in Photo Mode.	5	Bronze

NAME	GOAL/REQUIREMENT	POINT VALUE	TROPHY VALUE
Trend Setter	Finished a race with the fastest lap 100 times.	20	Silver
Contender	Won a Public Online Race.	20	Silver
Mano a Mano	Won a Driver Duel Invitational event.	25	Bronze
Champion	Won the Sprint Cup in Career Mode.	50	Gold
Taking Care Of Business	Signed a sponsor to each location on the car.	20	Bronze
Clock Watcher	Earned Gold at a Thunderlap Invitational event.	25	Bronze
Action Shot	Took a picture of the car with all four wheels off the track.	15	Bronze
Long Road Back	Won a Public Online Race after qualifying last.	20	Bronze
Consistent	Won a Gauntlet Invitational event.	25	Bronze
Brainiac	Answered 150 trivia questions correctly.	20	Bronze
Director	Saved a replay of a race.	5	Bronze
Gear Head	Created a custom setup.	15	Bronze
Lap It Up	Lapped an opponent in a Public Online Race.	20	Bronze
Maxed Out!	Fully upgraded the Career Car.	25	Silver
Serious	Won a race with no assists.	15	Bronze
Collector	Purchased everything in the Reward Store.	20	Silver
Hustler	Won a Public Online Race after passing 5 cars on the last lap.	25	Bronze
Slippery	Completed a race without touching another car.	25	Bronze
The King	Won the Sprint Cup in Career Mode while playing on Champion difficulty.	50	Silver
Perfect Day	Qualified in pole, led all laps, won the race.	25	Silver
Gambler	Ran out of fuel and coasted into pit road.	25	Bronze
Photo Finish	Won an offline race by less than 0.02 seconds.	15	Silver
Challenger	Completed an Inside Line Highlight Challenge.	20	Silver
Challenge Complete	Completed all Inside Line Highlight Challenges.	20	Silver
Platinum	Unlock every trophy in the game.	—	Platinum

SECRET ACHIEVEMENTS & TROPHIES

NAME	GOAL/REQUIREMENT	POINT VALUE	TROPHY VALUE
The Intimidator	Spun out an opponent.	10	Bronze
Ironman	Took part in 250 Public Online Races.	25	Bronze
Shake & Bake	Slingshotted to victory in the final straight.	15	Bronze
Pass in the Grass	Won a race after overtaking on grass.	20	Bronze
Polish Victory Lap	Completed a victory lap driving the opposite direction around the track.	15	Bronze
Too Much!	Won the race after crossing the finishing line backwards.	25	Silver

NBA 2K11

MJ: CREATING A LEGEND

In Features, select Codes from the Extras menu. Choose Enter Code and enter icanbe23.

2K CHINA TEAM

In Features, select Codes from the Extras menu. Choose Enter Code and enter 2kchina.

2K SPORTS TEAM

In Features, select Codes from the Extras menu. Choose Enter Code and enter 2Ksports.

NBA 2K TEAM

In Features, select Codes from the Extras menu. Choose Enter Code and enter nba2k.

VC TEAM

In Features, select Codes from the Extras menu. Choose Enter Code and enter vcteam.

ABA BALL

In Features, select Codes from the Extras menu. Choose Enter Code and enter payrespect.

2011 ALL-STAR UNIFORMS

In Features, select Codes from the Extras menu. Choose Enter Code and enter wydololoh.

SECONDARY ROAD UNIFORM

In Features, select Codes from the Extras menu. Choose Enter Code and enter ronoilnm. This unlocks the secondary road uniform for the Hornets, Magic, and Timberwolves.

ORANGE SPLIT DUNK

In Features, select Codes from the Extras menu. Choose Enter Code and enter SPRITEDUNK1. Go to Sprite Slam Dunk Showdown and use the help menu to find out more.

SPIN TOMMY DUNK

In Features, select Codes from the Extras menu. Choose Enter Code and enter SPRITEDUNK2. Go to Sprite Slam Dunk Showdown and use the help menu to find out more.

THE VILLAIN DUNK

In Features, select Codes from the Extras menu. Choose Enter Code and enter SPRITEDUNK3. Go to Sprite Slam Dunk Showdown and use the help menu to find out more.

2K CHINA TEAM

In Features, select Codes from the Extras menu. Choose Enter Code and key in 2kchina.

2K SPORTS TEAM

In Features, select Codes from the Extras menu. Choose Enter Code and key in 2Ksports.

NBA 2K TEAM

In Features, select Codes from the Extras menu. Choose Enter Code and key in nba2k.

VC TEAM

In Features, select Codes from the Extras menu. Choose Enter Code and key in vcteam.

ABA BALL

In Features, select Codes from the Extras menu. Choose Enter Code and key in payrespect.

NBA 2K12

ABA BALL

Select Extras from the Features menu. Choose Codes and enter payrespect. This can be toggled on and off from this Codes menu.

2K CHINA TEAM

Select Extras from the Features menu. Choose Codes and enter 2kchina.

2K SPORTS TEAM

Select Extras from the Features menu. Choose Codes and enter 2ksports.

UNLOCK NBA 2K TEAM

Select Extras from the Features menu. Choose Codes and enter nba2k.

VC TEAM

Select Extras from the Features menu. Choose Codes and enter vcteam.

JORDAN RETRO COLLECTION

Select Extras from the Features menu. Choose Codes and enter 23.

SECONDARY ROAD UNIFORMS

Select Extras from the Features menu. Choose Codes and enter hcsilapadatu. This unlocks uniforms for 76ers, Jazz, Kings, and Mavericks.

CHRISTMAS UNIFORMS

Select Extras from the Features menu. Choose Codes and enter ibyasmliancbhlald. This unlocks uniforms for Bulls, Celtics, Heat, Knicks, Lakers, and Mavericks.

HEAT BACK IN BLACK UNIFORM

Select Extras from the Features menu. Choose Codes and enter albkbinkcca.

RAPTORS MILITARY NIGHT UNIFORM

Select Extras from the Features menu. Choose Codes and enter liyrimta.

XBOX 360/PS3ABA BALL

Select Extras from the Features menu. Choose Codes and enter payrespect. This can be toggled on and off from this Codes menu.

2K CHINA TEAM

Select Extras from the Features menu. Choose Codes and enter 2kchina.

2K SPORTS TEAM

Select Extras from the Features menu. Choose Codes and enter 2ksports.

UNLOCK NBA 2K TEAM

Select Extras from the Features menu. Choose Codes and enter nba2k.

VC TEAM

Select Extras from the Features menu. Choose Codes and enter vcteam.

JORDAN RETRO COLLECTION

Select Extras from the Features menu. Choose Codes and enter 23.

SECONDARY ROAD UNIFORMS

Select Extras from the Features menu. Choose Codes and enter hcsilapadatu. This unlocks uniforms for 76ers, Jazz, Kings, and Mavericks.

CHRISTMAS UNIFORMS

Select Extras from the Features menu. Choose Codes and enter ibyasmliancbhlald. This unlocks uniforms for Bulls, Celtics, Heat, Knicks, Lakers, and Mavericks.

HEAT BACK IN BLACK UNIFORM

Select Extras from the Features menu. Choose Codes and enter albkbinkcca.

RAPTORS MILITARY NIGHT UNIFORM

Select Extras from the Features menu. Choose Codes and enter liyrimta.

PSP

ABA BALL

Select Cheats from the Features menu and enter payrespect.

BOBCATS NASCAR RACING UNIFORM

Select Cheats from the Features menu and enter agsntrccai.

CAVS CAVFANATIC UNIFORM

Select Cheats from the Features menu and enter aifnaatccv.

HARDWOOD CLASSICS UNIFORMS

Select Cheats from the Features menu and enter Wasshcicsl. This unlocks uniforms for the Cavaliers, Jazz, Magic, Raptors, Timberwolves, Trail Blazers, and Warriors.

MARDI GRAS UNIFORMS

Select Cheats from the Features menu and enter asrdirmga. This unlocks uniforms for the Bulls, Celtics, Knicks, and Raptors.

SECONDARY ROAD UNIFORMS

Select Cheats from the Features menu and enter eydonscar. This unlocks uniforms for the Grizzlies, Hawks, Mavs, and Rockets.

ST PATRICK'S DAY UNIFORMS

Select Cheats from the Features menu and enter riiasgerh. This unlocks uniforms for the Bulls, Celtics, Knicks, and Raptors.

TRAIL BLAZERS RIP CITY UNIFORM

Select Cheats from the Features menu and enter ycprtii.

NBA 2K13

NINTENDO WII U/XBOX 360/PS3

CHEAT PASSWORDS

These passwords can be used to unlock additional features and abilities.

EFFECT	PASSWORD
+3 to ball handles	SPRITEEFFECT
2013 All-Star Uniforms	MWPZOSLQOV
ABA Basketball	PAYRESPECT
Christmas Uniforms	MNSPXUWMDY
Heat White Hot Uniform	KQPXMZODQB
Secondary Uniforms	YPZBNWOLAW
UA Tourch Shoes	UNDERARMOUR

UNLOCKABLE SHOES

SHOE	REQUIREMENT
Under Armour Spine Bionic Shoe	Complete Training Camp
Under Armour Charge BB Shoe	Complete the "Raining 3's" achievement

CHEATS, ACHIEVEMENTS, AND TROPHIES

N

ACHIEVEMENTS & TROPHIES

NAME	GOAL/REQUIREMENT	POINT VALUE	TROPHY VALUE
Dawn of an Era	Get drafted as a lottery pick in the NBA draft in MyCAREER mode.	15	Silver
Serving Notice	Get 250,000 fans in MyCAREER mode.	15	Bronze
I'm Here to Stay	Get 1,000,000 fans in MyCAREER mode.	25	Bronze
Man of the People	Get 2,000,000 fans in MyCAREER mode.	40	Silver
Everyone is Special	Purchase and equip 1 Special Ability in MyCAREER mode.	15	Bronze
Some more Special than Others	Purchase and equip 5 Special Abilities simultaneously in MyCAREER mode.	30	Silver
Now Playing	Purchase a pre-game ritual in MyCAREER mode.	15	Bronze
Both Feet on the Ground	Sign an endorsement contract with either Nike or Jordan in MyCAREER mode.	30	Bronze
Come Fly with Me	Purchase Michael Jordan's dunk package (Historic Jordan) in MyCAREER mode.	15	Bronze
NBA Cares	Make a donation to the NBA Cares global community outreach initiative in MyCAREER mode.	15	Bronze
MyPLAYER of the Game	Be named Player of the Game (in an NBA game) in MyCAREER mode.	20	Bronze
My Every Day Player	Become a starter in the NBA in MyCAREER mode.	20	Bronze
My All-Star	Be named an NBA All-Star in MyCAREER mode.	25	Silver
Immortality	Make the Hall of Fame in MyCAREER mode.	30	Gold
Runneth Over	Obtain a balance of 20,000 VC.	30	Silver
Buzzer Beater	Make a game winning shot with no time left on the clock in a non-simulated game.	20	Bronze
Trip-Dub	Record a triple double with any player in a non-simulated game.	20	Bronze
Dub-Dub	Record two double doubles with any teammates in the same non-simulated game.	20	Bronze
Five by Five	Record 5 or more in 5 different stats with any player in a non-simulated game.	20	Bronze
It's Raining	Make 15 or more 3-pointers with any team in a non-simulated game.	20	Bronze
Block Party	Record 10 or more blocks with any team in a non-simulated game.	20	Bronze
Men of Steal	Record 10 or more steals with any team in a non-simulated game.	20	Bronze

NAME	GOAL/REQUIREMENT	POINT VALUE	TROPHY VALUE
Swat and Swipe	Record at least 5 blocks and 5 steals with any team in a non-simulated game.	20	Bronze
Smothering	Hold the opposing team's FG% below 40% with any team in a non-simulated game.	20	Bronze
Giveth and Taketh Away	Record 10 or more rebounds and assists with any player in a non-simulated game.	20	Bronze
Hold the Fat Lady	Start the 4th period losing by 10 or more points and win with any team in a non-simulated game.	20	Bronze
Wire to Wire	Do not allow your opponent to lead the game at any point with any team in a non-simulated game.	20	Bronze
The Closer	Hold the opposing team to zero points in the final two minutes of a non-simulated game.	20	Bronze
The Here and Now	Begin a "Today" Association.	15	Bronze
Puppet Master	Adjust your "Total Sim Control" strategy in The Association or Season mode.	10	Bronze
Not Your Father's Association	Join an Online Association.	10	Bronze
Another Day, Another Win	Win 5 NBA Today matchups.	20	Bronze
Don't Hate the Player	Win the championship in an Online Association.	30	Silver
Streaking	Win 5 non-simulated games in a row in The Association mode.	25	Bronze
Ticker Tape	Win an NBA Championship in The Association mode (playing every playoff game).	30	Silver
Shooting Star	Win the MVP award in the NBA: Creating a Legend mode.	30	Silver
Hey Mr. DJ	Create a 2K Beats Playlist.	10	Bronze
Maestro	Create a shoe in the 2K Shoe Creator.	15	Bronze
Raining 3's	Making at least 9 three-pointers in one game with Brandon Jennings to set a new career-high.	20	Silver
KD Unlimited	Score at least 52 points in one game with Kevin Durant to set a new career-high.	20	Silver
From the Ground Up	Purchase 15 Boosters in MyTEAM mode.	20	Bronze
To Good Use	Play a MyTEAM game online.	15	Bronze
On the Road Again	Play a MyPLAYER Blacktop game online.	15	Bronze
Remaking History	Play with an historic team online.	15	Bronze
This One Counts	Win one online Versus match.	15	Bronze
Back to Back to Back	Win 3 Versus matches in a row.	15	Bronze
You're Officially Hot	Win 5 Versus matches in a row.	20	Silver
Lincoln	Win 5 Versus matches total.	15	Bronze
Hamilton	Win 10 Versus matches total.	20	Silver
The Sum of Its Parts	Play a Team-Up Game.	15	Bronze

CHEATS, ACHIEVEMENTS, AND TROPHIES

ALL-STAR WEEKEND DLC

NAME	GOAL/REQUIREMENT	POINT VALUE	TROPHY VALUE
The Future is Now	Win the Rising Stars Challenge.	20	Bronze
All The Sprite Moves	Win the Sprite Slam Dunk Contest with at least one AI opponent.	20	Bronze
Home, Home on Long Range	Win the Three-Point Contest with at least one AI opponent.	20	Bronze
Starry, Starry Night	Win the All-Star Game.	30	Silver
I Came, I Saw…	Win all 4 All-Star events.	60	Gold

NBA JAM

PLAYSTATION 3

BEASTIE BOYS

At the title screen, press Up, Up, Down, Down, Left, Right, Left, Right, ●, ⊗. This team includes Ad Rock, MCA, and Mike D.

J. COLE AND 9TH WONDER

At the title screen, press Up, Left, Down, Right, Up, Left, Down, Right, ●, ⊗.

DEMOCRATS TEAM

At the title screen, press Left (x13), ⊗. This team includes Barack Obama, Joe Biden, Bill Clinton, and Hillary Clinton.

REPUBLICANS TEAM

At the title screen, press Right (x13), ⊗. The team includes George W. Bush, Sarah Palin, Dick Cheney, and John McCain.

ESPN'S SPORTSNATION

Select Play Now. When entering the initials, enter ESP for P1 and NSN for P2. Advance to the Choose Teams screen to find the team. This team includes the hosts of the show; Colin Cowherd and Michelle Beadle.

NBA MASCOTS

Select Play Now. When entering the initials, enter MAS for P1 and COT for P2.

ORIGINAL GENERATION JAM

Select Play Now. When entering the initials, enter MJT for P1. Advance to the Choose Teams screen to find the team. This team includes Mark Turmell and Tim Kitzrow.

XBOX 360

BEASTIE BOYS

At the title screen, press Up, Up, Down, Down, Left, Right, Left, Right, B, A. This team includes Ad Rock, MCA, and Mike D.

J. COLE AND 9TH WONDER

At the title screen, press Up, Left, Down, Right, Up, Left, Down, Right, Circle, A.

DEMOCRATS TEAM

At the title screen, press Left (x13), A. This team includes Barack Obama, Joe Biden, Bill Clinton, and Hillary Clinton.

REPUBLICANS TEAM

At the title screen, press Right (x13), A. The team includes George W. Bush, Sarah Palin, Dick Cheney, and John McCain.

ESPN'S SPORTSNATION

Select Play Now. When entering the initials, enter ESP for P1 and NSN for P2. Advance to the Choose Teams screen to find the team. This team includes the hosts of the show; Colin Cowherd and Michelle Beadle.

NBA MASCOTS

Select Play Now. When entering the initials, enter MAS for P1 and COT for P2.

ORIGINAL GENERATION JAM

Select Play Now. When entering the initials, enter MJT for P1. Advance to the Choose Teams screen to find the team. This team includes Mark Turmell and Tim Kitzrow.

NBA LIVE 10

PLAYSTATION 3/PSP

CHARLOTTE BOBCATS' 2009/2010 RACE DAY ALTERNATE JERSEYS

Select Options from My NBA Live and go to Select Codes. Enter ceobdabacarstcy.

NEW ORLEANS HORNETS' 2009/2010 MARDI GRAS ALTERNATE JERSEYS

Select Options from My NBA Live and go to Select Codes. Enter nishrag1rosmad0.

ALTERNATE JERSEYS

Select Options from My NBA Live and go to Select Codes. Enter ndnba1rooaesdc0. This unlocks alternate jerseys for Atlanta Hawks, Dallas Mavericks, Houston Rockets, and Memphis Grizzlies.

MORE HARDWOOD CLASSICS NIGHTS JERSEYS

Select Options from My NBA Live and go to Select Codes. Enter hdogdrawhoticns. This unlocks Hardwood Classics Nights jerseys for Cleveland Cavaliers, Golden State Warriors, Minnesota Timberwolves, Orlando Magic, Philadelphia 76ers.

ADIDAS EQUATIONS

Select Options from My NBA Live and go to Select Codes. Enter adaodqauieints1.

ADIDAS TS CREATORS WITH ANKLE BRACES

Select Options from My NBA Live and go to Select Codes. Enter atciadsstsdhecf.

ADIDAS TS SUPERNATURAL COMMANDERS

Select Options from My NBA Live and go to Select Codes. Enter andsicdsmatdnsr.

ADIDAS TS SUPERNATURAL CREATORS

Select Options from My NBA Live and go to Select Codes. Enter ard8siscdnatstr.

AIR MAX LEBRON VII

Select Options from My NBA Live and go to Select Codes. Enter ere1nbvlaoeknii, 2ovnaebnkrielei, 3rioabeneikenvl, ri4boenanekilve, ivl5brieekaeonn, or n6ieirvalkeeobn.

KOBE V

Select Options from My NBA Live and go to Select Codes. Enter ovze1bimenkoko0, m0kveokoiebozn2, eev0nbimokk3ozo, or bmo4inozeeo0kvk.

JORDAN CP3 IIIS

Select Options from My NBA Live and go to Select Codes. Enter iaporcdian3ejis.

JORDAN MELO M6S

Select Options from My NBA Live and go to Select Codes. Enter emlarmeoo6ajdsn.

JORDAN SIXTY PLUSES

Select Options from My NBA Live and go to Select Codes. Enter aondsuilyjrspxt.

NIKE HUARACHE LEGIONS

Select Options from My NBA Live and go to Select Codes. Enter aoieuchrahelgn.

NIKE KD 2S

Select Options from My NBA Live and go to Select Codes. Enter kk2tesaosepinrd.

NIKE ZOOM FLIP'NS

Select Options from My NBA Live and go to Select Codes. Enter epfnozaeminolki

NBA STREET HOMECOURT

XBOX 360

ALL TEAMS

At the Main menu, hold Right Bumper + Left Bumper and press Left, Right, Left, Right.

ALL COURTS

At the Main menu, hold Right Bumper + Left Bumper and press Up, Right, Down, Left.

BLACK/RED BALL

At the Main menu, hold Right Bumper + Left Bumper and press Up, Down, Left, Right.

NEED FOR SPEED CARBON: OWN THE CITY

PSP

UNLOCK EVERYTHING

At the Start menu, press X, X, Right, Left, ●, Up, Down.

JET CAR

At the Start menu, press Up, Down, Left, R1, L1, ●, ●.

LAMBORGINI MERCIALAGO

At the Start menu, press X, X, Up, Down, Left, Right, ●, ●.

TRANSFORMERS CAR

At the Start menu, press X, X, X, ●, ●, ●, Up, Down.

NEED FOR SPEED: MOST WANTED

XBOX 360

BURGER KING CHALLENGE

At the Title screen, press Up, Down, Up, Down, Left, Right, Left, Right.

CASTROL SYNTEC VERSION OF THE FORD GT

At the Title screen, press Left, Right, Left, Right, Up, Down, Up, Down.

MARKER FOR BACKROOM OF THE ONE-STOP SHOP

At the Title screen, press Up, Up, Down, Down, Left, Right, Up, Down.

JUNKMAN ENGINE

At the Title screen, press Up, Up, Down, Down, Left, Right, Up, Down.

PORSCHE CAYMAN

At the Title screen, press Left, Right, Right, Right, Right, Left, Right, Down.

ACHIEVEMENTS & TROPHIES

NAME	GOAL/REQUIREMENT	POINT VALUE	TROPHY VALUE
Most Wanted Rides	Own all the Most Wanted cars (Single Player)	100	Gold
Got to Smash Them All	Smashed every Billboard	25	Bronze
The Gatecrasher	Broke through every Security Gate	25	Bronze
Love Them and Leave Them	Drove every Car	30	Bronze
Networking	Found every Jack Spot	25	Bronze
Cameraman	Triggered every Speed Camera	25	Bronze
Go Pro or Go Home	Unlocked all the Pro mods on a car (Single Player)	15	Bronze
Feeling the Need	Emptied a full nitrous bar without hitting anything	5	Bronze
Fix Me Up	Used a Bodyshop to paint or repair your car for the first time	5	Bronze
Switcheroo	Used a Jack Spot in a Pursuit (Single Player)	10	Bronze
Kitchen Sink	Used a Billboard and a Jack Spot to successfully evade a pursuit (Single Player)	10	Bronze
The Heat is Off	Escaped successfully from all Heat levels	20	Silver
Social Climber	Have 5 or more NFS friends	10	Bronze
How Do You Like Me Now?	Beat a friend's Autolog recommendation	15	Bronze
Moving On Up	Moved up the Most Wanted List for the first time	10	Bronze
Nothing Personal	Took down a friend in Multiplayer	15	Bronze
After Market	Unlocked a mod for a car in Multiplayer	15	Bronze
Licensed to ill	Customized your license plate and number in Multiplayer	10	Silver
Mix Master	Played a Custom Speedlist you created (Multiplayer)	10	Bronze
The Modfather	Unlocked 3 Pro Mods in Multiplayer	25	Silver
Second is Nothing	Finished first in every race, in every car (Single Player)	80	Gold
Rim Shot	Escaped the cops with at least one blown tire	25	Silver
In Your Face	Smashed a friend's face on a billboard and beat their jump distance	20	Bronze
Pit Stop	Repaired a burst tire at a Bodyshop	10	Bronze
Alpha Dog	Shut down Most Wanted car number 10: Alfa Romeo 4C Concept (Single Player)	20	Bronze
Charming	Shut down Most Wanted car number 9: Shelby COBRA 427 (Single Player)	20	Bronze
Blackout	Shut down Most Wanted car number 8: Mercedes-Benz SL 65 AMG (Single Player)	20	Bronze
Lexus Ranger	Shut down Most Wanted car number 7: Lexus LFA (Single Player)	20	Bronze
Track Weapon	Shut down Most Wanted car number 6: McLaren MP4-12C (Single Player)	20	Bronze

NAME	GOAL/REQUIREMENT	POINT VALUE	TROPHY VALUE
Arachnophobic	Shut down Most Wanted car number 5: Porsche 918 Spyder Concept (Single Player)	20	Bronze
Main Avent	Shut down Most Wanted car number 4: Lamborghini Aventador (Single Player)	20	Bronze
White Gold	Shut down Most Wanted car number 3: Bugatti Veyron Super Sport (Single Player)	20	Bronze
Mighty Wind	Shut down Most Wanted car number 2: Pagani Huayra (Single Player)	20	Bronze
Don't Blink	Shut down Most Wanted car number 1: Koenigsegg Agera R (Single Player)	45	Silver
Gotcha	Got Busted for the first time	15	Bronze
First Strike	Took down your first Cop	5	Bronze
Troublemaker	Took down 50 Cops	30	Silver
Slip the Cuffs	Drove through a roadblock without crashing	10	Bronze
Sidewinder	Did a 250 yard (228.6 meter) drift	25	Bronze
Mauled	Wrecked 10 cops in a single pursuit in the Ford F-150 SVT Raptor	30	Silver
Beast from the East	Escaped from the cops in the Marussia B2	30	Silver
Iron Boots	Drove over 5 spike strips with re-inflates equipped	20	Bronze
Gladiator	Took down every racer at least once in a single race	25	Silver
Escape Velocity	Jumped over 200 yards (182.88 meters) through a Billboard	20	Bronze
Fast Forward	Triggered a speed camera at over 200mph (321.97km/h)	20	Bronze

ULTIMATE SPEED PACK DLC

NAME	GOAL/REQUIREMENT	POINT VALUE	TROPHY VALUE
Unstoppable	Finish first in every race in the Ultimate Speed Pack (Single Player)	20	Bronze
Snake Bite	Shut down the Hennessey Venom GT Spyder (Single Player)	20	Bronze
Uncanny	Unlock 'Supersonic', 'Super Powered', 'Super Natural' and 'Super Freak' License Plates	20	Bronze
Sidekicked	Takedown an opponent with 'Ultimate Fan' as your License Plate (Multiplayer)	20	Bronze

TERMINAL VELOCITY PACK DLC

NAME	GOAL/REQUIREMENT	POINT VALUE	TROPHY VALUE
Velocity: Terminal 5	Drive all 5 Terminal Velocity Pack cars (Single Player)	20	Bronze
Velocity: First Class	Finish first in every race in the Terminal Velocity Pack (Single Player)	20	Bronze
Velocity: On Final Approach	Unlock either Jump Nitrous PRO or Drift Tires PRO (Multi)	20	Bronze
Velocity: Terminal Addiction	Unlock Ram Chassis, Drift Tires and Jump Nitrous for all 5 Terminal Velocity Pack cars (Multi)	20	Bronze

MOVIE LEGENDS PACK DLC

NAME	GOAL/REQUIREMENT	POINT VALUE	TROPHY VALUE
Movies: It's a Wrap!	Finish first in every race in the Movie Legends Pack (Single Player)	20	Bronze
Movies: Gone!	Escape the cops in the Shelby GT500 (Single Player)	20	Bronze
Movies: Fan Friction	Get 5 Slam Takedowns while driving with the 'Movie Fan' License Plate (Multiplayer)	20	Bronze

NFS HEROES PACK DLC

NAME	GOAL/REQUIREMENT	POINT VALUE	TROPHY VALUE
NFS Hero: Need to Win	Finish first in every race in the NFS Heroes Pack (Single Player)	20	Bronze
NFS Hero: Six Underground	Unlock all 6 'Under' License Plates (Multiplayer)	20	Bronze
NFS Hero: Hero Worship	Win an event while driving with the 'NFS Hero' License Plate (Multiplayer)	20	Bronze

NEED FOR SPEED: PROSTREET

NINTENDO WII

$2,000

Select Career and then choose Code Entry. Enter 1MA9X99.

$4,000

Select Career and then choose Code Entry. Enter W2IOLL01.

$8,000

Select Career and then choose Code Entry. Enter L1IS97A1.

$10,000

Select Career and then choose Code Entry. Enter 1MI9K7E1.

$10,000

Select Career and then choose Code Entry. Enter CASHMONEY.

$10,000

Select Career and then choose Code Entry. Enter REGGAME.

AUDI TT

Select Career and then choose Code Entry. Enter ITSABOUTYOU.

CHEVELLE SS

Select Career and then choose Code Entry. Enter HORSEPOWER.

COKE ZERO GOLF GTI

Select Career and then choose Code Entry. Enter COKEZERO.

DODGE VIPER

Select Career and then choose Code Entry. Enter WORLDSLONGESTLASTING.

MITSUBISHI LANCER EVOLUTION

Select Career and then choose Code Entry. Enter MITSUBISHIGOFAR.

UNLOCK ALL BONUSES

Select Career and then choose Code Entry. Enter UNLOCKALLTHINGS.

CHEATS, ACHIEVEMENTS, AND TROPHIES

N

5 REPAIR MARKERS

Select Career and then choose Code Entry. Enter SAFETYNET.

ENERGIZER VINYL

Select Career and then choose Code Entry. Enter ENERGIZERLITHIUM.

CASTROL SYNTEC VINYL

Select Career and then choose Code Entry. Enter CASTROLSYNTEC. This also gives you $10,000.

NEED FOR SPEED: THE RUN

PLAYSTATION 3

AEM INTAKE CHALLENGE SERIES

Select Enter Cheat Code from Extras and enter aemintakes.

XBOX 360

AEM CHALLENGE

At the Extras menu enter aemintakes.

NEED FOR SPEED UNDERCOVER

PLAYSTATION 3

$10,000

Select Secret Codes from the Options menu and enter %%$3/.

DIE-CAST BMW M3 E92

Select Secret Codes from the Options menu and enter)B7@B=.

DIE-CAST LEXUS IS F

Select Secret Codes from the Options menu and enter 0;5M2;.

NEEDFORSPEED.COM LOTUS ELISE

Select Secret Codes from the Options menu and enter -KJ3=E.

DIE-CAST NISSAN 240SX (S13)

Select Secret Codes from the Options menu and enter ?P:COL.

DIE-CAST PORSCHE 911 TURBO

Select Secret Codes from the Options menu and enter >8P:I;.

SHELBY TERLINGUA

Select Secret Codes from the Options menu and enter NeedForSpeedShelbyTerlingua.

DIE-CAST VOLKSWAGEN R32

Select Secret Codes from the Options menu and enter!2ODBJ:.

XBOX 360

$10,000

Select Secret Codes from the Options menu and enter $EDSOC.

DIE-CAST BMW M3 E92

Select Secret Codes from the Options menu and enter)B7@B=.

DIE-CAST LEXUS IS F

Select Secret Codes from the Options menu and enter 0;5M2;.

NEEDFORSPEED.COM LOTUS ELISE

Select Secret Codes from the Options menu and enter -KJ3=E.

DIE-CAST NISSAN 240SX (S13)

Select Secret Codes from the Options menu and enter ?P:COL.

DIE-CAST PORSCHE 911 TURBO

Select Secret Codes from the Options menu and enter >8P:l;.

SHELBY TERLINGUA

Select Secret Codes from the Options menu and enter NeedForSpeedShelbyTerlingua.

DIE-CAST VOLKSWAGEN R32

Select Secret Codes from the Options menu and enter!2ODBJ:.

NERF: N-STRIKE

BLACK HEART VENGEANCE

Select Codes from the Main menu and enter BHDETA8.

CRUSHER SAD-G

Select Codes from the Main menu and enter CRUSH14.

FIREFLY ELITE

Select Codes from the Main menu and enter HELIOX6.

GOLIATHAN NITRO

Select Codes from the Main menu and enter FIERO2.

HABANERO

Select Codes from the Main menu and enter 24KGCON4.

HYDRA

Select Codes from the Main menu and enter HRANGEL3.

LONGSHOT STREET

Select Codes from the Main menu and enter LONGST5.

MAVERICK CRYSTAL

Select Codes from the Main menu and enter CRISTOL10.

MAVERICK MIDNIGHT

Select Codes from the Main menu and enter MAVMID7.

MERCURIO

Select Codes from the Main menu and enter RSMERC9.

SEMPER FIRE ULTRA

Select Codes from the Main menu and enter CROMO1.

SPARTAN NCS-12

Select Codes from the Main menu and enter THISIS12.

STAMPEDE

Select Codes from the Main menu and enter DOGIE15.

VULCAN MAGMA

Select Codes from the Main menu and enter MAGMA3.

NERF: N-STRIKE ELITE

Select Codebook and enter the following codes.

10 CANISTERS

Enter NERF.

UNLIMITED AMMO

Enter DART. This can be toggled on and off.

CERBERUS CS-12

Enter DUDE.

CRUSHER SAD-G

Enter RUSH.

GOLITHAN UB-1

Enter ROCK.

HAMMERHEAD GL-1
Enter PONG.

HYDRA SG-7
Enter WIDE.

ICARUS HM-7
Enter DOOM.

LONGSHOT CS-6
Enter IDOL.

LONGSTRIKE CS-6
Enter PING.

RECON CS-6
Enter DIRT.

SEMPERFIRE RF-100
Enter FLEX.

SPARTAN NCS-12
Enter ICON.

VULCAN EBF-25
Enter LOTS.

NEW SUPER MARIO BROS.

NINTENDO 3DS

PLAY AS LUIGI IN SINGLE-PLAYER MODE

At the Select a File screen, press and hold L + R while selecting a saved game.

SECRET CHALLENGE MODE

While on the map, pause the game and press L, R, L, R, X, X, Y, Y.

NEW SUPER MARIO BROS. U

NINTENDO WII U

PROPELLER HAT AND PENGUIN SUIT

After completing the game and unlocking Superstar Road the Propeller Hat and Penguin Suit power-ups become available from the Toad Houses there.

SAVE GAME AT ANY TIME

Finish Story Mode and "Quick-Save" will be replaced with "Save" in the pause menu.

VISIT TOAD HOUSES REPEATEDLY

Earn all five stars on your profile and you will be able to visit Toad Houses repeatedly.

FIREWORKS

If the last two digits on the timer match when the flagpole at the end of a level is touched fireworks will appear. You will also get an item depending on the number on the timer.

ITEM	TIMER
Fire Flower	33 or 44
Ice Flower	55
Star	88 or 99
Super Acorn	77
Super Mushroom	11 or 22
Tiny Mushroom	66

358

NFL BLITZ

Select Cheats from the Blitz Store to purchase the following cheats. They are entered with ●, ●, ●. Press these buttons until the three given icons are shown. The number indicates how many times each button is pressed. ● is the first number, ● the second, and ● is the third.

GAMEPLAY CHEATS

Buy these cheats to change the game to your advantage.

CHEAT	CODE
Tournament Mode	Goalpost, Goalpost, Goalpost (4 4 4)
Faster Passes	Helmet, NFL, NFL (5 1 1)
Speedster	Goalpost, NFL, EA Sports (4 1 0)
Fast Turbo Drain	Helmet, Headset, NFL (5 3 1)
More Fumbles	Helmet, Goalpost, NFL (5 4 1)
No First Downs	Goalpost, Headset, Goalpost (4 3 4)
No Fumbles	Helmet, EA Sports, Headset (5 0 3)
No Interceptions	Helmet, Helmet, EA Sports (5 5 0)
No Onside Kicks	Goalpost, Foam Finger, Foam Finger (4 2 2)
No Punting	Goalpost, Goalpost, EA Sports (4 4 0)
Power Defense	Goalpost, Whistle, Goalpost (4 8 4)
Power Offense	Helmet, Foam Finger, Helmet (5 2 5)
No Stepping out of Bounds	Helmet, EA Sports, EA Sports (5 0 0)
Unlimited Turbo	Helmet, NFL, Goalpost (5 1 4)

VISUAL CHEATS

Your team will get a Blitz makeover after you buy these cheats.

CHEAT	CODE
Big Head Player	Foam Finger, Helmet, EA Sports (2 5 0)
Big Head Team	Foam Finger, NFL, Foam Finger (2 1 2)
Tiny Head Team	Foam Finger, Goalpost, Headset (2 4 3)
Tiny Head Player	Headset, EA Sports, Foam Finger (3 0 2)
Huge Head Team	Headset, NFL, Foam Finger (3 1 2)
Huge Head Player	Foam Finger, EA Sports, NFL (2 0 1)
Super Ball Trail	EA Sports, NFL, Football (0 1 6)
Black & Red Ball	EA Sports, EA Sports, Foam Finger (0 0 2)
Camouflage Ball	EA Sports, EA Sports, Helmet (0 0 5)
Chrome Ball	EA Sports, Foam Finger, EA Sports (0 2 0)
Flames Ball	EA Sports, Goalpost, Foam Finger (0 4 2)
Ice Cream Ball	EA Sports, Foam Finger, Marker (0 2 7)
B-52 Ball	NFL, EA Sports, Goalpost (1 0 4)
Beachball	NFL, EA Sports, NFL (1 0 1)
Glow Ball	EA Sports, Marker, EA Sports (0 7 0)
Meat Ball	EA Sports, Football, EA Sports (0 6 0)
Pumpkin Ball	Whistle, Headset, NFL (8 3 1)
Soup Can Ball	Marker, NFL, EA Sports (7 1 0)
Blitz Team Ball	NFL, NFL, NFL (1 1 1)
USA Ball	Headset, NFL, Helmet (3 1 5)
Blitz Stadium	EA Sports, NFL, Goalpost (0 1 4)
Cardinals Stadium	EA Sports, Foam Finger, Foam Finger (0 2 2)
Falcons Stadium	EA Sports, Headset, EA Sports (0 3 0)
Ravens Stadium	EA Sports, Headset, Helmet (0 3 5)
Bills Stadium	EA Sports, Headset, Marker (0 3 7)
Panthers Stadium	EA Sports, Goalpost, Goalpost (0 4 4)
Bears Stadium	EA Sports, Goalpost, Football (0 4 6)

CHEAT	CODE
Bengals Stadium	EA Sports, Goalpost, Whistle (0 4 8)
Browns Stadium	EA Sports, Helmet, Headset (0 5 3)
Cowboys Stadium	EA Sports, Helmet, Helmet (0 5 5)
Broncos Stadium	EA Sports, EA Sports, Marker (0 0 7)
Lions Stadium	EA Sports, Helmet, Marker (0 5 7)
Packers Stadium	EA Sports, Football, Foam Finger (0 6 2)
Texans Stadium	EA Sports, Football, Goalpost (0 6 4)
Colts Stadium	EA Sports, Football, Football (0 6 6)
Jaguars Stadium	EA Sports, Marker, Foam Finger (0 7 2)
Chiefs Stadium	EA Sports, Whistle, EA Sports (0 8 0)
Dolphins Stadium	EA Sports, Marker, Marker (0 7 7)
Vikings Stadium	NFL, EA Sports, Football (1 0 6)
Patriots Stadium	NFL, NFL, Goalpost (1 1 4)
Saints Stadium	NFL, Foam Finger, Headset (1 2 3)
Giants Stadium	NFL, Headset, EA Sports (1 3 0)
Jets Stadium	NFL, EA Sports, Whistle (1 0 8)
Raiders Stadium	NFL, Foam Finger, Helmet (1 2 5)
Eagles Stadium	NFL, Headset, Headset (1 3 3)
Steelers Stadium	NFL, Headset, Helmet (1 3 5)
Chargers Stadium	NFL, Helmet, EA Sports (1 5 0)
Seahawks Stadium	Foam Finger, Foam Finger, EA Sports (2 2 0)
49ers Stadium	Foam Finger, NFL, EA Sports (2 1 0)
Rams Stadium	Foam Finger, Headset, EA Sports (2 3 0)
Bucs Stadium	Foam Finger, Goalpost, EA Sports (2 4 0)
Titans Stadium	Headset, EA Sports, Headset (3 0 3)
Redskins Stadium	Goalpost, EA Sports, NFL (4 0 1)
Day	EA Sports, Whistle, Foam Finger (0 8 2)
Twilight	NFL, NFL, Marker (1 1 7)
Night	NFL, Whistle, Marker (1 8 7)

SETTINGS CHEATS

Change certain game settings when you buy these cheats.

CHEAT	CODE
Hide Player Name	EA Sports, Foam Finger, Goalpost (0 2 4)
Extra Code Time	Helmet, Helmet, Helmet (5 5 5)
No Ball Target	EA Sports, Helmet, NFL (0 5 1)
Wide Camera	NFL, NFL, Foam Finger (1 1 2)
Show Field Goal Percentage	EA Sports, NFL, Foam Finger (0 1 2)
All-Time QB Coop	Headset, Headset, EA Sports (3 3 0)
All-Time WR Coop	EA Sports, Headset, Headset (0 3 3)
Icon Passing	Headset, Helmet, Headset (3 5 3)
No Player Icon	EA Sports, Goalpost, EA Sports (0 4 0)

FANTASY CHARACTERS

Buy these cheats to play as your favorite characters. Characters must be unlocked by defeating them in Blitz Gauntlet first.

UNLOCKABLE CHARACTERS

CHEAT	CODE
Bigfoot	Headset, Headset, Headset (3 3 3)
Bigfoot Team	Marker, EA Logo, EA Logo (7 0 0)
Cowboy	Headset, Foam Finger, Headset (3 2 3)
Cowboy Team	Goalpost, Marker, Goalpost (4 7 4)
Gladiator	Foam Finger, Whistle, Foam Finger (2 8 2)
Gladiator Team	Helmet, NFL, Marker (5 1 7)

CHEAT	CODE
Horse	NFL, Marker, NFL (1 7 1)
Horse Team	Foam Finger, Football, Foam Finger (2 6 2)
Hot Dog	NFL, Football, NFL (1 6 1)
Hot Dog Team	Foam Finger, Headset, Foam Finger (2 3 2)
Lion	Foam Finger, EA Sports, Foam Finger (2 0 2)
Lion Team	Headset, Goalpost, Headset (3 4 3)
Ninja	Foam Finger, Marker, Foam Finger (2 7 2)
Ninja Team	Football, NFL, Football (6 1 6)
Pirate	NFL, Foam Finger, NFL (1 2 1)
Pirate Team	Helmet, Headset, Helmet (5 3 5)

XBOX 360

Select Cheats from the Blitz Store to purchase the following cheats. They are entered with X, Y, and B. Press these buttons until the three given icons are shown. The number indicates how many times each button is pressed. X is the first number, Y the second, and B is the third.

GAMEPLAY CHEATS

Buy these cheats to change the game to your advantage.

CHEAT	CODE
Tournament Mode	Goalpost, Goalpost, Goalpost (4 4 4)
Faster Passes	Helmet, NFL, NFL (5 1 1)
Speedster	Goalpost, NFL, EA Sports (4 1 0)
Fast Turbo Drain	Helmet, Headset, NFL (5 3 1)
More Fumbles	Helmet, Goalpost, NFL (5 4 1)
No First Downs	Goalpost, Headset, Goalpost (4 3 4)
No Fumbles	Helmet, EA Sports, Headset (5 0 3)
No Interceptions	Helmet, Helmet, EA Sports (5 5 0)
No Onside Kicks	Goalpost, Foam Finger, Foam Finger (4 2 2)
No Punting	Goalpost, Goalpost, EA Sports (4 4 0)
Power Defense	Goalpost, Whistle, Goalpost (4 8 4)
Power Offense	Helmet, Foam Finger, Helmet (5 2 5)
No Stepping out of Bounds	Helmet, EA Sports, EA Sports (5 0 0)
Unlimited Turbo	Helmet, NFL, Goalpost (5 1 4)

VISUAL CHEATS

Your team will get a Blitz makeover after you buy these cheats.

CHEAT	CODE
Big Head Player	Foam Finger, Helmet, EA Sports (2 5 0)
Big Head Team	Foam Finger, NFL, Foam Finger (2 1 2)
Tiny Head Team	Foam Finger, Goalpost, Headset (2 4 3)
Tiny Head Player	Headset, EA Sports, Foam Finger (3 0 2)
Huge Head Team	Headset, NFL, Foam Finger (3 1 2)
Huge Head Player	Foam Finger, EA Sports, NFL (2 0 1)
Super Ball Trail	EA Sports, NFL, Football (0 1 6)
Black & Red Ball	EA Sports, EA Sports, Foam Finger (0 0 2)
Camouflage Ball	EA Sports, EA Sports, Helmet (0 0 5)
Chrome Ball	EA Sports, Foam Finger, EA Sports (0 2 0)
Flames Ball	EA Sports, Goalpost, Foam Finger (0 4 2)
Ice Cream Ball	EA Sports, Foam Finger, Marker (0 2 7)
B-52 Ball	NFL, EA Sports, Goalpost (1 0 4)
Beachball	NFL, EA Sports, NFL (1 0 1)
Glow Ball	EA Sports, Marker, EA Sports (0 7 0)
Meat Ball	EA Sports, Football, EA Sports (0 6 0)
Pumpkin Ball	Whistle, Headset, NFL (8 3 1)

CHEAT	CODE
Soup Can Ball	Marker, NFL, EA Sports (7 1 0)
Blitz Team Ball	NFL, NFL, NFL (1 1 1)
USA Ball	Headset, NFL, Helmet (3 1 5)
Blitz Stadium	EA Sports, NFL, Goalpost (0 1 4)
Cardinals Stadium	EA Sports, Foam Finger, Foam Finger (0 2 2)
Falcons Stadium	EA Sports, Headset, EA Sports (0 3 0)
Ravens Stadium	EA Sports, Headset, Helmet (0 3 5)
Bills Stadium	EA Sports, Headset, Marker (0 3 7)
Panthers Stadium	EA Sports, Goalpost, Goalpost (0 4 4)
Bears Stadium	EA Sports, Goalpost, Football (0 4 6)
Bengals Stadium	EA Sports, Goalpost, Whistle (0 4 8)
Browns Stadium	EA Sports, Helmet, Headset (0 5 3)
Cowboys Stadium	EA Sports, Helmet, Helmet (0 5 5)
Broncos Stadium	EA Sports, EA Sports, Marker (0 0 7)
Lions Stadium	EA Sports, Helmet, Marker (0 5 7)
Packers Stadium	EA Sports, Football, Foam Finger (0 6 2)
Texans Stadium	EA Sports, Football, Goalpost (0 6 4)
Colts Stadium	EA Sports, Football, Football (0 6 6)
Jaguars Stadium	EA Sports, Marker, Foam Finger (0 7 2)
Chiefs Stadium	EA Sports, Whistle, EA Sports (0 8 0)
Dolphins Stadium	EA Sports, Marker, Marker (0 7 7)
Vikings Stadium	NFL, EA Sports, Football (1 0 6)
Patriots Stadium	NFL, NFL, Goalpost (1 1 4)
Saints Stadium	NFL, Foam Finger, Headset (1 2 3)
Giants Stadium	NFL, Headset, EA Sports (1 3 0)
Jets Stadium	NFL, EA Sports, Whistle (1 0 8)
Raiders Stadium	NFL, Foam Finger, Helmet (1 2 5)
Eagles Stadium	NFL, Headset, Headset (1 3 3)
Steelers Stadium	NFL, Headset, Helmet (1 3 5)
Chargers Stadium	NFL, Helmet, EA Sports (1 5 0)
Seahawks Stadium	Foam Finger, Foam Finger, EA Sports (2 2 0)
49ers Stadium	Foam Finger, NFL, EA Sports (2 1 0)
Rams Stadium	Foam Finger, Headset, EA Sports (2 3 0)
Bucs Stadium	Foam Finger, Goalpost, EA Sports (2 4 0)
Titans Stadium	Headset, EA Sports, Headset (3 0 3)
Redskins Stadium	Goalpost, EA Sports, NFL (4 0 1)
Day	EA Sports, Whistle, Foam Finger (0 8 2)
Twilight	NFL, NFL, Marker (1 1 7)
Night	NFL, Whistle, Marker (1 8 7)

SETTINGS CHEATS

Change certain game settings when you buy these cheats.

CHEAT	CODE
Hide Player Name	EA Sports, Foam Finger, Goalpost (0 2 4)
Extra Code Time	Helmet, Helmet, Helmet (5 5 5)
No Ball Target	EA Sports, Helmet, NFL (0 5 1)
Wide Camera	NFL, NFL, Foam Finger (1 1 2)
Show Field Goal Percentage	EA Sports, NFL, Foam Finger (0 1 2)

CHEAT	CODE
All-Time QB Coop	Headset, Headset, EA Sports (3 3 0)
All-Time WR Coop	EA Sports, Headset, Headset (0 3 3)
Icon Passing	Headset, Helmet, Headset (3 5 3)
No Player Icon	EA Sports, Goalpost, EA Sports (0 4 0)

FANTASY CHARACTERS

Buy these cheats to play as your favorite characters. Characters must be unlocked by defeating them in Blitz Gauntlet first.

UNLOCKABLE CHARACTERS

CHEAT	CODE
Bigfoot	Headset, Headset, Headset (3 3 3)
Bigfoot Team	Marker, EA Logo, EA Logo (7 0 0)
Cowboy	Headset, Foam Finger, Headset (3 2 3)
Cowboy Team	Goalpost, Marker, Goalpost (4 7 4)
Gladiator	Foam Finger, Whistle, Foam Finger (2 8 2)
Gladiator Team	Helmet, NFL, Marker (5 1 7)
Horse	NFL, Marker, NFL (1 7 1)
Horse Team	Foam Finger, Football, Foam Finger (2 6 2)
Hot Dog	NFL, Football, NFL (1 6 1)
Hot Dog Team	Foam Finger, Headset, Foam Finger (2 3 2)
Lion	Foam Finger, EA Sports, Foam Finger (2 0 2)
Lion Team	Headset, Goalpost, Headset (3 4 3)
Ninja	Foam Finger, Marker, Foam Finger (2 7 2)
Ninja Team	Football, NFL, Football (6 1 6)
Pirate	NFL, Foam Finger, NFL (1 2 1)
Pirate Team	Helmet, Headset, Helmet (5 3 5)

NHL 12

3RD JERSEYS

Select NHL 12 Code Entry from My NHL 12 and enter 2wg3gap9mvrth6kq. This unlocks uniforms for Florida, New York Islanders, Ottawa, and Toronto.

NI NO KUNI: WRATH OF THE WHITE WITCH

TROPHIES

NAME	GOAL/REQUIREMENT	TROPHY VALUE
Boy Scout	Awarded for running 15 different errands.	Bronze
Familiarizer	Awarded for taming 20 different species.	Bronze
Glim Reaper	Awarded for gathering 2,000 glims.	Bronze
Globetrotter	Awarded for setting foot in all secluded regions.	Silver
Guildering the Lily	Awarded for amassing a fortune of half a million guilders.	Silver
Gunslinger	Awarded for learning all of Swaine's trickshots.	Bronze
Little Battler Experience	Awarded for winning 1,000 battles.	Silver
Magic Master	Awarded for learning all of Oliver's spells.	Silver
Man of Steal	Awarded for successfully stealing 50 times.	Bronze
New Sheriff in Town	Awarded for completing 10 different bounty hunts.	Bronze
Out of this World	Awarded for casting Gateway and traveling to another world.	Bronze
Overfamiliar	Awarded for maximizing a familiar's familiarity.	Bronze

NAME	GOAL/REQUIREMENT	TROPHY VALUE
Pedigree Breeder	Awarded for training a familiar to its full potential.	Bronze
Pop Pop Fizz Fizz	Awarded for alchemizing 10 different items.	Bronze
Prima Donna	Awarded for learning all of Esther's songs.	Bronze
Raising the Stakes	Awarded for collecting your first prize at the casino.	Bronze
Treasure Hunter	Awarded for finding all hidden treasure chests.	Silver
Viva the Evolution!	Awarded for managing 10 metamorphoses.	Bronze

SECRET TROPHIES

NAME	GOAL/REQUIREMENT	TROPHY VALUE
A Tonic for the Djinn	Awarded for defeating the Dark Djinn.	Bronze
Anchors Aweigh	Awarded for obtaining the Sea Cow.	Bronze
Bounty Hunter	Awarded for completing 40 different bounty hunts.	Silver
Council Trouncer	Awarded for freeing the other world from the clutches of the Zodiarchy.	Silver
En Guardian!	Awarded for defeating the Guardian of the Woods and bringing him back to his senses.	Bronze
Familiarologist	Awarded for taming 250 different species.	Gold
Fly the Friendlier Skies	Awarded for befriending Tengri.	Bronze
High Roller	Awarded for collecting all of the tickets for the Mem-O-Vision by winning big at the casino.	Silver
Humanitarian of the Year	Awarded for running 60 different errands.	Silver
King of the World	Awarded for defeating the Guardian of Worlds.	Gold
Mad Scientist	Awarded for alchemizing 120 different items.	Gold
Solosseum Slugger	Awarded for winning your first bout in the Solosseum Series.	Bronze
Solosseum Supremo	Awarded for becoming the champion of the Solosseum Series.	Gold
Super Hero	Awarded for collecting all the merit awards.	Gold
Wizardry Whiz	Awarded for becoming a master magician. Congratulations! You truly are a whiz at wizardry!	Platinum
Wonder Wand	Awarded for restoring the legendary wand Mornstar to its former glory.	Bronze

NICKTOONS: ATTACK OF THE TOYBOTS

NINTENDO WII

DAMAGE BOOST

Select Cheats from the Extras menu. Choose Enter Cheat Code and enter 456645.

INVULNERABILITY

Select Cheats from the Extras menu. Choose Enter Cheat Code and enter 313456.

UNLOCK EXO-HUGGLES 9000

Select Cheats from the Extras menu. Choose Enter Cheat Code and enter 691427.

UNLOCK MR. HUGGLES

Select Cheats from the Extras menu. Choose Enter Cheat Code and enter 654168.

UNLIMITED LOBBER GOO

Select Cheats from the Extras menu. Choose Enter Cheat Code and enter 118147.

UNLIMITED SCATTER GOO

Select Cheats from the Extras menu. Choose Enter Cheat Code and enter 971238.

UNLIMITED SPLITTER GOO

Select Cheats from the Extras menu. Choose Enter Cheat Code and enter 854511.

DANNY PHANTOM 2

Select Unlock Code from the Options and enter Tak, Jimmy, Zim, El Tigre.

SPONGEBOB 2

Select Unlock Code from the Options and enter Patrick, Jenny, Timmy, Tak.

NINJA GAIDEN 3

ACHIEVEMENTS & TROPHIES

NAME	GOAL/REQUIREMENT	POINT VALUE	TROPHY VALUE
Falcon Dive	Learn the Falcon Dive.	10	Bronze
Sliding	Learn how to slide.	10	Bronze
Kunai Climb	Learn the Kunai Climb.	10	Bronze
Wall Run	Learn the Wall Run.	10	Bronze
Flying Bird Flip	Learn the Flying Bird Flip.	10	Bronze
Rope Crossing	Learn how to cross a rope.	10	Bronze
Izuna Drop	Learn the Izuna Drop.	10	Bronze
Ultimate Technique	Learn the Ultimate Technique.	10	Bronze
Steel on Bone	Cut down 100 enemies with Steel on Bone attacks.	10	Bronze
I Got Your Back	Play a Co-op Ninja Trial with a partner.	10	Bronze
Initiation	Play a Clan Battle.	10	Bronze
Teamwork	Win 10 team battles.	10	Bronze
One Against the World	Win a battle royale match.	10	Bronze
Shady	Perform a betrayal.	10	Bronze
Sneaky	Perform a ghost kill.	10	Bronze
An Honorable Death	Perform harakiri.	10	Bronze
Snowman	Play the Snowfield stage 10 times.	10	Bronze
Guardian of the Village	Play the Hidden Village stage 10 times.	10	Bronze
Observer	Play the Watchtower stage 10 times.	10	Bronze
The Spice of Life	Get 10 customization parts.	10	Bronze
Walking Dictionary	Get 100 kanji.	50	Silver

SECRET ACHIEVEMENTS & TROPHIES

NAME	GOAL/REQUIREMENT	POINT VALUE	TROPHY VALUE
Inferno	Learned Ninpo.	10	Bronze
Steel on Steel	Destroyed the Steel Spider.	10	Bronze
The Grip of Murder	Finish Day 1.	10	Bronze
Mind the Gap	Escaped from the monorail.	10	Bronze
Bumpy Ride	Finish Day 2.	10	Bronze
Beyond the Flames	Made it through the fire.	15	Bronze
Antediluvian Slumber	Finish Day 3.	15	Bronze
Abysmal Creations	Escaped from the Chimera Disposal Facility.	15	Bronze
The Great Escape	Finish Day 4.	15	Bronze
The Acolyte	Successfully responded to Sanji's ambush.	15	Bronze
The Karma of a Shinobi	Finish Day 5.	15	Bronze
Evil Twin	Defeated the Epigonos.	15	Bronze

NAME	GOAL/REQUIREMENT	POINT VALUE	TROPHY VALUE
Waiting	Finish Day 6.	15	Bronze
Ahab	Land on the Black Narwhal.	15	Bronze
Advent of the Goddess	Finish Day 7.	15	Bronze
Brothers	Defeated Cliff.	15	Bronze
Atonement	Defeated Theodore.	15	Bronze
Hero	Cleared the game on Hero.	50	Silver
Shinobi	Cleared the game on Normal.	50	Silver
Mentor	Cleared the game on Hard.	60	Silver
Master Ninja	Cleared the game on Master Ninja.	100	Gold
Initiate	Cleared 10 Acolyte Trials.	10	Bronze
Veteran	Cleared 10 Mentor Trials.	10	Bronze
Prestige	Cleared 5 Leader Trials.	10	Bronze
Overlord	Cleared 5 Master Ninja Trials.	50	Silver
Ultimate Ninja	Cleared 3 Ultimate Ninja Trials.	100	Gold
Master of the Katana	Raised the katana to level 10.	15	Bronze
Hayabusa Style Grand Master	Reached level 50.	15	Bronze
Lone Ninja	Cleared 10 Solo Ninja Trials.	50	Silver

NINJA PACK 1

SECRET ACHIEVEMENTS & TROPHIES

NAME	GOAL/REQUIREMENT	POINT VALUE	TROPHY VALUE
Bloodied Talons	Defeat 100 opponents in Clan Battles with the Metal Claws.	15	Bronze
Warrior	Clear all Ninja Trials included in Ninja Pack 1.	45	Silver

NINJA PACK 2

SECRET ACHIEVEMENTS & TROPHIES

NAME	GOAL/REQUIREMENT	POINT VALUE	TROPHY VALUE
Grim Reaper	Defeat 100 opponents in Clan Battles with the Great Scythe.	15	Bronze
Sage	Clear all Ninja Trials included in Ninja Pack 2.	45	Silver

NINJA GAIDEN 3: RAZOR'S EDGE

NINTENDO WII U/XBOX 360/PS3

UNLOCKABLE COSTUMES

COSTUME	REQUIREMENT
Kasumi's 3rd Costume	Complete 25 Ninja Trials
Kasumi's 4th Costume	Complete 50 Ninja Trials
Momiji's 3rd Costume	Complete 25 Ninja Trials with Momiji
Momiji's 4th Costume	Complete 50 Ninja Trials with Momiji
Ryu & Ayane's 3rd Costume	Collect all 50 Scarabs
Ryu & Ayane's 4th Costume	Collect all 10 Crystal Skulls

ACHIEVEMENTS & TROPHIES

NAME	GOAL/REQUIREMENT	POINT VALUE	TROPHY VALUE
Falcon Dive	Successfully mastered the Falcon Dive technique.	5	Bronze
Sliding	Successfully mastered the Sliding technique.	5	Bronze
Flying Bird Flip	Successfully mastered the Flying Bird Flip technique.	5	Bronze
Kunai Climb	Successfully mastered the Kunai Climb technique.	5	Bronze
Wall Run	Successfully mastered the Wall Run technique.	5	Bronze
Izuna Drop	Successfully mastered the Izuna Drop technique.	5	Bronze
Obliteration Technique	Successfully mastered the Obliteration Technique.	5	Bronze
Ultimate Technique	Successfully mastered an Ultimate Technique.	5	Bronze
Ninpo Master	Successfully mastered a Ninpo spell.	5	Bronze
Steel on Bone	Successfully mastered the Steel on Bone technique.	5	Bronze
Bloody Rage	Reached the maximum karma multiplier during Bloody Rage.	10	Bronze
Feat of a Hundred Slashes	Achieved a 100-hit combo.	20	Bronze
Katana Master	Defeated 1,000 enemies with the Katana.	15	Bronze
Dual Sword Master	Defeated 1,000 enemies with Dual Swords.	15	Bronze
Falcon's Talons Master	Defeated 1,000 enemies with the Falcon's Talons.	15	Bronze
Lunar Staff Master	Defeated 1,000 enemies with the Lunar Staff.	15	Bronze
Kusari-gama Master	Defeated 1,000 enemies with the Kusari-gama.	15	Bronze
Eclipse Scythe Master	Defeated 1,000 enemies with the Eclipse Scythe.	15	Bronze
Fuma Kodachi Master	Defeated 1,000 enemies with the Fuma Kodachi.	15	Bronze
Heavenly Dragon Master	Defeated 1,000 enemies with the Heavenly Dragon.	15	Bronze
Shrouded Moon Master	Defeated 1000 enemies with the Shrouded Moon.	15	Bronze
Crystal Skull	Cleared all Tests of Valor.	50	Silver
Golden Scarab	Obtained all Golden Scarabs.	30	Silver
Kunoichi	Cleared all chapters with Ayane, Momiji, and Kasumi.	30	Bronze
You Got Skills	Unlocked all Ninja Skills for Hayabusa, Ayane, Momiji, Kasumi, and Unknown Ninja.	30	Silver
Dark Savior	Saved an ally.	10	Bronze
I Got Your Back	Completed a Co-op Ninjua Trial.	10	Bronze
Initiation	Played a Clan Battle.	5	Bronze
Teamwork	Won a Clan Battle.	15	Bronze
Master of the Secret Arts	Obtained all trophies.	—	Platinum

CHEATS, ACHIEVEMENTS, AND TROPHIES

SECRET ACHIEVEMENTS & TROPHIES

NAME	GOAL/REQUIREMENT	POINT VALUE	TROPHY VALUE
Steel on Steel	Destroyed the Spider Tank.	10	Bronze
The Grip of Murder	Finished Day 1.	10	Bronze
Bumpy Ride	Finished Day 2.	10	Bronze
Cooperation	Finished Day 2 – Ayane.	10	Bronze
Antediluvian Slumber	Finished Day 3.	15	Bronze
The Great Escape	Finished Day 4.	15	Bronze
The Karma of a Shinobi	Finished Day 5.	15	Bronze
Waiting	Finished Day 6.	15	Bronze
On Your Own	Finished Day 6 – Ayane.	10	Bronze
Advent of the Goddess	Finished Day 7.	15	Bronze
Shinobi	Cleared the game on Normal difficulty.	30	Bronze
Mentor	Cleared the game on Hard difficulty.	50	Silver
Master Ninja	Cleared the game on Master Ninja difficulty.	75	Gold
Ultimate Ninja	Cleared the game on Ultimate Ninja difficulty.	100	Gold
Hayabusa Style Grand Master	Reached Level 50.	15	Bronze
Lone Ninja	Cleared 10 Solo Trials.	30	Bronze
Initiate	Cleared 10 Acolyte Trials.	10	Bronze
Veteran	Cleared 10 Mentor Trials.	10	Bronze
Prestige	Cleared 5 Leader Trials.	10	Bronze
Overlord	Cleared 5 Master Ninja Trials.	50	Silver
Ultimate	Cleared 3 Ultimate Ninja Trials.	100	Gold

NINJA GAIDEN SIGMA

PLAYSTATION 3

5 EXTRA MISSIONS IN MISSION MODE.
At the mission mode screen, press Up, Down, Left, Down, Right, Up, ●.

NINJA GAIDEN SIGMA PLUS

NINTENDO 3DS

NINJA DOG DIFFICULTY
Die 3 times on Normal difficulty.

VERY HARD DIFFICULTY
Complete game on Hard.

MASTER NINJA DIFFICULTY
Complete game on Very Hard.

FORMAL ATTIRE (RACHEL)
Clear the game on Normal

BIKER (RACHEL)
Clear the game on Hard

LEGENDARY NINJA (RYU)
Clear the game on Normal

DOPPELGANGER (RYU)
Clear the game on Hard

THE GRIP OF MURDER (RYU)
Clear the game on Very Hard.

NINJA GAIDEN SIGMA PLUS 2

NINJA RACE MODE

Finish Chapter 1 in Story Mode in any difficulty to unlock Ninja Race mode.

TURBO MODE

To unlock Turbo Mode in Tag Missions, pass all 5 checkpoints in Ninja Race 01 and defeat both bosses.

UNLOCKABLE COSTUMES

COSTUME	REQUIREMENT
Momiji's Dynasty Warrior Costume	Complete 10 chapter challenges with a Master Ninja Ranking.
Momiji's Shrine Costume	Complete Momiji's Chapter 5.
Rachel's Blue Fiend Costume	Complete Rachel's Chapter 8.
Rachel's Dynasty Warrior Costume	Complete any 5 missions in Tag Mode.
Ryu's Dark Drakon Skin Costume	Complete 5 chapter challenges with a Master Ninja Ranking.
Ryu's Dynasty Warrior Costume	Complete the first 3 Ninja Races with Ryu.

NINTENDO LAND

DONKEY KONG'S CRASH COURSE—NEW COURSES

You can unlock additional courses by completing a Course twice. There are four total courses; complete Course 1, 2 and 3 twice each to unlock all of them.

LEGEND OF ZELDA BATTLE QUEST—EXTRA MISSIONS

Complete the first nine missions to unlock 5 additional missions.

LUIGI'S GHOST MANSION—EXTRA STAGES

Play 20 matches to unlock two additional stages.

LUIGI'S GHOST MANSION—MAGIC

When playing as the Ghost in Luigi's Mansion, hold L & R or ZL & ZR together at the same time to start charging. The ghost will become visible to all players and cannot move. Once the charge is complete, release the buttons and all the other players' flashlights' batteries will empty.

METROID BLAST—EXTRA MISSIONS

Complete the first 20 missions to unlock 10 additional missions.

PIKMIN ADVENTURE—ADDITIONAL ARENAS

Unlock the Warrior's Arena by playing five versus games in the Starter's Arena, then unlock the Hero's Arena by playing 5 games in the Warrior's Arena.

PIKMIN ADVENTURE—EXTRA MISSIONS

Complete the first 16 missions to unlock six additional missions.

STAMPS

Complete the following tasks to unlock stamps in every game.

STAMP	REQUIREMENT
Animal Crossing: Sweet Day—Double Takedown	Catch two animals at the same time.
Animal Crossing: Sweet Day—Serve and Protext x10	Win 10 times as the Gatekeepers.
Animal Crossing: Sweet Day—Sneaky Snatcher	Win without being caught once.
Animal Crossing: Sweet Day—So... Much... Candy...	Win with a head full of candy.
Animal Crossing: Sweet Day—Tackle Takedown	Perform a tackle.

STAMP	REQUIREMENT
Balloon Trip Breeze—30 Birds Down	Defeat 30 balloon birds.
Balloon Trip Breeze—Almost Fish Food	Escape from the fish.
Balloon Trip Breeze—Flawless Flight	Complete a perfect journey—don't use Wii Remote Assist and collect all balloons.
Balloon Trip Breeze—Island Hopper	Visit all islands.
Balloon Trip Breeze—Special Delivery	Complete two successful package deliveries.
Captain Falcon's Twister Race—4-Star Racer	Acquire four star items in one race.
Captain Falcon's Twister Race—5-Mistake Limit	Reach the goal with less than five mistakes.
Captain Falcon's Twister Race—Checkered Flag	Pass all areas.
Captain Falcon's Twister Race—Hang Time	First jump.
Captain Falcon's Twister Race—Racing Perfection	Complete a perfect run with no crashes. (No Assist Play allowed.)
Donkey Kong's Crash Course—Cutting Corners	Execute a shortcut.
Donkey Kong's Crash Course—Double Damsel Rescue	Save Pauline twice.
Donkey Kong's Crash Course—Perfect Run	Complete a perfect run. (No Assist Play allowed.)
Donkey Kong's Crash Course—Perfect Through Area 2	Get through area 2 with now mistakes.
Donkey Kong's Crash Course—Skip 30 Bananas	Leave 30 bananas behind.
Luigi's Ghost Mansion—Back from the Brink	Win as the Ghost with only a sliver of health left.
Luigi's Ghost Mansion—Battery Free Victory	Win without picking up any Batteries.
Luigi's Ghost Mansion—Ghostly Good Night	Win 10 times as the Ghost.
Luigi's Ghost Mansion—Magical Win	Win using magic.
Luigi's Ghost Mansion—Untouchable Roof Wraith	Win on Monita's Rooftop without taking any damage.
Mario Chase—1 Second on the Clock	Catch Mario with only one second remaining.
Mario Chase—10-Time Champion	Successfully escape as Mario 10 times.
Mario Chase—20-Second Catch	Catch Mario within the first 20 seconds of a match.
Mario Chase—Finish at the Start	Be sitting at the starting point as Mario when time runs out.
Mario Chase—Starless Getaway	Win a match as Mario without ever grabbing the Star.
Metroid Blast—Assault Mode—100 Enemies Down	Defeat 100 enemies total.
Metroid Blast—Assault Mode—Boss Blaster	Defeat the final boss.
Metroid Blast—Assault Mode—In the Belly of the Beast	Get inside a huge enemy's body.
Metroid Blast—Assault Mode—Master Bounty Hunter	Finish all missions, including Extra missions.
Metroid Blast—Assault Mode—Mission Accomplished	Earn Master Rank on all missions.
Metroid Blast—Ground Combat—10-Hit Hunter	Achieve 10 hits in a single match.
Metroid Blast—Ground Combat—100 Token Drop	Drop 100 Tokens in a single match.
Metroid Blast—Ground Combat—Max Token Victory	Win with 99 Tokens.
Metroid Blast—Ground Combat—Perfect Accuracy	Win with a 100% hit percentage.
Metroid Blast—Ground Combat—Thanks for the Tanks	Collect all Token Tanks in a single match.

STAMP	REQUIREMENT
Metroid Blast—Surface to Air—Free-Fall Finisher	Land the finishing blow to the Gunship while in free fall.
Metroid Blast—Surface to Air—Gunship Accuracy 100%	Win as the Gunship with 100% hit percentage.
Metroid Blast—Surface to Air—Gunship Bomber	Deal damage to the Gunship with a Charge Bomb.
Metroid Blast—Surface to Air—Last-Second Blast	Land the finishing blow with 1 second on the clock.
Metroid Blast—Surface to Air—Missile Strike	Land a direct blow on a Samus character with the Charge Missile.
Octopus Dance—3 Inky Moves	Perform 3 successful beats after being inked.
Octopus Dance—Flawless Fifty	Achieve 50 continuous perfects.
Octopus Dance—Perfect Perfect	Complete continuous perfects.
Octopus Dance—Perfect Streak x10	Perform 10 perfects in a row.
Octopus Dance—That's a Wrap	Clear the Extra Stage.
Pikmin Adventure—Challenge Mode—AI Mii Protector	Clear a Challenge stage without your AI controlled ally taking any damage.
Pikmin Adventure—Challenge Mode—Eyes of the Bulblord	Destroy the Bulblord's Eyes during his boss fight.
Pikmin Adventure—Challenge Mode—First Mastery	Master your first Challenge stage.
Pikmin Adventure—Challenge Mode—Great Explorer	Clear all challenge stages.
Pikmin Adventure—Challenge Mode—Master Explorer	Earn Master Completion on all Challenge stages: finish within the time limit and lose no hearts.
Pikmin Adventure—Versus Mode—Candy from a Pikmin	Make Mii Pikmin drop at least 10 candies in 15 attacks.
Pikmin Adventure—Versus Mode—Clobber Olimar	Land 10 blows on Olimar with a Mii Pikmin.
Pikmin Adventure—Versus Mode—Incredible Comeback	Achieve a miraculous comeback from a 30 candy deficit.
Pikmin Adventure—Versus Mode—Pacifist Victory	Win without attacking any opponents.
Pikmin Adventure—Versus Mode—Rock Your Foes x5	Hit opponents with a Rock 5 times in a single match.
Takamaru's Ninja Castle—10-Star Defense	Deflect 10 Throwing Stars.
Takamaru's Ninja Castle—First 100 Down	100 up, 100 down.
Takamaru's Ninja Castle—Princess Rescue	Rescue Princess Monita.
Takamaru's Ninja Castle—Unstoppable	Flawless victory: All enemies must be defeated in the Extra Stages and you cannot take any damage.
The Legend of Zelda: Battle Quest—Main Quest—1,000 Rupees	Collect 1,000 Rupees total.
The Legend of Zelda: Battle Quest—Main Quest—100 Rupees	Collect 100 Rupees total.
The Legend of Zelda: Battle Quest—Main Quest—Legendary Hero	Master all quests.
The Legend of Zelda: Battle Quest—Main Quest—Quest Master	Complete all quests.
The Legend of Zelda: Battle Quest—Main Quest—Triforce Collector	Finish all nine quests and claim the Triforces.
The Legend of Zelda: Battle Quest—Time Attack—Advanced: Finish Within 50 Seconds	Complete the final Time Trial stage in under 50 seconds.
The Legend of Zelda: Battle Quest—Time Attack—Beginner: Finish Within 50 Seconds	Complete the first Time Trial stage in under 50 seconds.
The Legend of Zelda: Battle Quest—Time Attack—Finish All Stages Within 45 Seconds	Complete all Time Trial stages in under 45 seconds.

STAMP	REQUIREMENT
The Legend of Zelda: Battle Quest—Time Attack—Intermediate: Finish Within 50 Seconds	Complete the second Time Trial stage in under 50 seconds.
The Legend of Zelda: Battle Quest—Time Attack—Speed Master	Earn Master Rank on all Time Attack stages.
Yoshi's Fruit Cart—3 Close Calls	Narrowly avoid three dangerous Obstacles.
Yoshi's Fruit Cart—5-Egg Exit	Reach a gate with five or more eggs in tow.
Yoshi's Fruit Cart—Gatekeeper	Clear all gates.
Yoshi's Fruit Cart—Gatemaster	Finish all 50 gates without using Assisted Play, Warp Gates or Check Marks.
Yoshi's Fruit Cart—Triple Bee Buffet	Use a Chili Plate to eat 3 bees.

STAR PLAYER

ATTRACTION	HOW TO UNLOCK
Animal Crossing: Sweet Day	Play 30 times.
Balloon Trip Breeze	Complete all standard days.
Captain Falcon's Twister Race	Complete all standard areas.
Donkey Kong's Crash Course	Complete all standard stages.
Legend of Zelda: Battle Quest	Complete all standard stages.
Luigi's Ghost Mansion	Play 30 times.
Mario Chase	Play 30 times.
Metroid Blast	Complete all standard stages.
Octopus Dance	Complete all standard stages.
Pikmin Adventure	Complete all standard stages.
Takamaru's Ninja Castle	Complete all standard scenes.
Yoshi's Fruit Cart	Complete all standard gates.

NINTENDOGS + CATS: FRENCH BULLDOG & NEW FRIENDS

NINTENDO 3DS

DOG BREEDS

Unlock the following breeds with the given amount of trainer points.

DOG BREED	TRAINER POINTS REQUIRED
Beagle	3400
Boxer	3400
Bull Terrier	600
Cocker Spaniel	2100
Golden Retriever	9800
Great Dane	5800
Jack Russell Terrier	7400
Labrador Retriever	5800
Maltese	3400
Miniature Dachshund	600
Miniature Pinscher	2100
Miniature Poodle	9800
Miniature Schnauzer	5800
Pembroke Welsh Corgi	2100
Pomeranian	5800
Pug	5800
Shiba Inu	9800
Shih Tzu	600

NINTENDOGS + CATS: GOLDEN RETRIEVER & NEW FRIENDS

DOG BREEDS

Unlock the following breeds with the given amount of trainer points.

DOG BREED	TRAINER POINTS REQUIRED
Bassett Hound	9800
Boxer	5800
Bull Terrier	3400
Cavalier King Charles Spaniel	5800
Chihuahua	600
Dalmatian	3400
French Bulldog	9800
German Shepherd	2100
Jack Russell Terrier	600
Labrador Retriever	3400
Miniature Poodle	9800
Miniature Schnauzer	2100
Pembroke Welsh Corgi	7400
Pomeranian	2100
Shetland Sheepdog	600
Shih Tzu	7400
Siberian Husky	5800
Yorkshire Terrier	7400

NINTENDOGS + CATS: TOY POODLE & NEW FRIENDS

DOG BREEDS

Unlock the following breeds with the given amount of trainer points.

DOG BREED	TRAINER POINTS REQUIRED
Basset Hound	3600
Beagle	3600
Cavalier King Charles	2000
Chihuahua	5800
Cocker Spaniel	3600
Dalmatian	7400
Daschund	5800
German Shepherd	7400
Great Dane	600
Husky	2000
Maltese	2000
Mini Pinscher	7400
Pug	600
Shetland	5800
Yorkshire	600

N

OKAMI HD

END GAME UNLOCKABLES

The ratings and items you find in the game will determine what extras you unlock.

UNLOCKABLE	REQUIREMENT
Art Gallery	Complete the game.
Invincibility	Find all 100 Stray Beads.
Jukebox	Complete the game.
Karmic Returner	Complete the game.
Karmic Transformer 1	Complete the game.
Karmic Transformer 2	Complete the game.
Karmic Transformer 3	S-Rating for "Deaths."
Karmic Transformer 4	S-Rating for "Enemies Defeated."
Karmic Transformer 5	S-Rating for "Money Gained."
Karmic Transformer 6	S-Rating for "Demon Fangs Found."
Karmic Transformer 7	S-Rating for "Praise Earned."
Karmic Transformer 8	S-Rating for "Praise Earned."
Karmic Transformer 9	S-Rating for "Praise Earned."
New Game+	Complete the game.
Secret Theater	Play the game for over 31 hours.
Stray Bead	Complete the game.

TROPHIES

NAME	GOAL/REQUIREMENT	TROPHY VALUE
All Creatures Great and Small	Complete your Animal Tome.	Bronze
Bakugami	Learn how to use Cherry Bomb.	Bronze
Barking Up the Cherry Tree	Earn a Cherry Tree rank for each item in the Total Results screen.	Gold
Diggin' It	Complete five digging mini games.	Bronze
Dog Eat Dog	Beat Hayabusa's turnip-digging record.	Bronze
Dog Gone Fast	Win the race against Kai.	Bronze
Dominate the Indomitable	Defeat Blight.	Bronze
Dragonian Dilemma	Meet Otohime.	Bronze
Eat My Flower Trail	Win the race against Ida and Hayate.	Bronze
Enemy in the Gates	Defeat enemies inside of a Devil Gate.	Bronze
Fox-Face	Defeat Evil Rao.	Bronze
Fox-Headed Wench	Defeat Ninetails.	Silver
From Imps to Demons	Complete your Bestiary.	Bronze
Gekigami	Learn how to use Thunderstorm.	Bronze
Give a Dog All the Bones	Complete your Treasure Tome.	Bronze
Grab Life by the Leash	Increase your Solar Energy, Ink Pot, and Astral Pouch levels to maximum capacity.	Bronze
Hasugami	Learn how to use Water Lily.	Bronze
Have Guides Will Travel	Complete your Travel Guide.	Bronze
Imp Exorcist	Defeat the imps that possessed Princess Fuse.	Bronze
Itegami	Learn how to use Blizzard.	Bronze
Kabegami	Learn how to use Catwalk.	Bronze
Kasugami	Learn how to use Veil of Mist.	Bronze
Kazegami	Learn how to use Galestorm.	Bronze
Leave No Chest Unopened	Collect all Stray Beads.	Gold

NAME	GOAL/REQUIREMENT	TROPHY VALUE
Lupine and Divine	Earn a Cherry Tree rank for each item in the Results screen.	Bronze
Moegami	Learn how to use Inferno.	Bronze
No Furball on the Menu	Make your way to shore without being swallowed by the Water Dragon.	Bronze
No More Fish in the Sea	Complete your Fish Tome.	Bronze
Nuregami	Learn how to use Watersprout.	Bronze
One Mean Dude	Defeat the Crimson Helm.	Bronze
Out of the Gate Swinging	Defeat all enemies at all three Devil Gate trial caves.	Silver
RIP Tobi	Win the final race against Tobi.	Bronze
Sakigami	Learn how to use Bloom.	Bronze
Sayonara	Board the Ark of Yamato.	Bronze
Serpent Breath	Defeat Orochi.	Silver
Sniff 'Em Out	Defeat all monsters on the Wanted List.	Silver
Tachigami	Learn how to use Power Slash.	Bronze
Teach an Old Dog New Tricks	Learn all god techniques to fill up your Technique Scroll.	Bronze
The Dark Lord	Defeat Yami.	Silver
To the Moon, Ammy!	Enter the Moon Cave.	Bronze
Top Dog	Acquire all trophies.	Platinum
True Serpent Breath	Defeat True Orochi.	Bronze
Tsutagami	Learn how to use Vine.	Bronze
Twin Birdbrains	Defeat the twin demons, Lechku and Nechku.	Bronze
Who Let the Dogs Out?	Defeat the Kusa 5.	Gold
Yomigami	Learn how to use Rejuvenation.	Bronze
Yumigami	Learn how to use Crescent.	Bronze

OMERTA: CITY OF GANGSTERS

XBOX 360

ACHIEVEMENTS

NAME	GOAL/REQUIREMENT	POINT VALUE
That's Got to Hurt	Inflicted 100 damage or more to an enemy with a single attack	20
Tactician	Won a combat encounter with 4 party members above 75% health	15
The Man with the Plan	Won a combat encounter with 4 party members at full health	35
Close and Personal	Won a combat encounter with 4 characters in your party wielding melee weapons	10
Spreading the Love	Hit 5 characters with an area attack	20
One Shot, One Kill	Killed an enemy at full health with a single attack	15
Last Man Standing	Won a combat encounter with three incapacitated gang members at the end	30
Lucky Rabbit's Foot	Hit with an attack that has 5% hit chance	20
Linxed	Missed with an attack that has 95% hit chance.	20
Three Birds with One Stone	Killed 3 enemies with a single attack	10
Fire in the Hole!	Hit an enemy with a grenade	25
Watch your Step!	Shoved an enemy within the area of a fire bomb	20
Home Run	Damaged 2 enemies with a single bat attack	15
Run, Coward!	Intimidated a panicked enemy	20

NAME	GOAL/REQUIREMENT	POINT VALUE
Back In Action	Bandaged an incapacitated character	10
Patched Up	Removed 2 negative conditions with First Aid	15
It's a Trap!	Damaged an enemy with a booby trap	15
Blood Red Eyes	Used Rage 3 times with the same character in a single battle	20
Knuckle Sandwich	Hit 3 different enemies in the same turn with knuckles	20
Slice and Dice	Hit an enemy with the Slice and Dice knife attacks in the same turn	10
Easy as One-Two	Killed 2 enemies in the same turn with a pistol	10
No Place to Hide	Destroyed 4 cover objects with a single shotgun attack	15
Do NOT Mess with Me!	Killed an enemy with a revolver retaliation shot	20
Shooting Fish in a Barrel	Hit 3 vulnerable enemies with a single Tommy Gun attack	20
Ruthless Efficiency	Had a building at 200% efficiency	10
Weapons Dealer	Stockpiled 200 Firearms	15
Money Launderer	Laundered $10,000 Dirty Money in a single mission	30
Hard Working	Completed 5 Jobs in a single mission	15
Go-To Man	Completed 15 Jobs in a single mission	25
Entrepreneur	Owned 10 businesses at the same time	20
An Offer You Can't Refuse	Bought out an independent business	10
Meet the Gang	Had a team of 6 gangsters in the campaign	15
Iron Fist	Gained 100 Feared Rating	15
Velvet Glove	Gained 100 Liked Rating	15
It's Getting Crowded Here	Unlocked 15 gang members	15
Scapegoat	Framed another criminal during a police investigation	20
This Ain't Your Daddy's Gun	Purchased a Unique Weapon in the Campaign	10
Weapons Collector	Purchased 13 unique Weapons in the Campaign	30
Firestarter	Burned 3 buildings in a single mission	20
Juggernaut	Had a gang member with 200 or more health.	20
Marathon Runner	Had a gang member with 20 or more Base Movement Points.	20
Nimble Fingers	Had a gang member with 16 or more Base Action Points	20
Go for the Eyes!	Had a gang member with 20 or more Critical Chance.	20
The Taste of Victory	Won a Competitive multiplayer mission.	30
Brothers in Arms	Won a Cooperative multiplayer mission.	30
Scarface	Won 25 multiplayer missions	50

SECRET ACHIEVEMENTS

NAME	GOAL/REQUIREMENT	POINT VALUE
The World's Playground	Completed the "Welcome to Atlantic City" mission	15
Capo	Completed Act 1	30
Capo Di Tutti Capi	Completed Act 2	30
Gone Clean	Finished the game	40

OPERATION FLASHPOINT: DRAGON RISING

AMBUSH BONUS MISSION

Select Cheats from the Options menu and enter AmbushU454.

CLOSE QUARTERS BONUS MISSION

Select Cheats from the Options menu and enter CloseQ8M3

COASTAL STRONGHOLD BONUS MISSION

Select Cheats from the Options menu and enter StrongM577

DEBRIS FIELD BONUS MISSION

Select Cheats from the Options menu and enter OFPWEB2

ENCAMPMENT BONUS MISSION

Select Cheats from the Options menu and enter OFPWEB1

NIGHT RAID BONUS MISSION

Select Cheats from the Options menu and enter RaidT18Z

THE ORANGE BOX

HALF-LIFE 2

The following codes work for Half-Life 2, Half-Life 2: Episode One, and Half-Life 2: Episode Two.

CHAPTER SELECT

While playing, press Left, Left, Left, Left, L1, Right, Right, Right, Right, R1. Pause the game and select New Game to skip to another chapter.

PORTAL

CHAPTER SELECT

While playing, press Left, Left, Left, Left, L1, Right, Right, Right, Right, R1. Pause the game and select New Game to skip to another chapter.

GET A BOX

While playing, press Down, ●, ✕, ●, ●, Down, ●, ✕, ●, ●.

ENERGY BALL

While playing, press Up, ●, ●, ●, ●, ●, ✕, ●, ●, ●, Up.

PORTAL PLACEMENT ANYWHERE

While playing, press ●, ✕, ●, ✕, ●, ●, ●, ✕, Left, Right.

PORTALGUN ID 0

While playing, press Up, Left, Down, Right, Up, Left, Down, Right, ●, ●.

PORTALGUN ID 1

While playing, press Up, Left, Down, Right, Up, Left, Down, Right, ●, ●.

PORTALGUN ID 2

While playing, press Up, Left, Down, Right, Up, Left, Down, Right, ✕, ✕.

PORTALGUN ID 3

While playing, press Up, Left, Down, Right, Up, Left, Down, Right, ●, ●.

UPGRADE PORTALGUN

While playing, press ●, ●, L1, R1, Left, Right, L1, R1, L2, R2.

RESTORE HEALTH (25 POINTS)

While playing, press Up, Up, Down, Down, Left, Right, Left, Right, ●, ⊗.

RESTORE AMMO FOR CURRENT WEAPON

While playing, press R1, ●, ●, ⊗, ●, R1, ●, ●, ⊗, ●, R1.

HALF-LIFE 2

The following codes work for Half-Life 2, Half-Life 2: Episode One, and Half-Life 2: Episode Two.

CHAPTER SELECT

While playing, press Left, Left, Left, Left, Left Bumper, Right, Right, Right, Right, Right Bumper. Pause the game and select New Game to skip to another chapter.

RESTORE HEALTH (25 POINTS)

While playing, press Up, Up, Down, Down, Left, Right, Left, Right, B, A.

RESTORE AMMO FOR CURRENT WEAPON

While playing, press Y, B, A, X, Right Bumper, Y, X, A, B, Right Bumper.

INVINCIBILITY

While playing, press Left Shoulder, Up, Right Shoulder, Up, Left Shoulder, Left Shoulder, Up, Right Shoulder, Right Shoulder, Up.

PORTAL

CHAPTER SELECT

While playing, press Left, Left, Left, Left, Left Bumper, Right, Right, Right, Right, Right Bumper. Pause the game and select New Game to skip to another chapter.

GET A BOX

While playing, press Down, B, A, B, Y, Down, B, A, B, Y.

ENERGY BALL

While playing, press Up, Y, Y, X, X, A, A, B, B, Up.

PORTAL PLACEMENT ANYWHERE

While playing, press Y, A, B, A, B, Y, Y, A, Left, Right.

PORTALGUN ID 0

While playing, press Up, Left, Down, Right, Up, Left, Down, Right, Y, Y.

PORTALGUN ID 1

While playing, press Up, Left, Down, Right, Up, Left, Down, Right, X, X.

PORTALGUN ID 2

While playing, press Up, Left, Down, Right, Up, Left, Down, Right, A, A.

PORTALGUN ID 3

While playing, press Up, Left, Down, Right, Up, Left, Down, Right, B, B.

UPGRADE PORTALGUN

While playing, press X, B, Left Bumper, Right Bumper, Left, Right, Left Bumper, Right Bumper, Left Trigger, Right Trigger.

ORCS MUST DIE!

AVATAR AWARDS

AVATAR	EARNED BY
OMD Logo Tee	Complete Act 1 of Orcs Must Die!
OMD Skull Hat	Kill 1,000 enemies in Orcs Must Dies!

THE OREGON TRAIL

HEIRLOOMS

HEIRLOOMS	HOW TO OBTAIN
Banjo	Finish the Gold Rush storyline.
Birch Pole	Catch 60 pounds of fish in one day.
Bugle	Bring the piano as your heirloom and complete the journey to Oregon.
Doctor's Bag	Get to the end of the trail without losing any family members.
Evil Eye	Score more than 150,000 points in a chapter.
Fine Suit	Score more than 120,000 points in a chapter.
Fine Whip Heirloom	Complete a trail segment without hitting an obstacle.
Fur Hat	Finish the Three Brave Brothers storyline.
Henry Rifle	Finish the Stuck in the Middle storyline.
Horseshoe	Get robbed 10 total times in one trip down the trail.
Piano	Finish the Family Affair storyline.

PAPER MARIO: STICKER STAR

LUIGI LOCATIONS

In the background of certain levels you can spot Luigi who can be peeled off by Paperizing. Each time you peel him off, you'll unlock a newspaper article in Decalburg's Residential Area.

STAGE	LOCATION
World 1-6	On the bridge leading to the central tower, he'll be in the background.
World 2-5	On the 4th floor of the tower in a window on the far right end of the second outdoor walkway.
World 3-12	On a rock formation sticking out of the ocean. He's only visible from the pier.
World 4-5	Near the end of the chair lift after enemies stop attacking.
World 5-5	In the background to the left of the hot springs.

MUSEUM EXHIBITION ROOMS

ROOM	REQUIREMENT
Enemy Exhibition Room	Collect all 96 battle stickers.
Music Exhibition Room	Collect all 64 thing stickers.

SUPER FLAG ACHIEVEMENTS & TROPHIES

Different achievements can be earned at any time. You'll find the Super Flags, indicating your progress, by checking the Super Flags in the Sticker Fest area of Decalburg.

FLAG	REQUIREMENT
Flag #1	Find every HP-Up Heart.
Flag #2	Collect every sticker type.
Flag #3	Make all secret doors appear.
Flag #4	Collect all Comet Pieces.
Flag #5	Spend 10,000 Coins at shops.
Flag #6	Achieve a Perfect Bonus in 500 or more battles.
Flag #7	Perform 1,000 "Excellent" Action Commands in battle.
Flag #8	Match three symbols on the Battle Spinner slots 50 times.

WIGGLER DIARY ENTRIES

When Wiggler segments are following you around World 3, you can unlock special Diary Entries by taking them to specific locations.

STAGE	REQUIREMENT
Surfshine Harbor	Obtained automatically.
World 3-2	Lead a segment to the dandelion in the area before the Comet Piece then walk through it.
World 3-6	Lead a segment to the overlook to the left of the shop.
World 3-8	Lead a segment to the poisoned hot springs.
World 3-10	Replay the game show while leading a segment.

MEGAFLASH STICKER LOCATIONS

These powerful stickers can only be found in certain locations and can be obtained at any time.

STICKER	LOCATION
Megaflash Baahammer	World 5-4: On the third floor through a warp pipe hidden to the right of the moving platforms.
Megaflash Burnhammer	World 5-5: In the first area, in a secret room behind a rock near the entrance to the second area.
Megaflash Chillhammer	World 4-6: On a platform in the second minecart area that requires you to Paperize the rail to reach.
Megaflash Clone Jump	World 5-6: On the third floor, pound the stake furthest to the right.
Megaflash Eekhammer	World 5-4: At the beginning of the level release the raft by hitting the stake with the hammer then ride it to the right.
Megaflash Hammer	World 2-2: Behind a secret panel below the balcony in the room with the Hammer Bros.
Megaflash Hopslipper	World 5-4: In the same room as the Megaflash Baahammer.
Megaflash Hurlhammer #1	World 5-1: Behind the Hammer Bro in the area with the second red flower.
Megaflash Hurlhammer #2	World 5-4: In the same room as the Megaflash Baahammer.
Megaflash Infinijump	World 5-3: In a secret area to the right of the pillars in the room with the Comet Piece, accessible from the loop in the river.

STICKER	LOCATION
Megaflash Iron Jump	World 5-5: In the fifth area under the "X" at the top of the hill. Stand on it until a shadow appears then move out of the way.
Megaflash Jump #1	World 6-2: Through the secret door in the ship's cabin.
Megaflash Jump #2	Any World: Get an "Excellent" rating using the Fish Hook Thing Sticker.
Megaflash Line Jump	World 4-6: On a ledge below and to the right of the boss. Return after getting the Royal Sticker.
Megaflash Slaphammer	World 5-5: In the fourth area under the "X" on the ground closest to the entrance. Stand on it until a shadow appears then move out of the way.

PEGGLE: DUAL SHOT

NINTENDO 3DS

Q LEVEL 10

Send the trial game to another DS.

PERFECT DARK

XBOX 360

PERFECT DARK ZERO SAVE CHEATS

If you have a save from Perfect Dark Zero on your hard drive, you get the following: All Guns (Solo), Cloaking Device, Hurricane Fists, and Weapon Stash Radar.

PERSONA 4 GOLDEN

PLAYSTATION VITA

SECRET MIDNIGHT CHANNEL

Set the clock of your Vita to 12:00 A.M. and go to the TV Listing section. Select the blinking channel with the flashing lights to find a mini-game starring Teddie.

PES 2011

XBOX 360

ACHIEVEMENTS

NAME	GOAL/REQUIREMENT	POINT VALUE
First Glory	Awarded for your first win.	10
Perfect 10	Awarded for winning 10 consecutive matches.	25
Come Back Win	Awarded for your first Come Back Win.	15
Last Gasp Winner	Awarded for scoring the Winner in Extra Time.	10
World Traveller	A Title awarded for playing at all featured Stadiums. (Excludes ones created in Edit Mode.)	20
The Gentleman	Awarded for committing less than 1 Foul per match on average in your last 10 Matches.	20
Possession Play	Awarded for having a Possession Rate of 60% or higher in your last 10 Matches.	25
Hat-trick Hero	Awarded for scoring 5 hat-tricks.	35
Predatory Striker	Awarded for playing over 20 Matches, averaging 2 plus goals per Match in your last 10.	40

CHEATS, ACHIEVEMENTS, AND TROPHIES

P

NAME	GOAL/REQUIREMENT	POINT VALUE
Dead-ball Expert	Awarded for scoring 5 Direct Free-Kicks.	40
Long Ranger	Awarded for scoring from 35m out or more.	50
League Winner	Awarded for winning one of the top leagues in [Master League]	15
European Elite 16	Awarded for making the Knockout phase of the UEFA Champions League in [Master League] .	20
Kings of Europe	Awarded for winning the Master League UEFA Champions League.	30
The Invincibles	Awarded for an undefeated season in Master League winning League, Cup and UEFA Champions League.	90
No.1 Club	Awarded for topping the Team Ranking in Master League.	50
World Footballer of the Year	Awarded if a member of your team wins World Footballer of the Year in Master League.	70
10 years of Service	An award to honor 10 years of service in Master League.	50
The Debutant	Awarded for your First Professional Appearance in Become a Legend.	10
International Cup Debut	Awarded for your First Appearance in the Become a Legend International Cup.	15
International Cup MVP	Awarded for being named International Cup Player of the Tournament in Become a Legend.	30
The Journeyman	A title awarded for playing at 10 different clubs across 6 countries in Become a Legend.	40
The Super Hero	A title awarded for being named World Footballer of the Year in BECOME A LEGEND.	50
Mr. Consistency (Online)	Awarded for winning 75% of your Last 20 Ranked matches Online.	50
Made the Knockout phase	Awarded for making the Knockout phase of the UEFA Champions League.	40
European Champions	Awarded when you win the UEFA Champions League.	70
Kings of Latin America	A title awarded for winning the Copa Santander Libertadores.	80

PEWPEW 2

MOBILE

AMALGAM STAGE

Complete 50% of Campaign.

CHROMATIC CONFLICT

Complete 100% of Campaign.

PHANTASY STAR PORTABLE 2

PSP

VISION PHONE

Use the Vision Phone to enter the following passwords:

NAME	PASSWORD
Akahara Reisou	24932278
Akahara Reisou	24932279
Akahara Reisou	24932280

NAME	PASSWORD
Alis Landale Poster	41325468
Angry Marshmellow	32549410
Art Javelin	72401990
Blank Epoch	48168861
Blank Epoch	48168862
Bullet Lancer	32091120
Clarita Visas	29888026
Crutches	98443460
Edelweiss Figurine	54333358
Hanhei Tsunagin	41761771
Hanhei Tsunagin	41761772
Hatsune Miku's Leek Wand	12344321
Kansho Bayuka	46815464
Longinus Lance	32143166
Lovely Feathers	72401991
Lovely Feathers	72401992
Magical Princess	55687361
Magical Princess	55687362
Maverick Rifle	53962481
Miku Hatsune Dress	39395341
Miku Hatsune Dress	39395342
Miku's Leek Rifle	39395345
Miku's Leek Saber	39395343
Miku's T. Leek Sabers	39395344
Mr. Ekoeko Stick	55687362
Ogi's Head	74612418
Pizza Shack D Box	89747981
Platinum Tiger	32549412
Platinum Tiger	32549414
Platinum Tiger	32549411
Platinum Tiger	32549413
Plug Suit Asuka	34336181
Plug Suit Asuka	34336182
Plug Suit Rei	46211351
Plug Suit Rei	46211352
Plug Suit Shinji	15644322
Puyo Pop Fever Gun	54186516
Puyo Pop Fists	11293398
Scouring Bubble	33286491
Sonic Knuckles	34819852
Special Pizza Cutter	34162313
Telltale Hearts	48168860
The Rappy of Hope	54684698
Toop Nasur	30495153
Trauma Bandages	98443462
Trauma Bandages	98443464
Trauma Bandages	98443461
Trauma Bandages	98443463
True Hash	41761770

PHANTASY STAR ZERO

PASSWORD MACHINE

Check out the vending machine on the far right side of the sewers. Type in special passwords here to find free items.

ITEM	PASSWORD
Selvaria's Spear	5703-8252
Selvaria's Shield	4294-2273
Blade Cannon	7839-3594
Caduceus's Rod	5139-6877
Game Master (Ge-maga)	7162-5792
CONSOLES+ (Famitsu)	9185-6189
INGame: Greg&Kiri (Nintendo Dream)	5531-0215
Nintendo Power (Dengeki DS)	3171-0109
Puyo Soul	3470-1424
Taupy Soul	9475-6843
Lassie Soul	4775-7197

PHANTOM BREAKER: BATTLE GROUNDS

UNLOCK CHARACTERS

CHARACTER	REQUIREMENT
Cocoa	Complete the game on Easy or Normal.
Infinity	Complete the game on Normal.
L	Complete the game on Hard.
M	Complete the game on Easy or Normal.
Nagi	Complete the game on Normal.
White Mikoto	Complete the game on Hard.

PHINEAS AND FERB

STOP CANDACE

At the Title screen, press X, Y, L, R, Select.

DOUBLE SPEED

At the Title screen, press A, B, L, R, Select.

PHINEAS AND FERB: ACROSS THE 2ND DIMENSION

SKIN FOR AGENT P: PERRY THE PLATYBORG

During a game, press the Minus button to bring up the pause menu. Select Enter Code from Extras and enter BAB121.

PHINEAS AND FERB: ACROSS THE 2ND DIMENSION

SKIN FOR AGENT P: PERRY THE PLATTYBORG

Pause the game, select Enter Code from Extras, and enter ●, ⊗, ●, ●, ●, ●.

PHOTO DOJO

FAST FIGHTERS

At the Title screen, hold Select and choose Head into Battle. Continue to hold Select and choose Vs. Mode.

PINBALL FX 2

AVATAR AWARDS

AWARD	EARNED BY
Pinball FX 2 T-Shirt	Achieve 5,000 Wizard Score.
Pinball Sorceress Dress (Female)	Achieve 100,000 Wizard Score.
Pinball Wizard Robe (Male)	Achieve 100,000 Wizard Score.

CAPTAIN AMERICA TABLE

ACHIEVEMENTS

NAME	GOAL/REQUIREMENT	POINT VALUE
The Cosmic Cube	Use the Cosmic Cube to your advantage on Captain America (Single player only).	5
Reunited	Find each member of the Howling Commandos on Captain America (Single player only.)	15
Stars and Stripes	Defeat the Red Skull in the Final Clash mission series on Captain America (Single player only).	30

EARTH DEFENSE

ACHIEVEMENTS

NAME	GOAL/REQUIREMENT	POINT VALUE
Artilleryman	You are the master of cannons on Earth Defense table.	5
Decorated Veteran	You got all medals or 10 Friends beaten on the Earth Defense table. Congratulations!	30
Eternal Hope	Fought back an alien invasion on the Earth Defense table.	15

EPIC QUEST TABLE

ACHIEVEMENTS

NAME	GOAL/REQUIREMENT	POINT VALUE
Did It for the Dowry	Start the Princess multiball on Epic Quest by hitting the locker wheel 3 times (Single player only.)	5
I Killed Everything	Defeat all 12 monsters and their fire breathing boss on Epic Quest (Single player only.)	15
Epic Win	Loot an Epic Helm, Weapon, Shield and Armor across multiple games on Epic Quest (Single player only)	30

EXCALIBUR

ACHIEVEMENTS

NAME	GOAL/REQUIREMENT	POINT VALUE
Glorious victory	Invasion of Camelot has been repelled on the Excalibur table.	15
Legend	A Knight's tale has been completed on the Excalibur table.	30
Renowned knight	Renown secured or 3 Friends beaten on the Excalibur table.	5

FANTASTIC FOUR TABLE

ACHIEVEMENTS

NAME	GOAL/REQUIREMENT	POINT VALUE
Doomsday	Lock 4 balls with Doctor Doom and start the Four-ball mode on Fantastic Four. (Single player only)	5
Flame on!	Ignite the sign of the Fantastic Four with the Human Torch on Fantastic Four. (Single player only)	15
Power Cosmic	Complete all the main missions and save the Earth on Fantastic Four. (Single player only)	30

MARS

ACHIEVEMENTS

NAME	GOAL/REQUIREMENT	POINT VALUE
Shuttle Pilot	Collect five samples with the Space Shuttle magnetic drain on Mars! (Single player only.)	5
Archaeologist	Deactivate the Pyramid defense system on Mars! (Single player only.)	15
Ancient Martian Map	Get the ancient Martian map by completing the Final Mission on Mars! (Single player only.)	30

MARVEL PINBALL

ACHIEVEMENTS

NAME	GOAL/REQUIREMENT	POINT VALUE
Tony Stark	You have completed all Tony Stark missions on the Iron Man table.	5
Iron Man	You have defeated Whiplash and Mandarin on the Iron Man table. Iron Man is Invincible!	15
Defeat Ultimo	You have defeated Ultimo on the Iron Man table. Congratulations!	30
Party Time	Aunt May's Dinner Party started on Spider-Man.	5
Maximum Clonage	Clone Chaos multiball unleashed on Spider-Man.	15
Clever Fighter	Doc Ock has been defeated by a pumpkin bomb on Spider-Man.	30
Clever Hand	Hand ninja defeated by a dumped ball on the Wolverine table.	5

NAME	GOAL/REQUIREMENT	POINT VALUE
Adamantium Skeleton	Adamantium bonded to Logan's bones on the Wolverine table!	15
Mutant Beater	Sabretooth has been defeated on the Wolverine table.	30
Golden Hoard	The ancient treasure trove on Blade is now liberated from the clutches of vampires.	5
Darkhold Chapter	A Darkhold chapter suppressed on Blade.	15
Lord of the Undead	With your victory on Blade, you defeated Dracula and scattered his vampires…for now.	30

MARVEL: VENGEANCE AND VIRTUE

ACHIEVEMENTS

NAME	GOAL/REQUIREMENT	POINT VALUE
Enemies Of Asgard	Accomplish all the Asgard missions on Thor! (Single player only.)	5
Worthy Warrior	Wield Mjolnir and defeat Surtur and the horde of Hela on Thor! (Single player only.)	15
The betrayer	Defeat the betrayer Loki on Thor! (Single player only.)	30
Moon Copter	Take off with the Moon Copter on Moon Knight (single-player only).	5
Fist of Khonshu	Defeat 100 thugs on Moon Knight (single-player only).	15
Lunar Eclipse	Survive the Lunar Eclipse and defeat Seth on Moon Knight (single-player only).	30
Stunt Rider	Complete at least three rounds in a row on the jump ramp on Ghost Rider (Single player only)	5
Hellfire Shells	Collect at least one Super Jackpot during Helluva Multiball on Ghost Rider (Single player only)	15
Medallion of Power	Beat all of the villains including the final boss on Ghost Rider (Single player only)	30
Assemble The Team	Collect 3 heroes to aid the Professor in his battle on X-Men. (Single player only.)	5
Bring Magneto To His Knees	Spell out X-MEN and finally conquer Magneto on X-Men. (Single player only.)	15
3-Ball Wizard	Defeat Magneto during Final Clash or destroy 2 Sentinels on X-Men. (Single player only.)	30

MS. SPLOSION MAN TABLE

ACHIEVEMENTS

NAME	GOAL/REQUIREMENT	POINT VALUE
Sploded!	Perform 100 Splodes on the Ms. Splosion Man table. (Single player only)	5
Kick it!	Make a Kicker combo on the Ms. Splosion Man table. (Single player only)	15
You are all-Mighty!	Defeat the Mighty Eternal on the Ms. Splosion Man table. (Single player only)	30

NIGHTMARE MANSION

ACHIEVEMENTS

NAME	GOAL/REQUIREMENT	POINT VALUE
Monster Hunter	All of the monsters are captured in the Monster Hunt mode of the Nightmare Mansion table.	30

CHEATS, ACHIEVEMENTS, AND TROPHIES

P

NAME	GOAL/REQUIREMENT	POINT VALUE
Monster Trees	Monster Trees mode activated on the Nightmare Mansion table.	15
Skull Shot	The skull of has been smacked up or 3 Friends beaten on the Nightmare Mansion table.	5

PARANORMAL
ACHIEVEMENTS

NAME	GOAL/REQUIREMENT	POINT VALUE
Ghost Sighting	Get up to the attic of the Haunted Mansion and banish a ghost on Paranormal! (Single player only.)	5
Cryptid Investigator	Start the Dizzy Hurry-up mode and make the chupacabra dizzy on Paranormal! (Single player only.)	15
Supernatural Phenomena	Start a Multiball Phenomenon with the cube on Paranormal! (Single player only.)	30

PINBALL FX CLASSIC
ACHIEVEMENTS

NAME	GOAL/REQUIREMENT	POINT VALUE
Bombardment	Multiplier reached by a complete bombardment on the Buccaneer table.	5
Cannonball Shower	Cannonballs rained or 5 Friends beaten on the Buccaneer table.	15
Infiltrator	Snuck into both the Oil Tanker and the Syscraper on the Agents table.	30
King of the Playground	Playground Multiball achieved or 5 Friends beaten on Extreme table.	15
Rampage	A super combo performed or 10 Friends beaten on the Speed Machine table.	30
Reliable	Always got the missions at the right time from the Command Base on the Agents table.	5
Safety First	You had Kickback and Ball Saver at the same time on Speed Machine table.	5
Skybencher	Reached the sky by hitting the Ollie ramp during multiball on the Extreme table.	30
Street Artist	TAG spelled on Extreme table.	5
Swashbuckler	A pirate adventure has been completed on the Buccaneer table.	30
Teamwork	Partnership Multiball earned or 5 Friends beaten on the Agents table.	15
The Heat Is On	All police stars were lit on the Speed Machine table.	15

PINBALL FX2 CORE COLLECTION
ACHIEVEMENTS

NAME	GOAL/REQUIREMENT	POINT VALUE
Abyss	50m depth reached or 10 friends beaten on the Secrets of the Deep table.	30
Centurion	50 million collected playing Romulus Multiball or 5 friends beaten on the Rome table.	15
Cookie Jar	A storehouse of monsterly pleasures, a Cookie Jar filled to the brim from the Biolab table!	30

NAME	GOAL/REQUIREMENT	POINT VALUE
Cozy Cookie	Awarded by the Mad Professor for not misbehaving too much on the Biolab table!	5
Desert explorer	You successfully led the caravan through the desert or beaten 3 friends on the Pasha table.	5
Diamond Plated Needle File	An escape completed or 5 friends beaten on the Biolab table!	15
Legatus Legionis	Seized control over the garrisons at least seven times or started FRENZY on the Rome table.	30
Legendary Swordsman	You defeated all of the guardians of the hidden mini-playfield on the Pasha table.	15
Munifex	Two sucessful shots completed against the galleon during Mock Warfare on the Rome table.	5
New Discovery	Probe launched successfully on the Secrets of the Deep table.	5
Story teller	All tales have been completed on the Pasha table.	30
Treasure Hunter	Shipwreck explored completely on the Secrets of the Deep table.	15

ROCKY & BULLWINKLE
ACHIEVEMENTS

NAME	GOAL/REQUIREMENT	POINT VALUE
Bullwinkle's Top Hat	Ball landed in a hat during the performance of Mr. Know-it-all on the Rocky & Bullwinkle table.	5
Counterfeit Box Tops	Wrongdoings of the Two Nogoodniks have been completed on the Rocky & Bullwinkle table.	30
Pilot Goggles	Super Combo achieved or 5 Friends beaten on the Rocky & Bullwinkle table.	15

SORCERER'S LAIR
ACHIEVEMENTS

NAME	GOAL/REQUIREMENT	POINT VALUE
Pathfinder	Complete a 6-way combo on Sorcerer's Lair (single player only)!	5
Sharpshooter	Take down the spiders in 20 seconds in the cellar on Sorcerer's Lair (single player only).	15
Secrets of the Lair	Conclude the final mode: Midnight Madness on Sorcerer's Lair (single player only).	30

STREET FIGHTER II
ACHIEVEMENTS

NAME	GOAL/REQUIREMENT	POINT VALUE
Focused Energy	Wall crumbler punch performed successfully on the Street Fighter II table.	5
Talented Fighter	You fought well on the Street Fighter II table.	15
The Final Round	M. Bison has been defeated or 10 Friends beaten on the Street Fighter II table.	30

PINBALL HALL OF FAME

CUSTOM BALLS OPTION

Enter CKF as a code.

TILT OPTION

Enter BZZ as a code.

PAYOUT MODE

Enter WGR as a code.

ACES HIGH IN FREEPLAY

Enter UNO as a code.

CENTRAL PARK IN FREEPLAY

Enter NYC as a code.

LOVE MACHINE IN FREEPLAY

Enter HOT as a code.

PLAYBOY TABLE IN FREEPLAY

Enter HEF as a code.

STRIKES 'N SPARES IN FREEPLAY

Enter PBA as a code.

TEE'D OFF IN FREEPLAY

Enter PGA as a code.

XOLTEN IN FREEPLAY

Enter BIG as a code.

PINBALL HALL OF FAME - THE GOTTLIEB COLLECTION

UNLOCK TABLES IN FREEPLAY, EXTRA OPTIONS, AND PAYOUT MODE

Select Enter Code from the Main Menu and enter the following:

EFFECTS	CODE
Aces High Freeplay	UNO
Big Shot Freeplay	UJP
Black Hole Freeplay	LIS
Central Park Freeplay	NYC
Goin' Nuts Freeplay	PHF
Love Machine Freeplay	HOT
Playboy Freeplay	HEF
Strikes 'N Spares Freeplay	PBA
Tee'd Off Freeplay	PGA
Xolten Freeplay	BIG
Custom Balls in Options	CKF
Optional Tilt in Options	BZZ
Payout Mode	WGR

PIRATES PLUNDARRR

CHEAT MENU

Press + to pause the game. Press Up, Up, Down, Down, Left, Right, Left, Right, 2, 1 to make a new Cheat option appear at the bottom of the menu.

AMAZON

Defeat Tecciztecatl, Witch Doctor.

SPECTRAL

Defeat Nanauatl, Hero of the Sun.

PLAGUE, INC.

UNLOCK CHEATS

To unlock the No Cure, No Action and Infinite DNA cheats complete all games modes on Brutal difficulty.

UNLOCK GAME TYPES

GAME TYPE	REQUIREMENT
Virus	Complete Bacteria on Normal or Brutal difficulty.
Fungus	Complete Virus on Normal or Brutal difficulty.
Parasite	Complete Fungus on Normal or Brutal difficulty.
Prion	Complete Parasite on Normal or Brutal difficulty.
Nano-Virus	Complete Prion on Normal or Brutal difficulty.
Bio-Weapon	Complete Nano-Virus on Normal or Brutal difficulty.
Neurax Worm	Complete all seven Plague types on Brutal difficulty.
Necroa Virus	Complete all eight Plague types on Brutal difficulty.
Hidden Plague	Complete all other Plague types on Brutal difficulty.
Immune Plague	Complete all other Plague types on Brutal difficulty.
Unlimited Plague	Complete all other Plague types on Brutal difficulty.

PLANTS VS. ZOMBIES

ZOMBIE YETI

Complete Adventure Mode. Then, play the mode again to 4-10.

QUICK PLAY

Complete Adventure Mode.

ACHIEVEMENTS

ACHIEVEMENT	REQUIREMENT
Home Lawn Security	Complete Adventure Mode.
Spudow!	Blow up a zombie using a Potato Mine.
Explodonator	Take out 10 full-sized zombies with a single Cherry Bomb.
Morticulturalist	Collect all 49 plants (including plants from Crazy Dave's Shop).
Don't Pea in the Pool	Complete a daytime pool level without using Pea Shooters of any kind.
Roll Some Heads	Bowl over 5 Zombies with a single Wall-nut.
Grounded	Defeat a normal Roof level without using any catapult plants.

ACHIEVEMENT	REQUIREMENT
Zombologist	Discover the Yeti Zombie.
Penny Pincher	Pick up 30 coins in a row on a single level without letting any disappear.
Sunny Days	Accumulate 8,000 sun during a single level.
Popcorn Party	Defeat 2 Gargantuars with Corn Cob missiles in a single level.
Good Morning	Complete daytime level by planting only Mushrooms and Coffee Beans.
No Fungus Among Us	Complete a nighttime Level without planting any Mushrooms.
Last Mown Standing	Defeat the last zombie in a level with a lawn mower.
20 Below Zero	Immobilize 20 full-sized zombies with a single Ice-shroom.
Flower Power	Keep 10 Twin Sunflowers alive in a single level.
Pyromaniac	Complete a level using only explosive plants to kill zombies.
Lawn Mower Man	Kill 10 zombies with a single lawn mower.
Chill Out	Feel the rhythm, feel the rhyme, you've one level to destroy 3 bobsleds, its jalapeno time!
Defcorn 5	Build 5 Cob Cannons in a single level.
Monster Mash	Crush 5 zombies with a single Squash.
Blind Faith	Complete an extremely foggy level without using Planterns or Blovers.
Pool's Closed	Complete a pool level without using water plants.
Melon-y Lane	Plant a Winter Melon on every lane.
Second Life	Complete Adventure Mode a second time.
Lucky Spin	Get 3 diamonds in Slot Machine.
Chilli Free	Complete Column Like You See 'Em without using Jalapenos.
Enlightened	Collect all Zen Garden, Mushroom Garden, and Aquarium Garden plants.
Diamond Beghouler	Upgrade all your plants in Beghouled.
Sultan of Spin	Upgrade all your plants in Beghouled Twist.
Green Fingers	Grow 10 Zen Garden plants to full size.
Wall-Not-Attack	Complete ZomBotany with no Wall-Nuts, Tall-Nuts or Pumpkins.
Beyond the Grave	Beat all 18 mini-games.
Down the Hole!	Dig your way to see the Chinese Zombies.
Thrilling the Zombies	Hypnotize the lead Dancer Zombie.
Alive and Planting	Survive 40 waves of pure zombie ferocity.

PLAYSTATION 3

If a code does not work, your Tree of Wisdom may not be tall enough. Try again later.

ALTERNATE LAWN MOWER

During a game, press R1 + R2 + L1 + L2 and enter trickedout.

ZOMBIE SHADES

During a game, press R1 + R2 + L1 + L2 and enter future.

ZOMBIES HAVE A MUSTACHE

During a game, press R1 + R2 + L1 + L2 and enter mustache.

ZOMBIES DANCE

During a game, press R1 + R2 + L1 + L2 and enter dance.

DEAD ZOMBIES LEAVE DAISIES BEHIND

During a game, press R1 + R2 + L1 + L2 and enter daisies.

CANDY SHOWER WHEN ZOMBIE DIES

During a game, press R1 + R2 + L1 + L2 and enter piñata.

CHANGES ZOMBIES SOUND

During a game, press R1 + R2 + L1 + L2 and enter sukhbir.

PLAYSTATION VITA

If a code does not work, your Tree of Wisdom may not be tall enough. Try again later.

ALTERNATE LAWN MOWER

During a game, press R1 + R2 + L1 + L2 and enter trickedout.

ZOMBIE SHADES

During a game, press R1 + R2 + L1 + L2 and enter future.

ZOMBIES HAVE A MUSTACHE

During a game, press R1 + R2 + L1 + L2 and enter mustache.

ZOMBIES DANCE

During a game, press R1 + R2 + L1 + L2 and enter dance.

DEAD ZOMBIES LEAVE DAISIES BEHIND

During a game, press R1 + R2 + L1 + L2 and enter daisies.

CANDY SHOWER WHEN ZOMBIE DIES

During a game, press R1 + R2 + L1 + L2 and enter piñata.

CHANGES ZOMBIES SOUND

During a game, press R1 + R2 + L1 + L2 and enter sukhbir.

XBOX 360

During a game, press Left Bumper, Right Bumper, Left Trigger, Right Trigger. Now you can enter the following codes. You must be given a code before it can be used.

MUSTACHES FOR ZOMBIE

Enter mustache.

SHADES FOR ZOMBIES

Enter future.

ZOMBIES DANCE

Enter dance.

CANDY WHEN ZOMBIE DIES

Enter piñata.

DEAD ZOMBIES LEAVE DAISIES

Enter daisies.

ALTERNATE LAWN MOWER

Enter trickedout.

PLAYSTATION ALL STARS BATTLE ROYALE

PLAYSTATION 3

ALTERNATE COSTUMES

To unlock Alternate Costumes, reach Rank 10 with a character.

EXTRA MINIONS

There are several extra Minions that can be unlocked by reaching a high Rank with multiple characters.

CHEATS, ACHIEVEMENTS, AND TROPHIES

P

MINION	REQUIREMENT
Curtis the Panda	Reach Rank 80 with 2 characters.
Dr. Nefarious	Reach Rank 80 with 3 characters.
Tag	Reach Rank 80 with 5 characters.
Chimera	Reach Rank 80 with 8 characters.

UNLOCK MINIONS

To unlock a Minion, reach Rank 8 with a character to unlock their associated Minion.

NAME	GOAL/REQUIREMENT	TROPHY VALUE
3x OVERTIME!!.	Enter 3x AP Overtime!	Silver
All-Star Legend – You've Only Done Everything	You have successfully earned all other trophies in the game. Congratulations!	Platinum
Ally of Larry Da Vinci	Perform a Level 3 Super with Sackboy on 'Dreamscape'	Bronze
Autarch of Helghan	Perform a Level 3 Super with Radec on 'Invasion'	Bronze
Cake, please!	Complete Arcade Mode with Fat Princess	Bronze
Calypso's Wishes	Perform a Level 3 Super with Sweet Tooth on 'Black Rock Stadium'	Bronze
Champion	Win a Versus Match against a team of three AI opponents	Silver
Character Mastery	Complete a Combo Tutorial	Bronze
Combo King	Land a 50+ AP Combo in Practice Mode	Bronze
Combo Virtuoso	Land a 70+ AP Combo in Practice Mode	Silver
Demon Hunter	Complete Arcade Mode with Dante	Bronze
Demon of Empire City	Complete Arcade Mode with Evil Cole	Bronze
Eco Master	Complete Arcade Mode with Jak	Bronze
First Blood	Earn a Kill in a match-made online game	Bronze
Friend of the People	Complete Arcade Mode with Toro	Bronze
Friendly Competition	Complete a Versus Match against an online player	Bronze
Fundamentals	Complete the Basic Tutorial	Bronze
Greatest Conduit	Complete Arcade Mode with Cole	Bronze
Heavenly Warrior	Complete Arcade Mode with Nariko	Bronze
Helghast Commander	Complete Arcade Mode with Radec	Bronze
Hero of Gallowmere	Complete Arcade Mode with Sir Daniel	Bronze
I Chose The Impossible	Perform a Level 3 Super with Big Daddy on 'Columbia'	Bronze
I Gotta Believe!	Complete Arcade Mode with PaRappa	Bronze
Intergalactic Heroes	Complete Arcade Mode with Ratchet	Bronze
Interpol HQ Break-In	Perform a Level 3 Super with Sly Cooper on 'Paris'	Bronze
Kerwan's Capital City	Perform a Level 3 Super with Ratchet on 'Metropolis'	Bronze
Let's Make a Scene	Complete Arcade Mode with Sackboy	Bronze
Master of the Ray Sphere	Perform a Level 3 Super with Cole or Evil Cole on 'Alden's Tower'	Bronze
Monkey Catcher	Complete Arcade Mode with Spike	Bronze
Mr. Bubbles	Complete Arcade Mode with Big Daddy	Bronze
Oh Boys and Girls	Complete Arcade Mode with Sweet Tooth	Bronze
Palace of the Underworld	Perform a Level 3 Super with Kratos on 'Hades'	Bronze
Revengeance	Complete Arcade Mode with Raiden	Bronze
REX versus RAY	Perform a Level 3 Super with Raiden on 'Franzea'	Bronze
Samos' Sacred Site	Perform a Level 3 Super with Jak on 'Sandover Village'	Bronze
Showing Off	Show off your Minion during a game	Bronze

NAME	GOAL/REQUIREMENT	TROPHY VALUE
Sic Parvis Magna	Perform a Level 3 Super with Nathan Drake on 'Stowaways'	Bronze
Student Becomes the Master	Perform a Level 3 Super with PaRappa on 'Dojo'	Bronze
Team Sweeper	Earn a Double Kill in a 2v2 match-made online game	Silver
The Doctor Is In...	Perform a Level 3 Super with Ratchet on 'San Francisco'	Bronze
The God of War	Complete Arcade Mode with Kratos	Bronze
The Iron Fist	Complete Arcade Mode with Heihachi	Bronze
The Legend	Complete Arcade Mode on Legend	Bronze
The Peak Point Helmet Blues	Perform a Level 3 Super with Spike on 'Time Station'	Bronze
Thievius Raccoonus	Complete Arcade Mode with Sly Cooper	Bronze
This is Living	Win a match-made online game without dying	Silver
Three for One	Earn a Triple Kill with a Level 1 Super Attack	Gold
Tournament Fighter	Complete an online Ranked Match	Bronze
Treasure Hunter	Complete Arcade Mode with Nathan Drake	Bronze
Trial Combatant	Complete a Combat Trial	Bronze
Triple Kill!	Earn a Triple Kill in a match-made online game	Silver
Two for One	Earn a Double Kill with a Level 1 Super Attack	Silver
Ultimate Power	Perform a Level 3 Super Attack	Silver
Victorious!	Win a match-made online game	Silver
We have Overtime! – Working Weekends?	Enter Overtime!	Bronze

PLAYSTATION VITA

ALTERNATE COSTUMES

To unlock Alternate Costumes, reach Rank 10 with a character.

EXTRA MINIONS

There are several extra Minions that can be unlocked by reaching a high Rank with multiple characters.

MINION	REQUIREMENT
Curtis the Panda	Reach Rank 80 with 2 characters.
Dr. Nefarious	Reach Rank 80 with 3 characters.
Tag	Reach Rank 80 with 5 characters.
Chimera	Reach Rank 80 with 8 characters.

UNLOCK MINIONS

To unlock a Minion, reach Rank 8 with a character to unlock their associated Minion.

POCKET GOD

MOBILE

OOGA JUMP JET PACK BONUS

At an island, click the arrow in the upper-left corner and then select the 3-star graphic. Tap the star and then Pocket God Comic Pre-Order Bonus. Enter journey to Uranus. You can participate in the promotion and get the jet pack, otherwise you need to score 6000 in Ooga

POCKET POOL

PSP

ALL PICTURES AND VIDEOS

At the Title screen, press L, R, L, L, R, R, R, L (x3), R (x3), L (x4), R (x4). jump.

POKÉDEX 3D PRO

HARD QUIZZES

In Quiz Numbers 37-39 you can enter a Keyword to enable various quizzes. Enter the Keyword UJFPJGAD to unlock Quizzes 40-69.

UNLOCK GENESECT DATA

In the Pokémon Challenge Menu, press "Delete" on one of the quizzes then enter PHSKUTDF to unlock a quiz which will unlock the data for Genesect when it's completed.

UNLOCK MELOETTA DATA

Delete one of the quiz codes from #37 onward and enter the code TTQALFHN. If you complete this quiz, Meloetta's data will become available.

UNLOCKABLES

REWARD	REQUIREMENT
PokéDex Text	50 correct answers
Pokémon Forms	70 correct answers
Perspectives	80 correct answers
Evolution	90 correct answers
Unown 1	100 correct answers
Categories	110 correct answers

POKÉMON DREAM RADAR

CHEAT CODES

Enter these codes on the main screen to unlock three Pokémon with special abilities.

EFFECT	CODE
Special Extension A (Beldum)	Up, Right, Down, Left, X, R, L
Special Extension B (Slowpoke)	Up, Down, Right, Left, Y, R, L
Special Extension C (Hoothoot)	R, L, Y, X, Left, Right, Y, X

LEGENDARY BATTLES

Insert the labeled DS game into the 3DS while playing Pokémon Dream Radar to unlock legendary battles for Pokémon Black and White 2.

EFFECT	REQUIREMENT
Diving Extension: Lugia	Insert Pokémon SoulSilver.
Rainbow Extension: Ho-Oh	Insert Pokémon HeartGold.
Renegade Extension: Giratina	Insert Pokémon Platinum.
Space Extension: Palkia	Insert Pokémon Pearl.
Time Extension: Dialga	Insert Pokémon Diamond.

POKÉMON MYSTERY DUNGEON: EXPLORERS OF DARKNESS/TIME

Select Wonder Mail before starting your game, and then enter the following passwords to add a mission to your Job List. These are listed by the reward you receive for completing the mission.

Each password can only be used once. There are many possible passwords, here we list some examples. These passwords work on Explorers of Darkness and Explorers of Time.

ACCESSORY

ACCESSORY	PASSWORD
Gold Ribbon	5+KPKXT9RYP754&M2-58&&1-
Golden Mask	@QYPSJ@-N-J%TH6=4-SK32CR
Joy Ribbon	597C6#873795@Q6=F+TSQ68J
Mobile Scarf	R2MQ0X0&&-RN+64#4S0R+&-1
Miracle Chest	FX199P@CW@-XK54Q%4628XT#
No-Stick Cap	1@484PJ7NJW@XCHC2&-+H=@P
Pecha Scarf	8%2R-T&T1F-KR5#08P#&T=@=
Persim Band	TCX#TJQ0%#46Q6MJYMH2S#C9
Power Band	FHSM5950-2QNFTH9S-JM3Q9F
Racket Band	-F773&1XM0FRJT7Y@PJ%9C40
Special Band	752PY8M-Q1NHY#QX92836MHT
Stamina Band	F9RM4Y6W1&2T7@%SWF=R0NK&
X-Ray Specs	C#7H-#P2J9QPHCFPM5F674H=
Wonder Chest	0@R#3-+&7SC2K3@4NQ0-JQX9
Zinc Band	@WWHK8X18@C+C8KTN51H#213

ITEM

ITEM	PASSWORD
Beauty Scarf	@+CWF98#5CPYR13RJ#3YWKS5
Calcium	Y=59NRNS-#M2%C25725NJMQQ
Coronet Rock	S%9@47NTYP#Y105SR#%QH9MX
Dawn Stone	N54=MK=FSH1FCR8=R@HN14#Y
Deepseascale	WT192-H2=K@-WTJ3=JJ64C16
Deepseatooth	WQCM0-H=QH&-W+JP7FKT4CP+
Dusk Stone	X0=-JQ&X1X4KRY=8Y=23M=FH
Electrilizer	4SJYCFNX0-N@JN%NQ#+7-Q7#
Frozen Rock	YT&8WY&+278+2QJT@53TM3M8
Heal Seed	TWTN%RFRK+39-P#M2X+CXQS#
Joy Seed	PQS39&-7WC+R&QJQM2Y@@1KN
Leaf Stone	NP96N4K0HW3CJX8#FNK%=F&+
Link Box	&%8FXT9C76F4Q4SP5F8X3RW%
Lost Loot	J%0+F18XW5%P-9@&17+F8P9M
Lunar Ribbon	%-94RKFY%505XXMMC=FYK45N
Magmarizer	=TK+0KH72MNJNRW5P@RS&Y6=
Max Elixir	4Q9F-K6X66YW5TJY6MXK+RX7
Metal Coat	NP3SMTH-T&TMQFY@N1Q&SFNK
Mossy Rock	@JH#ST1&S14W3T2XJ8=7KR+7
Mystery Part	PXJ634F44Q3FQW&KYRX538+=

ITEM	PASSWORD
Oval Stone	@&FYQ977C#0YN-77TM&=X&+Q
Razor Claw	6JK2T26&MPC7&%-HWRXK2&-W
Reviver Seed	W+P0MYKJFNN3&Q%&-J12J2QH
Secret Slab	K=&4Q=@908N7=X&XHQ+Q1-CS
Shiny Stone	69-HHQX%K@#%7+5SMSPSQP#2
Sun Ribbon	7C8W308RYJ2XM@&QTYSJ%3=9
Thunderstone	+4QQK3PY84Y39P&=KN3=@XYR
Vile Seed	8#8%4496C#=JKRX9M&RKQW4%
Zinc	X=S#N&RNYSP9R2S01HT4MP8&

TM

TM	PASSWORD
Attract	Y@=JC48#K4SQ0NS9#S7@/32%3
Blizzard	Y#ST42FMC4H+NM@M=T999#PR
Brick Break	@MF=%8400Y8X#T8FCTQC5XTS
Brine	9C04WP5XXN@=4NPFR08SS&03
Calm Mind	SH&YH&96C%&JK9Y0H99%3WM9
Dig	SQ96Y08RXJJXMJJ7=SSQK3K3
Embargo	1PQ7K%JX#4=HFHXPPK%7K04H
Energy Ball	5016-@1X8@&5H46#51M&+-XC
Fire Blast	W0T+NF98J13+F&NN=XNR&J-7
Flamethrower	JQ78%-CK%1PTP-77M740=F98
Flash	FS272Y61F1@MNN8FCSSTJ6TP
Gyro Ball	C#S@Y4%9YFQ+SQ6WRK36@1N0
Iron Tail	8+R006Y-&X57XX#&N-PT@R&6
Overheat	F=X5&K=FYJ3FC-N-@QXK34QJ
Payback	K3%0=W61FQCMN-FPHP=J5&W3
Poison Jab	S==YMX%92R54TSK6=F8%-%MN
Protect	Q#6762JK@967H#CMX#RQ3&M3
Psych Up	6=49WKH72&-JN%14SKNF&40N
Recycle	M@56C+=@H%K13WF4Q%RJ2JP9
Reflect	F=YTCK297HC02MT+MF13SQ4W
Rest	KR=WT#JC#@+HFS5K0JJM-0-2
Roar	C&0FWPTCRMKT&7NQ@N0&RQS+
Rock Slide	CN%+TMSHM0&3#&5YC4M1#C@2
Skill Swap	-H4TNNKY&1-P%4HSJY&XHW%Q
Sleep Talk	1M5972RY8X6NCC3CPPRS0K8J
Swords Dance	=633=JSY147RT=&0R9PJJ1FM
Thunder	WKY&7==@HR2%32YX6755JQ85
Vacuum-Cut	7PS2#26WN7HNX83M23J6F@C5
X-Scissor	S6P&198+-5QYR&22FJMKW1XF

NAME	GOAL/REQUIREMENT	POINT VALUE	TROPHY VALUE
Gesticul-8	Perform all 8 gestures of your own volition in co-op	15	Bronze
Confidence Building	Complete all test chambers in the Mass and Velocity co-op course	10	Bronze
Bridge Building	Complete all test chambers in the Hard-Light Surfaces co-op course	15	Bronze
Obstacle Building	Complete all test chambers in the Excursion Funnels co-op course	15	Bronze

POWER RANGERS SAMURAI

NINTENDO DS

PASSWORDS

Enter these passwords in the Passwords screen to unlock special effects which can be toggled on/off in the Bonus Settings menu.

EFFECT	PASSWORD
Blue Ranger's Mega Mode	BLUE736296
Boost Deker's Power	DEKER77530
Boost effect of Health Recovery Items	CYCLE98635
Boost effect of Symbol Power Recovery Items	CYCLE95627
Boost power of all Megazords	MEGAZORD56
Boost power of minor enemies	MORPHER854
Boost Ranger Attack	SMASHER000
Boost Ranger Defense	BLADE10001
Boost Ranger Symbol Power	BOW9999950
Counter attacks with timed blocking	OCTO729483
Gold Ranger's Mega Mode	GOLD842245
Green Ranger's Mega Mode	GREEN85452
Lengthen Secret Disc spin time	SHOGUN1867
Pink Ranger's Mega Mode	PINK987326
Red Ranger's Mega Mode	RED1826359
Yellow Ranger's Mega Mode	YELLOW8649

NINTENDO WII

ALL RANGERS IN EVERY LEVEL

Complete Mission 15 and go through the credits.

POWER RANGERS SUPER SAMURAI

XBOX 360

ACHIEVEMENTS

NAME	GOAL/REQUIREMENT	POINT VALUE
A Samurai in the making	Create an ID Card	10
You are a true Samurai Ranger!	Collect all badges	40
Power of the Ancestors	Complete all Super Samurai achievements	40
Gold Power	Train with the Gold Ranger	20
The new Red Ranger	Train with a secret Red Ranger	20
Now that's teamwork!	Use the 5-Disc Cannon	20

NAME	GOAL/REQUIREMENT	POINT VALUE
Bullzooka Blast!	Use the Bullzooka	20
Team Spirit	Defeat Splitface	20
Super Samurai Mode!	Become a Super Samurai	40
Quadruple Slash?	Defeat 4 or more enemies with one finishing move	40
Symbol Power!	Write a Samurai symbol for the first time	20
Symbol Master	Complete all the Ranger symbols	20
You can do anything as a team	Defeat Rofer with Red Ranger and Green Ranger (Co-op)	20
Rangers Together, Smile Forever!	Take a photo with all of the Rangers	20
Smile, we are united!	Take a photo with all of the Megazords	20
Samurai Perfection	Complete a Ranger mission without taking damage	10
The ultimate duel	Defeat Deker as the Red Ranger	20
Dayu's final song	Defeat Dayu as Pink Ranger	20
Power Disc	Defeat an enemy group that has an item in a Ranger mission	10
Hold it right there, Nighlok!	Defeat an enemy group that tried to mount a special attack in a Ranger mission	10
Megazord perfection	Complete a Megazord Battle without taking damage	10
Counter Victory	Defeat a MegaMonster using only counterattacks.	20
Two Rangers in perfect sync!	Do a Synchronized Attack on a MegaMonster	20
Defuse the situation	Prevent Splitface from exploding during a Ranger mission	10
Read the enemy's moves and react	Avoid Rofer's spin attack three times in a row in a Ranger mission	20
Perceive that not seen	Don't let the enemies that appeared during the power outage escape	10
Fast, brave and lucky	Successfully attack Deker 3 times in a row during a Ranger Battle	20
The great duel	Defeat Gigertox	20
Armed for battle!	Successfully attack Gigertox 3 times in a row during a Megazord Battle	20
Toxic Evader	Defeat Dayu in a Ranger mission without taking one hit from her poison bullets or mist	20
Strike first, finish later	Hit Serrator in a Ranger mission before taking an attack from him	20
Stroke of Fate	Defeat Serrator	10
VICTORY IS OURS!	Defeat Master Xandred	20
Untouchable	Avoid all Xandred's attacks in a Megazord Battle	20
Samurai Victory	Clear Game on Kids Level in Ranger Mode	10
Super Samurai Victory	Clear Game on Normal Level in Ranger Mode	20
Shogun Victory	Clear Game on Hard Level in Ranger Mode	40
Megazord mobilized!	Have a Megazord or MegaMonster appear during Training	10
Training just went Mega Mode!	Have a Megazord or MegaMonster appear five times during Training	10
Excellente!	Perform 10 or more Excellent moves while Training	20
Ranger Training Complete	Complete all Training Stages with all Rangers	40
Tameshiwari Expert	Set a Personal Record above 300 bricks	40
Samurai Chop!	Perform 5 top-speed chops in Breaking Challenge	20
Samurai Break!	Break more than 7 bricks at once	20
Breaking Training Complete	Complete Levels 1 through 4 in Breaking Challenge single player	40
Mooger Training… Complete?	Complete all Training Stages with the Nighlok	40

PRESS YOUR LUCK 2010 EDITION

NINTENDO WII

WARDROBE PIECES FOR AVATAR

Select the lock tab from the Wardrobe screen and enter SECRET.

THE PRICE IS RIGHT 2010 EDITION

NINTENDO WII

AVATAR UPGRADES

Select the lock tab from the Wardrobe screen and enter PRIZES.

PRINCE OF PERSIA

XBOX 360

SANDS OF TIME PRINCE/FARAH SKINS

Select Skin Manager from the Extras menu. Press Y and enter 52585854. This gives you the Sands of Time skin for the Prince and Farah from Sands of Time for the Princess. Access them from the Skin Manager

PRINCE ALTAIR IBN LA-AHAD SKIN

At the Main menu, press Y for Exclusive Content. Create an Ubisoft account. Then select "Altair Skin for Prince" to unlock.

PRINCE OF PERSIA RIVAL SWORDS

NINTENDO WII

BABY TOY WEAPON

Pause the game and enter the following code. Use the D-pad for the directions.

Left, Left, Right, Right, Z, Nunchuck down, Nunchuck down, Z, Up, Down

CHAINSAW

Pause the game and enter the following code. Use the D-pad for the directions.

Up, Up, Down, Down, Left, Right, Left, Right, Z, Nunchuck down, Z, Nunchuck down

SWORDFISH

Pause the game and enter the following code. Use the D-pad for the directions.

Up, Down, Up, Down, Left, Right, Left, Right, Z, Nunchuck down, Z, Nunchuck down

TELEPHONE SWORD

Pause the game and enter the following code. Use the D-pad for the directions.

Right, Left, Right, Left, Down, Down, Up, Up, Z, Nunchuck Down, Z, Z, Nunchuck Down, Nunchuck Down

CHEATS, ACHIEVEMENTS, AND TROPHIES

P

PRINCE OF PERSIA: THE SANDS OF TIME

PLAYSTATION 3

CLASSIC PRINCE OF PERSIA

Start a new game and while on the balcony, hold L3 and enter ✕, ●, ●, ●, ●, ✕, ●, ●.

CLASSIC PASSWORDS

LEVEL	PASSWORD
2	KIEJSC
3	DMKERC
4	ACCVQC
5	XRTLQC
6	UHLCQC
7	RXCTPC
8	KBJOOC
9	DFPJNC
10	SWJJLC
11	LAQEKC
12	ZMBTOC

PRINCESS NATASHA

NINTENDO 3DS

ALL GADGETS

Select Codes from the Extras menu and enter OLEGSGIZMO.

EXTRA LEVELS

Select Codes from the Extras menu and enter SMASHROBOT.

INFINITE LIVES

Select Codes from the Extras menu and enter CRUSHLUBEK.

PRINCESS TOMATO IN THE SALAD KINGDOM

NINTENDO WII

DEBUG BATTLE PASSWORD

Enter GG62 as a password.

PRINNY: CAN I REALLY BE THE HERO?

PSP

START A NEW GAME WITH THE ALTERNATE STORYLINE

At the Main menu, highlight New Game and press ●, ●, ●, ●, ●, ●, ✕.

PRINNY 2: DAWN OF OPERATION PANTIES, DOOD!

PSP

ASAGI WARS

Highlight New Game and press ●, ●, ●, ●, ●, ●, ●, ✕.

PROTOTYPE 2

NEW GAME +

Complete every story mission.

NEW GAME +

Complete every story mission.

AVATAR AWARDS

AVATAR	EARNED BY
James Heller Outfit	With RADNET activated, access the Events Screen for unlock details.
Heller Hoodie	With RADNET activated, access the Events Screen for unlock details.
Alex Mercer Outfit	With RADNET activated, access the Events Screen for unlock details.
Shield	With RADNET activated, access the Events Screen for unlock details.
T-Shirt	With RADNET activated, access the Events Screen for unlock details.

ACHIEVEMENTS & TROPHIES

NAME	GOAL/REQUIREMENT	POINT VALUE	TROPHY VALUE
Anger Management	Destroyed 5 vehicles using a Finisher.	20	Bronze
So Above It All	Spend at least 25 consecutive seconds in the air (helicopters don't count).	20	Bronze
Vitamin B-rains	Acquired 10 upgrades through Consumes.	10	Bronze
Eating Your Way to the Top	Acquired 30 upgrades through Consumes.	30	Bronze
Finally Full	Acquired all 46 upgrades through Consumes.	50	Bronze
Icarus	Reached the highest point in the world.	15	Bronze
Spindler's Search	Destroyed all Lairs.	40	Bronze
//BLACKNET Hacker	Completed all //BLACKNET dossiers.	40	Bronze
One by One	Stealth Consumed 50 Blackwatch troopers.	20	Bronze
Wanted Man	Triggered 50 alerts.	20	Bronze
All Growed Up	Fully upgraded Heller.	50	Bronze
Master Prototype	Completed the game on HARD difficulty.	50	Bronze
It's an Epidemic	Complete MEET YOUR MAKER.	10	Bronze
I Want Some More	Complete RESURRECTION.	10	Bronze
Religious Experience	Meet Father Guerra.	10	Bronze
This is a Knife	First Prototype Power aquired.	20	Bronze
Project Closed	Completed a //BLACKNET mission.	20	Bronze
The Mad Scientist	Complete NATURAL SELECTION.	30	Silver
Something to Live For	Complete FALL FROM GRACE.	30	Silver
What a Bitch	Complete LABOR OF LOVE.	30	Silver
Murder your Maker?	Complete the game.	100	Bronze

NAME	GOAL/REQUIREMENT	POINT VALUE	TROPHY VALUE
Follow Your Nose	Found all BlackBoxes.	30	Bronze
Up to No Good	Defeated all Field Ops teams.	30	Bronze
Strike, You're Out.	Destroyed a Strike Team in 15 seconds or less.	10	Bronze
Compulsive Eater	5 consumes in 10 seconds or less.	10	Bronze
Do the Evolution	Acquired 5 Mutations.	20	Bronze
Just a Flesh Wound	Dismembered a Brawler.	10	Bronze
All Together Now	10 or more kills with a single Black Hole attack.	20	Bronze
Back Atcha!	Deflected 5 missiles at enemies using Shield Block.	20	Bronze
Two for the Price of One	Simultaneously killed 2 Brawlers using a single Devastator.	20	Bronze
Lair to Rest	Destroyed a single Lair.	15	Bronze
Hijack Be Nimble	Stealth hijacked 5 tanks or APCs.	15	Bronze
Road Rage	Destroyed 10 Blackwatch tanks, APCs or helicopters using a single hijacked tank or APC.	20	Bronze
Who Watches the Watchers?	Consumed 10 //BLACKNET targets.	20	Bronze
Hard to Please	Acquired a Mutation in each of the 5 categories.	20	Bronze
The Floor is Lava	Traveled a half mile using only Wall Run, Glide, Jump and Air Dash.	15	Bronze
Cannonball!	20 or more kills with a single Hammerfist dive attack.	10	Bronze
You're the Bomb	10 or more kills using a single Bio-Bomb.	10	Bronze
Sic 'em!	Destroyed 5 helicopters using Pack Leader.	20	Bronze
Over-Equipped	Weaponized 10 vehicles.	20	Bronze
The Best Offense	Countered enemy attacks 20 times using Shield.	20	Bronze
Arcade Action	Karate kicked a helicopter.	10	Bronze
I Caught a Big One!	Mounted a helicopter using Whipfist.	10	Bronze

PUNCH-OUT!!

NINTENDO WII

REGAIN HEALTH IN BETWEEN ROUNDS

Press the Minus button between rounds to regain health at the start of the next round. Donkey Kong, Exhibition Mode

Fight Donkey Kong in Last Stand mode.

CHAMPIONS MODE

Win 10 bouts in Mac's Last Stand.

ACHIEVEMENTS

ACHIEVEMENT	DESCRIPTION
Magpie	Collect 25 pearls.
Hunter	Collect 50 pearls.
Hoarder	Collect 100 pearls.
Pearl Jammer	Collect 150 pearls.
Pearl Harboring	Collect 200 pearls.
Learnt the Ropes	Complete the 1928 shelf.
Apprentice	Complete the 1937 shelf.
Excellent	Complete the 1939 shelf.
Pro	Complete the 1941 shelf.
Expert	Complete the 1943 shelf.
Champion	Complete the 1945 shelf.
Complete	Complete every Quell level.
Minimalist	Complete 3 levels perfectly.
Accomplished	Complete 10 levels perfectly.
Flawless	Complete 20 levels perfectly.
Impeccable	Complete 40 levels perfectly.
Precise	Complete a stage in perfect moves.
Meticulous	Complete a shelf in perfect moves.
Perfect	Complete every Quell level in perfect moves.
Keep Going!	Play for 10 minutes.
Time Flies	Play for 30 minutes.
High Stamina	Play for 1 hour.
Suicidal	Die on a first move.
Ouch!	Spiked 3 times.
Fearless	Spiked 10 times.
Funeral Bill	Spiked 20 times.
Road to Nowhere	Get stuck in a loop 5 times.
Groundhog Day	Retry a level 20 times.
Matchmaker	Push 2 sets of blocks together.
Tired	Push 10 blocks.
Ring Leader	Use the ring 5 times.
Quick Thinking	Complete a level in under 5 seconds.
Defiant	Take over 10 minutes to complete a level.
Scenic Route	Take twice as many moves as necessary.

RABBIDS GO HOME

ASSASSIN RABBID

Finish Nick of Time to unlock the Rabbid customization option. Enter this option and select a Rabbid. Go to the menu and select Manage Figurines from the Figurines screen. Hold C + Z and press 2, 2, 1, 1, A, A, A, 1, 1.

BEST BUY RABBID

Finish Nick of Time to unlock the Rabbid customization option. Enter this option and select a Rabbid. Go to the menu and select Manage Figurines from the Figurines screen. Hold C + Z and press B, 1, 1, B, A, 2, 2, A.

GEEK SQUAD RABBID

Finish Nick of Time to unlock the Rabbid customization option. Enter this option and select a Rabbid. Go to the menu and select Manage Figurines from the Figurines screen. Hold C + Z and press A, A, 1, 1, 1, 1, 2, 2.

KANGAROO RABBID

Finish Nick of Time to unlock the Rabbid customization option. Enter this option and select a Rabbid. Go to the menu and select Manage Figurines from the Figurines screen. Hold C + Z and press 1, 1, 1, 1, 1, 2, 1, 2.

LEONARDO RABBID

Finish Nick of Time to unlock the Rabbid customization option. Enter this option and select a Rabbid. Go to the menu and select Manage Figurines from the Figurines screen. Hold C + Z and press 1, 1, 2, 2, A, A, 1, 1.

PRINCE RABBID

Finish Nick of Time to unlock the Rabbid customization option. Enter this option and select a Rabbid. Go to the menu and select Manage Figurines from the Figurines screen. Hold C + Z and press 1, 2, 1, 2, 1, 2, A, A.

SPLINTER CELL RABBID

Finish Nick of Time to unlock the Rabbid customization option. Enter this option and select a Rabbid. Go to the menu and select Manage Figurines from the Figurines screen. Hold C + Z and press B, B, B, B, A, A, A, A.

RABBIDS RUMBLE

NINTENDO 3DS

UNLOCKABLE CHARACTERS

CHARACTER	REQUIREMENT
Agent Bwah	Defeat his team then capture him in Bonus Arena at Rabbid in Space.
Armstwong	Defeat his team then capture him in Space Arena.
Atom Mick	Capture him in Power Plant AR Card Game.
Autobwahn	Defeat his team then capture him in Bonus Arena at Bwah Sports.
Bo Bwah	Defeat his team then capture him in Circus Arena.
Busby	Defeat his team then capture him in Bonus Arena at World Tour.
Buzz	Defeat his team then capture him in Space Arena.
Bwaahgette	Defeat his team then capture him in Bonus Arena at World Tour.
Bwahbarian	Defeat his team then capture him in Ancient Arena.
Bwahberella	Defeat her team then capture her in Space Arena.
Bwahbie	Defeat her team then capture her in FunFair Arena.
Bwahcula	Defeat his team then capture him in Haunted Arena.
Bwainiac	Capture him in Laboratory AR Card Game.
Bwian	Capture him in Rabbidhouse AR Card Game.
Day Taah	Defeat his team then capture him in Bonus Arena at Rabbid in Space.
Diablo	Defeat his team then capture him in Bonus Arena at Rabbident Evil.
Disco Stu	Defeat his team then capture him in Bonus Arena at Rabbid Party.
DJ Sniff	Defeat his team then capture him at FunFair Arena.
Dr.Dunno	Defeat his team then capture him in Bonus Arena at Rabbident Evil.
Durabbid	Defeat his team then capture him in Bonus Arena at Rabbid in Space.
Ednaah	Defeat her team then capture her in Bonus Arena at Rabbid Party.
Eggbert	Defeat his team then capture him in Bonus Arena at Cooking Rabbid.
Fido	Defeat his team then capture him in Haunted Arena.

CHARACTER	REQUIREMENT
Fwankie	Defeat his team then capture him in Haunted Arena.
Fwaraoh	Capture him in Pyramid AR Card Game.
Gingy	Capture him in Ginger House AR Card Game.
Gwadiataah	Defeat his team then capture him in Ancient Arena.
Gwim Weaper	Defeat his team then capture him in Bonus Arena at Rabbident Evil.
Hilda	Defeat her team then capture her in Bonus Arena at World Tour.
Inspectaah	Defeat his team then capture him in Bonus Arena at Rabbidville.
Jock	Defeat his team then capture him in Bonus Arena at Bwah Sports.
Judge Bwah	Defeat his team then capture him in Bonus Arena at Rabbidville.
Keef	Defeat his team then capture him in FunFair Arena.
Loco Libre	Defeat his team then capture him in Sports Arena.
Mastaah	Defeat his team then capture him in Circus Arena.
Misty	Defeat her team then capture him in Circus Arena.
Posh	Defeat her team then capture her in Bonus Arena at Bwah Sports.
Salty	Defeat his team then capture him in Diner Arena.
Senetaah	Defeat his team then capture him in Ancient Arena.
Spotz	Defeat his team then capture him in Diner Arena.
Sundae	Defeat his team then capture him in Bonus Arena at Cooking Rabbid.
Tigwah	Capture him in Mini Golf AR Card Game.
Tricksy	Capture him in Magic Party AR Card Game.
Twevaah	Defeat his team then capture him in Bonus Arena at Rabbidville.
Waitaah	Defeat his team then capture him in Diner Arena.
Weenah	Defeat his team then capture him in Bonus Arena at Cooking Rabbid.
Wocky	Defeat his team then capture him in Sports Arena.
Zunaah	Defeat his team then capture him in Sports Arena.

RACE DRIVER: CREATE & RACE

ALL CHALLENGES

Select Cheat Codes from Extras and enter 942785.

ALL CHAMPIONSHIPS

Select Cheat Codes from Extras and enter 761492.

ALL REWARDS

Select Cheat Codes from Extras and enter 112337.

FREE DRIVE

Select Cheat Codes from Extras and enter 171923.

NO DAMAGE

Select Cheat Codes from Extras and enter 505303.

EASY STEERING

Select Cheat Codes from Extras and enter 611334.

MINIATURE CARS

Select Cheat Codes from Extras and enter 374288.

MM VIEW

Select Cheat Codes from Extras and enter 467348.

RAGE

ACHIEVEMENTS & TROPHIES

NAME	GOAL/REQUIREMENT	POINT VALUE	TROPHY VALUE
Arts and Crafts	Construct 10 Engineering Items	10	Bronze
Tinkerer	Construct 50 Engineering Items	20	Bronze
Passive Aggressive	Get 3 kills with a single Sentry Bot	30	Silver
Three Birds, One Bomb Car	Kill 3 Enemies with one RC Bomb Car	30	Silver
Keep 'Em Coming	Get 5 kills with one deployed Sentry Turret	30	Silver
Mechanocide	Kill 100 Enemies with Sentry Bots, Sentry Turrets, or RC Bomb Cars	50	Silver
Jetpacker	Kill an Authority Enforcer during Jetpack descent	20	Bronze
Silent But Deadly	Stealth kill 10 Enemies with the Striker Crossbow	15	Bronze
Hat Trick	Kill at least 3 Enemies with a single Mind Controlled Enemy	15	Bronze
Decapathon	Get 10 Headshot kills with the Wingstick	15	Bronze
Open Minded	Get 10 Headshot kills with the Sniper Rifle	15	Bronze
Jumper	Perform all 18 Vehicle Jumps	20	Bronze
Gotta Have 'Em All	Collect all Playing Cards on one play-through	20	Bronze
Master Chef	Collect all Recipes and Schematics in one play-through	20	Bronze
Hardest Deck	Beat Teague's hardest Deck	25	Bronze
JACKPOT!	Roll 4 Targets in the first round of Tombstones	15	Bronze
Just a Flesh Wound	Complete the final round of 5 Finger Filet	15	Bronze
Deliverance	Complete the final round of Strum	15	Bronze
Minigamer	Win all Minigames	15	Bronze
Lead Foot	Win a Race in the Campaign	10	Bronze
Rage Cup	Win all Races in the Campaign	50	Silver
Demolition Man	Destroy 100 Enemy Cars	20	Bronze
It's Good!	Score each of the 3 Field Goals from the ATV	15	Bronze
Roadkill	Run over 10 Mutants	15	Bronze
Ghost Buster	Complete Ghost Hideout in the Campaign	10	Bronze
Waste Management	Complete Wasted Garage in the Campaign	10	Bronze
Gladiator	Complete Mutant Bash TV in the Campaign	10	Bronze
It's Alive!	Complete Dead City in the Campaign	10	Bronze
Wellness Plan	Complete The Well in the Campaign	10	Bronze
Debunked	Complete Shrouded Bunker in the Campaign	10	Bronze
ytiC daeD	Complete Dead City Reverse in the Campaign	10	Bronze
Jail Break	Complete Authority Prison in the Campaign	10	Bronze

NAME	GOAL/REQUIREMENT	POINT VALUE	TROPHY VALUE
Vault Assault	Complete Gearhead Vault in the Campaign	10	Bronze
Power Struggle	Complete Power Plant in the Campaign	10	Bronze
Decrypted	Complete Jackal Canyon in the Campaign	10	Bronze
Mutie Blues	Complete Blue Line Station in the Campaign	10	Bronze
Bringin' Home the Bacon	Earn 750 Dollars in one episode of Bash TV in the Campaign	20	Bronze
Mr. Oddjob	Complete 5 Job Board Quests in one play-through	40	Silver
Dev Graffiti	Find the secret Developer Graffiti Room	15	Bronze
Hey, not too rough	Finish the Campaign on any difficulty	50	Gold
Hurt me plenty	Finish the Campaign on at least Normal difficulty	25	Silver
Ultra-violence	Finish the Campaign on at least Hard difficulty	25	Silver
RAGE Nightmare	Finish the Campaign on Nightmare difficulty	25	Silver
Obsessive Compulsive	Reach 100% Completion in the Campaign	75	Gold
The Legend Begins…	Complete a Legend of the Wasteland	10	Bronze
Anthology	Complete all Legends of the Wasteland	20	Bronze
A True Legend	Complete a Legend of the Wasteland on Nightmare difficulty	25	Silver
No Room for Sidekicks	Complete a Legend of the Wasteland without any player(s) becoming incapacitated	15	Bronze
Fresh Meat	Complete a public Road RAGE match	10	Bronze
MVP	Get first place in a public Road RAGE match	20	Bronze

RASKULLS

I HATE YOU SHAPEASAURUS (PLAY AS SHAPEASAURUS)

Pause the game, press Y and enter Right Bumper, Up, Down, Right Bumper, Up, Down.

LE FILS DE l'HOMME (APPLE HEAD)

Pause the game, press Y and enter Up, Up, Up, Down, Down, Down.

EGOMANIACS (BIG HEADS)

Pause the game, press Y and enter Up, Down, Left, Right.

PAPER BAG (PAPER BAG HEAD)

Pause the game, press Y and enter Left, Right, Left, Right, Left.

GET FUNKY (AFRO)

Pause the game, press Y and enter X, X, X, Y, Y, Y.

TRANSIENT MODE (BEARD)

Pause the game, press Y and enter Up, Down, Up, Down, Up.

MOUSTACHE ENGAGE! (MUSTACHE)

Pause the game, press Y and enter Right Bumper, Right Bumper, Right Bumper, Left Bumper, Left Bumper, Left Bumper.

TOO BRIGHT! (SUNGLASSES)

Pause the game, press Y and enter Left Bumper, Right Bumper, Left Bumper, Right Bumper, Left Bumper.

AVATAR AWARDS

AWARD	EARNED BY
Raskulls T-Shirt	Complete a certain Mega-Challenge in Chapter 1.
A Giant King Mask	Complete a certain Mega-Challenge in Chapter 2.

RATATOUILLE

Select Gusteau's Shop from the Extras menu. Choose Secrets, select the appropriate code number, and then enter the code. Once the code is entered, select the cheat you want to activate it.

CODE NUMBER	CODE	EFFECT
1	Pieceocake	Very Easy difficulty mode
2	Myhero	No impact and no damage from enemies
3	Shielded	No damage from enemies
4	Spyagent	Move undetected by any enemy
5	Ilikeonions	Fart every time Remy jumps
6	Hardfeelings	Head butt when attacking instead of tailswipe
7	Slumberparty	Multiplayer mode
8	Gusteauart	All Concept Art
9	Gusteauship	All four championship modes
10	Mattelme	All single player and multiplayer minigames
11	Gusteauvid	All Videos
12	Gusteaures	All Bonus Artworks
13	Gusteaudream	All Dream Worlds in Gusteau's Shop
14	Gusteauslide	All Slides in Gusteau's Shop
15	Gusteaulevel	All single player minigames
16	Gusteaucombo	All items in Gusteau's Shop
17	Gusteaupot	5,000 Gusteau points
18	Gusteaujack	10,000 Gusteau points
19	Gusteauomni	50,000 Gusteau points

RATCHET & CLANK FUTURE: A CRACK IN TIME

DISCOUNT AT WEAPON VENDORS

Have a save game for Ratchet and Clank Future: Tools of Destruction.

PIRATE HAT SKIN

Have a save game for Ratchet and Clank Future: Quest for Booty.

BANCHO RATCHET SKIN

Pause the game and enter Up, Right, Down, Left, ●, ●, ✕, ●, R3.

RATCHET & CLANK FUTURE: TOOLS OF DESTRUCTION

PLAYSTATION 3

CHALLENGE MODE

After defeating the game, you can replay it in Challenge Mode with all of Ratchet's current upgraded weapons and armor.

SKILL POINTS

Complete the following objectives to earn skill points. Each one is worth 10 to 40 points and you can use these points to unlock Cheats in the Cheats menu. The list below lists the skill points with a location and description.

SKILL POINT	LOCATION	DESCRIPTION
Smashing Good Time	Cobalia	Destroy all crates and consumer bots in the trade port and gel factory.
I Should Have Gone Down in a Barrel	Cobalia	Jump into each of the two gel waterfall areas in Cobalia gel factory.
Giant Hunter	Cobalia	Kill several Basilisk Leviathans in the Cobalia wilderness.
Wrench Ninja 3	Stratus City	Use only the Omniwrench to get through the level to the Robo-Wings segment.
We Don't Need No Stinkin' Bridges!	Stratus City	Cross the tri-pad sequence using gel-cube bounces.
Surface-to-Air Plasma Beasts	Stratus City	Take out several flying targets using a specific weapon.
Been Around	Stratus City	Take off from every Robo-wing launch pad in Stratus City.
Collector's Addition	Voron	Be very thorough in your collection of goodies.
Minesweeper	Voron	Clear out a bunch of mines.
What's That, R2?	Voron	Barrel roll multiple times.
I Think I'm Gonna Be Sick	IFF	Ride the ferris wheel for 5 loops without getting off or taking damage.
Fast and the Fire-ious	IFF	Use the Charge Boots to cross the bridge to the arena without being burned.
One Heckuva Peephole	IFF	Return after receiving the Geo-laser and complete the Geo-laser setup.
Alphabet City	Apogee	Teleport to each of the six asteroids in alphabetical order.
Knock You Down to Size	Apogee	Wrench Slam 5 centipedes.
Dancin' with the Stars	Apogee	Make 5 enemies dance at once on an asteroid.
Taste o' Yer Own Medicine	Pirate Base	Destroy all of the Shooter Pirates with the Combuster.
Preemptive Strike	Pirate Base	Destroy all of the "sleeping bats" while they are still sleeping.
It's Mutant-E Cap'n!	Pirate Base	Change 5 pirates into penguins in one blast.
You Sunk My Battleship!	Rakar	Shoot down a large percentage of the big destroyers.
Pretty Lights	Rakar	Complete the level without destroying any of the snatchers that fire beams at Ratchet.
I've Got Places To Be	Rakar	Destroy the boss in under 2:30.
The Consumer Is Not (Always) Right	Rykan V	Destroy a bunch of consumer bots in the level.
Live Strong	Rykan V	Complete the Gryo Cycle in 1:45.
Untouchable	Rykan V	Don't take damage in the Gyro-Cycle.
It Sounded Like a Freight Train	Sargasso	Get 10 Swarmers in one tornado.
Head Examiner	Sargasso	Land on all of the dinosaur heads in Sargasso.
Extinction	Sargasso	Kill all of the Sargasso Predators.

R

SKILL POINT	LOCATION	DESCRIPTION
Lombaxes Don't Like Cold	Iris	Break all the breakable icicles.
Mow Down Ho-Down	Iris	Use turrets to destroy 10 dancing pirates.
Dancin' on the Ceiling	Zordoom	Successfully use a Groovitron while on a Magboot surface.
Seared Ahi	Zordoom	Use the Pyroblaster on 3 Drophid creatures after freeing them from their robotic suits.
Shocking Ascent	Zordoom	Destroy all enemies on the elevator using just the Shock Ravager.
Expert Marksman	Borag	Kill 75% of all of the enemies.
Can't Touch This	Borag	Don't take damage before fighting the boss.
Pyoo, Pyoo!	Borag	Complete the level without secondary fire.
Dead Aim	Kerchu	Destroy several destructible towers while on the pirate barge.
Fire With Fire	Kerchu	Kill a few Kerchu Flamethrowers with the Pyro Blaster.
Rocket Jump	Kerchu	Successfully jump over a row of three rockets while on the grindrail during the boss fight in Kerchu City.
Your Friendly Neighborhood…	Slag Fleet	Destroy 5 enemies while on the grav ramp before Slag's ship.
Turret Times Two	Slag Fleet	Destroy at least 2 pirates with each turret in the level.
Six Gun Salute	Slag Fleet	Get six pirates in a row to salute Ratchet while in the Pirate Disguise.
Gotta Catch 'Em All	Cragmite Ruins	Hit all Cragmite soldiers with the Mag-Net Launcher.
Ratchet and Goliath	Cragmite Ruins	Destroy multiple walkers using just the Nano-Swarmers.
Ratchet &…Not Clank?!	Cragmite Ruins	Use Mr. Zurkon in Cragmite's Ratchet-only segment.
Stay Still So I Can Shoot You!	Meridian	Use strafe-flip 10 times while fighting the Cragmite soldiers.
Now Boarding…	Meridian	Complete the Gyro-Cycle in 55 seconds.
Low Flying Howls	Meridian	Fly under an electrified barrier in the Robo-wings segment.
Extreme Alien Makeover	Fastoon2	Turn 10 Cragmites into penguins.
Empty Bag o' Tricks	Fastoon2	Complete the level without using any devices.
Nowhere to Hide	Fastoon2	Destroy every piece of breakable cover.
No, Up Your Arsenal	Global	Upgrade every weapon to the max.
Roflcopter	Global	Turn enemies into penguins, then use the Visicopter to destroy the penguins.
Stir Fry	Global	Kill 2 different enemy types using the Shock Ravager while they are trapped in a tornado.
Golden Children	Overall	Find all of the Gold Bolts.
Sacagawea	Global	Complete all of the maps 100%, leaving no area undiscovered.
Cheapskate	Global	Purchase a single Combustor round.
Everybody Dance Now	Global	Make every type of enemy in the game dance.
F5 on the Fujita Scale	Global	Pick up more than 10 enemies with one tornado.
Chorus line	Global	Get 10+ enemies to dance together.
Happy Feet	Global	Get several penguins to dance on-screen.
Disco Inferno	Global	Use the Groovitron followed by the Pyro Blaster.
Bolts in the Bank	Global	Sell a bunch of Leviathan Souls to the Smuggler.
It's Like the North Pole Here	Global	Have at least 12-15 enemies and/or citizens turned into penguins at one time.
Say Hello to My Little Friend	Global	Kill 15 enemies with one RYNO shot.

SKILL POINT	LOCATION	DESCRIPTION
For the Hoard!	Global	Get every item.
Promoted to Inspector	Global	Get every gadget.
Global Thermonuclear War	Global	Get every weapon.
It's Even Better the Second Time!	Global	Complete Challenge Mode.
The Hardest of Core	Global	Get all skill points and everything else in the game.

RAVING RABBIDS: ALIVE & KICKING

AVATAR AWARDS

AVATAR	EARNED BY
Rabbids A&K T-Shirt	The official T-Shirt supporting ravingness around the world.
Rabbid Helmet	A Rabbid helmet to stay incognito.
T.V. Helmet	A TV set that acts a stunning piece of headgear.

RAYMAN (DSIWARE)

Re-enter the code to toggle it off.

LEVEL SELECT (PAUSED ON THE WORLD MAP)

On the world map, enter R, Up, Left, Right, Down, Right, L.

INVINCIBILITY

Pause the game and enter L, Right, Up, Right, Left, Right, R.

99 LIVES

Pause the game and enter L Left, Right, Down, Right, Left, R.

ALL OF RAYMAN'S POWERS

Pause the game and enter R, Down, Left, Right, Left, Up, L.

10 HITPOINTS

Pause the game and enter L, Down, Up, Down, R.

25 BLUE TINGS

Pause the game and enter L, Up, Left, Right, Left, L.

RAYMAN ORIGINS

LAND OF THE LIVING DEAD LEVEL

Collect all ten Skull Teeth and turn them in.

RAYMAN RAVING RABBIDS 2

FUNKYTOWN

Play each game at least once.

RABBID COSTUMES

Costumes are unlocked as you score 12,000 points in certain games, as well as when you shoot the correct rabbid in the shooting games.

COSTUME	MINIGAME	HOW TO UNLOCK
Cossack	Chess	Earn 12,000 points
Crash Test Dummy	Shopping Cart Downhill	Earn 12,000 points
Cupid	Burgerinnii	Earn 12,000 points
Doctor	Anesthetics	Earn 12,000 points
Fireman	Paris, Pour Troujours	Shoot fireman rabbid
French Maid	Little Chemist	Earn 12,000 points
Fruit-Hat Dancer	Year of the Rabbids	Shoot rabbid wearing fruit hat
Gingerbread	Hot Cake	Earn 12,000 points
HAZE Armor	Big City Fights	Shoot rabbid with armor
Indiana Jones	Rolling Stone	Earn 12,000 points
Jet Trooper	Greatest Hits	Earn 12,000 points
Ken	RRR Xtreme Beach Volleyball	Earn 12,000 points
Martian	Bumper Cars	Earn 12,000 points
Party Girl	Paris, Mon Amour	Once inside boat, shoot girl rabbid
Raider's	American Football	Earn 12,000 points
Sam Fisher	Rabbid School	Earn 12,000 points
Samurai	The Office	Earn 12,000 points
Space	Year of the Rabbids	Earn 12,000 points
Spider-	Spider Rabbid	Play the "Spider Rabbid" Game
TMNT, Leonardo	Usual Rabbids	Earn 12,000 points
Transformer	Plumber Rabbids	Earn 12,000 points
Vegas Showgirl	Burp	Earn 12,000 points
Voodoo	Voodoo Rabbids	Earn 12,000 points
Wrestler	Greatest Hits	Shoot rabbid in green outfit

REALITY FIGHTERS

STORY MODE: FULL STEAM

Complete the regular Story Mode.

MR. MIYAGI

Defeat Mr. Miyagi in Story mode and Story Mode: Full Steam.

SURVIVAL EXTREME

In Survival Classic mode, win 15 fights.

RED DEAD REDEMPTION

CHEATS

Select Cheats from Options menu and enter the following codes. Note, though, that entering cheats will disable Trophies and saving.

NAME	ENTER
Invincibility	HE GIVES STRENGTH TO THE WEAK
Infinite Dead Eye	I DON'T UNDERSTAND IMNFINITY
Infinite Horse Stamina	MAKE HAY WHILE THE SUN SHINES
Infinite Ammo	ABUNDANCE IS EVERYWHERE
Money ($500)	THE ROOT OF ALL EVIL, WE THANK YOU!
Coach	NOW WHO PUT THAT THERE?
Horse	BEASTS AND MAN TOGETHER
Good Guy	IT AINT PRIDE. IT'S HONOR
Famous	I AM ONE OF THEM FAMOUS FELLAS
Diplomatic Immunity	I WISH I WORKED FOR UNCLE SAM
Decrease Bounty	THEY SELL SOULS CHEAP HERE
Gun Set 1	IT'S MY CONSTITUTIONAL RIGHT
Gun Set 2	I'M AN AMERICAN. I NEED GUNS
Who?	HUMILITY BEFORE THE LORD
Old School (Sepia)	THE OLD WAYS IS THE BEST WAYS
Man in Uniform (Bureau, US Army, and US Marshal uniforms)	I LOVE A MAN IN UNIFORM
Sharp Dressed Man (Gentleman's Suit)	DON'T YOU LOOK FINE AND DANDY
Lewis and Clark (All areas)	YOU GOT YOURSELF A FINE PAIR OF EYES
Gang Chic (Treasure Hunter outfit)	YOU THINK YOU TOUGH, MISTER?
Jack Attack (Play as Jack)	OH MY SON, MY BLESSED SON
Hic (Drunk)	I'M DRUNK AS A SKUNK AND TWICE AS SMELLY

PLAYSTATION HOME AVATAR ITEMS

ITEM	EARNED BY
Sombrero	Shooting the hat off an enemy.
Black on red RDR logo T-shirt (male & female)	Opening the chest in the burned out house in Riley's Charge.
Yellow Rockstar logo T-shirt (male & female)	Opening the chest in the attic of John Marston's Beechers Hope house.
Gentleman's attire/lady's finest	Completing Skin It To Win It Social Club Challenge
Posse T-shirt (male & female)	Getting the high score in Strike It Rich Social Club Challenge

ACHIEVEMENTS & TROPHIES

NAME	GOAL/REQUIREMENT	POINT VALUE	TROPHY VALUE
High Roller	Win over 2000 chips in a hand of Poker.	10	Bronze
No Dice	Complete a game of Liar's Dice without losing a single die.	10	Bronze
What About Hand Grenades?	Get a ringer in a game of Horseshoes.	10	Bronze
Austin Overpowered	Complete Twin Rocks, Pike's Basin, and Gaptooth Breach Hideouts in Single Player.	25	Silver

CHEATS, ACHIEVEMENTS, AND TROPHIES

R

NAME	GOAL/REQUIREMENT	POINT VALUE	TROPHY VALUE
Evil Spirits	Complete Tumbleweed and Tesoro Azul Hideouts in Single Player.	25	Silver
Instinto Asesino	Complete Fort Mercer and Nosalida Hideouts in Single Player.	25	Silver
Fightin' Around the World	Knock someone out in melee in every saloon in the game in Single Player.	5	Bronze
Strange Things are Afoot	Complete a task for a Stranger.	10	Bronze
People are Still Strange	Complete 15 tasks for Strangers.	25	Silver
Buckin' Awesome	Break the Kentucky Saddler, the American Standard-bred, and the Hungarian Half-bred.	10	Bronze
Clemency Pays	Capture a bounty alive.	10	Bronze
Exquisite Taste	Purchase a rare weapon from a gunsmith.	10	Bronze
Bearly Legal	Kill and skin 18 grizzly bears.	5	Bronze
He Cleans Up Well!	Obtain the Elegant Suit.	10	Bronze
More than a Fistful	Earn $10,000 in Single Player.	10	Bronze
Frontiersman	Obtain Legendary rank in any Single Player Ambient Challenge.	20	Bronze
The Gunslinger	Score a headshot on any enemy using Expert targeting mode.	5	Silver
Man of Honor / Chivalry's Dead	Attain highest Fame rank and either highest Honor rank or lowest Honor rank.	25	Bronze
Gold Medal	Earn a Gold Medal Rank for a combat mission in Single Player.	25	Bronze
On the Trail of de Vaca	Uncover every location on the map in Single Player.	10	Bronze
Friends in High Places	Use a pardon letter with more than $5000 bounty in Single Player.	10	Bronze
Redeemed	Attain 100% in the Single Player Game Completion stat.	100	Gold
Mowing Them Down	Kill 500 enemies with a mounted weapon in any game mode.	20	Silver
In a Hail of Bullets	Kill 500 enemies with any pistol or revolver in any game mode.	20	Silver
Long Arm of Marston	Kill 500 enemies with any rifle, repeater, or shotgun in any game mode.	20	Silver
Bullseye	Get 250 headshots in any game mode.	20	Bronze
Unnatural Selection	Kill one of every animal species in the game in any game mode.	20	Bronze
Have Gun Will Travel	Complete all Hideouts in a single public Free Roam session.	20	Silver
Slow on the Draw	Get 10 assists in a single Hideout in a public Free Roam session.	10	Bronze
Hit the Trail	Get from Blackwater to Escalera before sundown in a public Free Roam session.	10	Bronze
Posse Up!	Create a posse and get the maximum number of members.	10	Bronze
The Quick and Everyone Else...	Be the top scoring player in any three consecutive FFA games in public matches.	20	Silver
How the West Was Won	Reach the top rank for multiplayer experience.	20	Silver
Go Team!	Be on the winning team for four consecutive victories in any team based game in public matches.	20	Silver

NAME	GOAL/REQUIREMENT	POINT VALUE	TROPHY VALUE
Most Wanted	Become a Public Enemy for 10 minutes and escape alive in a public Free Roam session.	10	Bronze
Red Dead Rockstar	Kill a Rockstar or someone with this achievement in a public multiplayer match.	10	Bronze

SECRET ACHIEVEMENTS & TROPHIES

NAME	GOAL/REQUIREMENT	POINT VALUE	TROPHY VALUE
That Government Boy	Complete "Exodus in America".	10	Bronze
Land of Opportunity	Complete "The Assault on Fort Mercer".	30	Bronze
Sons of Mexico	Complete "The Gates of El Presidio".	40	Bronze
No More Fancy Words	Complete "An Appointed Time".	20	Bronze
A Savage Soul	Complete "At Home with Dutch".	10	Bronze
The Benefits of Civilization	Complete "And the Truth Will Set You Free".	90	Bronze
Into the Sunset	Complete "The Last Enemy That Shall Be Destroyed".	100	Bronze
Nurture or Nature?	Complete "Remember My Family".	50	Gold
Dastardly	Place a hogtied woman on the train tracks, and witness her death by train.	5	Bronze
Spurred to Victory	Complete 20 story missions without switching to a new horse at a hitching post.	10	Bronze
Heading South on a White Bronco	Evade the US Marshals while riding the Hungarian Half-Bred horse in Single Player.	5	Bronze
Manifest Destiny	Kill the last buffalo in the Great Plains in Single Player.	5	Bronze

DOWNLOADABLE CONTENT: OUTLAWS TO THE END

NAME	GOAL/REQUIREMENT	POINT VALUE	TROPHY VALUE
Well done	Complete a Co-Op mission.	5	Bronze
Have posse, will travel	Complete all Co-Op missions.	15	Bronze
2 guys, 1 Coop	Complete a Co-Op mission with just 2 people.	10	Bronze
Stake a claim	Gold medal any Co-Op mission.	5	Bronze
Struck gold	Gold medal all Co-Ops missions.	10	Bronze
Friends indeed	Complete a Co-Op mission without anyone dying.	5	Bronze
You rule!	Complete all Advanced Co-Op missions.	15	Bronze
The mother lode	Gold medal all Advanced Co-Op missions.	20	Bronze
Dodge this	Achieve a kill chain of 10 or more in any Advanced Co-Op mission.	10	Bronze
Bulletproof	Complete a Co-Op mission without dying.	5	Bronze

DOWNLOADABLE CONTENT: LEGENDS AND KILLERS

NAME	GOAL/REQUIREMENT	POINT VALUE	TROPHY VALUE
Call it a Comeback!	Come back from a 2-0 deficit and win a Hold Your Own game.	10	Bronze
Who needs Deadeye?	Kill 3 or more players in a standoff or showdown.	10	Bronze

NAME	GOAL/REQUIREMENT	POINT VALUE	TROPHY VALUE
Stick and Move	Get 3 kills with knives or throwing knives in a single competitive match.	10	Bronze
Double bagger	Double capture 3 times in a single Gold Rush map.	10	Bronze
Headhunter	Kill 5 players via headshot in a single Shootout or Gang Shootout.	10	Bronze
Legendary	Reach level 50 and pass into Legend.	10	Silver
Hail Mary	Get a kill greater than 35 yards with a Tomahawk.	10	Bronze
Axe Master	Complete all Tomahawk challenges in Single Player.	10	Bronze
Original Gunslinger	Get 25 Deadeye kills with Red.	10	Bronze
Reeeeal Good	Get 25 Dynamite kills with Pig Josh.	10	Bronze

DOWNLOADABLE CONTENT: LIARS & CHEATS

NAME	GOAL/REQUIREMENT	POINT VALUE	TROPHY VALUE
Master Exploder	Complete the Explosive Rifle Single Player Challenge	10	Bronze
Pa-Pa-Pa-Poker Ace	In a full Multiplayer Poker game, beat the table when blinds are at maximum	10	Silver
The Big Bluff	In a Multiplayer Poker game, win a hand by forcing someone with a better hand to fold	5	Bronze
In A Van Down By The River	In a Multiplayer Poker game, win a hand on the last card when you were losing prior	5	Bronze
Compulsive Liar	In a full Multiplayer Liar's Dice game, win without losing a single die	10	Bronze
Good Call	In a single Multiplayer Liar's Dice game, successfully make a spot-on call	5	Bronze
One Die to Rule Them All	In a Multiplayer Liar's Dice game, win with only one die left	5	Bronze
Triple Crown	Get first place in all races in any Grand Prix	10	Silver
Peacewalker	Finish a single race without getting shot or killed, and without shooting a bullet	5	Bronze
From Glue to Mon Dieu!	During a Grand Prix, finish a race in first after placing last in the previous race.	5	Bronze
We Must Protect This House!	While on defense, do not allow the attacking team to capture any of their objectives	10	Silver
Avatar of Death	Successfully complete either round of a Stronghold map without dying	5	Bronze
Legion of Boom	Get a triple kill while on the attacking team in Stronghold	5	Bronze
Over 9001	Attain over 9,001 points in a single Free Roam session	5	Bronze
Put the Posse on a Pedestal	Attain over 50,000 posse points in a single Free Roam session	5	Bronze

RED FACTION: GUERRILLA

WRECKING CREW MAPS

Select Extras from the Options menu, choose Enter Code, and enter MAPMAYHEM.

GOLDEN SLEDGEHAMMER, SINGLE-PLAYER MODE

Select Extras from the Options menu, choose Enter Code, and enter HARDHITTER.

ACHIEVEMENTS & TROPHIES

NAME	GOAL/REQUIREMENT	POINT VALUE	TROPHY VALUE
Welcoming Committee	Complete the Tutorial mission.	10	Bronze
Martian Tea Party	Complete 2 missions for the Red Faction.	10	Silver
Spread the Word	Liberate Parker Sector.	10	Bronze
Death From Above	Liberate Dust Sector.	20	Bronze
Friendly Skies	Liberate Badlands Sector.	30	Bronze
Don't Tread On Me	Liberate Oasis Sector.	40	Bronze
Coup D'etat	Liberate Eos Sector.	50	Bronze
Red Dawn	Liberate Mars.	100	Gold
Insurgent	Complete 5 Guerrilla Actions.	5	Bronze
Guerrilla	Complete 25 Guerrilla Actions.	10	Bronze
Freedom Fighter	Complete 50 Guerrilla Actions.	15	Bronze
Revolutionary	Complete all Guerrilla Actions.	25	Silver
Clean and Righteous!	Destroy 5 High Importance targets.	15	Bronze
Warp Speed	Beat all Transporter Pro times.	15	Bronze
Got Any Fingers Left?	Beat all Pro times in Demolitions Master.	15	Bronze
Lost Memories	Locate all missing radio tags.	25	Bronze
Working the Land	Mine all ore locations.	25	Bronze
Free Your Mind	Destroy all instances of propaganda.	25	Bronze
One Man Army	Complete 25 killing sprees during the Campaign.	25	Bronze
Disaster Area	Destroy 1 billion credits worth of EDF property.	50	Silver
Broken Supply Line	Destroy 250 EDF supply crates.	10	Bronze
Power to the People	Raise the Morale of 3 sectors to 100%.	10	Bronze
Tank Buster	Blow up 100 small hydrogen tanks.	10	Bronze
Best Friends Forever	Kill 100 EDF with the sledgehammer during the Campaign.	10	Silver
Coming Down!	Destroy 50 EDF owned buildings.	10	Bronze
Freed Space	Destroy 50 EDF flyers.	10	Bronze
Just the Beginning	Win a Matchmaking match.	5	Bronze
Start of Something Special	Play 5 Matchmaking matches.	5	Bronze
Doing Your Part	Kill 10 enemies in a Matchmaking Match.	10	Bronze
Juggernaut	Destroy a Siege target.	5	Bronze
Doozer	Reconstruct a Damage Control target.	5	Bronze
Grab Some Popcorn	Enter Spectator mode and enjoy the show!	5	Bronze
Try Anything Once	Finish a match in every mode.	10	Bronze

R

NAME	GOAL/REQUIREMENT	POINT VALUE	TROPHY VALUE
Check Your Map	Finish a match on every map in Multiplayer.	10	Bronze
Tools of the Trade	Score a kill with every weapon in Multiplayer.	10	Bronze
Field Tested	Earn 1,000 XP in Multiplayer.	10	Bronze
Battle Scarred	Earn 10,000 XP in Multiplayer.	25	Bronze
War Veteran	Earn 100,000 XP in Multiplayer.	50	Gold
A Winner is You!	Win 250 matchmaking games.	20	Bronze
Topher Would Be Proud	Play 250 matchmaking games.	20	Bronze
Courier of Pain	Score 5,000 kills in Multiplayer.	20	Bronze
Experimenter	Complete 4 hidden challenges in Multiplayer.	10	Bronze
Detective	Complete 8 hidden challenges in Multiplayer.	20	Bronze
Mad Genius	Complete 16 hidden challenges in Multiplayer.	40	Silver
Jack of all Trades	Score 10 kills while wearing each backpack.	10	Bronze
The High and Mighty	Kill a flying opponent using a remote charge stuck to them.	10	Bronze
Party Time	Play all Wrecking Crew modes once.	10	Bronze
Can't Get Enough	Play every mode on all maps in Wrecking Crew.	20	Bronze
Wrecking Ball	Score 25 million points worth of destruction in Wrecking Crew.	40	Bronze
Red Faction Member	Play online with another player who has completed the Campaign.	50	Gold
Bound By Blood	Complete Rescue.	30	Bronze
Family Vengeance	Complete Retribution.	40	Bronze
A Greater Purpose	Complete Redemption.	50	Bronze
Deliverance Defender	Complete Marauder Actions.	20	Bronze
Tumbling Down	Beat all Pro times in Mariner Valley Demo Masters and Transporters.	10	Bronze
Mobile Bombs	Destroy 100 EDF vehicles.	10	Bronze
Structural Integrity	Destroy all Medium and High Priority Targets in Mariner Valley.	20	Bronze
Purge the Valley	Break the EDF Control of the Mariner Valley.	30	Bronze
Ares' Bloodlust	Destroy the 4 Marauder War Totems.	20	Bronze
The Power of One	Collect 75 Marauder Power Cells.	20	Bronze

RED STEEL 2

.357 MAGNUM, THE TATARO

Select Preorder from Extras and enter 370402.

BARRACUDA

Select Preorder from Extras and enter 3582880.

THE LOST BLADE OF THE KUSAGARI CLAN

Select Preorder from Extras and enter 360378.

NIHONTO HANA SWORD

Select Preorder from Extras and enter 58855558.

SORA KATANA OF THE KATAKARA CLAN

Select Preorder from Extras and enter 360152.

RENEGADE OPS

XBOX 360

AVATAR AWARDS

AVATAR	EARNED BY
Renegade Ops Hoodie	Engage helicopter in Single Player.

RESIDENT EVIL 5

PLAYSTATION 3

MERCENARY CHARACTERS

Complete the following stages in The Mercenaries with at least an A-rank to unlock the corresponding character.

CHARACTER (OUTFIT)	STAGE
Jill (BSAA)	Public Assembly
Wesker (Midnight)	The Mines
Chris (Safari)	The Village
Sheva (Clubbin')	Ancient Ruins
Chris (S.T.A.R.S.)	Experimental Facility
Sheva (Tribal)	Missile Area
Jill (Battle Suit)	Ship Deck
Wesker (S.T.A.R.S.)	Prison

RESIDENT EVIL: OPERATION RACCOON CITY

XBOX 360/PS3

ACHIEVEMENTS & TROPHIES

NAME	GOAL/REQUIREMENT	POINT VALUE	TROPHY VALUE
Witness	Witness the beginning of the Raccoon City outbreak.	20	Bronze
Corrupted	Complete the second mission of the USS campaign.	20	Bronze
Danger, High Voltage!	Complete the third mission of the USS campaign.	20	Bronze
Rogue's Gallery	Complete the fourth mission of the USS campaign.	20	Bronze
Betrayal	Complete the fifth mission of the USS campaign.	20	Bronze
Down in the Labs	Complete the sixth mission of the USS campaign.	20	Bronze
Outbreak Survivalist	Complete all U.S.S. missions on Veteran.	25	Silver
Raccoon City Cleanser	Complete all U.S.S. missions on Professional.	35	Gold

NAME	GOAL/REQUIREMENT	POINT VALUE	TROPHY VALUE
Success	Complete all U.S.S. missions with an S Rank.	30	Silver
Great Success	Gain S+ on all U.S.S. mission on Professional/Veteran difficulty	45	Gold
On A Roll	Achieve a 5 kill streak in a Versus match.	15	Bronze
Skill... Or Luck?	Achieve a 10 kill streak in a Versus match.	25	Silver
Now That's G	Collect 3 G-Virus Samples in one Biohazard match.	15	Bronze
No Sample For You	Force 25 enemies to drop G-Virus Samples in Biohazard (lifetime).	30	Bronze
Supreme Survivors	In Survivors mode, have all 4 players on your team Survive the game.	20	Bronze
Fallen Idols	In Heroes mode, eliminate 4 Heroes in one game.	30	Silver
Sampler	Play at least one match in every Versus game type	20	Bronze
You Love to Hate my 98	Complete 98 Versus games	50	Bronze
Tongue Tied	Kill a Licker that is grappling a Teammate.	10	Bronze
Like a Butterfly	Kill 100 zombies with CQC (lifetime)	15	Bronze
Green Thumb	Heal with 101 Green Herbs (lifetime)	25	Bronze
Down Boy	Kill 13 zombie dogs (lifetime)	15	Bronze
These Will Do	Purchase 5 weapons.	10	Bronze
Choices Aplenty	Purchase 15 weapons.	15	Bronze
Quite The Collection	Purchase all available weapons.	30	Silver
One Trick Pony	Purchase an ability.	10	Bronze
Feelin' Stronger Every Day	Fully upgrade an ability.	15	Bronze
Look What I Can Do	Purchase all abilities for one character class.	20	Bronze
Ready To Dominate	Fully upgrade all abilities for one character class.	20	Bronze
So Many Choices	Purchase all abilities for all character classes.	30	Silver
Epic Standards	Upgrade all abilities for all characters to its maximum level.	40	Silver
Organic Shield	Kill 5 enemies consecutively while using a zombie as a shield.	20	Bronze
Baker's Dozen	Kill 13 zombified teammates.	30	Bronze
So Hot Right Now	Kill 103 enemies with incendiary rounds (lifetime)	15	Bronze
Bloody Good Time	Kill 5 enemies by causing Blood Frenzy in a single campaign game or multiplayer match.	20	Bronze
Up Close and Personal	Kill 5 players in one multiplayer game with CQC Kills.	10	Bronze
Chaos Averted	Kill an infected teammate with a headshot before they become a zombie in any mode.	5	Bronze
Like a Bee	Kill 10 enemy players in one Versus game with CQC.	20	Silver
A Gun by Any Other Name	Kill an enemy with each weapon type including special weapons.	15	Bronze
Raccoon City Mascot	Collect all 7 Raccoons.	15	Bronze

SECRET ACHIEVEMENTS & TROPHIES

NAME	GOAL/REQUIREMENT	POINT VALUE	TROPHY VALUE
Died Trying	Attempt "The Rescue" and fail.	15	Bronze
A Hero Spared!	Attempt "The Rescue" and survive.	15	Bronze
The Loyalists	Follow orders and defeat all liabilities	15	Bronze
Stop Squirming	17 Hunters Killed (lifetime)	10	Bronze
This Place Crawls	31 Parasites killed (lifetime)	15	Bronze
By Trail Of Dead	50 Versus opponents killed (lifetime)	10	Bronze
Hat Trick	3 Tyrants Killed (lifetime)	15	Bronze
Only Hurts For A While	Infected 13 times (lifetime)	10	Bronze
Clingy	13 Parasite Zombies killed (lifetime)	10	Bronze
Revival	Revive 31 team mates (lifetime)	20	Silver

ECHO SIX EXPANSION PACK 1
ACHIEVEMENTS & TROPHIES

NAME	GOAL/REQUIREMENT	POINT VALUE	TROPHY VALUE
Happy Trails	Complete By the Trail of Our Dead	20	Bronze
Hot Pants	Complete I Now Know Why You Cry	20	Bronze
Oh Yeah!!!	Complete Nothing is as it Seems	20	Bronze
Boom Worse than Bite	13 Bomb Dogs Detonated	30	Silver
Ticket to the Gun Show	As Tweed, use C4 to open door in Foundry	25	Bronze
Ladies Night	Beat an Echo Six Expansion Pack mission with the 3 female characters in your party.	30	Silver
Who needs guns?	Complete an Echo Six Expansion mission without killing anything with a gun.	30	Silver
Leave no Dead Man Behind	Kill every zombie in the Park before leaving.	25	Bronze
Burning Inside	Kill another player with Crucible in a Foundry Versus Match	15	Bronze

SECRET ACHIEVEMENTS & TROPHIES

NAME	GOAL/REQUIREMENT	POINT VALUE	TROPHY VALUE
Let Lounging Lickers Lie	Do not wake up Lickers in the Atrium encounter in By the Trail of Our Dead	35	Bronze

ECHO SIX EXPANSION PACK 2
ACHIEVEMENTS & TROPHIES

NAME	GOAL/REQUIREMENT	POINT VALUE	TROPHY VALUE
Rocket Socket	Kill 5 enemies with Rocket Launcher	15	Bronze
Bigger They Are	Complete Longest Yard	20	Bronze
Birth of An Abomination	Complete Root of All Evil	20	Bronze
Derailed	Complete The Places We're Meant to Die	20	Bronze

NAME	GOAL/REQUIREMENT	POINT VALUE	TROPHY VALUE
Tyranical	5 Tyrants Slain	15	Bronze
Delivery Specialist	Deliver all 5 virus samples for your team in Dispatch's Biohazard Mode	50	Bronze
Turrets Syndrome	Shut Down or Destroy 5 Turrets	20	Bronze
Boys Club	Beat an Echo Six Expansion Pack mission with 3 male characters in your party.	30	Silver
Supernaut	3 Super Tyrants Slain	30	Silver
Divided We Fall	Complete an Echo Six Expansion mission with no human player incapacitated from death or infection.	30	Silver

RESIDENT EVIL: THE MERCENARIES 3D

CHARACTERS

Complete the following missions with a B Rank to unlock the corresponding character.

CHARACTERS	CLEAR THIS MISSION
Claire	1-3
Rebecca	2-3
Krauser	3-5
Barry	4-5
Wesker	5-5

RESIDENT EVIL: THE UMBRELLA CHRONICLES

UNLIMITED AMMO

Earn S rank in all scenarios on hard difficulty.

ARCHIVE ITEMS

Defeat the following scenarios with the indicated rank to earn that item. Get an S rank to get both A and S items.

SCENARIO	A RANK	S RANK
Train Derailment 1	Mixing Set	Briefcase
Train Derailment 2	Statue of Evil/Good	Relief of Discipline/Obedience/Unity
Train Derailment 3	Blue/Green Leech Charm	Sterilizing Agent
Beginnings 1	Motherboard	Valve Handle
Beginnings 2	Fire/Water Key	Microfilm A/B
Mansion Incident 1	Lighter/Lockpick	Great Eagle/Wolf Medal
Mansion Incident 2	Sun/Star/Moon Crest	V-Jolt
Mansion Incident 3	MO Disc	Fuel Canteen
Nightmare 1	Cylinder Shaft	Hex Crank
Nightmare 2	Last Book, Vol. 1/2	Emblem/Gold Emblem
Rebirth 1	Clark/Gail X-Ray	Slide Cartridge
Rebirth 2	Blue/Red/Yellow Gemstone	Death Mask
Raccoon's Destruction 1	S.T.A.R.S. Card (Jill's)	Book of Wisdom/Future Compass

SCENARIO	A RANK	S RANK
Raccoon's Destruction 2	Joint N/S Plug	Lighter Fluid
Raccoon's Destruction 3	Crystal/Obsidian/Amber Ball	Chronos Key
Death's Door	Picture (Ada and Jon)	S.T.A.R.S. Card (Brad's)
Fourth Survivor	G-virus	Eagle/Serpent/Jaguar Stone
Umbrella's End 1	Plastic Bomb/Detonator	Square Crank
Umbrella's End 2	Blue/Red/Green Chemical	Ink Ribbon
Umbrella's End 3	Vaccine	Medium Base
Dark Legacy 1	King/Knight/Bishop/Rook Plug	Battery
Dark Legacy 2	Film A/B/D/C	Spade/Diamond/Club/Heart Key

RESISTANCE: FALL OF MAN

PLAYSTATION 3

HARD DIFFICULTY

Complete the game on Medium difficulty.

SUPERHUMAN DIFFICULTY

Complete the game on Hard difficulty.

SKILL POINTS

You can access the Skill Points and Rewards menus during gameplay by pressing START to access the Pause Menu, then selecting EXTRAS.

ENEMIES

NAME	LEVEL ACQUIRED	DESCRIPTION
Hybrid	The Gauntlet	After defeating first set of Hybrids.
Leaper	A Lone Survivor	After defeating first few Leapers.
Crawler	A Lone Survivor	After the cinematic and FPNICS.
Menial	Fate Worse Than Death	After the first room.
Cocoon	Conversion	At the third checkpoint.
Carrier	Fate Worse Than Death	At the window when you first see the Carriers.
Howler	Path of Least Resistance	After defeating the Howlers at the end of the level.
Steelhead	Cathedral	After defeating the first two Steelheads in the church.
Titan	Conduits	After defeating the Titan at the beginning of Conduits.
Slipskull	No Way Out	After defeating all three Slipskulls in the burrower room.
Leaper Pod	No Way Out or 61	After finding the Leaper Pods for the first time.
Gray Jack	Angel	After the cryo room.
Hardfang	Evacuation	After defeating the first Hardfang in the cafeteria.
Roller	Into the Depths	After defeating the Rollers in the room with the tunnel in the floor.
Widowmaker	Ice and Iron	After defeating the first Widowmaker.
Hybrid 2.0	Angel's Lair	After the first wave of Hybrids in the node.
Angel	Angel's Lair	After defeating the first Angel on the bridge.

R

VEHICLES

NAME	LEVEL ACQUIRED	DESCRIPTION
Hawk	The Gauntlet	Player automatically starts with this.
Kingfisher	Path of Least Resistance	At the start of the level.
Sabertooth	A Lone Survivor	After getting inside the tank.
Dropship	Hunted Down	After spotting a Dropship in the parking lot area.
Stalker	Outgunned	After spotting the first one in Outgunned.
Burrower	No Way Out	After spotting the first one in No Way Out.
Lynx	Common Ground	After getting inside the Lynx.
Goliath	Giant Slayer	After spotting the first one.

WEAPONS—1ST PLAYTHROUGH

NAME	LEVEL ACQUIRED	DESCRIPTION
M5A2 Carbine	The Gauntlet	Automatically unlocked at start of the game.
Frag Grenade	The Gauntlet	Automatically unlocked at start of the game.
Bullseye	The Gauntlet	In the alleyway after checkpoint 2.
Shotgun	Fate Worse Than Death or 32 or 40	Fate Worse Than Death: Behind the stairs in the outdoor area. Hunted Down: Behind the bar. Hunted Down: In the docks area. Path of Least Resistance: Forced here on the stairs between hill 1 and 2.
Auger	Cathedral	After defeating the first two advanced Hybrids.
Fareye	Conduits	After defeating the large Hybrid and reaching checkpoint 1.
Hailstorm	Search and Rescue	After leaving the first area.
Sapper	A Disturbing Discovery	At the back of the first mech factory.
LAARK	In a Darker Place	On the ground in the first room.
Bullseye Mark 2	Angel's Lair	After leaving the first room and going into the node.

WEAPONS—2ND PLAYTHROUGH

NAME	LEVEL ACQUIRED	DESCRIPTION
Reapers	The Gauntlet	Inside the house at the bottom of the hill.
Backlash Grenade	Cathedral	After crossing alley just past the cathedral; it's the first room on the left.
Arc Charger	No Way Out	At the end of the long hallway prior to the burrower.
L11-Dragon	Evacuation	Before the first elevator leading to the hangar.
Splitter	A Desperate Gambit	At checkpoint 1, near the big windows.

LOCATIONS

NAME	LEVEL ACQUIRED	DESCRIPTION
York	The Gauntlet	Unlocked at the start of the level.
Grimsby	Fate Worse Than Death	Unlocked at the start of the level.
Manchester	Path of Least Resistance	Unlocked at the start of the level.
Nottingham	Into the Fire	Unlocked at the start of the level.
Cheshire	No Way Out	Unlocked at the start of the level.
Somerset	Search and Rescue	Unlocked at the start of the level.
Bristol	Devil at the Door	Unlocked at the start of the level.
Bracknell	Into the Depths	Unlocked at the start of the level.
London	A Desperate Gambit	Unlocked at the start of the level.
Thames	Burning Bridges	Unlocked at the start of the level.
Tower	Angel's Lair	Unlocked at the start of the level.

REWARDS

NAME	HOW TO UNLOCK
Concept Art Pack 1	10 points
Concept Art Pack 2	20 points
The Mighty Wrench - Gives allies wrench	40 points
Flip Levels	70 points
Clank Backpacks	100 points
MP Mechanic Skin	126 points
MP Soldier Skin	Beat game on Superhuman mode.
MP Soldier head skin	Beat game on Superhuman mode and collect all Skill Points.
Movie player	Beat game once.

RESONANCE OF FATE

PLAYSTATION 3

Once you have reached Chapter 7, search Leanne's closet. As she speaks her first line enter the following codes to unlock more outfits.

8-BIT GIRL SHIRT

Up, Up, Down, Down, Left, Right, Left, Right, ●, ●

CLUB FAMITSU SHIRT

●, ●, Up, Up, ●, ●, Left, Left, L1, R1

GEMAGA SHIRT

R2, L2, L1, R1, ●, ●, ●, ●, ●, Up

HIRAKOU SHIRT

●, ●, L1, L1, R1, R1, L3, L3, Up, Down

PLATFORM LOGO SHIRT

R2, R1, R3, L3, L1, L2, Right, Left, ●, ●

POLITAN SUIT

R3, R3, R3, Right, Left, ●, ●, L2, R2, L1. This requires you to have the Reindeer Suit first.

XBOX 360

Once you have reached Chapter 7, search Leanne's closet. As she speaks her first line, enter the following codes to unlock more outfits.

8-BIT GIRL SHIRT

Up, Up, Down, Down, Left, Right, Left, Right, Y, X

CLUB FAMITSU SHIRT

Y, Y, Up, Up, X, X, Left, Left, Left Bumper, Right Bumper

GEMAGA SHIRT

Right Trigger, Left Trigger, Left Bumper, Right Bumper, Y, Y, Y, X, X, Up

HIRAKOU SHIRT

X, Y, Left Bumper, Left Bumper, Right Bumper, Right Bumper, Click Left Thumbstick, Click Left Thumbstick, Up, Down

PLATFORM LOGO SHIRT

Left, Up, Right, Down, Right Bumper, Right Bumper, Left Bumper, Left Bumper, Y, Click Left Thumbstick

POLITAN SUIT

Click Right Thumbstick (x3), Right, Left, Y, X, Left Trigger, Right Trigger, Left Bumper. This requires you to have the Reindeer Suit first.

CHEATS, ACHIEVEMENTS, AND TROPHIES

R

ACHIEVEMENTS & TROPHIES

NAME	GOAL/REQUIREMENT	POINT VALUE	TROPHY VALUE
First Contact	This is just the beginning.	10	Bronze
Maiden Mission	This is what pays the bills.	10	Bronze
Bonus Hitter	You can land one more hit.	15	Bronze
Tri-Attacker	You'll need to cooperate as a team of three.	15	Bronze
Hundred Plus Club	This is the natural product of having weathered countless battles.	15	Bronze
Bullet Barrage	It's all about positioning.	15	Bronze
Resonance Miser	It'll take all three of you to tackle this challenge.	15	Bronze
Hero Actor	Spend enough time in combat, and you'll cross this threshold.	15	Bronze
Spite Monger	Perfect the timing for landing a bonus hit.	15	Bronze
Extreme Spiker	There are more ways to deal extra damage than just a bonus hit.	15	Bronze
Professional Hunter	Their lives have not been given up in vain.	15	Bronze
Material Collector	They sometimes yield useful parts and materials.	15	Bronze
Thousand Pitcher	Throw as hard as your little arms can stand.	15	Bronze
The Iron Fist	A true warrior doesn't fear getting up close and personal.	15	Bronze
Big Shot	You'll have to put mind, spirit, and body into it to hit this hard.	15	Bronze
Material Creator	Become a regular down at the local shop.	15	Bronze
Shopaholic	It's your money. Spend it how you like!	15	Bronze
Customaestro	Laying out parts can become quite a puzzle.	15	Bronze
Basel's Repairman	There's a lot of world left out there.	15	Bronze
Four-Terminal Chain	Connect terminal effects to make them even more effective.	15	Bronze

SECRET ACHIEVEMENTS & TROPHIES

NAME	GOAL/REQUIREMENT	POINT VALUE	TROPHY VALUE
Prologue Complete	You've completed the prologue.	10	Bronze
Chapter 1 Complete	You've completed the first chapter.	10	Bronze
Chapter 2 Complete	You've completed the second chapter.	15	Bronze
Chapter 3 Complete	You've completed the third chapter.	15	Bronze
Chapter 4 Complete	You've completed the fourth chapter.	15	Bronze
Chapter 5 Complete	You've completed the fifth chapter.	15	Bronze
Chapter 6 Complete	You've completed the sixth chapter.	15	Bronze
Chapter 7 Complete	You've completed the seventh chapter.	15	Bronze
Chapter 8 Complete	You've completed the eighth chapter.	15	Bronze

NAME	GOAL/REQUIREMENT	POINT VALUE	TROPHY VALUE
Chapter 9 Complete	You've completed the ninth chapter.	15	Bronze
Chapter 10 Complete	You've completed the tenth chapter.	15	Bronze
Chapter 11 Complete	You've completed the eleventh chapter.	15	Bronze
Chapter 12 Complete	You've completed the twelfth chapter.	15	Bronze
Chapter 13 Complete	You've completed the thirteenth chapter.	15	Bronze
Chapter 14 Complete	You've completed the fourteenth chapter.	15	Bronze
Chapter 15 Complete	You've completed the fifteenth chapter.	15	Bronze
Game Complete	You've beat the game! Congratulations!	15	Bronze
An Unfortunate Accident	A party member has been caught in an explosion and died.	15	Bronze
Union Assault	You've defeated two or more enemies in a single attack.	15	Bronze
A New Beginning	You've begun your second playthrough!	15	Bronze
Tera-Driver	You've loaded over a terabit of data from the disc.	30	Silver
Disrespect Your Elders	You've defeated the Elderly Man. He's with the stars now!	30	Silver
Basel's Liberator	You've made all of Basel's hexes accessible again. Are you even human?!	30	Silver
Challenge Conqueror	You've defeated the top-ranked team, the Last Line! Amazing!	30	Silver
Kings of Neverland	You've cleared Neverland!	30	Silver
The Legendary Hunter	You've completed every mission in the game! The legend will never die!	90	Gold
Stardust Hunters	You've got a ★ in every rank!	90	Gold
Lap Two Complete	You've finished your second playthrough! Congratulations, and thank you!	90	Gold

RETRO CITY RAMPAGE

PLAYSTATION 3

ALL STAGES
Input the code Up, Up, X, Up, Up, X, Up, Up, X, O, O to unlock all stages.

ALL WEAPONS
Input the code Up, Up, Down, Down, Left, Right, Left, Right, X, O to instantly obtain all weapons.

EXTRA MONEY
Input the code Left, Right, Left, Right, Up, Up, Down, Down, R1, O to get extra money.

GAWD MODE
Input the code Up, Up, Left, Right, Left, Right, Down, Down, R1, X to become invincible.

LOSE THE COPS
Input the code Up, Up, Down, Down, R1, O, R1, O, X to immediately lose any pursuing cops.

SPEED SHOES
Input Right, Right, Up, Down, Left, Left, Up, Down, R1, X to move faster.

SUPER STOMP

Input Left, Left, Up, Down, Right, Right, Up, Down, R1, X to gain the Super Stomp ability.

UNLOCK ALL CHARACTERS

Input Up, Up, Up, Left, Right, R1, O, R1, O, R1 to unlock all characters.

UNLOCK ALL STYLES

Input Left, Left, Right, Right, Up, Down, Up, Down, X, O to instantly unlock all styles.

UNLOCK FACES

Go to the Face-R-Us store and input the following codes to unlock new faces.

FACE	CODE
Anthony Carboni	CARBONI
Destructoid Staff	DTOID
Electric Playground Staff	ELECPLAY
Epic Meal Time Staff	EMT
Gaijin Games Staff	GAIJIN
John Romero	ROMERO
Maxime's Friends	MAXIMEAMIS
Mojang Staff	MOJANG
Nintendo Power Staff	POWER
Phil Guerrero	PJFP
PlayStation Blog Staff	URNOTE
Polytron Staff	POLYTRON
Team Meat Staff	TEAMMEAT

PLAYSTATION VITA

ALL STAGES

Input the code Up, Up, X, Up, Up, X, Up, Up, X, O, O to unlock all stages.

ALL WEAPONS

Input the code Up, Up, Down, Down, Left, Right, Left, Right, X, O to instantly obtain all weapons.

EXTRA MONEY

Input the code Left, Right, Left, Right, Up, Up, Down, Down, R, O to get extra money.

GAWD MODE

Input the code Up, Up, Left, Right, Left, Right, Down, Down, R, X to become invincible.

LOSE THE COPS

Input the code Up, Up, Down, Down, R, O, R, O, X to immediately lose any pursuing cops.

SPEED SHOES

Input Right, Right, Up, Down, Left, Left, Up, Down, R, X to move faster.

SUPER STOMP

Input Left, Left, Up, Down, Right, Right, Up, Down, R, X to gain the Super Stomp ability.

UNLOCK ALL CHARACTERS

Input Up, Up, Up, Left, Right, R, O, R, O, R to unlock all characters.

UNLOCK ALL STYLES

Input Left, Left, Right, Right, Up, Down, Up, Down, X, O to instantly unlock all styles.

UNLOCK FACES

Go to the Face-R-Us store and input the following codes to unlock new faces.

FACE	CODE
Anthony Carboni	CARBONI
Destructoid Staff	DTOID
Electric Playground Staff	ELECPLAY
Epic Meal Time Staff	EMT
Gaijin Games Staff	GAIJIN
John Romero	ROMERO
Maxime's Friends	MAXIMEAMIS
Mojang Staff	MOJANG
Nintendo Power Staff	POWER
Phil Guerrero	PJFP
PlayStation Blog Staff	URNOTE
Polytron Staff	POLYTRON
Team Meat Staff	TEAMMEAT

XBOX 360

ALL STAGES

Input the code Up, Up, A, Up, Up, A, Up, Up, A, B, B to unlock all stages.

ALL WEAPONS

Input the code Up, Up, Down, Down, Left, Right, Left, Right, A, B to instantly obtain all weapons.

EXTRA MONEY

Input the code Left, Right, Left, Right, Up, Up, Down, Down, RB, B to get extra money.

GAWD MODE

Input the code Up, Up, Left, Right, Left, Right, Down, Down, RB, A to become invincible.

LOSE THE COPS

Input the code Up, Up, Down, Down, R1, O, R1, O, X to immediately lose any pursuing cops.

SUPER STOMP

Input Left, Left, Up, Down, Right, Right, Up, Down, RB, A to gain the Super Stomp ability.

UNLOCK ALL CHARACTERS

Input Up, Up, Up, Left, Right, RB, B, RB, B, RB to unlock all characters.

UNLOCK ALL STYLES

Input Left, Left, Right, Right, Up, Down, Up, Down, A, B to instantly unlock all styles.

UNLOCK FACES

Go to the Face-R-Us store and input the following codes to unlock new faces.

FACE	CODE
Anthony Carboni	CARBONI
Destructoid Staff	DTOID
Electric Playground Staff	ELECPLAY
Epic Meal Time Staff	EMT
Gaijin Games Staff	GAIJIN
John Romero	ROMERO
Maxime's Friends	MAXIMEAMIS
Mojang Staff	MOJANG
Nintendo Power Staff	POWER
Phil Guerrero	PJFP
PlayStation Blog Staff	URNOTE
Polytron Staff	POLYTRON
Team Meat Staff	TEAMMEAT

CHEATS, ACHIEVEMENTS, AND TROPHIES

R

AVATAR AWARDS

AWARD	REQUIREMENT
Manly Mullet	Complete all Slaughter Spree Arcade Challenges with gold medal scores.
Pixel Pants & Pumps	Complete Story Mode.
Pleather Pixel Jacket	Purchase the full game.

RETRO GAME CHALLENGE

COSMIC GATE

HARD MODE

At the Title screen, press Down, Down, B, B, A, A, Start.

POWERED-UP INFINITY

Pause the game and press Up, Up, A, B. This cheat can only be used once per game.

SHIP POWER-UP

Pause the game and press Up, Up, A, A, B, B.

CONTINUE GAME

At the Game Over screen, press Left + Start. You will continue the game with a score of 000.

HAGGLE MAN

FULL HEALTH

Pause the game and press Down, Right, Up, Left, B, B, B, B, A, A, A, A.

SCROLLS APPEAR

Pause the game and press Up, Right, Down, Left, A, A, A, A, B, B, B, B.

INFINITE TIME

Before a level, hold Up/Left and press A + B.

HAGGLE MAN 2

STAGE SELECT

At the Title screen, hold A and press Up, Up, Right, Right, Right, Down, Down, Left, Left, Left.

FULL POWER

Pause the game and press Up, Down, Up, Down, B, B, A, A.

SCROLLS APPEAR

Pause the game and press Down, Up, Down, Up, A, A, B, B.

CONTINUE

At the Game Over screen, hold Left and press Start.

HAGGLE MAN 3

99 LIVES

Pause the game and press A, B, A, B, Left, Right, Left, Right.

9999 GEARS

Pause the game and press B, A, B, A, Right, Left, Right, Left.

WARP TO BOSS

Pause the game and press B, B, A, A, Left, Left, Right, Right.

RALLY KING

INVINCIBILITY

At the Title screen, press Select + Left.

CARS DISAPPEAR

At the Title screen, hold Select and press Down/Right.

START AT COURSE 2

At the Title screen, press A, B, A, B, Up + Select.

START AT COURSE 3

At the Title screen, press A, B, A, B, Left + Select.

START AT COURSE 4

At the Title screen, press A, B, A, B, Down + Select.

STAR PRINCE

INVINCIBILITY

At the Title screen, hold Up and press A, A, A. Then hold Down and press B, B, B.

CONTINUE

At the Game Over screen, hold Left and press Start.

THE REVENGE OF SHINOBI

PLAYSTATION 3

STAGE PRACTICE

At the title screen, hold A + B + C and press Start. This unlocks the mode at the main menu.

RHYTHM HEAVEN

NINTENDO 3DS

RHYTHM TOYS — TELEPHONE NUMBERS

Enter the following numbers into the telephone in Rhythm Toys to unlock sounds from Rhythm Tengoku:

- 5553282338
- 5557325937
- 5557268724
- 5557625688

RIDGE RACER 3D

NINTENDO 3DS

CATEGORY 3 MACHINES

Complete Beginner Grand Prix Event No. 08

CATEGORY 2 MACHINES & ADVANCED GRAND PRIX

Complete Beginner Grand Prix Event No. 18

CATEGORY 1 MACHINES

Complete Advanced Grand Prix Event No. 26

EXPERT GRAND PRIX

Complete Advanced Grand Prix Event No. 36

KAMATA ANGL CONCEPT (SPECIAL CAT. 1 MACHINE)

Complete Expert Grand Prix Event No. 42

SOLDAT CRINALE (SPECIAL CAT. 1 MACHINE)

Complete Expert Grand Prix Event No. 43

AGE SOLO PETIT500 (SPECIAL CAT. 1 MACHINE)

Complete Expert Grand Prix Event No. 44

LUCKY & WILD MADBULL (SPECIAL CAT. 1 MACHINE)

Complete Expert Grand Prix Event No. 45

NAMCO PACMAN (SPECIAL CAT. 1 MACHINE) & PACMAN MUSIC CD

Complete Expert Grand Prix Event No. 46

NAMCO NEW RALLY-X (SPECIAL CAT. 1 MACHINE)

Complete Expert Grand Prix Event No. 47

MIRRORED & MIRRORED REVERSE COURSES

Complete Expert Grand Prix Event No. 48

RISE OF THE GUARDIANS: THE VIDEO GAME

XBOX 360/PS3

ACHIEVEMENTS & TROPHIES

NAME	GOAL/REQUIREMENT	POINT VALUE	TROPHY VALUE
Explorer – Burgess	Travel to Burgess by way of a Guardian Gate.	20	Bronze
Explorer – Tooth's Palace	Travel to Tooth's Palace by way of a Guardian Gate.	20	Bronze
Explorer – Bunnymund's Warren	Travel to The Warren by way of a Guardian Gate.	20	Bronze
Explorer – Sandman's Ship	Travel to the Sandman's Ship by way of a Guardian Gate.	20	Bronze
Explorer – North Pole	Travel to the North Pole by way of a Guardian Gate.	20	Bronze
Explorer – Pitch's Lair	Enter Pitch's Lair for the first time.	20	Bronze
Guardian Explorer	Travel to each realm in the whole world.	20	Silver
Gates of Burgess	Reclaim all gates at Burgess.	20	Bronze
Gates of Bunnymund's Warren	Reclaim all gates at The Warren.	20	Bronze
Gates of Sandman's Ship	Reclaim all gates at the Sandman's Ship.	20	Bronze
Gates of the North Pole	Reclaim all gates at the North Pole.	20	Bronze
Gates of Tooth's Palace	Reclaim all gates at Tooth's Palace.	20	Bronze
Keeper of the Gates	Complete all Gate Guardians missions in each realm.	20	Silver
Guardians Unite	Complete all Protectors of Belief missions in each realm.	20	Silver
Friends to the Rescue	Complete all Cage Break missions in each realm.	20	Silver
Nightmares Beware	Complete all Shadow Stompers missions in each realm.	20	Silver
Celebrate Your Center	Complete all Find Your Center missions in each realm.	20	Silver
Believe in the Magic	Level up for the first time.	20	Bronze
Elite Guardian	Reach Valor Level 20.	20	Silver
Shadow Spree	Destroy 100 Nightmare enemies.	20	Bronze
Shadow Take-Down	Destroy one of each Nightmare enemy.	20	Bronze
Magic is Everywhere	Destroy all Nightmares in all realms.	20	Bronze
Dig the Spring	Find and Collect all Painted Eggs scattered across all 5 realms.	20	Bronze

NAME	GOAL/REQUIREMENT	POINT VALUE	TROPHY VALUE
Memories Safe	Find and Collect all Tooth Boxes scattered across all 5 realms.	20	Bronze
Eternally Chill	Find and Collect all Snowballs scattered across all 5 realms.	20	Bronze
Toy Central	Find and Collect all Wooden Toys scattered across all 5 realms.	20	Bronze
Dreamer	Find and Collect all Dreamsand Capsules scattered across all 5 realms.	20	Bronze
Deliver Holiday Cheer	Perform a 10 point combo	20	Bronze
Never Stop Believing	Reach a 50 point combo.	20	Bronze
Cool Headed	Upgrade your weapon to Level 2.	20	Bronze
Ice Cold	Upgrade your weapon to Level 3.	20	Bronze
Cold Warrior	Upgrade your weapon to Level 4.	20	Bronze
My Kind of Element	Purchase all Gems.	20	Bronze
Crystal Champ	Collect 15000 Crystals.	20	Bronze
Guardians Deliver	Reach 100% World Belief	20	Gold
Co-op Captain	Instigate a co-operative attack move.	20	Bronze
Shadow Sifter	Destroy one of each type of Champion Nightmare.	20	Bronze
Beyond Belief	Defeat Pitch in the Final Showdown and reach 100% world belief.	40	Silver
This is Going to be Epic!	Defeat Pitch for the fifth and final time in his Lair.	20	Silver
Belief Spin	Turn the Globe of Belief 360 degrees on the Pause Screen.	20	Bronze
Bed Blaster	Destroy all beds that lead to Pitch's Realm portal.	20	Bronze
I Still Believe	Defeat Pitch in each of the five confrontations.	20	Silver
Glory of the Guardians	Defeat Pitch at the Final Showdown.	20	Gold
Tis' the Season to be Naughty	Destroy 40 piles of presents in North's Factory.	20	Bronze
Yeti Master	Hit a friendly Yeti ten times.	20	Bronze
Memories are Treasures	Destroy the circle of mushrooms in Tooth's Asia Temple.	20	Bronze
Workin' Hard Every Day	Destroy 20 vases in Tooth's realm.	20	Bronze
Riding the Wind	Hit 10 Mailboxes around the streets of Burgess.	20	Bronze
Gone Fishing	Destroy all 5 instances of fishing gear around the lake.	20	Bronze
Rise of the Guardians	Earn all trophies to unlock this platinum trophy.	—	Platinum

RISE OF NIGHTMARES

XBOX 360

AVATAR AWARDS

AVATAR	EARNED BY
Nightmarish T-Shirt	Clear Rise Of Nightmares.
Alchemy T-Shirt	Unlock all 50 achievements.

R

ROBERT LUDLUM'S
THE BOURNE CONSPIRACY

PLAYSTATION 3

AUTOMATIC SHOTGUNS REPLACE SEMI-AUTOS

Select Cheats from the Main menu, press ●, and then enter alwaysanobjective.

LIGHT MACHINE GUNS HAVE SILENCERS

Select Enter Code from the Cheats screen and enter whattheymakeyougive.

EXTRAS UNLOCKED – CONCEPT ART

Select Enter Code from the Cheats screen and enter lastchancemarie. Select Concept Art from the Extras menu.

EXTRAS UNLOCKED – MUSIC TRACKS

Select Enter Code from the Cheats screen and enter jasonbourneisdead. This unlocks Treadstone Appointment and Manheim Suite in the Music Selector found in the Extras menu.

XBOX 360

LIGHT MACHINE GUNS HAVE SILENCERS

Select Enter Code from the Cheats screen and enter whattheymakeyougive.

EXTRAS UNLOCKED — CONCEPT ART

Select Enter Code from the Cheats screen and enter lastchancemarie. Select Concept Art from the Extras menu.

EXTRAS UNLOCKED — MUSIC TRACKS

Select Enter Code from the Cheats screen and enter jasonbourneisdead. This unlocks Treadstone Appointment and Manheim Suite in the Music Selector found in the Extras menu.

ROCK BAND 2

XBOX 360

Most of these codes disable saving, achievements, and Xbox LIVE play.

UNLOCK ALL SONGS

Select Modify Game from the Extras menu, choose Enter Unlock Code and press Red, Yellow, Blue, Red, Red, Blue, Blue, Red, Yellow, Blue or Y, B, X, Y, Y, X, X, Y, B, X. Toggle this cheat on or off from the Modify Game menu.

SELECT VENUE SCREEN

Select Modify Game from the Extras menu, choose Enter Unlock Code and press Blue, Orange, Orange, Blue, Yellow, Blue, Orange, Orange, Blue, Yellow or X, Left Bumper, Left Bumper, X, B, X, Left Bumper, Left Bumper, X, B. Toggle this cheat on or off from the Modify Game menu.

NEW VENUES ONLY

Select Modify Game from the Extras menu, choose Enter Unlock Code and press Red, Red, Red, Red, Yellow, Yellow, Yellow, Yellow or Y (x4), B (x4). Toggle this cheat on or off from the Modify Game menu.

PLAY THE GAME WITHOUT A TRACK

Select Modify Game from the Extras menu, choose Enter Unlock Code and press Blue, Blue, Red, Red, Yellow, Yellow, Blue, Blue or X, X, Y, Y, B, B, X, X. Toggle this cheat on or off from the Modify Game menu.

AWESOMENESS DETECTION

Select Modify Game from the Extras menu, choose Enter Unlock Code and press Yellow, Blue, Orange, Yellow, Blue, Orange, Yellow, Blue, Orange or B, X, Left Bumper, B, X, Left Bumper, B, X, Left Bumper. Toggle this cheat on or off from the Modify Game menu.

STAGE MODE

Select Modify Game from the Extras menu, choose Enter Unlock Code and press Blue, Yellow, Red, Blue, Yellow, Red, Blue, Yellow, Red or X, B, Y, X, B, Y, X, B, Y. Toggle this cheat on or off from the Modify Game menu.

ROCK BAND 3

GUILD X-79 GUITAR

At the main menu, press Blue, Orange, Orange, Blue, Orange, Orange, Blue, Blue.

OVATION D-2010 GUITAR

At the main menu, press Orange, Blue, Orange, Orange, Blue, Blue, Orange, Blue.

STOP! GUITAR

At the main menu, press Orange, Orange, Blue, Blue, Orange, Blue, Blue, Orange.

ACHIEVEMENTS& TROPHIES

NAME	GOAL/REQUIREMENT	POINT VALUE	TROPHY VALUE
Tune Up	Calibrate your audio/video setup for the optimal Rock Band 3 experience.	4	Bronze
Self-Made Dude or Lady	Create a Character.	5	Bronze
Best. Name. Ever.	Rename your band.	5	Bronze
Well Connected	Connect your Rock Band 3 Band with rockband.com at http://www.rockband.com.	6	Bronze
You Ain't Seen Nothing Yet	Maintain overdrive for 60 seconds.	20	Bronze
Millionaire Club	Get 1,000,000 on one song.	25	Bronze
Rock Band Master	5 Star on Medium (or 3 Star on a higher difficulty) any 50 Rock Band 3 songs.	25	Bronze
Rock Band Legend	5 Star every song in Rock Band 3 on Hard.	30	Silver
Rock Band Immortal	5 Star every song in Rock Band 3 on Expert.	50	Silver
Alex's Luggage Combination	Beat a Rock Band 3 score of 12,345,678.	30	Bronze
Hometown Threwdown	Complete the "Hometown Threwdown" Road Challenge.	20	Bronze
Real Nor'easter	Complete "The Wicked Awesome Tour".	20	Bronze
Hell Defrosted	Win all rewards on the "Hell Freezes Over" Road Challenge.	25	Silver
Wilderness Survival	Complete the "Through the Wilderness, Eh?" Road Challenge.	20	Bronze
Major Mileage	Get 90 or more spades on "The Long Drive South" Road Challenge.	25	Silver
Party Animal	Completed the "Total Debauchery" Road Challenge.	20	Bronze
The Connoisseur's Connoisseur	Get 90 or more spades on "The European Connoisseur" Road Challenge.	25	Silver
Mile High Club	Complete the "Really Frequent Flyers" Road Challenge.	25	Bronze
Ultimate Road Warrior	Win all awards on the "Really Frequent Flyers" Road Challenge.	30	Silver
HOPO-cidal Maniac	Kill 53,596 Hammer-ons and Pull-offs.	25	Silver
Bleeding Fingers	Get 85% on all Guitar Solos in Rock Band 3 on Hard or Expert.	30	Silver
Guitar Perfectionist	Get 100% accuracy on Expert Guitar.	25	Bronze
Guitar Apprentice	5 Star on Easy Guitar (or 3 Star on a higher difficulty) any 25 Rock Band 3 songs.	20	Silver

R

NAME	GOAL/REQUIREMENT	POINT VALUE	TROPHY VALUE
Bass Streaker	Get a streak of 500 notes on Bass.	10	Bronze
Most Authentic Strummer	Hit 100% of the notes, only strumming up, on Hard Bass.	10	Bronze
Bass Apprentice	5 Starred on Easy Bass (or 3 Starred on a higher difficulty) 25 Rock Band 3 songs.	20	Silver
Drum Roll, Please!	Nail a drum roll.	10	Bronze
Fastest Feet	Hit 90% of the Kick notes in a song on Hard Drums.	15	Bronze
Drums Apprentice	5 Star on Easy Drums (or 3 Star on a higher difficulty) any 25 Rock Band 3 songs.	20	Silver
Keys Streaker	Get a streak of 350 notes on Keys.	15	Bronze
Keys Apprentice	5 Star on Easy Keys (or 3 Star on a higher difficulty) any 25 Rock Band 3 songs.	20	Silver
Pro Bass Apprentice	5 Star on Easy Pro Bass (or 3 Star on a higher difficulty) any 25 Rock Band 3 songs.	20	Silver
Drum Trainer Initiate	Complete the introductory Pro Drum Trainer lessons.	15	Bronze
Drum Trainer Graduate	Complete the final Pro Drum Trainer lessons.	30	Bronze
Play a Real Guitar Already!	Play "The Hardest Button to Button" on Pro Guitar.	15	Bronze
Pro Guitar to the Max	Max out your Score Multiplier meter on Pro Guitar.	15	Bronze
Power Chords	Complete the "Power Chords" lessons in the Pro Guitar trainer.	15	Bronze
Complex Chords	Complete the "More Chord Holding and Arpeggiation" Pro Guitar lessons.	25	Bronze
Pro Guitar Apprentice	5 Star on Easy Pro Guitar (or 3 Star on a higher difficulty) any 25 Rock Band 3 songs.	20	Silver
Pro Keyboardist	Hit at least 90% of the notes in 3 songs on Expert Pro Keys.	15	Bronze
Pro Keys Graduate	Complete the final Pro Keys trainers.	25	Bronze
Pro Keys to the Max	Max out your Score Multiplier meter on Pro Keys.	15	Bronze
Pro Keys Apprentice	5 Star on Easy Pro Keys (or 3 Star on a higher difficulty) any 25 Rock Band 3 songs.	20	Silver
Triple Awesome	Get a Triple Awesome while playing with Vocal Harmonies.	10	Bronze
Is This Just Fantasy?	Hit all triple awesomes in "Bohemian Rhapsody" on Medium or a higher difficulty.	25	Bronze
Vocals Showmanship	Deploy overdrive four times in a single song as a vocalist.	10	Bronze
Tambourine Master	Hit 100% of the notes in a percussion section.	10	Bronze
Vocal Virtuoso	Earn an Awesome rating on at least 90% of the phrases in 6 songs on Hard Vocals.	15	Bronze
Vocal Apprentice	5 Star on Easy Vocals (or 3 Star on a higher difficulty) any 25 Rock Band 3 songs.	20	Bronze
The Endless Setlist III	Successfully complete "The Endless Setlist III!"	50	Gold
Downloader	Play a downloaded song.	20	Bronze

NAME	GOAL/REQUIREMENT	POINT VALUE	TROPHY VALUE
Mercurial Vocalist	Earn 5 stars on Vocals on a downloaded Queen song.	30	Bronze
Live Free or Die	Beat all of the free downloadable songs for Rock Band.	25	Bronze
Fistful of Awesome	Beat 5 downloaded songs.	15	Bronze
Accountant's Dozen	Beat 12 downloaded songs.	15	Bronze
Decent Collection	Beat 20 downloaded songs.	15	Bronze
I Want It All	Play a downloaded Queen song.	15	Bronze
Shameless Self-Promotion	Download and play three songs from a band that has Harmonix team members in it.	15	Bronze
Just Another Band Out of Boston	5 Star any Boston song.	15	Bronze
Face Melter	Melt faces by beating any three '80s Metal songs.	25	Bronze
Dave Grohl Band	Beat 5 songs from any band that has had Dave Grohl as a member.	30	Bronze
The Perfect Drug	Get a 200 note streak on "The Perfect Drug".	30	Bronze

ROCK REVOLUTION

PLAYSTATION 3

ALL CHARACTERS

At the Main menu, press ●, ●, ●, ●, ●, ●, ●, ●, ●.

ALL VENUES

At the Main menu, press ●, ●, ●, ●, ●, ●, ●, ●, ●.

ROCKET KNIGHT

PLAYSTATION 3

ALL CHARACTER SKINS

At the Title screen, press Up, Up, Down, Down, Left, Right, Left, Right, ●, ●, Start.

XBOX 360

ALL CHARACTER SKINS

At the title screen, press Up, Up, Down, Down, Left, Right, Left, Right, B, A, Start.

ROCKET RACING

PSP

TRIGGER MODE

At the main menu or during a game, hold L and press Up, Down, Left, Right, ●, release L.

TRIGGER MODE (REVERSED)

At the main menu or during a game, hold L and press Up, Down, Left, Right, ●, release L.

STICK MODE (DEFAULT)

At the main menu or during a game, hold L and press Up, Down, Left, Right, R, release L

R

ROCKSMITH

UNLOCKABLE SONGS

As you achieve Double Encores, the following songs are unlocked randomly.

- Boss by Chris Lee
- Jules by Seth Chapla
- Ricochet by Brian Adam McCune
- Six AM Salvation by Versus Them
- Space Ostrich by Disonaur
- The Star Spangled Banner by Seth Chapla

ACHIEVEMENTS & TROPHIES

NAME	GOAL/REQUIREMENT	POINT VALUE	TROPHY VALUE
Duck Hunter	Play the Guitarcade game: Ducks	5	Bronze
Fret Fast	Beat 10,000,000 points in the Guitarcade game: Ducks	20	Bronze
Ducks x 6	Play the Guitarcade game: Super Ducks	5	Bronze
Just Super!	Beat 150,000,000 points in the Guitarcade game: Super Ducks	20	Bronze
Solo Foundations	Play the Guitarcade game: Scale Runner	5	Bronze
Scales Owned	Beat 50,000,000 points in the Guitarcade game: Scale Runner	20	Bronze
Challenge Harmonics	Play the Guitarcade game: Harmonically Challenged	5	Bronze
Beat Harmonics	Beat 1,000,000 points in the Guitarcade game: Harmonically Challenged	20	Bronze
Batter Up	Play the Guitarcade game: Big Swing Baseball	5	Bronze
Giant!	Beat 2,000,000 points in the Guitarcade game: Big Swing Baseball	20	Bronze
Slide Puzzle	Play the Guitarcade game: Super Slider	5	Bronze
Slide to Victory	Beat 15,000,000 points in the Guitarcade game: Super Slider	20	Bronze
Where Rainbows Come From	Play the Guitarcade game: Quick Pick Dash	5	Bronze
Furious Plucker	Beat 5,000,000 points in the Guitarcade game: Quick Pick Dash	20	Bronze
The One With Zombies	Play the Guitarcade game: Dawn of the Chordead	5	Bronze
Guitardead	Beat 1,000,000 points in the Guitarcade game: Dawn of the Chordead	20	Bronze
Happy Shopper	Visit the shop	5	Bronze
Singles Rock	Beat 100,000 points in a Single Note Arrangement	20	Bronze
Chordinated	Beat 100,000 points in a Chord Arrangement	20	Bronze
All Rounder	Beat 100,000 points in a Combo Arrangement	20	Bronze
The Basics	Complete Soundcheck (Reach Rank 1)	5	Bronze
New Act	Reach Rank 2	5	Bronze
Local Support Act	Reach Rank 3	10	Bronze
Local Headliner	Reach Rank 4	10	Bronze

NAME	GOAL/REQUIREMENT	POINT VALUE	TROPHY VALUE
National Support Act	Reach Rank 5	20	Bronze
National Headliner	Reach Rank 6	20	Bronze
International Support Act	Reach Rank 7	40	Bronze
International Headliner	Reach Rank 8	40	Silver
Elite Guitarist	Reach Rank 9	60	Silver
Super Elite Guitarist	Reach Rank 10	60	Silver
Rocksmith	Reach Rank 11	100	Gold
My 1st Gig	Play an Event	5	Bronze
My 1st Encore	Qualify for an Encore	10	Bronze
Better Than An Encore?	Qualify for a Double Encore	20	Silver
The Rocksmith Method	Earn all Bronze Technique Medals	20	Bronze
Tutorials My Axe	Earn all Gold Technique Medals	30	Silver
Tone is My Avatar	Create and save a custom tone	10	Bronze
Hear Me Now	Use the Amp	10	Bronze
D-licious	Use the Tuner to tune to Drop-D	10	Bronze
Cente-beater	Beat a 100 Note Streak	10	Bronze
Just Awesome	Beat a 750 Note Streak	40	Silver
Strummer	Beat a 5 Chord Streak	5	Bronze
No Dischord	Beat a 25 Chord Streak	20	Silver
Half-K	Beat a 500 Note Streak	25	Bronze
Art + Functionality	Collect all guitars	30	Silver
Tone Peddler	Collect 50 effects pedals	30	Silver
OK, I Learned	Beat 200,000 points in Master Mode	20	Bronze
Stage Ready	Complete a Master Event	40	Gold
Beneficial Friends	Play multiplayer with 2 guitars	20	Bronze
Just Singing?	Using a mic, sing along and achieve Nice Singing	10	Bronze

ROLLERCOASTER TYCOON 3D

NINTENDO 3DS

PARK DECODER UNLOCKABLES

Go to the Park Decoder under options and enter codes to unlock new items and abilities.

EFFECT	PASSWORD
Asteroid Splash	Splotch, splotch, splotch, crown
Atari Dragon	Crown, drink, crown, drink
Atari Ride Theme	Wrench, drink, wrench, drink
Bamboo Fence	Ferris wheel, wrench, wrench, wrench
Black Beard	Roller coaster, roller coaster, splotch, splotch
Boneyard	Splotch, Ferris wheel, mechanic, mechanic
Cemetery Fence	Crown, crown, mechanic, mechanic
Chute Drop	Wrench, mechanic, crown, crown
Coffin Bench	Mechanic, splotch, wrench, wrench
Combat Arena	Splotch, tree, wrench, wrench
Combat Mech	Mechanic, mechanic, mechanic, wrench
Dead Elm	Drink, drink, Ferris wheel, tree
Flying Carpet	Wrench, splotch, tree, tree
Fourth Dimension	Crown, drink, Ferris wheel, Ferris wheel

R

EFFECT	PASSWORD
Ginger Breads	Ferris wheel, Ferris wheel, tree, Ferris wheel
Griffin Bounce	Crown, crown, mechanic, drink
Hi Tech Sign	Mechanic, tree, mechanic, tree
Liquid Magic	Mechanic, mechanic, tree, mechanic
Mangrove	Splotch, tree, tree, splotch
Meteors	Ferris wheel, drink, tree, tree
Moai Head	Crown, crown, mechanic, crown
Outlaw Cactus	Splotch, Ferris wheel, splotch, Ferris wheel
Picket Fence	Splotch, drink, splotch, splotch
Pumpkin Slime	Drink, splotch, drink, splotch
Red Baron Refresh	Drink, mechanic, crown, wrench
Reverse	Ferris wheel, wrench, wrench, Ferris wheel
Robot Revolve	Ferris wheel, splotch, crown, crown
Robot Trash Can	Crown, crown, splotch, splotch
Rocket Repair	Drink, Ferris wheel, splotch, splotch
Standup Twister	Ferris wheel, Ferris wheel, splotch, splotch
String Theory	Mechanic, mechanic, splotch, splotch
Sundae Surprise	Drink, splotch, wrench, wrench
Sunflower	Drink, splotch, crown, crown
Suspended Swinging	Ferris wheel, Ferris wheel, Ferris wheel, tree
Tea Cups	Roller coaster, tree, roller coaster, tree
Techno Falls	Wrench, roller coaster, mechanic, splotch
Tropical Blends	Crown, Ferris wheel, crown, crown
Wing Seater	Splotch, wrench, crown, crown
Zipper	Drink, Ferris wheel, Ferris wheel, Ferris wheel

RPG ALPHADIA

MOBILE

CHEAT MODE

Defeat the game to unlock cheat mode. This gives you the ability to double experience, gold and skill points and skip enemy encounters.

RUBIK'S PUZZLE WORLD

NINTENDO 3DS

ALL LEVELS AND CUBIES

At the Main menu, press X, Y, Y, X, X.

NINTENDO WII

ALL LEVELS AND CUBIES

At the Main menu, press A, B, B, A, A.

RUGBY LEAGUE 3

$100,000,000 SALARY CAP

Go to Create a Player and enter SOMBRERO as the name.

UNLIMITED FUNDING

Go to Create a Player and enter Sugar Daddy as the name.

HUGE MUSCLES

Go to Create a Player and enter i'll be back as the name.

PRESS Z FOR MAX SPEED

Go to Create a Player and enter RSI as the name.

STRONG WIND

Go to Create a Player and enter Beans & Eggs as the name.

ONE TACKLE THEN HANDOVER

Go to Create a Player and enter Force Back as the name.

SAINTS ROW 2

CHEAT CODES

Select Dial from the Phone menu and enter these numbers followed by the Call button. Activate the cheats by selecting Cheats from the Phone menu. Enabling a cheat prevents the acquisition of Achievements.

PLAYER ABILITY

CHEAT	NUMBER
Give Cash	#2274666399
No Cop Notoriety	#50
No Gang Notoriety	#51
Infinite Sprint	#6
Full Health	#1
Player Pratfalls	#5
Milk Bones	#3
Car Mass Hole	#2
Infinite Ammo	#11
Heaven Bound	#12
Add Police Notoriety	#4
Add Gang Notoriety	#35
Never Die	#36
Unlimited Clip	#9

VEHICLES

CHEAT	NUMBER
Repair Car	#1056
Venom Classic	#1079
Five-0	#1055
Stilwater Municipal	#1072
Baron	#1047
Attrazione	#1043
Zenith	#1081
Vortex	#1080
Phoenix	#1064
Bootlegger	#1049

CHEAT	NUMBER
Raycaster	#1068
Hollywood	#1057
Justice	#1058
Compton	#1052
Eiswolf	#1053
Taxi	#1074
Ambulance	#1040
Backhoe	#1045
Bagboy	#1046
Rampage	#1067
Reaper	#1069
The Job	#1075
Quota	#1066
FBI	#1054
Mag	#1060
Bulldog	#1050
Quasar	#1065
Titan	#1076
Varsity	#1078
Anchor	#1041
Blaze	#1044
Sabretooth	#804
Sandstorm	#805
Kaneda	#801
Widowmaker	#806
Kenshin	#802
Melbourne	#803
Miami	#826
Python	#827
Hurricane	#825
Shark	#828
Skipper	#829
Mongoose	#1062
Superiore	#1073
Tornado	#713
Horizon	#711
Wolverine	#714
Snipes 57	#712
Bear	#1048
Toad	#1077
Kent	#1059
Oring	#1063
Longhauler	#1061
Atlasbreaker	#1042
Septic Avenger	#1070
Shaft	#1071
Bulldozer	#1051

WEAPONS

CHEAT	NUMBER
AR-50	#923
K6	#935
GDHC	#932
NR4	#942

CHEAT	NUMBER
44	#921
Tombstone	#956
T3K	#954
VICE9	#957
AS14 Hammer	#925
12 Gauge	#920
SKR-9	#951
McManus 2010	#938
Baseball Bat	#926
Knife	#936
Molotov	#940
Grenade	#933
Nightstick	#941
Pipebomb	#945
RPG	#946
Crowbar	#955
Pimp Cane	#944
AR200	#922
AR-50/Grenade Launcher	#924
Chainsaw	#927
Fire Extinguisher	#928
Flamethrower	#929
Flashbang	#930
GAL43	#931
Kobra	#934
Machete	#937
Mini-gun	#939
Pepperspray	#943
Annihilator RPG	#947
Samurai Sword	#948
Satchel Charge	#949
Shock Paddles	#950
Sledgehammer	#952
Stungun	#953
XS-2 Ultimax	#958
Pimp Slap	#969

WEATHER

CHEAT	NUMBER
Clear Skies	#78669
Heavy Rain	#78666
Light Rain	#78668
Overcast	#78665
Time Set Midnight	#2400
Time Set Noon	#1200
Wrath Of God	#666

WORLD

CHEAT	NUMBER
Super Saints	#8
Super Explosions	#7
Evil Cars	#16
Pedestrian War	#19
Drunk Pedestrians	#15
Raining Pedestrians	#20
Low Gravity	#18

SAINTS ROW: THE THIRD

XBOX 360

AVATAR AWARDS

AVATAR	EARNED BY
Oversized Gat Mask?	Completed the mission "When Good Heists…"
Saints Logo Shirt	Earned the "Flash the Pan" Achievement.
SR:TT Logo Shirt	Created and uploaded your first character to the community site!

XBOX 360/PS3

From the cell phone, select Cheats from Extras and enter the following. Using any of these cheats disables autosave and achievements.

GAMEPLAY CHEATS

CHEAT	CODE
Give $100,000	CHEESE
Give Respect	WHATITMEANSTOME
Heavenbound	FRYHOLE
Add Gang Notoriety	LOLZ
Add Police Notoriety	PISSOFPIGS
Infinite Sprint	RUNFAST
No Car Damage	VROOM
No Cop Notoriety	GOODY GOODY
No Gang Notoriety	OOPS
No Gang Notoriety	OOPS
No Police Notoriety	GOODYGOODY
Pedestrians become mascots	MASCOT
Pedestrians become pimps and prostitutes	HOHOHO
Pedestrians become zombies	BRAINS
Repair Car	REPAIRCAR

VEHICLES

VEHICLE	CODE
Ambulance	GIVEEMBULANCE
Anchor	GIVEANCHOR
Attrazione	GIVEATTRAZIONE
Bootlegger	GIVEBOOTLEGGER
Challenger	GIVECHALLENGER
Commander	GIVECOMMANDER
Condor	GIVECONDOR
Eagle	GIVEEAGLE
Estrada	GIVEESTRADA
Gatmobile	GIVEGATMOBILE

VEHICLE	CODE
Kanada	GIVEKANADA
Kenshin	GIVEKENSHIN
Knoxville	GIVEKNOXVILLE
Korbra	GIVEKOBRA
Krukov	GIVEKRUKOV
Miami	GIVEMIAMI
Municipal	GIVEMUNICIPAL
Nforcer	GIVENFORCER
Peacemaker	GIVEPEACEMAKER
Phoenix	GIVEPHOENIX
Reaper	GIVEREAPER
Repaircar	REPAIRCAR
RPG	GIVERPG
Sandstorm	GIVESANDSTORM
Satchel Charge	GIVESATCHEL
Shark	GIVESHARK
Sheperd	GIVESHEPERD
Spectre	GIVESPECTRE
Squasar	GIVESQUASAR
Status Quo	GIVESTATUSQUO
Taxi	GIVETAXI
Titan	GIVETITAN
Toad	GIVETOAD
Tornado	GIVETORNADO
Vortex	GIVEVORTEX
VTOL	GIVEVTOL
Vulture	GIVEVULTURE
Widowmaker	GIVEWIDOWMAKER
Woodpecker	GIVEWOODPECKER

WEAPON CHEATS

WEAPON	CODE
45 Sheperd	GIVESHEPERD
Air Strike	GIVEAIRSTRIKE
Apoca-fists	GIVEAPOCA
AR 55	GIVEAR
As3 Ultimax	GIVEULTIMAX
Baseball Bat	GIVEBASEBALL
Chainsaw	GIVECHAINSAW
Cyber Blaster	GIVECYBERSMG
Cyber Buster	GIVECYBER
D4th Blossom	GIVEBLOSSOM
Drone	GIVEDRONE
Electric Grenade	GIVEELECTRIC
Flamethrower	GIVEFLAMETHROWER
Grenade	GIVEGRENADE
Hammer	GIVEHAMMER
K-8 Krukov	GIVEKRUKOV
Minigun	GIVEMINIGUN
Molotov	GIVEMOLOTOV
RPG	GIVERPG

WEAPON	CODE
Satchel	GIVESATCHEL
Tek Z-10	GIVETEK

WEATHER CHEATS

WEATHER	CODE
Cloudy	OVERCAST
Rainy	LIGHTRAIN
Sunny	CLEARSKIES
Very Stormy	HEAVYRAIN

ACHIEVEMENTS & TROPHIES

NAME	GOAL/REQUIREMENT	POINT VALUE	TROPHY VALUE
Dead Presidents	Complete 'When Good Heists…'.	10	Bronze
The Welcome Wagon	Complete 'I'm Free - Free Falling'.	15	Bronze
We're Takin' Over	Complete 'We've Only Just Begun'.	20	Bronze
Tower Defense	Complete Act 1 in one way.	20	Bronze
Kuh, Boom.	Complete Act 1 in another way.	20	Bronze
Gotta Break Em In	Complete 'The Ho Boat'.	25	Bronze
I Heart Nyte Blayde	Complete 'STAG Party'.	25	Bronze
kill-deckers.exe	Complete 'http://deckers.die'.	25	Bronze
Titanic Effort	Complete Act 2.	40	Silver
Once Bitten… Braaaaaaains	Complete 'Zombie Attack!'.	25	Bronze
Murderbrawl 31	Complete 'Murderbrawl XXXI'.	25	Bronze
Mr. Fury Would Be Proud	Complete Act 3 in one way.	30	Silver
Gangstas… In Space!	Complete Act 3 in another way.	30	Silver
Hanging With Mr. Pierce	Complete all City Takeover gameplay in the Downtown district.	25	Silver
Mourning Stars	Complete all City Takeover gameplay in the New Colvin district.	25	Silver
Hack the Planet	Complete all City Takeover gameplay in the Stanfield district.	25	Silver
You're the Best…	Complete all City Takeover gameplay in the Carver Island district.	25	Silver
Bright Lights, Big City	Complete all City Takeover gameplay in the entire city of Steelport.	80	Gold
Ouch.	Complete all instances of Insurance Fraud.	20	Bronze
Tune In, Drop Off	Complete all instances of Trafficking.	20	Bronze
And Boom Goes the Dynamite	Complete all instances of Heli Assault.	20	Bronze
Fence Killa 2011	Complete all instances of Mayhem.	20	Bronze
Your Backseat Smells Funny	Complete all instances of Escort.	20	Bronze
Double Dose of Pimping	Complete all instances of Snatch.	20	Bronze
Porkchop Sandwiches	Complete all instances of Trail Blazing.	20	Bronze
Go Into the Light	Complete all instances of Guardian Angel.	20	Bronze
Tank You Very Much	Complete all instances of Tank Mayhem.	20	Bronze

NAME	GOAL/REQUIREMENT	POINT VALUE	TROPHY VALUE
Have A Reality Climax	Complete all instances of Professor Genki's Super Ethical Reality Climax.	20	Bronze
Everything is Permitted	Kill all of the hitman Assassination targets.	10	Bronze
Hi-Jack It	Steal and deliver all Vehicle Theft targets.	10	Bronze
Getting the Goods	Find 25% of all Collectibles.	10	Bronze
Life of the Party	Find 100% of all Collectibles.	20	Silver
Shake and Bake	Complete your first Challenge.	10	Bronze
You're My Hero!	Complete ALL Challenges.	30	Silver
Ow My Balls!	Do your first nutshot AND testicle assault.	10	Bronze
Gender Equality	Play for at least 2 hours as a male character AND 2 hours as a female character.	10	Bronze
Bo-Duke-En	Hijack 50 vehicles - Dukes style.	10	Bronze
Love/Hate Relationship	Taunt AND/OR Compliment 50 gang members.	10	Bronze
Gellin' Like Magellan	Explore every hood in Steelport.	20	Silver
Who Loves Ya Baby	Kill 50 brutes.	10	Bronze
A Better Person	Buy your first Upgrade from the Upgrade Store.	15	Bronze
Haters Gonna Hate	Kill 1000 Gang Members.	15	Bronze
Cowboy Up	Fully upgrade one Weapon in each slot.	10	Bronze
Pimped Out Pad	Upgrade one Stronghold to its full glory.	10	Bronze
Flash the Pan	Destroy all Gang Operations in Steelport.	10	Bronze
Third and 30	Spend over 30 hours in Steelport.	40	Gold
Jumped In	Create and share a character online.	10	Bronze
Opulence, You Has It	Complete 'Party Time'.	20	Bronze
Stay Classy Steelport	Kill 25 Gang Members each with 'the Penetrator' AND the Fart in a Jar.	10	Bronze
The American Dream	Customize 10 vehicles.	10	Bronze

GENKIBOWL VII

ACHIEVEMENTS & TROPHIES

NAME	GOAL/REQUIREMENT	POINT VALUE	TROPHY VALUE
Cooked To Perfection	Roast 50 peds with the car's flamethrower (in a single instance of Super Ethical PR Opportunity).	10	Bronze
Get off My Back	Destroy 5 chase vehicles (in a single instance of Super Ethical PR Opportunity).	5	Bronze
Stick the Landing	Land on Magarac Island (in Sad Panda Skyblazing).	5	Bronze
Cat on a Hot Tin Roof	Kill all of the rooftop mascots (in a single instance of Sad Panda Skyblazing).	10	Bronze
Flame On	Fly through all of the rings (in a single instance of Sad Panda Skyblazing).	10	Bronze
Feeding Time	Throw 5 mascots into the water (in a single instance of Apocalypse Genki).	10	Bronze

NAME	GOAL/REQUIREMENT	POINT VALUE	TROPHY VALUE
Murder in the Jungle	Finish both instances of Apocalypse Genki.	10	Bronze
Storm the Yarn	Destroy a mouse ATV during Sexy Kitten Yarngasm.	10	Bronze
C-C-C-Combo Breaker	Cause $150,000 worth of damage in a single Sexy Kitten Yarngasm combo.	10	Bronze
Genki Bowl Champ	Complete all activity instances in Genki Bowl VII.	20	Silver

GANGSTAS IN SPACE

ACHIEVEMENTS & TROPHIES

NAME	GOAL/REQUIREMENT	POINT VALUE	TROPHY VALUE
C-List Celebrity	Complete all missions for Gangstas in Space.	20	Silver
Do a Barrel Roll!	Perform all vehicle stunts with the Aegean.	10	Bronze
Revenge of the Navigator	Destroy 10 enemy spacecraft with the Aegean while filming.	10	Bronze
Warrior Princess	Kill 7 Space Amazons with melee attacks.	10	Bronze
Pew! Pew! Pew!	Kill 35 Space Amazons with the Laser Pistol.	10	Bronze
Lights! Camera! Action!	Collect all 6 hidden clapboards.	5	Silver
Xenaphobe	Kill Space Brutina.	10	Bronze
Union Buster	Kill 15 cameramen.	10	Bronze
First Contact	Destroy all enemy spacecraft during the chase scene.	10	Silver
I Do My Own Stunts	Land on the Parachute Target during the rescue scene.	5	Bronze

THE TROUBLE WITH CLONES

ACHIEVEMENTS & TROPHIES

NAME	GOAL/REQUIREMENT	POINT VALUE	TROPHY VALUE
B.A.M.F.	Defeat 15 enemies at Technically Legal using only melee attacks.	10	Bronze
Public Enemy #1	Destroy 45 Police and Swat Vehicles while protecting Jimmy's car.	10	Silver
Weird Science	Complete mission 'Weird Science'.	10	Bronze
Eye of the Bee-Holder	Spray 25 rabid fans with the Swarmitron.	10	Silver
Sting Operation	Destroy 5 Steelport Guard vehicles during mission 'Tour de Farce'.	5	Bronze
Tour de Farce	Complete mission 'Tour de Farce'.	10	Bronze
Supaa-Excellent!	Shoot down a helicopter with a Saints Flow fireball.	10	Bronze
Send in the Clones	Kill a Brute using only melee damage while under the influence of Saints Flow.	5	Bronze
The Johnnyguard	Prevent Johnny Tag from taking damage on the Magarac Bridge.	10	Bronze
My Pet, Monster	Complete all missions for "The Trouble With Clones…"	20	

SAMURAI SHODOWN 2

PLAY AS KUROKO IN 2-PLAYER

At the character select, press Up, Down, Left, Up, Down, Right + X.

SCARFACE: THE WORLD IS YOURS

MAX AMMO

Pause the game, select Cheats and enter AMMO.

REFILL HEALTH

Pause the game, select Cheats and enter MEDIK.

BULLDOZER

Pause the game, select Cheats and enter DOZER.

INCREASE GANG HEAT

Pause the game, select Cheats and enter GOBALLS.

DECREASE GANG HEAT

Pause the game, select Cheats and enter NOBALLS.

INCREASE COP HEAT

Pause the game, select Cheats and enter DONUT.

DECREASES COP HEAT

Pause the game, select Cheats and enter FLYSTRT.

FILL BALLS METER

Pause the game, select Cheats and enter FPATCH.

GRAY SUIT TONY WITH SUNGLASSES

Pause the game, select Cheats and enter GRAYSH.

TOGGLE RAIN

Pause the game, select Cheats and enter RAINY.

SCOOBY-DOO! AND THE SPOOKY SWAMP

BIG HEAD

Enter the clubhouse and select Codes from the Extras menu. Enter 2654.

CHIPMUNK TALK

Enter the clubhouse and select Codes from the Extras menu. Enter 3293.

DOUBLE DAMAGE

Enter the clubhouse and select Codes from the Extras menu. Enter 9991.

SLOW MOTION

Enter the clubhouse and select Codes from the Extras menu. Enter 1954.

SCOOBY-DOO! FIRST FRIGHTS

DAPHNE'S SECRET COSTUME

Select Codes from the Extras menu and enter 2839.

FRED'S SECRET COSTUME

Select Codes from the Extras menu and enter 4826.

SCOOBY DOO'S SECRET COSTUME

Select Codes from the Extras menu and enter 1585.

SHAGGY'S SECRET COSTUME

Select Codes from the Extras menu and enter 3726.

VELMA'S SECRET COSTUME

Select Codes from the Extras menu and enter 6588.

SCOTT PILGRIM VS. THE WORLD: THE GAME

PLAY AS SAME CHARACTER

At the title screen, press Down, R1, Up, L1, ●, ●.

POWER OF LOVE SWORD

At the title screen, press ●, ●, ●, ●, ●, ●, ●, ▲

HEARTS WHEN HITTING OPPONENT

At the title screen, press ✖, ●, ✖, ●, ●, ✖, ●, ●.

BLOOD MODE

At the title screen, press ✖, ●, ✖, ●, ✖, ●, ●.

BOSS RUSH MODE

Pause the game on the overworld and press Right, Right, ●, R1, Right, Right, ●, R1.

ZOMBIE MODE

At the title screen, press Down, Up, Right, Down, Up, Right, Down, Up, Right, Right, Right.

SOUND CHECK BONUS LEVEL

Pause the game on the overworld and press L1, L1, R1, R1, L1, L1, L1, R1, R1, R1, L1, R1.

CHANGE MONEY TO ANIMALS

At the title screen, press Up, Up, Down, Down, Up, Up, Up, Up.

PLAY AS SAME CHARACTER

At the title screen, press Down, Right Bumper, Up, Left Bumper, Y, B.

HEART SWORD

At the title screen, press X, X, X, A, B, A, Y, Y.

BLOOD MODE

At the title screen, press A, B, A, X, A, B, B.

BOSS RUSH MODE

Pause the game on the overworld and press Right, Right, B, Right Bumper, Right, Right, B, Right Bumper.

ZOMBIE MODE

At the title screen, press Down, Up, Right, Down, Up, Right, Down, Up, Right, Right, Right.

SOUND CHECK BONUS LEVEL

Pause the game on the overworld and press Left Bumper, Left Bumper, Left Bumper, Right Bumper, Right Bumper, Right Bumper, Left Bumper, Right Bumper.

CHANGE MONEY TO ANIMALS

At the title screen, press Up, Up, Down, Down, Up, Up, Up, Up.

SECRET AGENT CLANK

PSP

ACTIVATE CHALICE OF POWER

Press Up, Up, Down, Down, Left, Right, Left, Right to regain health once per level.

SCRIBBLENAUTS UNLIMITED

PC - STEAM

UNLOCK EDGAR AND JULIE AS AVATARS

Unlock Edgar and Julie, the parents, as avatars by collecting all 106 Starites in the game.

THE SECRET SATURDAYS: BEASTS OF THE 5TH SUN

NINTENDO WII

ALL LEVELS

Select Enter Secret Code from the Secrets menu and input Zon, Zon, Zon, Zon.

UNLOCK AMAROK TO BE SCANNED IN LEVEL 2

Select Enter Secret Code from the Secrets menu and input Fiskerton, Zak, Zon, Komodo.

UNLOCK BISHOPVILLE LIZARDMAN TO BE SCANNED IN LEVEL 3

Select Enter Secret Code from the Secrets menu and input Komodo, Zon, Zak, Komodo.

UNLOCK NAGA TO BE SCANNED IN LEVEL 7

Select Enter Secret Code from the Secrets menu and input Zak, Zak, Zon, Fiskerton.

UNLOCK RAKSHASA TO BE SCANNED IN LEVEL 8

Select Enter Secret Code from the Secrets menu and input Zak, Komodo, Fiskerton, Fiskerton.

UNLOCK BILOKO TO BE SCANNED IN LEVEL 9

Select Enter Secret Code from the Secrets menu and input Zon, Zak, Zon, Fiskerton.

PSP

ALL LEVELS

Select Enter Secret Code from the Secrets menu and input Zon, Zon, Zon, Zon.

UNLOCK AMAROK TO BE SCANNED IN LEVEL 2

Select Enter Secret Code from the Secrets menu and input Fiskerton, Zak, Zon, Komodo.

UNLOCK BISHOPVILLE LIZARDMAN TO BE SCANNED IN LEVEL 3

Select Enter Secret Code from the Secrets menu and input Komodo, Zon, Zak, Komodo.

UNLOCK NAGA TO BE SCANNED IN LEVEL 7

Select Enter Secret Code from the Secrets menu and input Zak, Zak, Zon, Fiskerton.

UNLOCK RAKSHASA TO BE SCANNED IN LEVEL 8

Select Enter Secret Code from the Secrets menu and input Zak, Komodo, Fiskerton, Fiskerton.

UNLOCK BILOKO TO BE SCANNED IN LEVEL 9

Select Enter Secret Code from the Secrets menu and input Zon, Zak, Zon, Fiskerton.

SECTION 8: PREJUDICE

XBOX 360

AVATAR AWARDS

AWARD	EARNED BY
T-Shirt	Complete the Answers level of the Campaign.
Gold Helmet	Reach level 20 or earn 46 Stars.

SEGA BASS FISHING

XBOX 360

AVATAR AWARDS

AVATAR	EARNED BY
Sega Bass Fishing Tee	Play the game for 5 hours.
Sega Bass Fishing Rod	Play the game for 10 hours.

SEGA GENESIS COLLECTION

PSP

Before using the following cheats, select the ABC Control option. This sets the controller to the following: ● is A, ● is B, ● is C.

ALTERED BEAST

OPTIONS MENU

At the Title screen, hold B and press Start.

LEVEL SELECT

After enabling the Options menu, select a level from the menu. At the Title screen, hold A and press Start.

BEAST SELECT

At the Title screen, hold A + B + C + Down/Left and then press Start.

SOUND TEST

At the Title screen, hold A + C + Up/Right and press Start.

COMIX ZONE

INVINCIBILITY

At the Jukebox screen, press C on the following sounds:

3, 12, 17, 2, 2, 10, 2, 7, 7, 11

LEVEL SELECT

At the Jukebox screen, press C on the following sounds:

14, 15, 18, 5, 13, 1, 3, 18, 15, 6

Press C on the desired level.

ECCO THE DOLPHIN

INVINCIBILITY

When the level name appears, hold A + Start until the level begins.

DEBUG MENU

Pause the game with Ecco facing the screen and press Right, B, C, B, C, Down, C, Up.

INFINITE AIR

Enter LIFEFISH as a password.

PASSWORDS

LEVEL	PASSWORD
The Undercaves	WEFIDNMP
The Vents	BQDPXJDS
The Lagoon	JNSBRIKY
Ridge Water	NTSBZTKB
Open Ocean	YWGTTJNI
Ice Zone	HZIFZBMF
Hard Water	LRFJRQLI
Cold Water	UYNFRQLC
Island Zone	LYTIOQLZ
Deep Water	MNOPOQLR
The Marble	RJNTQQLZ
The Library	RTGXQQLE
Deep City	DDXPQQLJ
City of Forever	MSDBRQLA
Jurassic Beach	IYCBUNLB
Pteranodon Pond	DMXEUNLI
Origin Beach	EGRIUNLB
Trilobite Circle	IELMUNLB
Dark Water	RKEQUNLN
City of Forever 2	HPQIGPLA
The Tube	JUMFKMLB
The Machine	GXUBKMLF
The Last Fight	TSONLMLU

FLICKY

ROUND SELECT

Begin a new game. Before the first round appears, hold A + C + Up + Start. Press Up or Down to select a Round.

GAIN GROUND

LEVEL SELECT

At the Options screen, press A, C, B, C.

GOLDEN AXE

LEVEL SELECT

Select Arcade Mode. At the character select, hold Down/Left + B and press Start. Press Up or Down to select a level.

RISTAR

Select Passwords from the Options menu and enter the following:

LEVEL SELECT

ILOVEU

BOSS RUSH MODE

MUSEUM

TIME ATTACK MODE

DOFEEL

TOUGHER DIFFICULTY

SUPER

ONCHI MUSIC

MAGURO. Activate this from the Sound Test.

CLEARS PASSWORD

XXXXXX

GAME COPYRIGHT INFO

AGES

SONIC THE HEDGEHOG

LEVEL SELECT

At the title screen, press Up, Down, Left, Right. Hold A and press Start.

SONIC THE HEDGEHOG 2

LEVEL SELECT

Select Sound Test from the options. Press C on the following sounds in order: 19, 65, 09, 17. At the title screen, hold A and press Start.

VECTORMAN

DEBUG MODE

At the options screen, press A, B, B, A, Down, A, B, B, A.

REFILL LIFE

Pause the game and press A, B, Right, A, C, A , Down, A, B, Right, A.

VECTORMAN 2

LEVEL SELECT

Pause the game and press Up, Right, A, B, A, Down, Left, A, Down.

EXTRA LIFE

Pause the game and press Right, Up, B, A, Down, Up, B, Down, Up, B. Repeat for more lives.

FULL ENERGY

Pause the game and press B, A, B, A, Left, Up, Up.

NEW WEAPON

Pause the game and press C, A, Left, Left, Down, A, Down. Repeat for more weapons.

SEGA SUPERSTARS TENNIS

PLAYSTATION 3

UNLOCK CHARACTERS

Complete the following missions to unlock the corresponding character.

CHARACTER	COMPLETE THIS MISSION
Alex Kidd	Mission 1 of Alex Kidd's World
Amy Rose	Mission 2 of Sonic the Hedgehog's World
Gilius	Mission 1 of Golden Axe's World
Gum	Mission 12 of Jet Grind Radio's World
Meemee	Mission 8 of Super Monkey Ball's World
Pudding	Mission 1 of Space Channel 5's World
Reala	Mission 2 of NiGHTs' World
Shadow The Hedgehog	Mission 14 of Sonic the Hedgehog's World

SEGA VINTAGE COLLECTION: ALEX KIDD & CO.

SUPER HANG-ON

START ARCADE MODE WITH $10,000

Highlight Arcade Mode and press Up, Left, A, B, Start.

THE REVENGE OF SHINOBI

STAGE PRACTICE

At the title screen, hold A + B + C and press Start. This unlocks the mode at the main menu.

SHANK

KUNG FU SHANK

Reach 1000 kills. Press Start to view your tally.

SHANK THE GIMP

Kill 500 creatures.

HORROR SHANK

Get 100 kills with the Chainsaw.

WHITE PAJAMAS SHANK

Perform a 100-hit combo.

RED PAJAMAS SHANK

Perform a 150-hit combo.

DANCE SHANK

Complete the single-player campaign on Normal mode.

WILDMAN SHANK

Complete the single-player campaign on Hard mode.

SHANK THE SPARTAN

Complete the Backstory Co-op mode.

ANY-S

After completing the single-player campaign, pause a game and press Up, Up, Down, Down, Left, Right, Left, Right, ●, ⊗.

DEATHSPANK

After completing the single-player campaign, pause a game and press Up, ●, Down, ●, Left, ●, Right, ⊗

SHANK 2

EVIL IN SURVIVAL MODE

At the character select, press Up, Up, Down, Down, Left, Right, Left, Right. This must be re-entered after quitting the game.

CHARACTERS FOR SURVIVAL MODE

CHARACTER	HOW TO UNLOCK
Boogie	Buy everything in survival mode.
Bubbles	Stay alive for 15 consecutive waves.
Cesar	Kill someone with the kitchen sink.
Chops	60 pistol counter kills.
Classic Shank	Kill a goon by throwing a bomber.
Defender	100 turret kills.
Falcone	Complete Campaign on hard.
Hobo	Complete all 30 waves on any survival map.
Horror	Reach the zombie wave (14) on each survival map.
Junior	50 fire trap kills.
Kats	100 grenade kills.
Rex	Complete campaign on normal.
Rin	Perform 20 bat counter kills.
Sunshine	Purchase any item in survival mode.

SHIN MEGAMI TENSEI: STRANGE JOURNEY

NINTENDO 3DS

SECRET DEMON PASSWORDS

Enter the following passwords when registering a demon in the Demon Compendium.

DEMON	PASSWORD
Alciel, the Black Sun	ALCARMOR
Beast Nekomata	Mai Namba
Brute Oni	Thick red skin
Cabracan	TRUSTIN SCALY ------- -----
Deity Prometheus	Yu Namba
Demonee-Ho	You can't laugh OR cry now!
Demonica-C	Special Password+Chaos
Demonica-L	Special Password+Law
Demonica-N	Special Password+Neutral
Fairy Pixie	Madoka Ueno
Fairy Silky	Soothing ice
Genma Cu Chulainn	Trust
Hare of Inaba	X-X!Ho!
Promethius	Yu Namba
Megami Ishtar	ISHTAR FIGHTS TAMMUZ ANGELS
Queen of the Faeries, Titania	summon smt.queen
Tyrant Mara	Nich Maragos
Vermin Mothman	Prophecy of wind
Vile Mishaguji	2000
Wilder Nue	James Kuroki
Yatagarasu	HELP ME
Yoma Koppa Tengu	Left hand freeze Right hand shock

SHINOBIDO 2: REVENGE OF ZEN

PLAYSTATION VITA

ITEM EATER

Pause the game, hold L + R and press Up, Down, Up, Down, Left, Right, ●.

RAGDOLL

Pause the game, hold L + R and press Down, Up, Right, Left, Down, Up, ●.

SHOCKMAN

NINTENDO WII

REFILL ENERGY

Pause the game and press Left + Select + 2

SOUND TEST

After completing the game and at the To Be Continued screen, hold Select and press Up or Down.

SID MEIER'S CIVILIZATION V

PC - STEAM

REVEAL THE MAP

Go to the directory "C:\Documents\My Games\Sid Meier's Civilization 5" and open up the "config.ini" file in Notepad and change "DebugPanel=0" to "DebugPanel=1". Then while in-game, hit the ~ key to in-game and select "Reveal All".

SILENT HILL: DOWNPOUR

XBOX 360/PS3

GREEN LOCKER PASSWORDS

At a green locker enter the following passwords:

WEAPONS	PASSWORD
Nail Gun and Double Axe	171678
Pistol 45 and Baseball Bat	353479
Rifle and Golf Club	911977

ACHIEVEMENTS & TROPHIES

NAME	GOAL/REQUIREMENT	POINT VALUE	TROPHY VALUE
Capital Punishment	Completed the game on the hard game difficulty setting, any ending.	100	Gold
Good Behavior	Completed the game on any difficulty without killing any monsters.	50	Silver
Silent Hill Tour Guide	Completed all side quests.	100	Gold
Useless Trinkets	Completed the "Digging up the Past" side quest.	5	Bronze
Birdman	Completed the "Bird Cage" side quest.	5	Bronze
Calling All Cars	Completed the "All Points Bulletin" side quest.	5	Bronze
Neighborhood Watch	Completed the "Stolen Goods" side quest.	5	Bronze
Art Appreciation	Completed "The Art Collector" side quest.	5	Bronze

NAME	GOAL/REQUIREMENT	POINT VALUE	TROPHY VALUE
Silent Alarm	Completed "The Bank" side quest.	5	Bronze
Will Work For Food	Completed the "Homeless" side quest.	5	Bronze
Cutting Room Floor	Completed the "Cinéma Vérité" side quest.	5	Bronze
Turn Back Time	Completed "The Gramophone" side quest.	5	Bronze
What's Your Sign?	Completed the "Shadow Play" side quest.	5	Bronze
Telltale Heart	Completed the "Dead Man's Hand" side quest.	5	Bronze
Dust to Dust	Completed the "Ashes to Ashes" side quest.	5	Bronze
Long Walk, Short Pier	Completed the "Ribbons" side quest.	5	Bronze
Spot the Difference	Completed the "Mirror, Mirror" side quest.	5	Bronze
Silence is Golden	Killed or incapacitated 10 Screamers.	20	Silver
Shadow Boxer	Killed or incapacitated 10 Dolls.	20	Silver
Piñata Party	Killed or incapacitated 10 Weeping Bats.	20	Silver
Lockdown	Killed or incapacitated 10 Prisoner Minions.	20	Silver
The Bigger They Are…	Killed or incapacitated 10 Prisoner Juggernauts.	20	Silver
Fight or Flight?	Escaped from 20 monsters.	20	Silver
Silent Hill Historic Society	Completed Murphy's Journal with all Mysteries.	50	Silver
Stay of Execution	Incapacitated 20 monsters without killing them.	25	Silver
Gun Control	Killed 25 monsters with the Pistol or Shotgun.	25	Bronze
Hypochondriac	Used 20 First Aid Kits.	10	Bronze
Puzzle Master	Completed the game on the hard puzzle difficulty setting, any ending.	100	Gold

SECRET ACHIEVEMENTS & TROPHIES

NAME	GOAL/REQUIREMENT	POINT VALUE	TROPHY VALUE
Now You're Cooking…	Survived the Diner Otherworld.	10	Bronze
Out of the Frying Pan	Rode the Sky Tram to Devil's Pit.	10	Bronze
Going off the Rails	Escaped from Devil's Pit.	10	Bronze
Found a Friend!	Met DJ Ricks in the Radio Station.	10	Bronze
Whatever Doesn't Kill You…	Escaped the Radio Station Otherworld.	10	Bronze
Ashes, Ashes	Collected 3 pages of the rhyme book.	10	Bronze
Broken Cycle	Defeated The Bogeyman.	10	Bronze
No Turning Back	Reached Overlook Penitentiary.	10	Bronze
Ending A	Achieved "Forgiveness" ending.	50	Silver
Ending C	Achieved "Full Circle" ending.	50	Silver
Ending B	Achieved "Truth & Justice" ending.	50	Silver
Ending D	Achieved "Execution" ending.	50	Silver
Ending E	Achieved "Surprise!" ending.	70	Silver

SILENT HILL: HOMECOMING

XBOX 360

YOUNG ALEX COSTUME

At the Title screen, press Up, Up, Down, Down, Left, Right, Left, Right, B.

SILENT HILL: ORIGINS

PSP

CODEBREAKER SUIT

During a game, press Up, Up, Down, Down, Left, Right, Left, Right, ✪, ◉. You must first finish the game to get this suit.

SIMANIMALS

NINTENDO WII

FERRET

Begin a game in an unlocked forest area, press 2 to pause, and select Enter Codes. Enter Ferret.

PANDA

Begin a game in an unlocked forest area, press 2 to pause, and select Enter Codes. Enter PANDA.

RED PANDA

Begin a game in an unlocked forest area, press 2 to pause, and select Enter Codes. Enter Red Panda.

SIMCITY CREATOR

NINTENDO 3DS

99999999 MONEY

Enter MONEYBAGS as a password.

AMERICAN PROSPERITY AGE MAP

Enter NEWWORLD as a password.

ASIA AGE MAP

Enter SAMURAI as a password.

ASIA AGE BONUS MAP

Enter FEUDAL as a password.

DAWN OF CIVILIZATION MAP

Enter ANCIENT as a password.

GLOBAL WARMING MAP

Enter MODERN as a password.

GLOBAL WARMING BONUS MAP

Enter BEYOND as a password.

RENAISSANCE BONUS MAP

Enter HEREANDNOW as a password.

CHEATS, ACHIEVEMENTS, AND TROPHIES

S

EGYPTIAN BUILDING SET

Name your city Mummy's desert.

GREEK BUILDING SET

Name your city Ancient culture.

JUNGLE BUILDING SET

Name your city Become wild.

SCI-FI BUILDING SET

Name your city Future picture.

THE SIMPSONS ARCADE GAME

ALL EXTRAS

At the title screen, press Up, Up, Down, Down, Left, Right, Left, Right, ●, ●.

ALL EXTRAS

At the title screen, press Up, Up, Down, Down, Left, Right, Left, Right, B, A.

THE SIMPSONS: TAPPED OUT

10 EXTRA DOUGHNUTS AND JEBEDIAH SPRINGFIELD STATUE

During a game, select Homer to get his task menu. Tap Homer ten times to get a message for performing the code correctly.

THE SIMS 2

PERK CHEAT

At the Buy Perks screen, hold L + R + ●. Buy the Cheat Perk to get some money, skills, and more.

THE SIMS 2: CASTAWAY

CHEAT GNOME

During a game, press B, Z, Up, Down, B. You can now use this Gnome to get the following:

MAX ALL MOTIVES

During a game, press Minus, Plus, Z, Z, A.

MAX CURRENT INVENTORY

During a game, press Left, Right, Left, Right, A.

MAX RELATIONSHIPS

During a game, press Z, Plus, A, B, 2.

ALL RESOURCES

During a game, press A, A, Down, Down, A.

ALL CRAFTING PLANS

During a game, press Plus, Plus, Minus, Minus, Z.

ADD 1 TO SKILL

During a game, press 2, Up, Right, Z, Right.

THE SIMS 2: CASTAWAY

PSP

CHEAT GNOME

During a game, press L, R, Up, ●, R. You can now use this Gnome to get the following during Live mode:

ALL PLANS

During a game, press ●, R, ●, R, ●.

ALL CRAFT AND RESOURCES

During a game, press ●, ●, R, Down, Down, Up.

MAX FOOD AND RESOURCES

During a game, press ●(x4), L.

THE SIMS 2: PETS

PSP

CHEAT GNOME

During a game, press L, L, R, ●, ●, Up. Now you can enter the following cheats:

ADVANCE TIME 6 HOURS

During a game, press Up, L, Down, R, R.

GIVE SIM PET POINTS

During a game, press ●, ●, ●, ●, L, R.

$10,000

During a game, press ●, Up, Left, Down, R.

THE SIMS 3

MOBILE

500 SIMOLEONS

Click the … in the corner and select Help & About. Go to Gardening Tips and shake your device. Repeat as desired.

PLAYSTATION 3

CHEATS

Load your family, press Start, and hold L1 + L2 + R1 + R2. The game will then prompt you to save another file before activating the cheats. After doing so, Spoot the Llama will be available in Misc Décor. Place it in your lot and click it to access the cheats. Note, however, that this disables Trophies and challenges.

XBOX 360

CHEATS

Load your family, press Start, and hold Left Bumper + Left Trigger + Right Bumper + Right Trigger. The game prompts you to save another file before activating the cheats. Spoot the Llama is now available in Misc Décor. Place it in your lot and click it to access the cheats. This disables Achievements and challenges.

THE SIMS 3: PETS

PLAYSTATION 3

CREATION MODE

Pause the game and press L2 + L1 + R2 + R1. This disables trophies.

XBOX 360

CREATION MODE

Pause the game and press Left Trigger + Left Bumper + Right Trigger + Right Bumper.
This disables achievements.

SINGULARITY

XBOX 360/PS3

ACHIEVEMENTS & TROPHIES

NAME	GOAL/REQUIREMENT	POINT VALUE	TROPHY VALUE
Time Master	Completed Singularity on Hard Mode	60	Bronze
Pistol Whipped	20 Centurion kills in single player campaign	10	Bronze
A Salt and Battery	40 AR9 Valkyrie kills in single player campaign	10	Bronze
Double Barrel	30 Volk S4 kills in single player campaign	10	Bronze
The Slower the Better	25 Kasimov SNV-E99 slo-mo kills in single player campaign	15	Bronze
No Time to Bleed	15 Autocannon kills without reloading in single player campaign	15	Silver
You're a Hit	20 Spikeshot kills in single player campaign	10	Bronze
Roller Derby	20 Dethex Launcher kills in single player campaign	15	Bronze
Drive By	15 Seeker kills in single player campaign	20	Bronze
Return to Sender	Kill 5 enemies by grabbing rockets and launching them back in single player campaign	20	Bronze
Put the Dead in Deadlock	Kill 10 enemies inside a Deadlock in single player campaign	15	Bronze
Up Close and Personal	Kill 20 enemies with Impulse in single player campaign	15	Bronze
Fire and Ice	Kill 10 enemies with Propane Tanks or Cryo Tanks in single player campaign	20	Bronze
Time Bandit	Grab 5 Shields from enemies in single player campaign	15	Bronze
Ashes to Ashes	Age 15 soldiers to Dust in single player campaign	20	Bronze
Night of the Living Revert	Turn 15 soldiers into Reverts in single player campaign	20	Bronze
Fully Armed	Fully Upgraded 1 Weapon in single player campaign	20	Bronze
E99 Tech Geek	Purchased 10 different Hero Upgrades in single player campaign	20	Bronze
Time's on My Side	Purchased 5 different TMD Equipment items in single player campaign	20	Bronze
Pen Pal	Used the TMD to find 15 Chrono-Notes in single player campaign	20	Bronze

NAME	GOAL/REQUIREMENT	POINT VALUE	TROPHY VALUE
Stay After Class	Used the TMD to revert 10 Chalkboards in single player campaign	20	Bronze
Revert Bomber	Killed 10 enemies by aging a Revert and having it explode near them in single player campaign	25	Silver
That Wheel?	Found the wheel. Will they ever explain this?	15	Bronze
Mother My Brain Hurts	Discovered the strange E99 specimen and what it morphs people into	15	Bronze
Extermination Expert	Play 5 public matches of Extermination	10	Bronze
Extermination Addict	Play 100 public matches of Extermination	40	Silver
Extermination Master	Win 25 public matches of Extermination	25	Silver
CvS Master	Win 25 public matches of Creatures Vs. Soldiers	25	Bronze
Creature Hater	Renew 25 beacons in Extermination (public match)	10	Bronze
Creature Lover	Kill 15 soldiers with each creature (public match)	10	Bronze
Fastball	Kill 15 soldiers with a Zek barrel (public match)	15	Bronze
Zekky Style	Kill 15 soldiers from behind with the Zek (public match)	15	Bronze
Hot Lunch Special	Kill 25 soldiers with the Revert puke (public match)	20	Bronze
Bombs over Katorga	Kill 25 soldiers with the Radion's lob attack (public match)	20	Bronze
In Yo Face	Possess 15 soldiers with tick leap attack (public match)	20	Silver
Talk to the Hand	Kill 25 creatures with the Bruiser's Impulse Power (public match)	20	Bronze
Dr. Time	Use the Healer's power to restore 25 soldiers to full health (public match)	20	Bronze
Don't Touch Me!	Kill 15 creatures with the Lurker's reflective shield damage from a melee hit (public match)	20	Bronze
The VP Treatment	Possess a soldier, then shoot another soldier in the face (public match)	10	Silver
Blitzkrieg	Travel 585 meters using the Blitzer's Teleport power (public match)	20	Bronze
Killer	Get highest number of kills in a public match	15	Bronze

SECRET ACHIEVEMENTS & TROPHIES

NAME	GOAL/REQUIREMENT	POINT VALUE	TROPHY VALUE
Workers' District	Completed the Workers' District Mission	25	Silver
Research Facility	Completed the Research Facility Mission	25	Silver
Rail Line	Completed the Rail Line Mission	25	Silver
Central Docks	Completed the Central Docks Mission	25	Silver
E99 Processing Complex	Completed the E99 Processing Complex Mission	25	Silver
Singularity	Completed Singularity	25	Silver

NAME	GOAL/REQUIREMENT	POINT VALUE	TROPHY VALUE
The Good of the Many	You sacrificed yourself to stop Demichev	30	Silver
One TMD to Rule Them All	You chose to live and rule the world alone	30	Silver
The Needs of the Few	You chose to live and join Demichev	30	Silver

SKATE 2

XBOX 360

BIG BLACK

Select Enter Cheat from the Extras menu and enter letsdowork.

3D MODE

Select Enter Cheat from the Extras menu and enter strangeloops.
Use glasses to view in 3D.

SKATE 3

PLAYSTATION 3

HOVERBOARD MODE

In Free Play, select Extras from the Options menu. Choose Enter Cheat Code and input mcfly.

MINI SKATER MODE

In Free Play, select Extras from the Options menu. Choose Enter Cheat Code and input miniskaters.

ZOMBIE MODE

In Free Play, select Extras from the Options menu. Choose Enter Cheat Code and input zombie.

ISAAC CLARK FROM DEADSPACE

In Free Play, select Extras from the Options menu. Choose Enter Cheat Code and input deadspacetoo.

DEM BONES

Defeat most of the Hall of Meat Challenges.

MEAT MAN

Complete all Hall of Meat Challenges.

RESET OBJECTS TO ORIGINAL POSITIONS

In Free Play, select Extras from the Options menu. Choose Enter Cheat Code and input streetsweeper.

SKULLGIRLS

PLAYSTATION 3

COLOR PALETTE 10

At the versus screen in local gameplay, press Down, R1, Up, L1, ●, ●.

XBOX 360

COLOR PALETTE 10

At the versus screen in local gameplay, press Down, Right Bumper, Up, Left Bumper, Y, B.

SKYLANDERS: GIANTS

NINTENDO WII U

SKYLANDERS SPECIFIC QUESTS

Skylanders Giants includes quests specific to each Skylander as a way to improve them. Here we list each Skylander with their quest and tips on how to complete it.

SKYLANDER	QUEST	HOW TO COMPLETE
Bash	On a Roll: Defeat 10 enemies with one roll attack.	If you have trouble completing this quest, opt for the Pulver-Dragon upgrade path.
Boomer	On a Troll: Defeat five enemies with one kicked Troll Bomb.	Once you have Troll Bomb Boot, look for a group of tight-knit Chompies. "Chapter 1: Time of the Giants" has several groupings of five Chompies.
Bouncer	Stay on Target!: Target enemies 100 times with laser-guided Shoulder Rockets.	You must purchase the Targeting Computer upgrade for Bouncer's Shoulder Rockets.
Camo	Garden Gorger: Eat 10 watermelons.	If you aren't in a rush to complete a level, switch to Camo when a watermelon appears.
Chill	Ice Sore: Defeat six enemies with one Ice Narwhal attack.	Try to find six enemies that are grouped together at a medium distance, such as in an arena.
Chop Chop	Stalwart Defender: Absorb 1,000 damage with your shield.	To complete this quest safely, block attacks from a small group of weaker enemies near a food item (just in case they sneak in some unexpected damage).
Crusher	High Roller: Defeat 100 enemies with boulders.	Use Rockslide to defeat enemies until you have completed this quest.
Cynder	On the Haunt: Defeat 50 enemies with your Ghost Ally.	Ghost Ally does not inflict much damage so focus on saving low-health enemies, like Chompies, for the ghost to attack. The Ghost attacks while Cynder is flying, so consider circling an area with Chompies.
Dino-Rang	Fooderang: Pick up 20 food items with boomerangs.	After acquiring Sticky Boomerangs, use it to grab any food found in the area. In the Arena Challenges on Flynn's Ship, the audience throws food items into the arena between rounds.
Double Trouble	Big Bomb Trouble: Defeat 10 enemies with one Magic Bomb attack.	Find a group of 10 or more Chompies and set off a bomb. A good place to earn this is any of Brock's Arena Challenges with regular Chompies.
Drill Sergeant	Drill Skill: Defeat Drill-X without changing Skylanders.	Drill Sergeant must defeat Drill-X (the final boss in "Chapter 11: Drill-X's Big Rig") solo. Use Adventure items (like Healing Potion) to survive the battle. You can complete it on Easy difficulty with a fully-upgraded Drill Sergeant.
Drobot	Feed the Burn: Defeat 50 enemies with Afterburners.	It's easier to hit enemies with Afterburners when Drobot first takes off.
Eruptor	Pizza Burp: Eat 10 Pizzas.	If you want to have a greater chance of encountering a pizza, equip Lucky Wheel of Health in the Luck-O-Tron.
Eye-Brawl	Gold Search: Collect 5,000 gold with the eyeball detached.	Remember to detach Eye-Brawl's eye before collecting any treasure from chests or enemies.
Flameslinger	Circular Combustion: Defeat 10 enemies with one column of Fire Flame Dash.	There are two upgrades you can get to help you on this quest. The first is Column of Fire. The second is Supernova in the Pyromancer Path.

SKYLANDER	QUEST	HOW TO COMPLETE
Flashwing	Let It Shine: Defeat 20 enemies with one Crystal Lighthouse.	Since Crystal Lighthouse is stationary, this is a tricky quest. The best candidate for this is one of the arena maps, particularly Kaos' Royal Flush (the second challenge, Birthday Bash). Set up the Lighthouse in the middle of the birthday cake.
Fright Rider	Delving Throw: Toss 50 enemies into the air.	The power to use for this quest is Burrow Bomber. Hit any medium or small enemy with the attack to pop them up in the air and register a toss.
Ghost Roaster	Grave Circumstances: Defeat 100 enemies with Skull Charge.	Repeatedly use Skull Charge to attack enemies and you should complete this quest in no time.
Gill Grunt	Anchors Away!: Defeat six enemies with one Anchor Attack.	Line up a group of Chompies with your Anchor Cannon and let loose to complete the quest. If you have Series 2 Gill Grunt, Anchors Away! Makes completing the quest easier.
Hex	Noggin Knocker: Knock away 100 enemies with your Skull Rain.	Once Hex has Skull Shield, allow enemies to get within melee range while Hex is charging that attack. If they get too close, they get knocked back, tallying a point for this quest.
Hot Dog	Animal Aggravator: Scare away 20 birds.	Look for the small birds pecking at the ground in each level. These birds are the ones you need to scare with Hot Dog for this achievement. Chapter 13: The Oracle and Chapter 1: Time of Giants both have plenty of birds.
Hot Head	Buggy Breakthrough: Destroy 20 walls in Hot Rod mode.	The walls this quest is referring to are the walls that can only be crushed by a Giant or a bomb. Whenever you encounter one of these walls, switch to Hot Head. A good spot with plenty of these types of walls is Chapter 2: Junkyard Isles.
Ignitor	Tinder Trekker: Travel 26,000 feet in Flame Form.	Use Flame Form often and this number will accumulate quickly.
Jet-Vac	Bird Cleaner: Suck up 50 birds in your Suction Gun.	Look for tiny birds on the ground throughout most levels with green grass. Cahpter 13: The Oracle and Chapter 1: Time of Giants both have plenty of birds.
Lightning Rod	Current Event: Defeat 10 enemies with one Grand Lightning strike.	You need to find a group of 10 Chompies in one area and use the Grand Lightning to blast them all. Choosing the Lord of Lightning Path makes this easier since the Grand Lightning attack lasts longer.
Ninjini	Bottle Beatdown: Defeat 5 enemies within five seconds of exiting your battle.	Transform Ninjini into the bottle and move into a large group of small enemies. Follow up the bottle attack with her swords.
Pop Fizz	Rampage: Do 200 HP of damage in a single run in Beast Form.	Transform into Beast Form in a large group of enemies and destroy everything in sight to complete the quest.
Prism Break	Bifurcation Sensation: Defeat 100 enemies with double refraction.	A beam must pass through two Shards before hitting an enemy to count. Unlock the Chained Refractions upgrade and place plenty of Crystal Shards. Fire an Energy Beam through them to indirectly take out nearby enemies.
Shroomboom	Lunching Launch: Eat a watermelon while performing a Self-Slingshot!	When you find a watermelon, blast Shroomboom through it with the Self-Slingshot power to complete the quest.
Slam Bam	Ice to Meet You: Trap 100 enemies in your Ice Blocks.	You do not need to damage or freeze enemies with Ice Block; it counts if you just hit them with the Ice Block.

SKYLANDER	QUEST	HOW TO COMPLETE
Sonic Boom	Sonic Squeak: Babies defeat 50 enemies.	Upgrade Sonic Boom's egg attack powers and keep babies summoned at all times.
Sprocket	Mined Your Step: Defeat 50 enemies using the Landmine Golf attack.	Once you unlock the Landmine Golf ability, use it often. A quick way to complete this quest is to load up one of the easier Arena levels.
Spyro	Full Charge: Collect 3 gold, eat 1 food item, and defeat 2 enemies in 1 Sprint Charge.	Look for two low-health enemies (Chompies are a good choice) as well as some food and gold on the screen. Purchase the Sprint Charge upgrade to increase the distance of Spyro's sprint.
Stealth Elf	Stealth Health: Gain 1,000 HP while stealthed.	You need to first purchase Sylvan Regeneration. Once you do, you get credit towards the 1,000 HP every time you heal while Stealth Elf is in the Stealthier Decoy mode.
Stump Smash	Meganut Bowling: Defeat five enemies with one Meganut.	Meganuts are powerful and bowling over five Chompies with one is no problem. The upgrade Acorn Croquet makes this much easier to achieve since you can whack the acorn directly at enemies.
Sunburn	Immolation Itinerant: Travel 1 mile using Immolation Teleport.	Use Immolation Teleport regularly to tally up the distance towards one full mile. The quickest way to complete this quest is to unlock the Flight of the Phoenix and the Guided Teleportation upgrades.
Swarm	Swarm Feelings: Defeat 100 enemies in Swarm Form.	While you can complete this quest without pursuing the Wasp Stormer Path, it's extremely difficult and you must focus on weaker enemies.
Terrafin	Land Lubber: Eat 20 food items while burrowing.	Once you have Surface Feeder, stay underground and collect Food Items as they drop.
Thumpback	Beached Whale: Defeat 8 enemies with one Belly Flop.	Upgrade Thumpback's Belly Flop attack with Slippery Belly. If you are having trouble getting this quest, invest in the Up Close and Personal path to further increase the strength of the Belly Flop attack.
Tree Rex	Timberrrrr!: Defeat 50 enemies by landing on them. Chompies don't count!	Unfortunately, Elbow Drop doesn't work for this quest. Tree Rex must crush enemies by landing on them. The best way to do this is to find a bounce pad in an area with plenty of Chompies.
Trigger Happy	Holding Gold: Save up 50,000 Gold.	This is one of the hardest quests any character has in the game. Not because it's difficult, but because it will take some time to collect 50,000 Gold.
Voodood	Trickwire: Defeat six enemies at once with your tripwire.	Find a group of six or more low-health enemies, like Bone Chompies, and set up the Tripwire near them. Chapter 1: Time of the Giants has several good spots to try for this quest.
Warnado	Chompy Catcher: Catch 100 Chompies in tornadoes.	The best place to do this is in the Arena Challenges. Head to any of the early challenges and there are plenty of Chompies. High Winds also helps gather up more Chompies at once.
Wham-Shell	Irate Invertebrate: Defeat 6 enemies with one Poseidon Strike.	To get the most out of Poseidon Strike, invest in the Captain Crustacean path. Once you have unlocked Mace of the Deep, go for this quest by finding a group of Chompies and blasting them.

SKYLANDER	QUEST	HOW TO COMPLETE
Whirlwind	What does it mean?: Create 50 double rainbows.	Unlock the Duel Rainbows ability, then fire out a Tempest cloud and following up with a Rainbow of Doom. Rainbows made via the Double Dose of Doom power don't count unless they hit a Tempest Cloud. Triple rainbows created via Triple Tempest count as one double rainbow.
Wrecking Ball	Competitive Eater: Swallow 100 enemies.	Purchase Enemy Slurp and swallow as many enemies as you can. Any medium-sized and smaller enemy can be eaten.
Zap	In the SLimelight: Defeat 50 enemies by electrifying them in Sea Slime.	Use Sea Slime to electrify enemies regularly and you'll complete this quest in no time.
Zook	Spore It On: Absorb 1,000 points of damage with a Foliage Barrier.	Use Foliage Barrier often and you will complete this quest quickly.

THE SLY COLLECTION

SLY 2: BAND OF THIEVES

RESTART CURRENT EPISODE

Pause the game and press Left, R1, Up, Down, Up, Left.

TUTORIAL

Pause the game and press Right, Left, Up, Up, Up, R1.

SKIP TO EPISODE 1

Pause the game and press Down, R1, Left, Right, R1, Down.

SKIP TO EPISODE 2

Pause the game and press R1, Left, Right, R1, Left, Down.

SKIP TO EPISODE 3

Pause the game and press Up, Left, Right, Left, Down, Up.

SKIP TO EPISODE 4

Pause the game and press Up, Right, Right, Up, Left, Left.

SKIP TO EPISODE 5

Pause the game and press Left, R1, Down, Down, Up, Right.

SKIP TO EPISODE 6

Pause the game and press Down, Up, R1, R1, Left, Down.

SKIP TO EPISODE 7

Pause the game and press Left, Left, Left, Down, Down, R1.

SKIP TO EPSIODE 8

Pause the game and press Down Up, Left, Left, R1, Right.

UNLOCK TOM GADGET

Pause the game and press Left, Left, Down, Right, Left, Right.

TIME RUSH ABILITY

Pause the game and press Down, Down, Up, Down, Right, Left.

SLY 3: HONOR AMONG THIEVES

FLY THE TOONAMI PLANE

While in the regular plane, pause the game and press R1, R1, Right, Down, Down, Right.

RESTART MISSIONS

Pause the game and enter the following codes to restart the corresponding missions:

RESTART THIS MISSION	ENTER THIS CODE
Episode 1, Day 1	Left, R2, Right, L1, R2, L1
Episode 1, Day 2	Down, L2, Up, Left, R2, L2
Episode 2, Day 1	Right, L2, Left, Up, Right, Down
Episode 2, Day 2	Down, Up, R1, Up, R2, L2
Episode 3, Day 1	R2, R1, L1, Left, L1, Down
Episode 3, Day 2	L2, R1, R2, L2, L1, Up
Episode 4, Day 1	Left, Right, L1, R2, Right, R2
Episode 4, Day 2	L1, Left, L2, Left, Up, L1
Episode 5, Day 1	Left, R2, Right, Up, L1, R2
Episode 5, Day 2	R2, R1, L1, R1, R2, R1
Operation Laptop Retrieval	L2, Left, R1, L2, L1, Down
Operation Moon Crash	L2, Up, Left, L1, L2, L1
Operation Reverse Double Cross	Right, Left, Up, Left, R2, Left
Operation Tar Be-Gone	Down, L2, R1, L2, R1, Right
Operation Turbo Dominant Eagle	Down, Right, Left, L2, R1, Right
Operation Wedding Crasher	L2, R2, Right, Down, L1, R2

SLY COOPER: THIEVES IN TIME

PLAYSTATION 3

SECRET ENDING

To see the Secret Ending, complete the game after earning the Sly Cooper: Thieves in Time Platinum Trophy.

UNLOCKABLES

To earn the unlockables in the Extras Menu, you'll need to collect a large number of Sly Masks.

UNLOCKABLE	REQUIREMENT
Monkey Paraglider	Collect 5 Sly Masks.
Camo Paraglider	Collect 10 Sly Masks.
Ultimate Sly	Collect 15 Sly Masks.
Ultimate Bentley	Collect 20 Sly Masks.
Ultimate Murray	Collect 30 Sly Masks.
Ultimate Carmelita	Collect 40 Sly Masks.
Ratchet's Wrench	Collect 50 Sly Masks.
Cole's Amp	Collect 60 Sly Masks.

TROPHIES

NAME	GOAL/REQUIREMENT	TROPHY VALUE
8-Bit Bentley Style	Beat every hideout arcade's top high score.	Gold
Airborne	Paraglide for at least 10 seconds without using any geysers!	Bronze
Ancient Warfare 3	Crackshot 10 enemies within 65 seconds.	Bronze
Apollo Wins	Have the perfect workout during the Training Montage.	Bronze
Arcade Operator	Repair any arcade machine.	Bronze
Bearcicle	Complete all the jobs and beat the boss in Episode 3.	Bronze

NAME	GOAL/REQUIREMENT	TROPHY VALUE
Bigfoot For Real	Track down Sly's long lost Cooper relative in Episode 3.	Bronze
Boom Stick	Introduce Sly to his long lost Cooper relative in Episode 4.	Bronze
Check Please	Unlock the Cooper Safe in Episode 5.	Bronze
Cheers	Don't miss a single glass of sarsaparilla in Saloon Bug.	Bronze
Child Of the 80's	Beat the top high score of one hideout arcade.	Bronze
Clockwerk Collector	Collect over 20 treasures.	Bronze
Cloud City	Defeat El Jefe on each tower without losing any health.	Silver
Cooper Calling Card	Collect your first hidden Sly mask.	Bronze
Costume Party	Obtain every costume in the game.	Silver
Crazed Climber	Scale the dragon lair in under 90 seconds.	Bronze
Downgrade	Complete any Alter Ego without leveling up once.	Bronze
Dust Bunnies	Complete all the jobs and beat the boss in Episode 2.	Bronze
Family Matters	Rescue Sly's long lost Cooper relative in Episode 1.	Bronze
Final Chapter?	Complete every job and beat every boss in all the episodes.	Gold
Get To the Chopper	Don't take any damage during Up In Smoke.	Bronze
Golden Arrow	Complete the archery minigame without hitting any friendly targets.	Bronze
Gunslinger	Reunite with Sly's long lost Cooper relative in Episode 2.	Bronze
Hassan Would Be Proud	Pickpocket a full collection of every item in the game.	Silver
Hero Tech	Battle with a secret weapon.	Bronze
Home Sick	Complete all the jobs and beat the boss in Episode 3.	Bronze
Hubba Hubba	Don't miss a beat in the Carmelita dance game.	Bronze
I Believe the Time Is Now	Complete all the jobs and beat the boss in Episode 4.	Bronze
I Need A Mouse Trap	Meet up with an old adversary.	Bronze
Keep Your Turban On	Make friends with Sly's long lost Cooper relative in Episode 5.	Bronze
Low Calorie Sushi	Complete all the jobs and beat the boss in Episode 1.	Bronze
Lunch Money	Slam 100 enemies with Murray.	Bronze
Mark Your Territory	Collect all the hidden Sly masks.	Gold
Mask and Stripes Forever	Collect every bronze, silver, and gold trophy.	Platinum
Navigate Like Drake	Take a look at every map in every episode.	Bronze
Oh Look It's Shiny	Pickpocket 10 unique items.	Bronze
Online Shopping	Make your first purchase on ThiefNet.	Bronze
PayDay	Purchase every item in ThiefNet.	Silver
Play It Safe	Unlock the Cooper Safe in Episode 1.	Bronze
Put It In Your 401K	Unlock the Cooper Safe in Episode 2.	Bronze
Quarter Cruncher	Unlock all 6 arcade machines.	Silver
Radical Ninja	Stealth kill 15 enemies without alerting anyone.	Bronze
Savings Account	Unlock the Cooper Safe in Episode 3.	Bronze
Sparrow Approves	Use the compass many times to navigate.	Bronze
The Cooper Open	Have a 20 hit rally with Bentley in each hideout.	Bronze
Unexpected Package	Place 60 bombs in enemy pockets with Bentley.	Bronze
Waddle Waddle	Shoot 40 penguins with Carmelita.	Bronze
Wardrobe Malfunction	Unlock your first change of clothing.	Bronze

NAME	GOAL/REQUIREMENT	TROPHY VALUE
What's Behind Door Number One?	Unlock a costume gate in any episode.	Bronze
Zenny, Gil, or Just Loot.	Unlock the Cooper Safe in Episode 4.	Bronze

SNIPER ELITE V2

ACHIEVEMENTS

NAME	GOAL/REQUIREMENT	POINT VALUE
Can Do!	Complete all co-op Overwatch Missions	20
Detonator	Career total of 50 shots on explosives	20
Bomb Happy	Survive 10 Games of bombing run	20
Bedpan Commando	Resuscitate your partner in coop 10 times	20
Target Eliminated!	As a sniper in Overwatch, snipe 50 enemies tagged by your partner	30
Target Spotted!	As a spotter in Overwatch, tag 50 enemies	30
Kilroy was Here	Make it through the tower to the winch room without being spotted	15
Fish Tank	Send the tank into the river by blowing up the bridge	15
High and Mighty	Wipe out the Elite Russian Sniper Team from the rooftops	15
Get Off the ground	Kill everyone in the convoy from ground level, except for Kreidl	15
Sniper Elite	Complete all missions on highest difficulty	100
Legendary Sniper	Prevent Wolff from escaping	65
Feared Sniper	Destroy the V2 rocket	20
Veteran Sniper	Discover the location of the V2 launch site	20
Master Sniper	Uncover Wolff's plan	20
Expert Sniper	Eliminate Müller	20
Pro Sniper	Collect intel from the church and make it out alive	20
Skilled Sniper	Stop the execution	20
Journeyman Sniper	Hold off the Russian advance	20
Apprentice Sniper	Destroy the V2 Facility and escape to safety	20
Novice Sniper	Stop the convoy	20
Trainee Sniper	Escape the German assault	20
Hide and Hope	Complete a level without being shot a single time	50
Make Every Bullet Count	Complete a level with 100% accuracy, using only rifles	25
Cooking Off	Snipe a grenade on an enemy's webbing from 100m	20
Double Dose	Snipe 2 people with one shot	20
Pass the Buck	Get a sniped ricochet headshot	30
Gold Rush	Find and retrieve all the stolen gold bars	50
Jungle Juice	Find and snipe all the hidden bottles throughout the game	50
Head Honcho	Get 100 sniped headshots	20
Gung Ho	Snipe 100 moving targets	20
World Record	Get 506 cumulative sniper kills	30
Potato Masher	Kill 100 enemies with explosives	20
Iron Lung	Hold your breath for a cumulative time of half an hour	20
Go the Distance	Get a cumulative sniped kill distance of a marathon	20
Deadeye	Snipe an enemy through his eye	10
Silent but deadly	Covertly kill 25 unaware enemies	10

NAME	GOAL/REQUIREMENT	POINT VALUE
Fuel Tank	Destroy a tank by sniping the fuel supply	10
Ear Plugs	Snipe an enemy while your rifle fire is masked by a loud sound	10
Mousetrap Fuse	Use a trip mine to kill an enemy who is trying to assault your position	10
Front and Center	Get a scoped headshot over 150m	10

SNIPER: GHOST WARRIOR 2

XBOX 360/PS3

ACHIEVEMENTS & TROPHIES

NAME	GOAL/REQUIREMENT	POINT VALUE	TROPHY VALUE
Operation Quarterback	Completed Act 1	10	Bronze
Operation Archangel	Completed Act 2	20	Bronze
Left No Man Behind	Completed the game on Casual	20	Bronze
My Rifle Is My Best Friend	Completed the game on Medium	50	Silver
Harvester Of Sorrow	Completed the game on Expert	75	Gold
Poking the Bush	Collected all secrets in Act 1	20	Bronze
Keepsakes Of War	Collected all secrets in Act 2	20	Bronze
In Search of Enlightenment	Collected all secrets in Act 3	20	Bronze
Hazardous Materials	Killed three or more enemies by shooting a grenade	25	Silver
Death's Scythe	Took 50 headshots in single player	30	Silver
Nerves Of Steel	Achieved 100% accuracy in any single player mission	30	Silver
Balls Of Steel	Completed any single player mission without using med kits, but taking damage	20	Bronze
Say Hello To My Little Friend	Killed 30 enemies using your sidearm	10	Bronze
Psst, Don't Look Behind You	Killed 15 enemies with a stealth kill	20	Bronze
Kill With Still	Killed 50 enemies while holding your breath	10	Bronze
Distance Matters Not	Killed 20 enemies from a distance of 600m or greater	20	Silver
Fisher King	Killed 25 enemies using thermal or night vision goggles	10	Bronze
Worlds Apart	Took a successful shot from a distance of 1 km or greater	20	Bronze
Bullets Can't Hurt Me	Completed any act without using medkits	25	Silver
I Never Bleed	Completed the Campaign using max one medkit per mission	75	Gold
Bloodstreak	Killed 25 opponents in multiplayer	10	Bronze
Pure Ownage	Killed 50 opponents in multiplayer	30	Silver
The Sniper Elite	Killed 100 opponents in multiplayer	50	Gold
Kill That F**ing Band!	Took 25 headshots in multiplayer	20	Bronze
Blood And Tears	Took 50 headshots in multiplayer	50	Silver
Unhappy Camper	Killed 10 opponents in multiplayer using your sidearm	10	Bronze
U Can't Touch This	Won 5 rounds in a row in Team Deathmatch	50	Silver

NAME	GOAL/REQUIREMENT	POINT VALUE	TROPHY VALUE
Wrath Child	Won 10 Team Deathmatch rounds	10	Bronze
Death Dealer	Won 25 Team Deathmatch rounds	30	Silver
Everything But The Kitchen Sink	In one multiplayer round killed an opponent with a sniper rifle, sidearm and melee attack	50	Silver
World Warrior	Participated in any multiplayer match	5	Bronze
Bullseye	Unlock all trophies	—	Platinum

SECRET ACHIEVEMENTS & TROPHIES

NAME	GOAL/REQUIREMENT	POINT VALUE	TROPHY VALUE
Hangman's Knot	Killed Major Vladic ("And Justice For All")	10	Bronze
Nemesis	Killed Maddox once and for all ("No Loose Ends")	10	Bronze
Laugh This Off	In the final duel with Maddox, killed him with the first shot ("No Loose Ends")	50	Gold
Back To School	Killed all enemy snipers in Sniper Alley without being hit ("Ghosts of Sarajevo")	30	Silver
Guardian Angel	Rescued the friendly ("From Out Of Nowhere")	15	Bronze
Karma Chameleon	Retrieved your weapon without being detected ("Burning Bridges")	20	Bronze
Solid Sandman	Killed all enemies in the beach houses without causing an alarm ("Leave No Man Behind")	20	Bronze

SIBERIAN STRIKE DLC

NAME	GOAL/REQUIREMENT	POINT VALUE	TROPHY VALUE
Once More Into The Fray	Begun the hunt	30	Bronze
Fool For The City	Completed "Operation Siberian Strike"	10	Bronze
With A Little Help From Friends	Completed "It Takes Two"	10	Bronze
Down Under	Completed "Last Rites"	10	Bronze
Getting Tail in Siberia	Collected all secrets in Siberian Strike campaign	50	Silver

SECRET ACHIEVEMENTS & TROPHIES

NAME	GOAL/REQUIREMENT	POINT VALUE	TROPHY VALUE
Easy Rider	Got the train moving again	30	Bronze
Taste of Your Own Medicine	Completed the first interrogation	20	Bronze
Learning To Fly	Completed the second interrogation	20	Bronze
Actions Speak Louder Than Words	Completed the third interrogation	20	Bronze
Shadow Man	Sneaked through the underground storehouse undetected	50	Silver

SOCOM: U.S. NAVY SEALS CONFRONTATION

AMELI MACHINE GUN

Select Spain as your clan country.

FAMAS G2 ASSAULT RIFLE

Select France as your clan country.

GMP SUBMACHINE GUN

Select Germany as your clan country.

IW-80 A2 ASSAULT RIFLE

Select U.K. as your clan country.

SCFR-LW ASSAULT RIFLE

Select U.S. as your clan country.

SONIC & ALL-STARS RACING TRANSFORMED

EXPERT DIFFICULTY

Win all five mirrored Grand Prix cups to unlock Expert Difficulty.

MIRRORED GRAND PRIX

Win all five standard Grand Prix cups to unlock mirrored Grand Prix cups.

UNLOCKABLE CHARACTERS

CHARACTER	REQUIREMENT
AGES	World Tour Mode: Super Star Showdown—Win Ranger Rush (Sprint) then purchase for 165 stars.
Alex Kidd	Automatically unlocked on December 25, 2012.
Amigo	World Tour Mode: Sunshine Coast—Win Studio Scrapes (Versus) then purchase for 8 stars.
Danica Patrick	World Tour Mode: Frozen Valley—Win Pirate Plunder (Race) and then purchase for 16 stars.
Doctor Eggman	Win all five mirrored Grand Prix cups.
Gilius Thunderhead	World Tour Mode: Moonlight Park—Win Molten Mayhem (Ring Race) and purchase for 120 stars.
Gum	World Tour Mode: Moonlight Park—Win Jet Set Jaunt (Boost Challenge) and purchase for 105 stars.
Joe Musashi	World Tour Mode: Twilight Engine—Win Shinobi Showdown (Versus) and purchase for 85 stars.
Mii	Win all five standard Grand Prix cups.
NiGHTS	World Tour Mode: Scorching Skies—Win Carrier Crisis (Sprint) and purchase for 80 stars.
Pudding	World Tour Mode: Twilight Engine—Win Hatcher Hustle (Sprint) and purchase for 50 stars.

CHARACTER	REQUIREMENT
Reala	World Tour Mode: Superstar Showdown—Win Nightmare Meander (Ring Race) and purchase for 160 stars.
Shadow the Hedgehog	World Tour Mode: Frozen Valley—Win Seaside Scrap (Versus) and then purchase for 35 stars.
Vyse	World Tour Mode—Scorching Skies—Win Rogue Rings (Ring Race) and then purchase for 30 stars.

NINTENDO WII U

EXPERT DIFFICULTY

Win all five mirrored Grand Prix cups to unlock Expert Difficulty.

MIRRORED GRAND PRIX

Win all five standard Grand Prix cups to unlock mirrored Grand Prix cups.

UNLOCKABLE CHARACTERS

CHARACTER	REQUIREMENT
AGES	World Tour Mode: Super Star Showdown—Win Ranger Rush (Sprint) then purchase for 165 stars.
Alex Kidd	Automatically unlocked on December 25, 2012.
Amigo	World Tour Mode: Sunshine Coast—Win Studio Scrapes (Versus) then purchase for 8 stars.
Danica Patrick	World Tour Mode: Frozen Valley—Win Pirate Plunder (Race) and then purchase for 16 stars.
Doctor Eggman	Win all five mirrored Grand Prix cups.
Gilius Thunderhead	World Tour Mode: Moonlight Park—Win Molten Mayhem (Ring Race) and purchase for 120 stars.
Gum	World Tour Mode: Moonlight Park—Win Jet Set Jaunt (Boost Challenge) and purchase for 105 stars.
Joe Musashi	World Tour Mode: Twilight Engine—Win Shinobi Showdown (Versus) and purchase for 85 stars.
Mii	Win all five standard Grand Prix cups.
NiGHTS	World Tour Mode: Scorching Skies—Win Carrier Crisis (Sprint) and purchase for 80 stars.
Pudding	World Tour Mode: Twilight Engine—Win Hatcher Hustle (Sprint) and purchase for 50 stars.
Reala	World Tour Mode: Superstar Showdown—Win Nightmare Meander (Ring Race) and purchase for 160 stars.
Shadow the Hedgehog	World Tour Mode: Frozen Valley—Win Seaside Scrap (Versus) and then purchase for 35 stars.
Vyse	World Tour Mode—Scorching Skies—Win Rogue Rings (Ring Race) and then purchase for 30 stars.

PLAYSTATION 3

EXPERT DIFFICULTY

Win all five mirrored Grand Prix cups to unlock Expert Difficulty.

MIRRORED GRAND PRIX

Win all five standard Grand Prix cups to unlock mirrored Grand Prix cups.

CHEATS, ACHIEVEMENTS, AND TROPHIES

UNLOCKABLE CHARACTERS

CHARACTER	REQUIREMENT
AGES	World Tour Mode: Super Star Showdown—Win Ranger Rush (Sprint) then purchase for 165 stars.
Alex Kidd	Automatically unlocked on December 25, 2012.
Amigo	World Tour Mode: Sunshine Coast—Win Studio Scrapes (Versus) then purchase for 8 stars.
Danica Patrick	World Tour Mode: Frozen Valley—Win Pirate Plunder (Race) and then purchase for 16 stars.
Doctor Eggman	Win all five mirrored Grand Prix cups.
Gilius Thunderhead	World Tour Mode: Moonlight Park—Win Molten Mayhem (Ring Race) and purchase for 120 stars.
Gum	World Tour Mode: Moonlight Park—Win Jet Set Jaunt (Boost Challenge) and purchase for 105 stars.
Joe Musashi	World Tour Mode: Twilight Engine—Win Shinobi Showdown (Versus) and purchase for 85 stars.
NiGHTS	World Tour Mode: Scorching Skies—Win Carrier Crisis (Sprint) and purchase for 80 stars.
Pudding	World Tour Mode: Twilight Engine—Win Hatcher Hustle (Sprint) and purchase for 50 stars.
Reala	World Tour Mode: Superstar Showdown—Win Nightmare Meander (Ring Race) and purchase for 160 stars.
Shadow the Hedgehog	World Tour Mode: Frozen Valley—Win Seaside Scrap (Versus) and then purchase for 35 stars.
Vyse	World Tour Mode—Scorching Skies—Win Rogue Rings (Ring Race) and then purchase for 30 stars.

PLAYSTATION VITA

EXPERT DIFFICULTY

Win all five mirrored Grand Prix cups to unlock Expert Difficulty.

MIRRORED GRAND PRIX

Win all five standard Grand Prix cups to unlock mirrored Grand Prix cups.

UNLOCKABLE CHARACTERS

CHARACTER	REQUIREMENT
AGES	World Tour Mode: Super Star Showdown—Win Ranger Rush (Sprint) then purchase for 165 stars.
Alex Kidd	Automatically unlocked on December 25, 2012.
Amigo	World Tour Mode: Sunshine Coast—Win Studio Scrapes (Versus) then purchase for 8 stars.
Danica Patrick	World Tour Mode: Frozen Valley—Win Pirate Plunder (Race) and then purchase for 16 stars.
Doctor Eggman	Win all five mirrored Grand Prix cups.
Gilius Thunderhead	World Tour Mode: Moonlight Park—Win Molten Mayhem (Ring Race) and purchase for 120 stars.
Gum	World Tour Mode: Moonlight Park—Win Jet Set Jaunt (Boost Challenge) and purchase for 105 stars.

CHARACTER	REQUIREMENT
Joe Musashi	World Tour Mode: Twilight Engine—Win Shinobi Showdown (Versus) and purchase for 85 stars.
NiGHTS	World Tour Mode: Scorching Skies—Win Carrier Crisis (Sprint) and purchase for 80 stars.
Pudding	World Tour Mode: Twilight Engine—Win Hatcher Hustle (Sprint) and purchase for 50 stars.
Reala	World Tour Mode: Superstar Showdown—Win Nightmare Meander (Ring Race) and purchase for 160 stars.
Shadow the Hedgehog	World Tour Mode: Frozen Valley—Win Seaside Scrap (Versus) and then purchase for 35 stars.
Vyse	World Tour Mode—Scorching Skies—Win Rogue Rings (Ring Race) and then purchase for 30 stars.

XBOX 360

EXPERT DIFFICULTY

Win all five mirrored Grand Prix cups to unlock Expert Difficulty.

MIRRORED GRAND PRIX

Win all five standard Grand Prix cups to unlock mirrored Grand Prix cups.

UNLOCKABLE CHARACTERS

CHARACTER	REQUIREMENT
AGES	World Tour Mode: Super Star Showdown—Win Ranger Rush (Sprint) then purchase for 165 stars.
Alex Kidd	Automatically unlocked on December 25, 2012.
Amigo	World Tour Mode: Sunshine Coast—Win Studio Scrapes (Versus) then purchase for 8 stars.
Avatar	Win all five standard Grand Prix cups.
Danica Patrick	World Tour Mode: Frozen Valley—Win Pirate Plunder (Race) and then purchase for 16 stars.
Doctor Eggman	Win all five mirrored Grand Prix cups.
Gilius Thunderhead	World Tour Mode: Moonlight Park—Win Molten Mayhem (Ring Race) and purchase for 120 stars.
Gum	World Tour Mode: Moonlight Park—Win Jet Set Jaunt (Boost Challenge) and purchase for 105 stars.
Joe Musashi	World Tour Mode: Twilight Engine—Win Shinobi Showdown (Versus) and purchase for 85 stars.
NiGHTS	World Tour Mode: Scorching Skies—Win Carrier Crisis (Sprint) and purchase for 80 stars.
Pudding	World Tour Mode: Twilight Engine—Win Hatcher Hustle (Sprint) and purchase for 50 stars.
Reala	World Tour Mode: Superstar Showdown—Win Nightmare Meander (Ring Race) and purchase for 160 stars.
Shadow the Hedgehog	World Tour Mode: Frozen Valley—Win Seaside Scrap (Versus) and then purchase for 35 stars.
Vyse	World Tour Mode—Scorching Skies—Win Rogue Rings (Ring Race) and then purchase for 30 stars.

CHEATS, ACHIEVEMENTS, AND TROPHIES

ACHIEVEMENTS & TROPHIES

NAME	GOAL/REQUIREMENT	POINT VALUE	TROPHY VALUE
Racing Transformed	Turned All-Star	15	Bronze
Parts Shop	Won an event with a Mod equipped	15	Bronze
Sonic Drift	Did a 10 second Drift as Sonic	10	Bronze
Tornado	Did a Level 3 Air-Drift	10	Bronze
Magic Second	Finished 0.5 seconds ahead of an opponent in a Race	15	Bronze
Spin Dash	Did a Boost-Start in each vehicle mode	10	Bronze
Scud Racer	Finished 1st in a Race without getting hit by weapons	15	Bronze
Blast Processing	Hit 2 opponents with a single Hot Rod Blast	15	Bronze
Fighting Viper	Evaded or Blocked a homing-weapon 3 times in a Race	10	Bronze
Catcher Pitcher	Absorbed a weapon with the Glove and fired it back at your attacker	15	Bronze
Eyes On The Road	Hit an opponent with a weapon while looking backwards	10	Bronze
Cosmic Smash	Detonated the Hot Rod at the very last second	10	Bronze
Nomad	Visited every location in the game	20	Bronze
Rank B	Earned your B Class License		Bronze
Rank A	Earned you're a Class License	20	Bronze
Rank S	Earned your S Class License	30	Bronze
SEGA All Star	Earned your Star License	50	Silver
SEGA Super Star	Earned your Triple-Star License	100	Gold
Hardcore	Completed a World Tour event on Expert difficulty	20	Bronze
Newtron	Player 10 Matchmaking games as a Random character	10	Bronze
SUMO Wrestled	Beat your first Staff Ghost in Time Attack	10	Bronze
Yokozuna	Beat all the Staff Ghosts in Time Attack	50	Silver
De Rol Le Credits	Unlocked Superstar Showdown in World Tour	20	Bronze
Takes AGES	Unlocked every Character in the game	30	Silver
Racing Hero	Got a Podium Finish in every Grand Prix tournament	30	Bronze
Welcome To The Fantasy Zone	Finished 1st in a Grand Prix tournament	15	Silver
Holosseum	Unlocked Mirror Grand Prix mode	20	Bronze
Gale Racer	Got a Podium Finish in every Grand Prix tournament on Expert difficulty	30	Bronze
Race Leader	Won a Matchmaking game	15	Bronze
House Party Of The Dead	Completed an event with 4 local friends	10	Bronze
Virtua Trickster	Rolled Left, Rolled Right, Backflipped, Forward Flipped and landed as a car or boat	15	Bronze
Link Chain	Completed the Dream Valley Ring Race and passed every Ring as NiGHTS or Reala	15	Bronze

NAME	GOAL/REQUIREMENT	POINT VALUE	TROPHY VALUE
Vyse The Legend	Beat 01:11.16 in Time Attack as Vyse in Rogue's Landing	15	Bronze
You Got The Horn	Leveled-up a character	15	Bronze
All Stars	Collected every Star in World Tour	50	Gold
Battle Outrunner	Did 5 overtakes in a single Drift	15	Bronze
Genesis	Triple-Stunted while transforming into a car or boat	15	Bronze
Drift More	Got a Perfect Drift score on a Drift Challenge event	15	Bronze
Mega Jet	Did a Reckless Boost	15	Bronze
Ax Battler	Finished a Battle Race without losing any lives	15	Bronze
Arrow Of Light	Froze an opponent with Ice from at least 100 meters away	15	Bronze
Buzz Bomber	Hit 1st, 2nd and 3rd place with a Swarm attack	10	Bronze
Lock On Sight	Scored 90% accuracy with aimed weapons in an event	20	Bronze
Welcome To Victory Lane	Finished 1st in every Grand Prix tournament on Expert difficulty	50	Gold
Meteor Strike	Collected 10 Stars in World Tour	15	Bronze
Justice Shot	Got 10 hits by firing weapons backwards in a single event	10	Bronze
Shadow Step	Did 10 Stunt Combos in a single event	15	Bronze
Crack Down	Got a total of 20 hits with weapons in a Race	10	Bronze
The King Of Speed	Finished 1st in a Grand Prix tournament at Expert difficulty	20	Silver
Team Sonic	Finished 1st, 2nd, 3rd and 4th with local friends in a 10 player Race	10	Bronze

SONIC CLASSIC COLLECTION

NINTENDO 3DS

SONIC THE HEDGEHOG

DEBUG MODE

At the title screen, press A, A, Up, Down, Left, Right, hold Y and press START.

LEVEL SELECT

At the title screen press Up, Down, Left, Right, hold Y and press START.

SONIC THE HEDGEHOG 2

LEVEL SELECT

At the title screen, press Up, Up, Up, Down, Down, Down, Left, Right, Left, Right, hold Y and press START.

SONIC THE HEDGEHOG 3

LEVEL SELECT

As the SEGA logo fades, quickly press Up, Up, Down, Down, Up, Up, Up, Up. Highlight Sound Test and press START.

SONIC KNUCKLES

LEVEL SELECT WITH SONIC THE HEDGEHOG 2

At the title screen, press Up, Up, Up, Down, Down, Down, Left, Right, Left, Right, hold A and press START.

SONIC COLORS

EXTRA LIVES

After completing a level, the results screen shows how well you did. Jump through the numbers until they break apart revealing gold rings and extra lives.

SONIC THE FIGHTERS

PLAY AS DR. EGGMAN

Press Start on Bean and press A to play as Dr. Eggman.

PLAY AS HONEY THE CAT

Press Start on Amy and press A to play as Honey.

PLAY AS METAL SONIC

Press Start on Sonic and press A to play as Metal Sonic.

PLAY AS SUPER SONIC

Defeat the first eight enemies without being defeated then defeat Metal Sonic in the first round. In the second round, press Back + Punch + Kick to transform into Super Sonic.

PLAY AS DR. EGGMAN

Press Start on Bean and press A to play as Dr. Eggman.

PLAY AS HONEY THE CAT

Press Start on Amy and press A to play as Honey.

PLAY AS METAL SONIC

Press Start on Sonic and press A to play as Metal Sonic.

PLAY AS SUPER SONIC

Defeat the first eight enemies without being defeated then defeat Metal Sonic in the first round. In the second round, press Back + Punch + Kick to transform into Super Sonic.

SONIC FREE RIDERS

AVATAR AWARDS

AWARD	EARNED BY
Sonic Free Riders Shirt	Watch the credits in their entirety.
E-10000 G Shirt	Place 1st on every course with E-10000 G.
Jet Shirt	Place 1st on every course with Jet.
Sonic Shirt	Place 1st on every course with Sonic.

CHAOS EMERALD BOARD

Get S-rank on all Story Missions.

PROFESSIONAL BOARD

Complete all Trial Missions.

SONIC GENERATIONS

XBOX 360/PS3

SECRET STATUE ROOM

In the Collection Room, hold Back for a few seconds. Sonic jumps into the statue room below. Once there, press Back and enter the following.

STATUE	CODE
Aero-Cannon	329 494
Amy Rose	863 358
Big the Cat	353 012
Blaze the Cat	544 873
Booster	495 497
Buzz Bomber	852 363
Capsule	777 921
Chao	629 893
Chaos Emerald	008 140
Charmy Bee	226 454
Chip	309 511
Chopper	639 402
Classic Eggman	103 729
Classic Sonic	171 045
Classic Tails	359 236
Cop Speeder	640 456
Crabmeat	363 911
Cream the Rabbit	332 955
Cucky/Picky/Flicky/Pecky	249 651
Dark Chao	869 292
Dr. Eggman	613 482
E-123 Omega	601 409
Egg Chaser	200 078
Egg Fighter	851 426
Egg Launcher	973 433
Egg Pawn	125 817
Eggrobo	360 031
Espio the Chameleon	894 526
Goal Plate	933 391
Goal Ring	283 015
Grabber	275 843
Gun Beetle	975 073
Gun Hunter	668 250
Hero Chao	507 376
Iblis Biter	872 910
Iblis Taker	513 929
Iblis Worm	711 268
Item Box	209 005
Jet the Hawk	383 870
Knuckles the Echidna	679 417
Metal Sonic	277 087
Miles "Tails" Prower	632 951
Moto Bug	483 990
Omochao	870 580

S

STATUE	CODE
Ring	390 884
Rouge the Bat	888 200
Sandworm	548 986
Shadow the Hedgehog	262 416
Silver the Hedgehog	688 187
Sonic the Hedgehog	204 390
Spinner	530 741
Spiny	466 913
Spring – Star	537 070
Spring	070 178
Vector the Crocodile	868 377

AVATAR AWARDS

AVATAR	EARNED BY
Classic Eggman Suit (Head)	Defeat the final boss on Hard Mode.
Classic Eggman Suit (Tops)	Defeat all bosses on Hard Mode.
Classic Eggman Suit (Bottoms)	Defeat all rivals on Hard Mode.

ACHIEVEMENTS & TROPHIES

NAME	GOAL/REQUIREMENT	POINT VALUE	TROPHY VALUE
The Opening Act	Race through the first stage.	10	Bronze
All Stages Cleared!	Clear Sonic Generations.	50	Silver
Greased Lightning	Clear GREEN HILL Act 1 within one minute.	10	Bronze
Bright Star	Get Rank S in an Act.	15	Bronze
Shooting Star	Get Rank S in three Acts.	20	Bronze
Blazing Meteor	Get Rank S in seven Acts.	30	Silver
Blue Comet	Get Rank S in twelve Acts.	40	Silver
Big Bang	Get Rank S in all Acts.	50	Gold
Trickstar	Pull off a seven or more trick combo or six trick combo ending in a finishing trick.	10	Bronze
Eradicator	Defeat 100 enemies.	15	Bronze
Ring King	Reach the goal without dropping any of the rings you collected in GREEN HILL Act 1.	15	Bronze
Action Hero	Perform all of Sonic's moves in Act 2.	10	Bronze
Bonds of Friendship	Complete all Challenge Acts featuring Sonic's friends.	10	Bronze
Walkie Talkie	Chat with each of Sonic's friends you have saved.	10	Bronze
Join the Ranks	Join the rankings.	20	Bronze
A 30-Second Test	Participate in a 30 Second Trial.	20	Bronze
Mad Skillz	Get all Skills.	30	Silver
(Hedge)Hogging It All Up!	Get all collectibles.	50	Gold
Time Attacker	Play Ranking Attack on all stages.	30	Silver
Red Ring Collector	Get all Red Star Rings.	30	Silver
Halfway Point	Clear half the Challenge Acts.	30	Silver
Mission Accomplished!	Clear all the Challenge Acts.	30	Silver

NAME	GOAL/REQUIREMENT	POINT VALUE	TROPHY VALUE
SKY SANCTUARY Restored!	Restored the SKY SANCTUARY Stage Gate.	15	Bronze
SPEED HIGHWAY Restored!	Restored the SPEED HIGHWAY Stage Gate.	15	Bronze
CITY ESCAPE Restored!	Restored the CITY ESCAPE Stage Gate.	15	Bronze
GREEN HILL Restored!	Restored the GREEN HILL Stage Gate.	15	Bronze
CHEMICAL PLANT Restored!	Restored the CHEMICAL PLANT Stage Gate.	15	Bronze
PLANET WISP Restored!	Restored the PLANET WISP Stage Gate.	15	Bronze
SEASIDE HILL Restored!	Restored the SEASIDE HILL Stage Gate.	15	Bronze
CRISIS CITY Restored!	Restored the CRISIS CITY Stage Gate.	15	Bronze
ROOFTOP RUN Restored!	Restored the ROOFTOP RUN Stage Gate.	15	Bronze
Treasure Hunter	Collected all the Chaos Emeralds.	20	Bronze
Shadow Boxing	Defeated Shadow.	25	Bronze
Silver Got Served	Defeated Silver.	30	Bronze
Scrap Metal	Defeated Metal Sonic.	20	Bronze
Perfect Punisher	Defeated Perfect Chaos.	25	Bronze
Boom Boom Dragoon	Defeated Egg Dragoon.	30	Bronze
Sunny Side Up	Defeated Death Egg Robot.	20	Bronze
Can't Touch This	Took no damage from the final boss and cleared the stage.	30	Silver
A Quick Breather	Got the Red Star Ring atop the highest spot in ROOFTOP RUN Act 2 and reached the goal.	10	Bronze
Color Power!	Got the Red Star Ring by using an Orange Wisp in PLANET WISP Act 2 and reached the goal.	10	Bronze
Supersonic!	Cleared a regular stage as Super Sonic.	20	Silver
Walk on Air	Cleared SKY SANCTUARY Act 1 without falling and losing a life.	20	Bronze
Demolition Derby	Wrecked 30 or more cars in CITY ESCAPE Act 2.	10	Bronze
Secret Sleuth	Got the Red Star Ring located in the hidden room in SEASIDE HILL Act 1 and reached the goal.	10	Bronze
Look Both Ways	Reached the goal in CRISIS CITY Act 2 without being hit by a tornado-carried cars or rocks.	10	Bronze
Walk on Water	Cleared CHEMICAL PLANT Act 2 without entering the water.	10	Bronze
Jump for Joy!	Found the spring hidden in GREEN HILL Act 1 and reached the goal with a Red Star Ring.	10	Bronze
The Byway or the Highway	Got the Red Star Ring located on the shortcut route in SPEED HIGHWAY Act 2 and reached the goal.	20	Bronze

SONIC THE HEDGEHOG 4: EPISODE I

XBOX 360

AVATAR AWARDS

AWARD	EARNED BY
Sonic Costume (Body)	After collecting the 7 Chaos Emeralds, defeat the final boss 1 more time
Sonic Costume (Head)	Collect all rings during ending after the final stage.

SONIC THE HEDGEHOG 4: EPISODE II

XBOX 360

AVATAR AWARDS

AVATAR	EARNED BY
Dr. Eggman Modern Costume (Body)	Defeat the last boss without taking damage.
Dr. Eggman Modern Costume (Legs)	Defeat the "Sylvania Castle Zone" boss without taking damage.

SOULCALIBUR V

PLAYSTATION 3

ALGOL FEAR AND TOWER OF GLORY: MOST HOLY DICHOTOMY STAGE

Defeat Algol Fear in Legendary Souls or Quick Battle

ALPHA PATROKLOS AND ASTRAL CHAOS: PATHWAY STAGE

Defeat Patrolklos in Quick Battle.

EDGE MASTER AND TOWER OF GLORY: SPIRAL OF GOOD AND EVIL

Complete chapter 17 of story mode to unlock Edge Master and his stage. You can also be obtained by defeating him in Arcade, Legendary Souls, or Quick Battle.

ELYSIUM AND UTOPIA OF THE BLESSED

Complete the final chapter of story mode.

KILIK AND THE PENITENTIARY OF DESTINY STAGE

Defeat Kilik in Arcade or Legendary Souls.

PYRRHA OMEGA AND DENEVER CASTLE: EYE OF CHAOS

Complete chapter 19 of story mode.

DEVIL JIN STYLE

Defeat Harada in Quick Battle or Legendary Souls.

Go to Customization and then to Original Characters. Select anyone male or female and enter size. Choose Weapons & Style and then to Style. At bottom of list is Devil Jin (Tekken).

SOUL SACRIFICE

ADDITIONAL BLACK RITES

Reach different Magic or Life levels to unlock additional Black Rite spells.

SPELL	REQUIREMENT
Gorgon	Level up Life to Lvl 20.
Vulcan	Level up Life to Lvl 40.
Gleipnir	Level up Magic to Lvl 20.
Excalibur	Level up Magic to Lvl 40.

A SPACE SHOOTER FOR TWO BUCKS!

INVINCIBILITY

At the credits screen, press Up, Up, Down, Down, Left, Right, Left, Right, ●, Start.

MAXIMUM CASH

At the credits screen, press Left, Right, Left, Right, +, Right, ●, ●, ●, Start.

DISABLE SHIP INERTIA

At the credits screen, press ●, ●, ●, ●, +,+,+,+,●, Start.

FULL OVERDRIVE

At the credits screen, press Down, Left, Up, Right, ●, ●, +, +, ●, Start.

HIGH SPEED

At the credits screen, press ●, +, ●, Left, Right, Left, Left, Up, ●, Start.

SLOW MOTION

At the credits screen, press +, ●, ●, Right, Left, Right, Right, ●, ●, Start.

SPECTROBES: ORIGINS

METALLIC LEO AND RYZA

At the Title screen and before creating a game save, press Up, Down, Left, Right, A.

SPIDER-MAN: EDGE OF TIME

SHATTERED DIMENSIONS BONUS SUITS

If you have a saved game data for Spider-Man: Shattered Dimensions on your system, new Alternate Suits become available in the Bonus Gallery.

BIG TIME SUIT (2099)

At the main menu, press Right, Down, Down, Up, Left, Down, Down, Right.

FUTURE FOUNDATION SUIT (AMAZING)

At the main menu, press Up, Down, Left, Up, Down, Left, Right, Left.

SHATTERED DIMENSIONS BONUS SUITS

If you have a saved game data for Spider-Man: Shattered Dimensions on your system, eight new Alternate Suits become available in the Bonus Gallery.

AMAZING SPIDER-MAN #500 SUIT (AMAZING)

Select Enter Code from VIP Unlock Code and enter laststand. Go to the Bonus Gallery to access the alternate suits.

POISON SUIT (2099)

Select Enter Code from VIP Unlock Code and enter innerspider. Go to the Bonus Gallery to access the alternate suits.

SPIDEY VS WOLVERINE SUIT (AMAZING) – WHAT IF? SPIDERMAN

Select Enter Code from VIP Unlock Code and enter coldhearted. Go to the Bonus Gallery to access the alternate suits.

2099 ARENA CHALLENGE AND AMAZING ARENA CHALLENGE

Select Enter Code from VIP Unlock Code and enter twospidersenter. Select Arenas from the Main Menu.

BIG TIME SUIT (2099)

At the main menu, press Right, Down, Down, Up, Left, Down, Down, Right.

FUTURE FOUNDATION SUIT (AMAZING)

At the main menu, press Up, Down, Left, Up, Down, Left, Right, Left.

SPIDER-MAN: FRIEND OR FOE

NEW GREEN GOBLIN AS A SIDEKICK

While standing in the Helicarrier between levels, press Left, Down, Right, Right, Down, Left.

SANDMAN AS A SIDEKICK

While standing in the Helicarrier between levels, press Right, Right, Right, Up, Down, Left.

VENOM AS A SIDEKICK

While standing in the Helicarrier between levels, press Left, Left, Right, Up, Down, Down.

5000 TECH TOKENS

While standing in the Helicarrier between levels, press Up, Up, Down, Down, Left,

NEW GREEN GOBLIN AS A SIDEKICK

While standing in the Helicarrier between levels, press Left, Down, Right, Right, Down, Left.

SANDMAN AS A SIDEKICK

While standing in the Helicarrier between levels, press Right, Right, Right, Up, Down, Left.

VENOM AS A SIDEKICK

While standing in the Helicarrier between levels, press Left, Left, Right, Up, Down, Down.

5000 TECH TOKENS

While standing in the Helicarrier between levels, press Up, Up, Down, Down, Left, Right.

NEW GOBLIN

At the stage complete screen, hold L + R and press ●, Down, ●, Right, ●, Up, ●, Left. Right.

SPIDER-MAN: SHATTERED DIMENSIONS

NINTENDO WII

The following can be entered after completing the tutorial.

IRON SPIDER SUIT

After completing the tutorial and at the Main menu, press Up, Right, Right, Right, Left, Left, Left, Down, Up.

NEGATIVE ZONE SUIT

After completing the tutorial and at the Main menu, press Left, Right, Right, Down, Right, Down, Up, Left.

SCARLET SPIDER SUIT

After completing the tutorial and at the Main menu, press Right, Up, Left, Right, Up, Left, Right, Up, Left, Right.

XBOX 360/PS3

The following codes can be entered after completing the tutorial. All the suits are found in the Bonus Gallery under Alternate Suits.

IRON SPIDER SUIT

At the Main menu, press Up, Right, Right, Right, Left, Left, Left, Down, Up.

NEGATIVE ZONE SUIT

At the Main menu, press Left, Right, Right, Down, Right, Down, Up, Left.

SCARLET SPIDER SUIT

At the Main menu, press Right, Up, Left, Right, Up, Left, Right, Up, Left, Right.

ACHIEVEMENTS & TROPHIES

NAME	GOAL/REQUIREMENT	POINT VALUE	TROPHY VALUE
Easy as pie!	Complete all levels on Easy	20	Bronze
Is this normal?	Complete all levels on Normal	50	Silver
Hard pressed	Complete all levels on Hard	100	Gold
Lead on, M-Dubs!	Complete the Tutorial	5	Bronze
End of Act 1	Complete Act 1 on any difficulty level	20	Bronze
End of Act 2	Complete Act 2 on any difficulty level	20	Bronze
End of Act 3	Complete Act 3 on any difficulty level	20	Bronze
Getting warmed up	Defeat 100 enemies	10	Bronze
In the zone	Defeat 500 enemies	20	Silver
Ain't no stoppin'!	Defeat 1000 enemies	50	Silver
Manifest Destiny	Complete the Web of Destiny	100	Gold
Bug collector	Collect all Hidden Spiders	50	Bronze
The complete package	Unlock all Character upgrades	20	Bronze
Smooth moves	Unlock all Combat upgrades	20	Bronze
Uncle Benjamin	Execute a 100-hit combo (except the Tutorial)	10	Bronze
Two hundo	Execute a 200-hit combo (except the Tutorial)	20	Bronze
Missed me!	Defeat a boss on any difficulty level without taking damage	20	Bronze
Close call!	Recover 10 times from a Critical Fall	10	Bronze
Amazing!	Complete 4 levels with the highest rank in Hard mode	20	Bronze
Sensational!!	Complete 8 levels with the highest rank in Hard mode	30	Silver
Spectacular!!!	Complete 12 levels with the highest rank in Hard mode	50	Gold

NAME	GOAL/REQUIREMENT	POINT VALUE	TROPHY VALUE
Hobbyist	Collect 125 Spider Emblems	10	Bronze
Enthusiast	Collect 250 Spider Emblems	15	Silver
Fanatic	Collect 500 Spider Emblems	20	Gold
The Spider's shadow	Complete a Noir level without triggering an alarm	10	Bronze
The Spider's bite	Keep Rage Mode active for one minute	10	Bronze
The Spider's grace	Complete a 2099 freefall section without taking damage	10	Bronze
The Spider's web	Defeat 50 enemies using the Amazing Charge Attack	10	Bronze

SECRET ACHIEVEMENTS & TROPHIES

NAME	GOAL/REQUIREMENT	POINT VALUE	TROPHY VALUE
Survival of the fittest	Defeat Kraven on any difficulty level	15	Bronze
Something CAN stop Juggernaut!	Defeat Juggernaut on any difficulty level	15	Bronze
Here's mud in your eye!	Defeat Sandman on any difficulty level	15	Bronze
Now there's a shock	Defeat Electro on any difficulty level	15	Bronze
Canceled!	Defeat Deadpool on any difficulty level	15	Bronze
Minimized Carnage	Defeat Carnage on any difficulty level	15	Bronze
Clipped wings	Defeat Hobgoblin on any difficulty level	15	Bronze
Took the sting out of him	Defeat Scorpion on any difficulty level	15	Bronze
Lay down your arms	Defeat Doc Ock on any difficulty level	15	Bronze
The caged bird squawks	Defeat Vulture on any difficulty level	15	Bronze
The hammer falls	Defeat Hammerhead on any difficulty level	15	Bronze
Circus freak	Defeat Goblin on any difficulty level	15	Bronze
Final curtain call	Defeat Mysterio on any difficulty level	50	Silver
No harm done	Complete any level without dying (except the Tutorial)	20	Silver

SPIDER-MAN: TOTAL MAYHEM HD

MOBILE

ULTIMATE DIFFICULTY

Defeat the game.

BLACK SUIT

Defeat the game. Access the suit on the level select with an icon in the upper-left corner.

SPIRIT CAMERA: THE CURSED MEMOIR

GOTHIC LOLITA COSTUME FOR MAYA

Complete the story mode.

PRINCESS PEACH COSTUME FOR MAYA

Complete all Battle Mode missions on Nightmare difficulty.

GOTHIC LOLITA COSTUME FOR PHOTO-OP

Complete the story mode on Nightmare difficulty.

BOY IN THE BOOK CURSED PAGES MINI-GAME

Complete all Four Strange Masks levels.

SPIRIT HOUSE CURSED PAGES MINI-GAME

Complete the first level of Boy in the Book.

SPLATTERHOUSE

ACHIEVEMENTS & TROPHIES

NAME	GOAL/REQUIREMENT	POINT VALUE	TROPHY VALUE
The Berserker	Complete Phase 2: The Doll that Bled.	10	Bronze
Be Garbage of Cesspool	Complete Phase 4: The Meat Factory.	20	Bronze
Experiment 765	Complete Phase 6: Beast with a Human Heart.	30	Bronze
Shattered Narcissus	Complete Phase 8: Reflections in Blood.	40	Silver
Pyre for the Damned	Complete Phase 10: The Wicker Bride.	50	Silver
Bride of the Corrupted	Complete the game on any difficulty.	100	Silver
I Walk with Death	Complete the game on "Savage" difficulty (or harder).	110	Silver
Dreams of the Dead	Complete the game on "Brutal" Difficulty.	120	Gold
Death Came Ripping	Kill an enemy with a Splatter Slash.	5	Bronze
Razor of Hell	Get 100 kills with Splatter Slash.	5	Bronze
Must Kill	Kill an enemy with Splatter Smash.	5	Bronze
Downpour of Blood	Get 100 kills with Splatter Smash.	5	Bronze
Flesh Re-animation!	Regenerate with Splatter Siphon.	5	Bronze
One Who Slays	Get 300 kills in Berserker Mode.	5	Bronze
Heavy Frikkin' Metal!	Get 50 kills with non-fleshy weapons.	5	Bronze
Triumph of Iron	Get 500 kills with non-fleshy weapons.	15	Silver
See you at the Party	Kill an enemy with an enemy's arm.	5	Bronze

NAME	GOAL/REQUIREMENT	POINT VALUE	TROPHY VALUE
None More Dead	Get 150 kills with enemy arms.	10	Bronze
Tongue in Cheek	Kill an enemy with an enemy's head.	5	Bronze
Head on Arrival	Get 50 kills with enemy heads.	10	Bronze
You Got Red on You	Splat an enemy on a wall with a weapon.	5	Bronze
Blood and Lightning	Splat 100 enemies on a wall with a weapon.	5	Bronze
The Blackest of Sundays	Splat 200 enemies on a wall with a weapon.	10	Silver
The Business of Killing	Perform a Splatterkill.	5	Bronze
South of Hell	Perform 75 Splatterkills.	5	Bronze
Vigorous Vengeance	Perform 150 Splatterkills.	10	Silver
Morbid Dismemberment	Kill an enemy with your own dismembered arm.	5	Bronze
Brain Dead	Tackle an enemy and pummel it 20 times.	5	Bronze
Bad Taste	Impale an enemy on a spike.	5	Bronze
Army of Dead Evil	Kill 6 enemies within one second.	5	Bronze
Headlong into Monsters	Kill 6 enemies in one ram attack.	5	Bronze
POW!	Launch an enemy straight up with "No Head Room".	5	Bronze
Barrels of Blood	Get 2000 or more BLOOD Points in one chain of attacks.	5	Bronze
Audiophile	Listen to all of Dr. West's gramophone records.	5	Bronze
Boreworm Massacre	Stomp on 1000 Boreworms.	10	Bronze
Killer of Killers	Get an S-rank in Survival Arena mode.	5	Bronze
Anvil Horror	Get three S-ranks in Survival Arena mode.	15	Bronze
Jason Schmason	Get six S-ranks in Survival Arena mode.	50	Silver
Dead on the Rise	Accomplish 5 Secret Missions in a single Survival Arena attempt.	5	Bronze
Too much Horror business	Accomplish all 10 Secret Missions in a single Survival Arena attempt.	10	Bronze
Hunger Pangs	Purchase a skill.	5	Bronze
Blood Lust	Unlock 25 skills.	25	Bronze
Lust for After Life	Unlock all skills.	50	Silver
Call of the Thule	Unlock 5% of Dr. West's journal.	10	Bronze
Nightmare in Arkham	Unlock 25% of Dr. West's journal.	20	Bronze
Lovecraft Baby	Unlock 50% of Dr. West's journal.	20	Bronze
The House that West Built	Unlock all pages of Dr. West's journal.	100	Gold
Jen Smells of Rot…of the Grave	Re-assemble one of Jen's sexy photos.	5	Bronze
Creepy Show	Re-assemble 8 of Jen's photos.	10	Bronze
Happy Ending?	Re-assemble all of Jen's photos.	20	Silver

THE SPLATTERS

XBOX 360

AVATAR AWARDS

AVATAR	EARNED BY
"Die With Style" T-Shirt	Unlock the Air-Strike move to receive this shirt.
"The Splatters" T-Shirt	Unlock the Flip move to receive this shirt.
Splatter-Head	Unlock the Ballistic move to earn this award!

SPONGEBOB SQUAREPANTS FEATURING NICKTOONS: GLOBS OF DOOM

NINTENDO 3DS

INFINITE HEALTH

Select Unlock Codes from the Options and enter Tak, Tlaloc, Jimmy Neutron, Beautiful Gorgeous.

INSTANT KO

Select Unlock Codes from the Options and enter Dib, Tak, Beautiful Gorgeous, Plankton.

EXTRA ATTACK

Select Unlock Codes from the Options and enter Dib, Plankton, Technus, Jimmy Neutron.

EXTRA DEFENSE

Select Unlock Codes from the Options and enter Zim, Danny Phantom, Plankton, Beautiful Gorgeous.

MAX DEFENSE

Select Unlock Codes from the Options and enter Plankton, Dib, Beautiful Gorgeous, Plankton.

ITEMS +

Select Unlock Codes from the Options and enter Danny Phantom, Beautiful Gorgeous, Jimmy Neutron, Technus.

ITEMS ++

Select Unlock Codes from the Options and enter SpongeBob, Tlaloc, SpongeBob, Danny Phantom.

NO HEALTH ITEMS

Select Unlock Codes from the Options and enter Tak, SpongeBob, Technus, Danny Phantom.

LOWER PRICES

Select Unlock Codes from the Options and enter Tlaloc, Zim, Beautiful Gorgeous, SpongeBob.

SUPER BEAUTIFUL GORGEOUS

Select Unlock Codes from the Options and enter Beautiful Gorgeous, Technus, Jimmy Neutron, Beautiful Gorgeous.

SUPER DANNY PHANTOM

Select Unlock Codes from the Options and enter Danny Phantom, Zim, Danny Phantom, Beautiful Gorgeous.

SUPER DIB

Select Unlock Codes from the Options and enter Zim, Plankton, Dib, Plankton.

S

SUPER JIMMY

Select Unlock Codes from the Options and enter Technus, Danny Phantom, Jimmy Neutron, Technus.

SUPER PLANKTON

Select Unlock Codes from the Options and enter Tak, Plankton, Dib, Technus.

SUPER SPONGEBOB

Select Unlock Codes from the Options and enter Technus, SpongeBob, Technus, Tlaloc.

SUPER TAK

Select Unlock Codes from the Options and enter Danny Phantom, Jimmy Neutron, Tak, Tlaloc.

SUPER TECHNUS

Select Unlock Codes from the Options and enter Danny Phantom, Technus, Tak, Technus.

SUPER TLALOC

Select Unlock Codes from the Options and enter Tlaloc, Beautiful Gorgeous, Dib, SpongeBob.

SUPER ZIM

Select Unlock Codes from the Options and enter Plankton, Zim, Technus, SpongeBob.

SUPER JETPACK

Select Unlock Codes from the Options and enter Beautiful Gorgeous, Tlaloc, Jimmy Neutron, Jimmy Neutron.

COLORLESS ENEMIES

Select Unlock Codes from the Options and enter Technus, Jimmy Neutron, Tlaloc, Plankton.

BLUE ENEMIES

Select Unlock Codes from the Options and enter Beautiful Gorgeous, Zim, Plankton, Technus.

RED ENEMIES

Select Unlock Codes from the Options and enter SpongeBob, Tak, Jimmy Neutron, Danny Phantom.

DIFFICULT ENEMIES

Select Unlock Codes from the Options and enter SpongeBob, Dib, Dib, Technus.

DIFFICULT BOSSES

Select Unlock Codes from the Options and enter Plankton, Beautiful Gorgeous, Technus, Tlaloc.

INVINCIBLE PARTNER

Select Unlock Codes from the Options and enter Plankton, Tak, Beautiful Gorgeous, SpongeBob.

NINTENDO WII

When entering the following codes, the order of the characters going down is: SpongeBob SquarePants, Nicolai Technus, Danny Phantom, Dib, Zim, Tlaloc, Tak, Beautiful Gorgeous, Jimmy Neutron, Plankton. These names are shortened to the first name in the following.

ATTRACT COINS

Using the Upgrade Machine on the bottom level of the lair, select "Input cheat codes here". Enter Tlaloc, Plankton, Danny, Plankton, Tak. Coins are attracted to you making them much easier to collect.

DON'T LOSE COINS

Using the Upgrade Machine on the bottom level of the lair, select "Input cheat codes here." Enter Plankton, Jimmy, Beautiful, Jimmy, Plankton. You don't lose coins when you get knocked out.

GOO HAS NO EFFECT

Using the Upgrade Machine on the bottom level of the lair, select "Input cheat codes here". Enter Danny, Danny, Danny, Nicolai, Nicolai. Goo does not slow you down.

MORE GADGET COMBO TIME

Using the Upgrade Machine on the bottom level of the lair, select "Input cheat codes here". Enter SpongeBob, Beautiful, Danny, Plankton, Nicolai. You have more time to perform gadget combos.

SPONGEBOB SQUAREPANTS: CREATURE FROM THE KRUSTY KRAB

NINTENDO WII

30,000 EXTRA Z'S

Select Cheat Codes from the Extras menu and enter ROCFISH.

PUNK SPONGEBOB IN DIESEL DREAMING

Select Cheat Codes from the Extras menu and enter SPONGE. Select Activate Bonus Items to enable this bonus item.

HOT ROD SKIN IN DIESEL DREAMING

Select Cheat Codes from the Extras menu and enter HOTROD. Select Activate Bonus Items to enable this bonus item.

PATRICK TUX IN STARFISHMAN TO THE RESCUE

Select Cheat Codes from the Extras menu and enter PATRICK. Select Activate Bonus Items to enable this bonus item.

SPONGEBOB PLANKTON IN SUPER-SIZED PATTY

Select Cheat Codes from the Extras menu and enter PANTS. Select Activate Bonus Items to enable this bonus item.

PATRICK LASER COLOR IN ROCKET RODEO

Select Cheat Codes from the Extras menu and enter ROCKET. Select Activate Bonus Items to enable this bonus item.

PATRICK ROCKET SKIN COLOR IN ROCKET RODEO

Select Cheat Codes from the Extras menu and enter SPACE. Select Activate Bonus Items to enable this bonus item.

PLANKTON ASTRONAUT SUIT IN REVENGE OF THE GIANT PLANKTON MONSTER

Select Cheat Codes from the Extras menu and enter ROBOT. Select Activate Bonus Items to enable this bonus item.

PLANKTON EYE LASER COLOR IN REVENGE OF THE GIANT PLANKTON MONSTER

Select Cheat Codes from the Extras menu and enter LASER. Select Activate Bonus Items to enable this bonus item.

PIRATE PATRICK IN ROOFTOP RUMBLE

Select Cheat Codes from the Extras menu and enter PIRATE. Select Activate Bonus Items to enable this bonus item.

HOVERCRAFT VEHICLE SKIN IN HYPNOTIC HIGHWAY - PLANKTON

Select Cheat Codes from the Extras menu and enter HOVER. Select Activate Bonus Items to enable this bonus item.

SPORTS CHAMPIONS 2

TROPHIES

NAME	GOAL/REQUIREMENT	TROPHY VALUE
All Heart	Come back to win after being knocked down in a single—player Boxing match (Silver or higher)	Silver
Allstar	Acquire 100 stars in Cup Play	Silver
Arrow Dynamic	Get 3 split arrows in a single Archery match	Bronze
Arrowbics	Last for 2 minutes in an Archery Challenge Mode match	Bronze
C-C-C-C-C-Combo!	Land a 6-hit combo in Boxing	Bronze
Clubbin'	Complete the Gold Cup in Golf	Silver
Double Deuce	Win a Tennis game after going deuce twice	Bronze
Fashion Forward	Equip your Champion with an unlockable item	Bronze
Flipping Crazy	Successfully land a jump with two forward flips and two back flips	Bronze
FORE!	Complete a round of Golf with four players	Bronze
Frost And The Flurrious	Pass another skier after drafting behind them for at least 5 seconds	Bronze
Game-Set-Match	Complete a game of Tennis	Bronze
Get The Point	Acquire 500,000 points in Cup Play with a single Champion.	Silver
Golf Carting	Win a game of Golf at each location in Free Play	Silver
Icy What You Did There	During a race, cause another skier to crash	Bronze
It's All Down Hill!	Complete the Gold Cup in Skiing	Silver
King Pins!	Complete the Gold Cup in Bowling	Silver
Legendary	Complete the Gold Cup in Boxing	Silver
Lesson Learned	Complete a training stage in any sport	Bronze
Make Some Racquet!	Complete the Gold Cup in Tennis	Silver
Most Improved	improve your score in a previously completed Cup Play match	Bronze
Mr. Z	Unlock all Bronze, Silver, and Gold Trophies	Platinum
Net Points	In Tennis, score 10 points at the net in a single match	Bronze
Party Monster!	Complete more than 1 Party Play playlist	Bronze
Pin Pal	Complete a game of Bowling	Bronze
Profilin'	Use two or more created Champions in a multiplayer game	Bronze
Quiver With Joy!	Complete the Gold Cup in Archery	Silver
Split Happens	In Bowling, pick up a split spare	Bronze
Sports Champions Champion	Complete the Gold Cup in all 6 sports	Gold
Star Bound	Acquire 25 stars in Cup Play	Bronze
Straight Shooter	Win a Silver difficulty level (or higher) Archery match without missing a shot	Bronze
Strike! A Pose	Accumulate 20 strikes in Bowling	Bronze
Stylin'	Customize an outfit for your Champion in all 6 sports	Bronze
Superstar	Acquire 250 stars in Cup Play	Gold
Take A Bow	Complete a game in Archery	Bronze

NAME	GOAL/REQUIREMENT	TROPHY VALUE
Tee Time	Complete a game of Golf	Bronze
The Challenger	Earn at least 2 stars on each Bronze Cup Challenge Mode	Bronze
To The Green	In Golf, hit the ball onto the green from the tee	Bronze
Two-Planker	Complete a game of Skiing	Bronze
Unbowlievable!	In Bowling, get above a 200 point game in Silver difficulty or higher	Silver
Upstart	Complete a game of Boxing	Bronze
What The Putt!?	In Golf, make a putt over 40 feet	Bronze
You Got Served	Score two aces in a single Tennis match	Bronze
You're A Piece Of Iron	Win a single-player Boxing match without being knocked down once (Silver or higher)	Bronze

SSX

ACHIEVEMENTS

NAME	GOAL/REQUIREMENT	POINT VALUE
This Gear Is Bronze	Collect all Bronze Gear Badges	10
This Gear Is Silver	Collect all Silver Gear Badges	25
This Gear Is Golden	Collect all Gold Gear Badges	50
The Bronze Campaign	Collect all Bronze World Tour Badges	10
The Silver Campaign	Collect all Silver World Tour Badges	25
The Silver Survival Guide	Collect all Silver Survive Badges	25
The Golden Survival Guide	Collect all Gold Survive Badges	50
Team SSX	Unlock every member of Team SSX through World Tour (or purchase in Explore or Global Events)	10
Tree Hugger	Survive Trees Deadly Descent without equipping armor (in World Tour)	25
The Apple Theory	Survive Gravity Deadly Descent without equipping a wingsuit (in World Tour)	25
Do You See What I See	Survive Darkness Deadly Descent without equipping a headlamp or pulse goggles (in World Tour)	25
Ice To See You	Survive Ice Deadly Descent without equipping ice axes (in World Tour)	25
Buried Alive	Survive Avalanche Deadly Descent without equipping armor (in World Tour)	25
Playing Favorites	Reach level 10 with any character	25
It's Cold Out Here	Survive Cold Deadly Descent without equipping a solar panel (in World Tour)	25
Rocky Road	Survive Rock Deadly Descent without equipping armor (in World Tour)	25
Caution Low Visibility	Survive Whiteout Deadly Descent without equipping pulse goggles (in World Tour)	25
That Was Easy	Unlock all Game Modes	5
I Am A Ghost	Upload your first personal ghost	5
Grindage	Grind your first rail (not achievable in Tutorial)	5

NAME	GOAL/REQUIREMENT	POINT VALUE
Around The World	Ride with all three Pilots with each member of Team SSX	10
I Ain't Afraid of Snow Ghost	Beat a Friend's Rival Ghost in every Range (in Explore)	10
The Golden Trick It	Earn your 1st Gold in a Trick Event (in Explore)	10
The Gold Standard	Earn your 1st Gold in a Race Event (in Explore)	10
Heart Of Gold	Earn your 1st Gold in a Survive Event (in Explore)	10
Peak-A-Boo	Participate in a Global Event in every Peak	10
Tag Team	Earn a Bronze in a Trick Event with every member of Team SSX (in Explore)	10
Pass The Baton	Earn a Bronze in a Race Event with every member of Team SSX (in Explore)	10
Leave No One Behind	Earn a Bronze in a Survive Event with every member of Team SSX (in Explore)	10
Überlesscious	Earn a Bronze Medal on a Trick Event in Explore without landing any Super Übers	20
Who Needs Boost	Earn a Bronze Medal on a Race Event in Explore without using any boost	20
I'm Alive!	Rewind out of Death for the First Time (not achievable in Tutorial)	5
I'm Flying!	Deploy your wingsuit for the first time (not achievable in Tutorial)	5
Gear Up!	Make your first Gear Purchase	5
Pass The Board Wax	Make your first Board Purchase	5
I Need A Boost	Make your first Mod Purchase	5
The Golden Campaign	Collect all Gold World Tour Badges	50
The Bronze Miner	Collect all Bronze Explore Badges	10
The Silver Miner	Collect all Silver Explore Badges	25
The Gold Miner	Collect all Gold Explore Badges	50
The Bronze Spender	Collect all Bronze Global Events Badges	10
The Silver Spender	Collect all Silver Global Events Badges	25
The Gold Spender	Collect all Gold Global Events Badges	50
The Bronze Badger	Collect all Bronze Tricky Badges	10
The Silver Boarder	Collect all Silver Tricky Badges	25
The Golden Tricker	Collect all Gold Tricky Badges	50
The Bronze Finish	Collect all Bronze Race Badges	10
The Silver Finish	Collect all Silver Race Badges	25
The Gold Finish	Collect all Gold Race Badges	50
The Bronze Survival Guide	Collect all Bronze Survive Badges	10

STAR TREK

ACHIEVEMENTS & TROPHIES

NAME	GOAL/REQUIREMENT	POINT VALUE	TROPHY VALUE
Well Done Captain	Completed the game on any difficulty setting	30	Silver
Into Darkness	Completed the game on hard difficulty setting	30	Silver
Captain's Phaser Master	Killed 100 enemies with the Captain's Phaser	10	Bronze
Vulcan Repeater Master	Killed 100 enemies with the Vulcan Repeater	10	Bronze
Starfleet Phaser Rifle Master	Killed 50 enemies with the Starfleet Phaser Rifle	10	Bronze
Vulcan Pulse Cannon Master	Killed 50 enemies with the Vulcan Pulse Cannon	10	Bronze
Starfleet Type III Rifle Master	Killed 20 enemies with the Starfleet Type III Rifle	10	Bronze
Ravager Master	Killed 50 enemies with the Ravager	10	Bronze
Marauder Master	Killed 50 enemies with the Marauder	10	Bronze
Pillager Master	Killed 50 enemies with the Pillager	10	Bronze
Railer Master	Killed 50 enemies with the Railer	10	Bronze
Striker Master	Killed 20 enemies with the Striker	10	Bronze
Arc Driver Master	Killed 50 enemies with the Arc Driver	10	Bronze
Plasma Grenade Master	Killed 20 enemies with Plasma Grenades	10	Bronze
Weapon Experimenter	Connected every weapon's alternate fire with enemies	30	Bronze
Listening In	Found half of all audio logs	20	Bronze
The Whole Story	Found all audio logs	50	Gold
Researcher	Found half of all research items	20	Bronze
Fascinating	Found all research items	50	Gold
Away Team: Mission Initiated	Completed one chapter in co-operative play	10	Bronze
Away Team: Mission In-Progress	Completed four chapters in co-operative play	20	Bronze
Away Team: Mission Accomplished	Completed all chapters in co-operative play	30	Silver
Captain's Phaser Tinkerer	Bought all upgrades for the Captain's Phaser	30	Bronze
Vulcan Repeater Tinkerer	Bought all upgrades for the Vulcan Repeater	30	Bronze
Tricorder Tinkerer	Bought all upgrades for the Tricorder	30	Bronze
Technologic	Cleared 30 mini-games including co-operative hacks, bypasses, and power reroutes	10	Bronze
Non-Lethal Master	Took down 30 enemies in a non-lethal manner	10	Bronze
Dagger of the Mind	Performed Mind Meld on 10 different enemies	10	Bronze
Live Long and Prosper	Revived your teammate (AI or co-op player) 20 times	10	Bronze
All Power to Forward Shields	Completed the Space Battle with a hull integrity of 85% or more	30	Bronze

NAME	GOAL/REQUIREMENT	POINT VALUE	TROPHY VALUE
Are You Not Entertained?	Won the brawl against your buddy in "The Trials" chapter	20	Bronze
Get to the Shuttle!	After the brawl, escaped in less than 6 minutes in "The Trials" chapter	20	Bronze
Exemplary Commendation	Completed all Optional Objectives	100	Gold
Honorary Commendation	Completed half of all Optional Objectives	60	Silver

SECRET ACHIEVEMENTS & TROPHIES

NAME	GOAL/REQUIREMENT	POINT VALUE	TROPHY VALUE
Beat Helios-1	Completed the Helios-1 chapter on any difficulty	20	Bronze
Beat New Vulcan	Completed the New Vulcan chapter on any difficulty	20	Bronze
Beat Space Battle	Completed the Space Battle chapter on any difficulty	20	Bronze
Beat Frontier Starbase	Completed the Frontier Starbase chapter on any difficulty	20	Bronze
Beat Volatile Cargo & Flashback	Completed the Volatile Cargo & Flashback chapters on any difficulty	20	Bronze
Beat Gorn Planet & The Trials	Completed the Gorn Planet & The Trials chapters on any difficulty	20	Bronze
Beat Enterprise Capture	Completed the Enterprise Capture chapter on any difficulty	20	Bronze
Beat Mothership	Completed the Mothership chapter on any difficulty	20	Bronze
Go Team!	Killed or took down an enemy that your teammate (AI or co-op player) has stunned	10	Bronze
My Robot Friend	Hacked an enemy drone to your side and have it kill another enemy	10	Bronze
I'll Cover You!	Ordered your teammate (AI or co-op player) and had him complete 5 bypasses in a row	10	Bronze
One Man Army	Killed 3 enemies while your teammate (AI or co-op player) was in a downed state	10	Bronze
Down But Not Out	Killed 3 enemies while in a single downed state	10	Bronze
Arena	As Kirk, had a Gorn enemy melee you	10	Bronze
I Shall Always Be Your Friend	As Spock, bled out during a downed state, leaving Kirk alone and failing the mission	10	Bronze

STAR WARS THE CLONE WARS: LIGHTSABER DUELS

COUNT DOOKU

Select Cheats from Extras and press 2, 2, +, 2, 2, +, 2, 2, -, A, -, C, -, Z, +, Z.

GENERAL GRIEVOUS

Select Cheats from Extras and press 2, 2, +, 2, 2, +, 2, 2, -, Z, -, A, -, C, +, C.

ALL STORY MODE STAGES

Select Cheats from Extras and press A, +, 2, 2, +, C, +, 2, 2, +, Z, +, 2, 2.

MUSTAFAR STAGE

Select Cheats from Extras and press Z (x5), +, Z (x5), +, 1.

RAXUS PRIME STAGE

Select Cheats from Extras and press A (x5), +, A (x5), +, , 2.

SEPARATIST DROID FACTORY STAGE

Select Cheats from Extras and press C (x5), +, C (x5), +, 1.

CREDITS

Select Cheats from Extras and press 1, 2, +, 1.

GALLERY ONE

Select Cheats from Extras and press -, A, +, 1.

GALLERY TWO

Select Cheats from Extras and press -, A, +, 2.

GALLERY THREE

Select Cheats from Extras and press +, A, +, 1, +, 2.

GALLERY FOUR

Select Cheats from Extras and press +, A, +, 2, +, 2.

STAR WARS THE CLONE WARS: REPUBLIC HEROES

BIG HEAD MODE

Pause the game, select Shop, and enter the following in Cheats: Up, Down, Left, Right, Left, Right, Down, Up.

MINI-GUN

Pause the game, select Shop, and enter the following in Cheats: Down, Left, Right, Up, Right, Up, Left, Down.

ULTIMATE LIGHTSABER

Pause the game, select Shop, and enter the following in Cheats: Right, Down, Down, Up, Left, Up, Up, Down.

LIGHTSABER THROW UPGRADE

Pause the game, select Shop, and enter the following in Combat Upgrades: Left, Left, Right, Right, Up, Down, Down, Up.

SPIDER DROID UPGRADE

Pause the game, select Shop, and enter the following in Droid-Jak Upgrades: Up, Left, Down, Left, Right, Left, Left, Left.

STAR WARS: THE FORCE UNLEASHED

CHEAT CODES

Pause the game and select Input Code. Here you can enter the following codes. Activating any of the following cheat codes will disable some unlockables, and you will be unable to save your progress.

CHEAT	CODE
All Force Powers at Max Power	KATARN
All Force Push Ranks	EXARKUN
All Saber Throw Ranks	ADEGAN
All Repulse Ranks	DATHOMIR
All Saber Crystals	HURRIKANE
All Talents	JOCASTA
Deadly Saber	LIGHTSABER

COMBOS

Pause the game and select Input Code. Here you can enter the following codes. Activating any of the following cheat codes will disable some unlockables, and you will be unable to save your progress.

COMBO	CODE
All Combos	MOLDYCROW
Aerial Ambush	VENTRESS
Aerial Assault	EETHKOTH
Aerial Blast	YADDLE
Impale	BRUTALSTAB
Lightning Bomb	MASSASSI
Lightning Grenade	RAGNOS
Saber Slam	PLOKOON
Saber Sling	KITFISTO
Sith Saber Flurry	LUMIYA
Sith Slash	DARAGON
Sith Throw	SAZEN
New Combo	FREEDON
New Combo	MARAJADE

ALL DATABANK ENTRIES

Pause the game and select Input Code. Enter OSSUS.

MIRRORED LEVEL

Pause the game and select Input Code. Enter MINDTRICK. Re-enter the code to return level to normal.

SITH MASTER DIFFICULTY

Pause the game and select Input Code. Enter SITHSPAWN.

COSTUMES

Pause the game and select Input Code. Here you can enter the following codes.

COSTUME	CODE
All Costumes	SOHNDANN
Bail Organa	VICEROY
Ceremonial Jedi Robes	DANTOOINE
Drunken Kota	HARDBOILED
Emperor	MASTERMIND
Incinerator Trooper	PHOENIX
Jedi Adventure Robe	HOLOCRON
Kashyyyk Trooper	TK421GREEN

COSTUME	CODE
Kota	MANDALORE
Master Kento	WOOKIEE
Proxy	PROTOTYPE
Scout Trooper	FERRAL
Shadow Trooper	BLACKHOLE
Sith Stalker Armor	KORRIBAN
Snowtrooper	SNOWMAN
Stormtrooper	TK421WHITE
Stormtrooper Commander	TK421BLUE

NINTENDO 3DS

INCREASED HEALTH

Select Unleashed Codes from the Extras menu and enter QSSPVENXO.

MAX OUT FORCE POWERS

Select Unleashed Codes from the Extras menu and enter CPLOOLKBF.

UNLIMITED FORCE ENERGY

Select Unleashed Codes from the Extras menu and enter TVENCVMJZ.

MORE POWERFUL LIGHTSABER

Select Unleashed Codes from the Extras menu and enter lightsaber.

UBER LIGHTSABER

Select Unleashed Codes from the Extras menu and enter MOMIROXIW.

ROM KOTA

Select Unleashed Codes from the Extras menu and enter mandalore.

CEREMONIAL JEDI ROBES

Select Unleashed Codes from the Extras menu and enter CURSEZRUX.

DAD'S ROBES

Select Unleashed Codes from the Extras menu and enter wookiee.

DARTH VADER'S COSTUME

Select Unleashed Codes from the Extras menu and enter HRMXRKVEN.

KENTO'S ROBE

Select Unleashed Codes from the Extras menu and enter KBVMSEVNM.

KOTA'S OUTFIT

Select Unleashed Codes from the Extras menu and enter EEDOPVENG.

SITH ROBE

Select Unleashed Codes from the Extras menu and enter ZWSFVENXA.

SITH ROBES

Select Unleashed Codes from the Extras menu and enter holocron.

SITH STALKER ARMOR

Select Unleashed Codes from the Extras menu and enter CPLZKMZTD.

PSP

CHEATS

Once you have accessed the Rogue Shadow, select Enter Code from the Extras menu. Now you can enter the following:

CHEAT	CODE
Invincibility	CORTOSIS
Unlimited Force	VERGENCE
1,000,000 Force Points	SPEEDER
All Force Powers	TYRANUS

CHEATS, ACHIEVEMENTS, AND TROPHIES

CHEAT	CODE
Max Force Power Level	KATARN
Max Combo Level	COUNTDOOKU
Amplified Lightsaber Damage	LIGHTSABER

COSTUMES

Once you have accessed the Rogue Shadow, select Enter Code from the Extras menu. Now you can enter the following:

COSTUME	CODE
All Costumes	GRANDMOFF
501st Legion	LEGION
Aayla Secura	AAYLA
Admiral Ackbar	ITSATWAP
Anakin Skywalker	CHOSENONE
Asajj Ventress	ACOLYTE
Ceremonial Jedi Robes	DANTOOINE
Chop'aa Notimo	NOTIMO
Classic stormtrooper	TK421
Count Dooku	SERENNO
Darth Desolous	PAUAN
Darth Maul	ZABRAK
Darth Phobos	HIDDENFEAR
Darth Vader	SITHLORD
Drexl Roosh	DREXLROOSH
Emperor Palpatine	PALPATINE
General Rahm Kota	MANDALORE
Han Solo	NERFHERDER
Heavy trooper	SHOCKTROOP
Juno Eclipse	ECLIPSE
Kento's Robe	WOOKIEE
Kleef	KLEEF
Lando Calrissian	SCOUNDREL
Luke Skywalker	T16WOMPRAT
Luke Skywalker (Yavin)	YELLOWJCKT
Mace Windu	JEDIMASTER
Mara Jade	MARAJADE
Maris Brook	MARISBROOD
Navy commando	STORMTROOP
Obi Wan Kenobi	BENKENOBI
Proxy	HOLOGRAM
Qui Gon Jinn	MAVERICK
Shaak Ti	TOGRUTA
Shadow trooper	INTHEDARK
Sith Robes	HOLOCRON
Sith Stalker Armor	KORRIBAN
Twi'lek	SECURA

STAR WARS THE FORCE UNLEASHED: ULTIMATE SITH EDITION

CHEAT CODES

Pause the game and select Input Code. Here you can enter the following codes. Activating any of the following cheat codes will disable some unlockables, and you will be unable to save your progress.

CHEAT	CODE
All Force Powers at Max Power	KATARN
All Force Push Ranks	EXARKUN
All Saber Throw Ranks	ADEGAN
All Repulse Ranks	DATHOMIR
All Saber Crystals	HURRIKANE
All Talents	JOCASTA
Deadly Saber	LIGHTSABER

COMBOS

Pause the game and select Input Code. Here you can enter the following codes. Activating any of the following cheat codes will disable some unlockables, and you will be unable to save your progress.

COMBO	CODE
All Combos	MOLDYCROW
Aerial Ambush	VENTRESS
Aerial Assault	EETHKOTH
Aerial Blast	YADDLE
Impale	BRUTALSTAB
Lightning Bomb	MASSASSI
Lightning Grenade	RAGNOS
Saber Slam	PLOKOON
Saber Sling	KITFISTO
Sith Saber Flurry	LUMIYA
Sith Slash	DARAGON
Sith Throw	SAZEN
New Combo	FREEDON
New Combo	MARAJADE

ALL DATABANK ENTRIES

Pause the game and select Input Code. Enter OSSUS.

MIRRORED LEVEL

Pause the game and select Input Code. Enter MINDTRICK. Re-enter the code to return level to normal.

SITH MASTER DIFFICULTY

Pause the game and select Input Code. Enter SITHSPAWN.

COSTUMES

Pause the game and select Input Code. Here you can enter the following codes.

COSTUME	CODE
All Costumes	SOHNDANN
Bail Organa	VICEROY
Ceremonial Jedi Robes	DANTOOINE
Drunken Kota	HARDBOILED
Emperor	MASTERMIND
Incinerator Trooper	PHOENIX
Jedi Adventure Robe	HOLOCRON

COSTUME	CODE
Kashyyyk Trooper	TK421GREEN
Kota	MANDALORE
Master Kento	WOOKIEE
Proxy	PROTOTYPE
Scout Trooper	FERRAL
Shadow Trooper	BLACKHOLE
Sith Stalker Armor	KORRIBAN
Snowtrooper	SNOWMAN
Stormtrooper	TK421WHITE
Stormtrooper Commander	TK421BLUE

STAR WARS: THE FORCE UNLEASHED II

NINTENDO WII

ALL COSTUMES

Select Story Mode and then choose Costumes from the Profile. Hold Z until you hear a sound and then press Left, Right, C, Left, Right, C, Up, Down.

XBOX 360

BOBA FETT COSTUME

Pause the game, select Cheat Codes from the Options, and enter MANDALORE.

DARK APPRENTICE COSTUME

Pause the game, select Cheat Codes from the Options, and enter VENTRESS.

GENERAL KOTA COSTUME

Pause the game, select Cheat Codes from the Options, and enter RAHM.

JUMP TROOPER COSTUME

Pause the game, select Cheat Codes from the Options, and enter AJP400.

NEIMOIDIAN COSTUME

Pause the game, select Cheat Codes from the Options, and enter GUNRAY.

REBEL COMMANDO COSTUME

Pause the game, select Cheat Codes from the Options, and enter SPECFORCE.

REBEL SOLDIER COSTUME

Pause the game, select Cheat Codes from the Options, and enter REBELSCUM.

SABER GUARD COSTUME

Pause the game, select Cheat Codes from the Options, and enter MORGUKAI.

SITH ACOLYTE COSTUME

Pause the game, select Cheat Codes from the Options, and enter HAAZEN.

STORMTROOPER COSTUME

Pause the game, select Cheat Codes from the Options, and enter TK421.

TERROR TROOPER COSTUME

Pause the game, select Cheat Codes from the Options, and enter SHADOW.

TRAINING DROID COSTUME

Pause the game, select Cheat Codes from the Options, and enter HOLODROID.

EXPERIMENTAL JEDI ARMOR

Pause the game, select Cheat Codes from the Options, and enter NOMI.

REPULSE FORCE POWER

Pause the game, select Cheat Codes from the Options, and enter MAREK.

JEDI MIND TRICK

Pause the game, select Cheat Codes from the Options, and enter YARAEL.

SABRE THROW

Pause the game, select Cheat Codes from the Options, and enter TRAYA.

DARK GREEN LIGHTSABER CRYSTAL

Pause the game, select Cheat Codes from the Options, and enter LIBO.

WISDOM LIGHTSABER CRYSTALS

Pause the game, select Cheat Codes from the Options, and enter SOLARI.

STAR WARS: LETHAL ALLIANCE

PSP

ALL LEVELS

Select Create Profile from the Profiles menu and enter HANSOLO.

ALL LEVELS AND REFILL HEALTH WHEN DEPLETED

Select Create Profile from the Profiles menu and enter JD1MSTR.

REFILL HEALTH WHEN DEPLETED

Select Create Profile from the Profiles menu and enter B0BAF3T.

STARCRAFT II: HEART OF THE SWARM

PC

SWARM CAMPAIGN CHEAT CODES

Bring up the chat interface and enter these codes to activate cheats in the campaign mode.

EFFECT	CODE
5,000 of each resource	whorunbartertown
Fast Build	catfoodforprawnguns
God Mode (Invincibility)	terribleterribledamage
Instant Win	whatisbestinlife
Remove the Supply Cap	bunker55aliveinside
Units & Structures for free	moredotsmoredots
Upgrade Weapons, Armor and Shields by 1	iamironman

STICKWARS

MOBILE

BONUS KILLS AND MONEY

Start a new game then immediately pause and tap the center of the screen six times. You will immediately gain 49 kills and $50,000.

ACHIEVEMENTS

ACHIEVEMENTS	REQUIREMENT
Big Money	Save $50,000.
Century of StickWars	Complete level 100 on any difficulty.
Effortless Slaughter	Train 100 archers.
Fireball Spammer	Train 50 wizards.
Forced Labor	Train 50 repairmen.
Half Century of StickWars	Complete level 50 on any difficulty.
Just Beginning	Complete level 1 on any difficulty.
Learning Fast	Complete level 5 on any difficulty.
Legendary Warrior	Complete level 50 on hard difficulty.
Never Give Up	Complete level 40 on any difficulty.

ACHIEVEMENTS	REQUIREMENT
Power Spellcaster	Train 100 wizards.
Rain of Arrows	Train 50 archers.
Simple Victory	Complete level 50 on easy difficulty.
Sugar Daddy	Save $10,000.
Thriving Industry	Train 100 repairmen.
Typical Hero	Complete level 50 on medium difficulty.
Wall St Ain't Got Nothin	Save $200,000.

STREET FIGHTER ALPHA 2

NINTENDO WII

AUSTRALIA STAGE

In versus mode, highlight Sagat, hold Start, and press any button.

CHUN-LI'S HIDDEN COSTUME

At the character select, highlight Chun-li, hold Start and press any button.

STREET FIGHTER IV

XBOX 360

ALTERNATE STAGES

At the stage select, hold Left Bumper or Right Bumper and select a stage.

STREET FIGHTER X TEKKEN

PLAYSTATION VITA

PANDORA MODE IN BURST KUMITE

After obtaining 10 wins consecutively, you can toggle Pandora mode on or off in Burst Kumite which puts both players in Pandora for the duration of the match.

STRIKERS 1945 PLUS PORTABLE

PSP

XP-55 ASCENDER

At the Random Select screen, press Down, Up, Down, Up, Down, Down, Down, Down, Up.

STRONG BAD'S COOL GAME FOR ATTRACTIVE PEOPLE EPISODE 1: HOMESTAR RUINER

NINTENDO WII

COBRA MODE IN SNAKE BOXER 5

At the Snake Boxer 5 title screen, press Up, Up, Down, Up, Plus.

STUNTMAN IGNITION

XBOX 360/PS3

3 PROPS IN STUNT CREATOR MODE

Select Cheats from Extras and enter COOLPROP.

ALL ITEMS UNLOCKED FOR CONSTRUCTION MODE

Select Cheats from Extras and enter NOBLEMAN.

MVX SPARTAN

Select Cheats from Extras and enter fastride.

ALL CHEATS

Select Cheats from Extras and enter Wearefrozen. This unlocks the following cheats: Slo-mo Cool, Thrill Cam, Vision Switcher, Nitro Addiction, Freaky Fast, and Ice Wheels.

ALL CHEATS

Select Cheats from Extras and enter Kungfoopete.

ICE WHEELS CHEAT

Select Cheats from Extras and enter IceAge.

NITRO ADDICTION CHEAT

Select Cheats from Extras and enter TheDuke.

VISION SWITCHER CHEAT

Select Cheats from Extras and enter GFXMODES.

SUBWAY SURFERS

MOBILE

UNLOCKABLE CHARACTERS

CHARACTER	REQUIREMENT
Brody	Collect 350,000 coins.
Frank	Collect 40,000 coins.
Fresh	Collect three Boomboxes.
Frizzy	Collect 150,000 coins.
King	Collect 80,000 coins.
Lucy	Collect 7,000 coins.
Ninja	Collect 20,000 coins.
Prince K	Collect 980,000 coins.
Spike	Collect three Guitars.
Tagbot	Collect 12,000 coins.
Tasha	Collect 30,000 coins.
Tony	Collect 95,000 coins.
Tricky	Collect three Caps.
Yutani	Collect three Spaceships.
Zoe	Collect 120,000 coins.

SUPER C

NINTENDO WII

RETAIN LIVES AND SCORE ON NEW GAME

After defeating the game, press A and then Start.

RETAIN SCORE ON NEW GAME

After defeating the game, press A, B, and then Start.

10 LIVES

At the Title screen, press Right, Left, Down, Up, A, B, Start.

SOUND TEST

At the Title screen, hold A + B and press Start.

SUPER HANG-ON

START ARCADE MODE WITH $10,000

Highlight Arcade Mode and press Up, Left, A, B, Start.

SUPER MARIO 3D LAND

SPECIAL WORLD

Complete World 8.

PLAY AS LUIGI

Complete the castle in Special World 1. Touch the L icon to switch to Luigi.

SUPER MARIO GALAXY

PLAY AS LUIGI

Collect all 120 stars and fight Bowser. After the credits you will get a message that Luigi is playable.

GRAND FINALE GALAXY

Collect all 120 stars with Luigi and beat Bowser.

STAR 121

Collect 100 purple coins.

SUPER MARIO GALAXY 2

ALL LUIGI GHOSTS

Collect 9999 coins.

BANKER TOAD

Depositing star bits with Banker Toad changes his outfit as indicated in the following table.

ITEM	# OF STAR BITS
Glasses	1000
Spear/Shield	2000
Pickaxe	4000
Scuba Suit	6000
Explorer Outfit	8000

GREEN STARS

Collect 120 stars to unlock 120 green stars.

WORLD S

After completing the game and watching the game ending, you'll unlock World S.

GRANDMASTER GALAXY

Collect 120 stars and 120 green stars.

GRANDMASTER GALAXY COMET—THE PERFECT RUN

Deposit 9999 star bits with Banker Toad.

SUPER MEAT BOY

PLAY AS BROWNIE

At the character select, press Right Bumper, Right Bumper, Right Bumper, B, B, B, X.

AVATAR AWARDS

AWARD	EARNED BY
Super Meat Boy	Beat the Light World.
Super Meat Boy T-Shirt	Play the first few levels.

CHEAT CODES

Entering these codes during the character select screen then selecting Meat Boy allows you to select hidden characters.

EFFECT	CODE
Brownie	Press "RB RB RB B B B X" (requires an Xbox 360 Controller connected to the PC
Goo Ball	Type "BALLGOO"
Tim (from Braid)	Type "outtatime"
Tofu Boy	Type "PETAPHILE"

SAVE REPLAYS

After you reach Bandage Girl in a Warp Zone level, press the space bar. You will see a replay of the stage that you can save.

UNLOCKABLE CHARACTERS

CHARACTER	REQUIREMENT
4 Bit Meat Boy	Collect 60 bandages
4 Color Meat Boy	Collect 80 bandages
8 Bit Meat Boy	Collect 40 bandages
Alien Hominid	Collect 30 bandages
Captain Viridian	Collect 90 bandages
Commander Video	Complete the warp zone in Chapter 1 level 12
Flywrench	Complete the warp zone in Chapter 4 level 18
Goo	Collect 10 bandages
Headcrab	Collect 10 bandages
Jill	Complete the warp zone in Chapter 2 level 8
Josef	Collect 30 bandages
Meat Ninja	Reach 100% completion, including Cotton Alley
Mr. Minecraft	Collect 100 bandages
Naija	Collect 50 bandages
Ogmo	Complete the warp zone in Chapter 3 level 16
Runman	Collect 70 bandages
The Kid	Complete the warp zone in Chapter 5 level 7

SUPER MONKEY BALL 3D

MONKEY FIGHT CHARACTERS

Complete the following series to unlock the characters in Monkey Fight

CHARACTER	COMPLETE THIS SERIES
W-MeeMee	Basic
P-YanYan	Super Fight

MONKEY RACE CHARACTERS

Complete the following cups in Grand Prix mode to unlock the characters in Monkey Race.

CHARACTER	FINISH GRAND PRIX IN GIVEN POSITION
N-Jam	1st in Sky-Way
A-Baby	2nd in Sky-Way
R-Doctor	3rd in Sky-Way
B-Jet	1st in Mt. Tyrano
P-YanYan	2nd in Mt. Tyrano
F-GonGon	3rd in Mt. Tyrano

MONKEY RACE CARS

To unlock more cars in Monkey Race, enter time trial mode and beat the given record for that track. If you beat it faster than that record, you unlock one car per level.

CAR	BEAT RECORD ON THIS TRACK
Robotron	Track 1 of Sky-Way
Mini Shooter	Track 2 of Sky-Way
Kitana	Track 3 of Sky-Way
G Caterpillar	Track 1 of Mt. Tyrano
Flying Carpet	Track 2 of Mt. Tyrano
Super Tops	Track 3 of Mt. Tyrano

SUPER PUZZLE FIGHTER II TURBO HD REMIX

PLAY AS AKUMA

At the character select, highlight Hsien-Ko and press Down.

PLAY AS DAN

At the character select, highlight Donovan and press Down.

PLAY AS DEVILOT

At the character select, highlight Morrigan and press Down.

PLAY AS ANITA

At the character select, hold L1 + R1 and choose Donovan.

PLAY AS HSIEN-KO'S TALISMAN

At the character select, hold L1 + R1 and choose Hsien-Ko.

PLAY AS MORRIGAN AS A BAT

At the character select, hold L1 + R1 and choose Morrigan.

PLAY AS AKUMA

At the character select, highlight Hsien-Ko and press Down.

PLAY AS DAN

At the character select, highlight Donovan and press Down.

PLAY AS DEVILOT

At the character select, highlight Morrigan and press Down.

PLAY AS ANITA

At the character select, hold Left Bumper + Right Bumper and choose Donovan.

PLAY AS HSIEN-KO'S TALISMAN

At the character select, hold Left Bumper + Right Bumper and choose Hsien-Ko.

PLAY AS MORRIGAN AS A BAT

At the character select, hold Left Bumper + Right Bumper and choose Morrigan.

PLAY AS ANITA

At the character select, hold Left Bumper + Right Bumper and choose Donovan.

PLAY AS HSIEN-KO'S TALISMAN

At the character select, hold Left Bumper + Right Bumper and choose Hsien-Ko.

PLAY AS MORRIGAN AS A BAT

At the character select, hold Left Bumper + Right Bumper and choose Morrigan.

SUPER ROBOT TAISEN OG SAGA: ENDLESS FRONTIER

NINTENDO 3DS

NEW GAME +

After you have finished the game and saved, load your save to start again with your items and money.

OG1 CHOKER

Start a new game or load a saved file with the GBA game Super Robot Taisen: Original Generation in the GBA slot. This item boosts your SP by 100.

OG2 PENDANT

Start a new game or load a saved file with the GBA game Super Robot Taisen 2: Original Generation in the GBA slot. This item boosts your HP by 250.

SUPER SPEED MACHINES

NINTENDO 3DS

UNLOCK VEHICLES

WIN GP	VEHICLE UNLOCKED
1	Haima (Rally)
2	Sandstrom (4x4)
3	Striker (Sports)
4	Copperhead (Muscle)
6	Gold Digger (Custom)
7	Blue Flame (Classic)

SUPER STICKMAN GOLF

ACHIEVEMENTS

ACHIEVEMENT	REQUIREMENT	POINTS
Sticky Ball	Unlocked the Sticky Ball	10
Ice Ball	Unlocked the Ice Ball	10
Hazard Swap	Unlock the Hazard Swap	20
Air Brakes	Unlock the Air Brakes	20
Super Ball	Unlock the Super Ball	30
Nitro Ball	Unlock the Nitro Ball—Get 30 Achievements	30
Thats A Bingo	Get a hole in one	10
Eagle	Get an eagle	10
Nothing But Net	Get a hole in one without touching the green	20
500 Strokes	Reach a combined 500 shots	10
Lunar Lander	Get a hole in one on the first hole in The Moon Base	10
Funky Dry	Score under par on Funky Town without getting wet	10
The Slew Sniper	Score under par on The Slew without hitting a sand trap	10
Parnage	Beat Dapper Dunes without getting a single bogey	
1000 Strokes	Take a combined 1000 shots	20
Jacob's Cabin	Can you find Jacob's Cabin? (Dapper Dunes—Hole 1)	10
The Tire Swing	Can you find The Tire Swing? (Lofstrom Links—Hole 8)	10
The Locksmith	Unlock all the courses	20
Cool It Down	Shoot a superball into a water hazard	10
The Trio	Bag three hole in one's in a row	10
2000 Strokes	Take a combined 2000 shots	30
3000 Strokes, Hardcore	Take a combined 3000 shots	50
The Impossible Shot	Get a hole in one on the second hole in The Ice Flows	20
Nil Score	Score a zero on a hole	20
Negative Score	Score a negative number on a hole	20
Purple Passion	Score a hole in one on hole 6 in Purple Haze	10
Purple Zero	Score a zero or less on hole 7 in Purple Haze	10
The Woodsman	Score a hole in one on hole 8 in The Woods	10
10 Clean Balls	Score under par on 10 courses without powerups	10
The Long One	Sink a super long putt	10
Look Up	Get a negative score on hole 3 in The Graveyard	10
Iced Temple	Freeze all the hazards on hole 3 in The Temple	10
Parkland Dry	Score under par on Parkland without getting wet	10
Freeze, Bounce, Drop	Beat hole 2 in Parkland in 3 strokes	10
Tropical Slide	Score a hole in one on hole 4 in The Tropics	10
Ride The Boundary	Score a hole in one on hole 3 in Key Lime Links	10
1 Multiplayer Win	Win 1 multiplayer game	10
5 Multiplayer Wins	Win 5 multiplayer games	10
10 Multiplayer Wins	Win 10 multiplayer games	20
10 Multiplayer Points	Reach a combined 10 awarded multiplayer points	10
50 Multiplayer Points	Reach a combined 50 awarded multiplayer points	10

ACHIEVEMENT	REQUIREMENT	POINTS
100 Multiplayer Points	Reach a combined 100 awarded multiplayer points	20
200 Multiplayer Points	Reach a combined 200 awarded multiplayer points	50
Haunted Hazards	Score under par on Haunted Hills without getting wet	10
Haunted Drop-in	Score a hole-in-one on hole 7 in the Haunted Hills	10
All Aces	Score all hole-in-one's in Parkland without powerups	50
Cinnamon Bounce	Score a hole-in-one on hole 7 in the Cinnamon Bluffs	20
Nitro Master	Score a hole-in-one on hole 7 on the Pipes	30
Food For Thought	Score a hole-in-one on hole 6 in the Belts	20
Belts Nil	Beat Belts hole 7 in zero or less strokes	20
Cinnamon Nil	Beat Cinnamon Bluffs hole 2 in zero or less strokes	20

SUPER STREET FIGHTER II TURBO HD REMIX

XBOX 360/PS3

The following codes give you the classic fighters in Classic Arcade Mode. Select the character, quickly enter the given code, and select him/her again.

CLASSIC BALROG

Right, Left, Left, Right

CLASSIC BLANKA

Left, Right (x3)

CLASSIC CAMMY

Up, Up, Down, Down

CLASSIC CHUN-LI

Down (x3), Up

CLASSIC DEE JAY

Down, Down, Up, Up

CLASSIC DHALSIM

Down, Up (x3)

CLASSIC E. HONDA

Up (x3), Down

CLASSIC FEI LONG

Left, Left, Right, Right

CLASSIC GUILE

Up, Down (x3)

CLASSIC KEN

Left (x3), Right

CLASSIC M. BISON

Down, Up, Up, Down

CLASSIC RYU

Right (x3), Left

CLASSIC SAGAT

Up, Down (x3), Up

CLASSIC T. HAWK

Right, Right, Left, Left

CLASSIC VEGA

Left, Right, Right, Left

CLASSIC ZANGIEF

Left, Right (x3)

SUPER STREET FIGHTER IV

BARREL BUSTER AND CAR CRUSHER BONUS STAGES

Beat Arcade Mode in any difficulty

COLORS AND TAUNTS

Colors 1 and 2 plus the first taunt for each fighter are available from the start. For colors 11 & 12, start a game with a Street Fighter IV save game on your system. To earn the rest of the colors and taunts, you need to fight a certain number of matches with that character.

COLOR	# OF MATCHES
3	2
4	4
5	6
6	8
7	10
8	12
9	14
10	16

TAUNT	# OF MATCHES
2	1
3	3
4	5
5	7
6	9
7	11
8	13
9	15
10	16

ACHIEVEMENTS & TROPHIES

NAME	GOAL/REQUIREMENT	POINT VALUE	TROPHY VALUE
Overachiever	Attain all the Achievements! The path of the warrior demands this from those who walk on it!	—	Bronze
Fashion Plate	Even a top rate fighter needs to coordinate properly! You gotta get all of the Colors first!	10	Bronze
Dan the Man	Mastery of the Saikyo arts requires mastery of the Personal Action! Collect 'em all, punk!	10	Bronze
Entitled	A Title does not tell all of a man, sir, but if I were to see one Title, I'd want them all...	50	Bronze
Iconoclast	Oh my gosh, those Icons are so adorable! I gotta find Don-chan and catch 'em all!	50	Silver
Special Movement	Do a Special Move 100 times! If you're a true student of the Rindo-kan dojo, it's your duty!	10	Silver
EXtra! EXtra!	Battle requires courage! Train by using your EX Gauge to successfully land 100 EX Moves!	10	Bronze
Super, Man!	To battle is to win a fight with overwhelming strength! Show me you can do 100 Super Combos!	10	Bronze

NAME	GOAL/REQUIREMENT	POINT VALUE	TROPHY VALUE
Ultra, Man!	If yer gonna fight, give it your all, pal. Performing 100 Ultra Combos oughta do it, eh?	10	Bronze
It Takes Focus	Your mission, should you wish to join Delta Red, is to connect with 100 Focus Attacks!	10	Bronze
Superior Super	Trust your instincts and winning will come easy. Let's begin with 50 Super Combo finishes!	10	Bronze
Ultimate Ultra	Candy always says you gotta win with style, so go out there and perform 50 Ultra Combo finishes!	10	Bronze
Sunspotter	Amigo, perform 365 Super or Ultra Combo finishes against your opponents! The dawn is coming!	10	Bronze
Absolute Perfection	Lauren's waiting, so how about you finish your fights quickly and get 30 Perfects. Sound good?	20	Bronze
Clear Headed	Hey! Got time to kill? Try to clear Arcade Mode on Medium or higher! That's all you gotta do!	10	Bronze
All Clear	To get strong takes lots of fighting! Clear Arcade Mode on Medium or higher with all characters!	10	Bronze
Herculean Effort	Can you finish Arcade Mode on Medium or higher without using a continue? Show me you can!	10	Bronze
Hard Times	To escape death is to beat the strongest of the strong. Finish Arcade Mode on Hardest, kid!	20	Bronze
Long Time No See	Do you wish for defeat? If so, complete Arcade Mode on Hardest difficulty and beat Gouken!	50	Bronze
Rival Schooled	See your future by clearing every Rival Battle on Medium or higher with every character.	20	Bronze
Speed Freak	Finish each round in Arcade Mode on Medium or higher in 20 seconds or less. Too easy.	30	Silver
Good Start	All of nature must withstand a trial. You must clear 10 trials in Trial Mode to succeed.	10	Bronze
Trail of Trials	There is no shortcut in the art of Yoga. Aim to clear any character's Trial Mode trials!	20	Bronze
Trial Athlete	I shall assimilate all and be all-powerful! Clear all Trial Mode challenges, and so can you!	50	Gold
Oh! My Car!	Hee hee, destruction is so much fun! Score 80,000 points or more in the Car Crusher bonus stage!	10	Bronze
Barrel of Laughs	No need for barrels without oil! Score 110,000 points or more in the Barrel Buster bonus stage!	10	Bronze
It Begins	The fight starts here! Set your Title and Icon, and begin fighting on Xbox Live!	10	Bronze
First Timer	I'll never forget my first time for Ryu's sake! Win one Ranked Match! Gotta aim for the top!	10	Bronze
Threepeat	You think being this good is easy? Let's see you win 3 Ranked Matches in a row, champ!	20	Bronze

NAME	GOAL/REQUIREMENT	POINT VALUE	TROPHY VALUE
Fivepeat	This is your real power, child? Show me it's not luck by winning 5 Ranked Matches in a row!	30	Bronze
Tenpeat	Don't hold back your true potential! Win 10 Ranked Matches in a row!	50	Silver
Moving On Up	Ya need to do anything to reach the top of the food chain! Let's see a Rank Up via Ranked Match!	10	Bronze
Now You C Me...	I wrestle only the strong! You shall rank up to C Rank if you wanna face me, comrade!	20	Bronze
From C to Shining C	You think you're good, don't you? Prove it by ranking up all characters to C Rank!	50	Silver
Road to Victory	You wanna get that fight money? You're gonna have to win 10 Xbox LIVE matches first, sucka!	10	Bronze
Battle Master	Only winners can attain such beauty. Win 30 Xbox LIVE matches and I may share my beauty secrets!	20	Bronze
Legendary Fighter	I shall make you the right hand of Shadaloo if you can win 100 Xbox LIVE matches!	50	Silver
Worldly Warrior	Let's do this, amigo! Fight 50 Xbox LIVE matches, because that's the only way to become strong!	10	Bronze
Bring it on!	No comrade, this will not do! We must become stronger, for our fans! Fight 100 Xbox LIVE matches!	20	Silver
This is Madness!	Fighting is fun, huh? Well then, let's aim for 300 Xbox LIVE matches fought, OK buddy?	50	Gold
Team Player	A 1-on-1 fight is fun, but it's more fun with friends! Try fighting in a Team Battle!	10	Bronze
Team Mate	Win 1 Team Battle match, and you will learn that teamwork can help you become stronger!	10	Bronze
Teamworker	A pro can win with any team. Win 10 Team Battles but don't forget, you have to win too!	30	Bronze
Keep on Truckin'	If you want to focus on nothing but the fight, entering an Endless Battle is for you!	10	Bronze
Three For The Road	In the pursuit of strength, one must have a goal! In Endless Battle win 3 matches in a row.	20	Bronze
Endless Ten	Throw away your fears and focus on the fight! Win 10 fights in a row in Endless Battle!	50	Silver
Replayer	Watch 30 Replays via the Replay Channel! Isn't it fun watching people go at it tooth and nail!?	10	Bronze
Endless Lobbyist	It's only natural for warriors to seek fights! Create 30 Endless Battle lobbies!	10	Bronze
Team Lobbyist	Hey mon, battlin' is fun, no? Go out and create 30 Team Battle lobbies and enjoy the rhythm!	10	Bronze
Quarter Up	Fight 30 opponents via Arcade Fight Request. It'd be easy with the right bait, he he.	10	Bronze

SUPER STREET FIGHTER IV: 3D EDITION

NINTENDO 3DS

FIGURINES

Select Password from the Figurine Collection and enter the following:

FIGURINE	PASSWORD
Silver Akuma	RYSsPxSbTh
Silver Balrog	PqUswOobWG
Silver Chun-Li	tLWkWvrblz
Silver Cody	naMkEQgbQG
Silver Dan	rDRkkSlbqS
Silver Dhalsim	JKbsOVHbVC
Silver E. Honda	uUDsTImbUN
Silver Hakan	rLPbyLgbUy
Silver Ibuki	ilMsRBabpB
Silver Juri	OfQkARpbJR
Silver Ken	NyosHgybuW
Silver Makoto	GHakWCTbsl
Silver Rose	GKkkXXtbSe
Silver Sakura	uzTsXzlbKn
Golden Blanka	DmdkeRvbxc
Golden Chun-Li	zAAkcHVbHk
Golden Guile	qeJkznDbKE
Golden M.Bison	CglsQNWbHu
Golden Ryu	KjckTnSbwK
Golden Vega	CglsQNWbHu
Golden Zangief	hinsVnebTu
Platinum Ryu	DPrkMnybCd
Special Akuma	uQHkWgYbJC

SUPREME COMMANDER 2

XBOX 360

ACHIEVEMENTS

NAME	GOAL/REQUIREMENT	POINT VALUE
Start Here	Complete both parts of the tutorial	10
Easy Going	Complete all three campaigns on 'Easy' difficulty	25
A Winner is You	Complete all three campaigns 'Normal' difficulty	75
Supremest Commander	Complete all three campaigns on 'Hard' difficulty	100
Knows it All	Complete all primary and secondary campaign objectives	25
Completist	Complete all hidden campaign objectives	25
Score Hoarder	Get a complete campaign score over 150,000	50
Replayer	Improve your score on any operation	5
Cakewalk	Win a skirmish or online match against any AI opponent	5
Good Game	Win a skirmish or online match against all AI opponents	20
Luddite	Win a skirmish or online match without building any Experimentals	10
To the Victor...	Win 25 skirmish or online matches	25

NAME	GOAL/REQUIREMENT	POINT VALUE
Rushin' Front	Win a skirmish or online match in less than five minutes	10
Sampling	Win a skirmish or online match with each faction	10
Dating	Play 10 skirmish or online matches with one faction	15
Committed Relationship	Play 25 skirmish or online matches with one faction	25
Sightseer	Win a skirmish or online match on every multiplayer map	20
Sharp Shooter	Destroy 10,000 units	25
Masster	Extract 1,000,000 mass	25
Master Builder	Build 10,000 units	25
Time Cruncher	Play the game for over 24 hours in total	50
Internet Commander	Win an online match	10
Friends	Win a co-op match vs AI	10
Ranker	Win a Ranked Match	10
Supreme Online Commander	Win 25 Ranked Matches	50
Good Friends	Win 10 co-op matches vs AI	20

SECRET ACHIEVEMENTS

NAME	GOAL/REQUIREMENT	POINT VALUE
Communication Breakdown	Complete the 'Prime Target' operation	10
Second Target	Complete the 'Off Base' operation	10
Deep Freeze	Complete the 'Strike While Cold' operation	10
Fatboy Parade	Complete the 'Titans of Industry' operation	15
Nuclear Strike	Complete the 'Factions or Family Plan' operation	15
Rodgers is Relievedis	Complete the 'End of an Alliance' operation	25
Barge Ahead	Complete the 'Delta Force' operationthe	10
Alarming	Complete the 'Lethal Weapons' operation	10
Prison Break	Complete the 'Back on the Chain Gang' operation	15
Hole in the Ground	Complete the 'Steamed' operation	15
Gorged	Complete the 'Cliff Diving' operation	20
Reunited	Complete the 'Prime Time' operation	25
Downloading	Complete the 'Fact Finder' operation	10
Bugs in the Systemthe	Complete the 'The Trouble With Technology' operation	20
Animal Magnetism	Complete the 'The Great Leap Forward' operation	10
Class Reunion	Complete the 'Gatekeeper' operation	20
Well Stocked	Complete the 'Surface Tension' operation	15
Terra Firma	Complete the 'The Final Countdown' operation	25
Survivor	Don't lose any units during the first attack in 'Prime Target'	10
Bot Lord	Complete 'Prime Time' with an army made up entirely of Assault Bots	15
Survivalist	Survive multiple waves after the download completes in 'Fact Finder'	15

SURF'S UP

ALL CHAMPIONSHIP LOCATIONS

Select Cheat Codes from the Extras menu and enter FREEVISIT.

ALL LEAF SLIDE STAGES

Select Cheat Codes from the Extras menu and enter GOINGDOWN.

ALL MULTIPLAYER LEVELS

Select Cheat Codes from the Extras menu and enter MULTIPASS.

ALL BOARDS

Select Cheat Codes from the Extras menu and enter MYPRECIOUS.

ASTRAL BOARD

Select Cheat Codes from the Extras menu and enter ASTRAL.

MONSOON BOARD

Select Cheat Codes from the Extras menu and enter MONSOON.

TINE SHOCKWAVE BOARD

Select Cheat Codes from the Extras menu and enter TINYSHOCKWAVE.

ALL CHARACTER CUSTOMIZATIONS

Select Cheat Codes from the Extras menu and enter TOPFASHION.

PLAY AS ARNOLD

Select Cheat Codes from the Extras menu and enter TINYBUTSTRONG.

PLAY AS ELLIOT

Select Cheat Codes from the Extras menu and enter SURPRISEGUEST.

PLAY AS GEEK

Select Cheat Codes from the Extras menu and enter SLOWANDSTEADY.

PLAY AS TANK EVANS

Select Cheat Codes from the Extras menu and enter IMTHEBEST.

PLAY AS TATSUHI KOBAYASHI

Select Cheat Codes from the Extras menu and enter KOBAYASHI.

PLAY AS ZEKE TOPANGA

Select Cheat Codes from the Extras menu and enter THELEGEND.

ALL VIDEOS AND SPEN GALLERY

Select Cheat Codes from the Extras menu and enter WATCHAMOVIE.

ART GALLERY

Select Cheat Codes from the Extras menu and enter NICEPLACE.

SYSTEM SHOCK 2

CHEAT CODES

Hold shift and press ; in shoot mode then enter one of these codes in the password box.

EFFECT	CODE
Adds ## cybernetic upgrade modules	add_pool ##
Display Version number	show_version
Max out PSI points	psi_full
Maximum stats	ubermensch
Summon an item	summon_obj (object name: see below)

SUMMON_OBJ CODES

In the cheat code password box, input "summon_obj XX" and replace XX with the codes below to spawn the item at your feet.

EFFECT	CODE
10 Nanites	10 nanites
12 AP bullets	ap clip
12 Standard bullets	standard clip
20 Nanites	20 nanites
20 Prisms	small prism
5 Nanites	5 nanites
50 Nanites	big nanite pile
50 Prisms	large prism
A disgusting pile of worms	wormgoo
Annelid Med Patch	annelid_medpatch
Annelid PSI Patch	annelid_psipatch
Annoying Worm	grub
Anti-Annelid Toxin	anti_annelid toxin
Anti-Toxin Hypo	detox patch
Antimony (Sb)	chem #4
Arachnid Organ	arach. Organ
Arsenic (As)	chem #11
Assault Rifle	assault rifle
Assult	assult
Baby Arachnid	baby arachnid
Bag of Chips	chips
Barium (Ba)	chem #18
Basketball	basketball
Big Arachnid	arachnightmare
BrawnBoost Implant	brawnboost
Bridge Access Card	bridge card
Caesium (Cs)	chem #12
Californium (Cf)	chem #7
Can of Soda	soda can
Cargo Bay 1A/1B Access Card	cargo bay 1a/1b
Cargo Bay 2A/2B Access Card	cargo bay 2a/2b
Copper (Cu)	chem #6
Crew Bed	crew bed
Crew Quarters Access Card	crew card
Crewman	crewman
Crewwoman	crewwoman
Cryo Access Card	cryo card
Crystal Shard	crystal shard
Dead Power Cell	power cell
Deck 2 Access Card	crew 2 card
Delacroix	Delacroix
Electro Shock	electro shock
EMP Grenade	emp grenade
EMP Projectile	emp shot
EMP Rifle	emp rifle
EndurBoost Implant	endurboost
Engine Override Key	eng override key
Female Apparition	female appar.
Fermium (Fm)	chem #1
Floor Pod	floor pod
French-Epstein Device	French-epstein device

EFFECT	CODE
Fusion Cannon	fusion cannon
Fusion Projectile	fusion shot
Gallium (Ga)	chem #3
Greater Overlord	greater over.
Greater Overlord Organ	gr. over. Organ
Grenade Launcher	gren launcher
Grenadier Hybrid	og-grenade
Grub Floor Pod	grub floor pod
Grub Wall Pod	grub wall pod
Hassium (Hs)	chem #13
Hazard Suit	vacc suit
HE Clip	he clip
Heavy Armor	heavy armor
Highly Explosive Barrel	explode barrel
Hydroponics A Access	hydro card a
Hydroponics B Access	hydro card b
Hydroponics C Access	hydro card c
Hydroponics D Access	hydro card d
ICE Pick	ice pick
Incendiary Grenades	incend. Grenade
Incomplete Surgical Unit	med bed
Interpolated Simulation Chip	chip c
Invincible Swarm	swarm
Invisible Arachnid	Invisible arachnid
Iridium (Ir)	chem #10
LabAssistant Implant	labassistant
Large Beaker of Worms	large worm beaker
Laser Pistol	laser pistol
Laser Turret (enemy)	laser turret
Light Armor	light armor
Linear Simulation Chip	chip b
Maintenance	maintenance
Maintenance Tool	maintenance tool
Male Apparition	male appar.
Med Access Key	med card
Med Annex Access Key	med annex key
Med Hypo	med patch
Medical Kit	medical kit
Medium Armor	medium armor
Melee Hybrid	og-pipe
Midwife	midwife
Midwife Organ	midwife organ
Mn. Overlord Organ	mn. over. Organ
Molecular Analyzer	molec. Analyzer
Molybdenum (Mo)	chem #15
Monkey	red monkey
Monkey	blue monkey
Monkey Brain	monkey brain
Ninja Assassin	assassin
Og Organ	og organ
Operations Override Key	ops override key
Osmium (Os)	chem #9
Overlord	overlord
Pistol	pistol

EFFECT	CODE
Portable Battery	portable battery
Protocol Droid	protocol droid
Proximity Grenade	prox. Grenade
PSI Amp	psi amp
PSI Booster	psi booster
PSI Hypo	psi trainer
Quantum Simulation Chip	chip a
Radiation Hypo	rad patch
Radioactive Barrel	rad barrel
Radium (Ra)	chem #17
Recreation Access Ky	rec crew key
Recycler	recycler
Reflex Armor	reflec armor
Research and Development Access Key	r and d card
Rickenbacker Access Card	rickenbacker card
Rickenbacker Key	rick room key
Rickenbacker Special Edition Defence Turret	rick turret
Rocket Turret	turret rocket
Rocket Turret (enemy)	blast turret
Rumbler	rumbler
Rumbler Organ	rumbler organ
Runfast	runfast
Science Access Key	science card
Security	security
Security Access Card	security card
Security Camera	security camera
Security Station	security comp
Selenium (Se)	chem #19
Shotgun	shotgun
Shotgun Shells	rifled slug box
Shotgunner Hybrid	og-shotgun
Shuriken-Wielding Assassin	red assassin
Shuttle Access Key	shuttle access key
Slug Turret	pellet shot box
Slug Turret #2	slug turret
SmartBoost Implant	smartboost
Sodium (Na)	chem #8
Some Random Machinery	wide machinery
Speed Booster	speed boost
Stasis Field Generator	stasis field generator
Stats Trainer	stats trainer
Strength Booster	strength boost
Surgical Unit Activation Key	med bed key
Swarm Organ	swarm organ
Swarmer Floor Pod	swarmer floor pod
Swarmer Wall Pod	swarmer wall pod
SwiftBoost Implant	swiftboost
Tech Trainer	tech trainer
Technetium (Tc)	chem #16
Tellerium (Te)	chem #14
Timed Grenades	timed grenade
Toxic Grenades	toxin grenade
Traits Machine	trait machine
Tri-Optium Mug	mug

EFFECT	CODE
Vanadium (V)	chem #2
Version 1 Hacking Software	hack soft v1
Version 1 Modification Software	modify soft v1
Version 1 Repair Software	repair soft v1
Version 1 Research Software	research soft v1
Version 2 Hacking Software	hack soft v2
Version 2 Modification Software	modify soft v2
Version 2 Repair Software	repair soft v2
Version 2 Research Software	research soft v2
Version 3 Hacking Software	hack soft v3
Version 3 Modification Software	modify soft v3
Version 3 Repair Software	repair soft v3
Version 3 Research Software	research soft v3
Viral Proliferator	viral prolif
Wall Pod	wall pod
Weapon Trainer	weapon trainer
Worm Launcher	worm launcher
WormBlood Implant	wormblood
WormHeart Implant	wormheart
WormSkin Armor	wormskin
Wrench	wrench
Yttrium (Y)	chem #5

TEKKEN 6

XBOX 360/PS3

ACHIEVEMENTS & TROPHIES

NAME	GOAL/REQUIREMENT	POINT VALUE	TROPHY VALUE
Give Your Fists a Rest	Defeat an enemy using a weapon in Scenario Campaign Mode.	15	Bronze
Night at the Movies	Unlock a movie in Scenario Campaign Mode.	15	Bronze
Item Connoisseur	Obtain a Rank S Item in Scenario Campaign Mode.	30	Silver
Treasure Amateur	Collect 50 treasures in Scenario Campaign Mode.	10	Bronze
Treasure Enthusiast	Collect 100 treasures in Scenario Campaign Mode.	20	Bronze
Treasure Master	Collect 200 treasures in Scenario Campaign Mode.	30	Silver
Enemy Hunting Amateur	Defeat 300 enemies in Scenario Campaign Mode.	10	Bronze
Enemy Hunting Enthusiast	Defeat 1000 enemies in Scenario Campaign Mode.	20	Bronze
Enemy Hunting Master	Defeat 2000 enemies in Scenario Campaign Mode.	30	Silver
Playing With Fire	Defeat 100 enemies with the Flamethrower in Scenario Campaign Mode.	15	Bronze
Heavy Artillery	Defeat 100 enemies with the Gatling Gun in Scenario Campaign Mode.	15	Bronze
Ready for Action	Pick up 300 health recovery items in Scenario Campaign Mode.	15	Bronze

NAME	GOAL/REQUIREMENT	POINT VALUE	TROPHY VALUE
Brute Force	Defeat 100 enemies with the Lead Pipe in Scenario Campaign Mode.	15	Bronze
Thirsty Fighter	Pick up 50 drink items in Scenario Campaign Mode.	15	Bronze
Crate Breaker	Destroy 100 wooden crates in Scenario Campaign Mode.	15	Bronze
Alien Hunter	Defeat 10 aliens in Scenario Campaign Mode.	20	Bronze
Scenario Expert	Clear all of the stages in Scenario Campaign Mode.	30	Silver
King of the Hill	Knock 10 enemies in the water in Scenario Campaign Mode.	20	Bronze
A Friend in Need	Rescue your downed partner 3 times in Scenario Campaign Mode (single player).	15	Bronze
Combo Amateur	Perform a 10 chain combo in Scenario Campaign Mode.	10	Bronze
Combo Enthusiast	Perform a 30 chain combo in Scenario Campaign Mode.	20	Bronze
Combo Master	Perform a 50 chain combo in Scenario Campaign Mode.	30	Silver
Upgraded Assistant	Upgrade Alisa to the highest possible level.	15	Bronze
What's So Special About It?	Obtain the Special Flag in Scenario Campaign Mode.	20	Bronze
No Key For Me	Clear the Millennium Tower stage without the boot-up key in Scenario Campaign Mode.	45	Gold
Learning is Fun	Clear the tutorial stage in Scenario Campaign Mode.	15	Bronze
Moving On Up	Win a Ranked Match in Online Mode.	20	Bronze
No Pressure	Win a Player Match in Online Mode.	20	Bronze
Fighting Amateur	Play 3 matches in Online Mode.	10	Bronze
Fighting Enthusiast	Play 10 matches in Online Mode.	20	Bronze
Fighting Master	Play 30 matches in Online Mode.	30	Silver
Arcade Addict	Clear the Arcade Battle in Offline Mode.	15	Bronze
Team Toppler	Defeat 3 teams in Team Battle in Offline Mode.	15	Bronze
Survival of the Fittest	Earn 10 consecutive wins in Survival in Offline Mode.	15	Bronze
Practice Makes Perfect	Inflict a total of 1000 damage in Practice in Offline Mode.	15	Bronze
Gallery Completionist	Complete the Gallery.	45	Gold
Ghost Vanquisher	Defeat 30 Ghosts.	20	Bronze
Love That Money	Collect more than 5,000,000 G.	15	Bronze
Machine Crusher	Defeat NANCY-MI847J.	30	Silver

SECRET ACHIEVEMENTS & TROPHIES

NAME	GOAL/REQUIREMENT	POINT VALUE	TROPHY VALUE
Tekken Fanatic	Complete all other objectives.	10	Bronze
Friend or Foe?	Reunite with your ally in Scenario Campaign Mode.	15	Bronze
Locate the Target	Learn the whereabouts of Heihachi Mishima in Scenario Campaign Mode.	15	Bronze
It's All Coming Back to Me	Recover your memory in Scenario Campaign Mode.	15	Bronze

NAME	GOAL/REQUIREMENT	POINT VALUE	TROPHY VALUE
The Key to Victory	Obtain the boot-up key in Scenario Campaign Mode.	15	Bronze
That's No Hero	Defeat the Hero in Scenario Campaign Mode.	15	Bronze
The Destroyer Has Fallen	Defeat the Destroyer of Worlds in Scenario Campaign Mode.	15	Bronze
Showdown	Win the final battle in Scenario Campaign Mode.	30	Silver
What a Nightmare	Clear the Nightmare Train stage in Scenario Campaign Mode.	30	Silver
Wooden Warrior	Clear the Subterranean Pavilion stage in Scenario Campaign Mode.	30	Silver
Eastern Explorer	Clear the Kigan Island stage in Scenario Campaign Mode.	30	Silver

TEMPLE RUN

MOBILE

PURCHASABLE CHARACTERS

CHARACTER	COST
Scarlett Fox	10,000
Barry Bones	10,000
Karma Lee	25,000
Montana Smith	25,000
Francisco Montoya	25,000
Zack Wonder	25,000

PURCHASABLE WALLPAPERS

WALLPAPER	COST
Temple Wall	5,000
Guy Dangerous	5,000
Evil Demon Monkeys	5,000

OBJECTIVES

OBJECTIVE	DESCRIPTION
Novice Runner	Run 500 meters
Pocket Change	Collect 100 coins
Adventurer	Scored 25,000 points
Sprinter	Ran 1,000 meters
Miser Run	500m collecting no coins
Piggy Bank	Collect 250 coins
Treasure Hunter	Scored 50,000 points
Mega Bonus	Fill the bonus meter 4x
Athlete	Ran 2,500 meters
Lump Sum	Collected 500 coins

CHEATS, ACHIEVEMENTS, AND TROPHIES

T

OBJECTIVE	DESCRIPTION
Resurrection	Resurrected after dying
Basic Powers	All level 1 Powerups
High Roller	Scored 100,000 points
Payday	Collected 750 coins
Head Start	Used a Head Start
Steady Feet	Ran 2,500m without tripping
Allergic to Gold	1,000m collecting no coins
5k Runner	Ran 5,000 meters
No Trip Runner	Ran 5,000 meters without tripping
1/4 Million Club	Scored 250,000 points
Double Resurrection	Resurrected twice in one run
Money Bags	Collected 1,000 coins
1/2 Million Club	Scored 500,000 points
Super Powers	All level 5 powerups
Dynamic Duo	Unlocked two characters
Million Club	Scored 1,000,000 points
Money Bin	Collected 2,500 coins
Fantastic Four	Unlocked Four Characters
Sexy Six	Unlocked 6 characters
Interior Decorator	Unlocked 3 wallpapers
10k Runner	Run 10,000 meters
Fort Knox	Collect 5,000 coins
2.5 Million Club	Scored 2,500,000 points
5 Million Club	Scored 5,000,000 points
The Spartan	1 million without power ups
10 Million Club	Score 10,000,000 points

TENCHU: SHADOW ASSASSINS

NINTENDO WII

ALL NORMAL ITEMS

At the Title screen, hold C + Z and quickly press Up, Left, Down, Right, Up, Left, Down, Right, Right, 1, 2.

ALL SECRET ITEMS

At the Title screen, hold C + Z and quickly press Up, Right, Down, Left, Up, Right, Down, Left, Left, 1, 2.

MAX ITEMS

At the Title screen, hold C + Z and quickly press Down, Up, Down, Up, Right, Left, Right, Left, Left, 1.

ALL MISSIONS/ASSIGNMENTS

At the Title screen, hold C + Z and quickly press Left, Left, Left, Left, Right, Right, Right, Right, 1, 2.

FULL SWORD GAUGE

At the Title screen, hold C + Z and quickly press Up, Down, Up, Down, Left, Right, Left, Right, Right, 1, 2.

TERMINATOR: SALVATION

ACHIEVEMENTS & TROPHIES

NAME	GOAL/REQUIREMENT	POINT VALUE	TROPHY VALUE
L.A. 2016	Complete Chapter 1—L.A. 2016 on any difficulty	80	Gold
Thank Heaven	Complete Chapter 2—Thank Heaven on any difficulty	80	Gold
New Acquaintances	Complete Chapter 3—New Acquaintances on any difficulty	80	Gold
The Sights	Complete Chapter 4—The Sights on any difficulty	80	Gold
Underground	Complete Chapter 5—Underground on any difficulty	80	Gold
Into the Wild	Complete Chapter 6—Into the Wild on any difficulty	80	Gold
Angie	Complete Chapter 7—Angie on any difficulty	80	Gold
Every life is sacred	Complete Chapter 8—Every life is sacred on any difficulty	80	Gold
For the Resistance	Complete Chapter 9—For the Resistance on any difficulty	80	Gold
Seasoned Commander	Complete the Game—Become a commander on Medium difficulty	100	Gold
Veteran Commander	Complete the Game—Become a commander on Hard difficulty	180	Gold

TEST DRIVE UNLIMITED 2

ACHIEVEMENTS & TROPHIES

NAME	GOAL/REQUIREMENT	POINT VALUE	TROPHY VALUE
Small Collection	Own 3 different cars	5	Bronze
One of each	Own a car from each category (A7-A6-A5-A4-A3-A2-A1, C4-C3, B4-B3)	30	Bronze
God of Cars	Own all purchasable cars	50	Gold
Mummy	Complete 20 multiplayer challenges with bandages	10	Bronze
My Beautiful Caravan	Own 1 house (caravan)	5	Bronze
Subprime crisis?	Own one house from each level	30	Silver
Fashion Victim	Change your clothes or hairstyle 40 times	10	Bronze
Hard earned money	Bank the maximum level of F.R.I.M. (10)	10	Bronze
Kangaroo	Make a 100 m (109 yd) jump (any game mode)	20	Bronze
Cruising	Drive 200 km (124 miles)	5	Bronze
Easy Money	Earn $100,000 with F.R.I.M.	10	Bronze
Car-tist	Decorate 5 different cars	15	Bronze
Big Spender	Spend 1 million dollars	50	Bronze
Reckless Driver	Drive around and hit 100 AI controlled cars and destructible objects	10	Bronze
The Beginner	Win a championship	5	Bronze
King of Ibiza	Win Ibiza Cup, area 1	25	Bronze

NAME	GOAL/REQUIREMENT	POINT VALUE	TROPHY VALUE
Coronation	Win all championships & cups	75	Gold
Racing School Master	Obtain all licenses	20	Bronze
Level 60	Reach level 60	100	Gold
Aloha!	Make it to Hawaii	20	Bronze
Learning	Obtain The C4 license	5	Bronze
Fast and Luxurious	Drive at 400 km/h (249 mph) for 5 sec. (any game mode)	10	Bronze
Say "Cheese!"	Get clocked by the radar 100 times (Speedtrap game mode)	10	Bronze
Tuning Addict	Tune a car to the max level	5	Bronze
Cockpit Addict	Drive 500 km (311 miles) using the cockpit view (any game mode)	20	Bronze
Get rich or try driving	Possess 1 million dollars	25	Bronze
Multi-Challenger	Win 5 challenges in each multiplayer mode (Race, Speed, Speedtrap)	25	Bronze
Instant challenge, easy cash!	Earn $10,000 in Instant Challenges	20	Bronze
Road Eater	Drive 1000 km (621 miles)	10	Bronze
Fugitive Wanted	Outrun the police 30 times in Online Chase Mode	10	Silver
My Club and Me	Drive 150 km (93 miles) in intra-Club challenges	15	Bronze
Club Basher	Win 30 Club vs. Club challenges	25	Silver
Marshall	Arrest 30 outlaws in Online Chase Mode	10	Bronze
Reporter	Find all viewpoints (photographer)	30	Silver
Hey! What's this car?!	Own 1 bonus car (treasure hunt)	5	Bronze
Tyrannosaurus wrecks	Own all 6 bonus cars (treasure hunt)	25	Silver
Ibiza Photographer	Find 5 viewpoints on Ibiza (photographer)	10	Bronze
The Explorer	Drive 5000 km (3107 miles)	50	Silver
Helping hand	Succeed in 10 missions	15	Bronze
Events Accomplished	Achieve all missions	40	Silver
Keep your distance	Drive for 15 sec. above 100 km/h (62 mph) with 8 players in "Keep Your Distance" mode	30	Bronze
Exclusive Car	Drive a Club car	10	Bronze
Exclusive CarS	Drive all Club cars	30	Silver
Co-op Challenger	Drive 150 km (93 miles) in "Keep Your Distance" and "Follow the Leader" modes	15	Bronze
Me against all of you	Play 40 challenges in the Community Racing Center	25	Bronze
Social Butterfly	Join and invite friends 100 times (any game mode)	10	Bronze
Better than a GPS	Invite 10 players to drive with you in your car.	10	Bronze

DOWNLOADABLE CONTENT: CASINO ONLINE

NAME	GOAL/REQUIREMENT	POINT VALUE	TROPHY VALUE
Risk Taker	Casino: Give up a Three of a Kind while playing Video Poker and win the next hand	10	Bronze
Island Caretaker	Casino: Wake up the Island caretaker	10	Bronze

NAME	GOAL/REQUIREMENT	POINT VALUE	TROPHY VALUE
Drinks	Casino: Have 10 cocktails at once at a poker table	10	Bronze
Casino Fashion Victim	Casino: Buy all clothes available in the Casino Clothes Shop	25	Silver
Socializing	Casino: Unlock all cocktails and emotes	25	Silver
V.I.P.	Casino: Become VIP of the Casino by reaching level 5	35	Silver
Ready to play TDU2?	Casino: Win the luxury car displayed in the entrance hall	20	Bronze
Western	Casino: Play the "duel" emote at the same time as your rival at a poker table for two	15	Bronze
Wanted	Casino: Get the right look to get the reward	25	Bronze
1-in-38 Chance	Casino: Win a straight-up bet at Roulette	20	Bronze

TERRARIA

XBOX 360/PS3

ACHIEVEMENTS & TROPHIES

NAME	GOAL/REQUIREMENT	POINT VALUE	TROPHY VALUE
Home Sweet Home	The Guide has moved in!	20	Bronze
All in the Family	Every NPC has moved in!	10	Bronze
Rock Bottom	You have reached the bottom of the World!	10	Bronze
Exterminator	You have defeated every boss!	25	Silver
Slimer	You have killed every type of slime!	10	Silver
Challenge Accepted	You have unlocked Hard Mode!	10	Gold
Maxed Out	You have the maximum health and mana!	15	Silver
Corruptible	Your World is Corrupt!	10	Silver
Hallowed Be Thy Name	Your World is Hallowed!	10	Silver
Ophthalmologist	You have defeated The Twins!	15	Silver
Bona Fide	You have defeated Skeletron Prime!	15	Silver
Ride the Worm	You have defeated The Destroyer!	15	Silver
Marathon Runner	You have traveled over 42km on the ground!	20	Bronze
Landscaper	You have removed more than 10,000 blocks!	15	Bronze
Crowd Control	You have defeated the Goblin Army!	15	Bronze
Survivor	You have survived the first night!	10	Bronze
Icarus	You can only go down from here!	10	Bronze
Vanity of Vanities	Looking good!	10	Bronze
Pet Hoarder	You seem to like pets.	10	Silver
Terraria Expert	You have completed the tutorial!	5	Bronze
Terraria Student	You have begun the tutorial!	5	Bronze
Be Prepared	You are ready for battle!	15	Bronze
Airtime!	Enjoy the view.	10	Bronze
Blacksmith	You are a master smith!	15	Silver

NAME	GOAL/REQUIREMENT	POINT VALUE	TROPHY VALUE
I'm Smelting!	You have smelted 10,000 bars of metal!	20	Silver
A Knight in Shining Armors	You have obtained every type of armor.	15	Silver
Engineer	You have placed 100 wires!	10	Bronze
Red Moon Rises	You have survived the Blood Moon!	10	Bronze
Crafty	You have used every crafting station!	20	Silver
To Hell and Back	You have gone to The Underworld and back without dying!	20	Silver
Completionist!	All the trophies have been earned.	—	Platinum

TEXAS HOLD 'EM

CHEAT MENU

Select New Player from the Options menu and enter YOUCHEAT as the player name. Hold down the center button until you get confirmation. This gives you a cheat menu with the following five options: Unlock All Tournaments, Start with $100,000, Show Tells and/or Down Cards, and Adjust AI Folding frequency.

APPLE CONFERENCE ROOM TOURNAMENT

Select New Player from the Options menu and enter THREEAMI as the player name. Hold down the center button until you get confirmation.

DOG TOURNAMENT

Select New Player form the Options menu and enter PLAYDOGS as the player name. Hold down the center button until you get confirmation.

FUTURISTIC TOURNAMENT

Select New Player form the Options menu and enter SPACEACE as the player name. Hold down the center button until you get confirmation.

ITUNES BAR TOURNAMENT

Select New Player form the Options menu and enter BARTUNES as the player name. Hold down the center button until you get confirmation.

STONEHENGE TOURNAMENT

Select New Player form the Options menu and enter BIGROCKS as the player name. Hold down the center button until you get confirmation.

SEE SECRET CHARACTERS

Select New Player form the Options menu and enter ALLCHARS as the player name. Hold down the center button until you get confirmation.

THRILLVILLE: OFF THE RAILS

$50,000

During a game, press ●, ●, ●, ●, ●, ●, ⊗. Repeat this code as much as desired.

ALL PARKS

During a game, press ●, ●, ●, ●, ●, ●, ●.

ALL RIDES

During a game, press ●, ●, ●, ● ●, ●, ●. Some rides still need to be researched.

COMPLETE MISSIONS

During a game, press ●, ●, ●, ●, ●, ●, ●. Then, at the Missions menu, highlight a mission and press ● to complete that mission. Some missions have Bronze, Silver, and Gold objectives. For these missions the first press of ● earns the Bronze, the second earns the Silver, and the third earns the Gold.

TIGER WOODS PGA TOUR 12: THE MASTERS

ALL BALLS AVAILABLE AT SHOP

Select Passwords from the Options and enter tour proving.

ALL CLUBS AVAILABLE AT SHOP

Select Passwords from the Options and enter clubsoda.

ADIDAS EQUIPMENT

Select Passwords from the Options and enter ClimaCool.

FOOTJOY EQUIPMENT

Select Passwords from the Options and enter Dry Joys.

ALL PING CLUBS

Select Passwords from the Options and enter rapture.

TIGER WOODS APPAREL

Select Passwords from the Options and enter gearoftheTiger.

JEWELRY

Select Passwords from the Options and enter Platinum.

TIGER WOODS PGA TOUR 12: THE MASTERS

50,000 XP

If you have a save game from Tiger Woods PGA Tour 2011, you receive 50,000 XP.

TIGER WOODS PGA TOUR 13

ACHIEVEMENTS & TROPHIES

NAME	GOAL/REQUIREMENT	POINT VALUE	TROPHY VALUE
Going Green with a Hybrid	Land on the green from over 175 yards away using a Hybrid	30	Bronze
Live from your couch	Play in a Live Tournament	25	Bronze
Tigers have FIR	Complete an 18 hole round with a 100 percent FIR. FIR = Fairway in Regulation	30	Bronze
That was GIRrrreat!	Complete an 18 hole round with a 100 percent GIR. GIR = Green in Regulation	15	Bronze

NAME	GOAL/REQUIREMENT	POINT VALUE	TROPHY VALUE
No Handouts Please	Actually get a hole in 1 in the 1982 First Hole in One event in Tiger Legacy Challenge	10	Bronze
Shouting at Amen Corner	Complete Amen Corner (Augusta 11,12,13) with a birdie or better on each in a single round.	10	Silver
It's a Start	Master 1 Course	15	Bronze
Now we're talking	Master 8 Courses	30	Bronze
Like a Boss	Master 16 Courses	60	Gold
So Much Easier than Putting	Make a hole in one	30	Silver
From the Ladies Tees	Complete an 18 hole round using the Red Tees	15	Bronze
When do we get paid?	Compete in an amateur championship	15	Bronze
Never leave home without it	Earn PGA TOUR card	15	Bronze
Top 50 Countdown	Break the top 50 in EA SPORTS Golf Rankings	15	Bronze
Top 10 Hits	Break the top 10 in EA SPORTS Golf Rankings	30	Bronze
King of the Hill	Become #1 in the EA SPORTS Golf Rankings	50	Bronze
Don't quit your day job	Win the Masters as an amateur	15	Bronze
It's all in the Hips	Sink a 40ft putt	15	Bronze
Like a Homing Pigeon	From the Fairway, land within 1 yard of the flagstick from 150 yards out	15	Bronze
I Own this Place	Defend your title in any Major	25	Silver
Small Tiger, Big Bite	Complete an 18 hole online head-to-head match with toddler Tiger	15	Bronze
Play Date	Play a Four Player online match with all players using toddlers	15	Bronze
Can you give me a Boost?	Play an 18 hole round with Boost Pins equipped	15	Bronze
Toddler Years	Complete Toddler Years in Tiger Legacy Challenge	15	Bronze
Early Years	Complete the Early Years in Tiger Legacy Challenge	15	Bronze
Junior Years	Complete the Junior Years in Tiger Legacy Challenge	15	Bronze
Amateur Years	Complete the Amateur Years in Tiger Legacy Challenge	15	Bronze
Rookie Years	Complete the Rookie Years in Tiger Legacy Challenge	15	Bronze
Tiger Slam	Complete the Tiger Slam in Tiger Legacy Challenge	20	Bronze
Pro Years	Complete the Pro Years in Tiger Legacy Challenge	20	Bronze
Present Day	Complete the Present Day in Tiger Legacy Challenge	30	Silver
The Future	Complete the Future in Tiger Legacy Challenge	30	Bronze
Dig Deep	Land within 1 yard of the flagstick from a bunker	15	Silver
He's going the distance	Hit a drive over 400 yards	30	Gold
Like a Metronome	Complete 10 perfect Tempo Swings with TOUR Pro Difficulty or better	15	Bronze
Check out my Custom Settings	Complete an 18 hole round using a Custom Difficulty	15	Bronze

NAME	GOAL/REQUIREMENT	POINT VALUE	TROPHY VALUE
I Finally Belong!	Create or Join a Country Club in Game	15	Bronze
Members Only	Play in a Country Club Tournament	15	Bronze
I Need a Commitment	Earn a Four Day loyalty Bonus	15	Bronze
Internal Conflict	Compete with a teammate in a head-to-head match launched from the Clubhouse lobby	15	Silver
Putt from the rough	Make a putt from the rough	15	Bronze
One Small Step for Mankind	Win the Green Jacket in Career Mode	35	Bronze
Unstoppable!	Win the Green Jacket for a Record 7 times in Career Mode	75	Bronze

SECRET ACHIEVEMENTS & TROPHIES

NAME	GOAL/REQUIREMENT	POINT VALUE	TROPHY VALUE
Swing and a miss	Whiff the ball	10	Bronze
Child's Play	Complete an 18 hole round with toddler Ricky	15	Silver
That was Easy	Beat the course record of 63 at the Masters (In Career Mode)	30	Gold

TIMESHIFT

PLAYSTATION 3

KRONE IN MULTIPLAYER

Select Multiplayer from the Options menu. Highlight Model and press ● to get to Krone. Press Y and enter RXYMCPENCJ.

TOM CLANCY'S SPLINTER CELL CHAOS THEORY HD

PLAYSTATION 3

TEAM PICTURE

At the main menu, press R2, ●, ●, ●, ●, ●, ●.

ALL LEVELS

Select your profile to play offline. Then, at the main menu, hold L1 + L2 + R1 + R2 and press ● (x5), ● (x5).

TOM CLANCY'S SPLINTER CELL PANDORA TOMORROW HD

PLAYSTATION 3

LEVEL SELECT

After defeating the game on hard, hold L1 + L2 at the game select and press ●, ●, ●, ●, Left, Right, Down, Down.

TOM CLANCY'S SPLINTER CELL: CONVICTION

ACHIEVEMENTS

NAME	GOAL/REQUIREMENT	POINT VALUE
Realistic Difficulty	Complete single player story on "Realistic" difficulty	50
Co-op Realistic Difficulty	Complete the co-op story on "Realistic" difficulty	50
Quality Time	Invite a friend to join and participate in a co-op story or game mode session	20
Hunter	Complete any 1 map in "Hunter" game mode in co-op	10
Last Stand	Complete any 1 map in "Last Stand" game mode in co-op	10
Hunter Completionist	Complete all maps in "Hunter" game mode on rookie or normal difficulty	20
Hunter Master	Complete all maps in "Hunter" game mode on realistic difficulty	50
Last Stand Completionist	Complete all maps in "Last Stand" game mode on rookie or normal difficulty	20
Last Stand Master	Complete all maps in "Last Stand" game mode on realistic difficulty	50
Face-Off Completionist	Complete all maps in "Face-Off" game mode using any connection type	20
Face Off	Win one match in "Face-Off" game mode on any difficulty	10
Preparation Master	Complete all prepare & execute challenges	30
Stealth Master	Complete all vanish challenges	30
Best Of The Best	Complete all Splinter Cell challenges	30
Well-Rounded	Complete all challenges	50
Weapon Upgraded	Purchase all 3 upgrades for any 1 weapon	10
Gadget Upgraded	Purchase all 3 upgrades for any 1 gadget	10
Weapons Expert	Purchase all 3 upgrades for all weapons	20
Gadgets Expert	Purchase both upgrades for all gadgets	20
Weapons Collector	Unlock all weapons in the weapon vault	20
Variety	Purchase any 1 uniform	10
Accessorizing	Purchase any 1 accessory for any 1 uniform	10
Ready For Anything	Purchase all 9 accessories for all uniforms	20
Fashionable	Purchase all 6 texture variants for all uniforms	20
Perfect Hunter	Complete any map in Hunter without ever having been detected on realistic difficulty	20
Last Man Standing	In Last Stand, survive all enemy waves of any map in one session without failing on any difficulty	50
Revelations	Discover Anna Grimsdottir's dark secret	10

SECRET ACHIEVEMENTS

NAME	GOAL/REQUIREMENT	POINT VALUE
Merchant's Street Market	Complete Single Player Story "Merchant's Street Market" on any difficulty	20
Kobin's Mansion	Complete Single Player Story "Kobin's Mansion" on any difficulty	20
Price Airfield	Complete Single Player Story "Price Airfield" on any difficulty	20
Diwaniya, Iraq	Complete Single Player Story "Diwaniya, Iraq" on any difficulty	20
Washington Monument	Complete Single Player Story "Washington Monument" on any difficulty	20

NAME	GOAL/REQUIREMENT	POINT VALUE
White Box Laboratories	Complete Single Player Story "White Box Laboratories" on any difficulty	20
Lincoln Memorial	Complete Single Player Story "Lincoln Memorial" on any difficulty	20
Third Echelon HQ	Complete Single Player Story "Third Echelon HQ" on any difficulty	20
Michigan Ave. Reservoir	Complete Single Player Story "Michigan Ave. Reservoir" on any difficulty	20
Downtown District	Complete Single Player Story "Downtown District" on any difficulty	20
White House	Complete Single Player Story "White House" on any difficulty	20
St. Petersburg Banya	Complete CO-OP Story "St. Petersburg Banya" on any difficulty	20
Russian Embassy	Complete CO-OP Story "Russian Embassy" on any difficulty	20
Yastreb Complex	Complete CO-OP Story "Yastreb Complex" on any difficulty	20
Modzok Proving Grounds	Complete CO-OP Story "Modzok Proving Grounds" on any difficulty	20
Judge, Jury and Executioner	Take down Tom Reed	10
Man of Conviction	Allow Tom Reed to live	10
Survivor	Battle your CO-OP teammate and survive	10

TOMB RAIDER

XBOX 360/PS3

ACHIEVEMENTS & TROPHIES

NAME	GOAL/REQUIREMENT	POINT VALUE	TROPHY VALUE
Bookworm	25% of all documents found.	10	Bronze
Historian	75% of all documents found.	15	Bronze
Relic Hunter	25% of all relics collected.	10	Bronze
Archaeologist	75% of all relics collected.	15	Bronze
Looking for Trouble	25% of all GPS caches found.	10	Bronze
Bag Full O' Cache	75% of all GPS caches found.	15	Bronze
No Stone Left Unturned	All documents, relics, and GPS caches found.	50	Gold
Picky	200 enemies looted.	15	Bronze
Clever Girl	Purchased all skills in one category.	25	Silver
Lethal	Purchased all skills in all categories.	50	Silver
Now We're Getting Serious	One weapon fully modded and completely upgraded.	25	Bronze
The Professional	All weapons fully modded and completely upgraded.	50	Silver
Big Game Hunter	10 large animals killed and looted.	15	Bronze
Tastes Like Chicken!	10 small animals killed and looted.	15	Bronze
Sharp Shooter	50 headshot kills performed in the single player campaign.	15	Bronze
Predator	50 enemies killed with the bow.	10	Bronze
Equalizer	75 enemies killed with the rifle.	10	Bronze
Widowmaker	40 enemies killed with the shotgun.	10	Bronze
Gunslinger	35 enemies killed with the pistol.	10	Bronze

NAME	GOAL/REQUIREMENT	POINT VALUE	TROPHY VALUE
Epic Fumble	Forced an enemy to drop dynamite that killed two people.	15	Bronze
Get Over Here!	5 enemies rope pulled off edges.	20	Bronze
Opportunist	25 unaware enemies killed.	15	Bronze
Down and Dirty	15 finishers performed.	15	Bronze
Deadeye	10 enemies shot off zip lines.	20	Bronze
Former Adventurer	25 enemies incapacitated with the dodge counter.	20	Bronze
One Smart Cookie	One optional tomb completed.	20	Bronze
Intellectually Superior	All optional tombs completed.	50	Gold
Unfinished Business	One challenge completed.	20	Bronze
Inconceivable!	All challenges complete.	50	Silver
A Survivor Is Born	Game completed.	75	Silver
Adventurer	Played a match to completion in all multiplayer modes.	20	Bronze
Artilleryman	20 enemy players killed with a turret in multiplayer.	20	Bronze
Down Boy!	Zip-lining enemy killed in multiplayer.	10	Bronze
Entrapment	Trapped an enemy in multiplayer.	10	Bronze
Escapist	Survived 10 explosions in multiplayer.	20	Bronze
Good Samaritan	Revived a teammate in a multiplayer match.	10	Bronze
I'm all that!	Won a ranked match in every multiplayer mode.	25	Silver
Sole Survivor	Sole survivor on your multiplayer team.	15	Bronze
Lights Out	10 multiplayer enemies killed with the melee attack.	15	Bronze
Master Blaster	Two multiplayer enemies killed with one explosive.	20	Bronze
Monkey Around	Survived 3 times in multiplayer by using the rope ascender.	15	Bronze
Narcissistic	New character purchased.	10	Bronze
On My Way Up	Multiplayer level 10 attained.	10	Bronze
Shopaholic	Purchased all upgrades and characters in multiplayer.	20	Bronze
True Commitment	Multiplayer level 60 attained.	30	Silver
True Survivor	Unlock every Tomb Raider trophy.	—	Platinum

SECRET ACHIEVEMENTS & TROPHIES

NAME	GOAL/REQUIREMENT	POINT VALUE	TROPHY VALUE
Boom Goes the Dynamite	Bundle of dynamite shot out of the air.	10	Bronze
Crab Cages	FeeFee the crab killed.	5	Bronze
Chatterbox	All conversations with the Endurance crew completed.	5	Bronze

TOMB RAIDER: LEGEND

PSP

You must unlock the following cheats before you can use them.

BULLETPROOF
During a game, hold L and press ⊗, R, ●, R, ●, R.

DRAW ENEMY HEALTH
During a game, hold L and press ●, ●, ⊗, R, R, ●.

INFINITE ASSUALT RIFLE AMMO
During a game, hold L and press ⊗, ●, ⊗, R, ●, ●.

INFINITE GRENADE LAUNCHER
During a game, hold L and press R, ●, R, ●, R, ●.

INFINITE SHOTGUN AMMO
During a game, hold L and press R, ●, ●, R, ●, ⊗.

INFINITE SMG AMMO
During a game, hold L and press ●, ●, R, R, ⊗, ●.

1-SHOT KILL
During a game, hold L and press ●, ⊗, ●, ●, R, ●.

TEXTURELESS MODE
Hold L and press R, ⊗, ●, ⊗, ●, R.

WIELD EXCALIBUR
During a game, hold L and press ●, ⊗, ●, R, ●, R.

XBOX 360

You must unlock the following codes in the game before using them.

BULLETPROOF
During a game, hold Left Trigger and press A, Right Trigger, Y, Right Trigger, X, Left Bumper.

DRAIN ENEMY HEALTH
During a game, hold Left Trigger and press X, B, A, Left Bumper, Right Trigger, Y.

INFINITE ASSAULT RIFLE AMMO
During a game, hold Left Bumper and press A, B, A, Left Trigger, X, Y.

INFINITE GRENADE LAUNCHER AMMO
During a game, hold Left Bumper and press Left Trigger, Y, Right Trigger, B, Left Trigger, X.

INFINITE SHOTGUN AMMO
During a game, hold Left Bumper and press Right Trigger, B, X, Left Trigger, X, A.

INFINITE SMG AMMO
During a game, hold Left Bumper and press B, Y, Left Trigger, Right Trigger, A, B.

EXCALIBUR
During a game, hold Left Bumper and press Y, A, B, Right Trigger, Y, Left Trigger.

SOUL REAVER
During a game, hold Left Bumper and press A, Right Trigger, B, Right Trigger, Left Trigger, X.

1-SHOT KILL
During a game, hold Left Trigger and press Y, A, Y, X, Left Bumper, B.

TEXTURELESS MODE
During a game, hold Left Trigger and press Left Bumper, A, B, A, Y, Right Trigger.

THE TOMB RAIDER TRILOGY

TOMB RAIDER: LEGEND

The following codes must be unlocked in the game before using them.

BULLETPROOF

During a game, hold L1 and press ✗, R1, ●, R1, ●, L2.

DRAIN ENEMY HEALTH

During a game, hold L1 and press ●, ●, ✗, L2, R1, ●.

INFINITE ASSAULT RIFLE AMMO

During a game, hold L2 and press ✗, ●, ✗, L1, ●, ●.

INFINITE GRENADE LAUNCHER AMMO

During a game, hold L2 and press L1, ●, R1, ●, L1, ●.

INFINITE SHOTGUN AMMO

During a game, hold L2 and press R1, ●, ●, L1, ●, ✗.

INFINITE SMG AMMO

During a game, hold L2 and press ●, ●, L1, R1, ✗, ●.

EXCALIBUR

During a game, hold L2 and press ●, ✗, ●, R1, ●, L1.

SOUL REAVER

During a game, hold L2. Then press: ✗, R1, ●, R1, L1, ●.

ONE SHOT KILL

During a game, hold L1 and press ●, ✗, ●, ●, L2, ●.

TEXTURELESS MODE

During a game, hold L1 and press L2, ✗, ●, ✗, ●, R1.

TOMB RAIDER: UNDERWORLD

INVINCIBLE

During a game, hold L2 and press ✗, R2, ●, R2, ●, L1.

ONE SHOT KILLS

During a game, hold L2 and press hold R2 and press ●, ✗, ●, ●, L1, ●.

SHOW ENEMY HEALTH

During a game, hold L2 and press ●, ●, ✗, L1, R2, ●.

TONY HAWK'S PROVING GROUND

Select Cheat Codes from the Options and enter the following cheats. Some codes need to be enabled by selecting Cheats from the Options during a game.

UNLOCK	CHEAT
Bosco	MOREMILK
Cam	NOTACAMERA
Cooper	THECOOP
Eddie X	SKETCHY
El Patinador	PILEDRIVER
Eric	FLYAWAY
Judy Nails	LOVEROCKNROLL
Mad Dog	RABBIES
MCA	INTERGALACTIC
Mel	NOTADUDE
Rube	LOOKSSMELLY
Spence	DAPPER

UNLOCK	CHEAT
Shayne	MOVERS
TV Producer	SHAKER
FDR	THEPREZPARK
Lansdowne	THELOCALPARK
Air & Space Museum	THEINDOORPARK
All Fun Items	OVERTHETOP
All Game Movies	WATCHTHIS
All Rigger Pieces	IMGONNABUILD
All specials unlocked and in player's special list	LOTSOFTRICKS
Full Stats	BEEFEDUP
Give player +50 skill points	NEEDSHELP

XBOX 360/PS3

Select Cheat Codes from the Options and enter the following cheats. Some codes need to be enabled by selecting Cheats from the Options during a game.

UNLOCK	CHEAT
Unlocks Boneman	CRAZYBONEMAN
Unlocks Bosco	MOREMILK
Unlocks Cam	NOTACAMERA
Unlocks Cooper	THECOOP
Unlocks Eddie X	SKETCHY
Unlocks El Patinador	PILEDRIVER
Unlocks Eric	FLYAWAY
Unlocks Mad Dog	RABBIES
Unlocks MCA	INTERGALACTIC
Unlocks Mel	NOTADUDE
Unlocks Rube	LOOKSSMELLY
Unlocks Spence	DAPPER
Unlocks Shayne	MOVERS
Unlocks TV Producer	SHAKER
Unlock FDR	THEPREZPARK
Unlock Lansdowne	THELOCALPARK
Unlock Air & Space Museum	THEINDOORPARK
Unlocks all Fun Items	OVERTHETOP
Unlocks all CAS items	GIVEMESTUFF
Unlocks all Decks	LETSGOSKATE
Unlock all Game Movies	WATCHTHIS
Unlock all Lounge Bling Items	SWEETSTUFF
Unlock all Lounge Themes	LAIDBACKLOUNGE
Unlock all Rigger Pieces	IMGONNABUILD
Unlock all Video Editor Effects	TRIPPY
Unlock all Video Editor Overlays	PUTEMONTOP
All specials unlocked and in player's special list	LOTSOFTRICKS
Full Stats	BEEFEDUP
Give player +50 skill points	NEEDSHELP

The following cheats lock you out of the Leaderboards:

UNLOCK	CHEAT
Unlocks Perfect Manual	STILLAINTFALLIN
Unlocks Perfect Rail	AINTFALLIN
Unlock Super Check	BOOYAH
Unlocks Unlimited Focus	MYOPIC
Unlock Unlimited Slash Grind	SUPERSLASHIN
Unlocks 100% branch completion in NTT	FOREVERNAILED
No Bails	ANDAINTFALLIN

You can not use the Video Editor with the following cheats:

UNLOCK	CHEAT
Invisible Man	THEMISSING
Mini Skater	TINYTATER
No Board	MAGICMAN

CHEATS, ACHIEVEMENTS, AND TROPHIES

T

The following cheats lock you out of the Leaderboards:

UNLOCK	CHEAT
Perfect Manual	STILLAINTFALLIN
Perfect Rail	AINTFALLIN
Unlimited Focus	MYOPIC

You can not use the Video Editor with the following cheats:

UNLOCK	CHEAT
Invisible Man	THEMISSING
Mini Skater	TINYTATER

TONY HAWK RIDE

NINTENDO WII

RYAN SHECKLER

Select Cheats from the Options menu and enter SHECKLERSIG.

QUICKSILVER 80S LEVEL

Select Cheats from the Options menu and enter FEELINGEIGHTIES.

TOP TRUMPS: DOCTOR WHO

NINTENDO WII

DATA CORE CARDS

Eight cards for the Data Core are unlocked by reaching 25,000 points in the different mini-games.

UNLOCKABLE	REQUIREMENT
Auton	Reach 25,000 points in Hi/Lo.
Brannigan	Reach 25,000 points in Cyber Sequence.
Judoon Captain	Reach 25,000 points in Cyber Sequence.
Novice Hame	Reach 25,000 points in Interrogation.
Ood	Reach 25,000 points in Memory Matrix.
Sisters of Plenitude	Reach 25,000 points in Interrogation.
Sycorax	Reach 25,000 points in Memory Matrix.
Tallulah	Reach 25,000 points in Hi/Lo.

TORCHLIGHT

XBOX 360

AVATAR AWARDS

AWARD	EARNED BY
Torchlight Logo Tee	Defeat the Overseer.
Robot Knit Cap	Defeat the game.

DESTROYER GAMERPIC

Earn the Tree Hugger Achievement.

TOY SOLDIERS: COLD WAR

COMMANDO GAMER PICTURE

Buy the game.

RUSSIAN GAMER PICTURE

Complete the game.

AVATAR AWARDS

AVATAR	EARNED BY
Flight Jacket	Complete the first section of Basic Training.
Mullet	Survive until Wave 9 in Basic Training.
Toy Soldiers T-Shirt	Play a survival match to Round 5.

TOY STORY 2: BUZZ LIGHTYEAR TO THE RESCUE!

LEVEL SELECT

At the Options menu, press Right, Left, ●, ●, ●.

ALL LEVELS

At the title screen, press Up (x4), Down, Down, Up, Up, Down (x3).

DEBUG MODE

At the title screen, press ✖, ●, ●.

TOY STORY 3

For the following Toy Story 3 codes, you must activate the cheat from the Pause menu after entering it.

BUZZ USES LASER (ALL STORY LEVELS)

Select Cheat Codes from the Bonus menu and enter BLASER.

WOODY'S BANDIT OUTFIT

Select Cheat Codes from the Bonus menu and enter BANDIT.

TOY ALIENS WITH 3D GLASSES

Select Cheat Codes from the Bonus menu and enter 3DGLAS.

OLD MOVIE EFFECT

Select Cheat Codes from the Bonus menu and enter OLDMOV.

TOY STORY MANIA!

ACHIEVEMENTS & TROPHIES

NAME	GOAL/REQUIREMENT	POINT VALUE	TROPHY VALUE
Clean as a whistle	Successfully dodge all the pies in a single shooting gallery.	20	Bronze
There's Pie in Your Face	Complete all of the Objectives in a shooting gallery without dodging a pie.	20	Bronze

NAME	GOAL/REQUIREMENT	POINT VALUE	TROPHY VALUE
Laser Blaster	Destroy 20 targets with the Laser power up in a single shooting gallery.	20	Bronze
Spread the Love	Destroy 20 targets with the Spread Shot power up in a single shooting gallery.	20	Bronze
Dyno-mite!	Destroy 20 targets with the Dynamite power up in a single shooting gallery.	20	Bronze
Slow Mo Joe	Destroy 20 targets while using the slow motion power up in a single shooting gallery.	20	Bronze
Double Up	Destroy 20 targets with the Double Points power up in a single shooting gallery.	20	Bronze
Earning Credit	Watch the credits to completion.	20	Bronze
Ticket to Ride	Get the train to come through town in Rootin' Tootin' Shootin'.	20	Bronze
Fly Me to the Moon	Earn 200,000 points during the UFO event in Rootin' Tootin' Targetin'.	20	Silver
Accuracy	Throw 20 balls in the distant holes in Wild West Alley Ball Challenge.	20	Bronze
Chug-a-lug	Knock down every mug in the back row throughout a single play session of Sarsaparilla Slide.	20	Bronze
Bats n' Pies	Score 5,000 points from hitting Bat Targets during the Pie Dodge Event of Mine Cart Spelunk.	20	Silver
Mine Alley	Throw 5 Balls into the mineshaft in Creaky Canyon Alley Ball Challenge.	20	Silver
High Moo-n	Complete the "Corral 3 Buffalo" objective as the Undertaker's clock reads Noon in Western Showdown.	20	Silver
Wrecking Crew	Let the town get destroyed in Please Do Feed the Animals.	20	Bronze
Zurg Rush	Shoot Zurg 30 times in Launched In Space.	20	Bronze
Pop n' Tops	Pop the tops off of the left and right moons in Launched in Deep Space.	20	Bronze
Bombs Away	Do not hit any bombs in Planetary Slash n' Defense.	20	Silver
Zaaaap!	Ring all the lasers in Flying Discs… in space!	20	Bronze
Master Terraformer	Terraform all terrain at the same time using the TNT Powerup in Terraformal Event.	20	Silver
Hack and Slash	Hit a multi-slash asteroid 12 times in Cosmic Slash n' Defense.	20	Bronze
Crack Shot	Take out the meteor and the UFO with a single rocket in Invasion of the Space Raiders.	20	Gold
Score Abduction	Ring a 5000 point UFO in Space Rescue.		Bronze
Bouquet Bonanza	Get the Big Flower to appear in Baaa-Loon Pop.	20	Bronze
Lead Air Balloon	Pop a hot air balloon in Pop Party.	20	Bronze
Rescuing Machine	Rescue more than 25 sheep in Flock of Sheep to Rescue.	20	Bronze

NAME	GOAL/REQUIREMENT	POINT VALUE	TROPHY VALUE
Basket Case	Score 15,000 points by popping basket balloons in Hot Air Balloon Show.	20	Silver
Flower Power	Pop every pink flower balloon at least once in Flight of the Balloons.	20	Bronze
My Hero!	Never miss hooking a sheep in Rescuing Fields of Sheep.	20	Silver
Cloudy Night	In Garden Grow, change the level from day to night. 20		Bronze
Pretty Red Balloons	Pop 100 balloons in Balloon Blast.	20	Bronze
The truck on the Left	Shoot all of the trucks on the left side of the screen in Shoot Camp.	20	Silver
Doing the Dishes	Break 25 stick targets in Plate Break.	20	Bronze
One and Done	Only hit a ball once and then never again in Midnight Breakout.	20	Silver
A Dish's Worst Enemy	Shatter 100 plates in Skeet Shoot.	20	Bronze
Thunderous Blue	Shoot all of the blue helicopters in Wayward Whirlybirds of Wonderment.	20	Silver
They're all mine!	Hit 20 different balls in Block Breakout Assault.	20	Silver
4-in-a-Row, All-in-One-Go!	Break all the plane plates in a single pass in Moving Target Madness.	20	Bronze
Quick Spotlight	Turn on all of the spotlights in Paratrooper Scooper in less than five seconds.	20	Silver
Streakin' Squeekin'	Hit the 5000 Point Mouse in Hamm and Eggs.	20	Bronze
Bow Ow!	Hit the dog 3 times in Bacon and Eggs.	20	Bronze
Finger Lickin' Good	Don't let any large chicken eggs fall to the ground in Fall-ing Eggs.	20	Silver
Hyper Hydra-sis	Shoot the Hydra target 8 times in Dino-Rama.	20	Bronze
Pleased Plesiosaurs	Knock down 25 plesiosaurs in The Jurassic Shore.	20	Bronze
Eggless Victor	Don't catch any eggs in It's an Egg Drop Spring.	20	Silver
Bird Feeder	Knock down 50 corn stalks in Farm Raising Fury.	20	Silver
Penguin Pusher	Knock down 50 penguins in Ice-berrrger and Fries.	20	Bronze
Partner Up	Play through any booth with a friend in Adventure Mode.	40	Bronze
Perfect Aim	Earn all trophies.	—	Platinum

TRANSFORMERS: DARK OF THE MOON

RATCHET IN MULTIPLAYER

Select Unlockables from the Extras and enter Up, Right, Down, Left, Up, Start.

CHEATS, ACHIEVEMENTS, AND TROPHIES

T

TRANSFORMERS: REVENGE OF THE FALLEN

LOW GRAVITY MODE

Select Cheat Code and enter ⬤, ⬤, ⬤, L3, ⬤, L3.

NO WEAPON OVERHEAT

Select Cheat Code and enter L3, ⬤, ⬤, L3, ⬤, L1.

ALWAYS IN OVERDRIVE MODE

Select Cheat Code and enter L1, ⬤, L1, ⬤, ⬤, R3.

UNLIMITED TURBO

Select Cheat Code and enter ⬤, L3, ⬤, R3, ⬤, ⬤

NO SPECIAL COOLDOWN TIME

Select Cheat Code and enter R3, ⬤, R3, R3, ⬤, ⬤.

INVINCIBILITY

Select Cheat Code and enter R3, ⬤, ⬤, L3, ⬤, ⬤.

4X ENERGON FROM DEFEATED ENEMIES

Select Cheat Code and enter ⬤, ⬤, ⬤, R3, ⬤, ⬤.

INCREASED WEAPON DAMAGE (ROBOT FORM)

Select the Cheat Code option and enter ⬤, ⬤, R3, ⬤, L1, ⬤.

INCREASED WEAPON DAMAGE (VEHICLE FORM)

Select Cheat Code and enter ⬤, ⬤, R1, ⬤, R3, L3.

MELEE INSTANT KILLS

Select the Cheat Code option and enter R3, ⬤. L1, ⬤, R3, L1.

LOWER ENEMY ACCURACY

Select Cheat Code and enter ⬤, L3, R3, L3, R3, R1.

INCREASED ENEMY HEALTH

Select Cheat Code and enter ⬤, ⬤, L1, ⬤, R3, ⬤.

INCREASED ENEMY DAMAGE

Select Cheat Code and enter L1, ⬤, ⬤, ⬤, R3, R3.

INCREASED ENEMY ACCURACY

Select Cheat Code and enter ⬤, ⬤, ⬤, ⬤, A, L1.

LOW GRAVITY MODE

Select Cheat Code and enter A, X, Y, Left Thumbstick, Y, Left Thumbstick.

NO WEAPON OVERHEAT

Select Cheat Code and enter Left Thumbstick, X, A, Left Thumbstick, Y, Left Bumper.

ALWAYS IN OVERDRIVE MODE

Select Cheat Code and enter Left Bumper, B, Left Bumper, A, X, Right Thumbstick.

UNLIMITED TURBO

Select Cheat Code and enter B, Left Thumbstick, X, Right Thumbstick, A, Y.

NO SPECIAL COOLDOWN TIME

Select Cheat Code and enter Right Thumbstick, X, Right Thumbstick, Right Thumbstick, X, A.

INVINCIBILITY

Select Cheat Code and enter Right Thumbstick, A, X, Left Thumbstick, X, X.

4X ENERGON FROM DEFEATED ENEMIES

Select Cheat Code and enter Y, X, B, Right Thumbstick, A, Y.

INCREASED WEAPON DAMAGE, ROBOT FORM

Select Cheat Code and enter Y, Y, Right Thumbstick, A, Left Bumper, Y.

INCREASED WEAPON DAMAGE, VEHICLE FORM

Select Cheat Code and enter Y, B, Right Bumper, X, Right Thumbstick, Left Thumbstick.

MELEE INSTANT KILLS

Select Cheat Code and enter Right Thumbstick, A, Left Bumper, B, Right Thumbstick, Left Bumper.

LOWER ENEMY ACCURACY

Select Cheat Code and enter X, Left Thumbstick, Right Thumbstick, Left Thumbstick, Right Thumbstick, Right Bumper.

INCREASED ENEMY HEALTH

Select Cheat Code and enter B, X, Left Bumper, B, Right Thumbstick, Y.

INCREASED ENEMY DAMAGE

Select Cheat Code and enter Left Bumper, Y, A, Y, Right Thumbstick, Right Thumbstick.

INCREASED ENEMY ACCURACY

Select Cheat Code and enter Y, Y, B, A, X, Left Bumper.

SPECIAL KILLS ONLY MODE

Select Cheat Code and enter B, B, Right Bumper, B, A, Left Thumbstick.

UNLOCK ALL SHANGHAI MISSIONS & ZONES

Select Cheat Code and enter Y, Left Thumbstick, Right Thumbstick, Left Bumper, Y, A.

UNLOCK ALL WEST COAST MISSIONS & ZONES

Select Cheat Code and enter Left Bumper, Right Bumper, Right Thumbstick, Y, Right Thumbstick, B.

UNLOCK ALL DEEP SIX MISSIONS & ZONES

Select Cheat Code and enter X, Right Bumper, Y, B, A, Left Bumper.

UNLOCK ALL EAST COAST MISSIONS & ZONES

Select Cheat Code and enter Right Thumbstick, Left Thumbstick, Right Bumper, A, B, X.

UNLOCK ALL CAIRO MISSIONS & ZONES

Select Cheat Code and enter Right Thumbstick, Y, A, Y, Left Thumbstick, Left Bumper.

UNLOCK AND ACTIVATE ALL UPGRADES

Select Cheat Code and enter Left Bumper, Y, Left Bumper, B, X, X.

XBOX 360/PS3

ACHIEVEMENTS & TROPHIES

NAME	GOAL/REQUIREMENT	POINT VALUE	TROPHY VALUE
Down to Chinatown	Medal in all Autobot Shanghai Missions	20	Bronze
West Side	Medal in all Autobot West Coast Missions	20	Bronze
Aerialbot Assault	Medal in all Autobot Deep Six Missions	20	Bronze
East Side	Medal in all Autobot East Coast Missions	20	Bronze
The Dagger's Tip	Medal in all Autobot Cairo Missions	20	Bronze
One Shall Stand	Defeat Megatron—Autobot Campaign	25	Bronze
Now I've Seen It All	Unlock all Autobot Unlockables	50	Bronze
Power to the People	Purchase All Autobot Upgrades	25	Bronze

CHEATS, ACHIEVEMENTS, AND TROPHIES

T

NAME	GOAL/REQUIREMENT	POINT VALUE	TROPHY VALUE
Awesome Achievement!	Eliminate 250 Decepticons—Autobot Campaign	25	Bronze
Do the Math	Acquire 2,000,000 Energon in the Autobot Campaign	20	Bronze
A True Autobot	Earn Platinum Medals on ALL Autobot Missions	75	Gold
Shanghai'd	Medal in all Decepticon Shanghai Missions	25	Bronze
West Coast For The Win!	Medal in all Decepticon West Coast Missions	25	Bronze
Rise of The Fallen	Medal in all Decepticon Deep Six Missions	25	Bronze
Coast to Coast	Medal in all Decepticon East Coast Missions	25	Bronze
Lies	Medal in all Decepticon Cairo Missions	25	Bronze
One Shall Fall	Defeat Optimus Prime—Decepticon Campaign	25	Bronze
Now I've Really Seen It All	Unlock all Decepticon Unlockables	50	Gold
Spoils of War	Purchase All Decepticon Upgrades	25	Bronze
Bad Boys	Eliminate 350 Autobots—Decepticon Campaign	25	Bronze
Break the Bank	Acquire 3,000,000 Energon in the Decepticon Campaign	25	Bronze
A True Decepticon	Earn Platinum Medals on ALL Decepticon Missions	75	Gold
Platty For The Win!	Earn a Platinum Medal—Either Campaign	20	Bronze
Golden Boy	Earn a Gold Medal—Either Campaign	15	Bronze
Not Gold Enough	Earn a Silver Medal—Either Campaign	10	Bronze
Cast in Bronze	Earn a Bronze Medal—Either Campaign	5	Bronze
On the Board	Make it into the Top 100000 on SP Leaderboards—Either Campaign	15	Bronze
Good Mojo	Make it into the Top 10000 on SP Leaderboards—Either Campaign	25	Silver
Bonecrusher	Make it into the Top 1000 on SP Leaderboards—Either Campaign	25	Gold
And So It Begins...	Unlock a Single Unlockable—Either Campaign	5	Bronze
Grind On	Purchase an Upgrade—Either Campaign	5	Bronze
Choices...	Unlock a New Zone—Either Campaign	5	Bronze
You've Got The Touch	Fill OVERDRIVE Meter—Either Campaign	25	Bronze
Choose a Side	Win one RANKED/PLAYER MATCH game as Autobots and one as Decepticons	15	Bronze
Hold!	Win a Control Point round without losing a control point in a RANKED/PLAYER MATCH game	15	Bronze
Follow the Leader	While playing One Shall Stand, as the leader, kill the opposing leader in a RANKED/PLAYER MATCH game	15	Bronze

NAME	GOAL/REQUIREMENT	POINT VALUE	TROPHY VALUE
Life of the Party	Host one game of each game type in a PLAYER MATCH game	15	Bronze
Smells Like Victory	Win a Match as Each of the 15 Default Characters	50	Silver

TRANSFORMERS: WAR FOR CYBERTRON

AUTOBOT SILVERBOLT (STORY & ARENA)

Select Cheats from the Main menu and enter 10141.

DECEPTICON RAMJET (IN ARENA)

Select Cheats from the Main menu and enter 99871.

DECEPTICON RAMJET (STORY & ARENA)

Select Cheats from the Main menu and enter 99871.

AUTOBOT SILVERBOLT (ARENA)

Select Cheats from the Main menu and enter 10141.

TRENCHED

AVATAR AWARDS

AVATAR	EARNED BY
Trenched T-Shirt	Complete Mobile Trench certification.
Trenchie	Wrest control of Europe back from the Northern Pylon.

TRON: EVOLUTION

THE ISLAND, TANK AND DISC BATTLE MAP

At the cheat menu, enter 25E0DE6B.

QUORRA COSTUME

At the cheat menu, enter c74f395f.

TWISTED METAL: HEAD-ON

Note that the following codes will not work for Multiplayer or Online modes.

HEALTH RECHARGED

Hold L + R and press ●, ⊗, ●, ●.

INFINITE AMMO

Hold L + R and press ●, ●, Down, Down, Left.

INVULNERABLE

Hold L + R and press Right, Left, Down, Up.

INFINITE WEAPONS

Hold L + R and press ●, ●, Down, Down.

KILLER WEAPONS

Hold L + R and press ✕, ✕, Up, Up.

MEGA GUNS

Hold L + R and press ✕, ●, ✕, ●

TWO WORLDS II

UNLOCKABLE ITEMS

Pause the game, select Bonus Code and enter the following:

ITEM	PASSWORD
Anathros Sword	6770-8976-1634-9490
Axe	1775-3623-3298-1928
Elexorien Two-handed Sword	3542-3274-8350-6064
Hammer	6231-1890-4345-5988
Lucienda Sword	9122-5287-3591-0927
Luciendar Sword	6624-0989-0879-6383
Two-handed Hammer	3654-0091-3399-0994
Dragon Scale Armor	4149-3083-9823-6545
Labyrinth Level	1797-3432-7753-9254
Scroll Bonus Map	6972-5760-7685-8477

UFC 2010 UNDISPUTED

BJ PENN (BLACK SHORTS)

At the main menu, press Left Bumper, Right Bumper, Left Trigger, Right Trigger, Right Trigger, Left Trigger, Right Bumper, Left Bumper, Y, X, X, Y, start.

SHAQUILLE O'NEAL

At the main menu, press Right, Up, Left, Right, Down, Left, Up, Right, Down, Left, X, Y, Y, X, Start.

TAPOUT CREW - MASK, PUNKASS, SKYSCRAPE

At the main menu, press Down, Down, Up, Right, Left, Down, Back, Start.

ACHIEVEMENTS & TROPHIES

NAME	GOAL/REQUIREMENT	POINT VALUE	TROPHY VALUE
Puppeteer	Create a fighter in Create A Fighter	10	Bronze
Puppetmaster	Win a fight against the CPU with a fighter you've created in Create A Fighter	15	Bronze
As Real As It Gets	Experience an entire 8 fight event card in Event Mode.	20	Bronze
White Belt	Win 10 Xbox LIVE Exhibition matches in total	15	Bronze
Baby Steps	Win an Xbox LIVE Exhibition Ranked match	10	Bronze

NAME	GOAL/REQUIREMENT	POINT VALUE	TROPHY VALUE
Hot Hands	Win 10 Xbox LIVE Exhibition Ranked matches consecutively	30	Silver
Olympic Mixed Martial Artist	Xbox LIVE Exhibition - Obtain all types of gold medals	20	Silver
Warriors, Come Out And Play	Join an Xbox LIVE Camp	10	Bronze
Under Your Wing	Act as a trainer in Xbox LIVE Camp Training	15	Bronze
Hall of Famer	Compete in a Champion vs. Champion fight and also make the UFC Hall of Fame in Career Mode	50	Gold
So Now You're A Fighter	Complete the Career Mode	150	Gold
Gotta Catch 'Em All	Collect all Topps® UFC trading cards	30	Silver
Submission Technician	Win a fight with a Submission Transition	20	Bronze
It's The Jits!	Win a fight by Submission against a non-CAF, Expert CPU in the first 60 seconds of Round 1.	15	Bronze
Steamroller	Win a fight by KO/TKO against a non-CAF, Expert CPU in the first 60 seconds of Round 1.	15	Bronze
Kay. Tee. Eff. Oh!	Win a fight by Flash KO against a CPU opponent.	15	Bronze
Veteran Champion	Complete the Title Defense Mode	50	Silver
Budding Champion	Complete the Title Mode	50	Silver
Learned Student	Go through all tutorials	20	Bronze
Tournament Title Holder	Win at least one championship in the Tournament mode	15	Bronze
Testing the Waters	Play all modes at least once, check the shop and all options	20	Bronze
Honorable Fighter	Touch gloves at the beginning of 10 matches.	20	Bronze
Ultimate Unlocks	Complete all A, B, and C class challenges (Red and Blue Corner)in a fight in Ultimate Fights Mode.	50	Silver
Pound For Pound Champ	Win a Champion vs. Champion fight in Career Mode	50	Gold
Yellow Belt	Win 25 Xbox LIVE Ranked Matches	20	Silver
Purple Belt	Win 50 Xbox LIVE Ranked Matches	30	Silver
Brown Belt	Win 75 Xbox LIVE Ranked Matches	40	Silver
Black Belt	Win 100 Xbox LIVE Ranked Matches	50	Gold
Coming Up Next...	Download an Event for Event Mode	10	Bronze
The Cessation Sensation!	Win by all methods of stoppage against the CPU. (KO, TKO, Submission, Doctor Stoppage)	25	Silver
Bobbin' And Weavin'	Dodge 3 consecutive strikes via sway (Outside of Tutorial Mode)	30	Silver
Blog Fodder	Complete a post-fight interview in Career Mode	15	Bronze
Move Mastery	Reach "World Class" (Level 3) status with a technique or move.	25	Silver

U

SECRET ACHIEVEMENTS & TROPHIES

NAME	GOAL/REQUIREMENT	POINT VALUE	TROPHY VALUE
Fighting with Pride	Now you're dirty boxing with Pride!	15	Bronze
Cocky S.O.B.	No respect for your opponent.	10	Bronze
It Slices, It Dices	Is there a doctor in the stadium!	15	Bronze

UFC PERSONAL TRAINER: THE ULTIMATE FITNESS SYSTEM

XBOX 360

AVATAR AWARDS

AVATAR	EARNED BY
UFC Trainer Gloves	Earn 10 Medals.
UFC Trainer Shorts	Earn 50 Medals.
UFC Trainer Shirt	Earn 150 Medals.

ULTIMATE MARVEL VS. CAPCOM 3

PLAYSTATION 3

PLAY AS GALACTUS

With a save game from Marvel vs. Capcom 3: Fate of Two Worlds on your system, Galactus becomes available. Otherwise, you need to accumulate 30,000 points on a player card. Now highlight Arcade Mode and press L1 + Select + ⬤.

PLAYSTATION VITA

PLAY AS GALACTUS

Accumulate 30,000 points on a player card. Now highlight Arcade Mode and press L + Select + ⬤.

XBOX 360/PS3

PLAY AS GALACTUS

With a save game from Marvel vs. Capcom 3: Fate of Two Worlds on your system, Galactus becomes available. Otherwise, you need to accumulate 30,000 points on a player card. Now highlight Arcade Mode and press Left Bumper + Back + A.

ACHIEVEMENTS & TROPHIES

NAME	GOAL/REQUIREMENT	POINT VALUE	TROPHY VALUE
The Ultimate	Unlock all achievements.	50	Bronze
Waiting for the Trade	View all endings in Arcade mode.	50	Gold
The Best There Is	Beat Arcade mode on the hardest difficulty.	10	Bronze
Saving My Quarters	Beat Arcade mode without using any continues.	10	Bronze
The Points Do Matter	Earn 400,000 points in Arcade mode.	20	Bronze
High-Score Hero	Earn 500,000 points in Arcade mode.	30	Silver
Missions? Possible.	Clear 120 missions in Mission mode.	20	Bronze
Up To The Challenge	Clear 240 missions in Mission mode.	30	Silver
Master of Tasks	Clear 480 missions in Mission mode.	40	Silver

NAME	GOAL/REQUIREMENT	POINT VALUE	TROPHY VALUE
Above Average Joe	Land a Viewtiful Combo. (Arcade/Xbox LIVE)	10	Bronze
Mutant Master	Land an Uncanny Combo. (Arcade/Xbox LIVE)	10	Bronze
Mega Buster	Use 1,000 Hyper Combo Gauge bars. (Arcade/Xbox LIVE)	20	Bronze
Defender	Block 100 times. (Arcade/Xbox LIVE)	10	Bronze
Advancing Guardian	Perform 100 Advancing Guards. (Arcade/Xbox LIVE)	10	Bronze
A Friend in Need	Perform 100 Crossover Assists. (Arcade/Xbox LIVE)	20	Bronze
First Strike	Land 50 First Attacks. (Arcade/Xbox LIVE)	10	Bronze
Savage Playing	Perform 50 Snap Backs. (Arcade/Xbox LIVE)	10	Bronze
Quick Change-Up	Perform 50 Crossover Counters. (Arcade/Xbox LIVE)	10	Bronze
Perfect X-ample	Use X-Factor 50 times. (Arcade/Xbox LIVE)	10	Bronze
Gravity? Please...	Land 50 Team Aerial Combos. (Arcade/Xbox LIVE)	10	Bronze
Mighty Teamwork	Land 30 Team Aerial Counters. (Arcade/Xbox LIVE)	10	Bronze
Big Bang Theory	Perform 30 Hyper Combo Finishes. (Arcade/Xbox LIVE)	15	Bronze
Hard Corps	Perform 30 Crossover Combination Finishes. (Arcade/Xbox LIVE)	15	Bronze
Training Montage	Play in Offline Mode for over 5 hours.	20	Bronze
Training in Isolation	Play in Offline Mode for over 30 hours.	30	Silver
Seductive Embrace	Play on Xbox LIVE for over 5 hours.	20	Bronze
Rivals Welcome	Play on Xbox LIVE for over 30 hours.	30	Silver
Brave New World	Participate in any mode over Xbox LIVE.	10	Bronze
Hellbent	Participate in 100 matches in Xbox LIVE.	20	Bronze
Dreaded Opponent	Participate in 200 matches in Xbox LIVE.	20	Bronze
Forged From Steel	Participate in 300 matches in Xbox LIVE.	30	Silver
Full Roster	Battle against all characters over Xbox LIVE.	30	Silver
Incredible	Win without calling your partners or switching out in a Xbox LIVE match.	20	Bronze
Need a Healing Factor	Win without blocking in an Xbox LIVE match.	20	Bronze
Crazy Good	Surpass the rank of Fighter.	10	Bronze
Mega Good	Surpass the 6th rank of any class.	40	Silver
Hotshot	Win 10 battles in Ranked Match.	15	Bronze
Slam Master	Win 50 battles in Ranked Match.	20	Bronze
Fighting Machine	Win 100 battles in Ranked Match.	40	Silver
Noble Effort	Get a 5-game win streak in Ranked Match.	15	Bronze
Assemble!	Participate in an 8 player Lobby over Xbox LIVE.	15	Bronze

CHEATS, ACHIEVEMENTS, AND TROPHIES

U

NAME	GOAL/REQUIREMENT	POINT VALUE	TROPHY VALUE
Dominator	Collect 100 titles.	30	Silver
A Warrior Born	Earn 5,000 Player Points (PP).	10	Bronze
Devil with a Blue Coat	Earn 30,000 Player Points (PP).	15	Bronze
Divine Brawler	Earn 100,000 Player Points (PP).	50	Silver
Comic Collector	Unlock all items in the Gallery.	50	Gold
Passport to Beatdown Country	Fight in all of the stages.	10	Bronze

ULTIMATE MORTAL KOMBAT

NINTENDO 3DS

VS CODES

At the VS screen, each player must use LP, BLK, and LK to enter the following codes:

EFFECT	PLAYER 1	PLAYER 2
You are now entering the realm	642	468
Blocking Disabled	020	020
Dark Kombat	448	844
Infinite Run	466	466
Play in Kahn's Kave	004	700
Play in the Kombat Temple	600	N/A
Play in the Soul Chamber	123	901
Play on Jade's Deset	330	033
Play on Kahn's Tower	880	220
Play on Noob Saibot Dorfen	050	050
Play on Rooftops	343	343
Play on Scislac Busorez	933	933
Play on Subway	880	088
Play on the Belltower	091	190
Play on the Bridge	077	022
Play on the Graveyard	666	333
Play on the Pit 3	820	028
Play on the Street	079	035
Play on the Waterfront	002	003
Play Scorpions Lair	666	444
Player 1 Half Power	033	N/A
Player 1 Quarter Power	707	N/A
Player 2 Half Power	N/A	033
Player 2 Quarter Power	N/A	707
Power Bars Disabled	987	123
Random Kombat	444	444
Revision 1.2	999	999
Sans Power	044	440
Silent Kombat	300	300
Throwing Disabled	100	100
Throwing Encouraged	010	010
Winner of round fights Motaro	969	141
Winner of round fights Noob Saibot	769	342
Winner of round fights Shao Kahn	033	564
Winner of round fights Smoke	205	205

UNLOCK ERMAC, MILEENA, CLASSIC SUB-ZERO

At the Ultimate Kombat Kode screen input the following codes:

CLASSIC SUB-ZERO

At the Ultimate Kombat Kode screen, enter 81835. You can reach this screen by losing and not continuing.

ERMAC

At the Ultimate Kombat Kode screen, enter 12344. You can reach this screen by losing and not continuing.

MILEENA

At the Ultimate Kombat Kode screen, enter 22264. You can reach this screen by losing and not continuing.

HUMAN SMOKE

Select ROBO Smoke. Hold Block + Run + High Punch + High Kick + Back before the fight begins.

ULTIMATE SHOOTING COLLECTION

NINTENDO WII

ROTATE DISPLAY ON SIDE IN TATE MODE

At the Main menu, press Left, Right, Left, Right, Up, Up, 1, 2.

UNCHARTED: DRAKE'S FORTUNE

PLAYSTATION 3

DRAKE'S BASEBALL T-SHIRT

At the costume select, press Left, Right, Down, Up, ●, R1, L1, ●.

MAKING A CUTSCENE—GRAVE ROBBING

At the rewards screen, highlight Making a Cutscene—Grave Robbing and press Left, R2, Right, Up, L2, ●, ●, Down.

MAKING A CUTSCENE—TIME'S UP

At the rewards screen, highlight Making a Cutscene—Time's Up and press L1, Right, ●, Down, Left, ●, R1, Up.

CONCEPT ART—BONUS 1

At the rewards screen, highlight Concept Art—Bonus 1 and press L2, Right, Up, ●, Left, ●, R1, Down.

CONCEPT ART—BONUS 2

At the rewards screen, highlight Concept Art—Bonus 2 and press ●, L1, Right, Left, Down, R2, ●, Up.

UNCHARTED: GOLDEN ABYSS

PLAYSTATION VITA

CRUSHING DIFFICULTY

Complete the game on Hard.

UNCHARTED 2: AMONG THIEVES

PLAYSTATION 3

In Uncharted 2: Among Thieves, upon opening the store you'll have the option to hit the Square button to check for Uncharted: Drake's Fortune save data. You'll obtain cash for having save data! This cash can be used in the single and multiplayer stores. Could be useful if you want a head start online!

$20,000

Have a saved game of Uncharted: Drake's Fortune.

$80,000

Have a saved game of Uncharted: Drake's Fortune with the story completed at least once.

UNCHARTED 3: DRAKE'S DECEPTION

PLAYSTATION 3

PIGGYBACK EMBLEM

Select Emblem from your Multiplayer Profile and then Image. Press Up, Right, Down, Left, Up, Left, Down, Right and Piggyback Frame appears at the end of the list. Each part of the logo is now unlocked, so next pick the Piggyback Base, followed by Piggyback Logo.

UP

NINTENDO 3DS

INVINCIBILITY

After completing the game, enter B, Y, B, Y, X, Y, X, Y, B, A at the title screen. This cheat disables saving.

VALKYRIA CHRONICLES II

PSP

TANK STICKERS

Enter the following codes in Extra Mode for the desired effect.

STICKER	ENTER
Alicia Gunther	K1C7XKLJMXUHRD8S
Blitz Logo	VWUYNJQ8HGSVXR7J
Edy Nelson	R5PT1MXEY3BW8VBE
Edy's Squad	CR6BG1A9LYQKB6WJ
SEGA Logo	6RK45S59F7U2JLTD
Skies of Arcadia	WVZLPTYXURS1Q8TV
Crazy Taxi	38WV17PK45TYAF8V
Faldio	GWNU95RSETW1VGNQ
Gallian Military	TXU14EUV74PCR3TE
Isara Gunther and Isara's Dream	37LRK5D214VQVFYH
Prince Maximilian and Imperial Flag	H73G4L9GLJR1CHJP
Selvaria	53K8FKGP1GHQ4SBN
Sonic the Hedgehog	CUP34ASEZ9WDKBYV
Super Monkey Ball	7JMNHZ83TGH7XFKT
Yakuza	QAKVXZTALF4TU7SK
Vanquish Tank	BUNLT4EXDS74QRCR

CHARACTERS

Enter the following codes in Extra Mode for the desired effect.

CHARACTER	ENTER
Alicia Gunther	KBAFLFHICAJTKMIY
Edy's Detachment	TKBHCNBERHRKJNFG
Julius Kroze	AMNKZKYTKNBNKYMT
Lamar/Ramal	LITSGAAMEORFRCRQ
Landzaat Farudio	KNWRJRGSMLASTNSQ
Maximillian	KBFHZRJTKMKSKNKP
Mintz	CKRJWNSXTYMNGZRT
Selvaria	KSNEGA56LPY7CTQ9
Support-Class Aliasse, Lancer-Class Cosette and Armor-Type Zeri	PZRJQM7SK4HPXTYM

VANQUISH

ACHIEVEMENTS & TROPHIES

NAME	GOAL/REQUIREMENT	POINT VALUE	TROPHY VALUE
One Day at DARPA	Complete all DARPA training exercises.	10	Bronze
Space Normandy	Complete Act 1.	15	Bronze
Storming Grand Hill	Complete Act 2.	15	Bronze
I Don't Speak Kreon!	Complete Act 3.	15	Bronze
My Way	Complete Act 4.	15	Bronze
End to Major Combat Operations	Complete Act 5.	15	Bronze
Survivor	Complete all Acts.	30	Silver
Operation Overlord II	Complete Act 1 on Hard difficulty or above.	25	Bronze
Ain't Life Grand?	Complete Act 2 on Hard difficulty or above.	25	Bronze
Cry on, Kreon!	Complete Act 3 on Hard difficulty or above.	25	Bronze
The High Way	Complete Act 4 on Hard difficulty or above.	25	Bronze
Mission Accomplished	Complete Act 5 on Hard difficulty or above.	25	Bronze
ARS Operator	Complete all Acts on Hard difficulty or above.	50	Gold
Gun Runner	Scan and acquire all weapons.	10	Bronze
King of the Hill	Level a weapon up to maximum operational capability.	20	Bronze
Fight or Flight	Manually trigger AR Mode and destroy an enemy robot.	10	Bronze
Adrenaline Rush	Manually trigger AR Mode and destroy three enemy robots in a row.	20	Bronze
Going in for the Kill	Destroy ten enemy robots with melee attacks.	10	Bronze
A Heartbreaker and Lifetaker	Destroy 100 enemy robots with melee attacks.	30	Silver
Helloooo, Nurse	Revive a friendly troop.	5	Bronze
Knight in Shining White Armor	Revive 20 friendly troops.	15	Bronze
Death Wish	Destroy three enemy robots while in damage-triggered AR Mode.	20	Bronze

NAME	GOAL/REQUIREMENT	POINT VALUE	TROPHY VALUE
40 Yard Dash	Maintain a Boost dash to the limit of the ARS reactor without overheating.	30	Bronze
Home Run	Destroy an incoming missile or grenade.	10	Bronze
Home Run God	Destroy ten incoming missiles or grenades.	10	Bronze
Brutality Bonus	Destroy a Romanov's arms and legs, then finish it with a melee attack.	10	Bronze
Romanov This!	Destroy a Romanov with a melee attack.	20	Bronze
The Hand of God	Destroy two Romanovs in a row using only melee attacks.	30	Silver
Robots Tend to Blow Up	Destroy three enemy robots at once with one hand grenade.	10	Bronze
Hole-in-One	Destroy a Chicane with a hand grenade.	5	Bronze
Short Circuit	Destroy ten enemy robots that have been disabled with an EMP emitter.	20	Bronze
Two Birds with One Stone	Destroy two or more enemy robots at once with the LFE gun.	20	Bronze
Trick Shot	Destroy three enemy robots at once with rocket launcher splash damage.	20	Bronze
Flash! King of the Impossible	Destroy four enemies simultaneously with the Lock-on Laser.	30	Silver
Piece by Piece	Destroy the arms, head, and back of an KNRB-0 Argus robot.	20	Bronze
That Ended Up Working Out Nicely	After taking control of the enemy transport in Act 2-2, do not let a single enemy escape.	10	Bronze
Failure Breeds Success	Destroy two Argus robots in Act 2-3 while they are in bipedal mode.	15	Bronze
Leibniz Defense Agency	Defend the Pangloss statue in Act 3-2.	10	Bronze
Tightrope Walker	Destroy two cannons in Act 3-3 and complete the mission.	10	Bronze
Fisher is the Other Sam	Proceed on the monorail in Act 3-4 without being spotted by the enemy troops or searchlights.	15	Bronze
Flyswatter	Destroy all the floating turrets in Act 3-4.	20	Bronze
Guardian	Do not allow any friendly armor to be destroyed during Act 3-5.	10	Bronze
Hurry the #@$% Up!	Destroy five or more enemy transports from atop the Kreon in Act 3-7.	10	Bronze
Civil Disobedience	Ignore the elevator start order in Act 4-1. Instead, hold position and destroy all reinforcements.	30	Bronze
Buzzard Beater	Destroy the Buzzard without allowing it to reach ground level in Act 5-1.	30	Bronze
Smoke 'em if ya got 'em!	Destroy 10 enemies distracted by cigarettes during one mission.	30	Bronze
Auld Lang Syne	Destroy two enemy robots who have been distracted by a cigarette.	15	Bronze
The Best of All Possible Worlds	Find and fire upon all of the Pangloss statues hidden on the colony.	30	Silver
Living Legend	Complete the game without dying, regardless of difficulty level.	50	Gold

SECRET ACHIEVEMENTS

NAME	GOAL/REQUIREMENT	POINT VALUE	TROPHY VALUE
Tactical Challenges	Complete all of the Tactical Challenges in VANQUISH	50	Gold

VIRTUA FIGHTER 2

XBOX 360/PS3

ALTERNATE COSTUMES

Hold Up while selecting your character to choose a different costume.

VIRTUA STRIKER

XBOX 360/PS3

BIG HEAD MODE

When the announcer is announcing teams, press Up, Down, Left, Right, Long Pass to unlock Big Head mode.

PLAY AS F.C. SEGA

When selecting your team, choose Spain and press Start, then move to England and press Start, then move to Germany and press Start and finally move to Argentina and press Start to unlock the F.C. Sega team.

VIRTUA TENNIS 3

PSP

ALL COURTS

At the Game Mode screen, press Up, Up, Down, Down, Left, Right, Left, Right.

ALL GEAR

At the Game Mode screen, press Left, Right, ●, Left, Right, ●, Up, Down.

KING & DUKE

At the Game Mode screen, press Up, Up, Down, Down, Left, Right, L, R.

VIRTUA TENNIS 4

NINTENDO WII

THERON TENNIEL

At the player select, select Load to access Custom Players. Next, press -.

VICKY BARNEY

At the player select, select Load to access Custom Players. Next, press +.

PLAYSTATION 3

THERON TENNIEL

At the player select, select Load to access Custom Players. Next, press L1.

VICKY BARNEY

At the player select, select Load to access Custom Players. Next, press R1.

XBOX 360

THERON TENNIEL

At the player select, select Load to access Custom Players. Next, press Left Bumper.

VICKY BARNEY

At the player select, select Load to access Custom Players. Next, press Right Bumper.

VIRTUAL ON: ORATORIO TANGRAM VER.5.66

PLAY AS ALPHA RAIDEN

After defeating Arcade Mode with Raiden, do the following at the Character Select screen: highlight Aphand B, press X, highlight Apharmd S, press X, highlight Dordray, press X, X, highlight Specineff, press X, X, highlight Fei-Yen, press X, X, highlight Cypher, press X (x3).

PLAY AS ALPHA TEMJIN

After defeating Arcade Mode with Temjin, do the following at the Character Select screen: highlight Temjin, press X, highlight Random, press X, highlight Raiden, press X, X, highlight Bal-Bados, press X, X, highlight Angelan, press X, X, highlight Grys-Vok, press X (x3).

VIVA PIÑATA: PARTY ANIMALS

CLASSIC GAMER AWARD ACHIEVEMENT

At the START screen, press Up, Up, Down, Down, Left, Right, Left, Right, B, A. This earns you 10 points toward your Gamerscore.

VIVA PIÑATA: TROUBLE IN PARADISE

CREDITS

Select Play Garden and name your garden Piñata People. This unlocks the ability to view the credits on the Main menu.

VOLTRON

AVATAR AWARDS

AVATAR	EARNED BY
Voltron Unlock T-Shirt	Purchase the game to unlock.

THE WALKING DEAD

ACHIEVEMENTS & TROPHIES

EPISODE 1

NAME	GOAL/REQUIREMENT	POINT VALUE	TROPHY VALUE
Out of the Frying Pan	Complete chapter 1 of episode 1.	10	Bronze
Adventures in Babysitting	Complete chapter 2 of episode 1.	10	Bronze
In Your Charge	Complete chapter 3 of episode 1.	10	Bronze
Rock and a Hard Place	Complete chapter 4 of episode 1.	10	Bronze
It's Just One Bullet	Complete chapter 5 of episode 1.	10	Bronze
Hey, Bud	Complete chapter 6 of episode 1.	10	Bronze
Two Enter, One Leaves	Complete chapter 7 of episode 1.	15	Silver
Everything's Going to be Okay	Complete Episode 1: A New Day.	25	Gold

EPISODE 2

NAME	GOAL/REQUIREMENT	POINT VALUE	TROPHY VALUE
Going Hungry	Complete chapter 1 of episode 2.	10	Bronze
Conversation Killer	Complete chapter 2 of episode 2.	10	Bronze
Thank You for Shopping!	Complete chapter 3 of episode 2.	10	Bronze
Guess Who's Coming to Dinner	Complete chapter 4 of episode 2.	10	Bronze
Too Much Salt Will Kill You	Complete chapter 5 of episode 2.	15	Silver
Taking Charlotte	Complete chapter 6 of episode 2.	10	Bronze
You Fight Like A Dairy Farmer	Complete chapter 7 of episode 2.	10	Bronze
It's Not Stealing If You Need It	Complete Episode 2: "Starved for Help"	25	Gold

EPISODE 3

NAME	GOAL/REQUIREMENT	POINT VALUE	TROPHY VALUE
Goodbye, She Quietly Says	Complete chapter 1 of episode 3.	10	Bronze
Bad Blood	Complete chapter 2 of episode 3.	10	Bronze
Hit the Road	Complete chapter 3 of episode 3.	10	Bronze
What now?	Complete chapter 4 of episode 3.	10	—
Handle It	Complete chapter 5 of episode 3.	10	—
Unexpected Delay	Complete chapter 6 of episode 3.	15	—
Look Behind You	Complete chapter 7 of episode 3.	10	—
Lend Me Your Ears	Complete Episode 3: "Long Road Ahead"	25	Gold
Woodbury Bound	Complete chapter 4 of episode 3.	—	Bronze
Rumbling Down the Track	Complete chapter 5 of episode 3.	—	Bronze
Can't Save 'em All	Complete chapter 6 of episode 3.	—	Silver
Tools for the Job	Complete chapter 7 of episode 3.	—	Bronze

EPISODE 4

NAME	GOAL/REQUIREMENT	POINT VALUE	TROPHY VALUE
Georgia's First City	Complete chapter 1 of episode 4.	10	Bronze
Down By The River	Complete chapter 2 of episode 4.	10	Bronze
Support Group	Complete chapter 3 of episode 4.	10	Bronze
Bedside Manor	Complete chapter 4 of episode 4.	10	Bronze
Georgia's Last City	Complete chapter 5 of episode 4.	10	Silver
For Whom The Bell Tolls	Complete chapter 6 of episode 4.	15	Bronze
The Morning After	Complete chapter 7 of episode 4.	10	Bronze
Penultimate	Complete Episode 4: "Around Every Corner"	25	Gold

EPISODE 5

NAME	GOAL/REQUIREMENT	POINT VALUE	TROPHY VALUE
Into The Fire	Complete chapter 1 of episode 5.	10	Bronze
Twice Shy	Complete chapter 2 of episode 5.	10	Bronze
There Ain't No Way	Complete chapter 3 of episode 5.	10	Bronze
Mercy	Complete chapter 4 of episode 5.	10	Bronze
The Marsh House	Complete chapter 5 of episode 5.	10	Bronze
What's in the bag?	Complete chapter 6 of episode 5.	10	Bronze
Stay Close To Me	Complete chapter 7 of episode 5.	15	Silver
What Remains	Complete Episode 5: "No Time Left"	25	Gold

THE WALKING DEAD: SURVIVAL INSTINCT

UNLOCKABLE RELICS

Relics are unlockable cheats that can be used after the first playthrough and only one can be activated at a time.

RELIC	REQUIREMENT
Bigger Clips	Complete the game once with Mia in your party.
Crossbow/Assault Rifle	Complete the game once.
Faster Stronger	Complete the game once with Sheila in your party.
Item Boost	Complete the game once with Swenson in your party.
Marksman Boost	Complete the game once with Harrison in your party.
Melee Boost	Complete the game once with Jane in your party.
Silenced Weapons	Complete the game once with Blake in your party.
Stealth Movement	Complete the game once with Warren in your party.
Survivor Success	Complete the game once with Noah in your party.
Unlimited Ammo	Unlock all other relics to unlock this relic.

ACHIEVEMENTS & TROPHIES

NAME	GOAL/REQUIREMENT	POINT VALUE	TROPHY VALUE
Oedipal Complex	Complete the First Location	5	Bronze
Sorry, Brother	Complete the First Act	10	Bronze
Nobody Can Kill Merle but Merle	Complete the Second Act	15	Bronze
Moving to the 'Burbs	Complete the Third Act	20	Bronze
Get Out of Dodge	Complete the Final Marked Destination on the Map	30	Bronze
Been Everywhere	Complete All Marked Destinations on the Map	50	Gold
On the Road Again	Explore an Unmarked Travel Location	5	Bronze
Zig-Zagging All Over the Road	Explore 25 Unmarked Travel Locations	50	Bronze
That's a Nice Swing You've Got	Kill Walkers Using Every Melee Weapon	15	Bronze
They Know Me at the Range	Kill Walkers Using Every Ranged Weapon	15	Bronze
Crash Course in Brain Surgery	Kill 100 Walkers while Grappling	25	Bronze
Need More Spots Up Front	Dismember 250 Limbs	35	Silver
Now Don't You Get Bit!	Prevent 50 Walkers from Grabbing You	30	Bronze
We Survive by Pulling Together	Recruit 1 Optional Survivor	5	Bronze
Every Man, Woman and Child	Choose to Travel at Least Once with Every Optional Survivor	30	Silver
No Down Payments	Find Every Useable Vehicle	30	Silver
No Stone Left Unturned	Collect Every Stuffed Squirrel	50	Gold
Good Samaritan	Complete 25 Optional Objectives	30	Bronze

NAME	GOAL/REQUIREMENT	POINT VALUE	TROPHY VALUE
Not a Scratch	Complete a Marked Destination on the Map without Taking Any Damage	30	Bronze
They're People, Too!	Complete a Marked Destination on the Map without Killing a Walker	30	Bronze
You're Just Not My Type	Complete a Marked Destination on the Map without Being Grabbed by a Walker	10	Bronze
I Can Handle This Myself	Enter Sherwood Without Any Survivors	30	Bronze
Say Hello to My Little Friend	Complete a Marked Map Destination Using Only Firearms	10	Bronze
True Dixon	Complete a Marked Destination on the Map Using Only the Crossbow	25	Bronze
Sneak Attack	Perform Execution Kills on 50 Walkers	35	Bronze
It's Gotta Be the Brain	Dismember All Limbs of 5 Walkers	45	Silver
Two Heads Are Better Than One	Kill Multiple Walkers with One Bullet	5	Bronze
Have a Nice Trip!	Kill a Walker That Is Falling Due to Dismemberment	20	Bronze
Mind if I Borrow This?	Pull a Bolt From a Walker Then Kill Them With It	15	Bronze
Ooh, Shiny!	Distract 50 Walkers with Items	15	Bronze
That Looks Like It Hurt	Restore Survivors 25 Times	30	Silver
Extreme Conditioning	Sprint Until You're Exhausted 10 Times in One Level	10	Bronze
It's Not Venison, but It'll Do	Consume 50 MREs	10	Bronze
Still Not Buying a Hybrid	Consume 250 Fuel	10	Bronze
Duct Tape Can Fix Anything	Survive 5 Breakdowns	10	Bronze
Next Step: Bullet Belt	Fire 300 Bullets	15	Bronze
Down to My Last	Complete the Game with Only 1 Firearm and 1 Bullet Left in Your Inventory	15	Bronze
Porcupine	Shoot a Walker with 10 Bolts without Killing It	15	Bronze
Guys Night Out	Arrive at Final Destination with Only Male Survivors	20	Bronze
Rosie the Rampager	Arrive at Final Destination with Only Female Survivors	20	Bronze
The Missing 8	Find Every Poster	50	Gold
I Used to Be a Human Like You	Shoot a Walker in the Knee with a Bolt	5	Bronze
This Is How Hot Dogs Are Made	10 Walkers Killed with Saw Blades in the Logging Camp	10	Bronze
BOOM! Who Needs a Headshot?	Kill Walkers with One Explosion	15	Bronze
Group Hug	Kill 4 Walkers in a Single Grapple Sequence	5	Bronze
Need a Hand?	Prevent a Walker from Damaging You by Severing Its Attacking Limb	5	Bronze
You Go Your Way, I'll Go Mine	Dismiss a Survivor	5	Bronze
PLATINUM	Get all other trophies.	—	Platinum

W

SECRET ACHIEVEMENTS & TROPHIES

NAME	GOAL/REQUIREMENT	POINT VALUE	TROPHY VALUE
Stay Together, Stay Safe	5 Survivors Were Killed While Scavenging	10	Bronze
The Hunted Becomes the Hunter	Killed 5 Walkers in the Cabot Ridge Creek Bed	10	Bronze
You're Doing It Wrong	Perished 13 Times	10	Bronze

WALL-E

The following cheats will disable saving. The five possible characters starting with Wall-E and going down are: Wall-E, Auto, EVE, M-O, GEL-A Steward.

ALL BONUS FEATURES UNLOCKED

Select Cheats from the Bonus Features menu and enter Wall-E, Auto, EVE, GEL-A Steward.

ALL GAME CONTENT UNLOCKED

Select Cheats from the Bonus Features menu and enter M-O, Auto, GEL-A Steward, EVE.

ALL SINGLE PLAYER LEVELS UNLOCKED

Select Cheats from the Bonus Features menu and enter Auto, GEL-A Steward, M-O, Wall-E.

ALL MULTIPLAYER MAPS UNLOCKED

Select Cheats from the Bonus Features menu and enter EVE, M-O, Wall-E, Auto.

ALL HOLIDAY COSTUMES UNLOCKED

Select Cheats from the Bonus Features menu and enter Auto, Auto, GEL-A Steward, GEL-A Steward.

ALL MULTIPLAYER COSTUMES UNLOCKED

Select Cheats from the Bonus Features menu and enter GEL-A Steward, Wall-E, M-O, Auto.

UNLIMITED HEALTH UNLOCKED

Select Cheats from the Bonus Features menu and enter Wall-E, M-O, Auto, M-O.

WALL-E: MAKE ANY CUBE AT ANY TIME

Select Cheats from the Bonus Features menu and enter Auto, M-O, Auto, M-O.

WALL-EVE: MAKE ANY CUBE AT ANY TIME

Select Cheats from the Bonus Features menu and enter M-O, GEL-A Steward, EVE, EVE.

WALL-E WITH A LASER GUN AT ANY TIME

Select Cheats from the Bonus Features menu and enter Wall-E, EVE, EVE, Wall-E.

WALL-EVE WITH A LASER GUN AT ANY TIME

Select Cheats from the Bonus Features menu and enter GEL-A Steward, EVE, M-O, Wall-E.

WALL-E: PERMANENT SUPER LASER UPGRADE

Select Cheats from the Bonus Features menu and enter Wall-E, Auto, EVE, M-O.

EVE: PERMANENT SUPER LASER UPGRADE

Select Cheats from the Bonus Features menu and enter EVE, Wall-E, Wall-E, Auto.

CREDITS

Select Cheats from the Bonus Features menu and enter Auto, Wall-E, GEL-A Steward, M-O.

KILL ALL

Select Cheats and then Secret Codes. Enter BOTOFWAR.

UNDETECTED BY ENEMIES

Select Cheats and then Secret Codes. Enter STEALTHARMOR.

LASERS CHANGE COLORS

Select Cheats and then Secret Codes. Enter RAINBOWLAZER.

CUBES ARE EXPLOSIVE

Select Cheats and then Secret Codes. Enter EXPLOSIVEWORLD.

LIGHTEN DARK AREAS

Select Cheats and then Secret Codes. Enter GLOWINTHEDARK.

GOGGLES

Select Cheats and then Secret Codes. Enter BOTOFMYSTERY.

GOLD TRACKS

Select Cheats and then Secret Codes. Enter GOLDENTRACKS.

THE WARRIORS

100% COMPLETION IN STORY MODE

During a game, press L, Select, ●, Down, L, Right.

COMPLETE CURRENT MISSION

During a game, press Down, ●, ✖, Select, R, Left.

UNLIMITED HEALTH

During a game, press Up, ●, R, Select, ✖, L.

UPGRADES STAMINA

During a game, press ✖, L, Down, ●, Up, ✖.

UNLIMITED RAGE

During a game, press ●, ●, ●, Select, ✖, Left.

BRASS KNUCKLES

During a game, press ●, ●, ●, L, Select, ●.

HANDCUFFS

During a game, press ✖, Up, Select, L, L.

HAND CUFF KEYS

During a game, press Left, ✖, ✖, R, L, Down.

KNIFE

During a game, press Down, Down, Select, Up, Up, L.

MACHETE

During a game, press L, ✖, R(x2), Select, R.

UNBREAKABLE BAT

During a game, press L, L, ●, Up, ●, Select.

ALL DEALERS

During a game, press right, R, ●, ✖, Select, ●.

UPGRADE FLASH CAPACITY

During a game, press L, ✖, R, L, L, ●.

99 CREDITS IN ARMIES OF THE NIGHT

During a game of Armie of the Night, press Up, Up, Down, Down, Left, Right.

WHAT DID I DO TO DESERVE THIS, MY LORD!? 2

PSP

WHAT DID I DO TO DESERVE THIS, MY LORD!?

At the Title screen, press L, R, L, R, L, R, L, R, L, R to play the first What Did I Do to Deserve This, My Lord!?

WHAT DID I NOT DO TO DESERVE THIS, MY LORD!?

After entering the previous code and the game loads, enter the same code again at the Title screen. This unlocks the Hard Mode of What Did I Do to Deserve This, My Lord!?.

WHERE'S MY WATER?

MOBILE

HIDDEN PLANETARIUM LEVEL

Go to the Achievements screen and scroll all the way to the top. Continue to scroll up until you see a drawing of a planet. Tap it to enter the level.

JELLY CAR BONUS LEVEL

If Jelly Car is installed on your device, view the credits. When a Jelly Car goes by, tap it to unlock this level.

COLLECTION SCREEN EASTER EGG

Go to the Collection screen and scroll all the way to the bottom. Continue to scroll and you will see someone carved a message into the wall.

EMBARRASSED ACHIEVEMENT

Clicking on Swampy during a level causes him to perform a random action. If he hides behind the curtain, this achievement is earned.

WII PARTY

NINTENDO WII

SPOT THE SNEAK IN MINI-GAMES

Play all of the 4-player mini-games.

WII SPORTS

NINTENDO WII

BOWLING BALL COLOR

After selecting your Mii, hold the following direction on the D-pad and press A at the warning screen:

DIRECTION	COLOR
Up	Blue
Right	Gold
Down	Green
Left	Red

NO HUD IN GOLF

Hold 2 as you select a course to disable the power meter, map, and wind speed meter.

BLUE TENNIS COURT

After selecting your Mii, hold 2 and press A at the warning screen.

WII SPORTS RESORT

MODIFY EVENTS

At the Select a Mii screen, hold 2 while pressing A while on "OK." This will make the following modifications to each event.

EVENT	MODIFICATION
Air Sports Island Flyover	No balloons or I points
Air Sports Skydiving	Play intro event
Archery	More difficult; no aiming reticule
Basketball Pickup Game	Nighttime
Frisbee Golf	No wind display or distance
Golf	No wind display or distance
Swordplay Duel	Evening
Table Tennis Match	11-point match

WIPEOUT: IN THE ZONE

AVATAR AWARDS

AWARD	EARNED BY
Wipeout Life Jacket	At the main menu, press Left, B, Down, Y, A, B, Right, Up.
Wipeout Safety Helmet	At the main menu, press Y, A, B, Up, Down, Left, Y, Right.

WIPEOUT: THE GAME

JOHN ANDERSON ALTERNATE OUTFIT

Play a single player game.

MAD COWGIRL, VALLEY GIRL (SECOND OUTFIT) AND GRASSHOPPER

Play a multiplayer game.

CHEF MUTTEN

Defeat Wipeout Zone within 1:00.

WIPEOUT 2

AVATAR AWARDS

AVATAR	EARNED BY
Winter Vest	Complete episode 6 to unlock this sweet avatar item.
Ice Helmet	Complete episode 8 to unlock this stylish avatar item.
Snow Helmet	Complete episode 8 to unlock this stylish avatar item.

WIPEOUT 2048

BOOST AT START

Use turbo just as the timer reaches Go.

THE WITCHER 2: ASSASSINS OF KINGS

ACHIEVEMENTS

NAME	GOAL/REQUIREMENT	POINT VALUE
To Aedirn!	Complete Chapter 1.	5
Alea Iacta Est	Complete Chapter 2.	10
Once Ain't Enough	Complete Chapter 3.	15
Apprentice	Use alchemy to brew five potions or oils.	10
Master Alchemist	Acquire the Mutant ability.	10
The Butcher of Blaviken	Kill 500 foes.	30
Miser	Collect 10000 orens.	10
Focus	Perform three successful ripostes in a row.	30
Craftsman	Hire a craftsman to create an item.	10
Pest Control	Finish all quests involing the destruction of monster nests.	20
Torn Asunder!	Kill more than one opponent using a single exploding bomb.	15
Gambler	Win an arm wrestling match, a dice poker game and a fist fight.	15
Gladiator	Defeat all opponents in the Kaedweni arena.	15
Madman	Finish the game while playing at the Dark difficulty level.	100
Journeyman	Achieve character level 10.	10
Guru	Achieve character level 35.	50
Master of Magic	Acquire the Sense of Magic ability.	10
Mutant!	Enhance abilities using mutagens at least five times.	30
Last Man Standing	Survive your 30th fight in the Arena	15
Perfectionist	Kill 10 foes in a row without losing any Vitality.	15
Poker!	Roll five-of-a-kind at dice poker.	30
Tried-and-True	Survive your 5th fight in the Arena	10
The Fugitive	Complete the Prologue.	5
Ricochet	Kill a foe by deflecting his own arrow at him.	10
Swordmaster	Acquire the Combat Acumen ability.	10
To Be Continued...	Finish the game at any difficulty level.	50
Threesome	Kill three foes at once by performing a group finisher.	15

SECRET ACHIEVEMENTS

NAME	GOAL/REQUIREMENT	POINT VALUE
Avenger	Finish the game by killing Letho.	30
Backbone	Craft a suit of armor from elements of the kayran's carapace.	20
Being Witcher George	Kill the dragon.	20
Fat Man	Kill the draug.	15
Eagle Eye	Hit Count Etcheverry using the ballista.	10
Heartbreaker	Seduce Ves.	10
Kingmaker	Help Roche rescue Anais from the Kaedweni camp.	15

NAME	GOAL/REQUIREMENT	POINT VALUE
Dragonheart	Spare or save Saskia.	20
Librarian	Find all additional information about the insane asylum's history.	30
Necromancer	Relive all of Auckes's memories in Dethmold's vision.	50
Old Friends	Finish the game by sparing Letho.	30
Sensitive Guy	Save Síle from dying in the unstable portal.	10
Intimidator	Intimidate someone.	15
Man of the Shadows	Successfully sneak through Loredo's garden and find the component of the kayran trap.	15
Black Ops	Sneak through the lower camp without raising the alarm.	20
Spellbreaker	Help Iorveth find the dagger needed to free Saskia from the spell that holds her.	15
Reasons of State	Stop Roche from killing Henselt.	15
Kayranslayer	Kill the kayran.	10
Artful Dodger	Cut off a tentacle using the kayran trap.	30
Tourist	Tour the camp with Zyvik.	10
Friend of Trolls	Spare all trolls in the game.	15
Trollslayer	Kill all the trolls in the game.	30
Witch Hunter	Leave Síle to die in the unstable portal.	10

WOLFENSTEIN

ACHIEVEMENTS & TROPHIES

NAME	GOAL/REQUIREMENT	POINT VALUE	TROPHY VALUE
Safe Keeping	Finish a match on Bank, spending the majority of your time on the winning team. (1 min minimum)	10	Bronze
Route Canal	Finish a match on Canals, spending the majority of your time on the winning team. (1 min minimum)	10	Bronze
Chemical Burn	Finish a match on Chemical, spending the majority of your time on the winning team. (1 min minimum)	10	Bronze
Facilitated	Finish a match on Facility, spending the majority of your time on the winning team. (1 min minimum)	10	Bronze
Hospitalized	Finish a match on Hospital, spending the majority of your time on the winning team. (1 min minimum)	10	Bronze
Mind your Manors	Finish a match on Manor, spending the majority of your time on the winning team. (1 min minimum)	10	Bronze
Pirate Radio	Finish a match on Rooftops, spending the majority of your time on the winning team. (1 min minimum)	10	Bronze
Shock and Awe	Finish a match on Tesla, spending the majority of your time on the winning team. (1 min minimum)	10	Bronze

NAME	GOAL/REQUIREMENT	POINT VALUE	TROPHY VALUE
Test Subject	Use every Veil ability once in multiplayer.	10	Bronze
Veilophile	Spend 5 minutes in the Veil in multiplayer.	10	Bronze
Ley Vacuum	Suck up 5 Veil Pools' worth of Veil energy in multiplayer.	10	Bronze
Surgical Striker	Kill 200 enemy players using the Veil Strike in multiplayer.	30	Silver
Sneaky Pete	Kill 100 enemy players with the Satchel Charge in multiplayer.	30	Silver
Unholy Lifeline	Revive 250 teammates, including 10 revives in a single match in multiplayer.	30	Silver
Focal Point	Restore 5000 points of health to teammates using the Healing Aura in multiplayer.	30	Silver
Quartermaster	Give 100 Health Packs to teammates in multiplayer.	30	Silver
Run-gineer	Use Veil Speed for 30 minutes in multiplayer.	30	Silver
Engineering Corps	Complete 30 primary objectives and 50 secondary objectives in multiplayer.	30	Silver
Beatdown	Kill 50 enemies with melee attacks in a single player campaign.	30	Bronze
Bubble Boy	Block 1000 shots with Shield power in a single player campaign.	20	Bronze
Buster	Destroy 1000 breakable objects in a single player campaign.	20	Bronze
Conservationist	Complete a story mission in the single player campaign without reloading a gun.	30	Silver
Endgame	Finish the single player campaign on any difficulty.	10	Bronze
Gadget Freak	Purchase all the upgrades for one of your weapons in the single player campaign.	20	Bronze
Game Hunter	Kill an enemy of every type in a single player campaign.	10	Bronze
Gold Digger	Collect all the valuables in a single player campaign.	30	Silver
Gun Nut	Collect all the weapons in a single player campaign.	10	Bronze
Honorary Geist	Spend two hours in the Veil in a single player campaign.	20	Bronze
Nerd Rage	Complete the single player campaign on Hard or Über difficulty.	20	Silver
Librarian	Collect all the Tomes of Power in a single player campaign.	20	Bronze
Man About Town	Complete all the Downtown missions in a single player campaign.	20	Bronze
Blitzkrieg	Complete the single player campaign in under 12 hours.	30	Silver
Master Spy	Collect all the Intel in a single player campaign.	20	Bronze
Monitor Tan	Collect every collectible in a single player campaign.	30	Silver
Newbie	Complete the Train Station mission in a single player campaign.	10	Bronze
Rampage	Kill 200 enemies with Empower in a single player campaign.	20	Bronze

NAME	GOAL/REQUIREMENT	POINT VALUE	TROPHY VALUE
Single Quarter	Complete the single player campaign with less than three deaths.	30	Silver
Slumming	Complete all the Midtown missions in a single player campaign.	10	Bronze
Super Soldier	Complete the single player campaign on Über difficulty.	30	Gold
Time Out	Use the Mire power for more than an hour in a single player campaign.	20	Bronze
Warchest	Collect more than $30,000 in a single player campaign.	20	Bronze
Enemies in a Barrel	Kill 3 floating enemies.	20	Bronze
Career Soldier	Reach Rank 25 in multiplayer.	15	Bronze
Das Big Man	Reach Rank 50 in multiplayer.	15	Bronze
Boot Camp	Get a kill with each Soldier weapon, the Satchel Charge and Veil Strike in multiplayer.	30	Bronze
Heavy-Handed	Kill 200 enemy players with either the Panzerschreck or the Flammenwerfer in multiplayer.	30	Silver
Med School	Revive a player, supply a Health Pack, and heal someone using Healing Aura in multiplayer.	30	Bronze
Basic Training	Complete a primary objective, supply an Ammo Pack, and use Veil Speed once in multiplayer.	30	Bronze
Johnny-on-the-spot	Give 100 Ammo Packs to teammates in multiplayer.	30	Bronze

WONDERBOOK: BOOK OF SPELLS

PLAYSTATION 3

TROPHIES

NAME	GOAL/REQUIREMENT	TROPHY VALUE
Accio!	Successfully cast the Summoning Charm.	Bronze
Aguamenti!	Successfully cast the Water-Making Spell.	Bronze
Alohomora!	Successfully cast the Unlocking Charm.	Bronze
Aparecium!	Successfully cast the Revealing Charm.	Bronze
Budding Herbologist	Re-pot the Mandrakes in the Levitation Charm practice.	Silver
Buried Treasure	Find some treasure buried by the Nifflers in the Gouging Spell practice.	Silver
By any means...	Pass Chapter 4 test and prove you know the fourth set of wizard values.	Gold
Checkmate	Summon the wizard chess pieces in the Summoning Charm practice.	Silver
Defodio!	Successfully cast the Gouging Spell.	Bronze
Diffindo!	Successfully cast the Severing Charm.	Bronze
Duellist	Defeat the wizards using the dueling spells in the practices for Shield Charm and Disarming Charm.	Silver
Expecto Patronum!	Successfully cast the Patronus Charm.	Bronze
Expelliarmus!	Successfully cast the Disarming Charm.	Bronze
Extra pumpkin pie	Successfully cast the Engorgement Charm and Shrinking Charm.	Bronze
Feathered friends	Successfully cast the Bird-Conjuring Charm.	Bronze
Fight fire with fire	Defeat the dragon in the Fire-Making Spell practice.	Silver

NAME	GOAL/REQUIREMENT	TROPHY VALUE
First Edition	Display the virtues required to master the 'Book of Spells'.	Platinum
Hard knocks	Successfully cast the Hardening Charm.	Bronze
If you've a ready mind	Pass Chapter 2 test and prove you know the second set of wizard values.	Gold
Impedimenta!	Successfully cast the Impediment Jinx.	Bronze
Incendio!	Successfully cast the Fire-Making Spell.	Bronze
Light relief	Fend off the Devil's Snare in the Wand-Lighting Charm practice.	Silver
Lumos!	Successfully cast the Wand-Lighting Charm.	Bronze
No need for Spellotape	Successfully cast the Mending Charm.	Bronze
On Solid Ground	Foil the Nifflers in the Hardening Charm practice.	Silver
Pick on someone your own size	Help the Knarls teach the Gnomes a lesson in the Engorgement Charm and Shrinking Charm practice.	Silver
Practical Household Magic	Successfully cast the Scouring Charm.	Bronze
Protego!	Successfully cast the Shield Charm.	Bronze
Pure nerve	Pass Chapter 5 test and prove you know the final set of wizard values.	Gold
Reducto!	Successfully cast the Reductor Curse	Bronze
Stop right there!	Stop the Gnome in the Impediment Jinx practice.	Silver
Stupefy!	Successfully cast the Stunning Spell.	Bronze
Swish and Flick	Successfully cast the Levitation Charm.	Bronze
Teach us something please	Pass Chapter 1 test and prove you know the first set of wizard values.	Gold
True Patronus	Make your Patronus appear in the safety of the classroom.	Silver
Unafraid of toil	Pass Chapter 3 test and prove you know the third set of wizard values.	Gold

WORLD CHAMPIONSHIP POKER

NINTENDO 3DS

UNLOCK CASINOS

At the Title screen, press Y, X, Y, B, L, R. Then press the following direction:

DIRECTION	CASINO
Left	Amazon
Right	Nebula
Down	Renaissance

WORLD OF GOO

MOBILE

WHISTLE ITEM

Complete Leap Hole level.

WORLD OF GOO CORPORATION MINI GAME

Complete Hang Low level.

A WORLD OF KEFLINGS

XBOX 360

AVATAR AWARDS

AWARD	EARNED BY
Baby Dragon	Make friends with the baby dragon released from an egg in the Ice Kingdom.
Winged Hat Of Kefkimo	Talk to the Chief at the great Hall in the Ice Kingdom.

WORLD OF OUTLAWS: SPRINT CARS

PLAYSTATION 3

$5,000,000

Enter your name as CHICMCHIM.

ALL DRIVERS

Enter your name as MITYMASTA.

ALL TRACKS

Enter your name as JOEYJOEJOE.

WORMS ULTIMATE MAYHEM

XBOX 360

AVATAR AWARDS

AVATAR	EARNED BY
Ultimate Mayhem Tee	Earn any Achievement in Worms: Ultimate Mayhem.
Worm Tee	Locate the 5 hidden Easter Eggs in Worms: Ultimate Mayhem.

WRC: FIA WORLD RALLY CHAMPIONSHIP

PSP

UNLOCK EVERYTHING

Create a new profile with the name PADLOCK.

EXTRA AVATARS

Create a new profile with the name UGLYMUGS.

GHOST CAR

Create a new profile with the name SPOOKY.

SUPERCHARGER

Create a new profile with the name MAXPOWER.

TIME TRIAL GHOST CARS

Create a new profile with the name AITRIAL.

BIRD CAMERA

Create a new profile with the name dovecam.

REVERSES CONTROLS

Create a new profile with the name REVERSE.

WRECK-IT RALPH

CHEAT CODES

Go to the Cheat Menu and select Enter Code, then enter these codes to unlock cheats.

EFFECT	CODE
Frozen Bugs	314142
Invincibility	132136
One Hit Kills	162226

WWE '12

WWE ATTITUDE ERA HEAVYWEIGHT CHAMPIONSHIP

Select Options from My WWE. Next, choose Cheat Codes and enter OhHellYeah!.

WWE '13

ACHIEVEMENTS & TROPHIES

NAME	GOAL/REQUIREMENT	POINT VALUE	TROPHY VALUE
A winner is you!	Win 10 ranked matches.	10	Bronze
The Streak Ends	Beat The Undertaker at WrestleMania with a Custom Superstar on Legend difficulty (single player).	50	Gold
King of the world	Achieve the maximum rank on Xbox LIVE.	50	Gold
Gold standard	Earn the WWE, WCW, and ECW Championship belts with a single Superstar.	45	Silver
Invincible man	Win at least 20 matches on Hard difficulty or higher (single player).	40	Silver
A man who wastes no opportunity	Cash in a Money in the Bank and win using a Custom Superstar in WWE Universe (single player).	35	Silver
Established veteran	Achieve the rank 10 on Xbox LIVE.	30	Silver
Berserker	Break a total of 50 tables, ladders, and chairs by attacking with them (single player).	25	Bronze
Mr. Money in the Bank	Win Money in the Bank using a Custom Superstar in WWE Universe mode (single player).	30	Silver
Comeback!	Successfully perform a Comeback Move (single player).	20	Bronze
A once in a lifetime event	Appear in Wrestlemania using a Custom Superstar in WWE Universe (single player)	20	Bronze
A winning combination!	Use a wake-up taunt, land a Finisher and immediately pin your opponent (single player).	25	Bronze
One of history's greats	Exhibition (Legend difficulty) – Defeat a Superstar with his Attitude Era version (single player).	25	Bronze

NAME	GOAL/REQUIREMENT	POINT VALUE	TROPHY VALUE
I just keep evolving!	Exhibition (Legend difficulty) – With a Superstar, defeat his Attitude Era version (single player).	20	Bronze
A legend begins	Win at least one match on Hard difficulty or higher (single player).	20	Bronze
Fighting smart	Exhibition – Attack the same body part 10 or more times in a single match (single player).	15	Bronze
Negotiatior	Exhibition – Force an opponent to quit in an "I Quit" Match (single player).	15	Bronze
All original baby!	Compete as a Custom Superstar in a Custom Arena for a Custom Championship.	15	Bronze
The ring is my home!	Play a match in an arena created in Create an Arena mode.	15	Bronze
Rising star	Achieve the rank 5 on Xbox LIVE.	20	Bronze
Made-up original story	Create a story including a Custom Superstar or a Custom Arena.	15	Bronze
Yes! Yes! Yes!	Use Daniel Bryan to defeat Sheamus (single player, Exhibition Mode only).	10	Bronze
Reached the ropes!	Crawl to the ropes during a submission (Single Player).	10	Bronze
A Superstar is born!	Win a match using a Custom Superstar in WWE Universe mode (single player).	10	Bronze
Arena designer	Create an arena in Create an Arena mode.	10	Bronze
Check out my Entrance Video!	Create an entrance movie in Create an Entrance mode	10	Bronze
Paint tool magician	Use the paint tool to create and add an original logo to any original creation.	10	Bronze
This is special!	Create a front, top-rope, and corner special move.	10	Bronze
The champ is here!	Create an original championship belt in the Championship Editor.	10	Bronze
Create and destroy	Exhibition (Title Match) – Attack your opponent with a custom belt (single player).	15	Bronze
Awesome!	Take a screenshot in Create a Highlight mode.	5	Bronze
A fresh beginning	Play in an Xbox LIVE match (Player match/Ranked match)	5	Bronze
Welcome to the creators' circle	Your Community Creations content has been reviewed at least 5 times.	5	Bronze
Critic	Review 5 or more user-created content items in Community Creations.	5	Bronze

SECRET ACHIEVEMENTS & TROPHIES

NAME	GOAL/REQUIREMENT	POINT VALUE	TROPHY VALUE
Off Script scenario cleared!	Clear the "Off Script" chapter.	45	Silver
Road to WrestleMania XV cleared!	Clear the "Road to WrestleMania XV" chapter.	40	Silver

W

NAME	GOAL/REQUIREMENT	POINT VALUE	TROPHY VALUE
Holy sh**t!!	Break the ring with an OMG Move (single player).	40	Silver
Mankind scenario cleared!	Clear the "Mankind" chapter.	30	Silver
Watch out!	Successfully reverse a Finisher (single player).	30	Silver
The Great One scenario cleared!	Clear the "The Great One" chapter.	25	Bronze
It's like a car crash!	Exhibition – Break the barricade in 2 places in the same match (single player).	20	Bronze
You can't let down your guard	Land a Catch Finisher (single player, Exhibition Mode only).	20	Bronze
Brothers of Destruction cleared!	Clear the "Brothers of Destruction" chapter.	20	Bronze
The rattlesnake is coming!?	Win by throwing an opponent through the window in Backstage Brawl (single player).	20	Bronze
Austin 3:16 scenario cleared!	Clear the "Austin 3:16" chapter.	15	Bronze
Ring hooligan	Break a total of 20 tables, ladders, and chairs by attacking with them (single player).	15	Bronze
Oh my!	Break the announcer table with an OMG Move (single player).	15	Bronze
Rise of D-X scenario cleared!	Clear the "Rise of D-X" chapter.	10	Bronze

WWE ALL STARS

NINTENDO 3DS

ALL CHARACTERS AND RING GEAR

At the main menu, press Left, Right, Left, Down, Up, Left, Right, Up.

PLAYSTATION 3

UNLOCK ARENAS, WRESTLERS, AND ATTIRE

At the main menu, press Left, ●, Down, Left, ●, ●, Left, ●, ●, Down, Right, ●, Left, Up, ●, Right.

AUSTIN AND PUNK ATTIRES

At the main menu, press Left, Left, Right, Right, Up, Down, Up, Down.

ROBERTS AND ORTON ATTIRES

At the main menu, press Up, Down, Left, Right, Up, Up, Down, Down.

SAVAGE AND MORRISON ATTIRES

At the main menu, press Down, Left, Up, Right, Right, Up, Left, Down.

PSP

UNLOCK EVERYTHING

At the main menu, press Left, Right, Left, Down, Up, Left, Right, Up.

STEVE AUSTIN AND CM PUNK ATTIRES

At the main menu, press Left, Left, Right, Right, Up, Down, Up, Down.

RANDY ORTON AND JAKE ROBERTS ATTIRES

At the main menu, press Up, Down, Left, Right, Up, Up, Down, Down.

JOHN MORRISON AND RANDY SAVAGE ATTIRES

At the main menu, press Down, Left, Up, Right, Right, Up, Left, Down.

UNLOCK ARENAS, WRESTLERS, AND ATTIRE

At the main menu, press Left, Y, Down, Left, Y, X, Left, X, Y, Down, Right, X, Left, Up, X, Right.

AUSTIN AND PUNK ATTIRES

At the main menu, press Left, Left, Right, Right, Up, Down, Up, Down.

ROBERTS AND ORTON ATTIRES

At the main menu, press Up, Down, Left, Right, Up, Up, Down, Down.

SAVAGE AND MORRISON ATTIRES

At the main menu, press Down, Left, Up, Right, Right, Up, Left, Down.

ACHIEVEMENTS & TROPHIES

NAME	GOAL/REQUIREMENT	POINT VALUE	TROPHY VALUE
Running Wild	Performed 50 successful finishers in any mode over the course of the game.	20	Silver
Born to Fly	Performed 10 successful regular aerial moves in a single match.	20	Bronze
Five Moves of Doom	Executed five signature moves in a single match.	20	Bronze
Dominating	Won a match against the CPU without losing any health.	20	Bronze
Layeth the Smacketh Down!	Won a match in under 2 minutes.	20	Bronze
Punch Drunk	Landed at least 100 strikes in a single match in any mode.	20	Bronze
Man of 1000 Holds	Won a match without using any strikes.	25	Bronze
Slobberknocker	Won a match without using any grapples.	25	Silver
Make Them Humble	Won 25 matches by knockout.	25	Bronze
Five Star Rating	Achieved a five star rating while facing the CPU.	20	Bronze
Mark of Excellence	Earned a gold medal while facing the CPU.	20	Bronze
The Apex Predator	Completed the Superstars Path of Champions.	20	Bronze
Breaking the Rules	Completed the Tag Team Path of Champions.	20	Bronze
Facing the Deadman	Completed the Legends Path of Champions.	20	Bronze
The New Generation	Defeated a Legend with a Superstar.	10	Bronze
Showing Them How It's Done	Defeated a Superstar with a Legend.	10	Bronze
Rising Star	Completed Path of Champions with a created Superstar.	20	Bronze
Reversal of Fortune	Performed at least 5 grapple reversals during a match.	15	Bronze
Chain Gang	Performed a combo at least 5 moves in length.	15	Bronze
The Next WWE Superstar	Made a created Superstar.	10	Bronze
Old School	Completed all Fantasy Warfare matches as a WWE Legend.	15	Silver
Legend Killer	Completed all Fantasy Warfare matches as a WWE Superstar.	15	Silver
Over the Top	Won a Steel Cage match.	15	Bronze
Suck It	Won a Tornado Tag Team match as Triple H and Shawn Michaels.	20	Bronze

CHEATS, ACHIEVEMENTS, AND TROPHIES

W

NAME	GOAL/REQUIREMENT	POINT VALUE	TROPHY VALUE
Mega Powers	Won a Tornado Tag Team match as Hulk Hogan and Randy Savage.	20	Bronze
The New Face of Cyberspace	Defeated a created Superstar in an Xbox LIVE match with your own created Superstar.	20	Bronze
Main Eventer	Won 50 Xbox LIVE matches.	50	Gold
You Can't See Me!	Won 10 consecutive Xbox LIVE matches.	50	Gold
Comeback of the Year	Won a match when your Superstar is at zero health.	20	Bronze
Beating the Odds	Won a Handicap match.	15	Bronze
Totally Extreme!	Won an Extreme Rules match.	15	Bronze
He's Got a Chair!	Landed at least 10 successful strikes with an object in a single match.	20	Bronze
In the Spotlight	Won an Xbox LIVE match.	15	Bronze
Last Man Standing	Won a Fatal 4 Way Elimination match.	15	Bronze
The Champ is Here!	Completed all three Path of Champions as John Cena.	50	Silver
Enhancement Talent	Won 10 Xbox LIVE matches.	20	Bronze
Mid Carder	Won 25 Xbox LIVE matches.	25	Bronze
The Bottom Line	Defeated the entire WWE All Stars roster with a single created Superstar.	50	Silver
The King of Kings	Defeated the entire WWE All Stars roster as Triple H.	50	Silver
The Ultimate Achievement	Defeated the entire Roster and all three Path of Champions as The Ultimate Warrior.	75	Gold

SECRET ACHIEVEMENTS & TROPHIES

NAME	GOAL/REQUIREMENT	POINT VALUE	TROPHY VALUE
Winner by Default	Won an Xbox LIVE match due to opponent's disqualification.	10	Bronze
Attitude Problem	Got disqualified in three consecutive matches.	10	Bronze
Booyaka Booyaka	Defeated Andre the Giant and Big Show in a Handicap Match as Rey Mysterio.	10	Bronze
I'm Your Papi!	Defeated Rey Mysterio in a Steel Cage match as Eddie Guerrero.	10	Bronze
The Pride of Scotland	Won a Tornado Tag Team match as Roddy Piper and Drew McIntyre.	10	Bronze

WWE SMACKDOWN VS. RAW 2010

NINTENDO WII/PS3

THE ROCK
Select Cheat Codes from the Options and enter The Great One.

VINCE'S OFFICE AND DIRT SHEET FOR BACKSTAGE BRAWL
Select Cheat Codes from the Options menu and enter BonusBrawl.

HBK/SHAWN MICHAEL'S ALTERNATE COSTUME
Select Cheat Codes from the Options menu and enter Bow Down.

JOHN CENA'S ALTERNATE COSTUME
Select Cheat Codes from the Options menu and enter CENATION.

RANDY ORTON'S ALTERNATE COSTUME
Select Cheat Codes from the Options menu and enter ViperRKO.

SANTINO MARELLA'S ALTERNATE COSTUME
Select Cheat Codes from the Options menu and enter Milan Miracle.

TRIPLE H'S ALTERNATE COSTUME
Select Cheat Codes from the Options menu and enter Suck It!.

XBOX 360/PS3

ACHIEVEMENTS & TROPHIES

NAME	GOAL/REQUIREMENT	POINT VALUE	TROPHY VALUE
Story Designer	Create an original story using WWE STORY DESIGNER Mode.	20	Bronze
2010 Hall of Fame Nominee	Induct a Superstar into the HALL OF FAME.	100	Gold
A Showman Like No Other	Have a total of 20 or more 5-star rated matches in your overall match history.	50	Silver
Mickie James Story	Complete the MICKIE JAMES story in ROAD TO WRESTLEMANIA mode.	20	Silver
Edge Story	Complete the EDGE story in ROAD TO WRESTLEMANIA mode.	20	Silver
HBK Story	Complete the HBK story in ROAD TO WRESTLEMANIA mode.	20	Silver
Orton Story	Complete the ORTON story in ROAD TO WRESTLEMANIA mode.	20	Silver
Brand Warfare Story	Complete the BRAND WARFARE story in ROAD TO WRESTLEMANIA mode.	20	Silver
Created Superstar Story	Complete the CREATE A SUPERSTAR story in ROAD TO WRESTLEMANIA mode.	20	Silver
Nothing More to Collect	Unlock all the playable characters and bonus items.	100	Gold
Face on the Big Screen	Convert a HIGHLIGHT REEL into an entrance movie.	15	Bronze
Developmental Graduate	Complete the TRAINING CHECKLIST.	50	Silver
Career Growth	Increase the overall rating of a CREATED SUPERSTAR character to a 90 or above.	50	Silver
Check Out the New Threads	Create ALTERNATE ATTIRE for a CREATED SUPERSTAR and new THREADS for a WWE SUPERSTAR.	15	Bronze

CHEATS, ACHIEVEMENTS, AND TROPHIES

NAME	GOAL/REQUIREMENT	POINT VALUE	TROPHY VALUE
Finisher of the Year Candidate	Create a dive finisher, in Create A Finisher mode, and use it in a match (single player only).	20	Silver
Ask Him Ref!	Win 10 matches by submission (single player only).	20	Silver
Ahead of the Pack	Win as tentative Champion from start to end in CHAMPIONSHIP SCRAMBLE. (single player only)	50	Silver
Royal Rumble Specialist	Win a 30-Man ROYAL RUMBLE as the first entrant without changing Superstars (single player only).	100	Gold
And STILL Champion...	Defend a Title in a Championship Scramble match on Legend difficulty (single player only).	100	Gold
Shoulders to the Mat	Win 50 matches by pinfall (single player only).	20	Silver
A Grappling Machine	In one match, perform all 16 STRONG GRAPPLE moves on your opponent (single player only).	20	Silver

SECRET ACHIEVEMENTS & TROPHIES

NAME	GOAL/REQUIREMENT	POINT VALUE	TROPHY VALUE
New Superstar Initiative	Create a SUPERSTAR in CREATE A SUPERSTAR Mode.	15	Bronze
An Original Design	Create an original image using the PAINT TOOL.	15	Bronze
Intermediate Technician	Succeed at a cumulative total of 50 reversals (single player only).	20	Silver
Technical Wizardry	Succeed at a cumulative total of 100 reversals (single player only).	100	Gold

WWE SMACKDOWN VS. RAW 2011

NINTENDO WII

JOHN CENA (ENTRANCE/CIVILIAN)

In My WWE, select Cheat Codes from the Options and enter SLURPEE.

ALL OF RANDY ORTON'S COSTUMES

In My WWE, select Cheat Codes from the Options and enter apexpredator.

TRIBUTE TO THE TROOPS ARENA

In My WWE, select Cheat Codes from the Options and enter 8thannualtribute.

XBOX 360/PS3/PSP

JOHN CENA (ENTRANCE/CIVILIAN)

In My WWE, select Cheat Codes from the Options and enter SLURPEE.

ALL OF RANDY ORTON'S COSTUMES

In My WWE, select Cheat Codes from the Options and enter apexpredator.

TRIBUTE TO THE TROOPS ARENA

In My WWE, select Cheat Codes from the Options and enter 8thannualtribute.

CRUISERWEIGHT TITLE, HARDCORE TITLE, AND MILLION DOLLAR TITLE

In My WWE, select Cheat Codes from the Options and enter Historicalbelts.

ACHIEVEMENTS & TROPHIES

NAME	GOAL/REQUIREMENT	POINT VALUE	TROPHY VALUE
The Excellence of Execution	Defeat 50 opponents using pin combination grapple moves (Offline).	10	Silver
Caught Slipping	Win a match in which you successfully use a leverage pin (Offline).	10	Bronze
Power Of The Punch	Win a match in which you successfully KO an opponent using a strong strike (Offline).	10	Bronze
Backstage Fisticuffs	During a backstage brawl, string 3 environmental grapple combos in succession (Offline).	10	Bronze
Talk About Resilient	Kick out of The Undertaker's Tombstone Piledriver finisher on Legend difficulty (Offline).	20	Silver
For Whom the Bell Tolls	Pin or submit Undertaker in the WrestleMania arena on Legend difficulty (Offline).	20	Silver
Thank You Shawn	Defeat Shawn Michaels in the WrestleMania arena on Legend difficulty as Undertaker (Offline).	20	Silver
THQ Storytellers	Create a story in Story Designer with at least 2 moments.	10	Bronze
Streak Breaker	Complete the Vs. Undertaker Road to WrestleMania story on any difficulty.	50	Silver
Randy's Fired	Complete John Cena's Road to WrestleMania story on any difficulty.	50	Silver
Runaway Champ	Complete Chris Jericho's Road to WrestleMania story on any difficulty.	50	Silver
5-Second Pose	Complete Christian's Road to WrestleMania story on any difficulty.	50	Silver
No More Mystery, Yo	Complete Rey Mysterio's Road to WrestleMania story on any difficulty.	50	Silver
Champion of Champions	Using a created character, hold either the WWE or World Heavyweight title (Offline).	50	Silver
US Champ	Using a created character, win the United States Championship in WWE Universe (Offline).	10	Bronze
Intercontinental Champ	Win the Intercontinental Championship in WWE Universe using a created character (Offline).	10	Bronze
Unified Tag Champs	Win the Unified Tag Team titles in WWE Universe using a created character (Offline).	10	Bronze
Mr. Money in the Bank	Win the Money In The Bank match in WWE Universe using a created character (Offline).	50	Silver
A Successful Cash In	Cash in Money In The Bank in WWE Universe and win using a created character (Offline).	20	Silver
A Student Of The Game	Complete 50% of the tips in the Practice Arena.	10	Bronze
Magna Cum Laude	Complete all of the tips in the Practice Arena.	50	Silver
The Last Man Standing	Win a Royal Rumble match on Xbox LIVE.	100	Gold

CHEATS, ACHIEVEMENTS, AND TROPHIES

W

NAME	GOAL/REQUIREMENT	POINT VALUE	TROPHY VALUE
Way To Contribute	Upload at least one item of created content to each category of Community Creations.	10	Bronze

SECRET ACHIEVEMENTS & TROPHIES

NAME	GOAL/REQUIREMENT	POINT VALUE	TROPHY VALUE
The Magic Number	Win a match in which you successfully pin an opponent (Offline)	10	Bronze
Well Scouted	Reverse an opponent's finishing move (Offline).	10	Bronze
Button Mash Expert	Win a collar and elbow mini-game (Offline).	10	Bronze
Worth Having To Re-Climb	Perform a successful ladder finishing move (Offline).	10	Bronze
That'll Shorten Your Career	During a Hell in a Cell match, perform a wall destroying finisher (Offline).	10	Bronze
Man of 1004 Holds	Perform a total of 1004 signature and finishing moves in any mode of play (offline)	100	Gold
Win Or Lose, At Least You Tried	Play a Royal Rumble match on Xbox LIVE to its conclusion.	20	Silver
Unhealthy Obsession With Wood	Destroy 50 tables (offline)	20	Silver
Sign Of The Times	Create an original crowd sign using the Paint Tool.	10	Bronze
Please Don't Try This at Home	Push an opponent off a ladder, so they fall out of the ring and through a table (Offline)	50	Silver
Creative With The Moves	Create a front, top rope and corner finishing move in Create A Finisher.	10	Bronze
Pinning's Not The Only Way	Win a match in which you successfully use a submission (Offline).	10	Bronze
Original Brand Logo	Create an original brand logo using the Paint Tool.	10	Bronze
One Step Closer To The Gold	Become No#1 contender for any title in WWE Universe using a Created Superstar (offline)	10	Bronze
Check for Splinters	Put an opponent through a table using a corner top grapple move (offline)	10	Bronze
Chairs Upside Your Head	Destroy 50 chairs (Offline).	20	Silver

X-MEN DESTINY

PLAYSTATION 3

JUGGERNAUT SUIT

At the title screen, hold L1 + R1 and press Down, Right, Up, Left, ●, ●.

XBOX 360

JUGGERNAUT SUIT

At the title screen, hold Left Bumper + Right Bumper and press Down, Right, Up, Left, Y, B.

EMMA FROST SUIT

At the title screen, hold Left Bumper + Right Bumper and press Up, Down, Right, Left, B, Y.

X-MEN ORIGINS: WOLVERINE

PLAYSTATION 3

CLASSIC WOLVERINE UNIFORM

During a game, press ✖, ●, ●, ●, ✖, ●, ●, ●, ✖, ●, ●, ●, ●, R3. Note that this code disables trophies.

INVINCIBLE

During a game, press ●, ✖, ●, ✖, ●, ●, ●, ●, ●, ●, ●, R3. Note that this code disables trophies.

INFINITE RAGE

During a game, press ●, ●, ●, ●, ●, ●, ●, ●, ✖, ✖, ●, R3. Note that this code disables trophies.

DOUBLES ENEMY REFLEX POINTS

During a game, press ✖, ✖, ●, ●, ●, ●, ●, ●, ●, ●, ●, ●, ✖, ✖, R3. Note that this code disables trophies.

CLASSIC WOLVERINE CHALLENGE/OUTFIT

Find any two Classic Wolverine action figures to unlock this challenge. Defeat Classic Wolverine in combat to unlock the Classic Wolverine outfit. Note that this code disables trophies.

ORIGINAL WOLVERINE CHALLENGE/OUTFIT

Find any two Original Wolverine action figures to unlock this challenge. Defeat Original Wolverine in combat to unlock the Original Wolverine outfit. Note that this code disables trophies.

X-FORCE WOLVERINE CHALLENGE/OUTFIT

Find any two X-Force Wolverine action figures to unlock this challenge. Defeat X-Force Wolverine in combat to unlock the X-Force Wolverine outfit. Note that this code disables trophies.

XBOX 360

CLASSIC WOLVERINE OUTFIT

During a game, press A, X, B, X, A, Y, A, Y, A, X, B, B, X, R3. This code disables achievements.

DOUBLE ENEMY REFLEX POINTS

During a game, press A, A, X, X, Y, Y, B, B, Y, Y, X, X, A, A, R3. This code disables achievements.

INFINITE RAGE

During a game, press Y, X, X, Y, B, B, Y, A, A, Y, R3. This code disables achievements.

INVINCIBLE

During a game, press X, A, A, X, Y, Y, X, B, B, X, R3. This code disables achievements.

CLASSIC WOLVERINE CHALLENGE/OUTFIT

Find any two Classic Wolverine action figures to unlock this challenge. Defeat Classic Wolverine in combat to unlock the Classic Wolverine outfit.

ORIGINAL WOLVERINE CHALLENGE/OUTFIT

Find any two Original Wolverine action figures to unlock this challenge. Defeat Original Wolverine in combat to unlock the Original Wolverine outfit.

X-FORCE WOLVERINE CHALLENGE/OUTFIT

Find any two X-Force Wolverine action figures to unlock this challenge. Defeat X-Force Wolverine in combat to unlock the X-Force Wolverine outfit.

CHEATS, ACHIEVEMENTS, AND TROPHIES

X

ACHIEVEMENTS &TROPHIES

NAME	GOAL/REQUIREMENT	POINT VALUE	TROPHY VALUE
Getting Started	Killed 100 enemies	10	Bronze
A Day's Work	Killed 500 enemies	20	Bronze
What I Do Best	Killed 2000 enemies	30	Silver
You Can't Hide	Lunged to 250 enemies	20	Bronze
Lunge	Lunged to 25 enemies	10	Bronze
Pounce	Lunged to 100 enemies	15	Bronze
Piggy Back Ride	Lunged to a W.E.N.D.I.G.0 prototype's back	10	Bronze
Quick Killer	Quick Killed 1 enemy	10	Bronze
Efficient Killer	Quick Killed 20 enemies	15	Bronze
Perfect Killer	Quick Killed 3 enemies in a row	20	Bronze
Drop Dead	Killed 10 enemies by throwing them off high areas	10	Bronze
Apprentice	Raised One Combat Reflex to Master Level	10	Bronze
Samurai	Raised All Combat Reflexes to Master Level	25	Silver
Mutant Lover	Raised one Mutagen to level 3	15	Bronze
Astonishing	Found 1/2 of all Dog Tags in the game	20	Bronze
Devil's Brigade	Found all Dog Tags in the game	30	Silver
Defensive	Performed 1 Counter move	10	Bronze
Untouchable	Performed 25 Counter moves	20	Bronze
Catch!	Killed 1 enemy with a reflected projectile	10	Bronze
Boomerang	Killed 25 enemies with a reflected projectile	20	Bronze
Aerial Assault	Performed 10 Air Grabs	10	Bronze
Ultimate Wolverine	Fought 4 W.E.N.D.I.G.0 prototypes at the same time and defeated them at Alkali lake.	15	Bronze
Hot Potato	Light 20 enemies on fire	20	Bronze
Shotgun Epic Fail	Killed 25 Ghosts with their own weapon	15	Bronze
James Howlett	Performed a Wolverine to Wolverine Lunge	15	Bronze
WoW!	You feel cold as you examine the skeleton and read the name "Arthas" etched into the nearby sword	15	Bronze
Aerial Master	Got 6 enemies airborne at once	15	Bronze
Fully Loaded	Maxed out all upgrades	35	Bronze
Slice n' Dice	Killed 6 enemies with a single attack	15	Bronze
Found!	You found a mysterious hatch!	15	Bronze
Slaughter House	Dismembered 100 enemies	15	Bronze
Blender	Killed 200 enemies with Claw Spin	25	Silver
Walking Death	Beat the game on Hard Difficulty	50	Gold
Heightened Senses	Killed 200 enemies in Feral Sense	20	Bronze
Environmentally Friendly	Killed 10 enemies using objects in the environment	15	Bronze
Whatever it Takes	Killed 30 enemies using objects in the environment	20	Bronze

NAME	GOAL/REQUIREMENT	POINT VALUE	TROPHY VALUE
Bloodlust	Killed 50 enemies while in Berserker mode	20	Bronze
Weapon X	Killed 150 enemies while in Berserker mode	25	Bronze
The Cake	You found the cake, yummy!	15	Bronze

SECRET ACHIEVEMENTS

NAME	GOAL/REQUIREMENT	POINT VALUE	TROPHY VALUE
Bar Fight	Defeated Victor Creed (Sabretooth)	30	Silver
Spillway Escape	Escapes from Weapon X	30	Bronze
Helicopter Ride	Defeated David Nord (Agent Zero)	30	Silver

YOU DON'T KNOW JACK

PLAYSTATION 3

ALL EPISODES

At the Episode Select, press Left, Left, Right, Left, ●.

XBOX 360

ALL EPISODES

At the Episode Select, press Left, Left, Right, Left, X.

AVATAR AWARDS

AVATAR	EARNED BY
A Classy Men's T-Shirt	Play any episode and score over $0.
A Trendy Ladies T-Shirt	Play any episode and score over $0.
A Fashionable Men's Pant	Play episode 9 and score over $0.
A Beautiful Ladies Pant	Play episode 9 and score over $0.
A "Bald-Headed" Ski Mask	Play episode 58 score over $0.
Billy O'Brien Replica Dummy	Find the episode 73 wrong answer of the game.

YOU'RE IN THE MOVIES

XBOX 360

ALL TRAILERS AND DIRECTOR'S MODE

At the options screen, press Left Bumper, Right Bumper, Left Bumper, Right Bumper, Y.

YU-GI-OH! GX TAG FORCE 2

PSP

MIDDDAY CONSTELLATION BOOSTER PACK

When buying booster packs, press Up, Up, Down, Down, Left, Right, Left, Right, ✕, ●.

CARD PASSWORDS

CARD	PASSWORD
4-Starred Ladybug of Doom	83994646
7 Colored Fish	23771716
A Cat of Ill Omen	24140059
A Deal With Dark Ruler	06850209
A Feather of the Phoenix	49140998
A Feint Plan	68170903
A Hero Emerges	21597117
A Legendary Ocean	00295517
A Man With Wdjat	51351302
A Rival Appears!	05728014
A Wingbeat of Giant Dragon	28596933
A-Team: Trap Disposal Unit	13026402
Abare Ushioni	89718302
Absolute End	27744077
Absorbing Kid From the Sky	49771608
Abyss Soldier	18318842
Abyssal Designator	89801755
Acid Trap Hole	41356845
Acrobat Monkey	47372349
Adhesion Trap Hole	62325062
Adhesive Explosive	53828396
After the Struggle	25345186
Agido	16135253
Airknight Parshath	18036057
Aitsu	48202661
Alkana Knight Joker	06150044
Alpha the Magnet Warrior	99785935
Altar for Tribute	21070956
Amazon Archer	91869203
Amazoness Archers	67987611
Amazoness Blowpiper	73574678
Amazoness Chain Master	29654737
Amazoness Paladin	47480070
Amazoness Swords Woman	94004268
Amazoness Tiger	10979723
Ambulance Rescueroid	98927491
Ambulanceroid	36378213
Ameba	95174353
Amphibian Beast	67371383
Amphibious Bugroth MK-3	64342551
Amplifier	00303660
An Owl of Luck	23927567
Ancient Elf	93221206
Ancient Gear	31557782
Ancient Gear Beast	10509340
Ancient Gear Cannon	80045583
Ancient Gear Castle	92001300

CARD	PASSWORD
Ancient Gear Drill	67829249
Ancient Gear Golem	83104731
Ancient Gear Soldier	56094445
Ancient Lamp	54912977
Ancient Lizard Warrior	43230671
Andro Sphinx	15013468
Anteatereatingant	13250922
Anti-Aircraft Flower	65064143
Anti-Spell	53112492
Apprentice Magician	09156135
Appropriate	48539234
Aqua Madoor	85639257
Aqua Spirit	40916023
Arcane Archer of the Forest	55001420
Archfiend of Gilfer	50287060
Archfiend Soldier	49881766
Archlord Zerato	18378582
Armaill	53153481
Armed Changer	90374791
Armed Dragon LV 3	00980973
Armed Dragon LV 5	46384672
Armed Dragon LV 7	73879377
Armed Dragon LV10	59464593
Armed Ninja	09076207
Armed Samurai - Ben Kei	84430950
Armor Axe	07180418
Armor Break	79649195
Armored Lizard	15480588
Armored Starfish	17535588
Armored Zombie	20277860
Array of Revealing Light	69296555
Arsenal Bug	42364374
Arsenal Robber	55348096
Arsenal Summoner	85489096
Assault on GHQ	62633180
Astral Barrier	37053871
Asura Priest	02134346
Aswan Apparition	88236094
Atomic Firefly	87340664
Attack and Receive	63689843
Attack Reflector Unit	91989718
Aussa the Earth Charmer	37970940
Autonomous Action Unit	71453557
Avatar of the Pot	99284890
Axe Dragonute	84914462
Axe of Despair	40619825
B. Skull Dragon	11901678
B.E.S. Covered Core	15317640
B.E.S. Crystal Core	22790789
B.E.S. Tetran	44954628

CARD	PASSWORD
Baby Dragon	88819587
Back to Square One	47453433
Backfire	82705573
Backup Soldier	36280194
Bad Reaction to Simochi	40633297
Bait Doll	07165085
Ballista of Rampart Smashing	00242146
Banisher of the Light	61528025
Bark of Dark Ruler	41925941
Barrel Dragon	81480460
Basic Insect	89091579
Battery Charger	61181383
Batteryman AA	63142001
Batteryman C	19733961
Batteryman D	55401221
Battle Footballer	48094997
Battle Ox	05053103
Battle-Scarred	94463200
Bazoo The Soul-Eater	40133511
Beast Soul Swap	35149085
Beaver Warrior	32452818
Beckoning Light	16255442
Beelze Frog	49522489
Begone, Knave	20374520
Behemoth the King of All Animals	22996376
Beiige, Vanguard of Dark World	33731070
Berserk Dragon	85605684
Berserk Gorilla	39168895
Beta the Magnet Warrior	39256679
Bickuribox	25655502
Big Bang Shot	61127349
Big Burn	95472621
Big Core	14148099
Big Koala	42129512
Big Shield Gardna	65240384
Big Wave Small Wave	51562916
Big-Tusked Mammoth	59380081
Bio-Mage	58696829
Birdface	45547649
Black Illusion Ritual	41426869
Black Luster Soldier - Envoy of the Beginning	72989439
Black Pendant	65169794
Black Tyranno	38670435
Blackland Fire Dragon	87564352
Blade Knight	39507162
Blade Rabbit	58268433
Blade Skater	97023549
Bladefly	28470714
Blast Held By a Tribute	89041555
Blast Magician	21051146

CARD	PASSWORD
Blast with Chain	98239899
Blasting the Ruins	21466326
Blazing Inpachi	05464695
Blind Destruction	32015116
Blindly Loyal Goblin	35215622
Block Attack	25880422
Blockman	48115277
Blowback Dragon	25551951
Blue-Eyes Shining Dragon	53347303
Blue-Eyes Toon Dragon	53183600
Blue-Eyes Ultimate Dragon	23995346
Blue-Eyes White Dragon	89631139
Blue-Winged Crown	41396436
Bokoichi the Freightening Car	08715625
Bombardment Beetle	57409948
Bonding - H2O	45898858
Boneheimer	98456117
Book of Life	02204140
Book of Moon	14087893
Book of Taiyou	38699854
Boss Rush	66947414
Bottom Dweller	81386177
Bottomless Shifting Sand	76532077
Bottomless Trap Hole	29401950
Bountiful Artemis	32296881
Bowganian	52090844
Bracchio-Raidus	16507828
Brain Control	87910978
Brain Jacker	40267580
Branch!	30548775
Breaker the Magical Warrior	71413901
Broww, Huntsman of Dark World	79126789
Brron, Mad King of Dark World	06214884
Bubble Blaster	53586134
Bubble Illusion	80075749
Bubble Shuffle	61968753
Bubonic Vermin	06104968
Burning Algae	41859700
Burning Beast	59364406
Burning Land	24294108
Burst Breath	80163754
Burst Return	27191436
Burst Stream of Destruction	17655904
Buster Blader	78193831
Buster Rancher	84740193
Butterfly Dagger - Elma	69243953
Byser Shock	17597059
Call of The Haunted	97077563

CARD	PASSWORD
Call of the Mummy	04861205
Cannon Soldier	11384280
Cannonball Spear Shellfish	95614612
Card of Safe Return	57953380
Card Shuffle	12183332
Castle of Dark Illusions	00062121
Cat's Ear Tribe	95841282
Catapult Turtle	95727991
Cathedral of Nobles	29762407
Catnipped Kitty	96501677
Cave Dragon	93220472
Ceasefire	36468556
Celtic Guardian	91152256
Cemetery Bomb	51394546
Centrifugal	01801154
Ceremonial Bell	20228463
Cetus of Dagala	28106077
Chain Burst	48276469
Chain Destruction	01248895
Chain Disappearance	57139487
Chain Energy	79323590
Chain Thrasher	88190453
Chainsaw Insect	77252217
Change of Heart	04031928
Chaos Command Magician	72630549
Chaos Emperor Dragon - Envoy of the End	82301904
Chaos End	61044390
Chaos Greed	97439308
Chaos Necromancer	01434352
Chaos Sorcerer	09596126
Chaosrider Gutaph	47829960
Charcoal Inpachi	13179332
Charm of Shabti	50412166
Charubin the Fire Knight	37421579
Chiron the Mage	16956455
Chopman the Desperate Outlaw	40884383
Chorus of Sanctuary	81380218
Chthonian Alliance	46910446
Chthonian Blast	18271561
Chthonian Polymer	72287557
Chu-Ske the Mouse Fighter	08508055
Clay Charge	22479888
Cliff the Trap Remover	06967870
Cobra Jar	86801871
Cobraman Sakuzy	75109441
Cold Wave	60682203
Collected Power	07565547
Combination Attack	08964854
Command Knight	10375182
Commander Covington	22666164

CARD	PASSWORD
Commencement Dance	43417563
Compulsory Evacuation Device	94192409
Confiscation	17375316
Conscription	31000575
Continuous Destruction Punch	68057622
Contract With Exodia	33244944
Contract With the Abyss	69035382
Contract with the Dark Master	96420087
Convulsion of Nature	62966332
Cost Down	23265313
Covering Fire	74458486
Crab Turtle	91782219
Crass Clown	93889755
Creature Swap	31036355
Creeping Doom Manta	52571838
Crimson Ninja	14618326
Criosphinx	18654201
Cross Counter	37083210
Crush D. Gandra	64681432
Cure Mermaid	85802526
Curse of Aging	41398771
Curse of Anubis	66742250
Curse of Darkness	84970821
Curse of Dragon	28279543
Curse of the Masked Beast	94377247
Curse of Vampire	34294855
Cyber Dragon	70095154
Cyber End Dragon	01546123
Cyber Twin Dragon	74157028
Cyber-Dark Edge	77625948
Cyber-Stein	69015963
Cyberdark Dragon	40418351
Cyberdark Horn	41230939
Cyberdark Keel	03019642
D - Shield	62868900
D - Time	99075257
D. D. Assailant	70074904
D. D. Borderline	60912752
D. D. Crazy Beast	48148828
D. D. Dynamite	08628798
D. D. M. - Different Dimension Master	82112775
D. D. Trainer	86498013
D. D. Trap Hole	05606466
D. D. Warrior Lady	07572887
Dancing Fairy	90925163
Dangerous Machine TYPE-6	76895648
Dark Artist	72520073
Dark Bat	67049542
Dark Blade	11321183

CARD	PASSWORD
Dark Blade the Dragon Knight	86805855
Dark Driceratops	65287621
Dark Dust Spirit	89111398
Dark Elf	21417692
Dark Energy	04614116
Dark Factory of Mass Production	90928333
Dark Flare Knight	13722870
Dark Hole	53129443
Dark Magic Attack	02314238
Dark Magic Ritual	76792184
Dark Magician	46986414
Dark Magician Girl	38033121
Dark Magician of Chaos	40737112
Dark Magician's Tome of Black Magic	67227834
Dark Master - Zorc	97642679
Dark Mirror Force	20522190
Dark Paladin	98502113
Dark Room of Nightmare	85562745
Dark Sage	92377303
Dark Snake Syndrome	47233801
Dark-Piercing Light	45895206
Darkfire Dragon	17881964
Darkfire Soldier #1	05388481
Darkfire Soldier #2	78861134
Darkworld Thorns	43500484
De-Spell	19159413
Deal of Phantom	69122763
Decayed Commander	10209545
Dedication Through Light And Darkness	69542930
Deepsea Shark	28593363
Dekoichi the Battlechanted Locomotive	87621407
Delinquent Duo	44763025
Demotion	72575145
Des Counterblow	39131963
Des Croaking	44883830
Des Dendle	12965761
Des Feral Imp	81985784
Des Frog	84451804
Des Kangaroo	78613627
Des Koala	69579761
Des Lacooda	02326738
Des Wombat	09637706
Desert Sunlight	93747864
Desertapir	13409151
Destiny Board	94212438
Destiny Hero - Captain Tenacious	77608643
Destiny Hero - Diamond Dude	13093792

CARD	PASSWORD
Destiny Hero - Doom Lord	41613948
Destiny Hero - Dreadmaster	40591390
Destiny Signal	35464895
Destroyer Golem	73481154
Destruction Ring	21219755
Dian Keto the Cure Master	84257639
Dice Jar	03549275
Dimension Distortion	95194279
Dimensional Warrior	37043180
Disappear	24623598
Disarmament	20727787
Disc Fighter	19612721
Dissolverock	40826495
Divine Dragon Ragnarok	62113340
Divine Wrath	49010598
DNA Surgery	74701381
DNA Transplant	56769674
Doitsu	57062206
Dokurorider	99721536
Dokuroyaiba	30325729
Don Turtle	03493978
Don Zaloog	76922029
Doriado	84916669
Doriado's Blessing	23965037
Dragon Seeker	28563545
Dragon Treasure	01435851
Dragon Zombie	66672569
Dragon's Mirror	71490127
Dragon's Rage	54178050
Dragoness the Wicked Knight	70681994
Draining Shield	43250041
Dream Clown	13215230
Drillago	99050989
Drillroid	71218746
Dunames Dark Witch	12493482
Dust Tornado	60082867
Earth Chant	59820352
Earthbound Spirit	67105242
Earthquake	82828051
Eatgaboon	42578427
Ebon Magician Curran	46128076
Electro-Whip	37820550
Elegant Egotist	90219263
Element Dragon	30314994
Elemental Burst	61411502
Elemental Hero Avian	21844576
Elemental Hero Bladedge	59793705
Elemental Hero Bubbleman	79979666
Elemental Hero Burstinatrix	58932615

CARD	PASSWORD
Elemental Hero Clayman	84327329
Elemental Hero Electrum/Erekshieler	29343734
Elemental Hero Flame Wingman	35809262
Elemental Hero Mariner	14225239
Elemental Hero Necroid Shaman	81003500
Elemental Hero Neos	89943723
Elemental Hero Phoenix Enforcer	41436536
Elemental Hero Shining Flare Wingman	25366484
Elemental Hero Shining Phoenix Enforcer	88820235
Elemental Hero Sparkman	20721928
Elemental Hero Thunder Giant	61204971
Elemental Mistress Doriado	99414158
Elemental Recharge	36586443
Elf's Light	39897277
Emblem of Dragon Destroyer	06390406
Embodiment of Apophis	28649820
Emergency Provisions	53046408
Emes the Infinity	43580269
Empress Judge	15237615
Empress Mantis	58818411
Enchanted Javelin	96355986
Enchanting Mermaid	75376965
Enemy Controller	98045062
Enraged Battle Ox	76909279
Enraged Muka Muka	91862578
Eradicating Aerosol	94716515
Eternal Draught	56606928
Eternal Rest	95051344
Exhausting Spell	95451366
Exile of the Wicked	26725158
Exiled Force	74131780
Exodia Necross	12600382
Exodia the Forbidden One	33396948
Fairy Box	21598948
Fairy Dragon	20315854
Fairy King Truesdale	45425051
Fairy Meteor Crush	97687912
Faith Bird	75582395
Fatal Abacus	77910045
Fenrir	00218704
Feral Imp	41392891
Fiber Jar	78706415
Fiend Comedian	81172176
Fiend Scorpion	26566878
Fiend's Hand	52800428

CARD	PASSWORD
Fiend's Mirror	31890399
Final Countdown	95308449
Final Destiny	18591904
Final Flame	73134081
Final Ritual of the Ancients	60369732
Fire Darts	43061293
Fire Eye	88435542
Fire Kraken	46534755
Fire Princess	64752646
Fire Reaper	53581214
Fire Sorcerer	27132350
Firegrass	53293545
Firewing Pegasus	27054370
Fireyarou	71407486
Fissure	66788016
Five God Dragon (Five Headed Dragon)	99267150
Flame Cerebrus	60862676
Flame Champion	42599677
Flame Dancer	12883044
Flame Ghost	58528964
Flame Manipulator	34460851
Flame Swordsman	45231177
Flame Viper	02830619
Flash Assailant	96890582
Flower Wolf	95952802
Flying Fish	31987274
Flying Kamakiri #1	84834865
Flying Kamakiri #2	03134241
Follow Wind	98252586
Foolish Burial	81439173
Forest	87430998
Fortress Whale	62337487
Fortress Whale's Oath	77454922
Frenzied Panda	98818516
Frozen Soul	57069605
Fruits of Kozaky's Studies	49998907
Fuh-Rin-Ka-Zan	01781310
Fuhma Shuriken	09373534
Fulfillment of the Contract	48206762
Fushi No Tori	38538445
Fusion Gate	33550694
Fusion Recovery	18511384
Fusion Sage	26902560
Fusion Weapon	27967615
Fusionist	01641883
Gadget Soldier	86281779
Gagagigo	49003308
Gaia Power	56594520
Gaia the Dragon Champion	66889139
Gaia the Fierce Knight	06368038
Gale Dogra	16229315

CARD	PASSWORD
Gale Lizard	77491079
Gamble	37313786
Gamma the Magnet Warrior	11549357
Garma Sword	90844184
Garma Sword Oath	78577570
Garoozis	14977074
Garuda the Wind Spirit	12800777
Gatling Dragon	87751584
Gazelle the King of Mythical Beasts	05818798
Gear Golem the Moving Fortress	30190809
Gearfried the Iron Knight	00423705
Gearfried the Swordmaster	57046845
Gemini Elf	69140098
Getsu Fuhma	21887179
Giant Axe Mummy	78266168
Giant Germ	95178994
Giant Kozaky	58185394
Giant Orc	73698349
Giant Rat	97017120
Giant Red Seasnake	58831685
Giant Soldier of Stone	13039848
Giant Trunade	42703248
Gift of the Mystical Elf	98299011
Giga Gagagigo	43793530
Giga-Tech Wolf	08471389
Gigantes	47606319
Gigobyte	53776525
Gil Garth	38445524
Gilasaurus	45894482
Giltia the D. Knight	51828629
Girochin Kuwagata	84620194
Goblin Attack Force	78658564
Goblin Calligrapher	12057781
Goblin Elite Attack Force	85306040
Goblin Thief	45311864
Goblin's Secret Remedy	11868825
Gogiga Gagagigo	39674352
Golem Sentry	82323207
Good Goblin Housekeeping	09744376
Gora Turtle	80233946
Graceful Charity	79571449
Graceful Dice	74137509
Gradius	10992251
Gradius' Option	14291024
Granadora	13944422
Grand Tiki Elder	13676474
Granmarg the Rock Monarch	60229110
Gravedigger Ghoul	82542267

CARD	PASSWORD
Gravekeeper's Cannonholder	99877698
Gravekeeper's Curse	50712728
Gravekeeper's Guard	37101832
Gravekeeper's Servant	16762927
Gravekeeper's Spear Soldier	63695531
Gravekeeper's Spy	24317029
Gravekeeper's Vassal	99690140
Graverobber's Retribution	33737664
Gravity Bind	85742772
Gray Wing	29618570
Great Angus	11813953
Great Long Nose	02356994
Great Mammoth of Goldfine	54622031
Green Gadget	41172955
Gren Maju Da Eiza	36584821
Ground Attacker Bugroth	58314394
Ground Collapse	90502999
Gruesome Goo	65623423
Gryphon Wing	55608151
Gryphon's Feather Duster	34370473
Guardian Angel Joan	68007326
Guardian of the Labyrinth	89272878
Guardian of the Sea	85448931
Guardian Sphinx	40659562
Guardian Statue	75209824
Gust Fan	55321970
Gyaku-Gire Panda	09817927
Gyroid	18325492
Hade-Hane	28357177
Hamburger Recipe	80811661
Hammer Shot	26412047
Hamon	32491822
Hand of Nephthys	98446407
Hane-Hane	07089711
Hannibal Necromancer	05640330
Hard Armor	20060230
Harpie Girl	34100324
Harpie Lady 1	91932350
Harpie Lady 2	27927359
Harpie Lady 3	54415063
Harpie Lady Sisters	12206212
Harpie's Brother	30532390
Harpies' Hunting Ground	75782277
Hayabusa Knight	21015833
Headless Knight	05434080
Heart of Clear Water	64801562
Heart of the Underdog	35762283
Heavy Mech Support Platform	23265594

CARD	PASSWORD
Heavy Storm	19613556
Helios - The Primordial Sun	54493213
Helios Duo Megistus	80887952
Helios Tris Megiste	17286057
Helping Robo for Combat	47025270
Hero Barrier	44676200
HERO Flash!!	00191749
Hero Heart	67951831
Hero Kid	32679370
Hero Ring	26647858
Hero Signal	22020907
Hidden Book of Spell	21840375
Hidden Soldier	02047519
Hieracosphinx	82260502
Hieroglyph Lithograph	10248192
High Tide Gyojin	54579801
Hiita the Fire Charmer	00759393
Hino-Kagu-Tsuchi	75745607
Hinotama Soul	96851799
Hiro's Shadow Scout	81863068
Hitotsu-Me Giant	76184692
Holy Knight Ishzark	57902462
Homunculus the Alchemic Being	40410110
Horn of Heaven	98069388
Horn of Light	38552107
Horn of the Unicorn	64047146
Horus The Black Flame Dragon LV4	75830094
Horus The Black Flame Dragon LV6	11224103
Horus The Black Flame Dragon LV8	48229808
Hoshiningen	67629977
House of Adhesive Tape	15083728
Howling Insect	93107608
Huge Revolution	65396880
Human-Wave Tactics	30353551
Humanoid Slime	46821314
Humanoid Worm Drake	05600127
Hungry Burger	30243636
Hydrogeddon	22587018
Hyena	22873798
Hyozanryu	62397231
Hyper Hammerhead	02671330
Hysteric Fairy	21297224
Icarus Attack	53567095
Illusionist Faceless Mage	28546905
Impenetrable Formation	96631852
Imperial Order	61740673
Inaba White Rabbit	77084837
Incandescent Ordeal	33031674

CARD	PASSWORD
Indomitable Fighter Lei Lei	84173492
Infernal Flame Emperor	19847532
Infernal Queen Archfiend	08581705
Inferno	74823665
Inferno Fire Blast	52684508
Inferno Hammer	17185260
Inferno Reckless Summon	12247206
Inferno Tempest	14391920
Infinite Cards	94163677
Infinite Dismissal	54109233
Injection Fairy Lily	79575620
Inpachi	97923414
Insect Armor with Laser Cannon	03492538
Insect Barrier	23615409
Insect Imitation	96965364
Insect Knight	35052053
Insect Princess	37957847
Insect Queen	91512835
Insect Soldiers of the Sky	07019529
Inspection	16227556
Interdimensional Matter Transporter	36261276
Invader From Another Dimension	28450915
Invader of Darkness	56647086
Invader of the Throne	03056267
Invasion of Flames	26082229
Invigoration	98374133
Iron Blacksmith Kotetsu	73431236
Island Turtle	04042268
Jack's Knight	90876561
Jade Insect Whistle	95214051
Jam Breeding Machine	21770260
Jam Defender	21558682
Jar of Greed	83968380
Jar Robber	33784505
Javelin Beetle	26932788
Javelin Beetle Pact	41182875
Jellyfish	14851496
Jerry Beans Man	23635815
Jetroid	43697559
Jinzo	77585513
Jinzo #7	32809211
Jirai Gumo	94773007
Jowgen the Spiritualist	41855169
Jowls of Dark Demise	05257687
Judge Man	30113682
Judgment of Anubis	55256016
Just Desserts	24068492
KA-2 Des Scissors	52768103
Kabazauls	51934376

CARD	PASSWORD
Kagemusha of the Blue Flame	15401633
Kaibaman	34627841
Kaiser Dragon	94566432
Kaiser Glider	52824910
Kaiser Sea Horse	17444133
Kaminari Attack	09653271
Kaminote Blow	97570038
Kamionwizard	41544074
Kangaroo Champ	95789089
Karate Man	23289281
Karbonala Warrior	54541900
Karma Cut	71587526
Kelbek	54878498
Keldo	80441106
Killer Needle	88979991
Kinetic Soldier	79853073
King Dragun	13756293
King Fog	84686841
King of the Skull Servants	36021814
King of the Swamp	79109599
King of Yamimakai	69455834
King Tiger Wanghu	83986578
King's Knight	64788463
Kiryu	84814897
Kiseitai	04266839
Kishido Spirit	60519422
Knight's Title	87210505
Koitsu	69456283
Kojikocy	01184620
Kotodama	19406822
Kozaky	99171160
Kozaky's Self-Destruct Button	21908319
Kryuel	82642348
Kumootoko	56283725
Kurama	85705804
Kuriboh	40640057
Kuwagata Alpha	60802233
Kwagar Hercules	95144193
Kycoo The Ghost Destroyer	88240808
La Jinn The Mystical Genie of The Lamp	97590747
Labyrinth of Nightmare	66526672
Labyrinth Tank	99551425
Lady Assailant of Flames	90147755
Lady Ninja Yae	82005435
Lady of Faith	17358176
Larvas	94675535
Laser Cannon Armor	77007920
Last Day of Witch	90330453
Last Turn	28566710
Launcher Spider	87322377

CARD	PASSWORD
Lava Battleguard	20394040
Lava Golem	00102380
Layard the Liberator	67468948
Left Arm of the Forbidden One	07902349
Left Leg of the Forbidden One	44519536
Legendary Black Belt	96438440
Legendary Flame Lord	60258960
Legendary Jujitsu Master	25773409
Legendary Sword	61854111
Leghul	12472242
Lekunga	62543393
Lesser Dragon	55444629
Lesser Fiend	16475472
Level Conversion Lab	84397023
Level Limit - Area A	54976796
Level Limit - Area B	03136426
Level Modulation	61850482
Level Up!	25290459
Levia-Dragon	37721209
Light of Intervention	62867251
Light of Judgment	44595286
Lighten the Load	37231841
Lightforce Sword	49587034
Lightning Blade	55226821
Lightning Conger	27671321
Lightning Vortex	69162969
Limiter Removal	23171610
Liquid Beast	93108297
Little Chimera	68658728
Little-Winguard	90790253
Lizard Soldier	20831168
Lord of D.	17985575
Lord of the Lamp	99510761
Lost Guardian	45871897
Luminous Soldier	57282479
Luminous Spark	81777047
Luster Dragon	11091375
Luster Dragon #2	17658803
M-Warrior #1	56342351
M-Warrior #2	92731455
Machine Conversion Factory	25769732
Machine Duplication	63995093
Machine King	46700124
Machine King Prototype	89222931
Machiners Defender	96384007
Machiners Force	58054262
Machiners Sniper	23782705
Machiners Soldier	60999392
Mad Dog of Darkness	79182538
Mad Lobster	97240270
Mad Sword Beast	79870141

CARD	PASSWORD
Mage Power	83746708
Magic Drain	59344077
Magic Jammer	77414722
Magical Cylinder	62279055
Magical Dimension	28553439
Magical Explosion	32723153
Magical Hats	81210420
Magical Labyrinth	64389297
Magical Marionette	08034697
Magical Merchant	32362575
Magical Plant Mandragola	07802006
Magical Scientist	34206604
Magical Thorn	53119267
Magician of Black Chaos	30208479
Magician of Faith	31560081
Magician's Circle	00050755
Magician's Unite	36045450
Magician's Valkyrie	80304126
Magnet Circle	94940436
Maha Vailo	93013676
Maharaghi	40695128
Maiden of the Aqua	17214465
Maji-Gire Panda	60102563
Maju Garzett	08794435
Makiu	27827272
Makyura the Destructor	21593977
Malevolent Nuzzler	99597615
Malfunction	06137095
Malice Ascendant	14255590
Malice Dispersion	13626450
Mammoth Graveyard	40374923
Man Eater	93553943
Man-Eater Bug	54652250
Man-Eating Black Shark	80727036
Man-Eating Treasure Chest	13723605
Man-Thro' Tro'	43714890
Manga Ryu-Ran	38369349
Manju of the Ten Thousand Hands	95492061
Manticore of Darkness	77121851
Marauding Captain	02460565
Marie the Fallen One	57579381
Marine Beast	29929832
Marshmallon	31305911
Marshmallon Glasses	66865880
Maryokutai	71466592
Masaki the Legendary Swordsman	44287299
Mask of Brutality	82432018
Mask of Darkness	28933734
Mask of Restrict	29549364
Mask of Weakness	57882509

CARD	PASSWORD
Masked Dragon	39191307
Masked of the Accursed	56948373
Masked Sorcerer	10189126
Mass Driver	34906152
Master Kyonshee	24530661
Master Monk	49814180
Master of Dragon Knight	62873545
Master of Oz	27134689
Mataza the Zapper	22609617
Mavelus	59036972
Maximum Six	30707994
Mazera DeVille	06133894
Mech Mole Zombie	63545455
Mecha-Dog Marron	94667532
Mechanical Hound	22512237
Mechanical Snail	34442949
Mechanical Spider	45688586
Mechanicalchaser	07359741
Meda Bat	76211194
Medusa Worm	02694423
Mefist the Infernal General	46820049
Mega Thunderball	21817254
Mega Ton Magical Cannon	32062913
Megamorph	22046459
Megarock Dragon	71544954
Melchid the Four-Face Beast	86569121
Memory Crusher	48700891
Mermaid Knight	24435369
Messenger of Peace	44656491
Metal Armored Bug	65957473
Metal Dragon	09293977
Metallizing Parasite	07369217
Metalmorph	68540058
Metalzoa	50705071
Metamorphosis	46411259
Meteor B. Dragon	90660762
Meteor Dragon	64271667
Meteor of Destruction	33767325
Meteorain	64274292
Michizure	37580756
Micro-Ray	18190572
Mid Shield Gardna	75487237
Mighty Guard	62327910
Mikazukinoyaiba	38277918
Millennium Golem	47986555
Millennium Scorpion	82482194
Millennium Shield	32012841
Milus Radiant	07489323
Minar	32539892
Mind Control	37520316
Mind Haxorz	75392615

CARD	PASSWORD
Mind on Air	66690411
Mind Wipe	52718046
Mine Golem	76321376
Minefield Eruption	85519211
Minor Goblin Official	01918087
Miracle Dig	06343408
Miracle Fusion	45906428
Miracle Kid	55985014
Miracle Restoring	68334074
Mirage Dragon	15960641
Mirage Knight	49217579
Mirage of Nightmare	41482598
Mirror Force	44095762
Mirror Wall	22359980
Misfortune	01036974
Mispolymerization	58392024
Mistobody	47529357
Moai Interceptor Cannons	45159319
Mobius the Frost Monarch	04929256
Moisture Creature	75285069
Mokey Mokey	27288416
Mokey Mokey King	13803864
Mokey Mokey Smackdown	01965724
Molten Behemoth	17192817
Molten Destruction	19384334
Molten Zombie	04732017
Monk Fighter	03810071
Monster Egg	36121917
Monster Eye	84133008
Monster Gate	43040603
Monster Reborn	83764718
Monster Recovery	93108433
Monster Reincarnation	74848038
Mooyan Curry	58074572
Morale Boost	93671934
Morphing Jar	33508719
Morphing Jar #2	79106360
Mother Grizzly	57839750
Mountain	50913601
Mr. Volcano	31477025
Mudora	82108372
Muka Muka	46657337
Multiplication of Ants	22493811
Multiply	40703222
Musician King	56907389
Mustering of the Dark Scorpions	68191243
Mysterious Puppeteer	54098121
Mystic Horseman	68516705
Mystic Lamp	98049915
Mystic Plasma Zone	18161786
Mystic Swordsman LV 2	47507260

CARD	PASSWORD
Mystic Swordsman LV 4	74591968
Mystic Swordsman LV 6	60482781
Mystic Tomato	83011277
Mystic Wok	80161395
Mystical Beast Serket	89194033
Mystical Elf	15025844
Mystical Knight of Jackal	98745000
Mystical Moon	36607978
Mystical Sand	32751480
Mystical Sheep #2	30451366
Mystical Shine Ball	39552864
Mystical Space Typhoon	05318639
Mystik Wok	80161395
Mythical Beast Cerberus	55424270
Nanobreaker	70948327
Necklace of Command	48576971
Necrovalley	47355498
Needle Ball	94230224
Needle Burrower	98162242
Needle Ceiling	38411870
Needle Wall	38299233
Needle Worm	81843628
Negate Attack	14315573
Nemuriko	90963488
Neo Aqua Madoor	49563947
Neo Bug	16587243
Neo the Magic Swordsman	50930991
Neo-Space	40215635
Neo-Spacian Aqua Dolphin	17955766
Newdoria	04335645
Next to be Lost	07076131
Night Assailant	16226786
Nightmare Horse	59290628
Nightmare Penguin	81306586
Nightmare Wheel	54704216
Nightmare's Steelcage	58775978
Nimble Momonga	22567609
Nin-Ken Dog	11987744
Ninja Grandmaster Sasuke	04041838
Ninjitsu Art of Decoy	89628781
Ninjitsu Art of Transformation	70861343
Nitro Unit	23842445
Niwatori	07805359
Nobleman of Crossout	71044499
Nobleman of Extermination	17449108
Nobleman-Eater Bug	65878864
Non Aggression Area	76848240

CARD	PASSWORD
Non-Fusion Area	27581098
Non-Spellcasting Area	20065549
Novox's Prayer	43694075
Nubian Guard	51616747
Numinous Healer	02130625
Nutrient Z	29389368
Nuvia the Wicked	12953226
O - Oversoul	63703130
Obnoxious Celtic Guardian	52077741
Ocubeam	86088138
Offerings to the Doomed	19230407
Ojama Black	79335209
Ojama Delta Hurricane	08251996
Ojama Green	12482652
Ojama King	90140980
Ojama Trio	29843091
Ojama Yellow	42941100
Ojamagic	24643836
Ojamuscle	98259197
Old Vindictive Magician	45141844
Ominous Fortunetelling	56995655
Oni Tank T-34	66927994
Opti-Camaflauge Armor	44762290
Opticlops	14531242
Option Hunter	33248692
Orca Mega-Fortress of Darkness	63120904
Ordeal of a Traveler	39537362
Order to Charge	78986941
Order to Smash	39019325
Otohime	39751093
Outstanding Dog Marron	11548522
Overdrive	02311603
Oxygeddon	58071123
Painful Choice	74191942
Paladin of White Dragon	73398797
Pale Beast	21263083
Pandemonium	94585852
Pandemonium Watchbear	75375465
Parasite Paracide	27911549
Parasitic Ticky	87978805
Patrician of Darkness	19153634
Patroid	71930383
Penguin Knight	36039163
Penumbral Soldier Lady	64751286
People Running About	12143771
Perfect Machine King	18891691
Performance of Sword	04849037
Petit Angel	38142739
Petit Dragon	75356564

CARD	PASSWORD
Petit Moth	58192742
Phantasmal Martyrs	93224848
Phantom Beast Cross-Wing	71181155
Phantom Beast Thunder-Pegasus	34961968
Phantom Beast Wild-Horn	07576264
Pharaoh's Servant	52550973
Pharonic Protector	89959682
Phoenix Wing Wind Blast	63356631
Photon Generator Unit	66607691
Pikeru's Circle of Enchantment	74270067
Pikeru's Second Sight	58015506
Pinch Hopper	26185991
Pineapple Blast	90669991
Piranha Army	50823978
Pitch-Black Power Stone	34029630
Pitch-Black Warwolf	88975532
Pitch-Dark Dragon	47415292
Poison Draw Frog	56840658
Poison Fangs	76539047
Poison Mummy	43716289
Poison of the Old Man	08842266
Polymerization	24094653
Possessed Dark Soul	52860176
Pot of Avarice	67169062
Pot of Generosity	70278545
Pot of Greed	55144522
Power Bond	37630732
Power Capsule	54289683
Precious Card from Beyond	68304813
Premature Burial	70828912
Prepare to Strike Back	04483989
Prevent Rat	00549481
Prickle Fairy	91559748
Primal Seed	23701465
Princess Curran	02316186
Princess of Tsurugi	51371017
Princess Pikeru	75917088
Protective Soul Ailin	11678191
Protector of the Sanctuary	24221739
Protector of the Throne	10071456
Proto-Cyber Dragon	26439287
Pumpking the King of Ghosts	29155212
Punished Eagle	74703140
Pyramid of Light	53569894
Pyramid Turtle	77044671
Queen's Knight	25652259
Rabid Horseman	94905343
Rafflesia Seduction	31440542

CARD	PASSWORD
Raging Flame Sprite	90810762
Raigeki	12580477
Raigeki Break	04178474
Rain Of Mercy	66719324
Rainbow Flower	21347810
Rallis the Star Bird	41382147
Rancer Dragonute	11125718
Rapid-Fire Magician	06337436
Rare Metalmorph	12503902
Raregold Armor	07625614
Raviel, Lord of Phantasms	69890967
Ray & Temperature	85309439
Ray of Hope	82529174
Re-Fusion	74694807
Ready For Intercepting	31785398
Really Eternal Rest	28121403
Reaper of the Cards	33066139
Reaper of the Nightmare	85684223
Reasoning	58577036
Reborn Zombie	23421244
Reckless Greed	37576645
Recycle	96316857
Red Archery Girl	65570596
Red Gadget	86445415
Red Medicine	38199696
Red Moon Baby	56387350
Red-Eyes B. Chick	36262024
Red-Eyes B. Dragon	74677422
Red-Eyes Black Metal Dragon	64335804
Red-Eyes Darkness Dragon	96561011
Reflect Bounder	02851070
Regenerating Mummy	70821187
Reinforcement of the Army	32807846
Release Restraint	75417459
Relinquished	64631466
Reload	22589918
Remove Trap	51482758
Rescue Cat	14878871
Rescueroid	24311595
Reshef the Dark Being	62420419
Respect Play	08951260
Return from the Different Dimension	27174286
Return of the Doomed	19827717
Reversal of Graves	17484499
Reversal Quiz	05990062
Revival Jam	31709826
Right Arm of the Forbidden One	70903634
Right Leg of the Forbidden One	08124921
Ring of Defense	58641905

CARD	PASSWORD
Ring of Destruction	83555666
Ring of Magnetism	20436034
Riryoku Field	70344351
Rising Air Current	45778932
Rising Energy	78211862
Rite of Spirit	30450531
Ritual Weapon	54351224
Robbin' Goblin	88279736
Robbin' Zombie	83258273
Robolady	92421852
Robotic Knight	44203504
Roboyarou	38916461
Rock Bombardment	20781762
Rock Ogre Grotto	68846917
Rocket Jumper	53890795
Rocket Warrior	30860696
Rod of the Mind's Eye	94793422
Roll Out!	91597389
Root Water	39004808
Rope of Life	93382620
Rope of Spirit	37383714
Roulette Barrel	46303688
Royal Command	33950246
Royal Decree	51452091
Royal Keeper	16509093
Royal Knight	68280530
Royal Magical Library	70791313
Royal Surrender	56058888
Royal Tribute	72405967
Ruin, Queen of Oblivion	46427957
Rush Recklessly	70046172
Ryu Kokki	57281778
Ryu Senshi	49868263
Ryu-Kishin Clown	42647539
Ryu-Kishin Powered	24611934
Saber Beetle	49645921
Sacred Crane	30914564
Sacred Phoenix of Nephthys	61441708
Saggi the Dark Clown	66602787
Sakuretsu Armor	56120475
Salamandra	32268901
Salvage	96947648
Samsara	44182827
Sand Gambler	50593156
Sand Moth	73648243
Sangan	26202165
Sanwitch	53539634
Sasuke Samurai	16222645
Sasuke Samurai #2	11760174
Sasuke Samurai #3	77379481
Sasuke Samurai #4	64538655
Satellite Cannon	50400231
Scapegoat	73915051

CARD	PASSWORD
Scarr, Scout of Dark World	05498296
Science Soldier	67532912
Scroll of Bewitchment	10352095
Scyscraper	63035430
Sea Serpent Warrior of Darkness	42071342
Sealmaster Meisei	02468169
Second Coin Toss	36562627
Second Goblin	19086954
Secret Barrel	27053506
Self-Destruct Button	57585212
Senri Eye	60391791
Serial Spell	49398568
Serpent Night Dragon	66516792
Serpentine Princess	71829750
Servant of Catabolism	02792265
Seven Tools of the Bandit	03819470
Shadow Ghoul	30778711
Shadow Of Eyes	58621589
Shadow Tamer	37620434
Shadowknight Archfiend	09603356
Shadowslayer	20939559
Share the Pain	56830749
Shield & Sword	52097679
Shield Crash	30683373
Shien's Spy	07672244
Shift	59560625
Shifting Shadows	59237154
Shinato's Ark	60365591
Shinato, King of a Higher Plane	86327225
Shining Abyss	87303357
Shining Angel	95956346
Shooting Star Bow - Ceal	95638658
Silent Insect	40867519
Silent Magician Lv4	73665146
Silent Magician Lv8	72443568
Silent Swordsman LV3	01995985
Silent Swordsman LV5	74388798
Silent Swordsman LV7	37267041
Sillva, Warlord of Dark World	32619583
Silpheed	73001017
Silver Fang	90357090
Simorgh, Bird of Divinity	14989021
Simultaneous Loss	92219931
Sinister Serpent	08131171
Sixth Sense	03280747
Skill Drain	82732705
Skilled Dark Magician	73752131
Skilled White Magician	46363422

CARD	PASSWORD
Skull Archfiend of Lightning	61370518
Skull Descovery Knight	78700060
Skull Dog Marron	86652646
Skull Invitation	98139712
Skull Lair	06733059
Skull Mariner	05265750
Skull Red Bird	10202894
Skull Servant	32274490
Skull Zoma	79852326
Skull-Mark Ladybug	64306248
Skyscraper	63035430
Slate Warrior	78636495
Smashing Ground	97169186
Smoke Grenade of the Thief	63789924
Snatch Steal	45986603
Sogen	86318356
Soitsu	60246171
Solar Flare Dragon	45985838
Solar Ray	44472639
Solemn Judgment	41420027
Solemn Wishes	35346968
Solomon's Lawbook	23471572
Sonic Duck	84696266
Sonic Jammer	84550200
Sorcerer of Dark Magic	88619463
Soul Absorption	68073522
Soul Exchange	68005187
Soul of Purity and Light	77527210
Soul Release	05758500
Soul Resurrection	92924317
Soul Reversal	78864369
Soul Tiger	15734813
Soul-Absorbing Bone Tower	63012333
Souleater	31242786
Souls Of The Forgotten	04920010
Space Mambo	36119641
Spark Blaster	97362768
Sparks	76103675
Spatial Collapse	20644748
Spear Cretin	58551308
Spear Dragon	31553716
Spell Canceller	84636823
Spell Economics	04259068
Spell Purification	01669772
Spell Reproduction	29228529
Spell Shield Type-8	38275183
Spell Vanishing	29735721
Spell-Stopping Statute	10069180
Spellbinding Circle	18807108
Spherous Lady	52121290
Sphinx Teleia	51402177
Spiral Spear Strike	49328340

CARD	PASSWORD
Spirit Barrier	53239672
Spirit Caller	48659020
Spirit Message A	94772232
Spirit Message I	31893528
Spirit Message L	30170981
Spirit Message N	67287533
Spirit of Flames	13522325
Spirit of the Breeze	53530069
Spirit of the Harp	80770678
Spirit of the Pharaoh	25343280
Spirit Reaper	23205979
Spirit Ryu	67957315
Spiritual Earth Art - Kurogane	70156997
Spiritual Energy Settle Machine	99173029
Spiritual Fire Art - Kurenai	42945701
Spiritual Water Art - Aoi	06540606
Spiritual Wind Art - Miyabi	79333300
Spiritualism	15866454
St. Joan	21175632
Stamping Destruction	81385346
Star Boy	08201910
Statue of the Wicked	65810489
Staunch Defender	92854392
Stealth Bird	03510565
Steam Gyroid	05368615
Steamroid	44729197
Steel Ogre Grotto #1	29172562
Steel Ogre Grotto #2	90908427
Stim-Pack	83225447
Stop Defense	63102017
Storming Wynn	29013526
Stray Lambs	60764581
Strike Ninja	41006930
Stronghold	13955608
Stumbling	34646691
Success Probability 0%	06859683
Summon Priest	00423585
Summoned Skull	70781052
Summoner of Illusions	14644902
Super Conductor Tyranno	85520851
Super Rejuvenation	27770341
Super Robolady	75923050
Super Roboyarou	01412158
Supply	44072894
Susa Soldier	40473581
Swarm of Locusts	41872150
Swarm of Scarabs	15383415
Swift Gaia the Fierce Knight	16589042
Sword Hunter	51345461
Sword of Deep-Seated	98495314

CARD	PASSWORD
Sword of Dragon's Soul	61405855
Sword of the Soul Eater	05371656
Swords of Concealing Light	12923641
Swords of Revealing Light	72302403
Swordsman of Landstar	03573512
Symbol of Heritage	45305419
System Down	18895832
T.A.D.P.O.L.E.	10456559
Tactical Espionage Expert	89698120
Tailor of the Fickle	43641473
Taunt	90740329
Tenkabito Shien	41589166
Terra the Terrible	63308047
Terraforming	73628505
Terrorking Archfiend	35975813
Terrorking Salmon	78060096
Teva	16469012
The Agent of Creation - Venus	64734921
The Agent of Force - Mars	91123920
The Agent of Judgment - Saturn	91345518
The Agent of Wisdom - Mercury	38730226
The All-Seeing White Tiger	32269855
The Big March of Animals	01689516
The Bistro Butcher	71107816
The Cheerful Coffin	41142615
The Creator	61505339
The Creator Incarnate	97093037
The Dark - Hex Sealed Fusion	52101615
The Dark Door	30606547
The Dragon Dwelling in the Cave	93346024
The Dragon's Bead	92408984
The Earl of Demise	66989694
The Earth - Hex Sealed Fusion	88696724
The Emperor's Holiday	68400115
The End of Anubis	65403020
The Eye Of Truth	34694160
The Fiend Megacyber	66362965
The Flute of Summoning Dragon	43973174
The Flute of Summoning Kuriboh	20065322
The Forceful Sentry	42829885
The Forces of Darkness	29826127
The Forgiving Maiden	84080938
The Furious Sea King	18710707

CARD	PASSWORD
The Graveyard in the Fourth Dimension	88089103
The Gross Ghost of Fled Dreams	68049471
The Hunter With 7 Weapons	01525329
The Illusionary Gentleman	83764996
The Immortal of Thunder	84926738
The Kick Man	90407382
The Last Warrior From Another Planet	86099788
The Law of the Normal	66926224
The League of Uniform Nomenclature	55008284
The Legendary Fisherman	03643300
The Light - Hex Sealed Fusion	15717011
The Little Swordsman of Aile	25109950
The Masked Beast	49064413
The Portrait's Secret	32541773
The Regulation of Tribe	00296499
The Reliable Guardian	16430187
The Rock Spirit	76305638
The Sanctuary in the Sky	56433456
The Second Sarcophagus	04081094
The Secret of the Bandit	99351431
The Shallow Grave	43434803
The Spell Absorbing Life	99517131
The Thing in the Crater	78243409
The Third Sarcophagus	78697395
The Trojan Horse	38479725
The Unhappy Girl	27618634
The Unhappy Maiden	51275027
The Warrior Returning Alive	95281259
Theban Nightmare	51838385
Theinen the Great Sphinx	87997872
Thestalos the Firestorm Monarch	26205777
Thousand Dragon	41462083
Thousand Energy	05703682
Thousand Needles	33977496
Thousand-Eyes Idol	27125110
Thousand-Eyes Restrict	63519819
Threatening Roar	36361633
Three-Headed Geedo	78423643
Throwstone Unit	76075810
Thunder Crash	69196160
Thunder Dragon	31786629
Thunder Nyan Nyan	70797118

CARD	PASSWORD
Thunder of Ruler	91781589
Time Seal	35316708
Time Wizard	71625222
Timeater	44913552
Timidity	40350910
Token Festevil	83675475
Token Thanksgiving	57182235
Tongyo	69572024
Toon Cannon Soldier	79875176
Toon Dark Magician Girl	90960358
Toon Defense	43509019
Toon Gemini Elf	42386471
Toon Goblin Attack Force	15270885
Toon Masked Sorcerer	16392422
Toon Mermaid	65458948
Toon Summoned Skull	91842653
Toon Table of Contents	89997728
Toon World	15259703
Tornado Bird	71283180
Tornado Wall	18605135
Torpedo Fish	90337190
Torrential Tribute	53582587
Total Defense Shogun	75372290
Tower of Babel	94256039
Tradgedy	35686187
Transcendent Wings	25573054
Trap Dustshoot	64697231
Trap Hole	04206964
Trap Jammer	19252988
Treeborn Frog	12538374
Tremendous Fire	46918794
Tri-Horned Dragon	39111158
Triage	30888983
Trial of Nightmare	77827521
Trial of the Princesses	72709014
Triangle Ecstasy Spark	12181376
Triangle Power	32298781
Tribe-Infecting Virus	33184167
Tribute Doll	02903036
Tribute to The Doomed	79759861
Tripwire Beast	45042329
Troop Dragon	55013285
Tsukuyomi	34853266
Turtle Oath	76806714
Turtle Tiger	37313348
Twin Swords of Flashing Light	21900719
Twin-Headed Beast	82035781
Twin-Headed Behemoth	43586926
Twin-Headed Fire Dragon	78984772
Twin-Headed Thunder Dragon	54752875

CARD	PASSWORD
Twin-Headed Wolf	88132637
Two Thousand Needles	83228073
Two-Man Cell Battle	25578802
Two-Mouth Darkruler	57305373
Two-Pronged Attack	83887306
Tyhone	72842870
Type Zero Magic Crusher	21237481
Tyranno Infinity	83235263
Tyrant Dragon	94568601
UFOroid	07602840
UFOroid Fighter	32752319
Ultimate Insect LV1	49441499
Ultimate Insect LV3	34088136
Ultimate Insect LV5	34830502
Ultimate Insect LV7	19877898
Ultimate Obedient Fiend	32240937
Ultimate Tyranno	15894048
Ultra Evolution Pill	22431243
Umi	22702055
Umiiruka	82999629
Union Attack	60399954
United Resistance	85936485
United We Stand	56747793
Unity	14731897
Unshaven Angler	92084010
Upstart Goblin	70368879
Uraby	01784619
Uria, Lord of Sealing Flames	06007213
V-Tiger Jet	51638941
Valkyrion the Magna Warrior	75347539
Vampire Genesis	22056710
Vampire Lord	53839837
Vampire Orchis	46571052
Vengeful Bog Spirit	95220856
Victory D	44910027
Vilepawn Archfiend	73219648
VW-Tiger Catapult	58859575
VWXYZ-Dragon Catapult Cannon	84243274
W-Wing Catapult	96300057
Waboku	12607053
Wall of Revealing Light	17078030
Wandering Mummy	42994702
Warrior Dai Grepher	75953262
Warrior of Zera	66073051
Wasteland	23424603
Water Dragon	85066822
Water Omotics	02483611
Wave Motion Cannon	38992735

CARD	PASSWORD
Weed Out	28604635
Whiptail Crow	91996584
Whirlwind Prodigy	15090429
White Dragon Ritual	09786492
White Horn Dragon	73891874
White Magical Hat	15150365
White Magician Pikeru	81383947
White Ninja	01571945
Wicked-Breaking Flameberge-Baou	68427465
Wild Nature's Release	61166988
Winged Dragon, Guardian of the Fortress #1	87796900
Winged Kuriboh	57116033
Winged Kuriboh LV10	98585345
Winged Minion	89258225
Winged Sage Falcos	87523462
Wingweaver	31447217
Witch Doctor of Chaos	75946257
Witch of the Black Forest	78010363
Witch's Apprentice	80741828
Witty Phantom	36304921
Wolf Axwielder	56369281
Woodborg Inpachi	35322812
Woodland Sprite	06979239
Worm Drake	73216412
Wroughtweiler	06480253
Wynn the Wind Charmer	37744402
X-Head Cannon	62651957
Xing Zhen Hu	76515293
XY-Dragon Cannon	02111707
XYZ-Dragon Cannon	91998119
XZ-Tank Cannon	99724761
Y-Dragon Head	65622692
Yamata Dragon	76862289
Yami	59197169
Yata-Garasu	03078576
Yellow Gadget	13839120
Yellow Luster Shield	04542651
Yomi Ship	51534754
YZ-Tank Dragon	25119460
Z-Metal Tank	64500000
Zaborg the Thunder Monarch	51945556
Zero Gravity	83133491
Zoa	24311372
Zolga	16268841
Zombie Tiger	47693640
Zombyra the Dark	88472456
Zure, Knight of Dark World	07459013

Y

ZERO ESCAPE: VIRTUE'S LAST REWARD

NINTENDO 3DS/PS VITA

SECRET PHONE NUMBERS

When investigating the Crew Quarters, enter these numbers on the telephone to hear secret messages.

EFFECT	NUMBER
Conversation with "Jenny"	5309
Erotic hotline	6969
The Origin of Pi	3141
Upside-down Message	8008

ZOMBIE APOCALYPSE

XBOX 360/PS3

7 DAYS OF HELL MODE

Complete Day 55.

CHAINSAW ONLY MODE

Complete a day only using the chainsaw.

HARDCORE MODE

Survive for seven straight days.

TURBO MODE

Get a 100 multiplier.

ZOMBIE DRIVER HD

XBOX 360

AVATAR AWARD

Defeat the first boss in Story Mode to unlock the Red Skull Avatar Award.

ZONE OF THE ENDERS HD COLLECTION

PLAYSTATION 3

ZONE OF THE ENDERS

FULL HEALTH AND AMMO

Pause the game and press LB, LB, LT, LT, LB, RB, LB, RB, RT, RB and you will go down a level but you will restore your health and ammo.

TWO EXTRA CHARACTERS AND STAGES IN VERSUS MODE

Complete the game on any difficulty to unlock Versus Mode, then complete the game again to unlock two additional characters and stages for Versus Mode.

UNLOCK VERSUS MODE

Complete the game on any difficulty to unlock versus mode.

ZONE OF THE ENDERS: THE 2ND RUNNER

UNLOCK EXTRA MISSIONS

Complete the game on any difficulty to unlock the Extra Missions mode.

UNLOCKABLE CHARACTERS

CHARACTER	REQUIREMENT
Aumaan Anubis	Complete the game once and then start a new game with all sub-weapons equipped. Get into Margrifier, the area with an unlockable gate, and go down the left route. Use the Vector Cannon to destroy the stones in your way to unlock a secret path. Defeat all the enemies to enter a one-on-one battle with Aumaan Anubis. When it is destroyed, pick up the small icon of Aumaan Anubis to unlock it.